Lecture Notes in Computer Science   11460

Commenced Publication in 1973
Founding and Former Series Editors:
Gerhard Goos, Juris Hartmanis, and Jan van Leeuwen

Editorial Board Members

David Hutchison, UK
Josef Kittler, UK
Friedemann Mattern, Switzerland
Moni Naor, Israel
Bernhard Steffen, Germany
Doug Tygar, USA

Takeo Kanade, USA
Jon M. Kleinberg, USA
John C. Mitchell, USA
C. Pandu Rangan, India
Demetri Terzopoulos, USA

Formal Methods

Subline of Lectures Notes in Computer Science

Subline Series Editors

Ana Cavalcanti, *University of York, UK*
Marie-Claude Gaudel, *Université de Paris-Sud, France*

Subline Advisory Board

Manfred Broy, *TU Munich, Germany*
Annabelle McIver, *Macquarie University, Sydney, NSW, Australia*
Peter Müller, *ETH Zurich, Switzerland*
Erik de Vink, *Eindhoven University of Technology, The Netherlands*
Pamela Zave, *AT&T Laboratories Research, Bedminster, NJ, USA*

More information about this series at http://www.springer.com/series/7408

Julia M. Badger · Kristin Yvonne Rozier (Eds.)

NASA
Formal Methods

11th International Symposium, NFM 2019
Houston, TX, USA, May 7–9, 2019
Proceedings

 Springer

Editors
Julia M. Badger
NASA
Houston, TX, USA

Kristin Yvonne Rozier (iD)
Iowa State University
Ames, IA, USA

ISSN 0302-9743   ISSN 1611-3349   (electronic)
Lecture Notes in Computer Science
ISBN 978-3-030-20651-2   ISBN 978-3-030-20652-9   (eBook)
https://doi.org/10.1007/978-3-030-20652-9

LNCS Sublibrary: SL2 – Programming and Software Engineering

This Springer imprint is published by the registered company Springer Nature Switzerland AG
The registered company address is: Gewerbestrasse 11, 6330 Cham, Switzerland

Preface

This volume contains the papers presented at the 11th NASA Formal Methods (NFM) Symposium held during May 7–9, 2019, at Rice University in Houston, Texas, USA.

The widespread use and increasing complexity of mission-critical and safety-critical systems at NASA and in the aerospace industry require advanced techniques that address these systems' specification, design, verification, validation, and certification requirements. The NASA Formal Methods Symposium (NFM) is a forum to foster collaboration between theoreticians and practitioners from NASA, academia, and industry. NFM's goals are to identify challenges and to provide solutions for achieving assurance for such critical systems.

New developments and emerging applications like autonomous software for uncrewed deep space human habitats, caretaker robotics, unmanned aerial systems (UAS), UAS traffic management (UTM), and the need for system-wide fault detection, diagnosis, and prognostics provide new challenges for system specification, development, and verification approaches. The focus of these symposiums are on formal techniques and other approaches for software assurance, including their theory, current capabilities and limitations, as well as their potential application to aerospace, robotics, and other NASA-relevant safety-critical systems during all stages of the software life-cycle.

The NASA Formal Methods Symposium is an annual event organized by the NASA Formal Methods (NFM) Steering Committee, comprising researchers spanning several NASA centers. NFM 2019 was co-hosted by Rice University and NASA-Johnson Space Center in Houston, TX. It was organized by a collaboration between Rice, NASA JSC, and Iowa State University.

NFM was created to highlight the state of the art in formal methods, both in theory and in practice. The series is a spinoff of the original Langley Formal Methods Workshop (LFM). LFM was held six times, in 1990, 1992, 1995, 1997, 2000, and 2008, near NASA Langley in Virginia, USA. The 2008 reprisal of LFM led to the expansion to a NASA-wide conference. In 2009 the first NASA Formal Methods Symposium was organized at NASA Ames Research Center in Moffett Field, CA. In 2010, the symposium was organized by NASA Langley Research Center and NASA Goddard Space Flight Center, and held at NASA Headquarters in Washington, D.C. The third NFM symposium was organized by the Laboratory for Reliable Software at the NASA Jet Propulsion Laboratory/California Institute of Technology, and held in Pasadena, CA, in 2011. NFM returned to NASA Langley Research Center in 2012 in nearby Norfolk, Virginia. NASA Ames Research Center organized and hosted NFM 2013, the fifth symposium in the series. NFM 2014 was organized via a collaboration between NASA Goddard Space Flight Center, NASA Johnson Space Center, and NASA Ames Research Center, and held at JSC. NASA JPL hosted the seventh NFM in 2015 in Pasadena, CA. In 2016, the eighth NFM Symposium visited the University of

Minnesota, hosted by a collaboration between academia and NASA. Then, 2017 brought the ninth NFM back to NASA Ames Research Center. NASA Langley hosted NFM's 10th anniversary edition in 2018.

NFM 2019 encouraged submissions on cross-cutting approaches that bring together formal methods and techniques from other domains such as probabilistic reasoning, machine learning, control theory, robotics, and quantum computing among others. The topics covered by the symposium include but are not limited to: formal verification, including theorem proving, model checking, and static analysis; advances in automated theorem proving including SAT and SMT solving; use of formal methods in software and system testing; run-time verification; techniques and algorithms for scaling formal methods, such as abstraction and symbolic methods, compositional techniques, as well as parallel and/or distributed techniques; code generation from formally verified models; safety cases and system safety; formal approaches to fault tolerance; theoretical advances and empirical evaluations of formal methods techniques for safety-critical systems, including hybrid and embedded systems; formal methods in systems engineering and model-based development; correct-by-design controller synthesis; and formal assurance methods to handle adaptive systems.

Two lengths of papers were considered: regular papers describing fully-developed work and complete results, and two categories of short papers: (a) tool papers describing novel, publicly-available tools; (b) case studies detailing complete applications of formal methods to real systems with publicly-available artifacts, or substantial work-in-progress describing results from designing a new technique for a new application, with appropriate available artifacts. Artifacts enabling reproducibility of the paper's major contributions were strongly encouraged and considered in PC evaluations. Artifacts may appear in online appendices; websites with additional artifacts, e.g., for reproducibility or additional correctness proofs, were encouraged.

The symposium received 102 abstract submissions, 72 of which resulted in full papers: 54 regular papers, and 18 short papers (ten tool papers and eight case studies) in total. Out of these, a total of 28 papers, 20 regular papers and eight short papers, were accepted, giving an overall acceptance rate of 39% (a 37% rate for regular papers and a 44% rate for short papers). All submissions went through a rigorous reviewing process, where each paper was read by at least three (and on average 3.8) reviewers.

In addition to the refereed papers, the symposium featured two invited talks and a NASA panel. Representing ONERA in France, Dr. Virginie Wiels delivered a keynote talk on "Integrating Formal Methods Into Industrial Processes." Professor Richard Murray from Caltech gave a keynote talk on "Safety-Critical Systems: Rapprochement Between Formal Methods and Control Theory." NFM 2019 included a NASA panel on "Challenges for Future Exploration" featuring four NASA civil servants: Dr. Kimberly Hambuchen, Space Technology Principle Technologist for Robotics; Emily Nelson, Deputy Chief, Flight Director Branch; Joe Caram, Gateway Systems Engineering and Integration Lead; Bill Othon, Gateway Verification and Validation Lead. The panel issued challenges to the formal methods research community as NASA pushes the state of the art in certifying the integrated systems required for human spaceflight, including unprecedented requirements for autonomy and safe operation in uniquely challenging environments.

The organizers are grateful to the authors for submitting their work to NFM 2019 and to the invited speakers and panelists for sharing their insights. NFM 2019 would not have been possible without the collaboration of the Steering Committee, the Program Committee, our many external reviewers who pitched in during a U.S. Government shutdown, and the support of the NASA Formal Methods community. We are also grateful to our collaborators at Rice University's Computer Science Department, including for financial support and local organization. The NFM 2019 website can be found at https://robonaut.jsc.nasa.gov/R2/pages/nfm2019.html.

March 2019

Kristin Yvonne Rozier
Julia Badger

Organization

Program Committee

Erika Abraham	RWTH Aachen University, Germany
Julia Badger	NASA, USA
Dirk Beyer	LMU Munich, Germany
Armin Biere	Johannes Kepler University of Linz, Austria
Nikolaj Bjorner	Microsoft, USA
Sylvie Boldo	Inria, France
Jonathan Bowen	London South Bank University, UK
Gianfranco Ciardo	Iowa State University, USA
Darren Cofer	Rockwell Collins, USA
Frederic Dadeau	FEMTO-ST, France
Ewen Denney	NASA, USA
Gilles Dowek	Inria and ENS Paris-Saclay, France
Steven Drager	AFRL, USA
Catherine Dubois	ENSIIE-Samovar, France
Alexandre Duret-Lutz	LRDE/EPITA, France
Aaron Dutle	NASA, USA
Marco Gario	Siemens Corporate Technology, USA
Alwyn Goodloe	NASA, USA
Arie Gurfinkel	University of Waterloo, Canada
John Harrison	Amazon Web Services, USA
Klaus Havelund	Jet Propulsion Laboratory, USA
Constance Heitmeyer	Naval Research Laboratory, USA
Marieke Huisman	University of Twente, The Netherlands
Shafagh Jafer	Embry-Riddle University, USA
Xiaoqing Jin	Apple Inc., USA
Rajeev Joshi	Amazon Web Services, USA
Laura Kovacs	Vienna University of Technology, Austria
Hadas Kress-Gazit	Cornell University, USA
Joe Leslie-Hurd	Intel, USA
Panagiotis Manolios	Northeastern University, USA
Cristian Mattarei	Stanford University, USA
Stefan Mitsch	Carnegie Mellon University, USA
Cesar Munoz	NASA, USA
Anthony Narkawicz	Amazon Web Services, USA
Necmiye Ozay	University of Michigan, USA
Corina Pasareanu	CMU/NASA Ames Research Center, USA
Lee Pike	Amazon Web Services, USA
Kristin Yvonne Rozier	Iowa State University, USA

Johann Schumann	NASA, USA
Cristina Seceleanu	Mälardalen University, Sweden
Bernhard Steffen	University of Dortmund, Germany
Stefano Tonetta	FBK-irst, Italy
Ufuk Topcu	University of Texas at Austin, USA
Christoph Torens	German Aerospace Center, Institute of Flight Systems, Germany
Michael Watson	NASA, USA
Huan Xu	University of Maryland, USA

Additional Reviewers

Al Ghazo, Alaa
Arechiga, Nikos
Asaadi, Erfan
Bainczyk, Alexander
Bharadwaj, Suda
Bonakdarpour, Borzoo
Chen, Xin
Chen, Yu-Ting
Cubuktepe, Murat
Devriendt, Jo
Dodds, Joey
Dureja, Rohit
Ehsan, Fauzia
Elliott, Trevor
Enoiu, Eduard Paul
Fedyukovich, Grigory
Filipovikj, Predrag
Foughali, Mohammed
Fried, Dror
Friedberger, Karlheinz
Frohme, Markus
Gallois-Wong, Diane
Garoche, Pierre-Loic
Haesaert, Sofie
Herlihy, Maurice
Heule, Marijn
Immler, Fabian
Jakobs, Marie-Christine
Jansen, Nils
Jeannin, Jean-Baptiste
Jiang, Shengbing
Jones, Benjamin
Kumar, Ankit
Kunnappilly, Ashalatha
Larus, James

Lathouwers, Sophie
Lemberger, Thomas
Li, Jianwen
Li, Meng
Liu, Zexiang
Mahmud, Nesredin
Melquiond, Guillaume
Micheli, Andrea
Moscato, Mariano
Müller, Andreas
Navas, Jorge A.
Neider, Daniel
Nilsson, Petter
Peled, Doron
Prez, Ivan
Raju, Dhananjay
Ravitch, Tristan
Ren, Hao
Renault, Etienne
Rieu-Helft, Raphaël
Rüthing, Oliver
Schieweck, Alexander
Schirmer, Sebastian
Schupp, Stefan
Seidl, Martina
Sogokon, Andrew
Spießl, Martin
Tabajara, Lucas
Urban, Caterina
Vardi, Moshe
Walter, Andrew
Xu, Zhe
Zhao, Ye
Zimmerman, Daniel M.

Challenges for Future Exploration (Panel Description)

A NASA Panel

NASA Johnson Space Center

Abstract. As NASA and the world look to exploration opportunities beyond low Earth orbit, several challenges have been identified. Spacecraft and other assets that will extend human presence beyond the vicinity of Earth will have unprecedented requirements for autonomy. These systems will be subject to new environments, latent and decreased communications bandwidth, sparse logistics support, and complex system requirements. New systems, such as vehicle system management, closed-loop environmental control and life support systems, and internal robotic caretakers, are proposed to close the technology gap between the current state of the art and future exploration needs. Current approaches to integration, testing, verification, and validation are likely to be insufficient to assure the operation of these vehicles and assets given their safety-critical functions. This panel will explore the challenges NASA is currently facing in the development of these systems, particularly from the standpoint of certifying the integrated system for human spaceflight.

Panelists

- **Joe Caram** leads the Systems Engineering and Integration Team for concept maturation of the cislunar spacecraft - Gateway. His agency wide team is responsible for refining the overall concepts for the Gateway. His work includes defining the integrated system requirements, concept of operations, and element functional allocations that make up the Gateway spacecraft.

  Prior to his current assignment, Joe has held key leadership roles in various projects, programs, and organizations including the lead Flight Dynamics Officer for the X-38 Project, Aerothermodynamics Team lead for the Columbia Accident Investigation, the Systems Engineering and Integration Chief Engineer for the Space Shuttle Return to Flight, Manager of the Integrated Systems Performance Office in Constellation SE&I Office, held Deputy Manager positions in both the Systems Architecture and Integration Office and the Technical Integration Office in the JSC Engineering Directorate, and was the manager of the Exploration Mission Planning Office of the JSC Exploration Integration and Science Directorate. He is the author or co-author of 24 technical papers.

- **Dr. Kimberly Hambuchen** is currently the NASA Space Technology Mission Directorate's (STMD) Principal Technologist for Robotics. As Principal Technologist, she serves as the STMD technical expert and advocate for robotics across all

NASA centers for STMD programs. Prior to this, she was the project manager for the Human Robotic Systems project, which focused on developing and advancing technologies to integrate robotics into human exploration missions.

As a robotics engineer in the Robotics Systems Technology branch of the Software, Robotics and Simulation division of engineering at NASA Johnson Space Center, Dr. Hambuchen developed expertise in novel methods for remote supervision of space robots over intermediate time delays and has proven the validity of these methods on various NASA robots, including JSC's Robonaut and Centaur robots. She participated in the development of NASA's Space Exploration Vehicle (SEV) and bipedal humanoid, Valkyrie (R5), to which she extended her work developing human interfaces for robot operations.

- **Emily Nelson** came to JSC as an employee of United Space Alliance (USA) in September of 1998 as an International Space Station (ISS) Thermal Operations and Resources Flight Controller (ThOR). She supported on-orbit operations in ISS Expeditions 0-15, and supported ISS assembly missions ISS 2A.2A (STS-101), ISS 4A (STS-97), ISS 5A (STS-98), ISS 6A (STS-100), ISS 7A.1 (STS-105) and ISS 11A (STS-113). Emily served as lead ThOR for ISS Expeditions 3, 5, 7 and 8 and the ISS 9A (STS-112) and ISS 12A.1 (STS-116) assembly flights. In 2004 she was hired by NASA and continued to support the ISS program as a ThOR and the Constellation program as a leader in information architecture development until May, 2007.

  In May of 2007, Emily was selected as a Flight Director and began ISS support with Expedition 16 in December 2007. Emily served as an ISS Flight Director in Houston's Mission Control during the ISS 1J (STS-124), ISS ULF2 (STS-126) and ISS ULF3 (STS-129) missions of the Space Shuttle to ISS. She also supported the ISS 1JA (STS-123) and ISS 2JA (STS-127) missions as an International Partner Liaison Flight Director from the Japanese Space Agency's SSIPC Control Center in Tsukuba, Japan. Emily served as lead Flight Director for ISS Expeditions 18, 27, 33, 46 and 49 and the lead ISS Flight Director for STS-132/ISS ULF4 and the third mission of the Orbital-ATK Cygnus vehicle (the OA-2 mission).

  Emily is currently serving as Deputy Chief of the Flight Director Office, is also the lead Flight Director for a series of spacewalks to repair the Alpha Magnetic Spectrometer research platform 2019, and continues to support continuous ISS operations in Mission Control Houston.

  Team Name Each NASA Flight Director chooses a symbol/color to represent his or her team. Ms. Nelson has chosen Peridot as the symbol for her flight control team because in addition to being a lovely stone, it's a gemstone known to be found in meteorites. This "space stone" represents all of the extraordinary things, familiar and unfamiliar, we're bound to find as we pursue exploration further and further from our beautiful blue planet.

- **Bill Othon** is the acting lead of Verification and Validation for the Gateway Program. Bill's team is responsible for verifying the performance of the integrated Gateway vehicle, assembled in cis-lunar space over a number of missions and with contributions from US and international partners.

Bill is also the lead for Ground Testing for the NextSTEP cis-lunar habitat activity in the AES program. The team will conduct evaluations on a number of ground habitat prototypes developed by US Industry partners, in preparation for exploration missions in the Proving Ground of cis-lunar space.

Bill has been at JSC for over 30 years, and involved in both spacecraft operations and technology development projects. Bill has a Bachelors in Aerospace Engineering from the University of Texas at Austin and a Masters in Computer Science from the University of Houston Clear Lake.

Abstracts of Invited Talks

Safety-Critical Systems: Rapprochement Between Formal Methods and Control Theory

Richard Murray

California Institute of Technology, USA
murray@cds.caltech.edu

Abstract. In computer science, formal methods provide a set of mathematically-based techniques for the specification, development, and verification of software and hardware systems. The field of control provides the principles and methods used to design engineering systems that maintain desirable performance by automatically adapting to changes in the environment. It turns out that both of these fields have been solving similar problems using different mathematical languages for the past 50 years or so. In this talk I will discuss how a convergent set of ideas from control theory and formal methods are coming together to provide useful frameworks for reasoning about the safety of these systems, motivated by applications in aerospace systems and self-driving cars.

Biography

Richard M. Murray received the B.S. degree in Electrical Engineering from California Institute of Technology in 1985 and the M.S. and Ph.D. degrees in Electrical Engineering and Computer Sciences from the University of California, Berkeley, in 1988 and 1991, respectively. He joined the faculty at Caltech in 1991 in Mechanical Engineering and helped found the Control and Dynamical Systems program in 1993.

In 1998–1999, Professor Murray took a sabbatical leave and served as the Director of Mechatronic Systems at the United Technologies Research Center in Hartford, CT. Upon returning to Caltech, Murray served as the Division Chair (dean) of Engineering and Applied Science at Caltech from 2000–2005, the Director for Information Science and Technology (IST) from 2006–2009, and interim Division Chair from 2008–2009. He is currently the Thomas E. and Doris Everhart Professor of Control & Dynamical Systems and Bioengineering at Caltech and an elected member of the National Academy of Engineering (2013).

Murray's research is in the application of feedback and control to networked systems, with applications in biology and autonomy. Current projects include analysis and design biomolecular feedback circuits, synthesis of discrete decision-making protocols for reactive systems, and design of highly resilient architectures for autonomous systems. Murray is a co-founder of Tierra Biosciences, a cell-free synthetic biology company, and a member of the Defense Innovation Board.

Integrating Formal Methods into Industrial Processes

Virginie Wiels

ONERA, France
Virginie.Wiels@onera.fr

Abstract. Formal techniques and tools have made significant progress for the last twenty years. However, industrial adoption of these techniques is still slow, despite some prominent successes. In this talk, I will identify missing bridges between formal verification research and potential industrial deployment, such as certification constraints or progressive shift between test and formal verification, and present work done at ONERA on these subjects.

Biography

Virginie Wiels is Director of the Information Processing and Systems Department (DTIS) at ONERA, the French aerospace laboratory. DTIS conducts study and research related to methods and tools for certification, autonomy, multidisciplinary design, systems of systems, intelligence and surveillance, applied mathematics. It gathers 300 persons including 80 PhD students. Virginie Wiels received her PhD in Computer Science from ISAE in 1997. Her expertise and research interest is on formal verification of critical systems and software, and the use of formal methods for the certification of avionics software.

She has served as principal investigator on government-sponsored research programs but also on industry-sponsored research programs (particularly in collaboration with Airbus). She served on EUROCAE committee WG-71 developing new certification guidance for airborne software (DO-178C/ED-12C) with significant contributions on the Formal Methods Supplement (DO-333/ED-216).

Contents

Learning-Based Testing of an Industrial Measurement Device

Bernhard K. Aichernig[1], Christian Burghard[1,2]($\boxtimes$), and Robert Korošec[2]

[1] Institute of Software Technology, Graz University of Technology, Graz, Austria
{aichernig,burghard}@ist.tugraz.at
[2] AVL List GmbH, Graz, Austria
{christian.burghard,robert.korosec}@avl.com

Abstract. Active automata learning algorithms have gained increasing importance in the field of model-based system verification. For some classes of systems - especially deterministic systems, like Mealy machines, a variety of learning algorithm implementations is readily available. In this paper, we apply this technique to a measurement device from the automotive industry in order to systematically test its behaviour. However, our system under learning shows sparse non-deterministic behaviour, preventing the direct application of the available learning tools.

We propose an implementation of the active automata learning framework which masks this non-determinism. We repeat a previous model-based testing experiment with faulty devices and show that we can detect all injected faults. Most importantly, our technique was also able to find unknown bugs.

Keywords: Active learning · Automata learning · Model inference · Testing · Mutation analysis · Automotive case study · Testbed

1 Introduction

Due to the ever increasing complexity of industrial software and mechatronical systems, *model-based testing* (MBT) techniques have seen a popularity gain in the past two decades [13,32]. The practice of model-based testing involves the creation of a system model, using an appropriate abstraction of the *system under test* (SUT). From this model, test cases are automatically derived according to a specific test selection method. These test cases can then be executed on the SUT to either strengthen the trust in its conformance to the system model or to disprove said conformance. The sub-discipline of *model-based mutation testing* (MBMT) [3] deserves special mentioning. In MBMT, a set of *mutants*, i.e. faulty variants of the system model, is generated. Test cases are selected in order to maximize the number of mutants which can be distinguished from the original. Hence, MBMT is able to rule out the presence of specific faults and, under certain circumstances, is also able to subsume other common test-selection criteria [27].

© Springer Nature Switzerland AG 2019
J. M. Badger and K. Y. Rozier (Eds.): NFM 2019, LNCS 11460, pp. 1–18, 2019.
https://doi.org/10.1007/978-3-030-20652-9_1

However, the feasibility of MBT techniques strongly depends on the presence of adequate system models which are not always available. *Learning-based testing* (LBT) [6] is a complementary approach to the conformance testing approaches described above. Here, a learning algorithm infers a system model through interaction with a black-box system. This learned model can then be checked for the fulfilment of requirements [15,16] or for conformance to a reference model [31]. Due to its objective to explore the entire space of system behaviours without regards to a specification (restricted only by the chosen abstraction), LBT can be used for *fuzzing*, i.e. robustness testing [2,29]. The fact that LBT does not require the presence of system models is an important factor in its industrial application.

Industrial Use Case. The AVL List GmbH is the world's leading supplier of automotive test systems with over 9.500 employees worldwide. Its portfolio comprises, among other things, a wide variety of measurement devices for engine exhaust, fuel consumption, engine torque, etc. These measurement devices are usually arranged in the form of a testbed (e.g. for engines, powertrains or entire vehicles) and integrated into a *testbed automation system* which controls each device, e.g., over an Ethernet connection. In the past, we have developed two MBMT approaches to test this integration for a specific measurement device. Our first approach [4,23] used UML [28] to specify the system model. The second approach [10,11] used a *domain-specific* modelling language called *MDML*.

Summary and Contributions. In the work at hand, we present a case study regarding the application of a learning-based testing approach to the same exhaust measurement device. We further present our approach to mask sparse non-deterministic behaviour of this device to enable the use of off-the-shelf automata learning algorithms. We perform a *mutation analysis* on our LBT approach—i.e. we evaluate its fault detection capability relative to a set of mutated devices. Finally, we compare the results of the mutation analysis with those of our MBMT approaches which have been evaluated against the same set of mutants.

Our contributions are threefold: (1) Our case study provides further evidence that LBT can be successfully applied in industry and, most importantly, that it helps in finding bugs. (2) The mutation analysis shows that LBT finds more injected faults than our previous approaches with model-based test-case generation. To the best of our knowledge this is the first comparison of this kind. (3) We provide details of a mapper that speeds-up learning and masks occurrences of non-determinism.

Structure. Section 2 defines used formalisms and gives a background on active automata learning. In Sect. 3, we describe the measurement device under test and the various components of our learning setup. The learning results based on these implementations are presented in Sect. 4. We discuss related work in Sect. 5 and draw our conclusions in Sect. 6.

2   Preliminaries

2.1   Notational Conventions and Mealy Machines

Let $a \in A$ be a symbol from an alphabet A. We define *words* or *sequences* over this alphabet as $\bar{a} = [a_1, a_2, \ldots, a_n] \in A^*$ with the *empty word* ϵ and $A^+ = A^* \setminus \{\epsilon\}$. We lift symbols $a \in A$ to words $[a] \in A^*$. The set of words over A within a defined length range is written as $A^{\{m \ldots n\}} = \{\bar{a} \in A^* \mid m \leq |\bar{a}| \leq n\}$. We write the concatenation of words as $\bar{a} = \bar{a}_1 \cdot \bar{a}_2$. We write the n-fold self-concatenation of a word as $\bar{a}^n$ with $n \in \mathbb{N}_{>0}$ and $\bar{a}^1 = \bar{a}$, as well as $\bar{a}^*$ for undefined finite n. We define $last(\bar{a}) : A^+ \to A$ to return the last symbol a_n from a sequence of length n. We furthermore define the set of non-empty prefixes of a sequence $pre(\bar{a} \in A^+) = \{\bar{a}_p \in A^+ \mid \exists \, \bar{a}_s \in A^* : \bar{a} = \bar{a}_p \cdot \bar{a}_s\}$.

Definition 1 (Finite-state transducer (FST)). *A finite-state transducer is a 6-tuple $\langle Q, q_0, I, O, \delta, \lambda \rangle$ with a sets of states Q, an initial state $q_0 \in Q$, an input alphabet I, an output alphabet O, a state transition relation $\delta \subseteq Q \times I \times Q$ and an output relation $\lambda \subseteq Q \times I \times O$.*

If $\langle q, i, q' \rangle \in \delta$ and $\langle q, i, o \rangle \in \lambda$, we write $q \xrightarrow{i/o} q'$.

Definition 2 (Mealy machine). *A Mealy machine is an FST $\mathcal{M} = \langle Q, q_0, I, O, \delta, \lambda \rangle$ with δ and λ restricted to functions: $\delta : Q \times I \to Q$ and $\lambda : Q \times I \to O$.*

If a Mealy machine $\mathcal{M}$ receives an input sequence $\bar{i} = [i_1, i_2, \cdots, i_n]$, such that $q_0 \xrightarrow{i_1/o_1} q_1 \xrightarrow{i_2/o_2} q_2 \cdots \xrightarrow{i_n/o_n} q_n$, producing an output sequence $\bar{o} = [o_1, o_2, \cdots o_n]$, we write $\mathcal{M}(\bar{i}) = \bar{o}$. Two Mealy machines $\mathcal{M}_1$ and $\mathcal{M}_2$ are called *equivalent* iff $\forall \, \bar{i} \in I^+ : \mathcal{M}_1(\bar{i}) = \mathcal{M}_2(\bar{i})$.

2.2   Active Automata Learning

Active automata learning [18] is the practice of inferring the internal behaviour of a black-box system by stimulating it with inputs and observing the produced outputs. One of the most important contributions in this field was made by Angluin [7] who proposed an algorithm called L* to infer regular sets of strings from a *minimally adequate teacher* (MAT). With slight modifications, the L* algorithm was later adapted to Mealy machines [26]. The MAT framework, depicted in Fig. 1, consists of a *learner* who implements the learning algorithm, and a *teacher* who usually encapsulates the *system under learning* (SUL). The learner is able to pose two types of questions to the teacher:

Output Query[1]: Here, the learner supplies an input word $\bar{i} \in I^+$ to the teacher who responds with an output word $\bar{o} \in O^+$ with $|\bar{o}| = |\bar{i}|$. Before an output query is executed, the teacher *resets* the SUL to a defined initial state. By posing output queries, the learner constructs a *hypothesis* $\mathcal{H}$ of the Mealy machine $\mathcal{S}$ which is

---

[1] Also known as *membership query* in literature.

assumed to be implemented in the SUL. Output queries may be handled by a component of the teacher called *output oracle* which resets the SUL, executes $\bar{\imath}$ symbol by symbol, records the SUL output and compiles it into $\bar{o}$. While this task is trivial by itself, its position in the data flow allows the output oracle to enact domain-specific performance-increasing caching operations as it is able to analyse each $\bar{\imath}$ before it is executed on the SUL.

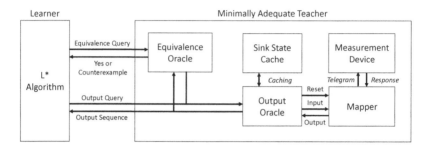

Fig. 1. *Minimally adequate teacher* (MAT) framework, including our specific implementation of the teacher.

Equivalence Query: When the learner has formed a hypothesis $\mathcal{H}$, it is forwarded to the teacher. If $\mathcal{H}$ is equivalent to $\mathcal{S}$, the teacher issues a positive response and the learning process concludes with $\mathcal{H}$ as its result. Otherwise, the teacher responds with a counterexample to equivalence $\langle \bar{\imath}, \bar{o} \rangle$ with $\mathcal{S}(\bar{\imath}) = \bar{o} \neq \mathcal{H}(\bar{\imath})$. The learner uses this counterexample and subsequent output queries to refine its hypothesis in a new round of learning. If the SUL is a black-box, equivalence queries cannot be executed directly. In this case, the teacher contains a component called *equivalence oracle*, which resolves an equivalence query into a series of output queries. In essence, the equivalence oracle performs a conformance test on the SUL with respect to the hypothesis [6]. As this approach to equivalence checking is subject to the inherent incompleteness of testing, it cannot guarantee that the learning result accurately captures the behaviour of a black-box SUL. In the work at hand, we use a guided random testing approach, described in Sect. 3.5.

2.3   Mapper

In most cases, an additional abstraction layer must be introduced between the SUL and the rest of the MAT framework, e.g., to reduce the size of an excessively large SUL state space or to augment the input or output alphabets [2]. For this purpose, Aarts et al. [1] have proposed a stateful *mapper* component to abstract the communication between the output oracle and the SUL.

Definition 3 (Mapper). *A mapper is an 8-tuple* $\langle R, r_0, C_I, C_O, I, O, \Delta, \nabla \rangle$ *with a set of states R, an initial state $r_0 \in R$, a concrete input alphabet C_I, a concrete output alphabet C_O, an abstract input alphabet I, an abstract output alphabet O, a state transition function $\Delta : R \times (C_I \cup C_O) \to R$ and an abstraction function $\nabla : (R \times C_I \to I) \cup (R \times C_O \to O)$.*

The output oracle operates on the mapper via the abstract alphabets I and O while the mapper uses the concrete alphabets C_I and C_O to interact with the SUL. If $\Delta(r, c) = r'$, we write $r \xrightarrow{c} r'$. We also use the mapper to reset the SUL to a defined initial state before performing an output query. Due to scope limitations and no direct relevance to our contribution, we cannot give a more detailed explanation of our reset operation in this work.

Definition 4 (Abstraction). *Let $\mathcal{S} = \langle Q, q_0, C_I, C_O, \delta, \lambda \rangle$ be an FST and let $\mathcal{A} = \langle R, r_0, C_I, C_O, I, O, \Delta, \nabla \rangle$ be a mapper. The abstraction of $\mathcal{S}$ via $\mathcal{A}$ is an FST $\alpha^{\mathcal{S}}_{\mathcal{A}} = \langle Q \times R, \langle q_0, r_0 \rangle, I, O \cup \{\bot\}, \delta_\alpha, \lambda_\alpha \rangle$ so that δ_α and λ_α satisfy the following inference rules:*

$$\frac{q \xrightarrow{c_i/c_o} q', \quad r \xrightarrow{c_i} r' \xrightarrow{c_o} r'', \quad \nabla(r, c_i) = i, \quad \nabla(r', c_o) = o}{(\langle q, r \rangle, i, \langle q', r'' \rangle) \in \delta_\alpha \ \wedge \ (\langle q, r \rangle, i, o) \in \lambda_\alpha}$$

$$\frac{\nexists c_i \in C_I : \nabla(r, c_i) = i}{(\langle q, r \rangle, i, \langle q, r \rangle) \in \delta_\alpha \ \wedge \ (\langle q, r \rangle, i, \bot) \in \lambda_\alpha}$$

If an abstract input $i \in I$ is received, a concrete input $c_i \in C_I$ is chosen non-deterministically, so that $\nabla(r, c_i) = i$. If no such c_i can be found, the mapper issues the output $\bot$. The abstraction of a concrete output $c_o \in C_O$ is straight-forward since ∇ contains exactly one abstract output for each c_o and $r' \in R$.

In general, it is possible that $\alpha^{\mathcal{S}}_{\mathcal{A}}$ introduces additional non-determinism through $\mathcal{A}$ that has not been present in $\mathcal{S}$. Aarts et al. [1] have defined an abstraction $\alpha^{\mathcal{S}}_{\mathcal{A}}$ to be *adequate* for a Mealy machine $\mathcal{S}$ if it introduces no non-determinism and is itself perceived as a Mealy machine. Our definition of an abstraction is based on non-deterministic SULs in the form of FSTs rather than on deterministic SULs in the form of Mealy machines. As we will explain in detail in Sect. 3, we use $\alpha^{\mathcal{S}}_{\mathcal{A}}$ to *mask* non-determinism present in our SULs. We refer to an abstraction as *sufficiently adequate* relative to a given learning algorithm[2] if the algorithm is unable in practice to distinguish the abstraction from a Mealy machine.

3 Learning Setup

We implemented our learning setup in Java using LearnLib [20], a popular open-source library for automata learning. LearnLib is available under the Apache License 2.0 and provides a multitude of implementations for different components of the MAT framework, including learning algorithms, output oracles and

---

[2] Including the equivalence oracle, since both components produce output queries.

equivalence oracles. With the exception of the learning algorithm, we have created our own concrete implementations of these components, as described in the remainder of this section. Unfortunately, LearnLib does not currently support a learning algorithm for FSTs. Therefore, we will define a mapper which masks the non-deterministic behaviour of our SULs to such an extent that the induced abstraction approximates a Mealy machine well enough for L* and related algorithms to perform successful, stable and repeatable learning runs.

3.1 System Under Learning: The AVL489 Particle Counter

The *AVL Particle Counter*—or AVL489 for short—is an automotive measurement device designed to measure the particle concentration in engine exhaust by means of laser scattering [8]. The device can be operated in one of several discrete states corresponding to different activities, abbreviated by single letters:

$$D_X = \left\{ \begin{array}{l} P \ (Pause), \ S \ (Standby), \ U \ (Purging), \ R \ (ResponseCheck), \\ Z \ (ZeroCheck), \ M \ (Measurement), \ I \ (Integ. \ Measurement), \\ L \ (LeakageCheck) \end{array} \right\}$$

The device can be remotely controlled by the testbed automation system via an Ethernet connection by means of the AK protocol [21]. The automation system always initiates the communication by sending an AK telegram, consisting of a 4-letter code. The device replies with an answer telegram, repeating back the code, followed by a data payload. Telegrams of the form S*** initiate state transitions while those of the form A*** are used to query specific device parameters or values. When transitioning between the operating states, the device may have to perform physical activities (e.g. opening/closing of valves) during which it may be unable to accept incoming commands. This behaviour is expressed by a second, orthogonal state dimension:

$$D_Y = \{R \ (Ready), \ B \ (Busy)\}$$

In the event of an operating state change, the device may simultaneously switch to *Busy*. In this case, incoming commands are refused until the device autonomously switches back to *Ready* after a few seconds. In addition, the device can be operated either remotely, as previously explained, or manually, as represented by a third state dimension:

$$D_Z = \{R \ (Remote), \ M \ (Manual)\}$$

The device can be switched to *Manual* control via the AK command SMAN. Usually, the only possible following interaction is a return to *Remote* via SREM. Neither are the commands SMAN and SREM refused during *Busy* phases, nor do they delay the return to *Ready*.

However, the *observable device state* $D = D_X \times D_Y \times D_Z$ does not uniquely identify the *actual device state* since the latter may also contain information dependent on its history or timing aspects. Generally, the properties described above are merely our expectations about the device's behaviour (based on common practice), which we intend to either confirm or refute.

We aim for an acceptable runtime of our learning setup in an industrial context. However, we also try to incorporate as little domain knowledge as possible into our learning setup, which limits our ability to perform domain-specific optimizations. Therefore, we based our learning approach on a few assumptions about our SUL which can be viewed as part of a *testing hypothesis* (cf. [17]):

Assumption 1. A: *All variants of the AVL489 measurement device examined in this work can be described as FSTs.* **B:** *The non-deterministic behaviours of each examined FST are limited to only a few isolated instances.*

Strictly speaking, we could regard each AK command as an input to our SUL and the data payload of its response as its output. For reasons described in Sect. 3.3, this is impractical. For each transition performed by our abstraction, we send multiple AK commands to the SUL. We use some of these commands to trigger a state transition and others to generate the output produced by the abstraction. Instead of substantially changing the relatively commonly used mapper definition [5,15] from Sect. 2.3, we will use the set of state setter actions $\mathcal{AK}_\mathrm{S}$, as well as the set of state retrieval actions $\mathcal{AK}_\mathrm{A}$ to describe our interactions with the device. Elements of both sets are composed of the command code and the data payload of the response. In the case of $\mathcal{AK}_\mathrm{S}$, the payload contains information about the success (Ok) or failure ($Error$)[3] of the action and in case of $\mathcal{AK}_\mathrm{A}$, it contains the observable device state D:

$$\mathcal{AK}_\mathrm{S} = \mathtt{S}\texttt{***} \times \{Ok, Error\}$$

$$\mathcal{AK}_\mathrm{A} = \{\mathtt{ASTA}\} \times D$$

Here, $\mathtt{S}\texttt{***}$ denotes the set of all S-telegrams. The $\mathtt{ASTA}$ telegram retrieves the observable device state D. Unless specified otherwise, we will use the symbols $x \in D_X$, $y \in D_Y$ and $z \in D_Z$ to refer to unspecified elements of their respective domains. We will abbreviate elements of D in the form xyz, e.g. PRR or UBz.

3.2 Masking Non-determinism with Sink States

Assumption 2. A: *If the SUL responds to an S-telegram with an Error message, the SUL state remains unchanged.* **B:** *If an $\mathtt{ASTA}$ response reveals no observable SUL state change after an S-telegram has been issued, no change of the actual SUL state has taken place.*

Based on Assumption 2, we introduced several optimizations to increase the performance and stability of the learning setup. In both cases of Assumption 2, we redirected the transition to a sink state. To cover case **B**, we introduce a dedicated output symbol *Inert* which is returned when the SUL performed a valid

---

[3] Simplified for the purpose of this work. In reality, the response to an S-command is either empty in the case of success or contains a specific error code.

self-transition. In both cases, *Error* or *Inert* are returned for all subsequent outputs until the SUL is reset. These behavioural augmentations are performed with the help of a mapper, which is described in detail in Sect. 3.3. Consequently, all self-transitions in the SUL are replaced with sink-transitions in the learned model. In a hypothetical post-processing step, these sink transitions can be easily turned back into self-transitions.

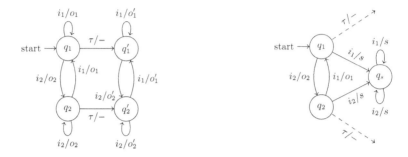

Fig. 2. Timing-induced non-determinism.   **Fig. 3.** Introducing a sink state q_s.

Our reasons for the introduction of sink states were twofold: on one hand, we attempted to prune the search space of the learning algorithm in order to increase its performance. On the other hand, the description of the measurement device as an FST yields instances of non-determinism like the one depicted in Fig. 2. These instances occur when a state q_1 exhibits both a self-transition as well as an internal transition $\tau/-$[4] to another state q_1' which is triggered after a certain amount of time has been spent in q_1. As the FST formalism does not account for the passing of time, the state q_1 is assumed to be unaltered after performing the self-transition. In reality however, each S-telegram sent to the measurement device takes several hundred milliseconds to process, effectively transitioning to a state with a reduced retention time until the timed transition is triggered. Therefore, a sequence of inputs i_1^* of sufficient length will eventually cause a transition to q_1'. The number of possible self-transitions before the time-out will most likely vary between experiments. If LearnLib encounters this behaviour repeatedly with different numbers of performed self-transitions, it will abort the learning process due to its inability to handle non-deterministic SULs.

This problem is mitigated by redirecting $\delta(q_1, i_1)$ to a sink state q_s, as depicted in Fig. 3. Once q_s has been reached, all transitions will output its specific sink label s. This modification was sufficient to keep the algorithm stable during hypothesis creation. However, in the case of loops of two or more transitions, the non-determinism cannot be masked by the introduction of a sink state. If the execution of a long *oscillating* sequence $[i_2, i_1]^*$ exceeds the time-out,

---

[4] In the notation for *labelled transition systems*, τ signifies an internal action which is not triggered via an external input. τ and inputs can be arbitrarily interleaved. "−" signifies *quiescence*—i.e. the absence of an output.

it will trigger a τ-transition in both Figs. 2 and 3. We will discuss our approach to this problem further in Sect. 3.5.

3.3 Mapper Implementation

Assumption 3. *The* ASTA *command always correctly retrieves the observable device state without influencing the actual device state.*

As explained in Sect. 3.1, the ASTA command retrieves the observable device state. According to Assumption 3, it behaves like a status message as described by Lee and Yannakakis [24]. Consequently, all interactions in $\mathcal{AK}_S$ are independent of those in $\mathcal{AK}_A$. To save further learning time, we directly incorporate Assumption 3 into the learning setup. For each individual step of the abstraction, we let the SUL perform both a state transition step, which is treated like an input, and a state retrieval step, which is treated like an output. The definition of the set of concrete input actions $C_I \subseteq \mathcal{AK}_S^{\{0,1\}} \cup \mathcal{AK}_A^{\{1\ldots n_p\}}$ allows for both S-telegrams as well as continuous polling for a timed device state change via ASTA. Hence, we may either send an S-telegram or actively wait and poll. With the maximum number of polls defined as $n_p = \lceil T_p \cdot f_p \rceil$, we choose the polling time-out $T_p = 25\,\mathrm{s}$ and the polling frequency $f_p = 10\,\mathrm{Hz}$. We choose the set of concrete output actions as $C_O \subseteq \mathcal{AK}_A^{\{0,1\}}$. With these definitions in place, an exemplary transition sequence on the concrete SUL $\mathcal{S}$ could look like this:

$$q_0 \xrightarrow{\langle \text{SPUL},Ok\rangle/\langle \text{ASTA},UBR\rangle} q_1 \xrightarrow{\langle \text{SPAU},Error\rangle/\epsilon_{\text{Error}}} q_1 \xrightarrow{\epsilon_{\text{STBY}}/\epsilon_{\text{Error}}} q_1$$

Note that, after $\mathcal{S}$ replies to SPAU with *Error*, only empty sequences of actions, i.e. no actions at all, are performed on $\mathcal{S}$. Simultaneously to this sequence performed by $\mathcal{S}$, we would like our abstraction $\alpha_{\mathcal{A}}^{\mathcal{S}}$ to perform

$$a_0 \xrightarrow{\text{SPUL}/UBR} a_1 \xrightarrow{\text{SPAU}/Error} a_{\text{Error}} \xrightarrow{\text{STBY}/Error} a_{\text{Error}}$$

Table 1. Abstractions and state transitions performed by the mapper.

Mapper state $r \in R$	Abstract symbol $\nabla(r,c)$	Concrete symbol $c \in (C_I \cup C_O)$	Successor state $\Delta(r,c)$
Input abstraction			
$\langle d, \bot \rangle$	$i \in \mathsf{S}{*}{*}{*}$	$\langle i, Ok \rangle$	$\langle d, \bot \rangle$
$\langle d, \bot \rangle$	$i \in \mathsf{S}{*}{*}{*}$	$\langle i, Error \rangle$	$\langle d, Error \rangle$
$\langle d, \bot \rangle$	$Wait$	$\overline{poll}(d)$	$\langle d, \bot \rangle$
$\langle d, s \in \{Error,\ Inert\} \rangle$	$i \in I$	ϵ_i	$\langle d, s \rangle$
Output abstraction			
$\langle d, \bot \rangle$	d' with $d' \neq d$	$\langle \text{ASTA}, d' \rangle$	$\langle d', \bot \rangle$
$\langle d, \bot \rangle$	$Inert$	$\langle \text{ASTA}, d \rangle$	$\langle d, Inert \rangle$
$\langle d, s \in \{Error,\ Inert\} \rangle$	s	ϵ_s	$\langle d, s \rangle$

Table 2. State transition and output behaviour of the sink cache.

Output $\lambda_K(K,\bar\imath)$	Successor State $\delta_K(K,\bar\imath)$	Condition
$\alpha^S_{\mathcal{A}}(\bar\imath)$	K	$\Lambda(K,\bar\imath) = \bot \wedge last(\alpha^S_{\mathcal{A}}(\bar\imath)) \notin S$
$\alpha^S_{\mathcal{A}}(\bar\imath)$	$K \cup \{\langle \bar\imath, \alpha^S_{\mathcal{A}}(\bar\imath)\rangle\}$	$\Lambda(K,\bar\imath) = \bot \wedge last(\alpha^S_{\mathcal{A}}(\bar\imath)) \in S$
$\bar{o}_p \cdot last(\bar{o}_p)^n$	K	$\Lambda(K,\bar\imath) = \bar{o}_p \in O^+ \wedge n = |\bar\imath| - |\bar{o}_p|$

Here, SPAU triggers a transition to a sink state a_{Error} which enforces the output symbol *Error* for all subsequent transitions. As suggested by this example, we choose the abstract input alphabet $I = \text{S***} \cup \{Wait\}$ as the set of S-telegrams plus an additional *Wait* symbol to abstract the polling for timed transitions. We choose our abstract output alphabet $O \subseteq D \cup S$ with the set of sink labels $S = \{Error, Inert\}$. To achieve this behaviour, we designed a mapper $\mathcal{A} = \langle R, r_0, C_I, C_O, I, O, \Delta, \nabla \rangle$. The mapper states $R \subseteq D \times (S \cup \{\bot\})$ comprise the last observed device state and either a sink label or, alternatively, $\bot$. We define the state transition function Δ and the abstraction function ∇ as per Table 1. We define the polling sequence for timed transitions as $\overline{poll}(d \in D) = [\langle \text{ASTA}, d_1\rangle \dots \langle \text{ASTA}, d_n\rangle]$ with $(n \leq n_p \wedge d_n \neq d \wedge \forall j \in \{1 \dots n-1\} : d_j = d) \vee n = n_p$.

3.4 Output Oracle Implementation

As previously mentioned in Sect. 2.2, an output oracle is ideally suited to perform caching operations on output queries to increase the performance of the learning setup[5]. In particular, we are interested in input words containing a prefix which in the past has been observed to lead to a sink state. We now know beforehand that each input word containing the same prefix will inevitably lead to the same sink state which allows us to emulate the output word without performing expensive SUL interactions. Therefore, we let our output oracle implement a sink cache, as it was previously done by Stone et al. [30]. This technique is very similar to the *prefix closure filter* for Discrete Finite Automata (DFAs) described by Margaria et al. [25] as well as Hungar et al. [19]. Emulating output words led to a substantial performance increase of our learning setup which allowed us to perform learning runs of the AVL489 device overnight.

Definition 5 (Sink Cache). *Let $\alpha^S_{\mathcal{A}} = \langle Q, q_0, I, O, \delta, \lambda \rangle$ be a Mealy machine, and let $S \subset O$ be a set of sink labels. A sink cache is a Mealy machine $\langle \mathcal{K}, \emptyset, I^+, O^+, \delta_K, \lambda_K \rangle$ with $\mathcal{K} \subset \mathcal{P}(I^+ \times O^+)$ being the set of possible cache states. δ_K and λ_K are defined in Table 2 utilizing the cache lookup function $\Lambda : \mathcal{K} \times I^+ \to O^+ \cup \{\bot\}$:*

$$\Lambda(K,\bar\imath) = \begin{cases} \bar{o}_p & \textbf{if } \exists! \; \bar\imath_p \in pre(\bar\imath), \bar{o}_p \in O^+ : \langle \bar\imath_p, \bar{o}_p\rangle \in K \\ \bot & \textbf{otherwise} \end{cases}$$

---

[5] In addition to the caching operations defined above, we also filter redundant output queries, as described by Margaria et al. [25].

3.5 Equivalence Oracle Implementation

Our equivalence oracle performs a random walk through the transitions of the hypothesis and compares the transition outputs with those produced by the abstract SUL. However, we were unable to use the standard random-walk oracle implementation of LearnLib due to two additional requirements: (1) We want to end the current sequence and start a new one when and only when the random walk chooses a transition to a sink state. Otherwise we would either waste oracle steps while being stuck in a sink state or squander the chance of testing a nearby sink transition before ending the sequence. (2) We need the ability to terminate a sequence early if the strict avoidance of sink transitions forces the random walk into an oscillating sequence. In essence, we need to *weaken* our learning setup for $\alpha_{\mathcal{A}}^{\mathcal{S}}$ to be sufficiently adequate. We mitigate this problem through an empirically chosen approach which we will describe informally due to scope limitations: After reaching a state q within the hypothesis, we assign probabilities $p_i \in [0,1]$ to each outgoing transition such that their sum equals 1. If the transition leads to a sink state, p_i is diminished relative to the other transition probabilities by a fixed factor. We also make p_i indirectly proportional to the number of times transition i has been chosen more often than the least-chosen transition originating in q. If the structure of the hypothesis funnels the random exploration into an oscillating sequence, this measure re-introduces an amount of fairness into the random choice and will eventually allow a sink transition to overrule the oscillating transitions. Dependent on the hypothesis, our equivalence oracle yielded a mean sequence length of around 30 ± 3 symbols and, within 3000 steps performed in total, a longest occurring sequence of about 100 ± 20 symbols.

3.6 Testbed Simulation Model

The AVL Test Center is tasked with testing the integration of various automotive measurement devices into the testbed automation system. As this integration needs to be tested for a multitude of different measurement device combinations and device firmware versions, it is infeasible to have all the actual devices present at the Test Center. Instead, the test engineers use a *Testbed Simulator* (TBSimu) which is able to emulate the AK interfaces of many different measurement devices over Ethernet. For our experiments, the test engineers provided us with a custom-made TBSimu model of AVL489 which can be configured to exhibit one of sixteen different implementation faults. This setup was previously used to evaluate the effectivity of both the UML-based and MDML-based MBMT approaches. Therefore, it stood to reason to use the same model for the evaluation of our LBT approach. Using the terminology of mutation testing, we will refer to the faulty configurations of the simulation model as *SUL mutants*. We named the respective mutants $\mathcal{S}_1$ to $\mathcal{S}_{16}$, as well as $\mathcal{S}_0$ for the error-free SUL. We refer to their respective learned models as $\mathcal{M}_0 - \mathcal{M}_{16}$. An overview of the individual SUL mutants is given in Table 3.

4   Results

4.1   Learned SUL Mutant Models

We ran the learning setup on each of the SUL mutants, as well as on $\mathcal{S}_0$. We then converted each learned model into a human-readable transition table. These transition tables were manually analysed and compared to the mutant specifications. Without exception, all learned mutant models showed differences to $\mathcal{M}_0$, thereby revealing the presence of errors. Some of the learned models showed partial deviations from the mutant specifications in Table 3 - either due to implementation errors or imprecise communication of the specification. Two of the learned models (specifically, $\mathcal{M}_{10}$ and $\mathcal{M}_{11}$) suggested the presence of highly unexpected behavioural anomalies within their respective SULs. These anomalies were later confirmed by manual experiments. All models, including $\mathcal{M}_0$, showed one common fault respective to our expectations from Sect. 3.1: Although the SULs were supposed to reject all commands except SMAN and SREM while in *Manual* mode, all *Manual* states accepted the same inputs as their *Remote* counterparts and reacted analogously. This effectively turned the *Manual* state space into a copy of the *Remote* state space.

Table 3. An overview of the SUL mutants, as well as mutant detection results of the LBT approach and both MBMT approaches.

ID	Mutant description	UML	MDML	LBT
1	SMAN (*Manual*) disabled in *Measurement*	✓	✓	✓
2	SMAN (*Manual*) disabled in *Integ. Measurement*	✓	✓	✓
3	SMAN (*Manual*) disabled in *Purging*	✓	✓	✓
4	No *Busy* phase when changing to *Pause*	✓	✓	✓
5	No *Busy* phase when changing to *Standby*	✓	✓	✓
6	No *Busy* phase when changing to *LeakageCheck*	✓	✓	✓
7	SREM (*Remote*) disabled in *ZeroCheck*	✗	✗	✓
8	SREM (*Remote*) disabled in *Purging*	✓	✗	✓
9	SREM (*Remote*) disabled in *LeakageCheck*	✗	✗	✓
10	Duration of *Busy* phases divided in half	✓	✓	(✓)
11	Duration of *Busy* phases doubled	✓	✓	✓
12	SMGA (*Measurement*) disabled	✓	✓	✓
13	SINT (*Integ. Measurement*) disabled	✓	✓	✓
14	SPUL (*Purging*) disabled	✓	✓	✓
15	SNGA (*ZeroCheck*) disabled	✓	✓	✓
16	Additional *Busy* phase when re-entering *Pause*	✓	✗	✓
Mutation Score (mutant detection ratio):		87.5%	75.0%	100.0%

Disregarding this common error, the models $\mathcal{M}_1 - \mathcal{M}_3$, $\mathcal{M}_7 - \mathcal{M}_9$ and $\mathcal{M}_{12} - \mathcal{M}_{15}$ were consistent with their respective mutant specifications. $\mathcal{M}_4 - \mathcal{M}_6$ showed the specified mutation for transitions triggered by $i \in$ S***, but not for $i = \mathit{Wait}$. In contrast to the specification, $\mathcal{M}_{16}$ exhibited a general mutation of all transitions $q \xrightarrow{i/PRz} q'$ to $q \xrightarrow{i/PBz} q''$. For $\mathcal{M}_{10}$ and $\mathcal{M}_{11}$, the analysis of the learning results was more complicated. We expected the algorithm to miss $\mathcal{S}_{10}$ due to its shorter Busy phases. We also expected $\mathcal{M}_{11}$ to have the latter transition of $q \xrightarrow{\text{SPUL}/UBz} q' \xrightarrow{\mathit{Wait}/PBz} q''$ changed to $q' \xrightarrow{\mathit{Wait}/\mathit{Inert}} q_{\text{Inert}}$ due to the Wait-transition exceeding our polling time-out T_p. Neither expectation was reflected in the learning results. Instead, a closer examination of the learned models and their respective SULs revealed an implementation error of the afore-mentioned timed transition. In $\mathcal{M}_{10}$, the transition was changed in a way that decoupled the timed transition from $\mathit{Purging}$ to Pause from the Busy time-out, resulting in $q \xrightarrow{\text{SPUL}/UBz} q' \xrightarrow{\mathit{Wait}/URz} q'' \xrightarrow{\mathit{Wait}/PBz} q'''$. Had $\mathcal{S}_{10}$ been imple-mented correctly, our LBT approach would most likely have missed it. In $\mathcal{S}_{11}$, the state $\mathit{Purging}$ did not exhibit a lengthened Busy phase when left via Wait but instead passed it on to Pause when prematurely left via SPAU. This caused a split of Pause into two states with different Wait-transitions (see Fig. 4).

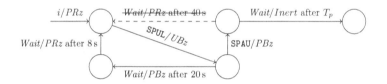

Fig. 4. Split of state $\langle Pause, Busy, z \rangle$ as captured by $\mathcal{M}_{11}$.

4.2 Discussion and Comparison to MBMT Approaches

In Table 4, we give an overview over a selection of learned mutant models with their number of states, the total number of non-redundant output queries, the number of queries executed on the SUL, the percentage of queries filtered by the sink cache, the same quantities regarding the individual steps and the total learning time. The percentage of filtered queries is consistent with the results of another case study utilizing a prefix-closure filter [25] as well as one on a version of L* optimized for prefix-closed automata [9]. With only few instances of hidden information, the device state is highly observable via the ASTA command. Therefore, the learning algorithm managed to capture their behaviour correctly in its initial hypothesis, without any counterexamples provided by the equiv-alence oracle. The only exception to this was $\mathcal{S}_{10}$ which contained states that could only be distinguished by at least two subsequent inputs. Hence, $\mathcal{M}_{10}$ was the only model to require counterexample processing, thereby yielding a high learning time despite the increased throughput of $\mathcal{S}_{10}$. In its particular case, the equivalence oracle would need to find the sequence [STBY, Wait, SPUL, Wait, Wait]

which constitutes the shortest possible counterexample to the initial hypothesis produced by L*. However, our equivalence oracle is not guaranteed to produce the shortest counterexample. Instead, it repeatedly produced longer and more indirect variants of the same counterexample.

Table 4. Comparison of selected learned mutant models in terms of state space and learning effort: C (first hypothesis correct), F (faster SUL), S (slower SUL).

ID	States	Queries			Steps			Time [hh:mm:ss]	Comment
		Total	SUL	Filtered	Total	SUL	Filtered		
0	32	4737	1593	66.4%	27972	11532	58.8%	09:52:30	C
4	32	4735	1615	65.9%	27972	11640	58.4%	09:48:01	C
6	30	4464	1512	66.1%	26100	10932	58.1%	09:51:11	C
10	36	9160	2849	68.9%	100255	34433	65.7%	15:35:40	F
11	34	5075	1667	67.2%	29268	11640	60.2%	17:15:15	C, S
12	22	3298	970	70.6%	17748	7164	59.6%	06:43:17	C
14	28	4178	1370	67.2%	25380	10500	58.6%	07:12:50	C

The LBT approach managed to distinguish all SUL mutants from the original, unlike both the UML- and MDML-based MBMT approaches. The UML-based approach suffered from performance bottlenecks in the test case generation algorithm and missed S_7 and S_9 due to its restricted exploration depth [4]. We show the combined results from all three test suites examined in the UML case study in Table 3. The MDML-based approach greatly improved upon the performance of the UML-based approach. However, at the time of its evaluation [10], it lacked an appropriate model *de-factoring* step which led to a detrimental relation between test model conciseness and test suite quality: If the system model was encoded very efficiently, small model mutations on the syntactic level could produce major changes on the semantic level. These coarse mutations led to the generation of weaker test suites. The generation of negative tests (i.e. testing the refusal of commands) was deliberately foregone in that case study to demonstrate the ability to generate useful test suites from underspecified MDML models. As a result, the common fault regarding the *Manual* mode was missed by the MDML-based approach. In contrast, automata learning techniques are only biased by the extent of the provided input alphabet and possible assumptions implemented in the mapper. The UML-based approach was evaluated against a different SUL implementation than both the MDML and LBT approaches, which may not have contained this fault. The above factors highlight the importance of careful mutant selection in MBMT approaches, as well as the relevance of *fuzzing* aspects in LBT approaches. While our learning runs take significantly more time than the execution of the generated test suites (29–96 min for UML and 12–15 min for MDML), they are still short enough to be performed overnight.

The AVL Test Center currently uses MDML models to generate test suites for measurement devices. While the use of MDML has drastically reduced the effort required for the creation and maintenance of test suites, it still requires an initial modelling effort which, in the absence of complete specifications, may involve a certain amount of guesswork. LBT on the other hand requires no a-priori modelling effort. Only the definition of an adequate abstraction is required, which can be re-used for similar SULs that share the same interface. It is also worth noting that our LBT approach is based on a significantly smaller technology stack than MDML-based test case generation, which comprised a substantial tool chain [10]. These factors make LBT attractive for our industrial use case.

5   Related Work

The most relevant related work for our use case is that of Stone et al. [30], who learned a common handshake protocol for Wi-Fi routers and had to deal with non-determinism caused by a lossy communication medium which manifested in time-out violations and message retransmissions. In contrast to our pre-emptive usage of sink states, they redirect the learning algorithm to a sink state after a non-deterministic re-transmission has already occurred. The non-determinisms were later discarded from the learning results through the repetition of output queries and a majority vote. Previously, Fiterău-Broştean et al. have employed a number of measures to deal with the same problem when learning the TCP protocol [14,15]. The authors masked time-outs by limiting the length of their output queries. De Ruiter and Poll [29] have utilized LBT to analyse TLS implementations. In their application domain, a sink state implicitly occurs when a TLS connection is closed. As their equivalence oracle, they used a modified variant of the W-Method [12] which filters prefixes navigating to this sink state. In their work on the inference of the Session Initiation Protocol [1], Aarts et al. introduced the technique of abstracting large SUL alphabets with the help of a mapper. All of the above approaches are either fully or partially based on LearnLib [20]. Both Hungar et al. [19] and Margaria et al. [25] present a number of query filtering techniques based on domain knowledge and evaluate different configurations thereof in their respective case studies. Berg et al. [9] have examined the scalability of L* on DFAs and modified the learning algorithm to perform prefix-closure filtering.

6   Conclusion and Outlook

We have created a learning setup based on LearnLib which offers a sufficiently adequate abstraction to the AVL489 measurement device and which can be executed within reasonable time. Our experiments have shown that the setup masks non-deterministic behaviour of our SUL reliably enough to enable the use of L* in AVLs industrial environment. We are confident that this method can be used to learn other systems which exhibit similar sparse (timing-induced) non-determinism. We have further shown that our learning setup is sensitive enough to uncover not only specified faults, but also unforeseen implementation errors within a measurement device simulation model. In contrast to the previously studied MBMT approaches, our LBT approach requires no initial modelling effort which makes it attractive to our industrial setting.

However, our masking of non-deterministic behaviour is still imperfect, since a hypothetical learning algorithm could issue membership queries containing sufficiently long oscillating sequences to circumvent our masking mechanism. In principle, our equivalence oracle is also able to produce oscillating sequences although we took measures to reduce their probability of occurrence.

In fact, the non-deterministic behaviour of our SUL is rooted in its description as an FST which lacks the concept of time. It is possible that AVL489 could be described as a *Mealy machine with timers*, as introduced by Jonsson and Vandraager [22] who also proposed a suitable learning algorithm. However, the absence of a respective implementation is still an issue. From an industrial point of view, LBT would lend itself to the automatic enhancement and maintenance of MDML models for regression testing. Alternatively, MDML models containing mere fragments of a device's behaviour could be used to specify requirements for the validation of learned device models.

Acknowledgements. Part of this work was supported by the TU Graz LEAD project "Dependable Internet of Things in Adverse Environments". We thank the four anonymous reviewers and Martin Tappler for their valuable feedback.

References

1. Aarts, F., Jonsson, B., Uijen, J.: Generating models of infinite-state communication protocols using regular inference with abstraction. In: Petrenko, A., Simão, A., Maldonado, J.C. (eds.) ICTSS 2010. LNCS, vol. 6435, pp. 188–204. Springer, Heidelberg (2010). https://doi.org/10.1007/978-3-642-16573-3_14
2. Aarts, F., de Ruiter, J., Poll, E.: Formal models of bank cards for free. In: Sixth IEEE International Conference on Software Testing, Verification and Validation, ICST 2013 Workshops Proceedings, Luxembourg, Luxembourg, 18–22 March 2013, pp. 461–468. IEEE (2013). https://doi.org/10.1109/ICSTW.2013.60
3. Aichernig, B.K.: Model-based mutation testing of reactive systems. In: Liu, Z., Woodcock, J., Zhu, H. (eds.) Theories of Programming and Formal Methods. LNCS, vol. 8051, pp. 23–36. Springer, Heidelberg (2013). https://doi.org/10.1007/978-3-642-39698-4_2
4. Aichernig, B.K., et al.: Model-based mutation testing of an industrial measurement device. In: Seidl, M., Tillmann, N. (eds.) TAP 2014. LNCS, vol. 8570, pp. 1–19. Springer, Cham (2014). https://doi.org/10.1007/978-3-319-09099-3_1
5. Aichernig, B.K., Bloem, R., Ebrahimi, M., Tappler, M., Winter, J.: Automata learning for symbolic execution. In: 2018 Formal Methods in Computer Aided Design, FMCAD 2018, Austin, TX, USA, 30 October–2 November 2018. IEEE (2018). https://doi.org/10.23919/FMCAD.2018.8602991

6. Aichernig, B.K., Mostowski, W., Mousavi, M.R., Tappler, M., Taromirad, M.: Model learning and model-based testing. In: Bennaceur, A., Hähnle, R., Meinke, K. (eds.) Machine Learning for Dynamic Software Analysis: Potentials and Limits. LNCS, vol. 11026, pp. 74–100. Springer, Cham (2018). https://doi.org/10.1007/978-3-319-96562-8_3

7. Angluin, D.: Learning regular sets from queries and counterexamples. Inf. Comput. **75**(2), 87–106 (1987). https://doi.org/10.1016/0890-5401(87)90052-6

8. AVL List GmbH: AVL Particle Counter - Product Guide, AT2858E, Rev. 08 (2013)

9. Berg, T., Jonsson, B., Leucker, M., Saksena, M.: Insights to Angluin's learning. Electron. Notes Theoret. Comput. Sci. **118**, 3–18 (2005). https://doi.org/10.1016/j.entcs.2004.12.015

10. Burghard, C.: Model-based testing of measurement devices using a domain-specific modelling language. Master's thesis, Graz University of Technology, Institute of Software Technology (2018). http://truconf.ist.tugraz.at/wp-content/uploads/2018/04/MastersThesis_ChristianBurghard.pdf

11. Burghard, C., Stieglbauer, G., Korošec, R.: Introducing MDML - a domain-specific modelling language for automotive measurement devices. In: Joint Proceedings of the International Workshop on Quality Assurance in Computer Vision and the International Workshop on Digital Eco-Systems Co-Located with the 28th International Conference on Testing Software and Systems (ICTSS), pp. 28–31. CEUR-WS.org (2016). http://ceur-ws.org/Vol-1711/paperDECOSYS1.pdf

12. Chow, T.S.: Testing software design modeled by finite-state machines. IEEE Trans. Software Eng. **4**(3), 178–187 (1978). https://doi.org/10.1109/TSE.1978.231496

13. Dias Neto, A.C., Subramanyan, R., Vieira, M., Travassos, G.H.: A survey on model-based testing approaches: a systematic review. In: Proceedings of the 1st ACM International Workshop on Empirical Assessment of Software Engineering Languages and Technologies: Held in Conjunction with the 22nd IEEE/ACM International Conference on Automated Software Engineering (ASE) 2007, pp. 31–36. ACM (2007). https://dl.acm.org/citation.cfm?id=1353681

14. Fiterău-Broştean, P., Janssen, R., Vaandrager, F.: Learning fragments of the TCP network protocol. In: Lang, F., Flammini, F. (eds.) FMICS 2014. LNCS, vol. 8718, pp. 78–93. Springer, Cham (2014). https://doi.org/10.1007/978-3-319-10702-8_6

15. Fiterău-Broştean, P., Janssen, R., Vaandrager, F.: Combining model learning and model checking to analyze TCP implementations. In: Chaudhuri, S., Farzan, A. (eds.) CAV 2016. LNCS, vol. 9780, pp. 454–471. Springer, Cham (2016). https://doi.org/10.1007/978-3-319-41540-6_25

16. Fiterau-Brostean, P., Lenaerts, T., Poll, E., de Ruiter, J., Vaandrager, F.W., Verleg, P.: Model learning and model checking of SSH implementations. In: Proceedings of the 24th ACM SIGSOFT International SPIN Symposium on Model Checking of Software, Santa Barbara, CA, USA, 10–14 July 2017, pp. 142–151. ACM (2017). https://doi.org/10.1145/3092282.3092289

17. Gaudel, M.-C.: Testing can be formal, too. In: Mosses, P.D., Nielsen, M., Schwartzbach, M.I. (eds.) CAAP 1995. LNCS, vol. 915, pp. 82–96. Springer, Heidelberg (1995). https://doi.org/10.1007/3-540-59293-8_188

18. Howar, F., Steffen, B.: Active automata learning in practice. In: Bennaceur, A., Hähnle, R., Meinke, K. (eds.) Machine Learning for Dynamic Software Analysis: Potentials and Limits. LNCS, vol. 11026, pp. 123–148. Springer, Cham (2018). https://doi.org/10.1007/978-3-319-96562-8_5

19. Hungar, H., Niese, O., Steffen, B.: Domain-specific optimization in automata learning. In: Hunt, W.A., Somenzi, F. (eds.) CAV 2003. LNCS, vol. 2725, pp. 315–327. Springer, Heidelberg (2003). https://doi.org/10.1007/978-3-540-45069-6_31

20. Isberner, M., Howar, F., Steffen, B.: The open-source LearnLib: A framework for active automata learning. In: Kroening, D., Păsăreanu, C.S. (eds.) CAV 2015. LNCS, vol. 9206, pp. 487–495. Springer, Cham (2015). https://doi.org/10.1007/978-3-319-21690-4_32

21. Jogun, K.: A universal interface for the integration of emissions testing equipment into engine testing automation systems: the VDA-AK SAMT-interface. Technical report, SAE Technical Paper (1994). https://doi.org/10.4271/940965

22. Jonsson, B., Vaandrager, F.W.: Learning Mealy machines with timers (2018). Preprint at http://www.sws.cs.ru.nl/publications/papers/fvaan/MMT/

23. Krenn, W., Schlick, R., Aichernig, B.K.: Mapping UML to labeled transition systems for test-case generation. In: de Boer, F.S., Bonsangue, M.M., Hallerstede, S., Leuschel, M. (eds.) FMCO 2009. LNCS, vol. 6286, pp. 186–207. Springer, Heidelberg (2010). https://doi.org/10.1007/978-3-642-17071-3_10

24. Lee, D., Yannakakis, M.: Principles and methods of testing finite state machines - a survey. Proc. IEEE **84**(8), 1090–1123 (1996). https://doi.org/10.1109/5.533956

25. Margaria, T., Raffelt, H., Steffen, B.: Knowledge-based relevance filtering for efficient system-level test-based model generation. Innovations Syst. Softw. Eng. **1**(2), 147–156 (2005). https://doi.org/10.1007/s11334-005-0016-y

26. Niese, O.: An integrated approach to testing complex systems. Ph.D. thesis, Technical University of Dortmund, Germany (2003). https://doi.org/10.17877/DE290R-14871

27. Offutt, A.J., Voas, J.M.: Subsumption of condition coverage techniques by mutation testing. Technical report, George Madison University, Fairfax, VA, USA (1996). http://citeseerx.ist.psu.edu/viewdoc/download?doi=10.1.1.83.8904&rep=rep1&type=pdf

28. OMG: OMG Unified Modeling Language (OMG UML), Version 2.5.1. Object Management Group, August 2017. http://www.omg.org/spec/UML/2.5.1

29. de Ruiter, J., Poll, E.: Protocol state fuzzing of TLS implementations. In: 24th USENIX Security Symposium, USENIX Security 15, Washington, D.C., USA, 12–14 August 2015, pp. 193–206. USENIX Association (2015). https://www.usenix.org/conference/usenixsecurity15/technical-sessions/presentation/de-ruiter

30. McMahon Stone, C., Chothia, T., de Ruiter, J.: Extending automated protocol state learning for the 802.11 4-way handshake. In: Lopez, J., Zhou, J., Soriano, M. (eds.) ESORICS 2018. LNCS, vol. 11098, pp. 325–345. Springer, Cham (2018). https://doi.org/10.1007/978-3-319-99073-6_16

31. Tappler, M., Aichernig, B.K., Bloem, R.: Model-based testing IoT communication via active automata learning. In: 2017 IEEE International Conference on Software Testing, Verification and Validation, ICST 2017, Tokyo, Japan, 13–17 March 2017, pp. 276–287. IEEE (2017). https://doi.org/10.1109/ICST.2017.32

32. Utting, M., Pretschner, A., Legeard, B.: A taxonomy of model-based testing approaches. Softw. Test. Verification Reliab. **22**(5), 297–312 (2012). https://doi.org/10.1002/stvr.456

ML_ν: A Distributed Real-Time Modal Logic

James Ortiz, Moussa Amrani$^{(\boxtimes)}$, and Pierre-Yves Schobbens

Namur Digital Institute, Computer Science Faculty,
University of Namur, Namur, Belgium
{james.ortizvega,moussa.amrani,pierre-yves.schobbens}@unamur.be

Abstract. Distributed Real-Time Systems (DRTS) can be characterized by several communicating components whose behavior depends on a large number of timing constraints and such components can basically be located at several computers spread over a communication network. Extensions of Timed Modal Logics (TML) such as, Timed Propositional Modal Logic (TPML), Timed Modal μ-calculus and L_ν have been proposed to capture timed and temporal properties in real-time systems. However, these logics rely on a so-called mono-timed semantics for the underlying Timed Labelled Transition Systems (TLTS). This semantics does not capture complex interactions between components with their associated local clocks, thus missing possible action sequences. Based on Multi-Timed Labelled Transition Systems (MLTS), which are an extension of TLTS in order to cope with the notion of distributed clocks, we propose ML_ν, an extension of L_ν that relies on a distributed semantics for Timed Automata (TA) instead of considering uniform clocks over the distributed systems, we let time vary independently in each TA. We define the syntax and the semantics of ML_ν over executions of MLTS with such a semantics and we show that its model checking problem against ML_ν is EXPTIME-complete.

1 Introduction

Distributed Real-Time Systems (DRTS) can be characterized by several communicating components (or processes) whose behavior depends on a large number of timing constraints. Such components can basically be located at several computers spread over a communication network. A DRTS can use *synchronous clocks*, i.e. they refer to a general clock; or *asynchronous clocks*, i.e. components have their own clocks, which are independent of each others and are therefore subject to clock drifts [9]. Synchronous and asynchronous models depict two forms of design, modeling and implementation of DRTS. However, the majority of current implementations of DRTS combines the advantages of both models in the so-called timed asynchronous models [9]. In such systems, the local clock of each component runs at a given rate of the global time; and components communicate with each other by passing messages that can take an unbounded time to be transmitted [9]. Formal verification methods have been used to verify the

© Springer Nature Switzerland AG 2019
J. M. Badger and K. Y. Rozier (Eds.): NFM 2019, LNCS 11460, pp. 19–35, 2019.
https://doi.org/10.1007/978-3-030-20652-9_2

logical correctness of DRTS with respect to their specification, e.g. in distributed vehicular coordination protocols [7], but also in various other areas [3,6,22,26].

To capture properties of interest in DRTS, several timed models and temporal logics (e.g., Timed Propositional Modal Logic (TPML); μ-calculus [12]; L_ν [15]; and Timed Computation Tree Logic (TCTL [24]), among others) have been used to specify sequential (mono-timed) systems. However, in these logics, the information about independent clocks and distributed components that constitute a DRTS are abstracted away, and modeled in a global setting [23]. Consequently, these logics fail at explicitly capturing timing properties related to local behavior, which shall hold only in selected parts of the whole system. In essence, this comes from the underlying semantics of the logic: since they consider automata that accept timed words, the logics adopt (variations of) Timed Labelled Transition Systems (TLTS).

Along the years, several logics appeared for explicitly taking into account distributed components and timing properties of DRTS (e.g., DRTL [17], APTL [25] and DECTL [21], among others). Roughly speaking, these logics allow for the definition of formulae whose truth values depend on (or are relative to) only part of their underlying mathematical models. In the case of APTL and DRTL, theses logics are an extension of First-Order and Second-Order Logics. In their full generality, these timed logics are generally undecidable; however, some fragments might become decidable when carefully drafted. For example for DECTL, a distributed real-time logic with independent time evolutions has been proposed, and automatically translated into a distributed event clock automaton for model-checking purposes [21]. A general limitation of these logics is the inability, at the semantic level, to distinguish transitions over different action labels and delays. Timed modal logics, on the other hand, can distinguish such transitions, and may consequently be useful for studying the behavioral equivalence by using bisimulation [18].

Timed Automata (TA) [5,15] assume clocks that progress at the same rate, and that are perfectly synchronized, with infinite precision. To achieve timed bisimulation of TA (e.g. to verify behavior preservation), several logics were proven decidable (e.g. TCTL [5] and L_ν [15]). However, this theoretical background cannot be used in the context of DRTS where different processes make use of clocks that may drift. We propose to capture DRTS as the composition of several TAs, which allows us to define Multi-Timed Automata (MTAs) [20] as the asynchronous clock product of TAs, where clocks are not synchronized. An MTA defines a common alphabet for all distributed processes, which can then interact in two ways: by synchronous discrete transitions and by asynchronous delay transitions. DRTS have another important characteristic: their behaviour may be unpredictable due to complex interactions between processes, making them sometimes non-deterministic. Since TAs are neither determinisable, nor complementable, and their inclusion is undecidable [5], we defined in [21] a formalism for capturing the behavior of non-deterministic DRTS that may be used for that purposes and are compatible with our MTAs.

ML$_\nu$ describes properties of states in a MLTS over a set of actions. We define its syntax and multi-timed semantics, and spotlight the most important features of ML$_\nu$ through the specification of DRTS.

Contributions. Our main contribution is the definition of ML$_\nu$, an extension of L$_\nu$ [15] that copes with the multi-timed semantics of MTAs and their distributed clocks, by describing properties of Multi-Timed Transition Systems' states over a set of actions. We define its syntax and (multi-timed semantics), and spotlight the most important features of ML$_\nu$ through the specification of DRTS. We show that the complexity of the model checking problem for our extended ML$_\nu$ formula interpreted over MTA is EXPTIME-complete. We focus in particular on their (multi-timed) bisimulation, and show that the extended ML$_\nu$ logic is sound and complete. Furthermore, we show several possible properties specified in the ML$_\nu$ logic for demonstrating its potential for specifying complex DRTS.

Structure of the Paper. Section 2 covers the background on multi-timed automata and their multi-timed semantics. Section 3 defines ML$_\nu$, the real-time modal logic appropriate for specifying properties of interest on multi-timed automata, and proves the decidability of the model-checking problem. Section 4 compares our work with existing contributions. Finally, Sect. 5 concludes by summarizing the results and describing future research directions.

2 Preliminaries

This section introduces the notion of multi-timed automata as an extension of the classical notion of Dill and Alur's Timed Automata [5]: instead of reading timed words denoting an action perceived by the automaton at a given time, a multi-timed automaton reads multi-timed words where actions are perceived at different times from each process composing the automaton.

2.1 Models of Time

Let $\mathbb{N}$, $\mathbb{R}$ and $\mathbb{R}_{\geq 0}$ respectively denote the sets of natural, real and non-negative real numbers. The set of all *finite words* over a finite alphabet of actions Σ is denoted by Σ^*. A timed word [5] over Σ is a finite sequence $\theta = (\sigma_i, t_i)_{1 \leq i \leq n} \in \Sigma \times \mathbb{R}_{\geq 0}$ of actions paired with nonnegative real numbers such that the timestamps sequence $t = (t_i)_{1 \leq i \leq n}$ is nondecreasing. Sometimes θ will be written as the pair $\theta = (\sigma, t)$ with $\sigma \in \Sigma^*$ and t a sequence of timestamps with the same length.

2.2 Clocks

A clock is a real-valued variable that increases with time. Thus, the value of a clock is the time elapsed since its last reset. Let X be a finite set of clock names. A clock constraint $\phi \in \Phi(X)$ is a conjunction of comparisons of a clock with a natural constant c: with $x \in X$, $c \in \mathbb{N}$, and $\sim \in \{<, >, \leq, \geq, =\}$, ϕ is defined by the following grammar:

$$\phi ::= true \mid x \sim c \mid \phi_1 \wedge \phi_2$$

A clock valuation $\nu \in \mathbb{R}_{\geq 0}^X$ over X is a mapping $\nu : X \to \mathbb{R}_{\geq 0}$. For a time value $t \in \mathbb{R}_{\geq 0}$, we note $\nu + t$ the valuation defined by $(\nu + t)(x) = \nu(x) + t$. Given a clock subset $Y \subseteq X$, we note $\nu[Y \to 0]$ the valuation defined as follows: $\nu[Y \to 0](x) = 0$ if $x \in Y$ and $\nu[Y \to 0](x) = \nu(x)$ otherwise. The projection of ν on Y, written $\nu\rfloor_Y$, is the valuation over Y containing only the values in ν of clocks in Y.

2.3   Rates

Let $Proc$ be a non-empty set of processes. A time function local to a process $q \in Proc$ is a function $\tau_q : \mathbb{R}_{\geq 0} \to \mathbb{R}_{\geq 0}$ that maps the reference time to the process' local time. Local functions must be continuous, strictly increasing, divergent, and satisfy $\tau_q(0) = 0$ for all $q \in Proc$. A rate is a tuple $\tau = (\tau_q)_{q \in Proc}$ of local time functions for each considered process. For $t \in \mathbb{R}_{\geq 0}$, $\tau(t)$ denotes the tuple $(\tau_q(t))_{q \in Proc}$ [2].

Several variants of timed automata have been proposed, extending the seminal proposal by Alur and Dill [5] in many directions. In the remaining part of this section, we briefly review multi-timed automata, with its associated notion of multi-timed bisimulation [20], and finish by introducing the L_ν [15] logic as the basis of our own logic ML_ν.

2.4   Timed Automata

Timed Automata (TA) extend Finite-State Automata with a finite set of clocks that are supposed to evolve synchronously [5]: time is thus global, and clocks are perfectly precise and synchronized. Clocks may be reset on transitions: at any instant, a clock's value denotes the time elapsed since the last reset. Transitions are guarded by clock constraints: a transition is enabled only if its associated timing constraint is satisfied by the current values of the clocks. State invariants are clock constraints assigned to locations that have to be satisfied while the location is active.

Definition 1. *A TA $\mathcal{A}$ is a tuple $\mathcal{A} = (\Sigma, X, S, s_0, \to_{ta}, I, F)$ where Σ is a finite alphabet, X a clock set, S a set of locations with $s_0 \in S$ the initial location and $F \subseteq S$ the set of final location, $\to_{ta} \subseteq S \times \Sigma \times \Phi(X) \times 2^X \times S$ is the automaton's transition relation, $I : S \to \Phi(X)$ associates to each location a clock constraint as invariant. For a transition $(s, \phi, a, Y, s') \in \to_{ta}$, we classically write $s \xrightarrow{a, \phi, Y} s'$ and call s and s' the source and target locations, ϕ is the guard, a the action or label, Y the set of clocks to be reset.*

During the execution of a TA $\mathcal{A}$, a *state* is a pair $(s, \nu) \in S \times \mathbb{R}_{\geq 0}^X$, where s denotes the current location with its accompanying clock valuation ν, starting at (s_0, ν_0) where ν_0 maps each clock to 0. We only consider *legal* states, i.e. states that satisfy $\nu \vDash I(s)$ (i.e. valuations that map clocks to values that satisfy the current invariant). The semantics of a timed automaton $\mathcal{A}$ traditionally given by a TLTS$(\mathcal{A}) = (Q, q_0, \Sigma \uplus \mathbb{R}_{\geq 0}, \rightarrow_{tlts})$ where Q is a set of legal states over $\mathcal{A}$ with initial state $q_0 = (s_0, \nu_0)$, Σ a finite alphabet and $\rightarrow_{tlts} \subseteq Q \times (\Sigma \uplus \mathbb{R}_{\geq 0}) \times Q$ is the TLTS transition relation defined by:

1. Delay transition: $(s, \nu) \xrightarrow{t} (s, \nu + t)$ for some $t \in \mathbb{R}_{\geq 0}$, iff $\nu + t \vDash I(s)$,
2. Discrete transition: $(s, \nu) \xrightarrow{a} (s', \nu')$, iff $\exists\, \phi, Y\ s \xrightarrow{a, \phi, Y} s'$, $\nu \vDash \phi$, $\nu' = \nu[Y \rightarrow 0]$ and $\nu' = I(s')$ and $a \in \Sigma$.

2.5   Multi-timed Word

A tuple $d \in \mathbb{R}_{\geq 0}^{Proc}$ is smaller than d', noted, $d < d'$ iff $\forall i \in Proc\ d_i \leq d'_i$ and $\exists i \in Proc\ d_i < d'_i$. A Monotone Sequence of Tuples (MST) is a sequence $d = d_1 d_2 \cdots d_n$ of tuples of $\mathbb{R}_{\geq 0}^{Proc}$ where: $\forall j \in 1 \cdots n-1$, $d_j \leq d_{j+1}$ [20]. This is the analog of a timed word [5].

Definition 2. *A multi-timed word [20] on Σ is a pair $\theta = (\sigma, d)$ where $\sigma = \sigma_1 \sigma_2 \ldots \sigma_n$ is a finite word $\sigma \in \Sigma^*$, where $d = d_1 d_2 \ldots d_n$ is a MST of the same length. A multi-timed word can equivalently be seen as a sequence of pairs in $\Sigma \times \mathbb{R}_{\geq 0}^{Proc}$.*

Example 1. In Fig. 1, the timestamps of the sequence of actions $\{a_1, a_2, a_3\}$ generated by the local clocks x^p, y^q, z^r associated to the processes $Proc = \{p, q, r\}$ are different for each action. A multi-timed word over $\Sigma \times \mathbb{R}_{\geq 0}^{Proc}$ is of the form $\theta = ((a_1, t_{p_1}, t_{q_1}, t_{r_1}), (a_2, t_{p_2}, t_{q_2}, t_{r_2}), (a_3, t_{p_3}, t_{q_3}, t_{r_3}))$ where $a_1, a_2, a_3 \in \Sigma$ and $t_{p_i}, t_{q_i}, t_{r_i} \in \mathbb{R}_{\geq 0}^{Proc}$ for all $i \in \{1, 2, 3\}$.

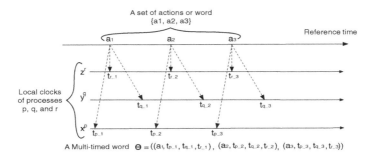

Fig. 1. Local clocks and reference time

2.6 Multi-timed Automata

Several variants and extensions of TA exists: we focus here on formalisms that allow a precise modeling of DRTS, namely Distributed Timed Automata (DTA) [14] and Timed Automata with Independent Clocks (icTA) [2]. In both formalisms, clocks may not necessarily be synchronized. However, the semantics of DTA and icTA are not expressive enough for fully modelling DRTS: their semantics rely on timed words, thus missing potential actions that may be perceived at different times by each components due to clock drifts.

We introduced in [20] the notion of Multi-timed Automata (MTA) to incorporate a multi-timed semantics, based on multi-timed words, for capturing and analyzing the local behavior of the processes and distributed clocks. An MTA is basically an icTA, but accepts multi-timed words and therefore rely on a multi-timed semantics. MTA may be used to model DTS, such as the Controller Area Network (CAN) [19], WirelessHART Networks [10], ARINC-659 protocol [11] and Distributed Vehicular Coordination Protocols [9].

Definition 3 (MTA). *A MTA is a pair $\mathcal{A} = (\mathcal{B}, \pi)$ over Proc where:*

1. $\mathcal{B}$ is a TA,
2. $\pi : X \rightarrow Proc$ maps each clock to a process.

Definition 4. *Given $\pi : X \rightarrow Proc$, a clock valuation $\nu : X \rightarrow \mathbb{R}_{\geq 0}$ and $\boldsymbol{d} \in \mathbb{R}_{\geq 0}^{Proc}$: the valuation $\nu +_{\pi} \boldsymbol{d}$ is defined by $(\nu +_{\pi} \boldsymbol{d})(x) = \nu(x) + \boldsymbol{d}_{\pi(x)}$ for all $x \in X$.*

The semantics of a multi-timed automaton is given by a MLTS [20].

Definition 5 (Semantics of MTA). *Given $\mathcal{A} = (\mathcal{B}, \pi)$ over Proc and $\tau \in$ Rates, the multi-timed semantics associated to an MTA is given by a family of MLTS over Proc, denoted by $MLTS(\mathcal{A}, \tau) = (Q, q_0, \Sigma, \rightarrow_{mlts})$. A state $q \in Q$ is composed of a location, a clock valuation and lastly the reference time, where is $Q = \{(s, \nu, t) \in S \times \mathbb{R}_{\geq 0}^{X} \times \mathbb{R}_{\geq 0} \mid \nu \models I(s)\}$. The starting state is $q_0 = (s_0, \nu_0, 0)$, where ν_0 is the valuation that assigns 0 to all the clocks. Σ is the alphabet of $\mathcal{A}$. The transition relation $\rightarrow_{mlts} \subseteq Q \times (\Sigma \uplus \mathbb{R}_{\geq 0}^{Proc}) \times Q$ is the MLTS transition relation defined by:*

1. *A transition $(q_i, \boldsymbol{d}, q_i')$ is denoted $q_i \xrightarrow{\boldsymbol{d}} q_i'$, and is called a delay transition, where $q_i = (s_i, \nu_i, t_i)$, $q_i' = (s_i, \nu_i +_{\pi} \boldsymbol{d}, t_{i+1})$, $\boldsymbol{d} = \tau(t_{i+1}) - \tau(t_i)$ and $\forall t \in [t_i, t_{i+1}] : \nu_i +_{\pi} (\tau(t) - \tau(t_i)) \models I(s_i)$.*
2. *A transition (q_i, a, q_{i+1}) is denoted $q_i \xrightarrow{a} q_{i+1}$, and is called a discrete transition, where $q_i = (s_i, \nu_i, t_i)$, $q_{i+1} = (s_{i+1}, \nu_{i+1}, t_{i+1})$, $a \in \Sigma$, there exists a transition $(s_i, a, \phi, Y, s_{i+1}) \in \rightarrow_{mlts}$, such that $\nu_i \models \phi$, $\nu_{i+1} = \nu_i[Y \rightarrow 0]$, $\nu_{i+1} \models I(s_{i+1})$, $t_i = t_{i+1}$.*

A run of a MTA $\mathcal{A}$ for $\tau \in$ Rates is an initial path in $MLTS(\mathcal{A}, \tau)$ where discrete and continuous transitions alternate.

Example 2. Figure 2 shows an MTA $\mathcal{M}$ over the finite alphabet $\Sigma = \{a, b, c, d\}$, on processes $Proc = \{p, q\}$, using clocks $X = \{x^p, y^q\}$ with the rate $\tau = (t^2, t)$ (i.e., $\tau_p(t) = t^2$ and $\tau_q(t) = t$)).

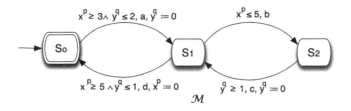

Fig. 2. A Multi-timed Automata $\mathcal{M}$ from [20]

2.7 Multi-timed Bisimulation

From a distributed approach, a mono-timed semantics is not adapted for modeling DRTS because the information about the evolution of the distributed clocks (which are not running at the same rate) over the different components is missing. In [20], the classical definition of timed bisimulation [8] has been extended towards a multi-timed semantics.

Let $\mathcal{M}_1$ and $\mathcal{M}_2$ be two MLTS over the same set of actions Σ and processes *Proc*. Let $Q_{\mathcal{M}_1}$ (resp., $Q_{\mathcal{M}_2}$) be the set of states of $\mathcal{M}_1$ (resp., $\mathcal{M}_2$). Let $\mathcal{R}$ be a binary relation over $Q_{\mathcal{M}_1} \times Q_{\mathcal{M}_2}$. We say that $\mathcal{R}$ is a strong multi-timed bisimulation whenever the following transfer property holds (note that technically this is simply strong bisimulation over $\Sigma \uplus \mathbb{R}_{\geq 0}^{Proc}$):

Definition 6 (Strong Multi-timed Bisimulation). *A strong multi-timed bisimulation over MLTS $\mathcal{M}_1$, $\mathcal{M}_2$ is a binary relation $\mathcal{R} \subseteq Q_{\mathcal{M}_1} \times Q_{\mathcal{M}_2}$ such that, for all $q_{\mathcal{M}_1} \mathcal{R} q_{\mathcal{M}_2}$, the following holds:*

1. *For every $a \in \Sigma$ and for every discrete transition $q_{\mathcal{M}_1} \xrightarrow{a}_{\mathcal{M}_1} q'_{\mathcal{M}_1}$, there exists a matching discrete transition $q_{\mathcal{M}_2} \xrightarrow{a}_{\mathcal{M}_2} q'_{\mathcal{M}_2}$ such that $q'_{\mathcal{M}_1} \mathcal{R} q'_{\mathcal{M}_2}$ and symmetrically.*

2. *For every $d = (d_1, \ldots, d_n) \in \mathbb{R}_{\geq 0}^{Proc}$, for every delay transition $q_{\mathcal{M}_1} \xrightarrow{d}_{\mathcal{M}_1} q'_{\mathcal{M}_1}$, there exists a matching delay transition $q_{\mathcal{M}_2} \xrightarrow{d}_{\mathcal{M}_2} q'_{\mathcal{M}_2}$ such that $q'_{\mathcal{M}_1} \mathcal{R} q'_{\mathcal{M}_2}$ and symmetrically.*

Two states $q_{\mathcal{M}_1}$ and $q_{\mathcal{M}_2}$ are multi-timed bisimilar, written $q_{\mathcal{M}_1} \approx q_{\mathcal{M}_2}$, iff there is a multi-timed bisimulation that relates them. $\mathcal{M}_1$ and $\mathcal{M}_2$ are multi-timed bisimilar, written $\mathcal{M}_1 \approx \mathcal{M}_2$, if there exists a multi-timed bisimulation relation $\mathcal{R}$ over $\mathcal{M}_1$ and $\mathcal{M}_2$ containing the pair of initial states.

The notion of multi-timed bisimulation extends to MTA and we have the following definition:

Definition 7 (Multi-timed Bisimilar). *Let $\mathcal{A}$ and $\mathcal{B}$ be two MTA. We say the automata $\mathcal{A}$ and $\mathcal{B}$ are multi-timed bisimilar, denoted $\mathcal{A} \approx \mathcal{B}$, iff $\forall \, \tau \in Rates$ $MLTS(\mathcal{A}, \tau) \approx MLTS(\mathcal{B}, \tau)$.*

Fig. 3. An example of multi-timed bisimulation from [20]

Example 3. Figure 3 depicts two MTA $\mathcal{A}_p$ (left) and $\mathcal{A}_q$ (right) over the alphabet $\Sigma = \{a\}$, on processes $Proc = \{p, q\}$, with clocks $X = \{x^p, y^q\}$. Suppose the rate given by $\tau = (t^2, 3t)$ (meaning that $\tau_p(t) = t^2$, and $\tau_q(t) = 3t$). Then $\mathcal{A}_p$ is bisimilar to $\mathcal{A}_q$.

2.8   Timed Modal Logic

The Timed Modal Logic L_ν is a real-time extension of the Hennessy-Milner Logic (HML) with greatest fixed-points [15]. L_ν is a modal logic that describes properties of states in a TLTS over the set of actions or symbols Σ. L_ν is specified with the following syntax:

Definition 8. *Let Σ be a finite alphabet of actions and X be a finite set of clocks, the formulae of L_ν over Σ, X and Id are defined by the grammar:*

$$\varphi ::= \; true \mid false \mid \varphi_1 \wedge \varphi_2 \mid \varphi_1 \vee \varphi_2 \mid [a]\varphi \mid \langle a \rangle \varphi \mid \exists \varphi \mid \forall \varphi \mid x \; \underline{in} \; \varphi \mid \phi \mid Z$$

where $a \in \Sigma$, $x \in X$, $\phi \in \Phi(X)$, $Z \in Id$, $[a]\varphi$, $\langle a \rangle \varphi$ are two modalities of the logic, and $\exists \, \varphi$ and $\forall \, \varphi$ are the two time modalities.

The meaning of the identifiers in Id is specified by a declaration $\mathcal{D}$ assigning an L_ν formula to every identifier in order to define properties with maximal fixpoints. A declaration is of the form $Z_i = \mathcal{D}(\overline{Z})$ where $\overline{Z} = (Z_1, \ldots, Z_n)$ and $\mathcal{D}(\overline{Z})$ is a formula over identifiers in $\overline{Z}$.

3   ML$_\nu$: A Distributed Real-Time Modal Logic

We now describe ML$_\nu$, a distributed real-time modal logic that extends L_ν [15] in order to deal with the distributed clocks that are part multi-timed automata. This allows the analysis of the local behavior of processes and clocks, as opposed to the mono-timed semantics of [15].

Syntactically, ML$_\nu$ extends L_ν by allowing to refer to local clocks in two modalities (namely, in $\underline{in}$ and $\sim$): clocks are related to their enclosing process (e.g., x^p says that clock $x \in X$ belongs to process $p \in Proc$). In that sense, ML$_\nu$ is a proper extension of L_ν: when there is only one process, formulas from ML$_\nu$ are compatible with formulas of L_ν with the same meaning.

We adopt a classical presentation by first detailing the syntax, then the semantics of ML$_\nu$, interpreted over MTAs. We then prove a theorem that state that bisimilar (semantic) states over the same clock valuation satisfy the same ML$_\nu$ formulas, opening the way to prove that MTAs are bisimilar iff they satisfy the same ML$_\nu$ formulae.

3.1 Syntax of ML$_\nu$

ML$_\nu$ is a multi-timed modal logic that extends the L$_\nu$ over distributed clocks. The syntax of ML$_\nu$ is given in the following definition.

Definition 9. *Let Σ be a finite alphabet, X be a finite set of clocks, Proc be a set of processes, $\pi : X \rightarrow$ Proc be a function mapping clocks to their owning process, and Id a set of identifiers. The set ML$_\nu$ of formulas over Σ, X, π and Id is defined by the following grammar:*

$$\varphi ::= \ true \mid false \mid \varphi_1 \wedge \varphi_2 \mid \varphi_1 \vee \varphi_2 \mid [a]\varphi \mid \langle a \rangle \varphi$$
$$\mid \exists \varphi \mid \forall \varphi \mid x^p \ \underline{in} \ \varphi \mid \phi \mid \ x^p + c \sim y^p + d \mid Z$$

where $a \in \Sigma$; $p \in$ Proc; $x^p, y^p \in X$; $c, d \in \{0, \cdots, k\}$ (with $k \in \mathbb{N}_{>0}$); $Z \in$ Id; $\phi \in \Phi(X)$ a clock constraint; $\sim \in \{=, >, \geq, <, \leq\}$.

The meaning of identifiers is captured by a declaration environment $\mathcal{D}$ assigning an ML$_\nu$ formula to each identifier. We abbreviate $Z \overset{\text{def}}{=} \varphi$ when $\mathcal{D}(Z) = \varphi$ and $\mathcal{D}$ is clear from context.

Let $\mathcal{A}$ be a MTA over *Proc* and $\tau \in$ Rates and assume that MLTS$(\mathcal{A}, \tau) = (Q, q_0, \Sigma, \rightarrow_{mlts})$ gives its semantics. Now, we interpret L$_\nu$ formulas over extended states. An extended state over Q is a pair (q, μ), where $q \in Q$ is a MLTS state (Definition 5) and μ a valuation for the formula clocks in X. An extended state satisfies an identifier Z if it belongs to maximal fixpoint of the equation $Z = \mathcal{D}(Z)$. The formal semantics of ML$_\nu$ formulas interpreted over MLTS$(\mathcal{A}, \tau)$ is given by the satisfaction relation $\models$ defined as the largest relation satisfying the equivalences in Definition 9.

Intuitively, a formula $x^p \ \underline{in} \ \varphi$ introduces a (formula) clock x^p (for process $p \in Proc$) and initializes it to 0: an extended state satisfies such a formula provided the modified state with x^p being reset to 0 satisfies φ. The introduced formula clocks are used inside formulas with comparison $\sim$: an extended state satisfies such a formula iff the values for clocks satifies the given comparison. The operators $\exists$ and $\forall$ denote existential and universal quantification over delay transitions: $\exists\varphi$ (resp. $\forall\varphi$) holds in an extended state if there is a (resp. if every) delay transition leads to a state satisfying φ. Similarly, the diamond and boxed modal operators denote existential and universal quantification over discrete transitions: $\langle a \rangle \varphi$ (resp. $[a]\varphi$) holds on an extended state from which it is possible to perform an a-action towards a state (resp. all states reachable from an a-action) where φ holds. An extended state satisfies Z if the state satisfies the declaration $\mathcal{D}(Z)$.

3.2 Semantics of ML$_\nu$

The following definition provides formal grounds for the intuitive explanation.

Definition 10. *Let Σ be a finite alphabet, X be a finite set of clocks and Proc be a set of processes. The semantics of formulae in ML$_\nu$ is implicitly given with respect to a given MLTS inductively as follows:*

$$
\begin{aligned}
(q,\mu) &\models & true && \Leftrightarrow\ true \\
(q,\mu) &\models & false && \Leftrightarrow\ false \\
(q,\mu) &\models & \varphi_1 \wedge \varphi_2 && \Leftrightarrow\ (q,\mu) \models \varphi_1 \ and\ (q,\mu) \models \varphi_2 \\
(q,\mu) &\models & \varphi_1 \vee \varphi_2 && \Leftrightarrow\ (q,\mu) \models \varphi_1 \ or\ (q,\mu) \models \varphi_2 \\
(q,\mu) &\models & \phi && \Leftrightarrow\ \mu \models \phi\ for\ \phi \in \Phi(X) \\
(q,\mu) &\models & [a]\varphi && \Leftrightarrow\ \forall q \xrightarrow{a}_{mlts} q',\ (q',\mu) \models \varphi \\
(q,\mu) &\models & \langle a\rangle\varphi && \Leftrightarrow\ \exists q \xrightarrow{a}_{mlts} q',\ (q',\mu) \models \varphi \\
(q,\mu) &\models & x^p\ \underline{in}\ \varphi && \Leftrightarrow\ (q,\mu[x^p \to 0]) \models \varphi \\
(q,\mu) &\models & \exists\varphi && \Leftrightarrow\ \exists \boldsymbol{d} \in \mathbb{R}^{Proc}_{>0},\ \exists q' \in Q,\ such\ that\ q \xrightarrow{d}_{mlts} q', \\
&&&& (q,\mu +_\pi \boldsymbol{d}) \models \varphi \\
(q,\mu) &\models & \forall\varphi && \Leftrightarrow\ \forall \boldsymbol{d} \in \mathbb{R}^{Proc}_{>0},\ \forall q' \in Q,\ such\ that\ q \xrightarrow{d}_{mlts} q', \\
&&&& (q,\mu +_\pi \boldsymbol{d}) \models \varphi \\
(q,\mu) &\models\ x^p + c \sim y^p + d &&\Leftrightarrow \mu(x^p) + c \sim \mu(y^p) + d \\
(q,\mu) &\models & Z && the\ maximal\ fixpoint\ in\ \mathcal{D}(Z)
\end{aligned}
$$

Two formulae are equivalent iff they are satisfied by the same set of extended states in every MLTS.

Definition 11. *A state q in a MLTS satisfies a formula φ, iff $(q,\mu_0) \models \varphi$ where μ_0 is the clock valuation that maps each formula clock to zero.*

Definition 12. *Let $\mathcal{A}$ be a MTA and $\varphi \in$ ML$_\nu$, then $\mathcal{A} \models \varphi$ iff $\forall \tau \in$ Rates, MLTS$(\mathcal{A}, \tau) \models \varphi$.*

Let φ be a closed formula, then the set of extended states satisfying φ is independent of the valuation μ for the formula clocks. Hence, if φ is closed then for each state q in a MLTS and valuations μ, μ' for the formula clocks, we can get that $(q,\mu) \models \varphi$ iff $(q,\mu') \models \varphi$. Therefore, when φ is closed it makes sense to speak of a state q satisfying φ.

Theorem 1. *Let Proc be a set of processes. Let $\mathcal{M} = (Q, q_0, \Sigma, \to_{mlts})$ be a MLTS and q_1, q_2 be multi-timed bisimilar states in Q. Let μ be a clock valuation for the formula clocks in X, then the extended states (q_1,μ) and (q_2,μ) satisfy exactly the same formulae in ML$_\nu$.*

Proof. Assume that q_1, q_2 are multi-timed bisimilar states in Q. Let μ be a clock valuation for the formula clocks in X. Assume that $(q_1,\mu) \models \varphi$ for some formula $\varphi \in ML_\nu$. Using structural induction on φ, we shall prove that $(q_2,\mu) \models \varphi$. By symmetry, this is enough to establish that (q_1,μ) and (q_2,μ) satisfy the same formulae in ML$_\nu$.

The proof proceeds by a case analysis on the form of φ. Here, we present the details only for four modalities $\forall\,\varphi_1$, the other modalities can be proved in the same way. Our inductive hypothesis is that, for all states r_1 and r_2, if r_1 and r_2 are multi-timed bisimilar and $(r_1, \mu') \models \varphi_1$ for some valuation μ' of the formula clocks, then $(r_2, \mu') \models \varphi_1$. Using this hypothesis, we shall prove that:

- $(q_2, \mu) \models \forall\,\varphi_1$: To this end, assume that, for every $d \in \mathbb{R}_{\geq 0}^{Proc}$, for all $q_2' \in Q$, $q_2 \xrightarrow{d}_{mlts} q_2'$. We wish to show that $(q_2', \mu +_\pi d) \models \varphi_1$. Now, since q_1 and q_2 are multi-timed bisimilar and $q_2 \xrightarrow{d}_{mlts} q_2'$, there is a state $q_1' \in Q$, $q_1 \xrightarrow{d}_{mlts} q_1'$ and q_1' is multi-timed bisimilar to q_2'. By our supposition that $(q_1, \mu) \models \varphi$, we have that $(q_1', \mu +_\pi d) \models \varphi_1$. The inductive hypothesis yields that $(q_2', \mu +_\pi d) \models \varphi_1$. Since q_2' and d were arbitrary we may conclude that $(q_2, \mu) \models \forall\,\varphi_1$, which was to be shown.

- $(q_2, \mu) \models \exists\,\varphi_1$: To this end, assume that, there is some $d \in \mathbb{R}_{\geq 0}^{Proc}$, there is some $q_2' \in Q$, $q_2 \xrightarrow{d}_{mlts} q_2'$. We wish to show that $(q_2', \mu +_\pi d) \models \varphi_1$. Now, since q_1 and q_2 are multi-timed bisimilar and $q_2 \xrightarrow{d}_{mlts} q_2'$, there is a state $q_1' \in Q$, $q_1 \xrightarrow{d}_{mlts} q_1'$ and q_1' is multi-timed bisimilar to q_2'. By our supposition that $(q_1, \mu) \models \varphi$, we have that $(q_1', \mu_\pi + d) \models \varphi_1$. The inductive hypothesis yields that $(q_2', \mu_\pi + d) \models \varphi_1$. Since q_2' and d were arbitrary we may conclude that $(q_2, \mu) \models \exists\,\varphi$, which was to be shown.

- $(q_2, \mu) \models y^p \; in \; \varphi_1$. To this end, assume that, for some $y^p \in X$, for $p \in Proc$, such that $(q_2, \mu[y^p \to 0]) \models \varphi_1$. Now, since q_1 and q_2 are multi-timed bisimilar and by our supposition that $(q_1, \mu) \models y^p \; in \; \varphi$ for some $y^p \in X$ for $p \in Proc$, we have that $(q_1, \mu[y^p \to 0]) \models \varphi$ reset y^p to 0.

- $(q_2, \mu) \models y^p \; + \; c \sim x^p \; + \; d$. To this end, assume that, for some $y^p, x^p \in X$ for $p \in Proc$, for some $c, d \in \mathbb{N}$ such that $\mu(y^p) + c \sim \mu(x^p) + d$. Now, since q_1 and q_2 are multi-timed bisimilar and by our supposition that $(q_1, \mu) \models y^p \; + \; c \sim x^p \; + \; d$ for some $y^p, x^p \in X$ for $p \in Proc$, for some $c, d \in \mathbb{N}$, we have that $\mu(y^p) + c \sim \mu(x^p) + d$.

As an immediate consequence of Theorem 1, by instantiating its results to the initial state of MLTS $\mathcal{M}_1$ and $\mathcal{M}_2$, we obtain the following result.

Lemma 1. *If $\mathcal{M}_1$ and $\mathcal{M}_2$ are multi-timed bisimilar, i.e. $\mathcal{M}_1 \approx \mathcal{M}_2$, and $\mathcal{M}_1 \models \varphi$ then $\mathcal{M}_2 \models \varphi$.*

Since MTA provide a formalism for the finite description of MLTS and the clock constraints are exactly the same as those present in the syntax of the logic ML$_\nu$, then we obtain the following result.

Theorem 2. *Let $\mathcal{A}_1$ and $\mathcal{A}_2$ be two MTA and $\varphi \in$ ML$_\nu$. If $(\mathcal{A}_1 \models \varphi$ iff $\mathcal{A}_2 \models \varphi)$ then $\mathcal{A}_1 \approx \mathcal{A}_2$.*

Proof (sketch). A proof of this theorem may be obtained from the characteristic property of TA [15].

As an immediate consequence of the above Theorem 2 and Lemma 1, we obtain the following result.

Lemma 2. *Given two MTA $\mathcal{A}_1$ and $\mathcal{A}_2$, if $\mathcal{A}_1 \approx \mathcal{A}_2$ and $\mathcal{A}_1 \models \varphi$ then $\mathcal{A}_2 \models \varphi$.*

3.3   Examples of Properties

Here, we use ML_ν formulas to express multi-timed properties.

Example 4. Consider the MTA $\mathcal{A}_q$ described in Fig. 3 right. The initial state (q_0, μ_0) (i.e., $q_0 = (T_0, \nu_0)$) satisfies the following ML_ν formula φ:

$$\varphi = y^q \ \underline{in} \ \exists (3 \geq y^q \geq 1 \ \wedge \ \langle a \rangle \ true)$$

Intuitively, this formula means that the action a can be performed by the process q after a delay between 1 and 3, for instance 2 time units.

Example 5. Consider the MTA $\mathcal{M}$ described in Fig. 2. The initial state (q_0, μ_0) (i.e., $q_0 = (S_0, \nu_0)$) satisfies the following ML_ν formula φ:

$$\varphi = y^q \ \underline{in} \ \exists (3 \geq y^q \geq 1 \ \wedge \ \langle a \rangle \ S_1) \wedge \ (x^p \geq 1 \ \wedge \ \langle a \rangle \ S_1)$$

Intuitively, this formula means that the action a can be performed by the process q after a delay between 1 and 3, for instance 2 and the action a can be performed by the process p after a delay 1 time units.

Example 6. Consider the MTA $\mathcal{A}$ described in Fig. 4. The state (q_1, μ_1) (i.e., $q_1 = (S_1, \nu_1)$) satisfies the following ML_ν formula φ:

$$Z_{S_1} = x^p \ \underline{in} \ \exists (x^p \leq 10 \ \wedge \ \langle b \rangle \ Z_{S_1}) \wedge [b] \ (x^p \leq 10 \ \wedge \ x^p \ \underline{in} \ Z_{S_1}) \wedge \forall \ Z_{S_1} \vee$$
$$y^q \ \underline{in} \ \exists (y^q \leq 9 \ \wedge \ \langle b \rangle \ S_0) \wedge \ x^p \ \underline{in} \ (\langle b \rangle \ S_0)$$

Intuitively, this formula means that the action b can be performed by the process p before a delay 10 time units (self-loop) or the action b can be performed by the process q before a delay 9 time units.

Example 7. The initial state (q_0, μ_0) satisfies the following ML_ν formula φ:

$$\varphi = x^p \ \underline{in} \ \exists (x^p \geq 1 \ \wedge \ (\langle a \rangle \ true \ \vee \ \langle b \rangle \ true))$$

Intuitively, this formula means that the action a or b can be performed by the process p before a delay 1 time units.

Example 8. Consider the two MTA $\mathcal{A}_p$ (left) and $\mathcal{A}_q$ (right) in Fig. 3 with the alphabet $\Sigma = \{a\}$, the set of processes $Proc = \{p, q\}$, the set of clocks $X = \{x^p, y^q\}$ and without invariants (i.e, all the invariants are true). We could combine two MTA to a single new one, where their interactions are determined by synchronous discrete transitions and asynchronous delay transitions (all clocks of the composition evolve independently with time). For sake of readability, we have renamed the action in Σ to a_p and a_q. Thus, we also could combine two formulas to a single new one, where the initial state (q_0, μ_0) is the conjunction the two initial state of $\mathcal{A}_p$ and $\mathcal{A}_q$. We could describe the multi-timed bisimulation with a single formula in ML$_\nu$. The initial state (q_0, μ_0) satisfies the following ML$_\nu$ formula φ:

$$\varphi = (\ [a_p]\langle a_q \rangle\ (x^p\ \underline{in}\ \exists (3 \geq x^p \geq 1\ \wedge\ \langle a_p \rangle\ true)))\wedge$$
$$(\ [a_q]\langle a_p \rangle\ (y^q\ \underline{in}\ \exists (3 \geq y^q \geq 1\ \wedge\ \langle a_q \rangle\ true))).$$

Intuitively, this formula means that the action a_p and a_q can be performed by the process p and q after a delay between 1 and 3, for instance 2 time units.

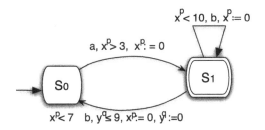

Fig. 4. A Multi-timed Automata $\mathcal{A}$

3.4   Reachability Problem

Region graph and zone graph constructions can be used for analyzing reachability and other properties in MTA (and TA) [5,20]. These graphs have sizes exponential in the number of clocks of the (multi)-timed automaton. The algorithms for model checking depend on the sizes of these graphs. Reachability algorithms based on zone graphs were extended to deal with the parallel composition of MTA [20]. Reachability problems for a single MTA as well as for a composition of MTA (or Network of TA) are both PSPACE-complete [1,20]. Using the zone graphs, we can define a symbolic multi-timed zone automaton for a MTA $\mathcal{A}$ (or the parallel composition of two MTA $\mathcal{A} \parallel \mathcal{B}$) which is a finite transition system, called the multi-timed zone graph [20], whose states are pairs $q = (s, \mathcal{Z})$ where s is a location of MTA $\mathcal{A}$ and $\mathcal{Z}$ a clock zone. Formulas in ML$_\nu$ can then be interpreted over the states of the zone graph as it is done for L$_\nu$ [15].

Theorem 3 ([1,20]). *The reachability problem is PSPACE-complete for MTA and TA.*

3.5   Model Checking

Here, we consider the model checking problem of ML_ν sentences on MTA models. This problem consists, given a ML_ν sentence φ and an MTA $\mathcal{A}$, in deciding whether the relation $\mathcal{A} \models \varphi$ holds.

Theorem 4. *The model checking problem of ML_ν on MTA is EXPTIME-complete.*

Proof. EXPTIME-hardness: The proof follows from the EXPTIME-hardness of the model-checking of the logic L_ν over TA [1], as MTA are an extension of TA and ML_ν is the corresponding extension of L_ν: If we use a single process, $ML_\nu = L_\nu$ and MTA = TA.

Proof. EXPTIME-membership: To prove EXPTIME-membership, we use the idea suggested in [15]. Let $\mathcal{A}$ be a MTA, $\varphi \in ML_\nu$, K the number of clocks of the automaton $\mathcal{A}$, C the maximal constant of $\mathcal{A}$ and φ, n the nesting depth of greatest fixpoint quantifier in φ. We consider the region graph $Regions(\mathcal{A}, \varphi)$ [5] associated with $\mathcal{A}$ and the formula φ with clocks X. The region graph depends on the maximal constants with which clocks are compared in $\mathcal{A}$ and φ. Using the region graph $Regions(\mathcal{A}, \varphi)$, model checking ML_ν formulas can be done in time that is exponential in the number of K, C and n. This can be shown in a similar fashion as [15].

Following [4], $\mathcal{A} \models \varphi$ iff $\mathcal{A}' \models \varphi$, where $\mathcal{A}' = untimed(\mathcal{A})$ is the untimed automaton associated with $\mathcal{A}$ and φ (the region graph $Regions(\mathcal{A}, \varphi)$). The size of $\mathcal{A}'$ is exponential in the length of the timing constraints of the given MTA automaton and in the length of the formula φ (assuming binary encoding of the constants), that is, $|\mathcal{A}'| = O((|S| + | \rightarrow_{ta} |) \cdot K! \cdot 2^K \cdot C^K)$. The region graph $\mathcal{A}'$ can be constructed in linear time, which is also bounded by $O((|S| + | \rightarrow_{ta} |) \cdot K! \cdot 2^K \cdot C^K)$ [4]. On the region graph, untimed model checking can be performed in time $O((|\varphi| \cdot |\mathcal{A}'|)$. Clearly we obtain an algorithm of time complexity $O(|\varphi| \cdot (|S| + | \rightarrow_{ta} |) \cdot K! \cdot 2^K \cdot C^K)^{|\varphi|}$.

4   Related Work

Similarly to the various extensions of Timed Automata for coping with distributed systems and their potential unsynchronized clocks, modal logics followed to be able to capture properties of interest adequately. Modal logic has been extended with time and recursion in [15]. The same authors showed that model-checking and satisfiability (for a bounded number of clocks and values of the constants) are decidable over TA. In [1], the model-checking problem for the logic L_ν over TA is PSPACE-complete. In [16], has been studied the Recursive Weighted Logic (RWL), a modal logic that expresses qualitative and quantitative properties. The satisfiability problem for RWL is decidable by applying a variant of the region technique developed for TA.

There are several logics that have been defined in order to capture aspects of quantitative timing information and distributed properties, such as DRTL [17], APTL [25] and DECTL [21]. In these logics it is possible to define formulae whose truth values depend on (or are relative to) only part of their underlying mathematical models. In the case of DRTL and APTL, theses logics are an extension of Second-Order Logic (SOL) and First-Order Logic (FOL) where the set of formulae are composed of constants, functions, predicates universal and existential quantifiers and logical connectives from FOL. In the case of DECTL, a distributed real-time logic with independent time evolutions is proposed. This logic can be model-checked by translating a DECTL formula into a distributed event clock automaton [21]. In general, this timed temporal logic do not make use of different action labels and delay i.e. it is interpreted over Timed Labelled Transition System (TLTS).

5   Conclusions

Distributed Real-Time Systems that are modeled with mono-timed semantics [10,11,19] may cause actions or events generated at the same instant of a reference time to have different timestamps given by local clocks of distributed processes. As a consequence, logics aligned with this semantics may not capture such subtle behaviors. In this paper, we have proposed the basis of a framework for specifying DRTS through of the introduction of distributed (or independent) clocks, inspired by MTA [20]. We presented ML$_\nu$, a logic interpreted on MTA, which have the capability to accept multi-timed words, and possess a multi-timed semantics [20]. ML$_\nu$ is an extension of the modal logic L$_\nu$ [15], tailored for multi-timed semantics over MTA. We defined its syntax and semantics, and showed that the model-checking problem over Multi-Timed Automata is EXP-TIME-complete, by analogy to L$_\nu$.

The *satisfiability checking* problem, which is the dual of the model checking problem, is to check whether a given φ formulae is satisfied by a multi-timed automaton $\mathcal{A}$. Formally, let φ be a ML$_\nu$ formula and $\mathcal{A}$ be a MTA, then the satisfiability problem ($\mathcal{A} \models \varphi$) is decidable.

Currently, the satisfiability problem for L$_\nu$ has been shown undecidable (in fact, even for its non-recursive fragment) [13]. The satisfiability problem for the Recursive Weighted Logic (RWL) has been shown decidable by applying a variant of the region technique developed for TA [16]. We could explore the possibility of using the technique presented in [16] in order to exploit a recent decidability result [13,16].

As a future work, we plan to specify and implement a prototype algorithm for model-checking, and envisage to study the satisfiability of ML$_\nu$, by exploiting recent decidability results on Recursive Weighted Logic [16], which presents similar features.

References

1. Aceto, L., Laroussinie, F.: Is your model checker on time? In: Kutyłowski, M., Pacholski, L., Wierzbicki, T. (eds.) MFCS 1999. LNCS, vol. 1672, pp. 125–136. Springer, Heidelberg (1999). https://doi.org/10.1007/3-540-48340-3_12
2. Akshay, S., Bollig, B., Gastin, P., Mukund, M., Narayan Kumar, K.: Distributed timed automata with independently evolving clocks. In: van Breugel, F., Chechik, M. (eds.) CONCUR 2008. LNCS, vol. 5201, pp. 82–97. Springer, Heidelberg (2008). https://doi.org/10.1007/978-3-540-85361-9_10
3. Al-Bataineh, O.I., Reynolds, M., French, T., Woodings, T.: Verifying real-time commit protocols using dense-time model checking technology. CoRR, volume 1201-3416 (2012)
4. Alur, R.: Techniques for automatic verification of real-time systems. Ph.D. thesis, Stanford University, CA, USA (1992)
5. Alur, R., Dill, D.L.: A theory of timed automata. Theor. Comput. Sci. **126**(2), 183–235 (1994). https://doi.org/10.1016/0304-3975(94)90010-8
6. Anier, A., Vain, J., Tsiopoulos, L.: DTRON: a tool for distributed model-based testing of time critical applications. Proc. Est. Acad. Sci. **66**, 75 (2017)
7. Asplund, M.: Automatically proving the correctness of vehicle coordination. ICT Express **4**, 51–54 (2018). SI: CI & Smart Grid Cyber Security
8. Čerāns, K.: Decidability of bisimulation equivalences for parallel timer processes. In: von Bochmann, G., Probst, D.K. (eds.) CAV 1992. LNCS, vol. 663, pp. 302–315. Springer, Heidelberg (1993). https://doi.org/10.1007/3-540-56496-9_24
9. Cristian, F.: Synchronous and asynchronous. Commun. ACM **39**, 273–297 (1996)
10. De Biasi, M., Snickars, C., Landernäs, K., Isaksson, A.: Simulation of process control with wirelesshart networks subject to clock drift. In: Proceedings of the 2008 32nd Annual IEEE International Computer Software and Applications Conference COMPSAC 2008 (2008)
11. Gwaltney, D.A., Briscoe, J.M.: Comparison of communication architectures for spacecraft modular avionics systems. Technical Report 214431, NASA (2006). http://www.sti.nasa.gov/
12. Henzinger, T.A., Nicollin, X., Sifakis, J., Yovine, S.: Symbolic model checking for real-time systems. Inf. Comput. **111**(2), 193–244 (1994)
13. Jaziri, S., Larsen, K.G., Mardare, R., Xue, B.: Adequacy and complete axiomatization for timed modal logic. Electr. Notes Theor. Comput. Sci. **308**, 183–210 (2014)
14. Krishnan, P.: Distributed timed automata. In: Workshop on Distributed Systems, vol. 28 (1999)
15. Laroussinie, F., Larsen, K.G., Weise, C.: From timed automata to logic — and back. In: Wiedermann, J., Hájek, P. (eds.) MFCS 1995. LNCS, vol. 969, pp. 529–539. Springer, Heidelberg (1995). https://doi.org/10.1007/3-540-60246-1_158
16. Larsen, K.G., Mardare, R.: Complete proof systems for weighted modal logic. Theor. Comput. Sci. **546**, 164–175 (2014)
17. Mall, R., Patnaik, L.: Specification and verification of timing properties of distributed real-time systems (1990)
18. Milner, R.: Communication and Concurrency. PHI Series in Computer Science. Prentice Hall, New York (1989)
19. Monot, A., Navet, N., Bavoux, B.: Impact of clock drifts on CAN frame response time distributions. In: 16th IEEE International Conference on Emerging Technologies and Factory Automation - ETFA, Toulouse, France, p. 2011, September 2011

20. Ortiz, J., Amrani, M., Schobbens, P.-Y.: Multi-timed bisimulation for distributed timed automata. In: Barrett, C., Davies, M., Kahsai, T. (eds.) NFM 2017. LNCS, vol. 10227, pp. 52–67. Springer, Cham (2017). https://doi.org/10.1007/978-3-319-57288-8_4

21. Ortiz, J., Legay, A., Schobbens, P.-Y.: Distributed event clock automata. In: Bouchou-Markhoff, B., Caron, P., Champarnaud, J.-M., Maurel, D. (eds.) CIAA 2011. LNCS, vol. 6807, pp. 250–263. Springer, Heidelberg (2011). https://doi.org/10.1007/978-3-642-22256-6_23

22. Ramasamy, H.V., Cukier, M., Sanders, W.H.: Formal specification and verification of a group membership protocol for an intrusion-tolerant group communication system. In: Pacific Rim International Symposium on Dependable Computing (2002)

23. Raynal, M.: Parallel computing vs. distributed computing: a great confusion? (position paper). In: Hunold, S., et al. (eds.) Euro-Par 2015. LNCS, vol. 9523, pp. 41–53. Springer, Cham (2015). https://doi.org/10.1007/978-3-319-27308-2_4

24. Tripakis, S., Yovine, S.: Analysis of timed systems using time-abstracting bisimulations. Formal Methods Syst. Des. **18**(1), 25–68 (2001)

25. Wang, F., Mok, A.K., Emerson, E.A.: Distributed real-time system specification and verification in APTL. ACM Trans. Softw. Eng. Methodol. **2**, 346–378 (1993)

26. Wang, X., Wang, J., Qi, Z.-C.: Automatic generation of run-time test oracles for distributed real-time systems. In: de Frutos-Escrig, D., Núñez, M. (eds.) FORTE 2004. LNCS, vol. 3235, pp. 199–212. Springer, Heidelberg (2004). https://doi.org/10.1007/978-3-540-30232-2_13

Local Reasoning for Parameterized First Order Protocols

Rylo Ashmore[✉], Arie Gurfinkel[✉], and Richard Trefler[✉]

University of Waterloo, Waterloo, Canada
{rjashmor,arie.gurfinkel,trefler}@uwaterloo.ca

Abstract. First Order Logic (FOL) is a powerful reasoning tool for program verification. Recent work on Ivy shows that FOL is well suited for verification of parameterized distributed systems. However, specifying many natural objects, such as a ring topology, in FOL is unexpectedly inconvenient. We present a framework based on FOL for specifying distributed multi-process protocols in a process-local manner together with an implicit network topology. In the specification framework, we provide an auto-active analysis technique to reason about the protocols locally, in a process-modular way. Our goal is to mirror the way designers often describe and reason about protocols. By hiding the topology behind the FOL structure, we simplify the modelling, but complicate the reasoning. To deal with that, we use an oracle for the topology to develop a sound and relatively complete proof rule that reduces reasoning about the implicit topology back to pure FOL. This completely avoids the need to axiomatize the topology. Using the rule, we establish a property that reduces verification to a fixed number of processes bounded by the size of local neighbourhoods. We show how to use the framework on two examples, including leader election on a ring.

1 Introduction

Auto-active [7] and automated verification engines are now commonly used to analyze the behavior of safety- and system-critical multi-process distributed systems. Applying the analysis techniques early in the design cycle has the added advantage that any errors or bugs found are less costly to fix than if one waits until the system is deployed. Therefore, it is typical to seek a proof of safety for *parametric* designs, where the number of participating program components is not yet determined, but the inter-process communication fits a given pattern, as is common in routing or communication protocols, and other distributed systems. Recently, Ivy [16] has been introduced as a novel auto-active verification technique (in the style of Dafny [7]) for reasoning about parameterized systems. Ivy models protocols in First Order Logic (FOL). The verification conditions are compiled (with user help) to a decidable fragment of FOL, called Effectively Propositional Reasoning (EPR) [17]. Ivy is automatic in the sense that the verification engineer only provides an inductive invariant. Furthermore, unlike Dafny,

© Springer Nature Switzerland AG 2019
J. M. Badger and K. Y. Rozier (Eds.): NFM 2019, LNCS 11460, pp. 36–53, 2019.
https://doi.org/10.1007/978-3-030-20652-9_3

$$\forall x, y, z \cdot btw(x, y, z) \Rightarrow btw(y, z, x)$$
$$\forall w, x, y, z \cdot btw(w, x, y) \land btw(w, y, z) \Rightarrow btw(w, x, z)$$
$$\forall w, x, y \cdot btw(w, x, y) \Rightarrow \neg btw(w, y, x)$$
$$\forall w, x, y \cdot distinct(w, x, y) \Rightarrow (btw(w, x, y) \lor btw(w, y, x))$$
$$\forall a, b \cdot (next(a, b) \iff \forall x \cdot x \neq a \land x \neq b \Rightarrow btw(a, b, x))$$

Fig. 1. A description of a unidirectional ring in FOL as presented by Ivy [16].

it guarantees that the verification is never stuck inside the decision procedure (verification conditions are decidable).

In representing a protocol in Ivy, an engineer must formally specify the entire protocol, including the topology. For instance, in verifying the leader election on a ring, Ivy requires an explicit axiomatization of the ring topology, as shown in Fig. 1. The predicate $btw(x, y, z)$ means that a process y is between processes x and z in the ring; similarly, $next(a, b)$ means that b is an immediate neighbour of a on the ring. All (finite) rings satisfy the axioms in Fig. 1. The converse is not true in general. For instance, take the rationals $\mathbb{Q}$ and let $btw(x, y, z)$ be defined as $x < y < z \lor y < z < x \lor z < x < y$. All axioms of btw are satisfied, but the only consistent interpretation of $next$ is an empty set. This satisfies all the axioms, but does not define a ring. For the axioms in Fig. 1, all *finite* models of btw and $next$ describe rings. This is not an issue for Ivy, since infinite models do not need to be considered for EPR. Such reasoning is non-trivial and is a burden on the verification engineer. As another example, we were not able to come up with an axiomatization of rings of alternating red and black nodes (shown in Fig. 2a) within EPR. In general, a complete axiomatization of the topology might be hard to construct.

In this paper, we propose to address this problem by specifying the topology independently of process behaviour. We present a framework which separates the two and provides a clean way to express the topology. We then specify our transitions locally, as this is a natural and common way to define protocols. Once these preliminaries are done, we provide a process-local proof rule to verify properties of the system. To generate the proof rule, we offload topological knowledge to an oracle that can answer questions about the topology. Finally, we prove various properties of the proof rule.

In summary, the paper makes the following contributions. First, in Sect. 3, we show how to model protocols locally in FOL. This is an alternative to the global modelling used in Ivy. Second, in Sect. 4, we show a proof rule with verification conditions (VC) in FOL, which are often in EPR. When the VC is in EPR, this gives an engineer a mechanical check of inductiveness. This allows reasoning about topology without axiomatizing it. Third, in Sect. 5, we show that our proof rule (a) satisfies a small model property, and (b) is relatively complete. The first guarantees the verification can be done on small process domains; the second ensures that our proof rule is relatively expressive.

We illustrate our approach on two examples. First, as a running example, motivated by [13], is a protocol on rings of alternating red and black nodes. These rings have only rotational symmetry, however, they have substantial local symmetry [8,12,13] consisting of two equivalence classes, one of red nodes, and one of black nodes. Second, in Sect. 6, we consider a modified version of the leader election protocol from Ivy [16]. This is of particular interest, since the local symmetry of [8,12,13] has not been applied to leader election. We thus extend [8,12,13] by both allowing more symmetries and infinite-state systems.

2   Preliminaries

FOL Syntax and Semantics. We assume some familiarity with the standard concepts of many sorted First Order Logic (FOL). A signature Σ consists of sorted predicates, functions, and constants. Terms are variables, constants, or (recursively) k-ary functions applied to k other terms of the correct sort. For every k-ary predicate P and k terms $t_1, \ldots, t_k$ of the appropriate sort for P, the formula $P(t_1, \ldots, t_k)$ is a well-formed formula (wff). Wffs are then boolean combinations of formulae and universally or existentially quantified formulae. Namely, if ψ and φ are wffs, then so are $(\psi \wedge \varphi)$, $(\psi \vee \varphi)$,$(\neg \psi)$, $(\psi \Rightarrow \varphi)$, $(\psi \iff \varphi)$, $(\forall x \cdot \psi)$, and $(\exists x \cdot \psi)$. A variable x in a formula ψ is bound if it appears under the scope of a quantifier. A variable not bound is free. A wff with no free variables is called a sentence. For convenience, we often drop unnecessary parenthesis, and use $\top$ to denote true and $\bot$ to denote false.

An FOL interpretation $\mathcal{I}$ over a domain D assigns every k-ary predicate P a sort-appropriate semantic interpretation $\mathcal{I}(P) : D^k \to \{T, F\}$; to every k-ary function f a sort-appropriate interpretation $\mathcal{I}(f) : D^k \to D$, and to every constant c an element $\mathcal{I}(c) \in D$. Given an interpretation $\mathcal{I}$ and a sentence ψ, then either ψ is true in $\mathcal{I}$ (denoted, $\mathcal{I} \models \psi$), or ψ is false in $\mathcal{I}$ (denoted $\mathcal{I} \not\models \psi$). The definition of the models relation is defined on the structure of the formula as usual, for example, $\mathcal{I} \models (\varphi \wedge \psi)$ iff $\mathcal{I} \models \varphi$ and $\mathcal{I} \models \psi$. We write $\models \varphi$ if for every interpretation $\mathcal{I}, \mathcal{I} \models \varphi$.

We write $\mathcal{I}(\Sigma')$ to denote a restriction of an interpretation $\mathcal{I}$ to a signature $\Sigma' \subseteq \Sigma$. Given disjoint signatures Σ, Σ' and corresponding interpretations $\mathcal{I}, \mathcal{I}'$ over a fixed domain D, we define $\mathcal{I} \oplus \mathcal{I}'$ to be an interpretation of $\Sigma \cup \Sigma'$ over domain D defined such that $(\mathcal{I} \oplus \mathcal{I}')(t) = \mathcal{I}(t)$ if $t \in \Sigma$, and $(\mathcal{I} \oplus \mathcal{I}')(t) = \mathcal{I}'(t)$ if $t \in \Sigma'$. Given interpretation $\mathcal{I}$ and sub-domain $D' \subseteq D$ where D' contains all constants, we let $\mathcal{I}(D')$ be the interpretation restricted to domain D'.

FOL Modulo Structures. We use an extension of FOL to describe structures, namely graphs. In this case, the signature Σ is extended with some pre-defined functions and predicates, and the interpretations are restricted to particular intended interpretations of these additions to the signature. We identify a structure class $\mathcal{C}$ with its signature $\Sigma^{\mathcal{C}}$ and an intended interpretation. We write $FOL^{\mathcal{C}}$ for First Order Logic over the structure class $\mathcal{C}$. Common examples are FOL over strings, FOL over trees, and other finite structures.

A structure $\mathcal{S} = (D, \mathcal{I})$ is an intended interpretation $\mathcal{I}$ for structural predicates/functions $\Sigma^{\mathcal{C}}$ over an intended domain D. A set of structures is denoted $\mathcal{C}$. The syntax of $FOL^{\mathcal{C}}$ is given by the syntax for FOL with signature $\Sigma \uplus \Sigma^{\mathcal{C}}$ (where Σ is an arbitrary disjoint signature). For semantics, any FOL interpretation $\mathcal{I}$ of signature Σ leads to an $FOL^{\mathcal{C}}$ interpretation $\mathcal{I} \oplus \mathcal{I}^{\mathcal{C}}$ of the signature $\Sigma \uplus \Sigma^{\mathcal{C}}$. We write $\models_{\mathcal{C}} \varphi$ iff every $FOL^{\mathcal{C}}$ interpretation $\mathcal{I}$ satisfies $\mathcal{I} \models \varphi$. We introduce a process sort $Proc$ and require the intended domain D to be exactly the set of $Proc$-sorted elements, so that we put our intended structure on the processes.

First Order Transition Systems. We use First Order Transitions Systems from Ivy [15,16]. While the original definition was restricted to the EPR fragment of FOL, we do not require this. A transition system is a tuple $Tr = (S, S_0, R)$, where S is a set of states, $S_0 \subseteq S$ is a set of initial states, and $R \subseteq S \times S$ is a transition relation. A trace π is a (finite or infinite) sequence of states $\pi = s_0 \cdots s_i \cdots$ such that $s_0 \in S_0$ and for every $0 \leq i < |\pi|$, $(s_i, s_{i+1}) \in R$, where $|\pi|$ denotes the length of π, or ∞ if π is infinite. A transition system may be augmented with a set $B \subseteq S$ of "bad" states. The system is safe iff all traces contain no bad states. A set of states I is inductive iff $S_0 \subseteq I$ and if $s \in I$ and $(s, s') \in R$, then $s' \in I$. Showing the existence of an inductive set I that is disjoint from bad set B suffices to show a transition system is safe.

A First-Order Transition System Specification (FOTSS) is a tuple $(\Sigma, \varphi_0, \tau)$ where Σ is an FOL signature, φ_0 is a sentence over Σ and τ is a sentence over $\Sigma \uplus \Sigma'$, where $\uplus$ denotes disjoint union and $\Sigma' = \{t' \mid t \in \Sigma\}$. The semantics of a FOTSS are given by First Order Transition Systems (FOTS). Let D be a fixed domain. A FOTSS $(\Sigma, \varphi_0, \tau)$ defines a FOTS over D as follows: $S = \{\mathcal{I} \mid \mathcal{I} \text{ is an FOL interpretation over } D\}$, $S_0 = \{\mathcal{I} \in S \mid \mathcal{I} \models \varphi_0\}$, and $R = \{(\mathcal{I}_1, \mathcal{I}_2) \in S \times S \mid \mathcal{I}_1 \oplus \mathcal{I}_2' \models \tau\}$, where $\mathcal{I}'$ interprets Σ'. We may augment a FOTSS with a FOL sentence Bad, giving bad states in the FOTS by $\mathcal{I} \in B$ iff $\mathcal{I} \models Bad$. A FOTSS is safe if all of its corresponding FOTS Tr are safe, and is unsafe otherwise. That is, a FOTSS is unsafe if there exists at least one FOTS corresponding to it that has at least one execution that reaches a bad state. A common way to show a FOTSS is safe is to give a formula Inv such that $\models \varphi_0 \Rightarrow Inv$ and $\models Inv \wedge \tau \Rightarrow Inv'$. Then for any FOTS over domain D, the set $I \subseteq S$ given by $I = \{\mathcal{I} \in S \mid \mathcal{I} \models Inv\}$ is an inductive set, and $\models Inv \Rightarrow \neg Bad$ then suffices to show that the state sets I, B in the FOTS are disjoint. Finding an invariant Inv satisfying the above proves the system safe.

Example 1. Consider the following FOTSS:

$$\Sigma \triangleq \{Even, +, 1, var\} \qquad\qquad \varphi_0 \triangleq Even(var)$$
$$\tau \triangleq (var' = (var + 1) + 1) \wedge Unch(Even, +, 1) \qquad Bad \triangleq \neg Even(var)$$

where $Unch(Even, +, 1)$ means that $Even$, $+$, and 1 have identical interpretations in the pre- and post-states of τ.

Our intention is to model a program that starts with an even number in a variable var and increments var by 2 at every transition. It is an error if var ever becomes odd. A natural invariant to conjecture is $Inv \triangleq Even(var)$. However, since the signature is uninterpreted, the FOTSS does not model our intention.

For example, let $D = \{0, 1, 2\}$, $\mathcal{I}_0(Even) = \{1, 2\}$, $\mathcal{I}_0(1) = 1$, $\mathcal{I}_0(+)(a, b) = a + b \mod 3$, and $\mathcal{I}_0(var) = 1$. Thus, $\mathcal{I}_0 \models \varphi_0$. Let $\mathcal{I}_1$ be the same as $\mathcal{I}_0$, except $\mathcal{I}_1(var) = 0$. Then, $\mathcal{I}_0 \oplus \mathcal{I}_1' \models \tau$ and $\mathcal{I}_1 \models Bad$. Thus, this FOTSS is unsafe.

One way to explicate our intention in Example 1 is to axiomatize the uninterpreted functions and relations in FOL as part of φ_0 and τ. Another alternative is to restrict their interpretation to a particular structure. This is the approach we take in this paper. We define a First-Order (relative to $\mathcal{C}$) Transition System Specification (FOCTSS).

We need to be able to talk about the structural objects in $\Sigma^{\mathcal{C}}$, and so we require that every FOCTSS $(\Sigma, \varphi_0, \tau)$ be an FOTSS with $\Sigma^{\mathcal{C}} \subseteq \Sigma$. Once we have these structural objects, any structure $(D, \mathcal{I}^{\mathcal{C}}) \in \mathcal{C}$ gives a FOCTS with states $\mathcal{I}$ where $\mathcal{I}(\Sigma^{\mathcal{C}}) = \mathcal{I}^{\mathcal{C}}$, initial states $\mathcal{I}$ where $\mathcal{I} \models \varphi_0$, transitions $(\mathcal{I}_1, \mathcal{I}_2)$ where $\mathcal{I}_1 \oplus \mathcal{I}_2' \models \tau$, and bad states $\mathcal{I}$ for which $\mathcal{I} \models Bad$.

3   First-Order Protocols

We introduce the notion of a *First-Order Protocol (FOP)* to simplify and restrict specifications in a FOTS. We choose restrictions to make our protocols asynchronous compositions of processes over static network topologies. Each process description is relative to its process neighbourhood. For example, a process operating on a ring has access to its immediate left and right neighbours, and transitions are restricted to these processes. This simplifies the modelling.

We begin with formalizing the concept of a network topology. As a running example, consider a Red-Black-Ring (RBR) topology, whose instance with 4 processes is shown in Fig. 2a. Processes are connected in a ring of alternating Red and Black processes. Each process is connected to two neighbours using two links, labelled *left* and *right*, respectively. From the example it is clear how to extend this topology to rings of arbitrary (even) size.

To formalize this, we assume that there is a unique sort *Proc* for processes. Define $\Sigma^{\mathcal{C}} = \Sigma_E^{\mathcal{C}} \uplus \Sigma_T^{\mathcal{C}}$ to be a *topological signature*, where $\Sigma_E^{\mathcal{C}}$ is a set of unary *Proc*-sorted functions and $\Sigma_T^{\mathcal{C}}$ is a set of distinct k-ary *Proc*-sorted predicates. Functions in $\Sigma_E^{\mathcal{C}}$ correspond to communication edges, such as *left* and *right* in our example. Predicates in $\Sigma_T^{\mathcal{C}}$ correspond to classes of processes, such as *Red* and *Black* in our example. For simplicity, we assume that all classes have the same arity k. We often omit k from the signature when it is contextually clear. We are now ready to define the concept of a network topology:

Definition 1. *A network topology $\mathcal{C}$ over a topological signature $\Sigma^{\mathcal{C}}$ is a collection of directed graphs $G = (V, E)$ augmented with an edge labelling dir : $E \to \Sigma_E^{\mathcal{C}}$ and k-node labelling kind : $V^k \to \Sigma_T^{\mathcal{C}}$. Given a node p in a graph $G = (V, E)$ from a network topology $\mathcal{C}$, the neighbourhood of p is defined as $nbd(p) = \{p\} \cup \{q \mid (p, q) \in E\}$, and a neighbourhood of a tuple $\boldsymbol{p} = (p_1, \ldots, p_k)$ is defined as $nbd(\boldsymbol{p}) = \bigcup_{i=1}^{k} nbd(p_i)$. A network topology is deterministic if for* *every distinct pair $q, r \in nbd(p) \setminus \{p\}$, $dir(p, q) \neq dir(p, r)$. That is, each neighbour of p corresponds to a distinct name in Σ_E.*

Given a deterministic network topology $\Sigma_T^C \cup \Sigma_E^C$, the intended interpretation of a predicate $P \in \Sigma_T^C$ is the set of all nodes in the network topology labelled by P, and the intended interpretation of a function $f \in \Sigma_E^C$ is such that $f(p) = q$ if an edge (p, q) is labelled by f and $f(p) = p$, otherwise.

Each graph G in a network topology C provides a possible intended interpretation for the sort of processes $Proc$, and the edge and node labelling provide the intended interpretation for predicates and functions in Σ^C.

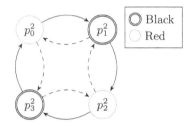

$$Init : \quad var := null$$
$$Tr : \quad black \Rightarrow right.var := r$$
$$red \Rightarrow right.var := b$$
$$Bad : \quad red \wedge var = b$$

(a) Red-Black-Ring of 4 process. Dashed arrows are *right*, and solid are *left*.

(b) A simple protocol over Red-Black-Ring topology.

Fig. 2. An example of a topology and a protocol. (Color figure online)

Example 2. For our running example, consider the protocol informally shown in Fig. 2b described by a set of guarded commands. The protocol is intended to be executed on the RBR topology shown in Fig. 2a. Initially, all processes start with their state variable var set to a special constant $null$. Then, at each step, a non-deterministically chosen process, sends a color to its right. Every black process sends a red color r, and every red process sends a black color b. It is bad if a Red process ever gets a black color.

To formalize the topology, for each $n > 1$, let $G_n = (V_n, E_n)$, where $V_n = \{p_i^n \mid 0 \leq i < 2n\}$, and $E_n = \{(p_i^n, p_j^n) \mid |i - j| \bmod 2n = 1\}$. The edge labelling is given by $dir(p_i^n, p_j^n) = right$ if $j = (i+1) \bmod n$ and $left$ if $j = (i-1) \bmod n$. Processes have colour $kind(p_i^n) = Red$ if i is even, and $Black$ if i is odd. Finally, we define $\mathcal{RBR} = \{G_n \mid n \geq 2\}$ as the class of Red-Black Rings (RBR). □

Note that any set of graphs $\mathcal{G}$ with an upper bound on the out-degree of any vertex can be given a finite labelling according to the above definition.

First-Order Protocols. Once we have specified the topology, we want to establish how processes transition. We define the syntax and semantics of a protocol.

A protocol signature Σ is a disjoint union of a topological signature Σ^C, a state signature Σ_S, and a background signature Σ_B. Recall that all functions and relations in Σ^C are of sort $Proc$. All elements of Σ_S have arity of at least 1 with the first and only the first argument of sort $Proc$. Elements of Σ_B do not allow arguments of sort *Proc* at all. Intuitively, elements of Σ^C describe how processes are connected, elements of Σ_S describe the current state of some process, and elements of Σ_B provide background theories, such as laws of arithmetic or uninterpreted functions.

For an interpretation $\mathcal{I}$, and a set of processes $P \subseteq \mathcal{I}(Proc)$, we write $\mathcal{I}(\Sigma_S)(P)$ for the interpretation $\mathcal{I}(\Sigma_S)$ restricted to processes in P. Intuitively, we look only at the states of P and ignore the states of all other processes.

Definition 2. *A* First-Order Protocol *(FO-protocol) is a tuple* $P = (\Sigma, Init(\boldsymbol{p}),$ $Mod(p), TrLoc(p), \mathcal{C})$, *where* Σ *is a protocol signature;* $Init(\boldsymbol{p})$ *is a formula with* k *free variables* $\boldsymbol{p}$ *of sort Proc;* $Mod(p)$ *is a set of terms* $\{t(p) \mid t \in dir(E)\} \cup \{p\}$; $TrLoc(p)$ *is a formula over the signature* $\Sigma \cup \Sigma'$ *with free process variable p, and* $\mathcal{C}$ *is a network topology. Furthermore,* $Init(\boldsymbol{p})$ *is of the form* $\bigwedge_{P \in \Sigma_T^C} (P(\boldsymbol{p}) \Rightarrow Init_P(\boldsymbol{p}))$, *and each* $Init_P$ *is a formula over* $\Sigma \setminus \Sigma_C$ *(an initial state described without reference to topology for each relevant topological class); and terms of sort Proc occurring in* $TrLoc(p)$ *are a subset of* $Mod(p)$.

Note that the *semantic* local neighbourhood $nbd(p)$ and the set of *syntactic* terms in $Mod(p)$ have been connected. Namely, for every edge $(p, q) \in E$, there is a term $t(p) \in Mod(p)$ to refer to q, and for every term $t(p) \in Mod(p)$, we will refer to some process in the neighbourhood of p.

$$Const = \{null_{/0}, r_{/0}, b_{/0}\} \qquad Func = \{left_{/1}, right_{/1}, var_{/1}\}$$
$$Pred = \{Red_{/1}, Black_{/1}, =_{/2}\} \qquad \Sigma = (Const, Func, Pred)$$
$$Init(p) = (Red(p) \Rightarrow var(p) = null) \wedge (Black(p) \Rightarrow var(p) = null)$$
$$Mod(p) = \{p, right(p), left(p)\}$$
$$t_r(p) = var'(right(p)) = b \wedge var'(p) = var(p) \wedge var'(left(p)) = var(left(p))$$
$$t_b(p) = var'(right(p)) = r \wedge var'(p) = var(p) \wedge var'(left(p)) = var(left(p))$$
$$TrLoc(p) = (Red(p) \Rightarrow t_r(p)) \wedge (Black(p) \Rightarrow t_b(p))$$

Fig. 3. A FO-protocol description of the system from Fig. 2.

$$\varphi_0 \triangleq \forall \boldsymbol{p} \cdot Init(\boldsymbol{p}) \qquad \tau \triangleq \exists p \cdot TrLoc(p) \wedge Frame(p)$$
$$Frame(p) \triangleq UnMod \wedge (\forall y \cdot y \notin Mod(p) \Rightarrow Unch(y))$$

$$Unch(y) \triangleq \left(\bigwedge_{P \in Preds_S} \forall \boldsymbol{v} \cdot P(y, \boldsymbol{v}) \iff P'(y, \boldsymbol{v}) \right) \wedge \left(\bigwedge_{f \in Funcs_S} \forall \boldsymbol{v} \cdot f(y, \boldsymbol{v}) = f'(y, \boldsymbol{v}) \right)$$

$$UnMod \triangleq \left(\bigwedge_{P \in Pred_B} \forall \boldsymbol{v} \cdot P(\boldsymbol{v}) \iff P'(\boldsymbol{v}) \right) \wedge \left(\bigwedge_{f \in Func_B} \forall \boldsymbol{v} \cdot f(\boldsymbol{v}) = f'(\boldsymbol{v}) \right)$$

Fig. 4. An FOTS of the protocol in Fig. 3.

A formal description of our running example is given in Fig. 3 as a FO-protocol. We define the signature including $\Sigma^{\mathcal{C}} = \{left, right, Red, Black\}$, the initial states $Init(p)$ in the restricted form, and modification set $Mod(p)$, where we allow processes to only write to their local neighbourhood. Next we specify two kinds of transitions, a red t_r and a black t_b transition. Each writes to their right neighbour the colour they expect that process to be. Each process p does not change the var states of p, $left(p) \in Mod(p)$. Finally, we specify our local transitions $TrLoc(p)$ by allowing each of the sub-transitions. Note that all process-sorted terms in $TrLoc(p)$ are in $Mod(p) = \{left(p), p, right(p)\}$, and we are allowed to call on topological predicates in $TrLoc$, finishing our specification.

The semantics of a protocol P are given be a FOCTSS as shown in Fig. 4. The protocol signature Σ is the same in the FOCTSS as in the FOP. Initially, φ_0 requires that all k-tuples of a given topology satisfy a topology-specific initial state. Second, to take a transition τ, some process takes a local transition $TrLoc(p)$ modifying states of processes that can be described using the terms in $Mod(p)$. $Frame(p), Unch(y)$ guarantee that the transition does not affect local state of processes that are outside of $Mod(p)$. Finally, $UnMod$ makes all functions and predicates in the background signature retain their interpretation during the transition. Overall, this describes a general multiprocess asynchronous protocol.

This definition of a FO-protocol places some added structure on the notion of FOTSS. It restricts how transition systems can be specified, which might seem like a drawback. On the contrary, the added structure provides two benefits. First, it removes the need for axiomatizing the network topology, since the topology is given semantically by $\mathcal{C}$. Second, the system guarantees that we model asynchronous composition of processes with local transitions – a common framework for specifying and reasoning about protocols.

To show safety of such a system, we will be concerned with invariants which only discuss a few processes, say $Inv(\boldsymbol{p})$ where $\boldsymbol{p} = p_1, \ldots, p_k$. Then our FO-invariants will be of the form $\forall \boldsymbol{p} \cdot Inv(\boldsymbol{p})$, and substituting φ_0 into our background, we find a natural check for when a given formula is inductive:

$$InvOk(Inv) \triangleq ((\forall \boldsymbol{p} \cdot Init(\boldsymbol{p})) \Rightarrow (\forall \boldsymbol{p} \cdot Inv(\boldsymbol{p}))) \wedge ((\forall \boldsymbol{p} \cdot Inv(\boldsymbol{p})) \wedge \tau \Rightarrow (\forall \boldsymbol{p} \cdot Inv'(\boldsymbol{p})))$$

Indeed, by unpacking definitions, one sees that $\models_{\mathcal{C}} InvOk$ means that every state on any trace of a FOCTS satisfies $\forall \boldsymbol{p} \cdot Inv(\boldsymbol{p})$, and thus it suffices to check that $\models_{\mathcal{C}} \forall \boldsymbol{p} \cdot Inv(\boldsymbol{p}) \Rightarrow \neg Bad$ to prove safety. We, however, will focus on the task of verifying a candidate formula as inductive or not.

To decide if a candidate is inductive or not requires reasoning in $FOL^{\mathcal{C}}$. However, reasoning about FOL extended with an arbitrary topology is difficult (or undecidable in general). We would like to reduce the verification problem to pure FOL. One solution is to axiomatize the topology in FOL – this is the approach taken by Ivy [16]. Another approach is to use properties of the topology to reduce reasoning about FO-protocols to FOL. This is similar to the use of topology to reduce reasoning about parameterized finite-state systems to reasoning about finite combinations of finite-state systems in [12]. In the next section, we show how this approach can be extended to FO-protocols.

4   Verifying FO-Protocols Using First Order Logic

In this section, we present a technique for reducing verification of FO-protocols over a given topology $\mathcal{C}$ to a decision problem in pure FOL. We assume that we are given a (modular) inductive invariant $\forall \boldsymbol{q} \cdot Inv(\boldsymbol{q})$ of the form $\left(\forall \boldsymbol{q} \cdot \bigwedge_{Top \in \Sigma_T^{\mathcal{C}}} Top(\boldsymbol{q}) \Rightarrow Inv_{Top}(\boldsymbol{q})\right)$. That is, Inv has a local inductive invariant $Inv_{Top(\boldsymbol{q})}$ for each topological class Top.

Given a First-Order Protocol and candidate invariant, we want to know if $\models_{\mathcal{C}} InvOk$. But deciding this is hard, and so we show that deciding validity of $InvOk$ can be done in pure FOL using modular verification conditions in the style of Owicki-Gries [14] and Parameterized Compositional Model Checking [12].

The input to our procedure is a formula Inv_{Top} over signature $\Sigma_B \uplus \Sigma_S$ for each topological class $Top \in \Sigma_T^{\mathcal{C}}$. The VC is a conjunction of sentences ensuring that for each tuple of processes $\boldsymbol{q}$ in a topological class Top, $Inv_{Top}(\boldsymbol{q})$ is true initially, is stable under a transition of one process in $\boldsymbol{q}$, and is stable under interference by any other process p whose execution might affect some $q_i \in \boldsymbol{q}$. If the VC is FOL-valid, an inductive invariant has been found. If not, there will be a local violation to inductiveness, which may correspond to a global violation.

Formally, $VC(Inv)$ is a conjunction of statements of the following two forms:

$$\forall \boldsymbol{q} \cdot (CrossInit_{Top}(\boldsymbol{q}) \Rightarrow Inv_{Top}(\boldsymbol{q})) \tag{1}$$

$$\forall p, \boldsymbol{q} \cdot ((CrossInv_{Top}(Mod(p), \boldsymbol{q}) \wedge \tau) \Rightarrow Inv'_{Top}(\boldsymbol{q})) \tag{2}$$

Statements of form (1) require that every local neighbourhood of $\boldsymbol{q}$ that satisfies all appropriate initial states also satisfies $\boldsymbol{q}$'s invariant. Statements of form (2) capture both transitions where $p = q_i$ for some i, or process p acts and modifies $q_i \in nbd(p)$, since p is quantified universally. All that remains is to formally construct the statements $CrossInit, CrossInv$. In order to do so, we construct a local characteristic formula $\chi(A, \boldsymbol{q})$ of a process $\boldsymbol{q}$ and neighbourhood A. Intuitively, we aim for $\chi(A, \boldsymbol{q})$ to encode the available local neighbourhoods of processes in A and $\boldsymbol{q}$ in $\mathcal{C}$.

Let $\chi_{Top}(A, \boldsymbol{q})$ be the strongest formula that satisfies $\models_{\mathcal{C}} \forall \boldsymbol{q} \cdot Top(\boldsymbol{q}) \Rightarrow \chi_{Top}(A, \boldsymbol{q})$, subject to the following syntactic restrictions. A formula is a candidate for $\chi_{Top}(A, \boldsymbol{q})$ when it is (1) over signature $\Sigma_T^{\mathcal{C}} \cup \Sigma_E^{\mathcal{C}} \cup \{=\}$, (2) contains only terms $A \cup \{q_i \mid q_i \in \boldsymbol{q}\}$, and (3) is in CNF and all literals from $\Sigma_T^{\mathcal{C}}$ appear in positive form. The syntactic restrictions are to capture when elements of $A, \boldsymbol{q}$ satisfy various topological notions given by signature $\Sigma_E^{\mathcal{C}} \cup \{=\}$. We also never force some processes to be outside of some topological class. Intuitively, χ is a formula that captures all topological knowledge derivable from the topology given that we know that $Top(\boldsymbol{q})$ holds. For instance, in $\mathcal{RBR}$, we have $\chi_{Red}(\emptyset, q) = Red(q)$, while expanding this for $A = \{left(p), p, right(p)\}$ results in the following formula. We drop some trivial statements. For instance, $left, right$ are inverse functions.

$$\chi_{Red}(\{left(p), p, right(p)\}, q) = Red(q) \wedge distinct(left(p), p, right(p)) \wedge$$
$$((Red(left(p)) \wedge Black(p) \wedge Red(right(p)) \wedge p \neq q) \vee$$
$$(Black(left(p)) \wedge Red(p) \wedge Black(right(p)) \wedge distinct(left(p), right(p), q)))$$

These characteristics are illustrated in Fig. 5. When we just look at $\chi_{Red}(\emptyset, q)$, we find q is red. However, if we expand our local reasoning to the characteristic $\chi_{Red}(Mod(p), q)$, we find that there are two options given by $\mathcal{RBR}$. One option is p is red, and $q = p$ is optional (dotted lines), while $q \neq left(p), right(p)$. Alternatively, p is black, and $q \neq p$, but q could be $left(p), right(p)$, or neither.

Once we have $\chi_{Top}(A, \boldsymbol{q})$, we can define our statements $CrossInit_{Top}$, $CrossInv_{Top}$. First, $CrossInit_{Top}(\boldsymbol{q})$ is obtained from $\chi_{Top}(\emptyset, \boldsymbol{q})$ by replacing every instance of $Top_i(\boldsymbol{q})$ with $Init_{Top_i}(\boldsymbol{q})$. We build our interference constraints in a similar way. We construct $CrossInv_{Top}(\boldsymbol{q})$ by modifying $\chi_{Top}(Mod(p), \boldsymbol{q})$. Namely, we obtain $CrossInv_{Top}(Mod(p), \boldsymbol{q})$ from $\chi_{Top}(Mod(p), \boldsymbol{q})$ by replacing every instance of $Top_i(\boldsymbol{q})$ with $Top_i(\boldsymbol{q}) \wedge Inv_{Top_i}(\boldsymbol{q})$.

Example 3. The VC generated by the $\mathcal{RBR}$ topology may be partitioned into VC_{Red} and VC_{Black}, each consisting of the statements whose conclusions are Inv_{Red}, Inv'_{Red} and $Inv_{black}, Inv'_{black}$, respectively. VC_{Red} is shown in Fig. 6. The conditions for VC_{Black} are symmetric. One can check that

$$Inv_{red}(p) \triangleq var(p) \neq b \qquad\qquad Inv_{black}(p) \triangleq \top$$

is an inductive invariant for the protocol in Fig. 2.   □

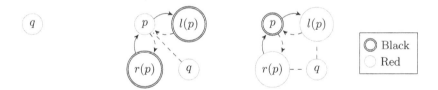

Fig. 5. Characteristics $\chi_{Red}(\emptyset, q)$ and $\chi_{Red}(Mod(p), q)$ for the $\mathcal{RBR}$ topology. (Color figure online)

$$\forall p \cdot Init_{red}(p) \Rightarrow Inv_{red}(p) \tag{3}$$

$$\forall p, q \cdot (Red(q) \wedge Inv_{red}(q) \wedge Red(left(p)) \wedge Inv_{red}(left(p)) \wedge$$
$$Black(p) \wedge Inv_{black}(p) \wedge Red(right(p)) \wedge Inv_{red}(right(p)) \wedge$$
$$p \neq q \wedge distinct(left(p), p, right(p))) \Rightarrow Inv'_{red}(q) \tag{4}$$

$$\forall p, q \cdot (Red(q) \wedge Inv_{red}(q) \wedge Black(left(p)) \wedge Inv_{black}(left(p)) \wedge$$
$$Red(p) \wedge Inv_{red}(p) \wedge Black(right(p)) \wedge Inv_{black}(right(p)) \wedge$$
$$distinct(left(p), right(p), q) \wedge distinct(left(p), p, right(p))) \Rightarrow Inv'_{red}(q) \tag{5}$$

$$VC_{P,1}(Inv_{red}, Inv_{black}) \triangleq (3) \wedge (4) \wedge (5) \tag{6}$$

Fig. 6. The verification conditions VC_{Red} for the red process invariant.

In practice, the role of the χ-computing oracle can be filled by a verification engineer. A description of local neighbourhoods starts by allowing all possible neighbourhoods. Then, a verifier may dismiss local configurations that cannot occur on the topology as they occur.

5   Soundness and Completeness

In this section, we present soundness and relative completeness of our verification procedure from Sect. 4.

Soundness. To show soundness, we present a model-theoretic argument to show that whenever the verification condition from Sect. 4 is valid in FOL, then the condition *InvOk* is valid in FOL extended with the given topology $\mathcal{C}$.

Theorem 1. *Given a FO-protocol P and a local invariant per topological class $Inv_{Top_1}(\boldsymbol{p}), \ldots, Inv_{Top_n}(\boldsymbol{p})$, if $\models VC(Inv)$, then $\models_{\mathcal{C}} InvOk(Inv)$.*

Proof. Assume $\models VC(Inv)$. We show that $InvOk(Inv)$ is valid in $FOL^{\mathcal{C}}$ by showing that any pair of $FOL^{\mathcal{C}}$ interpretations $\mathcal{I}$ and $\mathcal{I}'$ satisfy $VC(Inv)$ as FOL interpretations, and this is strong enough to guarantee $\mathcal{I} \oplus \mathcal{I}' \models InvOk(Inv)$.

Let $\mathcal{I}, \mathcal{I}'$ be $FOL^{\mathcal{C}}$ interpretations over some $G = (V, E) \in \mathcal{C}$. Then $\mathcal{I} \oplus \mathcal{I}' \models VC(Inv)$ because $VC(Inv)$ is valid and $\mathcal{I} \oplus \mathcal{I}'$ is an FOL interpretation.

We first show that $\mathcal{I} \models (\forall \boldsymbol{p} \cdot Init(\boldsymbol{p}) \Rightarrow \forall \boldsymbol{p} \cdot Inv(\boldsymbol{p}))$. Suppose that $\mathcal{I} \models \forall \boldsymbol{p} \cdot Init(\boldsymbol{p})$. Let $\boldsymbol{p}$ be an arbitrary tuple in G. If $\mathcal{I} \models \neg Top_i(\boldsymbol{p})$ for every $Top_i \in \Sigma_T$, then $Inv(\boldsymbol{p})$ follows vacuously. Otherwise, suppose $\mathcal{I} \models Top_i(\boldsymbol{p})$. Then by definition of χ, we obtain $\mathcal{I} \models \chi_{Top_i}(\emptyset, \boldsymbol{p})$ since $\mathcal{I} \models Top_i(\boldsymbol{p}) \Rightarrow \chi_{Top_i}(\emptyset, \boldsymbol{p})$. Since $\mathcal{I} \models \forall \boldsymbol{p} \cdot Init(\boldsymbol{p})$, this gives us that $\mathcal{I} \models CrossInit(\boldsymbol{p})$ (for any $Top_j(\boldsymbol{p}')$ in $\chi_{Top_i}(\emptyset, \boldsymbol{p})$, find that $Init(\boldsymbol{p}')$, and thus $Top_j(\boldsymbol{p}')$ implies $Init_{Top_j}(\boldsymbol{p}')$, giving $CrossInit$). Since $\mathcal{I} \models CrossInit_{Top_i}(\boldsymbol{p})$ and $\mathcal{I} \models VC$, we get $\mathcal{I} \models CrossInit_{Top_i}(\boldsymbol{p}) \Rightarrow Inv_{Top_i}(\boldsymbol{p})$, finally giving us $\mathcal{I} \models Inv_{Top_i}(\boldsymbol{p})$, as desired.

Second, we show that $\mathcal{I} \oplus \mathcal{I}' \models (\forall \boldsymbol{p} \cdot Inv(\boldsymbol{p})) \wedge \tau \Rightarrow (\forall \boldsymbol{p} \cdot Inv(\boldsymbol{p}))$. Suppose that $\mathcal{I} \models \forall \boldsymbol{p} \cdot Inv(\boldsymbol{p})$ and $\mathcal{I} \oplus \mathcal{I}' \models TrLoc(p) \wedge Frame(p)$ for some $p \in V$. We show that $\mathcal{I}' \models \forall \boldsymbol{q} \cdot Inv'(\boldsymbol{q})$. Let $\boldsymbol{q} \in V^k$ be an arbitrary process tuple. If $\mathcal{I}' \not\models Top_i(\boldsymbol{q})$ for all $1 \leq i \leq n$, then $\mathcal{I}' \models Inv'(\boldsymbol{q})$ vacuously. Suppose $\mathcal{I}' \models Top_i(\boldsymbol{q})$ for some $Top_i \in \Sigma_T$. Then $\mathcal{I} \models Top_i(\boldsymbol{q}) \Rightarrow \chi_{Top_i}(Mod(p), \boldsymbol{q})$, and so $\mathcal{I} \models \chi_{Top_i}(Mod(p), \boldsymbol{q})$. Again by instantiating $\forall \boldsymbol{p} \cdot Inv(\boldsymbol{p})$ on terms in $Mod(p), \boldsymbol{q}$, we may obtain that $\mathcal{I} \models CrossInv(Mod(p), \boldsymbol{q})$. Combined, we have $\mathcal{I} \oplus \mathcal{I}' \models CrossInv(Mod(p), \boldsymbol{q}) \wedge \tau$. Applying VC finally gives $Inv_{Top_i}(\boldsymbol{q})$. Thus both conjuncts of $InvOk(Inv)$ are satisfied, giving our result. □

Intuitively, the correctness of Theorem 1 follows from the fact that any interpretation under $FOL^{\mathcal{C}}$ is also an interpretation under FOL, and all preconditions generated for VC are true under $FOL^{\mathcal{C}}$ interpretation.

Small Model Property. Checking validity of universally quantified statements in FOL is in the fragment EPR, and thus we obtain a result saying that we only need to consider models of a given size. This means that a FOL solver needs to only reason about finitely many elements of sort *Proc*. It further means that topologies such as $\mathcal{RBR}$ may be difficult to compile to EPR in Ivy, but our methodology guarantees our verifications will be in EPR.

Theorem 2. *If* $\models VC(Inv)$ *for all process domains of size at most* $|Mod(p)|+k$, *then* $\models_C InvOk(Inv)$.

Proof. By contrapositive, suppose $\not\models_C InvOk(Inv)$. Then, by Theorem 1, $\not\models VC(Inv)$. Let $\mathcal{I} \oplus \mathcal{I}'$ be a falsifying interpretation. It contains an assignment to $Mod(p)$ and q, or to p that makes at least one statement in $VC(Inv)$ false. Then $\mathcal{I} \oplus \mathcal{I}'(Mod(p) \cup q)$ or $\mathcal{I}(p)$ is also a counter-model to $VC(Inv)$, but with at most $|Mod(p)| + k$ elements of sort *Proc*.

Relative Completeness. We show that our method is relatively complete for local invariants that satisfy the *completability* condition. Let $\varphi(p)$ be a formula of the form $\bigwedge_{i=1}^{n}(Top_i(p) \Rightarrow \varphi_{Top_i}(p))$ with $\varphi_{Top_i}(p)$ over the signature $\Sigma_S \cup \Sigma_B$. Intuitively, $\varphi(p)$ is *completable* if every interpretation $\mathcal{I}$ that satisfies $\forall p \cdot \varphi(p)$ and is consistent with some $\mathcal{C}$-interpretation $\mathcal{I}_G$ can be extended to a full $\mathcal{C}$-interpretation (not necessarily $\mathcal{I}_G$) that satisfies $\forall p \cdot \varphi(p)$. Formally, φ is *completable* relative to topology $\mathcal{C}$ iff for every interpretation $\mathcal{I}$ with domain $U \subseteq V$ for $G = (V,E) \in \mathcal{C}$ with an intended interpretation $\mathcal{I}_G$ such that $(\mathcal{I} \uplus \mathcal{I}_G)(U) \models \forall p \cdot \varphi(p)$, there exists an interpretation $\mathcal{J}$ with domain V s.t. $(\mathcal{J} \uplus \mathcal{I}_G) \models \forall p \cdot \varphi$ and $\mathcal{I}(U) = \mathcal{J}(U)$. In addition to relative completeness, we need a lemma for when a FOL interpretation can be lifted to a $\mathcal{C}$ interpretation.

Lemma 1. *If FOL interpretation* $\mathcal{I}$ *of signature* $\Sigma^{\mathcal{C}}$ *satisfies* $\mathcal{I} \models \chi_{Top}(A, q)$, *then there exists a* $\mathcal{C}$ *interpretation* $\mathcal{J}$ *of the same signature with* $\mathcal{J} \models \chi_{Top}(A, q)$ *and* $\mathcal{I} \models t_i = t_j$ *iff* $\mathcal{J} \models t_i = t_j$ *for terms* $t_i, t_j \in A \cup q$.

Proof. Let $\mathcal{I} \models \chi_{Top}(A, q)$. Let $\varphi(A, q)$ be the conjunction of all atomic formulae over the signature $\{=\}$ and statements $\neg Top_j(q')$ that is true of elements of A, q in interpretation $\mathcal{I}$. If no $\mathcal{C}$ interpretation $\mathcal{J} \models Top(q) \wedge \varphi(A, q)$, then we can add the clause $\neg\varphi(A, q)$ to $\chi_{Top}(A, q)$, thus strengthening it (this is stronger since $\mathcal{I} \models Top(q), \not\models \neg\varphi(A, q)$, and is true of every interpretation modelling $Top(q)$). However, this violates the assumptions that χ_{Top} is as strong as possible. Thus, some $\mathcal{J} \models Top(q) \wedge \varphi(A, q)$. Note that $\mathcal{J}$ already satisfies $t_i = t_j$ iff $\mathcal{I}$ satisfies $t_i = t_j$ since every statement of $=, \neq$ is included in $\varphi(A, q)$. Finally, since $\mathcal{J}$ is a $\mathcal{C}$ interpretation and $\mathcal{J} \models Top(q)$, then $\mathcal{J} \models \chi_{Top}(A, q)$ by definition. □

Theorem 3. *Given an FO-protocol P, if* $\models_C InvOk(Inv)$ *and both* $Inv(p)$ *and* $Init(p)$ *are completable relative to* $\mathcal{C}$, *then* $\models VC(Inv)$.

Proof. By contra-positive, we show that given a completable local invariant $Inv(p)$, if $VC(Inv)$ is falsifiable in FOL, then $InvOk(Inv)$ is falsifiable in $FOL^{\mathcal{C}}$.

Suppose $VC(Inv)$ is not valid, and let $\mathcal{I} \oplus \mathcal{I}'$ by such that $\mathcal{I} \oplus \mathcal{I}' \not\models VC(Inv)$. We consider two cases – a violation initially or inductively.

Case 1: Initialization: For some processes $\boldsymbol{p} = (p_1, \ldots, p_k)$ and $1 \leq i \leq |\Sigma_T^{\mathcal{C}}|$, $\mathcal{I} \models CrossInit_{Top_i}(\boldsymbol{p})$ and $\mathcal{I} \not\models Inv_{Top_i}(\boldsymbol{p})$. Modify $\mathcal{I}(\Sigma_T)$ for every $\boldsymbol{q}$ so that $Top_j(\boldsymbol{q})$ is interpreted to be true iff $Init_{Top_j}(\boldsymbol{q})$ is true. Noting that all initial conditions are outside of the signature $\Sigma_T^{\mathcal{C}}$, we observe that this is done without loss of generality. Since $\mathcal{I} \models CrossInit_{Top_i}(\boldsymbol{p})$, we conclude now that $\mathcal{I} \models \chi_{Top_i}(\emptyset, \boldsymbol{p})$. Applying Lemma 1 to $\mathcal{I}(\Sigma_{\mathcal{C}})$, we get a $\mathcal{C}$ interpretation $\mathcal{J} \models \chi_{Top_i}(\emptyset, \boldsymbol{p}^{\mathcal{C}})$. Since this model has the same equalities of terms $\boldsymbol{p}^{\mathcal{C}}$ in $\mathcal{J}$ as $\boldsymbol{p}$ in $\mathcal{I}$, we may copy the states $\mathcal{I}(\Sigma_S)(p_i)$ to $\mathcal{J}(\Sigma_S)(p_i^{\mathcal{C}})$. Set $\mathcal{J}(\Sigma_B) = \mathcal{I}(\Sigma_B)$. Since $Init$ is completable by assumption, we complete $\mathcal{J}(\Sigma_S \cup \Sigma_B)(\boldsymbol{p})$ to $\mathcal{J}(\Sigma_S \cup \Sigma_B)$, completing our construction of $\mathcal{J}$ interpreting $\Sigma^{\mathcal{C}} \cup \Sigma_S \cup \Sigma_B$. Note that $\mathcal{J} \models \forall \boldsymbol{p} \cdot Init(\boldsymbol{p})$, but $\mathcal{J} \models Top_i(\boldsymbol{p}^{\mathcal{C}}) \wedge \neg Inv_{Top_i}(\boldsymbol{p}^{\mathcal{C}})$, thus showing that $InvOk(Inv)$ is falsifiable in $FOL^{\mathcal{C}}$.

Case 2: Inductiveness: For some p, q, and $1 \leq i \leq |\Sigma_T^{\mathcal{C}}|$, we have $\mathcal{I} \models CrossInv_{Top_i}(Mod(p), q)$, $(\mathcal{I} \oplus \mathcal{I}') \models TrLoc(p) \wedge Frame(p)$, and $\mathcal{I}' \not\models Inv_{Top_i}(q)$. By construction, $\models CrossInv(Mod(p), q) \Rightarrow \chi_{Top_i}(Mod(p), q)$. Applying Lemma 1 to $\mathcal{I}(\Sigma_{\mathcal{C}}) \models \chi_{Top_i}(Mod(p), q)$, we get a $\mathcal{C}$ interpretation of $\Sigma_T^{\mathcal{C}}$, $\mathcal{J} \models \chi_{Top_i}(Mod(p^{\mathcal{C}}), q^{\mathcal{C}})$. We extend this to a full model $\mathcal{J} \oplus \mathcal{J}'$ of signature $\Sigma^{\mathcal{C}} \cup \Sigma_S \cup \Sigma_B$, and its primed copy. We set $\mathcal{J}'(\Sigma_{\mathcal{C}}) = \mathcal{J}(\Sigma_{\mathcal{C}})$. Then, since $\mathcal{J}$ and $\mathcal{I}$, and $\mathcal{J}'$ and $\mathcal{I}'$ share equalities across terms in $Mod(p) \cup q$ and $Mod(p^{\mathcal{C}}) \cup q^{\mathcal{C}}$, we can lift states from terms $t \in Mod(p) \cup q$ by $\mathcal{J}(\Sigma_S \cup \Sigma_B)(t^{\mathcal{C}}) \triangleq \mathcal{I}(\Sigma_S \cup \Sigma_B)(t)$ and $\mathcal{J}'(\Sigma_S)(t^{\mathcal{C}}) \triangleq \mathcal{I}'(\Sigma_S)(t)$. Since Inv is completable, we complete this interpretation with $\mathcal{J}(\Sigma_S \cup \Sigma_B)$ and clone the completion to $\mathcal{J}'(\Sigma_S \cup \Sigma_B)(V \setminus (Mod(p) \cup q))$. Overall, this completes the interpretation $\mathcal{J} \oplus \mathcal{J}'$.

Note that $\mathcal{J} \models \forall \boldsymbol{p} \cdot Inv(\boldsymbol{p})$ by construction. Similarly, $\mathcal{J} \oplus \mathcal{J}' \models \tau$ since $\mathcal{I} \oplus \mathcal{I}' \models \tau(p)$ and $Mod(p)$ terms are lifted directly from $\mathcal{I}$ and $\mathcal{I}'$ to $\mathcal{J}$ and $\mathcal{J}'$. Finally, $\mathcal{J}' \models \neg Inv'_{Top_i}(q)$ since $\mathcal{J}'(\Sigma_S)$ is lifted directly from $\mathcal{I}'(\Sigma_S \cup \Sigma_B)$, which is the language of invariants. Thus, we have shown that $InvOk(Inv)$ is falsifiable in $FOL^{\mathcal{C}}$ in this case as well. □

How restrictive is the requirement of *completability*? Intuitively, suppose a protocol is very restrictive about how processes interact. Then the system is likely sufficiently intricate that trying to reason locally may be difficult independent of our methodology. For instance, the invariant we later find for leader election is not completable. However, if equivalence classes are small, then most reasonable formulae satisfy the completability condition.

Theorem 4. *If $Inv_{Top_i}(p)$ is satisfiable over any domain for each $1 \leq i \leq n$ and topological predicates are of arity $k = 1$, then $Inv(p)$ is completable.*

Proof. Let $Inv_i(p)$ be satisfiable for each $1 \leq i \leq n$. Then let $\mathcal{I}(V')$ be an interpretation of $\Sigma_B \uplus \Sigma_S$ over domain $V' \subseteq V$ for $G = (V, E) \in \mathcal{C}$. For each $p \in V \setminus V'$, suppose $\mathcal{I}_G \models Top_i(p)$ for some $1 \leq i \leq n$. Then choose $\mathcal{J}(p) \models Inv_{Top_i}(p)$ since $Inv_{Top_i}(p)$ is satisfiable. Otherwise, if $\mathcal{I}_G \not\models Top_i(p)$ for all

$1 \leq i \leq n$, then $\mathcal{J}(p)$ is chosen arbitrarily. In either case, $\mathcal{J} \models Inv(p)$. Finally, define $\mathcal{J}(p) = \mathcal{I}(p)$ for $p \in V'$. Then $\mathcal{J}$ completes the partial interpretation $\mathcal{I}$.

Theorem 4 can be generalized to the case where the topological kinds Σ_T are non-overlapping, and individually completable, where by individually completable, we mean that if $Top(\mathbf{p})$ and process states of $\mathbf{p'} \subset \mathbf{p}$ are given, then there is a way to satisfy $Inv(\mathbf{p})$ without changing the states of $\mathbf{p'}$.

6 Example: Leader Election Protocol

In this section, we illustrate our approach by applying it to the well-known leader election protocol [3]. This is essentially the same protocol used to illustrate Ivy in [16]. The goal of the protocol is to choose a leader on a ring. Each process sends messages to its neighbour on one side and receives messages from a neighbour on the other side. Initially, all processes start with distinct identifiers, id, that are totally ordered. Processes pass ids around the ring and declare themselves the leader if they ever receive their own id.

We implement this behaviour by providing each process a comparison variable $comp$. Processes then pass the maximum between id and $comp$ to the next process. A process whose id and $comp$ have the same value is the leader. The desired safety property is that there is never more than one leader in the protocol.

In [16], the protocol is modelled by a global transition system. The system maintains a bag of messages for each process. At each step, a currently waiting message is selected and processed according to the program of the protocol (or a fresh message is generated). The network topology is axiomatized, as shown in Sect. 1. Here, we present a local model of the protocol and verify it locally.

Network Topology. The leader election protocol operates on a ring of size at least 3. For $n \geq 3$, let $G_n = (V_n, E_n)$, where $V_n = \{p_i^n \mid 0 \leq i < n\}$ and $E_n = \{(p_i^n, p_j^n) \mid 0 \leq i < n, j = i + 1 \bmod n\}$. Let $\Sigma_E = \{next\}$ and $\Sigma_T = \{btw\}$, where btw is a ternary relation such that $btw(p_i^n, p_j^n, p_k^n)$ iff $i < j < k$, $j < k < i$, or $k < i < j$. Finally, the network topology is $\mathcal{BTW} = \{G_n \mid n \geq 3\}$. Note that while $\mathcal{BTW}$ can be axiomatized in FOL, we do not require such an axiomatization. The definition is purely semantic, no theorem prover sees it.

$$Const \triangleq \{0_{/0}\} \quad Func \triangleq \{next_{/1}, id_{/1}, comp_{/1}\} \quad Pred \triangleq \{\leq_{/2}, =_{/2}, btw_{/3}\} \quad \mathcal{C} \triangleq \mathcal{BTW}$$

$$\Sigma \triangleq (Const, Func, Pred) \quad LO_0(\leq) \triangleq LO(\leq) \wedge \forall x \cdot 0 \leq x \quad Mod(p) \triangleq \{p, next(p)\}$$

$$Init(p) \triangleq (LO_0(\leq) \wedge btw(x, y, z) \Rightarrow (distinct(id(x), id(y), id(z)) \wedge 0 < id(x) \wedge comp(x) = 0))$$

$$\tau_1(p) \triangleq \big(id(p) \leq comp(p) \Rightarrow \big(comp'(next(p)) = comp(p)\big)\big)$$

$$\tau_2(p) \triangleq \big(comp(p) \leq id(p) \Rightarrow \big(comp'(next(p)) = id(p)\big)\big)$$

$$TrLoc(p) \triangleq \big(id(p) = id'(p) \wedge comp(p) = comp'(p) \wedge id'(next(p)) = id(next(p)) \wedge \tau_1(p) \wedge \tau_2(p)\big)$$

Fig. 7. A model of the Leader Election protocol as a FO-protocol.

$$(btw(x, y, z) \wedge id(y) = comp(x)) \Rightarrow (id(z) \leq id(y))$$
$$(btw(x, y, z) \wedge id(x) = comp(x)) \Rightarrow (id(y) \leq id(x) \wedge id(z) \leq id(x))$$
$$(btw(x, y, z) \wedge id(x) = comp(x) \wedge id(y) = comp(y)) \Rightarrow x = y$$

Fig. 8. Local inductive invariant $Inv_{lead}(x, y, z)$ for Leader Election from Fig. 7.

A formal specification of the leader election as an FO-protocol is shown in Fig. 7, where $LO(\leq)$ is an axiomatization of total order from [16], and $x < y$ stands for $x \leq y \wedge x \neq y$. The model follows closely the informal description of the protocol given above. The safety property is $\neg Bad$, where $Bad = btw(x, y, z) \wedge id(x) = comp(x) \wedge id(y) = comp(y)$. That is, a bad state is reached when two processes that participate in the btw relation are both leaders.

A local invariant Inv_{lead} based on the invariant from [16] is shown in Fig. 8. The invariant first says if an id passes from y to x through z, then it must witness $id(y) \geq id(z)$ to do so. Second, the invariant says that if a process is a leader, then it has a maximum id. Finally, the invariant asserts our safety property.

This invariant was found interactively with Ivy by seeking local violations to the invariant. Our protocol's btw is uninterpreted, while Ivy's btw is explicitly axiomatized. The inductive check assumes that the processes $p, next(p), q$ all satisfy a finite instantiation of the ring axioms (this could be done by the developer as needed if an axiomatization is unknown, and this is guaranteed to terminate as there are finitely many relevant terms), and $btw(q)$. Once the invariants are provided, the check of inductiveness is mechanical[1]. Overall, this presents a natural way to model protocols for engineers that reason locally.

An Uncompletable Invariant. The invariant for the leader election is not completable. To see this, we present a partial interpretation $\mathcal{I}$ over $\{p_0^3, p_2^3\} \subseteq V_3$ from G_3 with no extension. We choose $\mathcal{I}(\leq)$ to be $\leq$ over $\mathbb{N}$, as intended. Then we choose $\mathcal{I}(id)$ to map $p_0^3 \mapsto 1$ and $p_2^3 \mapsto 2$. We also choose $\mathcal{I}(comp)$ to map $p_0^3 \mapsto 0$ and $p_2^3 \mapsto 1$. Since no tuple satisfies btw, this vacuously satisfies all invariants thus far. Let $\mathcal{J}$ be a $\mathcal{BTW}$ interpretation agreeing on p_0^3, p_2^3. Consider $id(p_1^3)$. We know $id(p_1^3) \neq 0, 1, 2$ since we require distinct ids across the new btw relation. But we also have $id(p_0^3) = comp(p_2^3)$ and thus to satisfy Inv we must have $id(p_0^3) \geq id(p_1^3)$. Thus we seek an $n \in \mathbb{N}$ such that $1 \geq n$, but $n \neq 0, 1$, which cannot exist. Thus Inv is uncompletable.

7   Related Work

Finite-state parameterized verification is undecidable [2]. We have shown how analysis techniques for parametric distributed systems composed of components running on locally symmetric topologies, introduced in [8–10,12,13], can be generalized and applied within a First Order Logic based theorem proving engine.

---

[1] Ivy verifications for both examples, globally and locally, can be found at github.com/ashmorer/fopExamples.

We based our description of leader election on Ivy's [16]. However, the analysis carried out in Ivy [16] is global, while the analysis given in this paper is local, where the local structures reason about triples of processes in the ring.

There has been extensive work on proving properties of parametric, distributed protocols. In particular the work in [1] offers an alternative approach to parametric program analysis based on "views". In that work, cut off points are calculated during program analysis. As another example, in [8,12,13] the "cut-offs" are based on the program topology and the local structural symmetries amongst the nodes of the process interconnection networks.

The notion of a "cutoff" proof of safety for a parametric family of programs was first introduced by [5]. For example, in [5], if a ring of 3 processes satisfies a parametric property then the property must hold for all rings with at least three nodes. The technique used here is somewhat different; rather than needing to check a ring of 3 processes, we check all pseudo-rings of a given size.

Local symmetry reduction for multi-process networks and parametric families of networks generalizes work on "global" symmetry reduction introduced by [6] and [4]. Local symmetry is, in general, an abstraction technique that can offer exponentially more reduction than global symmetry. In particular, ring structures are globally rotationally symmetric, but for isomorphic processes may be fully-locally symmetric [12,13].

Recent work [18] has focused on *modular* reasoning in the proof or analysis of distributed systems. In the current work, the modularity in the proof is driven by a natural modularity in the program structures. In particular, for programs of several processes proofs are structured by modules that are local to a neighborhood of one or more processes [8,12,13].

8   Conclusion

We have presented a framework for specifying protocols in a process-local manner with topology factored out. We show that verification is reducible to FOL with an oracle to answer local questions about the topology. This reduction results in a decidable VC when the background theories are decidable. This cleanly separates the reasoning about the topology from that of the states of the processes.

Many open questions remain. We plan to investigate our methodology on other protocols and topologies, implement oracles for common topologies, and explore complexity of the generated characteristic formulae. Finally, we restricted ourselves to static topologies of bounded degree. Handling dynamic or unbounded topologies, for example in the AODV protocol [11], is left open.

Acknowledgements. The authors' research was supported, in part, by Individual Discovery Grants from the Natural Sciences and Engineering Research Council of Canada.

References

1. Abdulla, P., Haziza, F., Holík, L.: Parameterized verification through view abstraction. Int. J. Softw. Tools Technol. Transf. **18**(5), 495–516 (2016)
2. Apt, K.R., Kozen, D.C.: Limits for automatic verification of finite-state concurrent systems. Inf. Process. Lett. **22**(6), 307–309 (1986)
3. Chang, E., Roberts, R.: An improved algorithm for decentralized extrema-finding in circular configurations of processes. Commun. ACM **22**(5), 281–283 (1979)
4. Clarke, E.M., Enders, R., Filkorn, T., Jha, S.: Exploiting symmetry in temporal logic model checking. Form. Methods Syst. Des. **9**(1–2), 77–104 (1996)
5. Emerson, E.A., Namjoshi, K.S.: Reasoning about rings. In: Proceedings of the 22nd ACM SIGPLAN-SIGACT Symposium on Principles of Programming Languages, POPL 1995, pp. 85–94. ACM, New York (1995)
6. Emerson, E.A., Sistla, A.P.: Symmetry and model checking. Form. Methods Syst. Des. **9**(1–2), 105–131 (1996)
7. Leino, K.R.M.: Dafny: an automatic program verifier for functional correctness. In: Clarke, E.M., Voronkov, A. (eds.) LPAR 2010. LNCS (LNAI), vol. 6355, pp. 348–370. Springer, Heidelberg (2010). https://doi.org/10.1007/978-3-642-17511-4_20
8. Namjoshi, K.S., Trefler, R.J.: Local symmetry and compositional verification. In: Kuncak, V., Rybalchenko, A. (eds.) VMCAI 2012. LNCS, vol. 7148, pp. 348–362. Springer, Heidelberg (2012). https://doi.org/10.1007/978-3-642-27940-9_23
9. Namjoshi, K.S., Trefler, R.J.: Uncovering symmetries in irregular process networks. In: Giacobazzi, R., Berdine, J., Mastroeni, I. (eds.) VMCAI 2013. LNCS, vol. 7737, pp. 496–514. Springer, Heidelberg (2013). https://doi.org/10.1007/978-3-642-35873-9_29
10. Namjoshi, K.S., Trefler, R.J.: Analysis of dynamic process networks. In: Baier, C., Tinelli, C. (eds.) TACAS 2015. LNCS, vol. 9035, pp. 164–178. Springer, Heidelberg (2015). https://doi.org/10.1007/978-3-662-46681-0_11
11. Namjoshi, K.S., Trefler, R.J.: Loop freedom in AODVv2. In: Graf, S., Viswanathan, M. (eds.) FORTE 2015. LNCS, vol. 9039, pp. 98–112. Springer, Cham (2015). https://doi.org/10.1007/978-3-319-19195-9_7
12. Namjoshi, K.S., Trefler, R.J.: Parameterized compositional model checking. In: Chechik, M., Raskin, J.-F. (eds.) TACAS 2016. LNCS, vol. 9636, pp. 589–606. Springer, Heidelberg (2016). https://doi.org/10.1007/978-3-662-49674-9_39
13. Namjoshi, K.S., Trefler, R.J.: Symmetry reduction for the local Mu-Calculus. In: Beyer, D., Huisman, M. (eds.) TACAS 2018. LNCS, vol. 10806, pp. 379–395. Springer, Cham (2018). https://doi.org/10.1007/978-3-319-89963-3_22
14. Owicki, S.S., Gries, D.: Verifying properties of parallel programs: an axiomatic approach. Commun. ACM **19**(5), 279–285 (1976)
15. Padon, O., Hoenicke, J., Losa, G., Podelski, A., Sagiv, M., Shoham, S.: Reducing liveness to safety in first-order logic. PACMPL **2**(POPL), 26:1–26:33 (2018)
16. Padon, O., McMillan, K.L., Panda, A., Sagiv, M., Shoham, S.: Ivy: safety verification by interactive generalization. In: Proceedings of the 37th ACM SIGPLAN Conference on Programming Language Design and Implementation, PLDI 2016, Santa Barbara, CA, USA, 13–17 June 2016, pp. 614–630 (2016)

17. Piskac, R., de Moura, L.M., Bjørner, N.: Deciding effectively propositional logic using DPLL and substitution sets. J. Autom. Reason. **44**(4), 401–424 (2010)
18. Taube, M., et al.: Modularity for decidability of deductive verification with applications to distributed systems. In: Proceedings of the 39th ACM SIGPLAN Conference on Programming Language Design and Implementation, PLDI 2018, pp. 662–677. ACM, New York (2018)

Generation of Signals Under Temporal Constraints for CPS Testing

Benoît Barbot[1(✉)], Nicolas Basset[2(✉)], and Thao Dang[2(✉)]

[1] LACL, Université Paris-Est Créteil, Créteil, France
[2] VERIMAG/CNRS, Université Grenoble Alpes, Grenoble, France
benoit.barbot@lacl.fr, Nicolas.Basset1@univ-grenoble-alpes.fr,
thao.dang@imag.fr

Abstract. This work is concerned with validation of cyber-physical systems (CPS) via sampling of input signal spaces. Such a space is infinite and in general too difficult to treat symbolically, meaning that the only reasonable option is to sample a finite number of input signals and simulate the corresponding system behaviours. It is important to choose a sample so that it best "covers" the whole input signal space. We use timed automata to model temporal constraints, in order to avoid spurious bugs coming from unrealistic inputs and this can also reduce the input space to explore. We propose a method for low-discrepancy generation of signals under temporal constraints recognised by timed automata. The discrepancy notion reflects how uniform the input signal space is sampled and additionally allows deriving validation and performance guarantees. To evaluate testing quality, we also show a measure of uniformity of an arbitrary set of input signals. We describe a prototype tool chain and demonstrate the proposed methods on a Kinetic Battery Model (KiBaM) and a $\Sigma\Delta$ modulator.

1 Introduction

Cyber-physical systems (CPS) are integrations of computation with physical processes, and have become a predominant component of modern engineering systems. A major challenge in proving correct operations of industrial CPS is the absence of rigorous mathematical models, and even when such models are available they are often intractable by exhaustive formal verification techniques, due to computational complexity. Falsification methods, based on black-box testing, are often used for industrial-size complex systems. These methods rely on a tester that can execute/simulate the system under some input stimuli and observe the corresponding outputs; their goal is to search for the worst case behaviours by minimising robustness of satisfaction of some temporal logic formula (see for example [2,15,18,29]). The most popular tools are S-Taliro [3] and Breach [16]. Generally, a challenge in this approach is the limitation of global optimisation solvers which may converge to local optima. Also, most optimisers do not take into account input constraints and may lead to trivial solutions that do not correspond to realistic scenarios. Statistical model checking based on Monte Carlo

J. M. Badger and K. Y. Rozier (Eds.): NFM 2019, LNCS 11460, pp. 54–70, 2019.
https://doi.org/10.1007/978-3-030-20652-9_4

methods has also been applied to CPS [1,7,13]. The reader is referred to a survey on CPS validation approaches [8]. We defer a discussion on related work to Sect. 6 after our approach is described in detail.

It is clear that the efficiency of such a validation process depends on the class of input signals under consideration. On one hand, this class should be sufficiently expressive to capture all feasible configurations of the environment. On the other hand, such permissible classes can be very large; therefore, it is desirable to consider only the input stimuli which are realistic or relevant w.r.t. the operation context of the system. In this work, we are interested in classes of signals which satisfy temporal constraints modelled as timed automata (TA). Indeed, in a CPS, computation processes interact with physical processes via devices (such as sampling, measurement, actuation) the timing imprecision of which can be appropriately modelled using TA. We now formulate the problems we want to solve in order to address the above issues.

1. Generate a set of input signals satisfying some temporal constraints. Using these signals to simulate or execute the system, one expects to find a behaviour that falsifies the property. When no such behaviour is found, it is important to provide guarantees, such as the portion of correct behaviours, or the average robustness of property satisfaction.
2. Given an arbitrary set of input signals, determine its testing quality in terms of property checking or performance evaluation.

To address the first problem, we extend the method for uniform random generation of runs of timed automata [6] to propose a new method based on low discrepancy. The generated timed words are then mapped to input signals. To address the second problem, we employ the well-known Kolmogorov-Smirnov statistic [26] to measure the goodness of fit of a sample w.r.t. a given distribution. Interestingly, this statistic can be interpreted in terms of the star discrepancy [23] largely used in quasi-Monte Carlo methods.

The paper is organised as follows. Section 2 recalls important concepts, namely the star discrepancy, timed automata and timed polytopes, and quantitative guarantees. The next three sections assume that a timed automaton describing a class of input signals of interest is given, and focus on the problem of generation of timed words. Section 3 presents a transformation from the unit box to a timed polytope (corresponding to the constraints on time delays along a path). In the forward direction, by sampling over the unit box and then applying the transformation we obtain a sampling over the timed polytope. In Sect. 4, we describe a new method for low-discrepancy sampling which yields a quasi-Monte Carlo method. Section 5 presents a measure of uniformity degree of an arbitrary sample and discusses how this measure can be estimated, by using again the above-described transformation but in the backward direction (which is known as the Rosenblatt's transformation [26]). Finally, based on these results we propose in Sect. 6 a framework for testing CPS with guarantees. We include here a comparison with related work to highlight the novelty of our approach.

We describe a tool chain which integrates an implementation of these methods, and demonstrate the proposed methods on a Kinetic Battery Model and a $\Sigma\Delta$ modulator.

2 Preliminaries

Star Discrepancy. By the (n-dimensional) unit box we mean the set $[0,1]^n$. Given a point $\boldsymbol{b} = (b_1, \ldots, b_n)$ inside the unit box, we define the box $[\boldsymbol{0}, \boldsymbol{b}] = [0, b_1] \times \cdots \times [0, b_n]$. The star discrepancy of a finite set S of points in the unit box is defined as:

$$D_\star(S) = \sup_{\boldsymbol{b} \in [0,1]^n} \left| \mathtt{Vol}([\boldsymbol{0}, \boldsymbol{b}]) - \frac{|S \cap [\boldsymbol{0}, \boldsymbol{b}]|}{|S|} \right|.$$

Intuitively, the star discrepancy is a measure of how equi-distributed a set of points is over the unit box, or how different its distribution is compared to the uniform distribution. This notion is used in number theoretic and quasi-Monte Carlo methods. The lower the discrepancy is, the better the space is "filled" with points. Asymptotically a sequence of uniform random points will homogeneously fill the space $\mathcal{P}$ that is sampled such that for every subset of $\mathcal{P}$, the density of points in this subset will be proportional to its volume. In this work we use two well-known low-discrepancy sequences: Halton [19] and Kronecker [25]. The star discrepancy is a way of quantifying how homogeneously a sample covers the sampling space for finite sequences. Its link with the n-dimensional Kolmogorov-Smirnov statistic is provided later (see Sect. 5.2).

Timed Automata and Timed Polytopes. Let X be a finite set of non-negative real-valued variables called *clocks*, which are assumed bounded by a constant $M \in \mathbb{N}$. A *clock constraint* has the form $x \sim c$ or $x - y \sim c$ where $\sim \in \{\leq, <, =, >, \geq\}$ with $x, y \in X$, $c \in \mathbb{N}$. A *guard* is a finite conjunction of clock constraints. For a clock vector $\boldsymbol{x} \in [0, M]^X$ and a non-negative real t, we denote by $\boldsymbol{x} + t$ the vector $\boldsymbol{x} + (t, \ldots, t)$. A *timed automaton* (TA) $\mathcal{A}$ is a tuple $(\Sigma, X, Q, i_0, \mathcal{F}, \Delta)$ where Σ is a finite set of events; X is a finite set of clocks; Q is a finite set of *locations*; i_0 is the initial location; $\mathcal{F} \subseteq Q$ is a set of final locations; and Δ is a finite set of *transitions*. A transition $\delta \in \Delta$ has an *origin* $\delta^- \in Q$, a *destination* $\delta^+ \in Q$, a label $a_\delta \in \Sigma$, a *guard* $\mathfrak{g}_\delta$ and a *reset* function $\mathfrak{r}_\delta$ determined by a subset of clocks $B \subseteq X$; this transition resets to 0 all the clocks in B and does not modify the other clocks. A *state* $s = (q, \boldsymbol{x}) \in Q \times [0, M]^X$ is a pair of a location and a clock vector. The initial state of $\mathcal{A}$ is $(i_0, \boldsymbol{0})$. A *timed transition* is a pair (t, δ) of a time *delay* $t \in [0, M]$ followed by a discrete transition $\delta \in \Delta$. The delay t represents the time before firing the transition δ. A run is an alternating sequence $(q_0, \boldsymbol{x}_0) \xrightarrow{t_1, \delta_1} (q_1, \boldsymbol{x}_1) \ldots \xrightarrow{t_n, \delta_n} (q_n, \boldsymbol{x}_n)$ of states and timed transitions with the following updating rules: q_i is the successors of q_{i-1} by δ_i, the vector $\boldsymbol{x}_{i-1} + t$ must satisfy the guard $\mathfrak{g}_\delta$ and $\boldsymbol{x}_i = \mathfrak{r}_\delta(\boldsymbol{x}_{i-1} + t)$. This run is *labelled* by the *timed word* $(t_1, a_1) \cdots (t_n, a_n)$ where for every $i \leq n$,

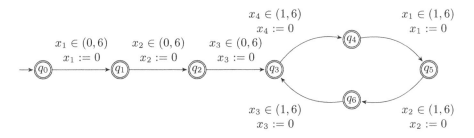

Fig. 1. A timed automaton for the running example.

a_i is the label of δ_i. The set of timed words that label all the runs leading from the initial state $(i_0, \mathbf{0})$ to a final state $(q_n \in \mathcal{F})$ is called the *timed language* of $\mathcal{A}$. Given a discrete path $\alpha = \delta_1 \cdots \delta_n$ of $\mathcal{A}$ the set of timed vectors $\mathbf{t} \in [0, M]^n$ such that $(i_0, \mathbf{0}) \xrightarrow{t_1, \delta_1} (q_1, t_1) \ldots \xrightarrow{t_n, \delta_n} (q_n, t_n)$ is called the *timed polytope* associated to the path α.

Example 1 (Running example). We consider the TA in Fig. 1. This automaton has the property that after entering the cycle the time between 4 consecutive events is between 1 and 6. Intuitively, they are loosely periodic as transitions cannot be taken too early or too late. This automaton is used to model a quasi-periodic pattern of signals with uncertain period ranging between 1 and 6. Its first three locations before the cycle model the uncertain phase of the signals. To illustrate the timed polytope notion, we consider the path of length 2 starting at location q_0 and ending at q_2. The timed polytope corresponding to this path is the triangle $\{(t_1, t_2) \mid t_1 + t_2 < 6, t_1 > 0, t_2 > 0\}$. Its 2-dimensional volume is $6^2/2 = 18$. Uniform sampling in this polytope is depicted in Fig. 2 (b_1). More generally, the timed polytope associated to the (unique) path of length n is defined by $0 < t_{k-3} + t_{k-2} + t_{k-1} + t_k < 6$, for $k = 1, \ldots, 3$ with the convention that $t_j = 0$ for $j < 1$, and $1 < t_{k-3} + t_{k-2} + t_{k-1} + t_k < 6$, for $k = 4, \ldots, n-3$. The kth constraint is due to the guard $x_i \in (1, 6)$ (to be precise, with $i = (k \bmod 4) + 1$) because the clock x_i contains the sum of the 4 last delays before taking the kth transition. Computing the volume of such a timed polytope requires dynamic programming algorithms (involving an integral operator per transition) which can be found in [4, 6].

Quantitative Guarantees and Sampling-Based Estimation. Quantitative properties of CPS can be expressed by averaging some function f defined on the set of input signals. For instance, such a function can be the indicator function of the set of input stimuli that lead to incorrect behaviours, and the average gives the probability that an input signal falls in this set. This is more generally the problem of estimating a sub-language volume. In addition, given a property expressed using temporal logics, f can be the (satisfaction) robustness which is a function of the input. Such properties can thus be evaluated by sampling in the input signal space, as in Monte Carlo and quasi-Monte Carlo methods. To obtain

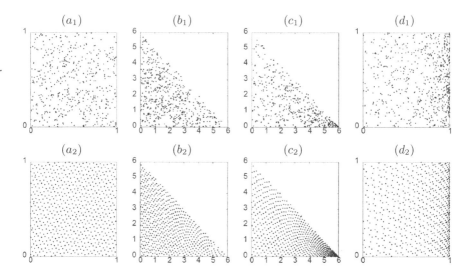

Fig. 2. First line, left to right. (a_1): we first draw 450 points uniformly at random in the unit box; (b_1): we then apply the inverse sampling method with the CDF of the uniform sampling (see Theorem 1) to get 450 timed vectors in the timed polytope; (c_1): we do the same as for (b_1) but using the CDF of the isotropic sampling; (d_1): the sample in (c_1) is mapped back to the unit box with the CDF of the uniform sampling to check its star discrepancy. Second line, we do the same as for the first line, but starting with a low-discrepancy sequence of 450 points in the unit box (a_2).

accurate results, the sampling process should generate the signals as uniformly as possible to cover well the input signal space with high probability. In other words, the probability that a generated signal falls in a set should be proportional to the volume of this set. To solve this problem for timed automata we need a transformation from the unit box to a timed polytope, which is explained in the next section. We also use this transformation for a low-discrepancy generation method presented in Sect. 4. We further exploit this transformation in Sect. 5 to estimate a measure of uniformity degree for an arbitrary sample of timed words.

3   Transformation from the Unit Box to a Timed Polytope

Defining Probability Distributions to Sample Timed Languages. We first emphasise that we want to sample uniformly timed words of a given length from the timed language of a given TA. This *uniform sampling* is such that every timed word of the language has the "same chance" of being sampled. Note that the sampled space is uncountably infinite since the delays are real numbers. This uniform sampling should not be confused with an intuitive sampling method, called *isotropic*, which at each discrete step makes a uniform choice among the possible delays. This isotropic sampling method is used as a "default" sampling in several work (see [10] and references therein). The difference between the two sampling methods will be illustrated in Example 2.

For a given TA, our previous work [6] proposes a method for generating uniformly timed words of a given length. Such a uniform sampling is done by adding probability distributions on time delays along a run of the automaton. In [9] we treat the case of generating infinite timed words, based on the notion of maximal entropy. Let us now explain the essence of these ideas. The constraints on the delays along a discrete path define a timed polytope; sampling runs along a discrete path thus reduces to sampling over a timed polytope. For simplicity of presentation, we will explain only the generation of timed vectors in a timed polytope, or in a sequence of timed polytopes along a single path. Discrete branching can be handled similarly as in [6].

Given a discrete path $\alpha = \delta_1 \cdots \delta_n$ of the TA $\mathcal{A}$, let $\mathcal{P}$ be the timed polytope associated to this path. We want to evaluate $\int_{\mathcal{P}} f(t)dt / \mathtt{Vol}(\mathcal{P})$, the average over $\mathcal{P}$ of a function $f : \mathcal{P} \rightarrow \mathbb{R}$ (used to express a quantitative property). Here the normalising constant $\mathtt{Vol}(\mathcal{P}) = \int_{\mathcal{P}} 1 dt$ is the n-dimensional volume of $\mathcal{P}$. More generally, we can give different weights to different timed vectors of $\mathcal{P}$ by using a *probability density function* (PDF), namely a function $\omega : \mathcal{P} \rightarrow \mathbb{R}^+$ such that $\int_{\mathcal{P}} \omega(t)dt = 1$. Then the integral we want to evaluate becomes $\int_{\mathcal{P}} f(t)\omega(t)dt$, which is also called the expectation $E(f(T))$ of the random variable $T = (T_1, \ldots, T_n)$ distributed according to the PDF ω (and that takes values as timed vectors in $\mathcal{P}$).

The uniform distribution assigns the density of probability $\omega(t) = 1/\mathtt{Vol}(\mathcal{P})$ to every timed vector $t \in \mathcal{P}$. A sampled timed vector t thus falls in a given subset A of the timed polytope $\mathcal{P}$ with probability $\mathtt{Vol}(A)/\mathtt{Vol}(\mathcal{P})$. If we define f as the indicator function 1_B of a set B of "bad" behaviours, and if T is distributed according to the uniform distribution, then the expectation $E(1_B(T))$ measures the portion of bad behaviours in $\mathcal{P}$, formally $E(1_B(T)) = \mathtt{Vol}(B)/\mathtt{Vol}(\mathcal{P})$.

To define the random variables T, it suffices to give its n-dimensional cumulative distribution function (CDF) $F(t) = \mathrm{Prob}(T \leq t)$ where the partial order $\leq$ is defined by $(T_1, \ldots, T_n) \leq (t_1, \ldots, t_n)$ iff $T_i \leq t_i$ for every $i = 1 \ldots n$. This CDF is usually given by the following sequence of conditional CDF: $F_i(t_i \mid t_1, \ldots, t_{i-1}) = \mathrm{Prob}(T_i \geq t_i \mid T_1 = t_1, \ldots, T_{i-1} = t_{i-1})$. The following chain rule gives the relation between the conditional CDF and the CDF of T:

$$F(t_1, \ldots, t_n) = F_1(t_1)F_2(t_2 \mid t_1) \ldots F_n(t_n \mid t_1, \ldots, t_{n-1}).$$

In [6] and in some other work, the conditional CDF $F_i(t_i \mid t)$, used to sample t_i, depends only on the current state (q_{i-1}, x_{i-1}), that is $F_i(t_i \mid t) = G_i(t_i \mid (q_{i-1}, x_{i-1}))$ for some conditional CDF G_i. For the uniform distribution on a timed polytope, the conditional CDF are characterised in [6], via the definition of the conditional PDF (which are the derivatives of the CDF). These conditional CDF for uniform sampling play a particular role in our subsequent development, and is denoted specifically by $\mathfrak{F} = (\mathfrak{F}_1, \ldots, \mathfrak{F}_n)$. Theorem 1 summarises the characterisation of the CDF for the uniform sampling of timed words. These CDF can be effectively computed and their computation was implemented in the tool chain of [6].

Theorem 1 ([6]). *Given a path in a TA one can compute the CDF $\mathfrak{F}_i$ in polynomial time w.r.t. the length of the path. These CDF can be written in the following form $\mathfrak{F}_i(t_i \mid t_1, \ldots, t_{i-1}) = \pi_i(t_1, \ldots, t_{i-1})/\gamma_i(t_1, \ldots, t_i)$ with π_i and γ_i polynomials of degree at most i.*

Example 2 (Example 1 continued). To show the difference between the isotropic and uniform methods, we consider again the path $q_0\, q_1\, q_2$ of the automaton of Example 1. We sample timed vectors (t_1, t_2) in the 2-dimensional timed polytope associated to this path (shown in the first line of Fig. 2). Using the isotropic sampling, t_1 is chosen uniformly in $(0, 6)$ and then t_2 is chosen uniformly in $(0, 6 - t_1)$. This is why in Fig. 2-(c_1) the set of points generated by the isotropic sampling gets more and more dense along the t_1-axis. In particular, with the isotropic sampling the set $\{(t_1, t_2) \mid t_1 \in (0, 1), t_1 + t_2 < 6\}$ has the same probability as the small triangle $\{(t_1, t_2) \mid t_1 \in (5, 6), t_1 + t_2 < 6\}$, while the former is 11 times bigger than the latter. This is in contrast with the uniform sampling where the chance of falling in a set is proportional to its area. With the uniform sampling (see Fig. 2-(b_1)), t_1 is chosen according to the probability density function (PDF) $t_1 \mapsto (1 - t_1)/18$, and t_2 according to $t_2 \mapsto 1/(1 - t_1)$. The PDF of a timed vector (t_1, t_2) is hence $((1 - t_1)/18)1/(1 - t_1) = 1/18 = 1/\mathtt{Vol}(\mathcal{P})$, as expected.

Transformation from the Unit Box to a Timed Polytope. We observe further that if we use the conditional CDF $F = (F_i)_{i=1..n}$ to transform a timed vector $\boldsymbol{t}$ to a vector $\boldsymbol{u}$ as follows: $u_1 = F_1(u_1)$, and for $i = 2, \ldots, n$ $u_i = F_i(t_i \mid t_1, \ldots, t_{i-1})$, then $\boldsymbol{u} = (u_1, \ldots, u_n)$ is in $[0, 1]^n$. The following theorem allows going back and forth between a timed polytope and the unit box.

Theorem 2 (Rosenblatt's transformation [26]). *Let $F = (F_i)_{i=1..n}$ be a sequence of conditional CDF. Define the transformation $\boldsymbol{U} = F(\boldsymbol{T})$ between the random vectors $\boldsymbol{U}$ and $\boldsymbol{T}$ by $U_1 = F_1(T_1)$, $U_i = F_i(T_i \mid T_1, \ldots, T_{i-1})$ for every $i = 2 \ldots n$. Then $\boldsymbol{T}$ is distributed according to the CDF F iff $U_1, \ldots, U_n$ are i.i.d uniformly distributed random variables on $[0, 1]$.*

This theorem allows us to make use of the transformation $\mathfrak{F}^{-1}$ for generating timed words, similarly to random sampling according to CDF as in *inverse transform sampling*. Once $t_1, \ldots, t_{i-1}$ are sampled, the next delay t_i is randomly sampled as follows. A real number u_i is drawn uniformly in $[0, 1]$, and then one finds the unique t_i such that $\mathfrak{F}_i(t_i \mid t_1, \ldots, t_{i-1}) = u_i$ using for instance the Newton's method. Ultimately, from n i.i.d uniformly distributed random numbers $u_1, \ldots, u_n$ in the unit interval, we get a timed vector $(t_1, \ldots, t_n) = \mathfrak{F}^{-1}(u_1, \ldots, u_n)$. This transformation $\mathfrak{F}^{-1}$ implicitly underlies the uniform sampling method presented in [6]. We can now use it for the two problems stated in the introduction:

- *In a forward manner for low-discrepancy generation (see Sect. 4).*
- *In a backward manner to evaluate the generation quality (see Sect. 5.2).*

4   Low-Discrepancy Generation and Quasi-Monte Carlo Methods for Timed Polytopes

We exploit the forward use of $\mathfrak{F}^{-1}$ (from the unit box to a timed polytope), to generate points in a timed polytope with low discrepancy. To this end, it suffices to start with a low-discrepancy set of points in the unit box and then apply to it the transformation $\mathfrak{F}^{-1}$. To obtain a low discrepancy point set in the unit box, in this work we use, as mentioned earlier, the well-known low-discrepancy sequences Halton [19] and Kronecker [25].

The use of low-discrepancy generation is motivated by the fact that when considering finite sequences, some (deterministic) low-discrepancy sequences behave better than uniform sequences in terms of homogeneous space-filling. Our generation procedure indeed yields a quasi-Monte Carlo method [24] for estimating or averaging integral functions which express quantitative properties of interest. Note that using the uniform random generation, one can only provide statistical guarantees, as Monte Carlo methods. This new generation method, in contrast, allows characterising *deterministic* error bounds (that is, without probabilistic uncertainty) in approximating the multi-dimensional integral of a function by the average of the function values on a sample of points. A popular characterisation is the Koksma-Hlawka (KH) inequality [20]. Formally, given a function $g : [0, 1]^n \rightarrow \mathbb{R}$ and a sample $S = (\boldsymbol{p}^{(k)})_{k=1..N}$, the Koksma-Hlawka inequality is

$$\left| \frac{1}{N} \sum_{n=1}^{N} g(\boldsymbol{p}^{(n)}) - \int_{[0,1]^n} g(\boldsymbol{r})d\boldsymbol{r} \right| \leq V^*(g)(D_\star(S))^{1/n} \tag{1}$$

where $D_\star(S)$ is the star discrepancy of the set S, $V^*(g)$ is the variation in the sense of Hardy and Krause, which does not depend on S, so it is constant when we fix g. Using low-discrepancy sequences yields an upper-bound $D_\star(S) \leq C_n \log(N)^n/N$ where the constant C_n depends on the point dimension n and on the type of the sequence but not on the number N of sampled points.

We now show how the above result can be applied to our testing context where f is the function expressing the guarantee. Each timed word corresponds to an input signal. To average f, we can use the quasi-Monte Carlo approach for $g = f \circ \mathfrak{F}^{-1}$ (where $\mathfrak{F}$ is the above-described CDF of the uniform generation in a timed polytope $\mathcal{P}$) as follows. We first generate a low-discrepancy sequence of vectors in the unit box, next we apply $\mathfrak{F}^{-1}$ and then f to the sequence, compute the average to get an estimate of the expectation $\int_{\mathcal{P}} f(\boldsymbol{t})d\boldsymbol{t}/\texttt{Vol}(\mathcal{P})$. Another application is to estimate the size (volume measure) of a subset E of the timed polytope $\mathcal{P}$ (corresponding for instance to the set of input stimuli leading to incorrect behaviours). To this end, it suffices to define $g = \chi_{\mathfrak{F}(E)}$ where χ_A is the indicator function of a set A.

Providing different types of guarantees (statistical vs. deterministic), the uniform random and low-discrepancy generation methods are complementary. It is important to emphasise that the low-discrepancy generation method does not require estimating the star discrepancy, which is indeed computationally costly. Only after the testing process is done, the star discrepancy or more generally the

Kolmogorov-Smirnov statistic (which will be introduced in the next section) are estimated to evaluate the testing results. This information is useful for deciding whether additional test cases are needed.

5   Evaluating the Uniformity Degree

To evaluate the level of confidence in the testing results, we now address the second problem stated in the introduction. In the sampling-based framework described thus far, this problem can be formulated as evaluating the quality of an arbitrary sample in estimating a quantitative guarantee. Since the approximation quality of both Monte Carlo and quasi-Monte Carlo methods depends on the uniformity degree of the sampled point set (which indicates how close the distribution of this set is to the uniform distribution), we are interested in evaluating the uniformity degree of a given point set.

5.1   Visualising n-dimensional Uniformity Degree via Histograms

One practical way to evaluate the uniformity degree is visualisation. For 2-dimensional samples, we have already visualised in Fig. 2, the difference in the uniformity degree between the sets sampled using different methods. For clouds of points in dimensions higher than 2, we propose the following visualisation method based on histograms.

Example 3. We modify slightly the TA of Fig. 1 to ensure that every delay is bounded by 2. To do so, it suffices to add a clock y that is reset at each transition and must satisfy the condition $y < 2$ for the transition to be taken. This ensures that the timed polytope associated to the discrete path of length n is included in the box $[0, 2]^n$. We draw timed words (using a sampling method) and for each box $\prod_{i=1}^{n}[b_i, b_{i+1}]$ we count the number of times this box is *hit* by a sampled timed word. Since each box has volume 1, every box that is fully included in the language has probability to be hit equal to $1/\text{Vol}(L_n)$. The other have a lower probability which is proportional to the volume of their intersection with the language. To visualise the boxes, we number each box with a binary representation given by the lower bounds of the box. Formally, $\prod_{i=1}^{n}[b_i, b_i + 1]$ is numbered by $\sum_{i=1}^{n} b_i 2^{n-i}$. For instance with $n = 5$, the number 25, the binary representation of which is 11001, is assigned to the box $[1, 2] \times [1, 2] \times [0, 1] \times [0, 1] \times [1, 2]$. Figure 3 shows the histograms of the hitting count for each box included in $[0, 2]^5$ after drawing $5,000,000$ timed words. All the boxes intersect the language, and the purple bars correspond to the boxes fully included in the language that we call hereafter purple boxes. We can observe from the histograms a great similarity between the uniform and low-discrepancy sampling methods. As expected, when restricted to the purple bars, their histograms are flat because the probability for each purple box to be hit is the same and equal to $1/\text{Vol}(L_5)$. We can see that the isotropic sampling is clearly not uniform on the purple boxes and it over-samples the green boxes.

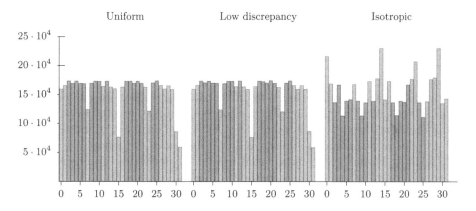

Fig. 3. Histograms for Example 3 (Color figure online)

5.2 Measuring the Uniformity Degree

Another evaluation method is to characterise the uniformity degree using the Kolmogorov-Smirnov (KS) test, which is a statistical test to measure how well a sample S of points fits a distribution given by a known CDF F. We first point out the relation between this test and the star discrepancy, which allows us to exploit the backward use of $\mathfrak{F}^{-1}$ (from a timed polytope to the unit box) to estimate the KS statistic. The Kolmogorov-Smirnov statistic is defined by the following value (which is a random variable when the sample is drawn at random):

$$\mathbf{KS}(F,S) = \sup_{p \in \mathbb{R}^n} |F(p) - \tilde{F}_S(p)|$$

where $\tilde{F}_S$ is the empirical CDF associated with the sample S defined as $\tilde{F}_S(p) = |\{p' \in S \mid p' \leq p\}|/|S|$, which is the ratio of the number of points in S that falls in the box $[-\infty, p_1] \times \ldots \times [-\infty, p_n]$. Let F_U be the CDF associated to n i.i.d. uniform random variables on $[0, 1]$, then $F_U(p)$ is the volume of the box $[\mathbf{0}, p]$, and the KS statistic $\mathbf{KS}(F_U, S)$ is nothing else than $D_\star(S)$, that is the *star discrepancy* introduced in the preliminaries and used in the Koksma-Hlawka inequality (1). This connection is known (see for example [21,23]). Theorem 2 is a basis for the following observation. Given a sample S, one can translate $\mathbf{KS}(F,S)$ into $\mathbf{KS}(F_U, F(S))$. The former is the multi-dimensional KS statistic of S w.r.t. a CDF F, and the latter is the KS statistic of the transformed sample $F(S) = \{F(p) \mid p \in P\}$ w.r.t. the uniform distribution F_U on the unit box. The latter is, as mentioned before, the star discrepancy of $F(S)$. Applying this observation to the CDF $\mathfrak{F}$ of the uniform distribution on a timed polytope, we have $\mathbf{KS}(\mathfrak{F}, S) = D_\star(\mathfrak{F}(S))$. Note that when S is obtained via uniform (resp. low-discrepancy) sampling then $S = \mathfrak{F}^{-1}(S')$ where S' is a sample of uniform random vectors (resp. a low-discrepancy sample). So in that case $\mathbf{KS}(\mathfrak{F}, S) = D_\star(\mathfrak{F}(\mathfrak{F}^{-1}(S'))) = D_\star(S')$ and the KS test that requires the KS statistic to be below a threshold passes with high probability (resp. for sure).

Example 4. For the running example, we compute $D_\star(\mathfrak{F}(S))$ of a sample S of timed words drawn using the three sampling methods. After mapping the generated timed vectors back to the unit box, we estimate the star discrepancy of the resulting points. The estimation based on a grid provides a lower and an upper bound on the star discrepancy value [28]. For the set generated by the low-discrepancy method (Fig. 2-(b_1)), the star discrepancy estimation interval is $[0.009, 0.020]$, by the uniform method (Fig. 2-(a_1)) $[0.040, 0.047]$; by the isotropic method with a uniform random sequence (Fig. 2-(a_4)) $[0.256, 0.266]$, and by the isotropic method with a low-discrepancy sequence (Fig. 2-(b_4)) $[0.250, 0.257]$. From these results, regarding the KS statistics, we observe that the low-discrepancy and uniform methods are clearly better than the isotropic method. It is worth noting that although the points in the unit box generated by the isotropic method from the low-discrepancy sequence look in the figure more "regular", their discrepancy is far larger.

6   Application to CPS Testing

6.1   CPS Testing

Our development thus far focuses on timed words, which can be thought of as an abstraction of real-valued signals. In order to achieve a procedure for CPS testing with guarantees, we show how to define real-valued signals from timed words. We also discuss how timed automata can be used to specify temporal constraints of input signals. Before continuing, let us sketch our procedure.

1. Specifying the temporal constraints on input signals by a timed automaton.
2. Generating a sample of timed words of the timed automaton, using either the uniform method or the low-discrepancy method.
3. Mapping the generated timed words to input signals.
4. Simulating the model or executing the system under the input signals.
5. Determining the guarantees: the uniform method produces statistical guarantees (such as, probability of satisfaction) while the low-discrepancy method produces deterministic ones (such as, error bound on the ratio of correct behaviours or on the satisfaction robustness).

If the testing process uses an arbitrary sample of timed words we can still evaluate its generation quality by the step 5. The steps 2 and 5 have been discussed in the previous sections. Before proceeding with the remaining steps, we point out the novelty of our approach. The existing approaches, such as S-Taliro [3] and Breach [16], use a parametrisation of input signals to reduce the involved infinite dimensional optimisation problem to a finite dimensional one. Such a parametrisation (based on a fixed time discretisation producing to a fixed sequence of time stamps) does not directly capture temporal constraints on input signals. This may lead to a large number of non-realistic test scenarios that are explored by the optimiser but then need to be discarded. With the ability of generating valid signals satisfying temporal constraints, our approach can consider a larger variety of time discretisations leading to better coverage. Also, our approach can reduce the search space and aim at good coverage only over the valid signal space. Furthermore, our generation methods can generate parametric signals; for example, the signal values for the time intervals between the transitions need not be fixed but are represented as parameters over which optimisation can be used, as in the existing optimisation-based approaches. In terms of complexity, if we use the existing optimisation-based approaches, the number of the parameters (that is the number of the optimisation variables) corresponds to the path length in our approach. Both of the generation methods (low-discrepancy and uniform) require computing the CDF which, as mentioned earlier, can be done in polynomial time w.r.t. the path length. In other words, compared to these methods, our signal generation methods do not add much computation efforts and enable more efficient search since all the generated signals are relevant.

Specifying Temporal Constraints on Signals Using Timed Automata. Timed automata are a popular tool for specifying temporal properties of various types of systems [8]. In this section, we only illustrate the usefulness of timed automata in specifying two common properties of signals arising in CPS applications. The first is *bounded variability*, meaning that within any time period of duration T_p there cannot be more than m events. Another definition is to state that for every integer $1 \leq k \leq n - m$ the sum of delays $t_k + \ldots + t_{k+m-1}$ is always greater than T_p. This can be measured by a clock that can be reused every m transitions, so it suffices to have m clocks (one per congruence class modulo m). This is illustrated in our running example: every sequence of $m = 4$ delays needs more than $T_p = 1$ time units to occur.

The second property is a perturbed periodic pattern, which specifies that some m events occur during a period of $[T_p, T_p + \Delta_p]$ time units and that during this period the delays are in the prescribed intervals. This perturbed periodic pattern is used in the sequel to create input signals to a model of $\Sigma\Delta$ modulator.

From Timed Words to Signals. A mapping can be directly defined when the timed words yield directly Boolean signals which switch between True or False values after a time delay. As we will show later, such Boolean signals can model the fact that a battery is turned on or off in the KiBaM model used in our experimentation. Another straightforward mapping can be defined to obtain signals that are piecewise constant taking values in a finite set. In the above-described case of uncertain periodic pattern, during a period the signals take a predefined sequence of values (this can model for instance a discretised sinus function) and each change of value occurs after a time delay. A more general way of mapping is to use *retiming* functions, motivated by sampled-data systems and more generally embedded control systems. A retiming function can specify perturbation in terms of imprecision and delay in sampling and communication.

6.2   Experimentation

Our Tool Chain. We implemented our workflow using 4 tools: PRISM [22], SageMath [27], Cosmos [5] and Simulink®. The workflow is depicted in Fig. 4. The first steps are similar to those in [6], their output is a stochastic process generating timed words in the language of the automaton. Cosmos then simulates

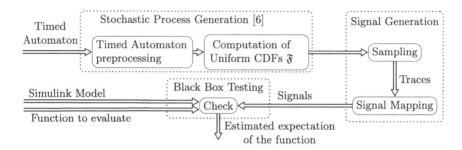

Fig. 4. Tool chain for black-box CPS validation with input temporal constraints.

the stochastic process using Monte Carlo or quasi-Monte Carlo sampling (box "Signal Generation" in Fig. 4). The obtained timed traces are used to generate real-valued signals which are then fed to the Simulink model we want to test.

Example 1 - KiBaM Model. We first illustrate our workflow on an example of a micro-controller powered by a battery using a Kinetic Battery Model (KiBaM) depicted in Fig. 5. The goal is to show that if the micro-controller follows its specification in terms of energy usage pattern then the battery will last a certain amount of time. The KiBaM battery model is easily described by a system of ODE. The main feature of this model is that it reflects well the ability of the battery to "self-recharge" when idle. The controller oscillates between two states: the idle state where it consumes a very small amount of power and the active state where it consumes more. The energy usage pattern specification is that the controller may not stay active for more than τ_1 time units but needs to be active every τ_3 time units and when it is idle it waits at least τ_2 time units until it becomes active again. During the operation, the controller drains the battery if it stays active for too long, but the battery restores itself when the controller is idle. Eventually the battery will be completely drained. The property we want to check is that the battery lasts more than T time units: `always_[0,T] (BatteryCharge > 0)`. Figure 6 depicts a simulation trace of the battery and the controller. One can observe that when the controller is active, the

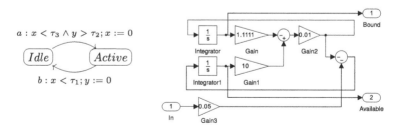

Fig. 5. KiBaM model: Simulink diagram and 2-state controller. When the state of the controller is *Idle* (resp. *Active*), the input port (In) receives the value 0 (resp. 1).

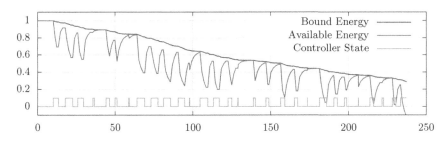

Fig. 6. Co-simulation of the automaton with uniform sampling and the KiBaM model. The energy unit is a fraction of initial capacity.

available charge quickly drops, but as the controller quickly returns to the idle state, the battery is able to self-recharge. This trace was sampled with uniform sampling. We performed experiments with the three sampling methods using 10,000 trajectories. For $T = 271$, the property holds on every trajectory for all methods. For $T = 272$, the estimated satisfaction probability is in $[0.948, 0.959]$ for the uniform sampling and $[0.953, 0.963]$ for the low-discrepancy sampling using Halton's sequence. The confidence level is 0.99 and the total computation time is around 1 min, where a dominating part of 45 s was used for the CPS simulation, and 15 s for the stochastic process simulation and signal generation. The CPS simulation requires to numerically solve differential equations which is costly.

Example 2 - $\Sigma\Delta$ Modulator. $\Sigma\Delta$ analog-to-digital converters are widely used for analog signals of a large range of frequencies. This is a typical mixed-signal circuit comprising of an analog component (modulator) and a digital component (digital signal processor for filter and decimation). The most basic architecture of the modulator contains a 1-bit DAC (comparator), a 1-bit DAC (switch), and one or more integrators. $\Sigma\Delta$ modulator stability analysis is a challenging problem. When instability occurs, low frequency signal at the input port of the quantizer alternates between the minimum and maximum magnitudes, which causes the quantizer output to get saturated and the modulator can no longer track the input signal. This constitutes a major non-linearity of the modulator. In this work we apply our methods of signal generation to test if a saturation can occur in a $\Sigma\Delta$ modulator. We use a behavioral model of a second-order modulator specified using Simulink®, which takes into account most non-idealities [11] (see Fig. 7), including sampling jitter, integrator noise, op-amp parameters (finite gain, finite bandwidth, slew-rate and saturation voltages). In terms of model complexity, this Simulink model is heterogeneous including embedded Matlab code and mixing discrete-time and continuous-time components, which goes beyond the applicability of the existing formal verification tools. We also remark that formal verification has previously applied to check the saturation occurrence for a much simpler discrete-time $\Sigma\Delta$ modulator model without non-idealities, for which it is possible to derive its dynamics equations and thus

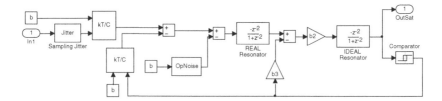

Fig. 7. High-level view of the $\Sigma\Delta$ model with non-idealities [11]

optimization can be formulated and solved [14]. This simple model was also treated by a statistical model-checking approach which picks uniformly an input value at random at each time step [12]. We consider a class of quasi-periodic signals with the frequency spectrum satisfying the nominal range required for the correct operation of the modulator. The temporal pattern of the considered signals is specified by a variant of the automaton in Fig. 1. Each period ranges between 10 et 16, and the delay between two transitions between 1 and 3. The signal value range is discretised into 4 integer values from 0 to 3. We generate a set of 100 timed words of length 300 with the uniform sampling and low-discrepancy methods. The signals are constructed by linear interpolation between the values at the time stamps and then fed to the Breach tool [16], which evaluates the robustness of simulation traces. The STL specification [17] expressing the absence of saturation is `always_[0, sim_time] (abs(OutSat1[t]) < 2)`. Note that we focus on the first integrator since its non-idealities cannot be attenuated by the noise shaping. To test different frequency range, we scale the time stamps with different factors. For the scaling factors $\kappa \geq 0.8 \times 10^{-7}$, the two methods detected a saturation situation. With $\kappa = 0.6 \times 10^{-7}$ the low-discrepancy method detected a saturation while the uniform method did not. For $\kappa \leq 0.5 \times 10^{-7}$, both methods did not detect a saturation, which can be explained by these high frequencies getting closer to the oversampling frequency ($F_s = 42\,\text{MHz}$). This experiment showed the interest of the low-discrepancy generation method. The timed word and signal generation took about 30 s, while the average Simulink simulation time was 58 s for simulating 100 trajectories.

7 Conclusion

We have extended the work on uniform random generation of runs of timed automata, leading to two new contributions. The first one is a new method for low-discrepancy generation, which is an alternative to the uniform random generation, providing deterministic guarantees. The second contribution is a method for validation of complex CPS models which go beyond the scalability of formal verification and are treated in our approach as black boxes. The ability to handle temporal constraints on input signals is also a novelty in this context. This work opens a number of directions for future work. First, the star discrepancy calculation is a difficult problem. The grid-based estimation method used in this work becomes expensive in high dimensions when a good estimate is needed. We plan to explore methods based on the points in the sample to identify points with jumps in the empirical CDF that affect the supremum result. Additionally, we plan to combine the sampling-based approach with optimisation within the signal value space.

Acknowledgements. This work is partially supported by the IDEX project SYMER, funded by Université Grenoble Alpes.

References

1. Abbas, H., Fainekos, G., Sankaranarayanan, S., Ivančić, F., Gupta, A.: Probabilistic temporal logic falsification of cyber-physical systems. ACM Trans. Embed. Comput. Syst. **12**(2s) (2013)
2. Adimoolam, A., Dang, T., Donzé, A., Kapinski, J., Jin, X.: Classification and coverage-based falsification for embedded control systems. In: Majumdar, R., Kunčak, V. (eds.) CAV 2017. LNCS, vol. 10426, pp. 483–503. Springer, Cham (2017). https://doi.org/10.1007/978-3-319-63387-9_24
3. Annpureddy, Y., Liu, C., Fainekos, G., Sankaranarayanan, S.: S-TaLiRo: a tool for temporal logic falsification for hybrid systems. In: Abdulla, P.A., Leino, K.R.M. (eds.) TACAS 2011. LNCS, vol. 6605, pp. 254–257. Springer, Heidelberg (2011). https://doi.org/10.1007/978-3-642-19835-9_21
4. Asarin, E., Basset, N., Degorre, A.: Entropy of regular timed languages. Inf. Comput. **241**, 142–176 (2015)
5. Ballarini, P., Barbot, B., Duflot, M., Haddad, S., Pekergin, N.: HASL: a new approach for performance evaluation and model checking from concepts to experimentation. Perform. Eval. **90**, 53–77 (2015)
6. Barbot, B., Basset, N., Beunardeau, M., Kwiatkowska, M.: Uniform sampling for timed automata with application to language inclusion measurement. In: Agha, G., Van Houdt, B. (eds.) QEST 2016. LNCS, vol. 9826, pp. 175–190. Springer, Cham (2016). https://doi.org/10.1007/978-3-319-43425-4_13
7. Barbot, B., Bérard, B., Duplouy, Y., Haddad, S.: Integrating simulink models into the model checker cosmos. In: Khomenko, V., Roux, O.H. (eds.) PETRI NETS 2018. LNCS, vol. 10877, pp. 363–373. Springer, Cham (2018). https://doi.org/10.1007/978-3-319-91268-4_19
8. Bartocci, E., et al.: Specification-based monitoring of cyber-physical systems: a survey on theory, tools and applications. In: Lectures on Runtime Verification - Introductory and Advanced Topics, pp. 135–175 (2018)
9. Basset, N.: A maximal entropy stochastic process for a timed automaton. In: Fomin, F.V., Freivalds, R., Kwiatkowska, M., Peleg, D. (eds.) ICALP 2013. LNCS, vol. 7966, pp. 61–73. Springer, Heidelberg (2013). https://doi.org/10.1007/978-3-642-39212-2_9
10. Bohlender, D., Bruintjes, H., Junges, S., Katelaan, J., Nguyen, V.Y., Noll, T.: A review of statistical model checking pitfalls on real-time stochastic models. In: Margaria, T., Steffen, B. (eds.) ISoLA 2014. LNCS, vol. 8803, pp. 177–192. Springer, Heidelberg (2014). https://doi.org/10.1007/978-3-662-45231-8_13
11. Brigati, S., Francesconi, F., Malcovati, P., Tonietto, D., Baschirotto, A., Maloberti, F.: Modeling sigma-delta modulator non-idealities in simulink(r). In: Proceedings of the 1999 IEEE International Symposium on Circuits and Systems VLSI, ISCAS 1999, vol. 2, pp. 384–387, May 1999

12. Clarke, E.M., Donzé, A., Legay, A.: On simulation-based probabilistic model checking of mixed-analog circuits. Formal Methods Syst. Des. **36**(2), 97–113 (2010)
13. Clarke, E.M., Zuliani, P.: Statistical model checking for cyber-physical systems. In: Bultan, T., Hsiung, P.-A. (eds.) ATVA 2011. LNCS, vol. 6996, pp. 1–12. Springer, Heidelberg (2011). https://doi.org/10.1007/978-3-642-24372-1_1
14. Dang, T., Donzé, A., Maler, O.: Verification of analog and mixed-signal circuits using hybrid system techniques. In: Hu, A.J., Martin, A.K. (eds.) FMCAD 2004. LNCS, vol. 3312, pp. 21–36. Springer, Heidelberg (2004). https://doi.org/10.1007/978-3-540-30494-4_3
15. Deshmukh, J., Jin, X., Kapinski, J., Maler, O.: Stochastic local search for falsification of hybrid systems. In: Finkbeiner, B., Pu, G., Zhang, L. (eds.) ATVA 2015. LNCS, vol. 9364, pp. 500–517. Springer, Cham (2015). https://doi.org/10.1007/978-3-319-24953-7_35
16. Donzé, A.: Breach, a toolbox for verification and parameter synthesis of hybrid systems. In: Touili, T., Cook, B., Jackson, P. (eds.) CAV 2010. LNCS, vol. 6174, pp. 167–170. Springer, Heidelberg (2010). https://doi.org/10.1007/978-3-642-14295-6_17
17. Donzé, A., Maler, O.: Robust satisfaction of temporal logic over real-valued signals. In: Chatterjee, K., Henzinger, T.A. (eds.) FORMATS 2010. LNCS, vol. 6246, pp. 92–106. Springer, Heidelberg (2010). https://doi.org/10.1007/978-3-642-15297-9_9
18. Dreossi, T., Dang, T., Donzé, A., Kapinski, J., Jin, X., Deshmukh, J.V.: Efficient guiding strategies for testing of temporal properties of hybrid systems. In: Havelund, K., Holzmann, G., Joshi, R. (eds.) NFM 2015. LNCS, vol. 9058, pp. 127–142. Springer, Cham (2015). https://doi.org/10.1007/978-3-319-17524-9_10
19. Halton, J.H.: Algorithm 247: radical-inverse quasi-random point sequence. Commun. ACM **7**(12), 701–702 (1964)
20. Hlawka, E.: Discrepancy and riemann integration. Stud. Pure Math., 121–129 (1971)
21. Justel, A., Peña, D., Zamar, R.: A multivariate Kolmogorov-Smirnov test of goodness of fit. Stat. Probab. Lett. **35**(3), 251–259 (1997)
22. Kwiatkowska, M., Norman, G., Parker, D.: PRISM 4.0: verification of probabilistic real-time systems. In: Gopalakrishnan, G., Qadeer, S. (eds.) CAV 2011. LNCS, vol. 6806, pp. 585–591. Springer, Heidelberg (2011). https://doi.org/10.1007/978-3-642-22110-1_47
23. Liang, J.-J., Fang, K.-T., Hickernell, F., Li, R.: Testing multivariate uniformity and its applications. Math. Comput. **70**(233), 337–355 (2001)
24. Niederreiter, H.: Random Number Generation and Quasi-Monte Carlo Methods. Society for Industrial and Applied Mathematics, Philadelphia (1992)
25. Roberts, M.: The unreasonable effectiveness of quasirandom sequences. http://extremelearning.com.au/unreasonable-effectiveness-of-quasirandom-sequences/
26. Rosenblatt, M.: Remarks on a multivariate transformation. Ann. Math. Stat. **23**(3), 470–472 (1952)
27. Stein, W.A., et al.: Sage Mathematics Software (Version 6.9). The Sage Development Team (2015). http://www.sagemath.org
28. Thiémard, E.: An algorithm to compute bounds for the star discrepancy. J. Complex. **17**(4), 850–880 (2001)
29. Yaghoubi, S., Fainekos, G.: Falsification of temporal logic requirements using gradient based local search in space and time. In: 6th IFAC Conference on Analysis and Design of Hybrid Systems, ADHS 2018, Oxford, UK, 11–13 July 2018, pp. 103–108 (2018)

Traffic Management for Urban Air Mobility

Suda Bharadwaj[1(✉)], Steven Carr[1], Natasha Neogi[2], Hasan Poonawala[3], Alejandro Barberia Chueca[1], and Ufuk Topcu[1]

[1] The University of Texas at Austin, Austin, TX 78712, USA
{suda.b,stevencarr,utopcu}@utexas.edu
[2] NASA-Langley Research Center, Hampton, VA, USA
natasha.a.neogi@nasa.gov
[3] University of Kentucky, Lexington, KY 40506, USA
hasan.poonawala@uky.edu

Abstract. Urban air mobility (UAM) refers to on-demand air transportation services within an urban area. We seek to perform mission planning for vehicles in a UAM fleet, while guaranteeing system safety requirements such as traffic separation. In this paper, we present a localized hierarchical planning procedure for the traffic management problem of a fleet of (potentially autonomous) UAM vehicles. We apply decentralized policy synthesis for route planning on individual vehicles, which are modeled by Markov decision processes. We divide the operating region into sectors and use reactive synthesis to generate local runtime enforcement modules or shields, each of which satisfies its own assume-guarantee contract that encodes requirements of conflict management, safety, and interactions with neighbouring sectors. We prove that the realization of these contracts ensures that the entire network of shields satisfies the safety specifications with each shield limited to acting in its local sector of operation.

Keywords: Reactive synthesis · System safety · Air traffic management

1 Introduction

There is growing interest in on-demand aerial mobility over urban centers, for both passenger and cargo carrying missions [2,18]. However, the airspace above urban areas is rapidly evolving into a dynamic and complex environment, and the urban air mobility (UAM) ecosystem will be characterized by a set of competing requirements and priorities. Thus, UAM operations will likely be comprised of a complex network of vehicles with a large range of traffic management and control options. Planning for UAM fleet operations over a dense, complex airspace may suit a localized, hierarchical approach. Centralized planning approaches typically suffer computational costs that grow exponentially with the number of vehicles

© Springer Nature Switzerland AG 2019
J. M. Badger and K. Y. Rozier (Eds.): NFM 2019, LNCS 11460, pp. 71–87, 2019.
https://doi.org/10.1007/978-3-030-20652-9_5

in the system [15]. Furthermore, the UAM ecosystem will encompass multiple UAM service suppliers (USS), and for those vehicles that fly in uncontrolled airspace (e.g., Class G [10]), there is currently no civil aviation authority brokering information exchange and providing control guidance. Thus, the ability to provide separation services will likely rest with the UAM vehicles and USS.

In this paper, we present a localized hierarchical planning procedure for the traffic management problem of a fleet of (potentially autonomous) UAM vehicles. We divide the planning problem into: (1) onboard route planning for the individual vehicles, and (2) shielding airspace regions to enforce safety constraints. We divide the airspace into regions or sectors, and use *localized shield synthesis* to generate a shield for each sector. We employ a separation-of-concerns approach to the traffic management problem. That is, we assume that the planner is unaware of the state of the whole fleet and can thus take actions that may result in a violation of a safety requirement. In such cases, there needs to be an enforcement module that can interfere with the local plans of the vehicles at runtime. We use localized shield synthesis to provide runtime enforcement and present a decentralized synthesis procedure for shield generation.

1.1   Related Work

Currently, there is no established infrastructure to safely manage the widespread use of low-altitude airspace over dense urban cores, under diverse piloting modes. A traffic management system called UTM for unmanned aerial systems (UAS) has been proposed to handle small unmanned aerial systems, and takes a volumetric approach to ensuring airspace access [23]. This approach will likely enable the incorporation of multiple safety oriented services [20] such as aircraft separation [21] and geo-fencing [22]. However, this centralized volumetric approach is not scalable to projected UAM traffic densities, and leaves a need for a localized approach to UAM traffic management, possibly employing runtime enforcement techniques.

Runtime verification is an active area of research, for example [3,5] allow for checking whether a run of a system satisfies a given specification. An extension to verification is *runtime enforcement* [11,26] of a specified property, by not only detecting violations, but also altering the behaviour of the system in a way that maintains the desired property. An existing approach called shielding [7,17] uses reactive synthesis and assumes that the shield has full knowledge and control of the whole system—in this case the entire UAM system and the vehicles it handles.

A technique for synthesizing quantitative shields for multi-agent systems in a fully centralized manner was presented in [6]. All these approaches rely on restrictive assumptions on runtime communication (i.e., full network coverage) and the extent of awareness and control authority of the shield (e.g., the shield can affect any agent in the network instantaneously). Removing these assumptions requires a version of distributed synthesis. However, except for a few restricted classes of architectures, the distributed synthesis problem is undecidable [25]. The decidable versions of the problem lack practical solutions due to their non-elementary complexity [24]. Significant effort in runtime monitoring in this area is focused on providing efficient solutions by exploiting the structure of the system [8,12] or the specification [4,13]. In approaching the UAM problem, we propose to avoid the undecidability of distributed synthesis by leveraging the infrastructure in the geography to divide the region into sectors, and separately synthesizing a shield for each sector. Each shield is then only concerned with the behaviours of neighbouring sectors. Similarly, we assume that specifications are decomposed such that each shield is only responsible for safety violations in its own sector.

1.2   Contributions of the Paper

This work is the first that considers a quantitative, decentralized synthesis procedure for runtime enforcement modules (referred to as shields) for use in traffic management on a UAM system. We break down our contributions as follows: (1) We use a decentralized Markov decision process (MDP) policy synthesis procedure to plan routes for individual vehicles in the UAM and dynamically update routes on the fly if conflicts between vehicles occur. (2) We divide up the operating region of the vehicles into *sectors* and synthesize a shield for each sector that enforces local safety properties as well as assume-guarantee *contract-induced safety properties* in their respective sectors. (3) We use these contracts to prove correctness of the decentralized approach to synthesize shields that, when all composed together, are correct with respect to the conjunction of all local specifications.

2   Preliminaries

Basic Notations. We consider reactive systems with a finite set I (O) of Boolean *inputs (outputs)*. The input alphabet is $\Sigma_I = 2^I$, the output alphabet is $\Sigma_O = 2^O$, and $\Sigma = \Sigma_I \times \Sigma_O$. The set of finite (infinite) words over Σ is denoted by Σ^* (Σ^ω), and we define $\Sigma^\infty = \Sigma^* \cup \Sigma^\omega$. We will also refer to words as *(execution) traces*. We write $|\overline{\sigma}|$ for the length of a trace $\overline{\sigma} \in \Sigma^*$. For an infinite trace $\overline{\sigma} \in \Sigma^\omega$ we define $|\overline{\sigma}| = \infty$. For $\overline{\sigma}_I = x_0 x_1 \ldots \in \Sigma_I^\infty$ and $\overline{\sigma}_O = y_0 y_1 \ldots \in \Sigma_O^\infty$, we write $\overline{\sigma}_I \parallel \overline{\sigma}_O$ for the composition $(x_0, y_0)(x_1, y_1) \ldots \in \Sigma^\infty$. For $i \in \mathbb{N}$ and a word $\overline{\sigma} = \sigma_0 \sigma_1 \ldots \in \Sigma^\infty$, we define $\overline{\sigma}[i] = \sigma_i$, and we define $\overline{\sigma}[i,j) = \sigma_i \sigma_{i+1} \ldots \sigma_{j-1}$ if $j \in \mathbb{N}$ and $\overline{\sigma}[i,j) = \sigma_i \sigma_{i+1} \ldots$ if $j = \infty$. A *language* is a set $L \subseteq \Sigma^\infty$ of words.

Reactive Systems. A *reactive system* is defined by a 6-tuple $\mathcal{D} = (Q, q_0, \Sigma_I, \Sigma_O, \delta, \lambda)$, where Q is a finite set of states, $q_0 \in Q$ is the initial state, Σ_I is the input alphabet, Σ_O is the output alphabet, $\delta : Q \times \Sigma_I \to Q$ is the complete transition function, and $\lambda : Q \times \Sigma_I \to \Sigma_O$ is the output function. Given an input trace $\overline{\sigma}_I = x_0 x_1 \ldots \in \Sigma_I^\infty$, a reactive system $\mathcal{D}$ produces an output trace $\overline{\sigma}_O = \mathcal{P}(\overline{\sigma}_I) = \lambda(q_0, x_0)\lambda(q_1, x_1) \ldots \in \Sigma_O^\infty$ with $q_{i+1} = \delta(q_i, x_i)$ for all $i \geq 0$. The set of words produced by $\mathcal{D}$ is denoted $L(\mathcal{P}) = \{\overline{\sigma}_I \parallel \overline{\sigma}_O \in \Sigma^\infty \mid \mathcal{D}(\overline{\sigma}_I) = \overline{\sigma}_O\}$.

Specifications. A *specification* φ defines a set $L(\varphi) \subseteq \Sigma^\infty$ of allowed traces. A reactive system $\mathcal{D}$ *realizes* φ, denoted by $\mathcal{D} \models \varphi$, iff $L(\mathcal{D}) \subseteq L(\varphi)$. Given a set of propositions AP, a formula in *linear temporal logic* (LTL) describes a language in $(2^{AP})^\omega$. In this paper we deal with fragment of LTL referred to as *safety specifications*. φ is called a *safety specification* if every trace $\bar{\sigma}$ that is not in $L(\varphi)$ has a prefix τ such that all words starting with τ are also not in the language $L(\varphi)$. We represent a safety specification φ by a safety automaton $\varphi = (Q, q_0, \Sigma, \delta, F)$, where $F \subseteq Q$ is a set of safe states.

Games. A game is a tuple $\mathcal{G} = (G, g_0, \Sigma, \delta, \mathsf{Acc})$, where G is a finite set of states, $g_0 \in G$ is the initial state, $\delta : G \times \Sigma \to G$ is a complete transition function, $\mathsf{Acc} : (G \times \Sigma \times G)^\omega \to \mathbb{B}$ is a winning condition and defines the qualitative objective of the game. The game is played by two players: the system and the environment. In every state $g \in G$ (starting with g_0), the environment chooses an input $\sigma_I \in \Sigma_I$, and then the system chooses some output $\sigma_O \in \Sigma_O$. These choices define the next state $g' = \delta(g, (\sigma_I, \sigma_O))$, and so on. The resulting (infinite) sequence $\bar{\pi} = (g_0, \sigma_I, \sigma_O, g_1)(g_1, \sigma_I, \sigma_O, g_2)\ldots$ is called a *play*. A deterministic *strategy* for the environment is a function $\rho_e : G^* \to \Sigma_I$. A non-deterministic *strategy* for the system is a relation $\rho_s : G^* \times \Sigma_I \to 2^{\Sigma_O}$ and a deterministic strategy for the system is a function $\rho_s : G^* \times \Sigma_I \to \Sigma_O$.

A play $\bar{\pi}$ is *won* by the system iff $\mathsf{Acc}(\bar{\pi}) = \top$. A strategy is *winning* for the system if all plays $\bar{\pi}$ that can be constructed when defining the outputs using the strategy result in $\mathsf{Acc}(\bar{\pi}) = \top$. The *winning region* Win is the set of states from which a winning strategy exists. A *maximally permissive* winning strategy $\rho_s : G^* \times \Sigma_I \to 2^{\Sigma_O}$ is a strategy that is not only winning for the system, but also contains all deterministic winning strategies. Simply, if a play $\bar{\pi}$ can be constructed from a deterministic strategy it can also be constructed from the maximally permissive strategy.

A *safety game* defines Acc via a set $F \subseteq G$ of safe states: $\mathsf{Acc}(\bar{\pi}) = \top$ iff $g_i \in F$ for all $i \geq 0$, i.e., if only safe states are visited in the play $\bar{\pi}$. Otherwise, $\mathsf{Acc}(\bar{\pi}) = \bot$. The quantitative objective of the system is to minimize $\mathsf{Val}(\bar{\pi})$, while the environment tries to maximize it.

Markov Decision Processes. We define a *single-agent* MDP as a tuple $\mathcal{M}_z = (S_z, s_I, Act_z, P_z, \mathcal{R}_z, \mathcal{T}_z)$ with a finite set S_z states, an initial state $s_I \in S_z$ a finite set Act_z of actions, a transition function $P_z : S_z \times Act_z \times S_z \to [0, 1]$ such that $\forall s \in S_z \, \forall a \in Act_z : \sum_{s' \in S_z} P_z(s, a, s') \in \{0, 1\}$ and a cost function $\mathcal{R}_z : S \times Act \to \mathbb{R}$ such that $\mathcal{R}_z(s, a)$ represents the cost of taking action a in state s and a target operator (or operators) $\mathcal{T}_z \subset S_z$.

Given n agents, the overall MDP is formed from the product of the MDPs describing each individual MDP: $\mathcal{M} = (S, s_I, Act, P, \mathcal{R}, \mathcal{T})$, where $S = \prod_{z \in [1,n]} S_z$, $Act = \prod_{z \in [1,n]} Act_z$, P and $\mathcal{R}$ are the transition and reward functions for the new product state space as defined in a similar manner above and the set of goal conditions for all agents is defined by $\mathcal{T} = \prod_{z \in [1,n]} \mathcal{T}_z \subset S$.

3   Problem Setting

Consider an environment motivated by the setting for SkyGrid [2] consisting of an operating space and a network formed from a series of k urban air mobility (UAM) sectors labeled $V_1, \cdots, V_k$. Figure 1 depicts an example environment.

A set of UAM vehicles (henceforth referred to as vehicles) are tasked with completing trips between origin-destination pairs in this environment. Each sector is a designated region of control, wherein all vehicles have coordinated responses and maintain the required separation minima between themselves (e.g., collision avoidance). If two vehicles are projected to lose separation, the sector controller acts tactically to separate the vehicles, by issuing a rerouting command, or by blocking a vehicle's entry to the sector (e.g., conflict management). Note that, for example, sector controller V_6 in Fig. 1 controls the operational area defined by $V_6 - (V_6 \cap V_5)$, and the area of overlap $V_5 \cap V_6$ is the region where the handoff takes place, wherein the sector controller of the region the vehicle is about to enter takes control of the vehicle. The sectors are distributed such that the union of their regions cover the entire operating space.

The number of vehicles allowed inside each sector is upper bounded by the separation standards between the vehicles, along with the complexity of the airspace (e.g., intersection with general aviation traffic etc.). Sectors cannot accept vehicles (i.e., accept a handoff) if the maximum operational density will be exceeded, or if a conflict will ensue. However, sectors must ensure that if a vehicle needs to pass through its region, it is eventually allowed to do so in order to make progress towards its goal. Thus, a sector can send an idle vehicle out of its region by requesting a handoff with a neighbour in order to make room for transiting vehicles to enter. However, this action can cause violations of safety requirements for the neighbouring regions. Hence, we propose the use of a runtime monitor or *shield* that can correct the decisions of the sector as necessary to avoid such violations.

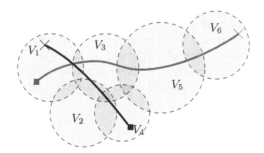

Fig. 1. Example UAM operating environment. Green circles correspond to local sectors. UAM vehicles (blue and black) start at the squares and finish at the crosses. (Color figure online)

In the following section, we formulate the set of vehicles moving in the environment as an MDP. We then synthesize a policy in this MDP for each vehicle to transit from its origin to its destination with minimal cost and dynamically update the policy to avoid conflicts. We then formally define shields and their composition with sector control in order to guarantee the individual vehicle policies do not violate safety specifications of the sectors it transits.

3.1 MDP Formulation of the Environment

First consider the case of a single vehicle labelled $\mathcal{G}_z$ transiting in the environment. We can model its behavior using a Markov decision process, defined by a tuple $\mathcal{M}_z = (S_z, s_I, Act_z, P_z, \mathcal{R}_z, \mathcal{T}_z)$. We define a state $s_i \in S_z$ as the condition where sector controller V_i has authority over the vehicle. For each state s_i there are two types of actions: *loiter* $a_i \in Act_z$ or *hand-off request* $a_{ij} \in Act_z$ to state s_j. The loiter in state s_i corresponds to a self-transition with probability 1. We define p as the probability of a successful hand-off, i.e. a transition from sector V_i to sector V_j. Formally, we denote $P_z(s_i, a_{ij}, s_j) = p \in [0, 1]$. An unsuccessful hand-off can occur from events such as authority-responsibility mismatches between the two sector controllers, communications interference, or the shield of the sector denying entry. This results in the agent remaining inside its previous states $P_z(s_i, a_{ij}, s_i) = 1 - p$.

Extending the problem to n vehicles, the overall model is formed from the product of the MDPs describing each individual vehicle: $\mathcal{M} = (S, s_I, Act, P, \mathcal{R}, \mathcal{T})$, where $S = \prod_{z \in [1,n]} S_z$, $Act = \prod_{z \in [1,n]} Act_z$, P and $\mathcal{R}$ are the transition and reward functions for the new product state space as defined in a similar manner above and the set of goal operators for all vehicles is defined by $\mathcal{T} = \prod_{z \in [1,n]} \mathcal{T}_z \subset S$. This product system scales exponentially with the number of vehicles, $|S| = |S_z|^n$ and $|Act| = |Act_z|^n$. Instead of calculating the optimal centralized policy, we decentralize through each agent computing (offline) an optimal individual policy based upon its knowledge of the environment and coordinating (online) with other agents as they interact [14] (see Sect. 4).

Since the policy is computed in a decentralized manner, we assume each vehicle has only limited information on the status of the entire UAM airspace. This limited information can result in vehicles potentially violating safety requirements that they are not aware of by trying to move into a sector that is at capacity, thereby causing a conflict. A shield is needed to guarantee that a sector does not accept a vehicle that will create a conflict within its region.

3.2 Shields

Sector Model. We model the controller of each sector V_i as a reactive system $\mathcal{D}_i = (Q_i, q_{0_i}, \Sigma_{I_i}, \Sigma_{O_i}, \delta_i, \lambda_i)$ and form a connected system which we define as set of reactive systems $\mathcal{D} = [\mathcal{D}_1 \cdots \mathcal{D}_n]$ with a corresponding *connectivity graph* $G_{\mathcal{D}}$.

We define a connectivity graph as a directed graph with each vertex corresponding to a reactive system. We say two reactive systems are *connected* if they share an edge in the graph. Let $connect(\mathcal{D}_i)$ be the set of reactive systems

$\mathcal{D}_j \in \mathcal{D}$, $i \neq j$ that share an edge with $\mathcal{D}_i$. For example, in Fig. 1, overlapping operational regions share an edge in the corresponding directed graph in Fig. 2 and therefore the corresponding reactive systems are connected. The inputs to the reactive system $\mathcal{D}_i$ denoted as Σ_{I_i} are produced by the strategy synthesized in the MDP $\mathcal{M}$ and can correspond to the numbers of vehicles entering or leaving the sector of the distributed system $\mathcal{D}_i$. In this example, the output Σ_{O_i} takes one of the following three actions: allow vehicles to enter, move vehicles inside the sector to a neighboring sector, or force vehicles to loiter until the sector is ready to allow them to enter.

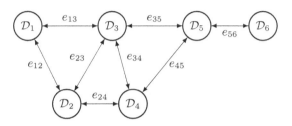

Fig. 2. The connectivity graph $G_{\mathcal{D}}$ of the UAM sector controllers $\mathcal{D}$ modeling the sectors V in Fig. 1. Each edge e_{ij} corresponds to $\mathcal{D}_i$ and $\mathcal{D}_j$ being connected, i.e., the outputs of $\mathcal{D}_i$ are inputs to $\mathcal{D}_j$ and vice versa.

Attaching a Shield. A shield $\mathcal{S}_i = (Q', q'_0, \overline{\Sigma_{I_i}} \times \Sigma_{O_i}, \Sigma_{O_i}, \delta', \lambda')$ corresponding to sector V_i is a reactive system that is composed with the sector controller $\mathcal{D}_i$ where $\overline{\Sigma_{I_i}} = \Sigma_{I_i} \times \Sigma_{O_j}$ for $\mathcal{D}_j \in connect(\mathcal{D}_i)$. Simply, the outputs from all neighbouring sectors is an input to $\mathcal{S}_i$. For example, if sector controller $\mathcal{D}_j \in connect(\mathcal{D}_i)$ sends a vehicle to $\mathcal{D}_i$, this output Σ_{O_j} functions as an input to $\mathcal{S}_i$. In response the shield produces a possibly corrected output Σ_{O_i}. This architecture is shown in Fig. 3. Each shield will need to make assumptions or *contracts* with its neighbours in order to guarantee they will all be able to satisfy their individual specifications (see Sect. 5).

Formally, we define the composition of $\mathcal{S}_i$ and $\mathcal{D}_i$ as $\mathcal{D}_i \circ \mathcal{S}_i = (\hat{Q}, \hat{q}_0, \hat{\Sigma}_I, \hat{\Sigma}_O, \hat{\delta}, \hat{\lambda})$, with states $\hat{Q}_i = Q_i \times Q'_i$, $\hat{q}_{0_i} = (q_{0_i}, q'_{0_i})$, transition function $\hat{\delta}_i((q_i, q'_i), \hat{\sigma}_I) = (\delta(q_i, \sigma_{I_i}), \delta'(q'_i, (\overline{\sigma}_{I_i}, \sigma'_{O_i})))$, and output function $\hat{\lambda}((q_i, q'_i), \sigma_{I_i}) = \lambda'_i(q'_i, \lambda(q_i, (\sigma_{I_i}, \sigma_{O_i})))$.

3.3 Requirements on the Shield

Now we define the basic requirements that a shield must satisfy: namely it should enforce correctness without deviating from the system's output unnecessarily.

Correctness. We say that $\mathcal{S} = (Q', q'_0, \Sigma'_I \times \Sigma'_O, \Sigma_O, \delta', \lambda')$ *ensures correctness* with respect to a safety specification φ if for any reactive system $\mathcal{D} = (Q, q_0, \Sigma_I, \Sigma_O, \delta, \lambda)$ it holds that $(\mathcal{D} \circ \mathcal{S}) \models \varphi$.

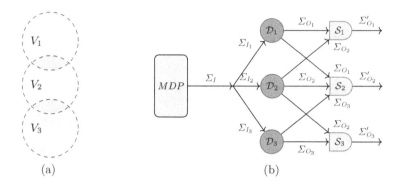

Fig. 3. (a) Example region space and (b) Corresponding sector controllers and shielding architecture.

No Unnecessary Interference. A shield is only allowed to interfere when the output of the reactive system is not *correct*. Formally, given a safety specification φ, a reactive system $\mathcal{S} = (Q', q'_0, \Sigma'_I \times \Sigma'_O, \Sigma_O, \delta', \lambda')$ *does not interfere unnecessarily* if for any reactive system $\mathcal{D} = (Q, q_0, \Sigma_I, \Sigma_O, \delta, \lambda)$ and any trace $(\bar{\sigma}_I \parallel \bar{\sigma}_O) \in (\Sigma_I \times \Sigma_O)^\infty$ of $\mathcal{D}$ that is not wrong, we have that $\mathcal{S}(\bar{\sigma}_I \parallel \bar{\sigma}_O) = \bar{\sigma}_O$.

Localized Shields. A set of localized *shields* $\mathcal{S} = [\mathcal{S}_1 \cdots \mathcal{S}_n]$ for a conjunction of specifications $\varphi = \bigwedge_i^n \varphi$ is a set of reactive systems such that for $\mathcal{S}_i \in \mathcal{S}$, where $\mathcal{S}_i = (Q', q'_0, \overline{\Sigma}_{I_i} \times \Sigma_{O_i}, \Sigma_{O_i}, \delta', \lambda')$, for any set of connected reactive systems $\mathcal{D} = [\mathcal{D}_1 \cdots \mathcal{D}_n]$ where $\mathcal{D}_i = (Q_i, q_{0_i}, \Sigma_{I_i}, \Sigma_{O_i}, \delta_i, \lambda_i)$ with connectivity graph $G_\mathcal{D}$, it holds that $\mathcal{D}_i \circ \mathcal{S}_i \models \varphi_i$ with no unnecessary deviation. Additionally, it must hold that the global composition is correct with respect to the conjunction of specifications. Formally, $(\mathcal{D}_1 \circ \mathcal{S}_1) \circ \cdots \circ (\mathcal{D}_n \circ \mathcal{S}_n) \models \varphi_1 \wedge \cdots \wedge \varphi_n$.

Problem Statement. Given a conjunction of safety specifications $\varphi = \bigwedge_i^n \varphi_i$, synthesize a set of localized shields $\mathcal{S} = [\mathcal{S}_1 \cdots \mathcal{S}_n]$ for any set of reactive systems $\mathcal{D} = [\mathcal{D}_1 \cdots \mathcal{D}_n]$ with connectivity graph $G_\mathcal{D}$, such that each $\mathcal{S}_i$ is (1) correct with respect to φ_i, (2) can only correct the outputs of $\mathcal{D}_i$, (3) can only observe the outputs of sectors in $connect(\mathcal{D}_i)$, and (4) global composition of the shields and design is correct with respect to the conjunction of safety specifications. Informally (4) states that $\mathcal{S}_i$ must not only be correct with respect to φ_i, but also must not prevent all connected shields from satisfying their safety specifications.

4   Decentralized Vehicle Policy Synthesis

We describe the process for decentralized synthesis of the optimal policies for the individual UAM vehicles. The MDP $\mathcal{M}$ described in Sect. 3.1 serves as a model for the coordination of n vehicles. The reward in $\mathcal{M}$ consists of a global payoff function $\mathsf{Val}: Act \to \mathbb{R}$. Since each action $a \in Act$ is a collective action for the vehicles, solving the MDP $\mathcal{M}$ for an optimal policy yields an optimal coordination strategy for the agents. Solving for the optimal policy in $\mathcal{M}$ with this large action space Act is a centralized approach and is computationally expensive.

In practice each vehicle interacts with only few other vehicles relative to the total number of vehicles at any time. The concept of a coordination graph [14] captures this sparsity of mutual influence of actions on the global payoff Val. The sparse coordination graph implies that one can decompose Val as a sum of local payoff functions Val_j for each vehicle $\mathcal{G}_j$ so that the global coordination problem can be replaced by a number of smaller local coordination problems. This decomposition implies that the optimal collective action a is $\arg\max_{a \in Act}(\sum_j Val_j(a))$.

The implemented algorithm from [14] involves the following steps: (1) Compute an approximate value function $\mathcal{V}$ for the MDP $\mathcal{M}$; (2) compute local payoff functions Val_j for agent $\mathcal{G}_j$ using value iterations involving $\mathcal{V}$ with one-step lookahead; (3) instantiate for each $\mathcal{G}_j$, its local payoff value Val_j using its current state s and the states of a limited set of vehicles defined by the coordination graph; and (4) compute a locally optimal collective action for the MDP $\mathcal{M}$ via a variable elimination algorithm and message passing. The first two steps are performed offline, the last two are performed online.

The topology of the coordination graph determines the decomposition of Val. The construction of a sparse coordination graph for the n vehicles is as follows. The nodes of the coordination graph consist of the vehicles. We seek to penalize the situation where two agents will act to occupy the same sector in the next time instant. Therefore, an edge exists between vehicle $\mathcal{G}_i$ and vehicle $\mathcal{G}_j$ in the coordination graph if both agents can take an action to move to the same sector V_k. A necessary condition for two agents to be connected in the coordination graph is that the sectors, which are nodes in graph $G_{\mathcal{D}}$, corresponding to their current state be at distance two or less in the graph $G_{\mathcal{D}}$.

The local payoff functions that achieve the desired penalty given this topology for the coordination graph are as follows. Let $Neighbor[z]$ be vehicles in sectors that are two edges away from the current sector occupied by $\mathcal{G}_z$. Then, $Val_z = \sum_{j \in Neighbor[z]} Val_{jz}(a_{jk}, a_{zl})$, where $Val_{jz}(a_{jk}, a_{zl}) = -q$ if $l = k$ and $Val_{jz}(a_{jk}, a_{zl}) = 0$ otherwise, for some penalty value $q > 0$.

5   Localized Shield Synthesis Framework

In this section, we present a correct-by-design approach to localized shield synthesis with assume-guarantee contracts. We first formalize the notion of assume-guarantee contracts that we use in the synthesis process. We then demonstrate the incorporation of these contracts into a safety game, which we solve using GR(1) synthesis.

5.1 Assume-Guarantee Contracts

An assume-guarantee contract for a shield expresses the assumptions on the outputs of neighbouring sectors under which the shield provides the corresponding individual guarantees for its own sector.

We employ a localized synthesis process, such that the synthesis process for each shield is unaware of the specification and implementation details of both the vehicles in the fleet, as well as the shields in connected sectors. The only guarantees that the shield provides concern the duration and frequency of vehicle entrance (and rejection) periods from neighbouring sectors. These guarantees can in turn be taken into account in the shield synthesis process for neighbouring sectors. Alternatively, one can use the contract to verify if the controller implementation still satisfies its desired specification under the shield, and in fact under any shield that meets the guarantees in the contract.

For ease of notation, the following definitions are with respect to the assumptions and guarantees of the ith shield. An *assume-guarantee contract* for a shield $\mathcal{S}_i$ attached to $\mathcal{D}_i$ is a set of tuples $\mathcal{C}_{\mathcal{S}_j}^{\mathcal{S}_i} = (A_{\mathcal{S}_j}^{\mathcal{S}_i}, B_{\mathcal{S}_j}^{\mathcal{S}_i})$:

- $A_{\mathcal{S}_j}^{\mathcal{S}_i}$ is the assumption on the outputs of $\mathcal{S}_j$ as it pertains to $\mathcal{S}_i$.
- $B_{\mathcal{S}_j}^{\mathcal{S}_i}$ describes the guarantees which $\mathcal{S}_i$ provides to $\mathcal{S}_j$.

where $\mathcal{S}_j$ is the shield attached to $\mathcal{D}_j \in connect(\mathcal{D}_i)$

The guarantees $B_{\mathcal{S}_j}^{\mathcal{S}_i}$ that $\mathcal{S}_i$ provides to $\mathcal{S}_j$ bound the length of time $\mathcal{S}_i$ can refuse to accept vehicles from $\mathcal{S}_j$ when requested. Formally, we define $B_{\mathcal{S}_j}^{\mathcal{S}_i} = (b_{\mathcal{S}_j}^{\mathcal{S}_i}) \in \overline{\mathbb{N}}$ as the maximal length of a (contiguous) period of refusal for accepting UVs from $\mathcal{S}_j$. The assumptions that $\mathcal{S}_i$ makes on the output of $\mathcal{S}_j$, given by $A_{\mathcal{S}_j}^{\mathcal{S}_i} = (a_{\mathcal{S}_j}^{\mathcal{S}_i}) \in \overline{\mathbb{N}}$ are symmetric to the guarantees $B_{\mathcal{S}_j}^{s}$ and will function as guarantees for $\mathcal{S}_j$. Formally we will have $A_{\mathcal{S}_j}^{\mathcal{S}_i} = B_{\mathcal{S}_i}^{\mathcal{S}_j}$.

Remark: We note that the values in the assume-guarantee contracts are heavily dependent on the topology of the environment and the connections. For example, a shielded sector with many connecting sectors may not be able to guarantee quick transit of vehicles through its regions, i.e., $b_{\mathcal{S}_i}^{\mathcal{S}_j}$ may need to be large. Generating these contracts automatically based on the given graph $G_\mathcal{D}$ is a subject of future work. In this paper, the contract values are chosen manually.

5.2 Synthesis Overview

We first present an overview of the synthesis procedure. The synthesis procedure for a shield consists of the following three steps:

(1) For each shield $\mathcal{S}_i$, we construct a game $\mathcal{G}^{\mathcal{S}_i}$ from the safety specification φ_i, augmented with the contracts $C_{\mathcal{S}_j}^{\mathcal{S}_i}$ for the shields of all connected sectors.
(2) We then compute the permissive winning strategy $\rho^{\mathcal{S}_i}$, such that any shield $\mathcal{S}_i$ that implements $\rho^{\mathcal{S}_i}$ ensures *correctness* $(\mathcal{D}_i \circ \mathcal{S}_i \models \varphi_i \wedge_j B_{\mathcal{S}_j}^{\mathcal{S}_i})$ given the assumptions $A_{\mathcal{S}_j}^{\mathcal{S}_i}$ for all shields $\mathcal{S}_j$ of connected sectors. This construction is similar to the one in [17].

(3) We compute a locally optimal deterministic strategy that implements $\rho^{\mathcal{S}_i}$ using GR(1) synthesis for each $\mathcal{S}_i$ using a procedure detailed in [6].

5.3   Game Construction with Contract Guarantees

Let φ_i be a safety specification represented as a safety automaton $\varphi_i = (Q, q_0, \Sigma_I, \delta, F)$. For each $\mathcal{S}_i$, we construct a game $\mathcal{G}^{\mathcal{S}_i}$ such that its maximally permissive strategy subsumes all possible shields that are correct w.r.t. φ_i as well as the contract safety guarantees, given that the contract safety assumptions hold. Let J be the set of indices of sectors connected to $\mathcal{S}_i$. We first define two boolean variables t_j and u_j for all $j \in J$:

- t_j is true when a vehicle attempts to move from the sector shielded by $\mathcal{S}_j$ to the sector of $\mathcal{S}_i$, and $\mathcal{S}_i$ does not allow it to enter.
- u_j is true when $\mathcal{S}_i$ attempts to move a vehicle to a sector shielded by $\mathcal{S}_j$ and $\mathcal{S}_j$ does not allow it to enter.

Given the contracts $C_{\mathcal{S}_j}^{\mathcal{S}_i}$, the shield must additionally satisfy contract-induced safety guarantees $B_{\mathcal{S}_j}^{\mathcal{S}_i}$ given assumptions $A_{\mathcal{S}_i}^{\mathcal{S}_j}$. To encode these contracts, the state space $G^{\mathcal{S}_i}$ of $\mathcal{G}^{\mathcal{S}_i}$ is constructed by augmenting the states Q of φ with two tuples of integer variables: (v_j) and (w_j) for all $j \in J$, as is explained below.

We construct a game $\mathcal{G}^{\mathcal{S}_i} = (G^{\mathcal{S}_i}, g_0^{\mathcal{S}_i}, \Sigma_I, \Sigma_O, \delta^{\mathcal{S}_i}, \mathsf{Acc}^{\mathcal{S}_i})$ such that $G^{\mathcal{S}_i} = \{(g \bigotimes_j (v_j, w_j) \mid g \in Q, j \in J\}$ is the state space, $g_0^{\mathcal{S}_i} = (g_0, (0,0), \ldots, (0,0))$ is the initial state δ^s is the next-state function, such that $\delta^s((g, (v_j, w_j)), (\sigma_I, \sigma_O), \sigma_O') = (\delta(g, \sigma_I, \sigma_O'), (v_j', w_j'))$. The transitions of variables v_j and w_j depend on the values of the boolean variables t_j and u_j. Explicitly, we construct for all $j \in J$:

- if $v_j \leq b_{\mathcal{S}_j}^{\mathcal{S}_i}$, $t_j' = \top$, then $v_j' = v_j + 1$,
- if $v_j \leq b_{\mathcal{S}_j}^{\mathcal{S}_i}$, and $t_j' = \bot$, then $v_j' = 0$,
- if $v_j = b_{\mathcal{S}_j}^{\mathcal{S}_i} + 1$, then $v_j' = b_{\mathcal{S}_j}^{\mathcal{S}_i} + 1$,
- if $w_j \leq a_{\mathcal{S}_j}^{\mathcal{S}_i}$, and $u_j' = \top$, then $w_j' = w_j + 1$,
- if $w_j \leq a_{\mathcal{S}_j}^{\mathcal{S}_i}$ and $t_j' = \bot$, then $w_j' = 0$,
- if $w_j = a_{\mathcal{S}_j}^{\mathcal{S}_i} + 1$, then $w_j' = a_{\mathcal{S}_j}^{\mathcal{S}_i} + 1$.

Intuitively, the counter w_j tracks the number of consecutive times $\mathcal{S}_j$ refuses to accept a vehicle, and is reset to 0 when the vehicle is accepted. If w_j exceeds the bound $A_{\mathcal{S}_j}^{\mathcal{S}_i} + 1$, it remains $A_{\mathcal{S}_j}^{\mathcal{S}_i} + 1$ forever. Similarly, the counter v_j tracks the number of consecutive times $\mathcal{S}_i$ refuses to accept a vehicle from $\mathcal{S}_j$ and is reset to 0 when a vehicle is accepted. Given a run in the game $\overline{\pi}$, the acceptance condition $\mathsf{Acc}^{\mathcal{S}_i}(\overline{\pi}) = \top$ iff for $g_t^{\mathcal{S}_i} = (g_t, (v_{j_t}, w_{j_t}))$, we have $g_t \subseteq F$ for all t and one of the following conditions holds for (v_{j_t}, w_{j_t}) for all $j \in J$:

$$\exists\, t \geq 0 \text{ with } w_{j_t} > a_{\mathcal{S}_j}^{\mathcal{S}_i} \tag{1}$$

$$\forall\, t \geq 0 : \bigwedge_j v_{j_t} \leq b_{\mathcal{S}_j}^{\mathcal{S}_i} \tag{2}$$

Using the counter w_j, we encode the assumption $\mathcal{S}_i$ makes on the behaviour of $\mathcal{S}_j$. This is captured in condition 1 which says that if at some point in the play, the assumption made on $\mathcal{S}_j$ is violated. Specifically if $\mathcal{S}_j$ refuses to accept a UAV from $\mathcal{S}_i$ for more than $a_{\mathcal{S}_j}^{\mathcal{S}_i}$ consecutive times, then the play is winning as the assumption has been violated.

Similarly, we use v_j to encode the guarantee $\mathcal{S}_i$ must give to $\mathcal{S}_j$. This is captured in condition 2 which states that $\mathcal{S}_i$ has to accept a UAV from $\mathcal{S}_j$ in fewer than $b_{\mathcal{S}_j}^{\mathcal{S}_i}$ time steps.

Lemma 1. *Encoding the integers in this manner means* $\mathsf{Acc}^{\mathcal{S}_i}$ *is a safety acceptance condition and* $\mathcal{G}^{\mathcal{S}_i}$ *is a safety game.*

We use standard algorithms for safety games (e.g. [19]) to compute the maximally permissive winning strategy $\rho^{\mathcal{S}_i} : G^{\mathcal{S}_i} \times \Sigma_I \to 2^{\Sigma_O}$ of $\mathcal{G}^s$.

5.4   Synthesis of Locally-Optimal Shields

Next, we propose a procedure to synthesize shields that minimize the cost per deviation period, assuming that contract assumptions are satisfied. This allows the user to specify a cost function $c(\sigma_O, \sigma'_O)$ to tailor behaviour such as prioritizing vehicles entering from some sectors compared to others. More details of possible cost functions can be found in [6].

We start with the game graph $\mathcal{G}^{\mathcal{S}_i} = (G^{\mathcal{S}_i}, g_0^{\mathcal{S}_i}, \Sigma, \Sigma_O, \delta^{\mathcal{S}_i}, \mathsf{Acc}^{\mathcal{S}_i})$ and construct a new game $\mathcal{G}_{opt}^{\mathcal{S}_i} = (G^{\mathcal{S}_i}, g_0^{\mathcal{S}_i}, \Sigma, \Sigma_O, \delta^{\mathcal{S}_i}, \mathsf{Acc}^{\mathcal{S}_i}, \mathsf{Val}_{opt}^{\mathcal{S}_i})$ with value function $\mathsf{Val}_{opt}^{\mathcal{S}_i}(\overline{\pi})$ which is an *accumulated cost objective* using c as edge labeling: $cost^{opt}(g^a, (\sigma_I, \sigma_O), \sigma'_O) = c(\sigma_O, \sigma'_O)$.

Using the procedure described in [6,16], we synthesize shields, that are winning according to $\mathsf{Acc}^{\mathcal{S}_i}$ and optimize Val^{opt}.

5.5   Proof of Correctness

In this section we prove that if there exists a set of localized shields synthesized using the construction detailed earlier, they must correct with respect to the conjunction of all safety properties for k UAM sectors φ_i where $i = 1, \ldots, k$.

Theorem 1. $(\mathcal{D}_1 \circ \mathcal{S}_1) \circ \ldots \circ (\mathcal{D}_k \circ \mathcal{S}_k) \models \varphi_1 \wedge \ldots \wedge \varphi_k.$

Proof. Recall we will have that if a $\mathcal{S}_i$ is generated from the safety game then we must have $\mathcal{D}_i \circ \mathcal{S}_i \models \varphi_i$. There are two cases where the joint system will violate the conjunction of specifications.

Case 1: Suppose the following holds for shield $\mathcal{S}_i$:

$$\mathcal{D}_i \circ \mathcal{S}_i \not\models \varphi_i \bigwedge_{j \in J} B_{\mathcal{S}_j}^{\mathcal{S}_i}.$$

By construction, if assumptions $\bigwedge_{j \in J} A_{\mathcal{S}_j}^{\mathcal{S}_i}$ hold, each shield is synthesized from the corresponding safety game $\mathcal{G}^{\mathcal{S}_i}$, whose acceptance condition is augmented to become $\varphi_i \wedge_{j \in J} B_{\mathcal{S}_j}^{\mathcal{S}_i}$. Contradiction.

Case 2: Suppose assumption $\bigwedge_{j \in J} A_{\mathcal{S}_j}^{\mathcal{S}_i}$ is violated. If so, there is no guarantee that $(\mathcal{D}_i \circ \mathcal{S}_i)$ is correct with respect to φ_i and the contract-induced safety requirements $\bigwedge_{j \in J} B_{\mathcal{S}_j}^{\mathcal{S}_i}$. However, by design, $A_{\mathcal{S}_j}^{\mathcal{S}_i} = B_{\mathcal{S}_i}^{\mathcal{S}_j}$. Hence, if $\bigwedge_{j \in J} A_{\mathcal{S}_j}^{\mathcal{S}_i}$ is violated, there exists $j \in J$ such that $\mathcal{S}_j \nvDash \varphi_j \wedge B_{\mathcal{S}_i}^{\mathcal{S}_j}$. As showed in case 1, this is a contradiction.   □

We remark that this construction guarantees correctness if a set of localized shields can be synthesized. However, since it requires the contract-induced guarantees to be manually constructed, the construction cannot always guarantee that such a set of shields exists.

6 Validation via Simulation

We use the reactive synthesis tool Slugs [9] to compute the shields using the procedure described in Sect. 5. All experiments were performed on an Intel i5-5300U 2.30 GHz CPU with 8 GB of RAM.

6.1 Shield Synthesis Comparison

We compare the localized synthesis procedure presented in this paper with the centralized procedure detailed in [6]. In a centralized setting, the synthesis time grows exponentially with the number of sectors present.

In each sector the safety specification φ_i is to not exceed an upper bound of vehicles in each sector. For simplicity, we use the same contract values $\mathcal{C}_{\mathcal{S}_j}^{\mathcal{S}_i} = (A_{\mathcal{S}_j}^{\mathcal{S}_i}, B_{\mathcal{S}_j}^{\mathcal{S}_i})$ referred to as C in Table 1 and maximum vehicle upper bound for the referred to as N for all sectors, though, in principle, this is not necessary.

Again, we use the same N for each sector. We compare the two procedures for increasing numbers of sectors in Table 1. We report synthesis times for computing the permissive strategy, along with the time for computing the cost-optimal strategy from the permissive strategy. We use a cost function that assigns a cost whenever the shield moves an idle vehicle out of its region in order to disincentivize shields from moving vehicles when it is not required. Note that the synthesis time in the decentralized procedure significantly outperforms that of the centralized case. In the last two trials, the centralized shield synthesis timed out unsuccessfully.

6.2 Traffic Management Case Study

In order to demonstrate empirical performance and behaviour of the proposed system, we also implement the synthesis framework on an example environment of 9 UAM sectors and 5 UAM vehicles (see Fig. 4). Each region has an upper

Table 1. Synthesis time comparison between centralized and localized methods.

	Sectors	N	C	Perm. strategy time (s)	Opt. strategy time (s)
Centralized	3	2	2	43	17
	5	3	3	1840	1489
	7	4	4	Time out	Time out
	9	5	5	Time out	Time out
Localized	3	2	2	13	10
	5	3	3	123	32
	7	4	4	219	111
	9	5	5	470	286

bound $N = 1$, except for sector V_9 that has $N = 2$. Three of the vehicles ($\mathcal{G}_1$, $\mathcal{G}_2$ and $\mathcal{G}_3$) have been assigned tasks, while two are loitering inside sector V_9. The MDP planner approaches this problem as a composed system $\mathcal{M}$ of the MDPs associated with $\mathcal{G}_1$, $\mathcal{G}_2$ and $\mathcal{G}_3$, and a policy is synthesized for each one and executed on-board each agent. We present two cases—an execution of the system with and without a local shield in each region.

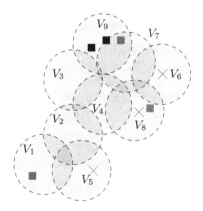

Fig. 4. Example UAM environment with 9 regions ($V_1, \cdots, V_9$), 5 UAM vehicles and 3 destinations. The initial locations and desired destinations of $\mathcal{G}_1$ (blue), $\mathcal{G}_2$ (red) and $\mathcal{G}_3$ (magenta) are given by the squares and crosses respectively. Agents $\mathcal{G}_4$ and $\mathcal{G}_5$ (black squares) are initially loitering in sector V_9 with no task requirement. (Color figure online)

Figure 5 shows the evolution of the decentralized strategy as the system progresses in time, in both the shielded and unshielded cases. Videos comparing the policies in an open-air traffic simulator [1] are shown at: https://bit.ly/2CjrET5. The initial trajectories of $\mathcal{G}_1$ (blue) and $\mathcal{G}_2$(red) are in conflict, and after one time-step the agents' on-board planners coordinate and re-route such that $\mathcal{G}_1$ moves to V_3 and $\mathcal{G}_2$ loiters until $\mathcal{G}_1$ has cleared V_2.

$\mathcal{G}_1$'s new route takes it through V_9 as shown in Fig. 5b. However, since V_9 already has two vehicles loitering, $\mathcal{G}_1$ cannot enter. In Fig. 5c, the sector controller $\mathcal{D}_9$ allows $\mathcal{G}_1$ to enter, which will lead to a violation of φ_9 that requires fewer than 2 vehicles in V_9 at all times. .

The local shield $\mathcal{S}_9$ ensures that the one of the vehicles ($\mathcal{G}_4$ or $\mathcal{G}_5$) in V_9 exits from the sector so that the $\mathcal{G}_1$ can transit. $\mathcal{G}_1$ is forcéd to loiter while $\mathcal{S}_9$ can move a vehicle out to make room as shown in Figs. 5d–f. At the next time interval, $\mathcal{S}_7$ moves the vehicle again so that $\mathcal{G}_1$ can transit through V_7.

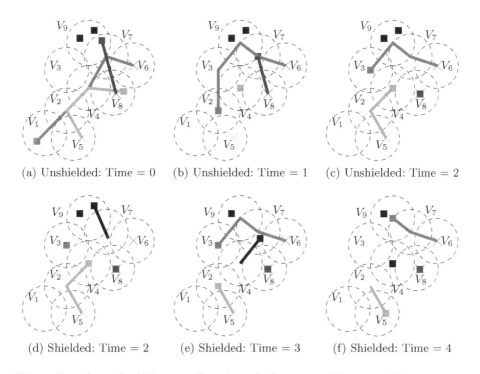

(a) Unshielded: Time = 0   (b) Unshielded: Time = 1   (c) Unshielded: Time = 2

(d) Shielded: Time = 2   (e) Shielded: Time = 3   (f) Shielded: Time = 4

Fig. 5. Snapshots of vehicles travelling through the sectors. The top and bottom rows show the vehicle policies without and with shielded sectors respectively.

7   Conclusion

We presented a localized shield synthesis method to generate runtime enforcement modules to perform traffic management for a UAM system. We exploit the geographic separation of the traffic management problem to avoid the full distributed synthesis problem and focus on *localized* shield synthesis where shields can observe the outputs of neighbours. We make use of assume-guarantee contracts between neighbouring shields to ensure that each shield can still satisfy its safety requirement without violating the ability of neighbours to satisfy theirs. In this paper, these contracts are manually generated. For future work we aim to generate or learn these contracts in an automated way. We also aim to use this framework to perform *shielded multi-agent reinforcement learning* where the agents will have to learn and adjust their optimal policy during runtime.

Acknowledgement. The authors would like to thank Ali Husain and Dr. Bruce Porter from Spark-Congition Inc. for inspiring discussions. This work was supported in part by grants AFRL FA 8650-15-C-2546 and DARPA W911NF-16-1-0001.

References

1. Bluesky - the open air traffic simulator. https://github.com/ProfHoekstra/bluesky
2. Skygrid Technology. https://skygrid.com/technology/. Accessed 11 Dec 2018
3. Bartocci, E., Falcone, Y. (eds.): Lectures on Runtime Verification. LNCS, vol. 10457. Springer, Cham (2018). https://doi.org/10.1007/978-3-319-75632-5
4. Bauer, A., Falcone, Y.: Decentralised LTL monitoring. Formal Methods Syst. Des. **48**(1–2), 46–93 (2016). https://doi.org/10.1007/s10703-016-0253-8
5. Bauer, A., Leucker, M., Schallhart, C.: Runtime verification for LTL and TLTL. ACM Trans. Softw. Eng. Methodol. **20**(4), 14:1–14:64 (2011). https://doi.org/10.1145/2000799.2000800
6. Bharadwaj, S., Bloem, R., Dimitrova, R., Könighofer, B., Topcu, U.: Synthesis of minimum-cost shields for distributed systems. In: 2019 Annual American Control Conference, ACC 2019. IEEE, Philadelphia, 10–12 July (2019)
7. Bloem, R., Könighofer, B., Könighofer, R., Wang, C.: Shield synthesis: In: Baier, C., Tinelli, C. (eds.) TACAS 2015. LNCS, vol. 9035, pp. 533–548. Springer, Heidelberg (2015). https://doi.org/10.1007/978-3-662-46681-0_51
8. Cassar, I., Francalanza, A.: On implementing a monitor-oriented programming framework for actor systems. In: Ábrahám, E., Huisman, M. (eds.) IFM 2016. LNCS, vol. 9681, pp. 176–192. Springer, Cham (2016). https://doi.org/10.1007/978-3-319-33693-0_12
9. Chaudhuri, S., Farzan, A. (eds.): CAV 2016 Part II. LNCS, vol. 9780. Springer, Cham (2016). https://doi.org/10.1007/978-3-319-41540-6
10. FAA: Order JO 7400.9Y Air Traffic Organization Policy (2014). https://www.faa.gov/documentLibrary/media/Order/JO_7400.9Y.pdf
11. Falcone, Y.: You should better enforce than verify. In: Barringer, H., et al. (eds.) RV 2010. LNCS, vol. 6418, pp. 89–105. Springer, Heidelberg (2010). https://doi.org/10.1007/978-3-642-16612-9_9
12. Falcone, Y., Jaber, M., Nguyen, T., Bozga, M., Bensalem, S.: Runtime verification of component-based systems in the BIP framework with formally-proved sound and complete instrumentation. Softw. Syst. Model. **14**(1), 173–199 (2015). https://doi.org/10.1007/s10270-013-0323-y
13. Francalanza, A., Seychell, A.: Synthesising correct concurrent runtime monitors. Formal Methods Syst. Des. **46**(3), 226–261 (2015). https://doi.org/10.1007/s10703-014-0217-9
14. Guestrin, C., Koller, D., Parr, R.: Multiagent planning with factored MDPS. In: Advances in Neural Information Processing Systems, pp. 1523–1530 (2002)

15. Hopcroft, J.E., Schwartz, J.T., Sharir, M.: On the complexity of motion planning for multiple independent objects; pspace- hardness of the "warehouseman's problem". Int. J. Robotic Res. IJRR **3**, 76–88 (1984). https://doi.org/10.1177/027836498400300405
16. Jing, G., Ehlers, R., Kress-Gazit, H.: Shortcut through an evil door: optimality of correct-by-construction controllers in adversarial environments. In: 2013 IEEE/RSJ International Conference on Intelligent Robots and Systems, Tokyo, Japan, pp. 4796–4802, 3–7 November 2013. https://doi.org/10.1109/IROS.2013.6697048
17. Könighofer, B., et al.: Shield synthesis. Formal Methods Syst. Des. **51**(2), 332–361 (2017). https://doi.org/10.1007/s10703-017-0276-9
18. Kottasová, I.: Uber invests millions to build flying taxis in France. CNN Business, May 2018. https://www.cnn.com/2018/10/01/tech/uber-flying-taxi-france/index.html
19. Mazala, R.: Infinite games. In: Grädel, E., Thomas, W., Wilke, T. (eds.) Automata Logics, and Infinite Games. LNCS, vol. 2500, pp. 23–38. Springer, Heidelberg (2002). https://doi.org/10.1007/3-540-36387-4_2
20. Moore, A., et al.: Testing enabling technologies for safe UAS urban operations. In: Proceedings of the 2018 Aviation, Technology, Integration, and Operations Conference. No. AIAA-2018-3200, Atlanta, Georgia, June 2018
21. Narkawicz, A., Muñoz, C., Dutle, A.: Sensor uncertainty mitigation and dynamic well clear volumes in DAIDALUS. In: Proceedings of the 37th Digital Avionics Systems Conference (DASC). London, England, UK, September 2018
22. Neogi, N., Cuong, C., Dill, E.: A risk based assessment of a small UAS cargo delivery operation in proximity to urban areas. In: Proceedings of the 37th Digital Avionics Systems Conference (DASC). London, England, UK, September 2018
23. Prevot, T., Rios, J., Kopardekar, P., Robinson, J.E., Johnson, M., Jung, J.: UAS Traffic Management (UTM) concept of operations to safely enable low altitude flight operations. In: Proceedings of the 2018 Aviation, Technology, Integration, and Operations Conference. No. AIAA-2016-3292, Washington, DC, June 2016
24. Schewe, S.: Synthesis of distributed systems. Ph.D. thesis, Saarland University, Saarbrücken, Germany (2008)
25. Schewe, S.: Distributed synthesis is simply undecidable. Inf. Process. Lett. **114**(4), 203–207 (2014). https://doi.org/10.1016/j.ipl.2013.11.012, http://www.sciencedirect.com/science/article/pii/S0020019013002925
26. Schneider, F.B.: Enforceable security policies. ACM Trans. Inf. Syst. Secur. **3**(1), 30–50 (2000). https://doi.org/10.1145/353323.353382

Towards Full Proof Automation in Frama-C Using Auto-active Verification

Allan Blanchard[1]([⊠]) [iD], Frédéric Loulergue[2] [iD], and Nikolai Kosmatov[3] [iD]

[1] Inria Lille—Nord Europe, Villeneuve d'Ascq, France
allan.blanchard@inria.fr
[2] School of Informatics Computing and Cyber Systems, Northern Arizona University, Flagstaff, USA
frederic.loulergue@nau.edu
[3] CEA, List, Software Reliability and Security Lab, PC 174, Gif-sur-Yvette, France
nikolai.kosmatov@cea.fr

Abstract. While deductive verification is increasingly used on real-life code, making it fully automatic remains difficult. The development of powerful SMT solvers has improved the situation, but some proofs still require interactive theorem provers in order to achieve full formal verification. Auto-active verification relies on additional guiding annotations (assertions, ghost code, lemma functions, etc.) and provides an important step towards a greater automation of the proof. However, the support of this methodology often remains partial and depends on the verification tool. This paper presents an experience report on a complete functional verification of several C programs from the literature and real-life code using auto-active verification with the C software analysis platform FRAMA-C and its deductive verification plugin WP. The goal is to use automatic solvers to verify properties that are classically verified with interactive provers. Based on our experience, we discuss the benefits of this methodology and the current limitations of the tool, as well as proposals of new features to overcome them.

1 Introduction

Formal verification enables obtaining a high level of assurance in software reliability, but requires significant expertise and is still very costly to apply on real-world use cases. The purpose of this experience report is to investigate how to achieve a higher level of automation of formal verification. We address this problem in the context of FRAMA-C.

Context and Motivation. FRAMA-C [19] is a source code analysis platform that aims at conducting verification of industrial-size programs written in C. FRAMA-C offers a large range of analyzers, such as abstract interpretation based value analysis, deductive verification, dependence analysis, program slicing, runtime verification, test generation, etc., as well as a common specification language: ACSL [3].

WP is the deductive verification plugin of FRAMA-C. It is based on the weakest precondition calculus [11]. WP can be used to prove functional correctness of C programs with respect to a specification written in the form of ACSL annotations. Given an annotated program, WP computes *verification conditions* (VCs) or *proof obligations*, that

J. M. Badger and K. Y. Rozier (Eds.): NFM 2019, LNCS 11460, pp. 88–105, 2019.
https://doi.org/10.1007/978-3-030-20652-9_6

is, properties that must be proved to ensure that the program respects its specification. These verification conditions can then be proved either automatically by SMT solvers (for example, by Alt-Ergo [10], or—through the Why3 [14] platform—by CVC4 [2] or Z3 [24]) or by interactive provers (like the Coq proof assistant [28]).

Generally, the verification engineer wants to achieve a maximal level of automation, thus relying on SMT solvers whenever possible. In practice, it is not always possible. For example, when the proof of some properties requires reasoning by induction, SMT solvers often remain inefficient. Thus, most of the time the solution is to introduce generic lemmas that can be directly instantiated by SMT solvers to prove verification conditions, and to prove those lemmas using interactive provers like Coq. However, producing a Coq proof often requires extensive background in formal methods, can be time consuming and can increase the maintenance cost when a new version of the verification condition generator is released. It makes the proof much harder for many verification engineers.

Approach and Goals. Leino and Moskal [21] proposed the notion of *auto-active verification* to qualify verification approaches that suggest to enrich the code with more annotations than just necessary to express function contracts. They are available to the verification tool before the generation of the verification conditions, and so can be used to optimize this generation. However, depending on the tools, auto-active features are more or less developed and lead to different levels of automation.

In this experience report, we investigate the use of auto-active verification with FRAMA-C/WPand apply it to verify the following three case studies[1]:

1. a memory allocation module [22],
2. a linked list module [5],
3. all examples of an independent benchmark called *ACSL by Example* [7].

The first two examples are taken from recent real-life case studies on formal verification of the Contiki operating system [13]. The third artifact contains a rich set of annotated programs verified with FRAMA-C/WP, maintained by Fraunhofer FOKUS. Previous proofs of these programs essentially relied on some interactive proofs in Coq.

Our goal was to increase the level of automation and to demonstrate that, thanks to auto-active verification, interactive proof was not needed anymore to achieve full formal verification. Based on our experience, we analyze the results in terms of necessary annotations and proof effort. We identify some features that are currently not available in FRAMA-C, but appear to be necessary for a better auto-active verification. We also provide some discussion and comparison with existing approaches.

Contributions. The contributions of this work include:

- a formal specification and a *fully automatic proof* of the aforementioned programs using the auto-active verification approach;
- analysis of the effort that was needed to achieve this goal;
- identification of several features that could be helpful (and some workarounds we used to overcome their absence);
- a comparison with existing work that could be integrated into FRAMA-C to improve auto-active verification.

---

[1] All source code available at: http://allan-blanchard.fr/code/auto-active-nfm-2019.zip.

```
1  struct memb {
2    unsigned short size;
3    unsigned short num;
4    char *busy;
5    void *mem;
6  };
7
8  /*@ requires valid_memb(m);
9      assigns m->busy[0 .. (m->num - 1)];
10     behavior free_found:
11       assumes ∃ ℤ i; 0 ≤ i < m->num ∧ m->busy[i] == 0;
12       ensures _memb_numfree(m) == \old(_memb_numfree(m)) - 1;
13     behavior full:
14       assumes ∀ ℤ i; 0 ≤ i < m->num ⇒ m->busy[i] ≠ 0;
15       ensures _memb_numfree(m) == \old(_memb_numfree(m));
16     complete behaviors; disjoint behaviors; */
17 void * memb_alloc(struct memb *m){
18   /*@ loop invariant 0 ≤ i ≤ m->num;
19       loop invariant ∀ ℤ j; 0 ≤ j < i ⇒ m->busy[j] ≠ 0;
20       loop assigns i;
21       loop variant m->num - i; */
22   for(int i = 0; i < m->num; ++i) {
23     if(m->busy[i] == 0) {
24       m->busy[i] = 1 ;
25       /*@ assert one_change{Pre, Here}(i, m->busy, 0, m->num); */
26       return address_of_block(m, i);
27     }
28   }
29   return NULL;
30 }
```

Fig. 1. The memory allocation function of MEMB and its (partial) specification

Outline. The paper is organized as follows. Section 2 presents a running example verified using a classic combination of automatic and interactive proof. Section 3 explains how to avoid interactive proofs. Section 4 further details the results of our experiments. Section 5 compares our approach with other tools. Section 6 discusses some lessons learned and necessary features. Section 7 gives a conclusion and future work.

2   Classic Lemma-Based Verification in Frama-C

In this section, we briefly present ACSL, the specification language of FRAMA-C, its deductive verification plugin WP and the way it is generally used to prove a particular program. We illustrate it on a running example (shown in Fig. 1) taken from the Contiki operating system: function memb_alloc of the memory management module MEMB. This module simulates memory (de-)allocation using a set of pre-allocated blocks that can be attributed (or released) on demand. Function memb_alloc iterates over blocks and if it finds an available block, it marks it as allocated and returns its address.

Running Example. The memb structure contains the data required to manage a set of memory blocks. The size field (line 2 in Fig. 1) indicates the size of a block in bytes, while num (line 3) indicates the maximal number of allocable blocks. The pointer mem (line 5) refers to the pre-allocated array of blocks (of total size num*size). The main invariant to maintain in the module is the fact that it correctly keeps track of allocated (i.e. attributed) and free (i.e. released) blocks. This is done in the busy field (line 4), which contains an array of length num whose i-th cell indicates for the i-th block whether it is busy (value 1) or not (value 0). In the verification, we simply consider that

```
1  /*@ axiomatic OccArray{
2       logic Z occ{L}(Z e, char *a, Z from, Z to)
3          reads a[from .. (to - 1)];
4       axiom end_occ{L}:
5       ∀ Z e, char *a, Z from, to;
6          from ≥ to ⇒ occ{L}(e, a, from, to) == 0;
7       axiom iter_occ_true{L}:
8       ∀ Z e, char *a, Z from, to;
9          (from < to ∧ a[to-1] == e) ⇒
10         occ{L}(e, a, from, to) == occ{L}(e, a, from, to-1) + 1;
11      axiom iter_occ_false{L}:
12      ∀ Z e, char *a, Z from, to;
13         (from < to ∧ a[to-1] ≠ e) ⇒
14         occ{L}(e, a, from, to) == occ{L}(e, a, from, to-1);
15   }
16   logic Z _memb_numfree(struct memb *m) =
17      occ(0, m->busy, 0, m->num);
18  */
```

Fig. 2. The axiomatic definition of occurrence counting

a block of index i is free when the corresponding value at the cell of index i of busy is 0, and allocated otherwise. From a specification point of view, this knowledge is also used to ensure that after an allocation fewer memory blocks are available (and dually, that after a free, more blocks are available). In this example, we will focus on this last simple property and ignore some other aspects of the proof (for more detail see [22]).

In an ACSL contract, a precondition is specified in a **requires** clause. Here, the function requires (line 8) that the received memb structure be valid (in the sense of the memb invariant). There exist two kinds of postconditions. An **assigns** clause specifies a list of memory locations that the function is allowed to modify. An **ensures** clause specifies properties that should be verified after the function call. Here, the function can potentially assign (cf. line 9) any memory cell of the busy array (even though we know it will actually assign at most one)—the **assigns** clause has only to give a correct over-approximation. The unmodified values can be further constrained by other postconditions. We can specify different behaviors (or cases) for the function. Here, when the function is called, either there exists a free block (lines 10–12), or not (lines 13–15). The condition that defines each case is stated using an **assumes** clause. Each behavior can have its own postconditions. In this example we only consider postconditions on the number of free blocks. If some free blocks are available (line 11), the function ensures that one more block is allocated, that is, one less block is free (line 12). Otherwise, if all blocks are busy (line 14), the number of free blocks does not change (line 15). Line 16 states that the specified behaviors are complete and disjoint, that is, cover all possible cases and do not overlap. Notice that for convenience of the reader, the ACSL annotations in this paper are slightly pretty-printed (using e.g. mathematical notation $\mathbb{Z}$, $\forall$, $\exists$, $\Rightarrow$, $\neq$ instead of ACSL notation **integer**, \forall, \exists, ==>, !=, respectively).

To refer to program states at different program points in ACSL predicates, in addition to the usual *labels* of C language (see e.g. line 7 in Fig. 5), ACSL predefines a few additional labels, such as the current program point **Here** (used by default), the pre-state **Pre** on entry and the post-state **Post** on exit of the current function.

```
1  /*@
2  lemma occ_split{L}:
3    ∀ ℤ e, char *t, ℤ from, cut, to;
4    from ≤ cut ≤ to ⇒ occ{L}(e,t,from,to) ==
5                      occ{L}(e,t,from,cut)+occ{L}(e,t,cut,to);
6
7  predicate same_elems{L1,L2}(char *t, ℤ from, ℤ to) =
8    ∀ ℤ j; from ≤ j < to ⇒ \at(t[j], L1) == \at(t[j], L2);
9
10 lemma same_elems_means_same_occ{L1, L2}:
11   ∀ ℤ e, char *t, ℤ from, to;
12   same_elems{L1,L2}(t,from,to) ⇒
13     occ{L1}(e, t, from, to) == occ{L2}(e, t, from, to);
14
15 predicate one_change{L1,L2}(ℤ index, char *t, ℤ from, ℤ to) =
16   from ≤ index < to ∧
17   same_elems{L1,L2}(t, from, index) ∧ same_elems{L1,L2}(t, index+1, to) ∧
18   \at(t[index], L1) ≠ \at(t[index], L2);
19
20 lemma one_change_means_inc_and_dec{L1, L2}:
21   ∀ ℤ index, char *t, ℤ from, to;
22     \let old_val = \at(t[index],L1); \let new_val = \at(t[index],L2);
23     (one_change{L1,L2}(index, t, from, to)) ⇒ (
24       occ{L1}(old_val, t, from, to)-1 == occ{L2}(old_val, t, from, to) ∧
25       occ{L1}(new_val, t, from, to)+1 == occ{L2}(new_val, t, from, to) ∧
26       (∀ ℤ other; other ≠ old_val ∧ other ≠ new_val ⇒
27         occ{L1}(other, t, from, to) == occ{L2}(other, t, from, to))
28     );
29 */
```

Fig. 3. Predicates and lemmas to reason about occurrence counting

The definition of the _memb_numfree is provided in Fig. 2 (line 16–17). It consists in counting the number of occurrences of value 0 in the busy array of the MEMB structure. The counting operation occ{L}(e,a,from,to) is defined axiomatically (lines 1–15): it counts the number of occurrences of value e in array a at program label L, from an index from to an (excluded) index to. Label L can be omitted (cf. line 18) and is then by default **Here**, the current program point. The definition considers three cases. If the index range is empty then the number of occurrences is 0 (lines 4–6). If there is at least one cell to visit then the number of occurrences is (recursively) the number of occurrences in the array prefix of indices from from to to--1 (excluded), incremented or not depending if the last value included in the initial range (that is, a[to-1]) is equal to e (lines 8–10) or not (lines 12–14). The **reads** clause (line 3) indicates the values that impact the result of the function and thus determines when a memory modification invalidates the property.

Lines 18–21 of Fig. 1 define in a classic way a loop contract specifying which variables can be modified (line 20) and what other properties remain valid (lines 18–19) after any number of complete loop iterations (i.e. *each time the loop condition is evaluated*), as well as a loop variant used to prove termination (line 21).

Lemmas and Assertions. Consider the instruction on line 24 of Fig. 1. It assigns a particular value of the busy array inside a loop. This value was previously 0 (line 23) and becomes 1. Thus the number of 0's decreases by 1. However, proving this property requires some kind of reasoning by induction, to show how the counting can be split into three segments: segment $[0, i)$ preceding the value (possible empty), the modified value itself, and segment $[i + 1, \text{m->num})$ that follows it (possibly empty again). We also need to reason by induction to show that since the first and the last array segments remain unchanged, the number of occurrences in them does not change either.

SMT solvers are not good at reasoning by induction. In our example, they cannot prove the contract of the function if we do not give them more help. The classic approach with WP is to provide lemmas that capture the inductive reasoning. These lemmas can be directly instantiated by SMT solvers to deduce the required conclusion from the premises without reasoning by induction.

Let us illustrate it with the three lemmas presented in Fig. 3. We state the lemma one_change_means_inc_and_dec to prove our property on the number of occurrences after a change in the array. This lemma states that if one (and only one) value changes in an array from a label L1 to another label L2, then the number of occurrences of the old value decreases, the number of occurrences of the new value increases and the number of occurrences of other values does not change. While we could directly prove this property in Coq, it is easier to state two more lemmas to ease the process. Lemma occ_split allows splitting the total range of indices into two subranges (segments). Lemma same_elems_means_same_occ states that when all the values of an array remain unchanged between two labels, the number of occurrences does not change either. All these lemmas cannot be proved directly by most SMT solvers, so classically they are proved using an interactive prover, e.g. the Coq proof assistant.

Once these lemmas have been stated, they can be automatically used by SMT solvers to discharge the different verification conditions generated by WP. However, depending on the property that needs to be proved, and on the proof context (i.e., the different properties known about the program at the corresponding program point), SMT solvers can fail to automatically *trigger* the use of these lemmas. For example, in the case when the function modifies the array, the ensures clause on line 12 will not be proved because of the complexity of the proof context. In this case, we use a first feature of auto-active verification: we add an assertion (line 25 in Fig. 1) that makes the link between the current state (label **Here**) and the state before the function starts (label **Pre**). It directly states the premise of Lemma one_change_means_inc_and_dec (cf. line 23 in Fig. 3) and will allow SMT solvers to trigger its application and to deduce that the number of 0's decreased (i.e. to deduce line 12 in Fig. 1 from line 24 in Fig. 3).

The more complex the proof context is, the harder is the automatic triggering of lemmas. So it is common to add assertions, but sometimes, even with assertions, triggering of lemmas can be hard to predict. The question is then to know whether we can further increase proof automation, both in efficient triggering of SMT solvers and in the ability to prove complex properties without interactive provers. Since this approach can require adding more annotations, the question is also whether these annotations are more costly to add compared to an interactive proof or not.

3 Auto-active Verification Illustrated for the Running Example

As many other verification tools, FRAMA-C provides the ability to add *ghost code* in annotations of the source code being analyzed. Ghost code is regular C code, except that it is only visible by the verification tools. Ghost code must not interfere with the behavior of the program: it can basically observe the real world but cannot influence it.

Lemma functions are a particular form of ghost code. They consist of ghost functions that serve the same purpose as lemmas: to deduce some conclusions from some general premises. Like for lemmas, the properties are proved separately—here as function contracts—and can then be used in a particular context by simply calling the corresponding lemma function. Moreover, in lemma functions, some tricks can help to avoid the limitations of SMT solvers, for example, on reasoning by induction.

Let us illustrate on our running example how to completely remove the need for the Coq proof assistant. Basically, we can provide a way of performing the reasoning of the Coq proof of our lemma but using ghost code. The first step of the proof is to split our array again into three segments, the first and the last being unchanged, and the second containing the modified cell. We define a function that mimics the previously introduced `occ_split` lemma as shown in Fig. 4.

```
1  /*@ requires from ≤ cut ≤ to;
2      ensures occ(e,a,from,to) == occ(e,a,from,cut)+occ(e,a,cut,to);
3      assigns \nothing; */
4  void occ_split(int e, char * a, int from, int cut, int to){
5      /*@ loop invariant cut ≤ i ≤ to;
6          loop invariant occ(e,a,from,i) == occ(e,a,from,cut)+occ(e,a,cut,i);
7          loop assigns i;
8          loop variant to - i; */
9      for(int i = cut ; i < to ; i++){ }
10 }
```

Fig. 4. The lemma function `occ_split` with its proving code

The contract of the function expresses the lemma. The premise of the lemma is specified in a precondition, and the conclusion as a postcondition. A lemma function is pure, and thus **assigns \nothing**. The **for** loop provides, thanks to its loop invariant (lines 5–6), a way to reason by induction on the distance between `cut` and `to`. Indeed, the VC generation for this invariant creates the two cases to prove: either the distance is zero, or the relation is known for rank i and must be verified for $i + 1$. The function is fully proved by SMT solvers.

The lemma can then be instantiated in the `memb_alloc` function by calling it with suitable parameters, as illustrated in Fig. 5, on lines 4–5 and 13–14. The first call splits the global range of counting into segments $[0, i)$ and $[i, \text{m->num})$, and then the latter is split again into $[i, i + 1)$ and $[i + 1, \text{m->num})$. Notice that we need to split the range before and after the assignment since it invalidates any knowledge about `occ` over the whole array (as defined by the **reads** clause on line 3 of Fig. 2).

```
1 void * memb_alloc(struct memb *m){
2   /*@ ... */ // loop contract as in Fig.1
3   for(int i = 0; i < m->num; ++i) {
4     /*@ ghost occ_split(0, m->busy, 0, i, m->num); */
5     /*@ ghost occ_split(0, m->busy, i, i+1, m->num); */
6     if(m->busy[i] == 0) {
7       BA:
8         m->busy[i] = 1 ;
9
10      /*@ ghost same_elems_means_same_occ(BA, Here, 0, m->busy, 0, i) ; */
11      /*@ ghost same_elems_means_same_occ(BA, Here, 0, m->busy, i+1, m->num) ; */
12
13      /*@ ghost occ_split(0, m->busy, 0, i, m->num); */
14      /*@ ghost occ_split(0, m->busy, i, i+1, m->num); */
15
16      return address_of_block(m, i);
17    }
18  }
19  return NULL;
20 }
```

Fig. 5. Function memb_alloc fully proved in auto-active fashion

To prove that the unmodified segments $[0, i)$ and $[i + 1, $m->num$)$ contain the same number of 0's before and after the assignment, the notion of labels must be taken into account, as is done for the lemma on lines 10–13 of Fig. 3. Therefore, we cannot use a lemma function here since *we cannot specify arbitrary labels in a function call.*

```
1 #define same_elems_means_same_occ(_L1, _L2, _value, _array, _from, _to) \
2   /@                                                                     \
3     loop invariant _from ≤ _k ≤ _to ;                                    \
4     loop invariant occ{_L1}(_value, _array, _from, _k) ==                \
5                    occ{_L2}(_value, _array, _from, _k) ;                 \
6     loop assigns _k ;                                                    \
7     loop variant _to - _k ; @/                                           \
8   for(int _k = _from ; _k < _to ; ++ _k) ;                               \
9   /@ assert occ{_L1}(_value, _array, _from, _to) ==                      \
10             occ{_L2}(_value, _array, _from, _to) ; @/
```

Fig. 6. The same_elems_means_same_occ lemma macro

As a workaround, we directly *inject* proof-carrying code at the program point where we want to prove that the number of occurrences did not change (cf. lines 10–11 of Fig. 5) between labels BA and **Here**. This is done via a C macro[2]. This macro is defined in Fig. 6, it receives two labels _L1 and _L2, the counted _value, and the _array with the bounds of the considered segment. The assertion on lines 9–10 states the equality to be proved, and the **for** loop enables this proof thanks to the invariant on lines 3–4. We use the term *lemma macro* for such a proof-carrying macro.

Notice however that with this workaround, the proof is done each time we need an instance of the lemma: each instance of the lemma macro generates annotations to be

---

[2] Given a macro **#define** name(p1,...,pN) text, the C preprocessor replaces any occurrence name(e1,...,eN) by text where named parameters are replaced accordingly.

proved. In contrast, the original `occ_split` lemma is proved once and for all, and then instantiated as many times as necessary.

Another issue in creating a lemma macro in more complex cases is that it can be difficult to design and to prove directly for a large proof context (where the proof can be sensitive to other annotations). We propose to use a wrapper function that creates the smallest possible relevant context for such a lemma macro.

Let us illustrate this point with the helper function (given by Fig. 7) that we used to build the lemma macro `same_elems_means_same_occ`. The purpose of the function on lines 9–13 is to create a sufficiently generic context that only establishes the premises of the original lemma, in order to validate that our lemma macro can indeed prove our property of interest in isolation of any other context. The lemma `same_elems_means_same_occ` (Fig. 3, lines 10–13) states that if `same_elems` holds for an array for two program labels L1 and L2 then the number of occurrences does not change between L1 and L2. Let us consider that L1 is the **Pre** label of the function, and L2, the **Post** label. We have to create a context that assures that the **Pre** and **Post** labels of the function are two different memory states related by `same_elems`, and that our lemma macro can assure the conclusion of the lemma.

We first use a function call `side_effect_to_L2` (line 10) to introduce a different state before the use of the lemma macro. The function is specified (and does not need an implementation) on lines 1–3. It assigns the array to invalidate any previous knowledge about it (line 1) and ensures the premise that relates the two labels of the lemma (line 2). By calling this function in the wrapper function, we ensure that there exist two program states **Pre** (that corresponds to L1 in the lemma) and `SideEffectHappened` (that corresponds to L2 in the lemma) that are different because some side effect happened in between, and related by the predicate `same_elems`. Since the remaining part of the code is the call to the lemma macro which is pure, the label **Post** is equivalent to `SideEffectHappened`. Finally, the role of this wrapper function is thus to create a context where some labels L1 (= **Pre**) and L2 (= `SideEffectHappened` = **Post**) are related by `same_elems` in order to deduce, using the lemma macro we want to create, that the number of occurrences between these two labels did not change (lines 6–7). Using this wrapper function, we can now design the lemma macro of Fig. 7 and prove the wrapper function with it.

```
1  /*@ assigns array[from .. to-1] ;
2      ensures same_elems{Pre, Post}(array, from, to) ; */
3  void side_effect_to_L2(char* array, int from, int to) ;
4
5  /*@ assigns array[from .. to-1] ;
6      ensures occ{Pre}(value, array, from, to) ==
7              occ{Post}(value, array, from, to) ;
8  */
9  void prove_same_elems_means_same_occ(int value, int* array, int from, int to){
10   side_effect_to_L2(array, from, to) ;
11 SideEffectHappened:
12   //@ ghost same_elems_means_same_occ(Pre, Here, value, array, from, to) ;
13 }
```

Fig. 7. Code produced to build the `same_elems_means_same_occ` macro (Fig. 6)

As the attentive reader might notice, this wrapper function is not pure anymore, and the labels considered by the lemma macro are supposed to be ordered (while specified labels in ACSL lemmas are not). We further discuss these aspects in Sect. 6.

4 Experiments Using Auto-active Verification

In order to evaluate the use of auto-active verification with FRAMA-C/WP and to compare it to the classic lemma-based approach, we applied the auto-active approach to verify several previously verified examples from the literature and real-life code: (1) the memory allocation module MEMB (briefly presented in Sect. 2) and (2) the linked list module [5] of Contiki, as well as (3) all programs of an independent benchmark *ACSL by Example* [7]. For case studies (1) and (3), auto-active proofs were done without knowing the earlier Coq proofs. The list module appears to be the most complex case study. *In all these case studies, we managed to achieve a fully automatic proof with the auto-active approach*, except only for two lemmas explained below.

Approach. For each case study, we begin with the annotated code previously verified using interactively proved lemmas. First, we remove all lemmas from the annotations. Then, we identify the assertions that are not proved anymore. For each assertion, we consider the lemma(s) that are required to enable the verification. If such a lemma can be fully automatically proved (without relying on other lemmas that require interactive proof), it is preserved. Otherwise, we replace such a lemma by a lemma function or a lemma macro necessary to enable the verification, and adapt the annotations of the functions to verify.

For case studies (1) and (2), we also separately expressed and verified, in an auto-active style, the lemmas that were not required anymore (and thus were not preserved) with the auto-active approach. Our goal was to measure the time to verify all lemmas of these case studies. (For *ACSL by Example*, this was not done because of the large number of such lemmas.) In other statistics presented in the tables below for the auto-active approach we count only lemmas that were *required* for the verification.

Table 1. Statistics for the considered case studies

	Lemmas, incl. lemma functions & lemma macros	Generated goals	Goals proved with Coq	Lines of code		Execution time
				Lemmas, incl. l.fun./macros	Guiding annotations	
Case study (1). The memory management module MEMB (70 lines of C code)						
Classic	15	134	15	33	20	47 s
Auto-active	3	217	1	25	25	19 s
Case study (2). The linked list module (176 lines of C code)						
Classic	24	805	19	163	708	24 min
Auto-active	17	1631	1	366	629	21 min
Case study (3). *ACSL by Example*, v. 17.2.0 (630 lines of C code)						
Classic	87	1398	40	594	485	92 min
Auto-active	53	1790	0	670	611	78 min

Measured Indicators and Statistics. The MEMB module is composed of 5 functions; we needed to adapt the proofs for 2 of them. This adaptation to the auto-active app-roach took about 6 person-hours (including the proof of lemma functions that were not required). The verified version of the list module is composed of 11 functions and 2 auxiliary functions. We had to write one more auxiliary function, and to adapt the veri-fication for 9 functions. In total, the adaptation took about 20 person-hours. This effort includes the time to validate that the proof remains valid on different list data-types (see [5] for more detail). The *ACSL by Example* repository contains 76 proved examples (some functions are proved with two different contracts, methods, or implementations), 12 of which needed to be adapted. This adaptation took about 30 person-hours.

Table 1 sums up the amount of annotation required by each approach for each use case. The second column indicates the number of declared lemmas (including lemma functions or lemma macros if any). The third column gives the number of proof obliga-tions generated by WP from the annotated program. The fourth column indicates how many of these goals required an interactive proof. The fifth column indicates how many lines of code were required to write the lemma functions/macros (including function bodies, assertions, and loop invariants for them). The sixth column corresponds to the number of lines written to guide the proof, including loop invariants, and excluding the lines needed to prove lemma functions/macros (as we count them in column 5). The last column indicates the time needed to replay entirely the proofs of the goals[3].

Analysis of Results. We notice that in each case study, *we need fewer lemmas (including lemma functions) in the full auto-active approach.* The main reason for this result is that for complex proofs it is common to "duplicate" a lemma with slightly different premises or conclusions in order to make them easier to trigger by SMT solvers in the context of a particular proof. Each version must be separately proved in Coq. In the auto-active approach, since lemmas are manually instantiated, this duplication is not needed.

Furthermore, in the auto-active approach it is easier to know exactly which lemmas, and in particular lemma functions, are used during the verification. An instance of a lemma function is explicit: this is a function call (or an occurrence of a lemma macro). On the contrary, to detect the required lemmas in the classic approach, we need to proceed iteratively: (1) remove a lemma; (2) re-run all proofs to see whether some of them fail; (3) if that is the case, put the lemma back; and (4) go back to (1). This process is time-consuming, and it cannot be done before everything has been proved because triggering of lemmas can be impacted e.g. when we add more assertions in the code to prove. Thus, most of the time it is not done.

While the auto-active approach needs fewer lemmas/lemma-functions, *lemma func-tions often require more code to be written.* This was expected: we need to express a function contract, which is already longer than a lemma due to the format of the con-tract. We also need to provide a body for each lemma function that basically carries out the proof of the lemma. In our study, we noticed that we spent less time producing the auto-active proofs of the lemmas that were previously proved with Coq. For both case studies on Contiki modules, we proved all lemma function versions of the lemmas used

---

[3] Executed on a Core i7 6700HQ with 16 GB DDR4. Versions of the tools: Frama-C 18 Argon, Why3 0.88.3, Alt-Ergo 2.2, CVC3 2.4.1, CVC4 1.6, Z3 4.8.1, E Prover 2.1, Coq 8.7.2.

in the classic approach (even those that we removed later since they were not required), it took about a day, while the corresponding Coq proofs took at least a week.

The Number of Generated Proof Obligations is Greater for the Auto-active Approach. For the first two case studies, this number doubles. This increase was expected. Indeed, in the classic approach, the proof of a lemma generates a single proof obligation. In the auto-active approach, we need a proof obligation for the postcondition, but the body of the function also generates other proof obligations (for assertions, function calls, loop invariants or variants). The strong advantage is that *all these obligations are automatically verified by SMT solvers.*

Moreover, as we already mentioned, we use lemma macros to inline the proof-carrying code for lemmas that require multiple labels. Each time we use an instance of such a lemma, we perform a new complete proof of its statement. This significantly increases the number of proof obligations. The experiment on *ACSL by Example*, where the number of proof obligations increased less significantly, tends to confirm this intuition. Indeed, the semantic properties of the **reads** clause—stating that arrays with unmodified values between two labels have the same properties—were simply stated as axioms in the *ACSL by Example* case study, whereas we chose to prove them as lemmas in the other two case studies. These lemmas required creating additional lemma macros, resulting in more proof obligations.

Regarding guiding annotations needed in the verified code (that include assertions, loop invariants and ghost code), the results of the first and the third case studies indicate that *the auto-active approach needs more guiding annotations*. This is consistent with the idea that lemmas must be triggered manually. For the list module the opposite situation is observed. To explain that, we presume that during the adaptation of the proofs, we aggressively removed a lot of assertions to get faster results from SMT solvers. In this way, we removed some assertions that were superfluous in the classic approach.

Overall, *we expect that auto-active proofs will be easier to achieve for non-experts.* Using the auto-active approach does not require more expertise in FRAMA-C/WP than needed for the classic approach (proving a lemma function is just like proving any other C function). On the other hand, in the interactive approach, one also needs a strong expertise in Coq to prove the Coq goals generated from ACSL lemmas by WP, which involve a (relatively technical) encoding of the C memory model in Coq as well.

Resisting Lemmas. We were able to prove the great majority of lemmas without interactive proof. *Only two lemmas had to be proved in Coq.* The first one, used in the MEMB module, states: $\forall a, b \in \mathbb{Z}, a \geq 0 \Rightarrow b > 0 \Rightarrow (a * b)/b = a$. Indeed, the reasoning of SMT solvers can become harder here since WP encodes the division with a particular logic function that represents the C semantics of the division.

The second resisting lemma, used in the linked list module, is related to the encoding of inductive definitions by WP. We illustrate the issue with a simple inductive predicate (checking if a given vector a of length size contains only zeroes):

```
inductive null_vector(int* a, size_t size){
case len_0: ∀ int* a;
  null_vector(a, 0);
case len_n: ∀ int* a, size_t s;
  s > 0 ⇒ (null_vector(a+1, s-1) ∧ a[0] == 0) ⇒ null_vector(a, s);
}
```

To reason about the cases of such an inductive definition, we need the following fact:

```
axiom empty_or_not: ∀ int* a, size_t s;
  null_vector(a, s) ⇒ ( (s == 0) ∨ (s > 0 ∧ null_vector(a+1, s-1) ∧ a[0] == 0) );
```

Such a property is readily provided by Coq, but not by WP. This is why we have to explicitly state it as a lemma and establish it with a simple one-line proof[4] in Coq.

5 Related Work

The term *auto-active verification* was coined by Leino and Moskal [21] to designate methods of verification that rely on specific annotations added into the source code to help the generation of verification conditions. Auto-active is there pointed out as one of the most efficient solutions to verify real-life programs.

This observation mainly came from several projects that involved some auto-active verification. They include VCC [8], a verifier for concurrent C code where annotations are extensively used to manipulate concurrency or ownership related properties, and Spec# [1] for the object-oriented C# language. The latter strongly influenced the language Dafny [20] and its verifier, which were specifically designed to ease verification yet enabling the construction of realistic systems. It was for example used to verify the secure execution of applications [16]. In object-oriented verification, AutoProof [15], part of EVE (Eiffel Verification Environment), targets Eiffel language. It was used to verify a container library [25]. OpenJML [9], for verification of Java programs, also supports introducing lemma functions and assertions to assist an automatic proof.

In the field of functional languages, the tools Leon [4] for Scala and Why3 [14] for the WhyML language are both based on auto-active features, in particular lemma functions. The Why3 platform has for example been used to verify binary heaps [27]. It is also used as a backend for FRAMA-C/WP to enable the use of different SMT solvers.

With FRAMA-C, we target the C programming language, mostly for critical applications. In addition to VCC that we already cited, the closest tool is the GNATprove [17] verifier, used to prove programs written in SPARK 2014 [23]. The auto-active features of GNATprove are extensively used for SPARK, in particular ghost code. It was for example used to verify a red-black tree data structure [12]. Verifast [18] is a verifier for C and Java based on separation logic, which is particularly powerful to verify heap-related properties, the counterpart being an extensive use of code annotations that are not related to the application of lemma functions or ghost code.

The closest work to the present study has been done recently in VerKer project [30]. In this work Volkov et al. use another deductive verification plugin of FRAMA-C, called AstraVer, which is a fork of the Jessie plugin. They introduce the notion of lemma function in FRAMA-C and the corresponding verification process. The main idea consists in giving the ability to declare a function as a "lemma" with a specific syntax, the contract of the corresponding function being then automatically converted into a lemma. This work also takes advantage of the fact that the AstraVer plugin supports function variant clause **decreases** to prove recursion termination that makes the verifying code easier to write. They tested the approach on a set of 8 functions, all of them being related to string manipulations.

---

[4] By introducing the variables and hypotheses, inverting the inductive hypothesis and automatically verifying all remaining proof goals.

Our work continues these efforts and performs a large verification study over 23 different functions, proved almost fully automatically with FRAMA-C/WP, some of which are related to array manipulations (in MEMB module and *ACSL by Example*), others to linked-list manipulations, and yet others to intricate axiomatic definitions (in *ACSL by Example* again). A particular focus of our work is a detailed comparison with an earlier classic lemma-based verification of the same case studies based on our personal experience and the discussion of the difficulties encountered and possible solutions.

6 Discussion

Logic Types. As pointed out by Volkov et al. [30], lemma functions in the particular case of FRAMA-C often lead to a loss of generality. Indeed, contrary to other languages that allow the use of logic types in the code, FRAMA-C does not, even in ghost code. That means that we cannot use logic types when we declare lemma functions. For example, if we compare the occ_split lemma (lines 2–5 of Fig. 3) and its equivalent lemma function (Fig. 4), we can notice that the bounds are no longer mathematical integers but machine integers. In all the cases we have currently verified, this is not a big problem. It often suffices to declare functions with the same types as the ones used in the program under verification (or with the largest one when multiple types exist), or to simply duplicate the lemma with the suitable type, which is not really elegant, but works.

However, the current support of ghost code by FRAMA-C limits the ability to use auto-active style depending on the needed ACSL features. For example, in a recent work, we verified the linked list module of Contiki with another formalization, using ACSL logic lists [6]. As some lemmas rely on purely logic types (the logic list), we would be unable to express them as lemma functions in FRAMA-C, and to use them in ghost code. The ACSL language allows the use of logic types in ghost code, however, adding support to FRAMA-C for this feature would require a significant implementation effort.

Lemmas with Unique Labels. For the particular case of lemma functions with a single label, a solution was proposed in the AstraVer tool. A function is declared as follows:

```
1 /*@ lemma
2   requires premise_1 ; ... requires premise_N ;
3   ensures conclusion ; */
4 void lemma_func_name(type_1 p1, ... type_M pM){ /* pure proof-carrying code */}
```

The **lemma** keyword indicates that the following function is a lemma, and consequently that it must be pure (which has to be proved). From this function, the plugin automatically generates an ACSL lemma supposed to be valid as soon as the lemma function is proved:

```
1 /*@ lemma lemma_func_name{L}: ∀ type_1 p1, ... type_M pM ;
2        premise_1 ∧ ... ∧ premise_N ⇒ conclusion ; */
```

Lemmas with Multiple Labels. Our study allowed us to identify this point as an important challenge used for many considered functions. In the case of multi-label lemmas, the translation into a lemma function is still an open problem. Unlike other tools like Why3 or SPARK/GNATprove, FRAMA-C and ACSL support the use of C labels in annotations, including lemmas and predicates, and this notion is often used to specify the behavior of a section of code that involves a memory modification. Currently, we use lemma macros (cf. Sect. 3 and Fig. 6) to directly inject the proof when it is needed. However, this is not completely satisfactory. Indeed, first, the system has to prove the lemma again each time it is used, which is not modular, and second, it makes the proof context bigger. In complex proofs, it can make the job of SMT solvers more difficult, meaning that we need more time to get results during verification and, since SMT solvers are sensitive to the context, making the proof less robust to new versions of the VC generator.

As mentioned in the end of Sect. 3, to create and prove a lemma macro more easily before inserting it in a more complex function. As a workaround we proposed to use a wrapper function to prepare the lemma macro in isolation of the rest of the proof.

The first important observation is the fact that contrary to a lemma function, the wrapper function we use to build the lemma macro should not be pure. For example, it Fig. 7, the wrapper function can modify the whole array (line 5). This is not a problem: the wrapper is not meant to be called, it is a helper to build the lemma macro. If it was pure, the states before and after the call would, from a memory point of view, correspond to the same memory state, and we precisely do not want to have the same memory state to validate that our lemma macro can indeed relate to different program labels. However, the role of the `side_effect_to_L2` function is not really to produce side-effects. It is just meant to create a new memory state and to invalidate the knowledge we had at the beginning of the function and at the same time to establish that we have some new knowledge that relates previous labels and the new label we reached. The proof-carrying code is still pure.

Second, in a wrapper function, the labels are ordered, while this is not the case for the labels specified in a lemma. In our study, since the code of the proof is directly injected, it does not introduce a risk of unsoundness. However, if we want to provide a lemma function mechanism that considers multiple labels, we must ensure that the VC generation does not take into account a specific ordering, or at least force the labels to be ordered at the calling point, which can be checked using the control flow graph.

Let Us Sum Up the Difficulties on Multi-label Lemma Functions. First, adapting ghost functions to multiple labels would probably require modifying the kernel of FRAMA-C. Second, since preconditions of a usual function contract describe only one state (**Pre**), taking into account multi-label premises will require a new way to generate the VCs. On the side of the proof-carrying code of the lemma function itself, we will have to consider different memory states related by some predicates. On the call site, the verification of the multi-label premises will require us to provide a suitable verification condition at each label considered by the premises of the lemma. It radically differs from the way WP currently generates those conditions.

Remaining Interactive Proofs. As two of our case studies show, with the current versions of the tools, it is not always possible to completely remove interactive proofs. The first resisting lemma is about arithmetic properties. Its proof in Coq basically proceeds in two steps. First, it relates the Coq encoding of the type of FRAMA-C logic integers to the Z type of the Coq standard library. Then it applies a lemma that states the same property for multiplication and division on $\mathbb{Z}$. In this respect, it seems that this lemma could be part of a standard library of FRAMA-C lemmas. The second lemma was necessary only because WP currently does not generate the axiom we mentioned. WP could be extended to generate this kind of axiom for any inductive definition. This extension would avoid the need for interactive proof for the second resisting lemma as well.

Soundness. Soundness of axioms and inductive definitions is crucial for the verification both for the classic and auto-active approach, so we do not discuss it in this comparison. We put maximal effort in using sound statements for the case studies in this work.

7   Conclusion and Future Work

This experience report makes a step forward towards a better proof automation with FRAMA-C/WP. While the classic approach still allows to get good results with a combination of automatic and interactive proofs, we are convinced that auto-active verification can provide a usable solution for users that do not have a strong background in formal methods. While writing contracts can still remain relatively difficult, proving and calling lemma functions to deduce necessary properties seems to be easier than interactive proof since it avoids the need for a double expertise in both WP and Coq.

In this work, following the auto-active approach, we verified 23 functions from two real-life modules and a rich suite of examples proved with FRAMA-C and WP. These programs include functions that manipulate linked data-structures which are known to be hard to verify with WP. The corresponding proofs were adapted rather fast, even for examples that we had never verified by ourselves. This paper also reports on the recorded results and identified limitations. In particular, we pointed out the problem of multi-label lemmas, often needed for verification of real-life C programs involving non-trivial memory manipulations, and proposed lemma macros as a workaround.

Regarding future work, while implementing the extension proposed in AstraVer [30] is appealing, we plan to directly consider multi-label lemmas that would be more general than the AstraVer extension. On the long run, allowing logic types in ghost code seems to be another important feature to implement if we want to have more general and more easily reusable lemmas. Future work also includes creating a detailed methodology for auto-active verification, realizing an extensive user study to compare the auto-active and classic approaches, as well as experiments on real-life code verification applying the recently improved capacities of solvers to perform induction (e.g. [26,29]).

Acknowledgment. This work was partially supported by a grant from CPER DATA and the project VESSEDIA, which has received funding from the European Union's Horizon 2020 research and innovation programme under grant agreement No. 731453. The authors thank the FRAMA-C team for providing the tools and support, as well as Patrick Baudin, François Bobot and Loïc Correnson for fruitful discussions and advice. Many thanks to David Cok, Denis Efremov, Marieke Huisman and the anonymous referees for their helpful comments.

References

1. Barnett, M., Fähndrich, M., Leino, K.R.M., Müller, P., Schulte, W., Venter, H.: Specification and verification: the Spec# experience. Commun. ACM **54**(6), 81–91 (2011)
2. Barrett, C., et al.: CVC4. In: Gopalakrishnan, G., Qadeer, S. (eds.) CAV 2011. LNCS, vol. 6806, pp. 171–177. Springer, Heidelberg (2011). https://doi.org/10.1007/978-3-642-22110-1_14
3. Baudin, P., et al.: ACSL: ANSI/ISO C specification language. http://frama-c.com/acsl.html
4. Blanc, R., Kuncak, V., Kneuss, E., Suter, P.: An overview of the Leon verification system: verification by translation to recursive functions. In: Proceedings of the 4th Workshop on Scala, SCALA@ECOOP 2013, pp. 1:1–1:10 (2013)
5. Blanchard, A., Kosmatov, N., Loulergue, F.: Ghosts for lists: a critical module of Contiki verified in Frama-C. In: Dutle, A., Muñoz, C., Narkawicz, A. (eds.) NFM 2018. LNCS, vol. 10811, pp. 37–53. Springer, Cham (2018). https://doi.org/10.1007/978-3-319-77935-5_3
6. Blanchard, A., Kosmatov, N., Loulergue, F.: Logic against ghosts: comparison of two proof approaches for a list module. In: Proceedings of the 34th Annual ACM Symposium on Applied Computing, SAC 2019. ACM (2019, to appear)
7. Burghardt, J., Gerlach, J., Lapawczyk, T.: ACSL by example (2016). https://github.com/fraunhoferfokus/acsl-by-example/blob/master/ACSL-by-Example.pdf
8. Cohen, E., et al.: VCC: a practical system for verifying concurrent C. In: Berghofer, S., Nipkow, T., Urban, C., Wenzel, M. (eds.) TPHOLs 2009. LNCS, vol. 5674, pp. 23–42. Springer, Heidelberg (2009). https://doi.org/10.1007/978-3-642-03359-9_2
9. Cok, D.R.: OpenJML: software verification for Java 7 using JML, OpenJDK, and Eclipse. In: F-IDE (2014)
10. Conchon, S., Contejean, E., Iguernelala, M.: Canonized rewriting and ground AC completion modulo Shostak theories: design and implementation. Logical Methods in Computer Science (2012)
11. Dijkstra, E.W.: A constructive approach to program correctness. BIT Numer. Math. **8**(3), 174–186 (1968). https://doi.org/10.1007/BF01933419
12. Dross, C., Moy, Y.: Auto-active proof of red-black trees in SPARK. In: Barrett, C., Davies, M., Kahsai, T. (eds.) NFM 2017. LNCS, vol. 10227, pp. 68–83. Springer, Cham (2017). https://doi.org/10.1007/978-3-319-57288-8_5
13. Dunkels, A., Gronvall, B., Voigt, T.: Contiki - a lightweight and flexible operating system for tiny networked sensors. In: LCN 2014. IEEE (2004)
14. Filliâtre, J.-C., Paskevich, A.: Why3—where programs meet provers. In: Felleisen, M., Gardner, P. (eds.) ESOP 2013. LNCS, vol. 7792, pp. 125–128. Springer, Heidelberg (2013). https://doi.org/10.1007/978-3-642-37036-6_8
15. Furia, C.A., Nordio, M., Polikarpova, N., Tschannen, J.: AutoProof: auto-active functional verification of object-oriented programs. STTT **19**(6), 697–716 (2017)
16. Hawblitzel, C., et al.: Ironclad apps: end-to-end security via automated full-system verification. In: 11th USENIX Symposium on Operating Systems Design and Implementation, OSDI 2014, pp. 165–181 (2014)
17. Hoang, D., Moy, Y., Wallenburg, A., Chapman, R.: SPARK 2014 and GNATprove - a competition report from builders of an industrial-strength verifying compiler. STTT **17**(6), 695–707 (2015)
18. Jacobs, B., Piessens, F.: The VeriFast program verifier. Technical report. CW-520, KU Leuven (2008)
19. Kirchner, F., Kosmatov, N., Prevosto, V., Signoles, J., Yakobowski, B.: Frama-C: a software analysis perspective. Formal Asp. Comput. **27**(3), 573–609 (2015). http://frama-c.com

20. Leino, K.R.M.: Dafny: an automatic program verifier for functional correctness. In: Clarke, E.M., Voronkov, A. (eds.) LPAR 2010. LNCS (LNAI), vol. 6355, pp. 348–370. Springer, Heidelberg (2010). https://doi.org/10.1007/978-3-642-17511-4_20

21. Leino, K.R.M., Moskal, M.: Usable auto-active verification (2010). http://fm.csl.sri.com/UV10/

22. Mangano, F., Duquennoy, S., Kosmatov, N.: Formal verification of a memory allocation module of Contiki with FRAMA-C: a case study. In: Cuppens, F., Cuppens, N., Lanet, J.-L., Legay, A. (eds.) CRiSIS 2016. LNCS, vol. 10158, pp. 114–120. Springer, Cham (2017). https://doi.org/10.1007/978-3-319-54876-0_9

23. McCormick, J., Chapin, P.: Building High Integrity Applications with SPARK. Cambridge University Press, Cambridge (2015). https://books.google.fr/books?id=Yh9TCgAAQBAJ

24. de Moura, L., Bjørner, N.: Z3: an efficient SMT solver. In: Ramakrishnan, C.R., Rehof, J. (eds.) TACAS 2008. LNCS, vol. 4963, pp. 337–340. Springer, Heidelberg (2008). https://doi.org/10.1007/978-3-540-78800-3_24

25. Polikarpova, N., Tschannen, J., Furia, C.A.: A fully verified container library. Formal Asp. Comput. **30**(5), 495–523 (2018)

26. Reynolds, A., Kuncak, V.: Induction for SMT solvers. In: D'Souza, D., Lal, A., Larsen, K.G. (eds.) VMCAI 2015. LNCS, vol. 8931, pp. 80–98. Springer, Heidelberg (2015). https://doi.org/10.1007/978-3-662-46081-8_5

27. Tafat, A., Marché, C.: Binary heaps formally verified in Why3. Research report RR-7780, INRIA (2011). https://hal.inria.fr/inria-00636083

28. The Coq Development Team: The Coq proof assistant. http://coq.inria.fr

29. The Imandra Team: The Imandra verification tool. https://docs.imandra.ai/

30. Volkov, G., Mandrykin, M., Efremov, D.: Lemma functions for Frama-C: C programs as proofs. In: Proceedings of the 2018 Ivannikov ISPRAS Open Conference (ISPRAS-2018), pp. 31–38 (2018)

Using Standard Typing
Algorithms Incrementally

Matteo Busi[1] , Pierpaolo Degano[1] , and Letterio Galletta[2](✉)

[1] Dipartimento di Informatica, Università di Pisa, Pisa, Italy
{matteo.busi,degano}@di.unipi.it
[2] IMT School for Advanced Studies, Lucca, Italy
letterio.galletta@imtlucca.it

Abstract. Modern languages are equipped with static type checking/inference that helps programmers to keep a clean programming style and to reduce errors. However, the ever-growing size of programs and their continuous evolution require building fast and efficient analysers. A promising solution is *incrementality*, aiming at only re-typing the *diffs*, i.e. those parts of the program that change or are inserted, rather than the entire codebase. We propose an algorithmic schema that drives an incremental usage of existing, standard typing algorithms with no changes. Ours is a *grey-box* approach: just the shape of the input, that of the results and some domain-specific knowledge are needed to instantiate our schema. Here, we present the foundations of our approach and the conditions for its correctness. We show it at work to derive two different incremental typing algorithms. The first type checks an imperative language to detect information flow and non-interference, and the second infers types for a functional language. We assessed our proposal on a prototypical implementation of an incremental type checker. Our experiments show that using the type checker incrementally is (almost) always rewarding.

1 Introduction

Most of the modern programming languages are equipped with mechanisms for checking or inferring types. Such static analyses prescribe programmers a clean programming style and help them to reduce errors. The ever-growing size of programs requires building fast and efficient analyzers. This quest becomes even more demanding because many companies are recently adopting development methodologies that advocate a continuous evolution of software, e.g. *perpetual development model* [4]. In such a model a shared code base is altered by many programmers submitting small code modifications (*diffs*). Software systems are no longer monolithic pieces of code, to which only new components/modules can be compositionally added, rather their components grow and change incrementally.

The first two authors have been partially supported by U. Pisa project PRA_2018_66 *DECLware: Declarative methodologies for designing and deploying applications*. The last author is supported by IMT project *PAI VeriOSS*.

J. M. Badger and K. Y. Rozier (Eds.): NFM 2019, LNCS 11460, pp. 106–122, 2019.
https://doi.org/10.1007/978-3-030-20652-9_7

Consequently, analyses and verification should only consider the *diffs*, rather than the entire codebase. As recently observed by [7], it becomes crucial defining algorithms that require an amount of work on the size of the *diffs* instead of the whole codebase. The idea is to store summaries of the analysis results for program components, and to only reanalyze changed parts, re-using the cached summaries. Here we formalise this idea focussing on type systems.

The literature reports on some techniques, briefly surveyed below, which introduce *new* typing algorithms that work incrementally. Instead, we propose a method that takes an *existing* typing algorithm and *uses it incrementally*, without re-doing work already done, but exploiting available summaries, through caching and memoization. An advantage of our proposal is that it consists of an algorithmic schema *independent* of any specific language and type system. In addition, we put forward a mild condition on the summaries that guarantees that the results of incremental typing match those of the original algorithm.

Roughly, our schema works as follows. We start from the abstract syntax tree of the program, where each node is annotated with the result R provided by the original typing algorithm $\mathcal{A}$. We build then a cache, containing for each subterm t the result R and other relevant contextual information needed by $\mathcal{A}$ to type t (typically a typing environment binding the free variables of t). When the program changes, its annotated abstract syntax tree changes accordingly and typing the subterm associated with the changed node is done incrementally, by reusing the results in the cache whenever possible and by suitably invoking $\mathcal{A}$ upon need. Clearly, the more local the changes, the more information is reused.

Technically, our proposal consists of a set of rule schemata that drive the usage of the cache and of the original algorithm $\mathcal{A}$, as sketched above. Actually, the user has to define the shape of caches and to instantiate a well-confined part of the rule schemata. If the instantiation meets an easy-to-check criterion, the typing results of $\mathcal{A}$ and of the incremental algorithm are guaranteed to be coherent, i.e. the incremental algorithm behaves as the non-incremental one. All the above provides us with the guidelines to develop a framework that makes incremental the usage of a given typing algorithm.

Summing up, the main contributions of this paper include:

- a parametric, language-independent algorithmic schema that uses an existing typing algorithm $\mathcal{A}$ incrementally (Sect. 3);
- a formalisation of the steps that instantiate the schema and yield the incremental version of $\mathcal{A}$: the resulting typing algorithm only types the *diffs* and those parts of the code affected by them (Sect. 3);
- a characterisation of the rule format of standard typing algorithms in terms of two functions *tr* and *checkJoin* (Sect. 3);
- a theorem that under a mild condition guarantees the coherence of results between the original algorithm and its incremental version (Sect. 3);
- the instantiation of the schema for type checking and type inference algorithm for an imperative (Sect. 4) and a functional language (Sect. 5);

- a prototype of the incremental version of the type checker for MinCaml [20],[1] showing that implementing the schema is doable (Sect. 6); and
- experimental results showing that the cost of using the type checker incrementally depends on the size of *diffs*, and its performance increases as these become smaller (Sect. 6).

All the proofs of our theorems, some additional material and the tables with the experimental results on the time and space overheads are in the extended version available online [3].

Related Work. To the best of our knowledge, the literature has some proposals for incrementally typing programs. However, these approaches heavily differ from ours, because all of them propose a *new* incremental algorithm for typing, while we *incrementally* use *existing* algorithms as they are. Additionally, none of the approaches surveyed below use a uniform characterisation of type judgements as we do through the metafunctions *tr* and *checkJoin*.

Meertens [13] proposes an incremental type checking algorithm for the language B. Johnson and Walz [9] treat incremental type inference, focussing on identifying where type errors precisely arise. Aditya and Nikhil [1] propose an incremental Hindley/Milner type system supporting incremental type checking of top-level definitions. Our approach instead supports incremental type-checking for all kinds of expressions, not only the top-level ones. Miao and Siek [14] introduce an incremental type checker leveraging the fact that, in multi-staged programming, programs are successively refined. Wachsmuth et al. [23] propose a task engine for type checking and name resolution: when a file is modified a task is generated and existing (cached) results are re-used where possible. The proposal by Erdweg et al. [5] is the most similar to ours, but, given a type checking algorithm, they describe how to obtain a *new* incremental algorithm. As in our case, they decorate an abstract syntax tree with types and typing environments, represented as sets of constraints, to be suitably propagated when typing. In this way there is no need of dealing with top-down context propagation while types flow bottom-up. Recently, Facebook released Pyre [6] a scalable and incremental type checker specifically designed for `Python`.

Incrementality has also been studied for static analysis other than typing. IncA [21] is a domain-specific language for the definition of incremental program analyses, which represents dependencies among the nodes of the abstract syntax tree of the target program as a graph. Infer [8] uses an approach similar to ours in which analysis results are cached to improve performance [2]. Ryder and Paull [18] present two incremental update algorithms, ACINCB and ACINCF, that allow incremental data-flow analysis. Yur et al. [26] propose an algorithm for an incremental *points-to* analysis. McPeak et al. [12] describe a technique for incremental and parallel static analysis based on *work units* (self-contained atoms of analysis input). The solutions are computed by a sort of processes called *analysis workers*, all coordinated by an *analysis master*. Also, there are papers that use memoization with a goal similar to the one of our cache, even if they

---

[1] Available at https://github.com/mcaos/incremental-mincaml.

consider different analysis techniques. In particular, Mudduluru et al. propose, implement, and test an incremental analysis algorithm based on memoization of (equivalent) boolean formulas used to encode paths on programs [15]. Leino et al. [11] extend the verification machinery of Dafny with a way to cache the results from earlier runs of the verifier, so as to only verify those parts of the program most recently modified. Their cache mechanism is similar to ours, but no formal condition is explicitly stated guaranteeing a safe re-use of cached data, as we do. Also other authors apply memoization techniques to incremental model-checking [10,24] and incremental symbolic execution [17,25].

2   An Overview of the Incremental Schema

In this section we illustrate how the algorithmic schema we propose can type check a simple program using incrementally the *standard* algorithm for non-interference by Volpano-Smith-Irvine [19,22] (see also Sect. 4). Suppose there is a large program P including the following code snippet that causes no leaks

$$x := y + z; \text{if } y + z \geq 42 \text{ then } result := y + z \text{ else } result := 42 \qquad (1)$$

where $y, z, result$ are public and x is secret. After a shallow glance one may optimise it obtaining the following code that leaks the value of x

$$x := y + z; \text{if } x \geq 42 \text{ then } result := x \text{ else } result := 42 \qquad (2)$$

Rather than re-typing the whole program P, one would like to detect the unsafe optimization by only type checking the *diff*, i.e. the if-then-else. To re-use as much as possible the typing information of P, we consider the abstract syntax tree of (1), we annotate its nodes with types, and we use this information to type (2). More precisely, we proceed as follows.

First, we build a *cache* C associating each statement with its type and the typing environment needed to obtain it. Then we *incrementally* use this information to decide which existing results in the cache can be re-used and which are to be recomputed for typing (2). This process is divided into four steps. For the moment, we omit the last one that consists in proving the correctness of the resulting algorithm, which is established by showing that a component of our construction (the predicate $compat_{env}$ used below) meets a mild condition.

Defining the Shape of Caches. The cache is a set of triples that associate with each statement the typing environment needed to close its free variables, and its type. For example, the first statement has the following entry in the cache, recording in the environment the types of the variables (H and L for secret and public) and the type $H\,cmd$ of the assignment (it is a command of type H),

$$(x := y + z, \{x \mapsto H\,var, y \mapsto L\,var, z \mapsto L\,var\}, H\,cmd) \qquad (3)$$

Table 1. Tabular representation of the cache C for the program (1).

Expression	Environment	Type
(1)	$\{x \mapsto H \; var, \; y \mapsto L \; var, \; z \mapsto L \; var, \; result \mapsto L \; var\}$	$L \; cmd$
$x := y + z$	$\{x \mapsto H \; var, \; y \mapsto L \; var, \; z \mapsto L \; var\}$	$H \; cmd$
x	$\{x \mapsto H \; var\}$	H
y	$\{y \mapsto L \; var\}$	L
z	$\{z \mapsto L \; var\}$	L
$result$	$\{result \mapsto L \; var\}$	L
42	$\{\}$	L
$y + z$	$\{y \mapsto L \; var, \; z \mapsto L \; var\}$	L
if $y + z \geq 42$ then $result := y + z$ else $result := 42$	$\{y \mapsto L \; var, \; z \mapsto L \; var, \; result \mapsto L \; var\}$	$L \; cmd$
$y + z \geq 42$	$\{y \mapsto L \; var, \; z \mapsto L \; var\}$	L
$result := y + z$	$\{y \mapsto L \; var, \; z \mapsto L \; var, \; result \mapsto L \; var\}$	$L \; cmd$
$result := 42$	$\{result \mapsto L \; var\}$	$L \; cmd$

Building Caches. We visit the given annotated abstract syntax tree of (1) in a depth-first order and we cache the relevant triples for it and for its (sub-)trees. Consider again the first assignment for which the cache records the triple in (3), among others. All the entries for (1) are in Table 1.

Incremental Typing. The selected typing algorithm $\mathcal{S}$ is used to build the incremental algorithm $\mathcal{IS}$ as follows. A judgement inputs an environment Γ, a cache C and a statement c and it incrementally computes the type ς (see Sect. 4) and C', with possibly updated cache entries for the sub-terms of c:

$$\Gamma, C \vdash_{\mathcal{IS}} c : \varsigma \triangleright C'$$

The incremental algorithm is expressed as a set of inductively defined rules. Most of these simply mimic the structure of the rules defining $\mathcal{S}$. Consider the assignment that requires two rules. The first rule says that we can reuse the information available if the statement is cached and the environments Γ and Γ' coincide on the free variables of c (checked by the predicate $compat_{env}(\Gamma, \Gamma', c)$):

$$\frac{C(x := a) = \langle \Gamma', \varsigma \rangle \quad compat_{env}(\Gamma, \Gamma', x := a)}{\Gamma, C \vdash_{\mathcal{IS}} x := a : \varsigma \triangleright C}$$

The second rule is for when nothing is cached (the side condition *miss* holds), or the typing environments are not compatible. In this case, to obtain C', the new cache, is obtained from C by inserting in it the triples for x, for the expression a and for the assignment itself through $\mathcal{IS}$.

$$\frac{\begin{array}{c} \Gamma, C \vdash_{\mathcal{IS}} x : \tau_x \triangleright C'' \quad \Gamma, C \vdash_{\mathcal{IS}} a : \tau_a \triangleright C''' \quad \tau_a = \tau_x \\ \varsigma = \tau_a \; cmd \quad C' = C'' \cup C''' \cup \{(x := a, \Gamma_{\mid FV(x:=a)}, \varsigma)\} \end{array}}{\Gamma, C \vdash_{\mathcal{IS}} x := a : \varsigma \triangleright C'} \; miss(C, x := a, \Gamma)$$

Back to our example, to discover the leak it suffices to type $x \geq 42$ and $result := x$ having already in the cache the types of x and $result$, while no re-typing is needed for all the other statements of the whole program P.

3   Formalizing the Incremental Schema

Here we formalise our algorithmic schema for incremental typing, exemplified in Sect. 2. Remarkably, it is independent of both the specific type system and the programming language (for that we use below $t \in Term$ to denote an expression or a statement). We only assume to have variables $x, y, \ldots \in Var$, types $\tau, \tau', \ldots \in Type$, typing environments $\Gamma \colon Var \to Type \in Env$; and in addition that the original typing algorithm $\mathcal{A}$ is syntax-directed and defined through inference rules; that it is invoked by writing $\Gamma \vdash_{\mathcal{A}} t \colon R$, where $R \in Res$ is the result (not necessarily a type only).

Below we express the rules of $\mathcal{A}$ according to the following format. It is convenient to order the subterms of t, by stipulating $i \leq j$ provided that t_j requires the result of t_i to be typed $(i, j \leq n_t)$.

$$\frac{\forall i \in \mathbb{I}_t \,.\, tr^t_{t_i}(\Gamma, \{R_j\}_{j < i \wedge j \in \mathbb{I}_t}) \vdash_{\mathcal{A}} t_i : R_i \quad checkJoin_t(\Gamma, \{R_i\}_{i \in \mathbb{I}_t}, \mathsf{out}\ R)}{\Gamma \vdash_{\mathcal{A}} t : R}$$

where $\mathbb{I}_t \subseteq \{1, \ldots, n_t\}$. The function $tr^t_{t_i}$ maps Γ and a set of typing results R_i into the typing environment needed by t_i. The (conjunction of) predicate(s) $checkJoin_t$ checks that the subterms have compatible results R_i and combines them in the overall result R. (Both tr and $checkJoin$ are easily defined when typing rules in the usual format are rendered in the format above.)

For example the standard typing rule for variables:[2]

$$\frac{x \in dom(\Gamma) \quad \tau = \Gamma(x)}{\Gamma \vdash_{\mathcal{A}} x : \tau}$$

is rendered in our format as follows (note that $\mathbb{I}_x = \emptyset$ just as the function tr)

$$\frac{checkJoin_x(\Gamma, \emptyset, \mathsf{out}\ \tau)}{\Gamma \vdash_{\mathcal{A}} x : \tau} \quad \text{where } checkJoin_x(\Gamma, \emptyset, \mathsf{out}\ \tau) \triangleq x \in dom(\Gamma) \wedge \tau = \Gamma(x)$$

As a further example consider the rule for the expression **let** $x = e_2$ **in** e_3 below

$$\frac{\Gamma \vdash_{\mathcal{A}} e_2 : \tau_2 \quad \Gamma[x \mapsto \tau_2] \vdash_{\mathcal{A}} e_3 : \tau_3}{\Gamma \vdash_{\mathcal{A}} \textbf{let } x = e_2 \textbf{ in } e_3 : \tau_3}$$

that becomes as follows (we abuse the set notation, e.g. omitting $\emptyset$ or $\{$ and $\}$).

$$\frac{tr^{\textbf{let } x = e_2 \textbf{ in } e_3}_{e_2}(\Gamma, \emptyset) \vdash_{\mathcal{A}} e_2 : \tau_2 \qquad}{tr^{\textbf{let } x = e_2 \textbf{ in } e_3}_{e_3}(\Gamma, \tau_2) \vdash_{\mathcal{A}} e_3 : \tau_3 \quad checkJoin_{\textbf{let } x = e_2 \textbf{ in } e_3}(\Gamma, \tau_2, \tau_3, \mathsf{out}\ \tau)} {\Gamma \vdash_{\mathcal{A}} \textbf{let } x = e_2 \textbf{ in } e_3 : \tau}$$

---

[2] Instead with the axiom $\Gamma'[x \mapsto \tau] \vdash_{\mathcal{A}} x : \tau$ one has $\mathbb{I}_x = \emptyset$ and the same $checkJoin_x$, where $\Gamma = \Gamma'[x \mapsto \tau]$.

Note that the definition of function tr is immediate; that we need the type of e_2 for typing e_3; and that the second parameter of $tr_{e_2}^{\mathbf{let}\ x\, =\, e_2\ \mathbf{in}\ e_3}$ is empty, because we only need the environment to type e_2.

$$tr_{e_2}^{\mathbf{let}\ x\, =\, e_2\ \mathbf{in}\ e_3}(\Gamma, \emptyset) \triangleq \Gamma \qquad\qquad tr_{e_3}^{\mathbf{let}\ x\, =\, e_2\ \mathbf{in}\ e_3}(\Gamma, \tau) \triangleq \Gamma[x \mapsto \tau] \qquad (4)$$

Also the following definition is immediate

$$checkJoin_{\mathbf{let}\ x\, =\, e_2\ \mathbf{in}\ e_3}(\Gamma, \tau_2, \tau_3, \mathbf{out}\ \tau) \triangleq (\tau = \tau_3)$$

To enhance readability, we will hereto highlight the occurrences of $\boxed{tr_{t'}^t}$ (red in the pdf) and $\overline{checkJoin_t}$ (blue in the pdf).

Defining the Shape of Caches. The shape of the cache is crucial for re-using incrementally portions of the available typing results. A cache associates the input data t and Γ with the result R, rendered by a set of triples (t, Γ, R), as done in Sect. 2. More formally, the set of caches C is defined as:

$$Cache = \wp(Terms \times Env \times Res)$$

We write $C(t) = \langle \Gamma, R \rangle$ if the cache has an entry for t, and $C(t) = \bot$ otherwise.

Building Caches. Given a term, we assume that the nodes of its abstract syntax tree (called *annotated abstract syntax tree* or *aAST*) are annotated with the result of the typing for the subterm they represent (written $t : R$, possibly $t : \bot$ if t does not type). Let $\mathbb{I}_t$, $\{t_i\}_{i \in \mathbb{I}_t}$, and $tr_{t_i}^t$ be as above, and let $\Gamma_{|FV(t)}$ be the restriction of Γ to the free variables of t. Then the following procedure visits the aAST in a depth-first manner and builds the cache.

$$buildCache\ (t : R)\ \Gamma\ = \{(t, \Gamma_{|FV(t)}, R)\} \cup$$
$$\bigcup_{i \in \mathbb{I}_t} \left(buildCache\ (t_i : R_i)\ \boxed{tr_{t_i}^t(\Gamma, \{R_j\}_{j < i \wedge j \in \mathbb{I}_t})} \right)$$

The following theorem ensures that each entry of a cache returned by *buildCache* represents correct typing information.

Theorem 1 (Cache correctness). *For all* t, R, Γ

$$(t, \Gamma, R) \in (buildCache\ (t : R)\ \Gamma) \iff \Gamma \vdash_{\mathcal{A}} t : R$$

Incremental Typing. The third step consists of instantiating the rule templates that make typing incremental. We remark that no change to the original algorithm $\mathcal{A}$ is needed: it is used as a *grey-box*—what matters are just the shape of the original judgements, the rules and some domain-specific knowledge. The judgements for the incremental typing algorithm $\mathcal{IA}$ have the form:

$$\Gamma, C \vdash_{\mathcal{IA}} t : R \triangleright C'$$

We have three different rule templates defining the incremental typing algorithm. The first template is for the case when there is a cache hit:

$$\frac{C(t) = \langle \Gamma', R \rangle \quad compat_{env}(\Gamma, \Gamma', t)}{\Gamma, C \vdash_{\mathcal{I}\mathcal{A}} t : R \triangleright C}$$

where $compat_{env}(\Gamma, \Gamma', t)$ is a predicate testing the compatibility of typing environments for the term t and means that Γ' includes the information represented by Γ for t and that they are compatible (see the example in Sect. 2). Note that this predicate must be defined for *each* algorithm $\mathcal{A}$ and, as discussed below, it must meet a mild requirement to make the algorithm $\mathcal{I}\mathcal{A}$ coherent with $\mathcal{A}$.

The second rule template is for when there is a cache miss and the term in hand has no subterms:

$$\frac{\Gamma \vdash_{\mathcal{A}} t : R \quad C' = C \cup \{(t, \Gamma_{\restriction FV(t)}, R)\}}{\Gamma, C \vdash_{\mathcal{I}\mathcal{A}} t : R \triangleright C'} \; miss(C, t, \Gamma)$$

where $\Gamma \vdash_{\mathcal{A}} t : R$ is the invocation to $\mathcal{A}$, and the predicate *miss* is defined below with the intuition that either there is no association for t in C, or if an association (t, Γ', R) exists the typing environment Γ' is not compatible with the current Γ.

$$miss(C, t, \Gamma) \triangleq \nexists \Gamma', R. \; \big(C(t) = \langle \Gamma', R \rangle \wedge compat_{env}(\Gamma, \Gamma', t) \big)$$

Finally, the last template applies when there is a cache miss, but the term t is inductively defined starting from its subterms. In this case the rule invokes the incremental algorithm on the subterms, by composing the results available in the cache (if any):

$$\frac{\forall i \in \mathbb{I}_t . \boxed{tr_t^{t_i}(\Gamma, \{R_j\}_{j<i \wedge j \in \mathbb{I}_t})}, C \vdash_{\mathcal{I}\mathcal{A}} t_i : R_i \triangleright C^i}{\boxed{checkJoin_t(\Gamma, \{R_i\}_{i\in\mathbb{I}_t}, \mathbf{out}\; R)} \quad C' = \{(t, \Gamma_{\restriction FV(t)}, R)\} \cup \bigcup_{i\in\mathbb{I}_t} C^i}{\Gamma, C \vdash_{\mathcal{I}\mathcal{A}} t : R \triangleright C'} \; miss(C, t, \Gamma)$$

Typing Coherence. The resulting algorithm $\mathcal{I}\mathcal{A}$ preserves the correctness of the original one $\mathcal{A}$, provided that the rule templates above, and especially the predicate $compat_{env}$ are carefully instantiated.

The following definition characterises when two environments are compatible, and it helps in proving that our incremental typing correctly implements the given non-incremental one.

Definition 1 (Typing environment compatibility). *A predicate $compat_{env}$ expresses compatibility iff*

$$\forall \Gamma, \Gamma', t . \; compat_{env}(\Gamma, \Gamma', t) \wedge \Gamma' \vdash_{\mathcal{A}} t : R \implies \Gamma \vdash_{\mathcal{A}} t : R$$

Note that the notion of compatibility guarantees that Γ and Γ' share all the information needed to correctly type the term t. This is the basic condition to ensure that the incremental typing algorithm is concordant with the original one. In particular, the following theorem suffices to establish the correctness of the incremental algorithm $\mathcal{IA}$, provided that the original algorithm $\mathcal{A}$ is such. In its statement, the cache is universally quantified because $\mathcal{IA}$ re-uses $\mathcal{A}$ to re-build the needed cache as soon as a cache miss occurs.

Theorem 2 (Typing coherence). *If compat$_{env}$ expresses compatibility, then for all terms t, caches C, typing environments Γ, and typing algorithm $\mathcal{A}$*

$$\Gamma \vdash_{\mathcal{A}} t : R \iff \Gamma, C \vdash_{\mathcal{IA}} t : R \triangleright C'.$$

4   Incremental Type Checking for Non-interference

Here we use incrementally the typing algorithm $\mathcal{S}$ of Volpano-Smith-Irvine [19, 22] for checking non-interference policies, obtaining the algorithm $\mathcal{IS}$. We assume that the variables of programs are classified either as high, H, or low L. Intuitively, a program enjoys the non-interference property when the values of low level variables do not depend on those of high level ones.

As usual, assume a simple imperative language WHILE, whose syntax is below (*Var* denotes the set of program variables).

$$
\begin{aligned}
AExpr \ni a &::= n \mid x \mid a_1 \; \mathsf{op_a} \; a_2 & n \in \mathbb{N}, \quad \mathsf{op_a} \in \{+, *, -, \ldots\}, \quad x \in Var \\
BExpr \ni b &::= \mathtt{true} \mid \mathtt{false} \mid b_1 \; \mathtt{or} \; b_2 \mid \mathtt{not} \; b \mid a_1 \leq a_2 \\
Stmt \ni c &::= \mathtt{skip} \mid x := a \mid c_1; c_2 \mid \mathtt{if} \; b \; \mathtt{then} \; c_1 \; \mathtt{else} \; c_2 \mid \mathtt{while} \; b \; \mathtt{do} \; c \\
Phrase \ni p &::= a \mid b \mid c \\
DType \ni \tau &::= H \mid L \quad PType \ni \varsigma ::= \tau \mid \tau \; var \mid \tau \; cmd \quad Env \ni \Gamma ::= \emptyset \mid \Gamma[p \mapsto \varsigma]
\end{aligned}
$$

The type checking algorithm has judgements of the form

$$\Gamma \vdash_{\mathcal{S}} p : \varsigma$$

where $\varsigma \in PType = Res$, and its rules are in the extended version [3]. We have coloured and framed the results of $\boxed{tr}$ and $\lceil \overline{checkJoin} \rfloor$. In the following we assume that the initial typing environment Γ contains the security level of each variable occurring in the program at hand.

Defining the Shape of Caches. The shape of the caches is:

$$C \in Cache = \wp(Phrase \times Env \times PType)$$

Building Caches. We build the cache by visiting the aAST and "reconstructing" the typing environment. The function *buildCache* is in Fig. 1, where for brevity we have directly used the results of tr rather than writing the needed invocations.

Incremental Typing. In Fig. 2 we display the rules defining the algorithm $\mathcal{IS}$ with judgements of the following form

$buildCache\ (c:L)\ \Gamma \triangleq \{(c,\emptyset,L)\}\qquad c \in \mathbb{N} \cup \{true, false\}$

$buildCache\ (x:\tau)\ \Gamma \triangleq \{(x, [x \mapsto \tau\ var], \tau)\}$

$buildCache\ (a_1\ \mathrm{op}\ a_2:\tau)\ \Gamma \triangleq \{(a_1\ \mathrm{op}\ a_2, \Gamma_{\mid FV(a_1\mathrm{op}a_2)}, \tau)\}$
$\qquad \cup\,(buildCache\ (a_1:\tau_1)\ \boxed{\Gamma}) \cup (buildCache\ (a_2:\tau_2)\ \boxed{\Gamma})$

$buildCache\ (a_1 \le a_2:\tau)\ \Gamma \triangleq \{(a_1 \le a_2, \Gamma_{\mid FV(a_1\le a_2)}, \tau)\}$
$\qquad \cup\,(buildCache\ (a_1:\tau_1)\ \boxed{\Gamma}) \cup (buildCache\ (a_2:\tau_2)\ \boxed{\Gamma})$

$buildCache\ (b_1\ \mathrm{or}\ b_2:\tau)\ \Gamma \triangleq \{(b_1\ \mathrm{or}\ b_2, \Gamma_{\mid FV(b_1\mathrm{or}b_2)}, \tau)\}$
$\qquad \cup\,(buildCache\ (b_1:\tau_1)\ \boxed{\Gamma}) \cup (buildCache\ (b_2:\tau_2)\ \boxed{\Gamma})$

$buildCache\ (\mathrm{not}\ b:\tau)\ \Gamma \triangleq \{(\mathrm{not}\ b, \Gamma_{\mid FV(\mathrm{not}b)}, \tau)\} \cup (buildCache\ (b:\tau)\ \boxed{\Gamma})$

$buildCache\ (skip:H\ cmd)\ \Gamma \triangleq \{(skip, \emptyset, H\ cmd)\}$

$buildCache\ (x:=a:\tau\ cmd)\ \Gamma \triangleq \{(x:=a, \Gamma_{\mid FV(x:=a)}, \tau\ cmd)\}$
$\qquad \cup\,(buildCache\ (x:\tau_x)\ \boxed{\Gamma}) \cup (buildCache\ (a:\tau_a)\ \boxed{\Gamma})$

$buildCache\ (\mathrm{if}\ b\ \mathrm{then}\ c_1\ \mathrm{else}\ c_2:\tau\ cmd)\ \Gamma \triangleq \{(\mathrm{if}\ b\ \mathrm{then}\ c_1\ \mathrm{else}\ c_2, \Gamma_{\mid FV(\mathrm{if}\ b\ \mathrm{then}\ c_1\ \mathrm{else}\ c_2)}, \tau\ cmd)\}$
$\qquad \cup\,(buildCache\ (b:\tau_b)\ \boxed{\Gamma}) \cup (buildCache\ (c_1:\tau_1\ cmd)\ \boxed{\Gamma}) \cup (buildCache\ (c_2:\tau_2\ cmd)\ \boxed{\Gamma})$

$buildCache\ (\mathrm{while}\ b\ \mathrm{do}\ c:\tau\ cmd)\ \Gamma \triangleq \{(\mathrm{while}\ b\ \mathrm{do}\ c, \Gamma_{\mid FV(\mathrm{while}\ b\ \mathrm{do}\ c)}, \tau\ cmd)\}$
$\qquad \cup\,(buildCache\ (b:\tau_b)\ \boxed{\Gamma}) \cup (buildCache\ (c:\tau_c\ cmd)\ \boxed{\Gamma})$

$buildCache\ (c_1;c_2:\tau\ cmd)\ \Gamma \triangleq \{(c_1;c_2, \Gamma_{\mid FV(c_1;c_2)}, \tau\ cmd)\}$
$\qquad \cup\,(buildCache\ (c_1:\tau_1\ cmd)\ \boxed{\Gamma}) \cup (buildCache\ (c_2:\tau_2\ cmd)\ \boxed{\Gamma})$

Fig. 1. Definition of $buildCache$ for the incremental type checking of WHILE.

$$\Gamma, C \vdash_{\mathcal{IS}} p : \varsigma \triangleright C'$$

Most of the rules are trivial instantiations of rules in Sect. 3 that mimic those of the original type checking algorithm. Of course, $\mathcal{IS}$ inherits unchanged the subtyping relation of $\mathcal{S}$ and applies it when needed.

Typing Coherence. To prove that $\mathcal{IS}$ is coherent with $\mathcal{S}$, we first show that $compat_{env}$ satisfies Definition 1.

Lemma 1. *The predicate $compat_{env}$ of Eq. (1) in Fig. 2 expresses compatibility.*

The above lemma suffices to prove the following theorem, which is an instance of Theorem 2.

Theorem 3. $\forall \Gamma, C, e.\ \Gamma \vdash_{\mathcal{S}} e : \tau \iff \Gamma, C \vdash_{\mathcal{IS}} e : \tau \triangleright C'$

5   Incremental Type Inference for a Functional Language

In this section we instantiate our schema in order to use incrementally the type inference algorithm of a simple functional programming language, called FUN. The syntax, the types and the semantics of FUN are standard, see e.g. [16]. Types are also now augmented with type variables $\alpha, \beta, \ldots \in TVar$. We only recall some relevant aspects below.

$(\mathcal{IS}\text{-}\textsc{Hit})$
$$\frac{C(p) = \langle \Gamma', \varsigma \rangle \quad compat_{env}(\Gamma, \Gamma', p)}{\Gamma, C \vdash_{\mathcal{IS}} p : \varsigma \triangleright C}$$

$(\mathcal{IS}\text{-}\textsc{Const-Miss})$
$$\frac{\emptyset \vdash_S c : \varsigma \quad C' = C \cup \{(c, \emptyset, \varsigma)\}}{\Gamma, C \vdash_{\mathcal{IS}} c : \varsigma \triangleright C'} \quad miss(C, c, \Gamma)$$

$(\mathcal{IS}\text{-}\textsc{Var-Miss})$
$$\frac{\Gamma \vdash_S x : \varsigma \quad C' = C \cup \{(x, \Gamma_{|x}, \varsigma)\}}{\Gamma, C \vdash_{\mathcal{IS}} x : \varsigma \triangleright C'} \quad miss(C, x, \Gamma)$$

$(\mathcal{IS}\text{-}\textsc{Skip-Miss}) \qquad miss(C, \textbf{skip}, \Gamma)$
$$\frac{\Gamma \vdash_S \textbf{skip} : \varsigma \quad C' = C \cup \{(\textbf{skip}, \emptyset, \varsigma)\}}{\Gamma, C \vdash_{\mathcal{IS}} \textbf{skip} : \varsigma \triangleright C'}$$

$(\mathcal{IS}\text{-}\textsc{Op-Miss})$
$$\frac{\Gamma, C \vdash_{\mathcal{IS}} a_1 : \tau_1 \triangleright C'' \quad \Gamma, C \vdash_{\mathcal{IS}} a_2 : \tau_2 \triangleright C'''}{\lceil \tau_1 = \tau_2 \wedge \varsigma = \tau_1 \rceil \quad C' = C'' \cup C''' \cup \{(a_1 \textbf{ op } a_2, \Gamma_{|FV(a_1 op a_2)}, \varsigma)\}}{\Gamma, C \vdash_{\mathcal{IS}} a_1 \textbf{ op } a_2 : \varsigma \triangleright C'} \quad miss(C, a_1 \textbf{ op } a_2, \Gamma)$$

$(\mathcal{IS}\text{-}\textsc{BOp-Miss})$
$$\frac{\Gamma, C \vdash_{\mathcal{IS}} b_1 : \tau_1 \triangleright C'' \quad \Gamma, C \vdash_{\mathcal{IS}} b_2 : \tau_2 \triangleright C'''}{\lceil \tau_1 = \tau_2 \wedge \varsigma = \tau_1 \rceil \quad C' = C'' \cup C''' \cup \{(b_1 \textbf{ or } b_2, \Gamma_{|FV(b_1 or b_2)}, \varsigma)\}}{\Gamma, C \vdash_{\mathcal{IS}} b_1 \textbf{ or } b_2 : \varsigma \triangleright C'} \quad miss(C, b_1 \textbf{ or } b_2, \Gamma)$$

$(\mathcal{IS}\text{-}\textsc{Not-Miss})$
$$\frac{\Gamma, C \vdash_{\mathcal{IS}} b : \tau \triangleright C'' \quad C' = C'' \cup \{(\textbf{ not } b, \Gamma_{|FV(not b)}, \tau)\}}{\Gamma, C \vdash_{\mathcal{IS}} \textbf{not } b : \tau \triangleright C'} \quad miss(C, \textbf{ not } b, \Gamma)$$

$(\mathcal{IS}\text{-}\textsc{Leq-Miss})$
$$\frac{\Gamma, C \vdash_{\mathcal{IS}} a_1 : \tau_1 \triangleright C'' \quad \Gamma, C \vdash_{\mathcal{IS}} a_2 : \tau_2 \triangleright C'''}{\lceil \tau_1 = \tau_2 \wedge \varsigma = \tau_1 \rceil \quad C' = C'' \cup C''' \cup \{(a_1 \leq a_2, \Gamma_{|FV(a_1 \leq a_2)}, \varsigma)\}}{\Gamma, C \vdash_{\mathcal{IS}} a_1 \leq a_2 : \varsigma \triangleright C'} \quad miss(C, a_1 \leq a_2, \Gamma)$$

$(\mathcal{IS}\text{-}\textsc{Assign-Miss})$
$$\frac{\Gamma, C \vdash_{\mathcal{IS}} x : \tau_x \, var \triangleright C'' \quad \Gamma, C \vdash_{\mathcal{IS}} a : \tau_a \triangleright C'''}{\lceil \tau_a = \tau_x \wedge \varsigma = \tau_a \, cmd \rceil \quad C' = C'' \cup C''' \cup \{(x := a, \Gamma_{|FV(x:=a)}, \varsigma)\}}{\Gamma, C \vdash_{\mathcal{IS}} x := a : \varsigma \triangleright C'} \quad miss(C, x := a, \Gamma)$$

$(\mathcal{IS}\text{-}\textsc{If-Miss}) \qquad miss(C, \textbf{if } b \textbf{ then } c_1 \textbf{ else } c_2, \Gamma)$
$$\frac{\Gamma, C \vdash_{\mathcal{IS}} b : \tau_b \triangleright C''}{\Gamma, C \vdash_{\mathcal{IS}} c_1 : \tau_1 \, cmd \triangleright C''' \quad \Gamma, C \vdash_{\mathcal{IS}} c_2 : \tau_2 \, cmd \triangleright C^{iv} \quad \lceil \tau_1 = \tau_2 = \tau_b \wedge \varsigma = \tau_1 \, cmd \rceil}{C' = C'' \cup C''' \cup C^{iv} \cup \{(\textbf{if } b \textbf{ then } c_1 \textbf{ else } c_2, \Gamma_{|FV(\textbf{if } b \textbf{ then } c_1 \textbf{ else } c_2)}, \varsigma)\}}{\Gamma, C \vdash_{\mathcal{IS}} \textbf{if } b \textbf{ then } c_1 \textbf{ else } c_2 : \varsigma \triangleright C'}$$

$(\mathcal{IS}\text{-}\textsc{While-Miss})$
$$\frac{\Gamma, C \vdash_{\mathcal{IS}} b : \tau_b \triangleright C''}{\Gamma, C \vdash_{\mathcal{IS}} c : \tau_1 \, cmd \triangleright C'' \quad \lceil \tau_1 = \tau_b \wedge \varsigma = \tau_1 \, cmd \rceil}{C' = C'' \cup C''' \cup \{(\textbf{while } b \textbf{ do } c, \Gamma_{|FV(\textbf{while } b \textbf{ do } c)}, \varsigma)\}}{\Gamma, C \vdash_{\mathcal{IS}} \textbf{while } b \textbf{ do } S : \varsigma \triangleright C'} \quad miss(C, \textbf{while } b \textbf{ do } c, \Gamma)$$

$(\mathcal{IS}\text{-}\textsc{Seq-Miss})$
$$\frac{\Gamma, C \vdash_{\mathcal{IS}} c_1 : \tau_1 \, cmd \triangleright C'' \quad \Gamma, C \vdash_{\mathcal{IS}} c_2 : \tau_2 \, cmd \triangleright C'''}{\lceil \tau_1 = \tau_2 \wedge \varsigma = \tau_1 \, cmd \rceil \quad C' = C'' \cup C''' \cup \{(c_1; c_2, \Gamma_{|FV(c_1;c_2)}, \varsigma)\}}{\Gamma, C \vdash_{\mathcal{IS}} c_1; c_2 : \varsigma \triangleright C'} \quad miss(C, c_1; c_2, \Gamma)$$

with $compat_{env}(\Gamma, \Gamma', p) \triangleq dom(\Gamma) \supseteq FV(p) \wedge dom(\Gamma') \supseteq FV(p) \wedge \forall y \in FV(p) . \Gamma(y) = \Gamma'(y)$ (5)

Fig. 2. Rules defining the incremental algorithm $\mathcal{IS}$ to type check WHILE.

$buildCache\ (c : (\tau_c, \theta))\ \Gamma \triangleq \{(c, \emptyset, (\tau_c, \theta))\}$

$buildCache\ (x : (\tau_x, \theta))\ \Gamma \triangleq \{(x, [x \mapsto \tau_x], (\tau_x, \theta))\}$

$buildCache\ (\lambda_f\ x.e : (\tau_f, \theta_f))\ \Gamma \triangleq \{(\lambda_f\ x.e, \Gamma_{|FV(\lambda_f\ x.e)}, (\tau_f, \theta_f))\} \cup (buildCache\ (f : (\tau_f, \theta_f))\ \boxed{\Gamma})$

$\qquad \cup (buildCache\ (x : (\tau_x, \theta_x))\ \boxed{\Gamma}) \cup (buildCache\ (e : (\tau_e, \theta_e))\ \boxed{\Gamma[x \mapsto \tau_x, f \mapsto \tau_f]})$

$buildCache\ (\textbf{let}\ x = e_2\ \textbf{in}\ e_3 : (\tau_{let}, \theta_{let}))\ \Gamma \triangleq \{(\textbf{let}\ x = e_2\ \textbf{in}\ e_3, \Gamma_{|FV(\textbf{let}\ x = e_2\ \textbf{in}\ e_3)}, (\tau_{let}, \theta_{let}))\}$

$\qquad \cup (buildCache\ (x : (\tau_x, \theta_x))\ \boxed{\Gamma}) \cup (buildCache\ (e_2 : (\tau_2, \theta_2))\ \boxed{\Gamma})$

$\qquad \cup (buildCache\ (e_3 : (\tau_3, \theta_3))\ \boxed{\Gamma[x \mapsto \tau_x]})$

$buildCache\ (e_1\ op\ e_2 : (\tau_{op}, \theta_{op}))\ \Gamma \triangleq \{(e_1\ op\ e_2, \Gamma_{|FV(e_1\,op\,e_2)}, (\tau_{op}, \theta_{op}))\}$

$\qquad \cup (buildCache\ (e_1 : (\tau_1, \theta_1))\ \boxed{\Gamma}) \cup (buildCache\ (e_2 : (\tau_2, \theta_2))\ \boxed{\Gamma})$

$buildCache\ (e_1\ e_2 : (\tau_{app}, \theta_{app}))\ \Gamma \triangleq \{(e_1\ e_2, \Gamma_{|FV(e_1\ e_2)}, (\tau_{app}, \theta_{app}))\}$

$\qquad \cup (buildCache\ (e_1 : (\tau_1, \theta_1))\ \boxed{\Gamma}) \cup (buildCache\ (e_2 : (\tau_2, \theta_2))\ \boxed{\Gamma})$

Fig. 3. Definition of *buildCache* for the incremental type inference of FUN.

$$Val \ni v ::= c \mid \lambda_f\ x.e \qquad\qquad op \in \{+, *, =, \leq\}$$
$$Expr \ni e ::= v \mid x \mid e_1\ op\ e_2 \mid e_1\ e_2 \mid \textbf{if}\ e_1\ \textbf{then}\ e_2\ \textbf{else}\ e_3 \mid \textbf{let}\ x = e_2\ \textbf{in}\ e_3$$
$$AType \ni \tau ::= \texttt{int} \mid \texttt{bool} \mid \tau_1 \to \tau_2 \mid \alpha \qquad Env \ni \Gamma ::= \emptyset \mid \Gamma[x \mapsto \tau]$$

where in the functional abstraction f denotes the name of the (possibly) recursive function we are defining. The judgements of the type inference algorithm $\mathcal{W}$ are

$$\Gamma \vdash_{\mathcal{W}} e : (\tau, \theta)$$

where $\theta : (TVar \to AType) \in Subst$ is a substitution mapping type variables into augmented types. As usual, we write $\theta\tau$ to indicate the application of the substitution θ to τ, and $\theta_2 \circ \theta_1$ stands for the composition of substitutions.

Hereafter, we assume to use the inference algorithm $\mathcal{W}$ (see e.g. [16]), where constants c have a fixed and known type, and $\mathcal{U}$ denotes the standard type unification algorithm.

Defining the Shape of Caches. Entries in the cache are $(e, \Gamma, (\tau, \theta))$ and a cache is

$$C \in Cache = \wp(Expr \times Env \times (AType \times Subst))$$

Building Caches. The function *buildCache* is easily defined in Fig. 3.

Incremental Typing. In Fig. 4 we display the rules defining the algorithm $\mathcal{IW}$ with judgements of the following form

$$\Gamma, C \vdash_{\mathcal{IW}} e : (\tau, \theta) \triangleright C'$$

Most of the rules mimic the behaviour of algorithm $\mathcal{W}$, following the templates of Sect. 3. Consider for example the rule ($\mathcal{IW}$-LET-MISS): first, the types of e_1 and e_2 are incrementally inferred in the environments prescribed by the relevant calls to the function tr. The result associated with the whole expression **let-in** is then the pair $(\tau_2, \theta_2 \circ \theta_1)$, where θ_1 and θ_2 are the substitutions obtained recursively from e_1 and e_2, respectively.

Typing Coherence. To prove the incremental algorithm $\mathcal{IW}$ coherent with $\mathcal{W}$, we first show that $compat_{env}$ satisfies Definition 1.

Lemma 2. *The predicate $compat_{env}$ of Eq. (6) in Fig. 4 expresses compatibility.*

Again, the following theorem is an instance of Theorem 2, and follows from the above lemma.

Theorem 4. $\forall \Gamma, C, e.\ \Gamma \vdash_{\mathcal{W}} e : (\tau, \theta) \iff \Gamma, C \vdash_{\mathcal{IW}} e : (\tau, \theta) \triangleright C'$

6   Implementation and Some Experiments

We have implemented in OCaml our proposal making incremental the usage the type-checker of MinCaml [20].[3] A formalization of MinCaml in our framework and all tables and results of our experiments are available online in the extended version [3]. In detail, caches and type environments are implemented as hash-tables, so their handling is done almost in constant time. The memory overhead due to the cache is $\mathcal{O}(n \times m)$, where n is the size of the program under analysis and m is the number of variables therein.

The other possible time consuming part concerns checking environment compatibility. The key idea to make $compat_{env}$ efficient is to compute the sets of the free variables beforehand, and to store them as additional annotations on the aAST. Summing up, implementing our schema is not too demanding, since it can be done with standard data structures.

Next, we show that (i) the cost of using the type checker incrementally depends on the size of *diffs*; (ii) its performance increases as these become smaller; and (iii) the incremental usage is almost always faster than re-using the standard one. The comparison is done by type checking synthetic programs with (binary and complete) aAST of increasing depth from 8 to 16, and with a number of variables ranging from 1 to 2^{15}. All the internal nodes are binary operators and the leaves are free variables. This test suites are intended to stress our incremental algorithm in the worst, yet artificial case. The measures are obtained using the library *Benchmark* that takes into account the overhead of OCaml runtime.[4]

To test the efficiency of caching we first re-typed twice the program with no changes, starting with an empty cache. We considered (binary and complete) aAST of depth 16, and we collected the number of re-typings per second in function of the number of variables in the program, ranging from 1 to 2^{15}.

The experiments show not only that the overhead for caching is negligible but also that caching is beneficial when the number of free variables is not too large w.r.t. the aAST depth because the results of common subtrees are re-used.

Then, we have simulated program changes by invalidating parts of caches that correspond to the rightmost subexpression at different depths. Note that invalidating cache entries for the *diff* subexpression e' of e requires to invalidate

---

[3] Available at https://github.com/mcaos/incremental-mincaml.
[4] Available at https://github.com/Chris00/ocaml-benchmark.

$(\mathcal{IW}\text{-Hit})$
$$\frac{C(e) = \langle \Gamma', (\tau, \theta)\rangle \quad compat_{env}(\Gamma, \Gamma', e)}{\Gamma, C \vdash_{\mathcal{IW}} e : (\tau, \theta) \triangleright C}$$

$(\mathcal{IW}\text{-Const-Miss})$ $\qquad\qquad miss(C, c, \Gamma)$
$$\frac{\Gamma \vdash_W c : (\tau, \theta) \quad C' = C \cup \{(c, \emptyset, (\tau, \theta))\}}{\Gamma, C \vdash_{\mathcal{IW}} c : (\tau, \theta) \triangleright C'}$$

$(\mathcal{IW}\text{-Var-Miss})$
$$\frac{\Gamma \vdash_W x : (\tau, \theta) \quad C' = C \cup \{(x, \Gamma_{\restriction x}, (\tau, \theta))\}}{\Gamma, C \vdash_{\mathcal{IW}} x : (\tau, \theta) \triangleright C'} \; miss(C, x, \Gamma)$$

$(\mathcal{IW}\text{-Abs-Miss})$
$$\frac{\begin{array}{c} \Gamma[x \mapsto \alpha_x, f \mapsto \alpha_x \to \alpha_e], C \vdash_{\mathcal{IW}} e : (\tau_e, \theta_e) \triangleright C'' \\ \theta_1 = \mathcal{U}(\tau_e, \theta_e \alpha_e) \wedge (\tau, \theta) = ((\theta_1 (\theta_e \alpha_x)) \to (\theta_1 \tau_e), \theta_1 \circ \theta_e) \\ C' = C'' \cup \{(\lambda_f x : \tau_x.e, \Gamma_{\restriction FV(\lambda_f x:\tau_x.e)}, (\tau, \theta))\} \end{array}}{\Gamma, C \vdash_{\mathcal{IW}} \lambda_f x.e : (\tau, \theta) \triangleright C'} \; miss(C, \lambda_f x.e, \Gamma) \wedge \alpha_x, \alpha_e \; fresh$$

$(\mathcal{IW}\text{-Op-Miss})$ $\qquad\qquad miss(C, e_1 \; op \; e_2, \Gamma) \wedge \tau_{op}, \tau_{res} = \{\texttt{int}, \texttt{bool}\}$
$$\frac{\begin{array}{c} \Gamma, C \vdash_{\mathcal{IW}} e_1 : (\tau_1, \theta_1) \triangleright C'' \qquad \theta_1 \Gamma, C \vdash_{\mathcal{IW}} e_2 : (\tau_2, \theta_2) \triangleright C''' \\ \theta_3 = \mathcal{U}(\theta_2 \tau_1, \tau_{op}) \wedge \theta_4 = \mathcal{U}(\theta_3 \tau_2, \tau_{op}) \wedge (\tau, \theta) = (\tau_{res}, \theta_4 \circ \theta_3 \circ \theta_2 \circ \theta_1) \\ C' = C'' \cup C''' \cup \{(e_1 \; op \; e_2, \Gamma_{\restriction FV(e_1 op e_2)}, (\tau, \theta))\} \end{array}}{\Gamma, C \vdash_{\mathcal{IW}} e_1 \; op \; e_2 : (\tau, \theta) \triangleright C'}$$

$(\mathcal{IW}\text{-App-Miss})$
$$\frac{\begin{array}{c} \Gamma, C \vdash_{\mathcal{IW}} e_1 : (\tau_1, \theta_1) \to \tau_e \triangleright C'' \qquad \theta_1 \Gamma, C \vdash_{\mathcal{IW}} e_2 : (\tau_2, \theta_2) \triangleright C''' \\ \theta_3 = \mathcal{U}(\theta_2 \tau_1, \tau_2 \to \alpha) \wedge (\tau, \theta) = (\theta_3 \alpha, \theta_3 \circ \theta_2 \circ \theta_1) \\ C' = C'' \cup C''' \cup \{(e_1 e_2, \Gamma_{\restriction FV(e_1 e_2)}, (\tau, \theta))\} \end{array}}{\Gamma, C \vdash_{\mathcal{IW}} e_1 e_2 : (\tau, \theta) \triangleright C'} \; miss(C, e_1 e_2, \Gamma) \wedge \alpha \; fresh$$

$(\mathcal{IW}\text{-If-Miss})$ $\qquad\qquad miss(C, \texttt{if } e_1 \texttt{ then } e_2 \texttt{ else } e_3, \Gamma)$
$$\frac{\begin{array}{c} \Gamma, C \vdash_{\mathcal{IW}} e_1 : (\tau_1, \theta_1) \triangleright C'' \\ \theta_1 \Gamma, C \vdash_{\mathcal{IW}} e_2 : (\tau_2, \theta_2) \triangleright C''' \qquad \theta_2(\theta_1 \Gamma), C \vdash_{\mathcal{IW}} e_3 : (\tau_3, \theta_3) \triangleright C^{iv} \\ \theta_4 = \mathcal{U}(\theta_3(\theta_2 \tau_1), \texttt{bool}) \wedge \theta_5 = \mathcal{U}(\theta_4 \tau_3, \theta_4(\theta_3 \tau_1)) \wedge (\tau, \theta) = (\theta_5(\theta_4 \tau_3), \theta_5 \circ \theta_4 \circ \theta_3 \circ \theta_2) \\ C' = C'' \cup C''' \cup C^{iv} \cup \{(\texttt{if } e_1 \texttt{ then } e_2 \texttt{ else } e_3, \Gamma_{\restriction FV(\texttt{if } e_1 \texttt{ then } e_2 \texttt{ else } e_3)}, (\tau, \theta))\} \end{array}}{\Gamma, C \vdash_{\mathcal{IW}} \texttt{if } e_1 \texttt{ then } e_2 \texttt{ else } e_3 : (\tau, \theta) \triangleright C'}$$

$(\mathcal{IW}\text{-Let-Miss})$ $\qquad\qquad miss(C, \texttt{let } x = e_1 \texttt{ in } e_3, \Gamma)$
$$\frac{\begin{array}{c} \Gamma, C \vdash_{\mathcal{IW}} e_2 : (\tau_2, \theta_2) \triangleright C'' \qquad (\theta_1 \Gamma)[x \mapsto \tau_2], C \vdash_{\mathcal{IW}} e_3 : (\tau_3, \theta_3) \triangleright C''' \\ (\tau, \theta) = (\tau_3, \theta_3 \circ \theta_1) \qquad C' = C'' \cup C''' \cup \{(\texttt{let } x = e_2 \texttt{ in } e_3, \Gamma_{\restriction FV(\texttt{let } x = e_2 \texttt{ in } e_3)}, (\tau, \theta))\} \end{array}}{\Gamma, C \vdash_{\mathcal{IW}} \texttt{let } x = e_2 \texttt{ in } e_3 : (\tau, \theta) \triangleright C'}$$

with $compat_{env}(\Gamma, \Gamma', e) \triangleq dom(\Gamma) \supseteq FV(e) \wedge dom(\Gamma') \supseteq FV(e) \wedge \forall y \in FV(e) . \mathcal{U}(\Gamma(y), \Gamma'(y))$ (6)

Fig. 4. Rules defining incremental algorithm $\mathcal{IW}$ to infer FUN types.

(i) all the entries for the nodes in the path from the root of the aAST of e to e' and (ii) all the entries for e' and its subexpressions, recursively. We collected the number of re-typings per second vs. the size of the *diff* for a few choices of aAST depth (from 12 tp 16) and number of variables (from 2^7 to 2^{16}). The experimental results show that our caching and memoization is faster than re-typing twice. An exception is when aAST have the maximum number of variables and the considered changes exceed 25% of the nodes. All in all, the advantage of using incrementally a type checker decreases, as expected, when there is a significant growth of the number of variables or in the size of the program. However, these cases only show up with very big numbers, which are not likely to occur often.

We also measured the number of MBs allocated by our implementation for the standard type checking and by its incremental usage with respect to the size of the synthetic aAST and the number of free variables.[5] We considered aAST of depth ranging from 10 to 16 and the number of variables ranging from 2^9 and 2^{15}, and the results show that the ratio standard/incremental is .99, almost constant.

7   Conclusions

We have presented an algorithmic schema for incrementally using existing type checking and type inference algorithms. Since only the shape of the input, the output, and some domain-specific knowledge of the original algorithms are relevant, our schema considers them as grey-boxes. Remarkably, the only real effort for defining the incremental algorithm is required for establishing the notion of compatibility between parts of the environments relevant for re-typing. We have introduced the basic bricks of our approach and proved a theorem guaranteeing the coherence of *any* original algorithm with its incremental version, and *vice versa*. As a matter of fact, coherence follows from easily checking a mild condition on the environment compatibility. To illustrate the approach we have then instantiated our proposal for checking non-interference within an imperative language and for type inference within a functional language.

We have implemented the incremental version of the type checker of Min-Caml, and we have assessed it on synthetic programs with varying size and number of variables. The experiments have shown our proposal worth using within a continuous software development model where fast responsiveness is needed, because only *diffs* are typed, possibly with those parts of the code affected by them. Additionally, the cost of using the type checker incrementally depends on the size of *diffs*, and its performance increases as these become smaller, a typical situation when applying local transformations, e.g. code motion, dead code elimination, and code wrapping.

Future Work. We are confident that little extensions to our proposal are needed to cover also type and effect systems. Also, other programming paradigms should be easily accommodated in our incremental schema, as preliminary results on process calculi suggest. More work is instead required to apply our ideas to other syntax-directed static analyses, e.g. control flow analysis because of fixed-point computations. We also plan to carry our proposal on Abstract Interpretation, where the rich structure of the abstract domains poses some serious challenges. Presently, we are extending our prototype with an incremental type inference for MinCaml. Moreover, we plan to further automatize our proposal by mechanically deducing the relation $compat_{env}$, based on the syntax and on some relevant aspects of types, e.g. sub-typing. Since *tr* and *checkJoin* are directly inherited from the given type checking or inference algorithm, one can implement a generator that automatically produces its corresponding incremental version.

More experiments on real programs are also in order to better assess the performance of our proposal, as well as its scalability.

Finally, we would also like to apply the incremental schema to real-world languages, e.g. OCaml.

---

[5] As measured by the Landmarks library https://github.com/LexiFi/landmarks.

References

1. Aditya, S., Nikhil, R.S.: Incremental polymorphism. In: Hughes, J. (ed.) FPCA 1991. LNCS, vol. 523, pp. 379–405. Springer, Heidelberg (1991). https://doi.org/10.1007/3540543961_19
2. Blackshear, S., Di Stefano, D., Luca, M., O'Hearn, P., Villard, J.: Finding inter-procedural bugs at scale with infer static analyzer, September 2017. https://code.facebook.com/posts/1537144479682247/finding-inter-procedural-bugs-at-scale-with-infer-static-analyzer/
3. Busi, M., Degano, P., Galletta, L.: Using standard typing algorithms incrementally. Extended Version http://arxiv.org/abs/1808.00225
4. Calcagno, C., et al.: Moving fast with software verification. In: Havelund, K., Holzmann, G., Joshi, R. (eds.) NFM 2015. LNCS, vol. 9058, pp. 3–11. Springer, Cham (2015). https://doi.org/10.1007/978-3-319-17524-9_1
5. Erdweg, S., Bracevac, O., Kuci, E., Krebs, M., Mezini, M.: A co-contextual formulation of type rules and its application to incremental type checking. In: Proceedings of the 2015 ACM SIGPLAN International Conference on Object-Oriented Programming, Systems, Languages, and Applications, pp. 880–897 (2015)
6. Facebook: Pyre - a performant type-checker for Python 3. https://pyre-check.org/
7. Harman, M., O'Hearn, P.: From start-ups to scale-ups: opportunities and open problems for static and dynamic program analysis. In: IEEE International Working Conference on Source Code Analysis and Manipulation (2018)
8. Infer, F.: Infer static analyzer. http://fbinfer.com/
9. Johnson, G.F., Walz, J.A.: A maximum-flow approach to anomaly isolation in unification-based incremental type inference. In: Proceedings of the 13th Symposium on Principles of Programming Languages, pp. 44–57. ACM (1986)
10. Lauterburg, S., Sobeih, A., Marinov, D., Viswanathan, M.: Incremental state-space exploration for programs with dynamically allocated data. In: 30th International Conference on Software Engineering, ICSE 2008, pp. 291–300 (2008)
11. Leino, K.R.M., Wüstholz, V.: Fine-grained caching of verification results. In: Kroening, D., Păsăreanu, C.S. (eds.) CAV 2015. LNCS, vol. 9206, pp. 380–397. Springer, Cham (2015). https://doi.org/10.1007/978-3-319-21690-4_22
12. McPeak, S., Gros, C., Ramanathan, M.K.: Scalable and incremental software bug detection. In: Joint Meeting of the European Software Engineering Conference and the ACM SIGSOFT Symposium on the Foundations of Software Engineering, ESEC/FSE 2013, pp. 554–564 (2013)
13. Meertens, L.G.L.T.: Incremental polymorphic type checking in B. In: Wright, J.R., Landweber, L., Demers, A.J., Teitelbaum, T. (eds.) Proceedings of the 10th ACM Symposium on Principles of Programming Languages, pp. 265–275. ACM (1983)
14. Miao, W., Siek, J.G.: Incremental type-checking for type-reflective metaprograms. In: Visser, E., Järvi, J. (eds.) Proceedings of the Ninth International Conference on Generative Programming and Component Engineering, pp. 167–176. ACM (2010)
15. Mudduluru, R., Ramanathan, M.K.: Efficient incremental static analysis using path abstraction. In: Gnesi, S., Rensink, A. (eds.) FASE 2014. LNCS, vol. 8411, pp. 125–139. Springer, Heidelberg (2014). https://doi.org/10.1007/978-3-642-54804-8_9
16. Nielson, F., Nielson, H.R., Hankin, C.: Principles of Program Analysis. Springer, Heidelberg (1999). https://doi.org/10.1007/978-3-662-03811-6
17. Qiu, R., Yang, G., Pasareanu, C.S., Khurshid, S.: Compositional symbolic execution with memoized replay. In: 37th IEEE/ACM International Conference on Software Engineering, ICSE 2015, vol. 1, pp. 632–642 (2015)

18. Ryder, B.G., Paull, M.C.: Incremental data-flow analysis. ACM Trans. Program. Lang. Syst. **10**(1), 1–50 (1988)
19. Smith, G.: Principles of secure information flow analysis. In: Christodorescu, M., Jha, S., Maughan, D., Song, D., Wang, C. (eds.) Malware Detection, vol. 27, pp. 291–307. Springer, Boston (2007). https://doi.org/10.1007/978-0-387-44599-1_13
20. Sumii, E.: MinCaml: a simple and efficient compiler for a minimal functional language. In: Findler, R.B., Hanus, M., Thompson, S. (eds.) Proceedings of the 2005 Workshop on Functional and Declarative Programming in Education, pp. 27–38. ACM (2005)
21. Szabó, T., Erdweg, S., Voelter, M.: IncA: a DSL for the definition of incremental program analyses. In: Proceedings of the 31st IEEE/ACM International Conference on Automated Software Engineering, pp. 320–331 (2016)
22. Volpano, D.M., Irvine, C.E., Smith, G.: A sound type system for secure flow analysis. J. Comput. Secur. **4**(2/3), 167–188 (1996)
23. Wachsmuth, G.H., Konat, G.D.P., Vergu, V.A., Groenewegen, D.M., Visser, E.: A language independent task engine for incremental name and type analysis. In: Erwig, M., Paige, R.F., Van Wyk, E. (eds.) SLE 2013. LNCS, vol. 8225, pp. 260–280. Springer, Cham (2013). https://doi.org/10.1007/978-3-319-02654-1_15
24. Yang, G., Dwyer, M.B., Rothermel, G.: Regression model checking. In: 25th IEEE International Conference on Software Maintenance, ICSM 2009, pp. 115–124 (2009)
25. Yang, G., Person, S., Rungta, N., Khurshid, S.: Directed incremental symbolic execution. ACM Trans. Softw. Eng. Methodol. **24**(1), 3:1–3:42 (2014)
26. Yur, J., Ryder, B.G., Landi, W.: An incremental flow- and context-sensitive pointer aliasing analysis. In: Proceedings of the 1999 International Conference on Software Engineering, pp. 442–451 (1999)

Using Binary Analysis Frameworks: The Case for BAP and angr

Chris Casinghino[1], J. T. Paasch[1], Cody Roux[1(✉)], John Altidor[2], Michael Dixon[3], and Dustin Jamner[4]

[1] Draper, Cambridge, USA
{ccasinghino,jpaasch,croux}@draper.com
[2] Cambridge Semantics Inc., Boston, USA
john.altidor@cambridgesemantics.com
[3] Los Alamos National Laboratory, Los Alamos, USA
mdixon@lanl.gov
[4] Northeastern University, Boston, USA
jamner.d@husky.neu.edu

Abstract. Binary analysis frameworks are critical tools for analyzing software and assessing its security. How easy is it for a non-expert to use these tools? This paper compares two popular open-source binary analysis libraries: BAP and angr, which were used by two of the top three teams at the DARPA Cyber Grand Challenge. We describe a number of experiments to evaluate the capabilities of the two tools. We have implemented a value-set analysis and a call graph comparison algorithm with each tool, and report on their performance, usability, and extensibility for real-world applications.

Keywords: BAP · angr · Binary analysis · Differential analysis · Cyber security

1 Introduction

If you want to analyze the version of your program that actually gets executed, you may need to examine its binary code directly. There are a variety of tools to help with this task. Some of these tools are general libraries that can help you build your own custom program analyses.

In this paper, we compare two popular, open-source binary analysis libraries: BAP [5] and angr [13]. We examine how each library constructs call graphs (CGs) and control flow graphs (CFGs). We have implemented a value-set analysis (VSA) and an algorithm to compare call graphs in both BAP and angr, and assess how easy it is to build real-world program analyses using each.

Our contributions include the following:

This work is sponsored by ONR/NAWC Contract N6833518C0107. Its content does not necessarily reflect the position or policy of the US Government and no official endorsement should be inferred.

J. M. Badger and K. Y. Rozier (Eds.): NFM 2019, LNCS 11460, pp. 123–129, 2019.
https://doi.org/10.1007/978-3-030-20652-9_8

- We detail some technical differences in the way BAP and angr identify function starts, as well as how they construct CGs and CFGs.
- We provide a first-hand account of building custom analyses with these libraries, and we profile the tools we built.
- We conclude by identifying the strengths and weaknesses of each tool, and give our impression of their suitability for building sound, static program analyses.

The data from our analyses is publicly accessible at https://github.com/draperlaboratory/cbat_tools/tree/master/bap-angr.

2   BAP and angr Overview

BAP and angr both begin by lifting a binary program to an intermediate representation (IR), and then analyzing that IR. BAP lifts to its own IR, the BAP Intermediate Language (BIL), while angr lifts to VEX, which is the IR used by Valgrind. The differences between BIL, VEX, and other potential IR choices are not the focus of this paper, but have been studied elsewhere [9].

Once a binary has been lifted to the IR, you can use built-in BAP or angr program analyses, or write your own tools to explore the lifted program. BAP is written in OCaml and angr is written in Python; it is easiest to write your own tools in the host language.

The idiomatic use of each tool is similar: first you load a binary into a "project," and then perform your own analysis. For example, you might begin by generating a CFG. In angr:

```
import angr

exe = "/bin/true"
project = angr.Project(exe)
cfg = project.analyses.CFGFast()
# Now do something with the CFG...
```

In BAP, the process is similar. In the following example, we select byteweight [4] to identify function starts, then we load the program into a project, retrieve the lifted IR program, and generate a CG:

```
open Core_kernel.Std;;
open Bap.Std;;

let exe = Project.Input.file "/bin/true";;
let byteweight = Rooter.Factory.find "byteweight";;
let Ok proj = Project.create exe ?rooter:byteweight;;
let lifted_prog = Project.program proj;;
let cg = Program.to_graph lifted_prog;;
(* Now do something with the CG... *)
```

Both libraries are easy to use in a REPL. For instance, you can import angr in a Jupyter console to explore a particular binary, and you can import BAP into utop, or the baptop REPL that BAP provides.

For batch mode, angr analyses can be written as straight-forward Python scripts that import `angr` and proceed from there. BAP offers a modular plugin architecture: each plugin makes a pass over the program, where it extracts information, alters the IR, or performs other tasks. Passes can be chained together.

Both tools offer a reasonably easy point of entry into programmatic binary analysis, with library functions for common tasks such as generating a CG or CFG. The communities for both projects are extremely helpful and responsive, to the extent that most of our technical questions about the tools were immediately answered.

For the experiments below, we worked on an Ubuntu 16.04.4 VM (Linux 4.4.0-87 and GCC 5.4.0) with 16 Gb of memory and eight 2.2 GHz Broadwell family 6, 61 processors. We report results for angr 7.8.9 with vanilla Python 2.7, BAP 1.5.0 with OCaml 4.05.0. We also experimented with running angr with PyPy 6.0 rather than Python. We found PyPy to be less efficient for small programs and more efficient for larger ones. We ran BAP with a `--no-cache` flag, but normally BAP caches disassembly and other information, so repeat runs are significantly faster.

We estimated each library's resource overhead by loading an empty C program into a new project. On average, BAP took a half second with a max resident set size (RSS) of 84 MB, while angr took one second with a max RSS of 82 MB.

3   Extracting and Using Control Flow Data

A basic requirement for analyzing or transforming code in any non-trivial manner involves getting data and control flow information. For binary code, this can be a complex operation, and both BAP and angr offer built-in support. In this section, we compare the CFGs and CGs recovered by each tool, and describe a CG-based analysis that we implemented in both BAP and angr as a comparison of their capabilities and performance.

3.1   Control Flow Graphs

Both tools make CGs and CFGs easy to generate and manipulate. However, they make different choices about how to lift various binary constructs, making a direct comparison challenging.

First, angr generates a CFG for the whole program, while BAP generates one per function. Additionally, the two tools represent binary control flow differently. BAP's CFGs include "dummy nodes" at branch points that do have a direct analogue in the original binary but are created to make uplifting more convenient. angr does not create similar nodes, but sometimes coalesces basic blocks. Neither angr nor BAP resolve most indirect jumps, with the notable exceptions of jump tables in angr, which are resolved using a heuristic. Some of these issues, and a detailed analysis of the accuracy of CFG construction for several binary analysis tools including (older versions of) BAP and angr is explored in detail by Andriesse *et al.* [1].

3.2   Call Graphs

We compared BAP and angr's features for working with CGs in two ways. First, we developed a script to directly compare the CGs produced by each tool, and report here on their similarity. Second, we selected a CG-based program analysis from the literature and implemented it twice, using each tool as a library.

Comparing CG Accuracy. Both tools make it simple to recover a program's CG and output it in the DOT graph description language. We implemented a simple algorithm for comparing this output:

- Start with the program entry point of both graphs.
- Recursively fetch the reachable nodes from that point, excluding already seen nodes.
- Compare the reachable nodes at step n as sets between the graphs.

While the tools agree well on small examples, differences appear quite early in the CGs of larger programs. For example, we get around 6% difference 1 step below `main` in the CG for the `grep` executable, and the errors snowball at lower levels up to a significant fraction. The cause for these discrepancies is unclear, but may be related to disagreements between what the tools consider to be reachable function calls during CFG construction (see again [1]).

Implementing a CG-Based Program Analysis. One common use of CFGs and CGs is to judge the similarity of two programs [6]. As a basis on which to evaluate the usability and performance of each tool, we selected a well-regarded algorithm for estimating the similarity of two CGs [7] and implemented it both as a BAP plugin and as an angr script.

Implementation of this algorithm was mostly straightforward. One obstacle was that the BAP's plugin interface is designed to manipulate a single program at a time. However, BAP does support saving a program's `Project` data structure to disk. Thus, we designed our plugin to take one binary from the command line and compare with a previously saved `Project` structure.

For evaluation, we took 11 GNU applications of varying sizes and compiled them on two optimization levels (`-O0` and `-O1`). We used the analysis to compare the two versions of each program. Table 1 contains the results. Each column lists BAP's and angr's results respectively, separated by a slash. A long dash indicates that the analysis did not complete within 35 min.

The results show that our BAP OCaml implementation runs approximately 15% faster than our angr Python implementation on average, despite constructing larger CGs. Profiling revealed that the running time in both cases is dominated by a standard graph matching algorithm that the analysis uses, and thus speaks more to differences in the efficiency of OCaml and Python code than to differences in BAP and angr. The running time scales with the size of the graphs (reported as a sum of the number of nodes and edges). Substantial differences in graph sizes are a result of the discrepancies in CG recovery described above, and the similarity scores computed by the algorithm also differed as a result.

Table 1. CG construction performance (BAP/angr)

Exe	Time (s)	Max RSS (Kb)	Graph size
bison	1181/824	15182/16847	7717/6078
gawk	158/2004	20253/25680	5760/8661
grep	89/581	7184/7528	3339/4002
gnuchess	158/82	20253/10815	5760/868
gzip	58/162	7391/6122	2065/1706
less	113/—	3741/—	4142/—
make	313/552	15812/10440	4835/4436
nano	729/454	8060/10620	6500/4618
screen	699/964	12980/12054	7466/6094
sed	27.6/—	4536/—	2320/—
tar	—/1321	—/8139	—/6520

4   Value-Set Analysis

As an example of a standard, more complex use of a binary analysis toolkit, we experimented with value-set analysis (VSA) in both BAP and angr [2,3]. The angr tools include an experimental Value Flow Graph (VFG) module that performs a VSA. It annotates the CFG with sets of values that registers and memory locations can take on at various points during execution. At the time of writing, BAP does not ship with a comparable module, so we implemented our own VSA plugin using BAP's built-in support for abstract interpretation.

Both implementations perform abstract interpretation, but use slightly different abstract domains. Our VSA plugin for BAP uses *circular linear progressions* [8,12]. The implementation found in angr uses an extension of *wrapped strided intervals* [3,10,11]. These two representations are similar, and the distinction made little difference for our purposes.

To evaluate the two VSA implementations, we used them to resolve indirect jumps that BAP and angr CFG construction missed. We profiled runs on four small test programs that contain indirect jumps that require some insight to resolve. The results are in Table 2.

Table 2. Indirect jump resolution via VSA (BAP/angr)

Exe	Time (s)	Max RSS (Mb)	Resolved jumps
Prog A	0.73/1.21	124/88	5 of 5 (100%)/4 of 5 (80%)
Prog B	0.72/1.59	124/91	8 of 8 (100%)/7 of 8 (88%)
Prog C	0.71/1.85	124/93	8 of 8 (100%)/7 of 8 (88%)
Prog D	0.70/4.20	124/104	8 of 8 (100%)/8 of 8 (100%)

We found that our BAP VSA plugin resolved all jump targets, while angr's missed one in all but the last case. On further inspection, it looks like angr's VFG module has a bug that causes it to discard the contents of previous value sets after successive iterations, thereby resulting in an under approximation. By stopping after each iteration, we were able to observe that angr actually resolved some of the missing jumps before discarding the results for the next iteration.

The BAP plugin runs faster, but uses more memory at a constant level for our toy programs, while angr runs more slowly, but uses less memory. Neither implementation scales well to larger programs. When run on the GNU utilities described in the previous section, we typically encountered issues ranging from memory exhaustion to unsupported constructs before the analysis completes.

As implementors, we found that BAP gave us more confidence in the VSA results than angr. The simple Python interface and VFG module in angr made it easy to get started and obtain initial results. However, the lack of documentation and the presence of apparent bugs made it difficult to verify the correctness of the analysis we built on angr's capabilities. By contrast, since BAP ships with no VSA, it was a fair amount of work to build our own. Nevertheless, BAP's module-based documentation and the static checking provided by its use of the OCaml type system gave us more confidence that we were using it correctly.

5   Conclusion

Both BAP and angr enable analysis of binaries, providing a convenient interface that hides the technical details of the binary formats and ISAs. In addition, they each supply a suite of pre-built analyses to jump start the process.

We compared these tools in several ways. We described the process of implementing program analyses using them, and differences in the call graphs and control flow graphs they recover from binary programs. We implemented two representative program analyses using each tool, and examined their usability and performance.

In terms of resource usage, BAP is often more efficient, but not drastically so. We found that angr was easier than BAP to pick up quickly and begin experimenting with, and includes more-built in analyses. By contrast, BAP required us to do more work to get started, but its comprehensive module-based documentation gave us more confidence that we were using the tool correctly, even as new users.

References

1. Andriesse, D., Chen, X., van der Veen, V., Slowinska, A., Bos, H.: An in-depth analysis of disassembly on full-scale x86/x64 binaries. In: 25th USENIX Security Symposium (USENIX Security 2016), pp. 583–600. USENIX Association, Austin (2016)
2. Balakrishnan, G., Reps, T.: Analyzing memory accesses in x86 executables. In: Duesterwald, E. (ed.) CC 2004. LNCS, vol. 2985, pp. 5–23. Springer, Heidelberg (2004). https://doi.org/10.1007/978-3-540-24723-4_2

3. Balakrishnan, G., Reps, T.: WYSINWYX: what you see is not what you execute. ACM Trans. Program. Lang. Syst. **32**(6), 23:1–23:84 (2010)
4. Bao, T., Burket, J., Woo, M., Turner, R., Brumley, D.: BYTEWEIGHT: learning to recognize functions in binary code. In: USENIX Security Symposium (2014)
5. Brumley, D., Jager, I., Avgerinos, T., Schwartz, E.J.: BAP: a binary analysis platform. In: Gopalakrishnan, G., Qadeer, S. (eds.) CAV 2011. LNCS, vol. 6806, pp. 463–469. Springer, Heidelberg (2011). https://doi.org/10.1007/978-3-642-22110-1_37
6. Chan, P.P.F., Collberg, C.: A method to evaluate CFG comparison algorithms. In: 2014 14th International Conference on Quality Software, pp. 95–104, October 2014
7. Hu, X., Chiueh, T.-c., Shin, K.G.: Large-scale malware indexing using function-call graphs. In: Proceedings of the 16th ACM Conference on Computer and Communications Security, CCS 2009, pp. 611–620. ACM, New York (2009)
8. Källberg, L.: Circular linear progressions in SWEET. Technical report, Mälardalen University, Embedded Systems (2014)
9. Kim, S., et al.: Testing intermediate representations for binary analysis. In: Proceedings of the 32nd IEEE/ACM International Conference on Automated Software Engineering, ASE 2017, pp. 353–364. IEEE Press, Piscataway (2017)
10. Lee, J., Avgerinos, T., Brumley, D.: TIE: principled reverse engineering of types in binary programs. In: Network and Distributed Systems Security Symposium (NDSS). Internet Society, January 2011
11. Navas, J.A., Schachte, P., Søndergaard, H., Stuckey, P.J.: Signedness-agnostic program analysis: precise integer bounds for low-level code. In: Jhala, R., Igarashi, A. (eds.) APLAS 2012. LNCS, vol. 7705, pp. 115–130. Springer, Heidelberg (2012). https://doi.org/10.1007/978-3-642-35182-2_9
12. Sen, R., Srikant, Y.N.: Executable analysis using abstract interpretation with circular linear progressions. In: Proceedings of the 5th IEEE/ACM International Conference on Formal Methods and Models for Codesign, MEMOCODE 2007, pp. 39–48. IEEE Computer Society, Washington, DC (2007)
13. Shoshitaishvili, Y., et al.: SOK: (state of) the art of war: offensive techniques in binary analysis. In: IEEE Symposium on Security and Privacy, SP 2016, San Jose, CA, USA, 22–26 May 2016, pp. 138–157 (2016)

Automated Backend Selection for PROB Using Deep Learning

Jannik Dunkelau[1]([✉])[iD], Sebastian Krings[1,2][iD], and Joshua Schmidt[1][iD]

[1] Heinrich-Heine-University, Düsseldorf, Germany
{dunkelau,krings,schmidt}@cs.hhu.de
[2] Niederrhein University of Applied Sciences, Mönchengladbach, Germany

Abstract. Employing formal methods for software development usually involves using a multitude of tools such as model checkers and provers. Most of them again feature different backends and configuration options. Selecting an appropriate configuration for a successful employment becomes increasingly hard. In this article, we use machine learning methods to automate the backend selection for the PROB model checker. In particular, we explore different approaches to deep learning and outline how we apply them to find a suitable backend for given input constraints.

Keywords: Formal methods · Model checking ·
Automated configuration · Deep learning

1 Introduction and Motivation

The typical workflow when using formal methods consists of requirements engineering, writing specifications and analysing them using proof techniques and model checking. For all three tasks a variety of tools exists, each featuring a multitude of configuration options.

However, selecting the best tool for a task or choosing the optimal configuration is not trivial, even for domain experts. This is in alignment with the *No Free Lunch* theorem [42,43], and also affirmed by empirical evaluation on verification tasks as shown by Krings et al. [23] for the B method.

For instance, when solving constraints involving relations over sets, a SAT solver often provides a better performance than an SMT solver or a solver based on constraint logic programming [25]. However, especially when using integers, an SMT solver is often preferable to a SAT solver: a SAT solver needs to restrict the bitwidth which might result in integer overflows. Furthermore, an SMT solver directly supports integers without translation into propositional logic.

However, one cannot easily generalise on which constraints different solvers are efficient as it is impossible to set up universal selection rules. Consequently,

Computational support and infrastructure was provided by the "Centre for Information and Media Technology" (ZIM) at the University of Düsseldorf (Germany).

J. M. Badger and K. Y. Rozier (Eds.): NFM 2019, LNCS 11460, pp. 130–147, 2019.
https://doi.org/10.1007/978-3-030-20652-9_9

we decided to use statistical models in order to predict the constraint solver which most likely provides the best performance for a given constraint.

In this paper, we present our work towards using machine learning for the automated configuration of PROB [29–31], a model-checker and constraint solver for the B method [1]. In particular, we try to automate the selection of backends used for constraint solving in various places, e.g. for computing suitable parameters to operations or for symbolic model checking.

2   Related Work

Using heuristics, statistics or machine learning for configuration or selection of algorithms has been tried both for theorem provers and constraint solvers.

For the SETHEO theorem prover [28], Goller [16] employed folded architecture networks [17] to learn heuristic evaluation functions, i.e. performance measures for individual inference steps within a proof. While the results were promising, experiments were run for simple problems, with Goller stating that 'the next step is to experiment in a more realistic application domain' [16].

In the work of Bridge [7], support vector machines were used to automate the heuristic selection for the theorem solver E [39]. Here, the problem was limited to first order logic with equality. Bridge was able to improve E with his heuristic selection as it outperformed fixed heuristics as well as the already implemented auto-mode of E.

In the works of Healy [20,21], an SMT solver portfolio was conducted for Why3. Why3 [4,13] is a platform for deductive program verification, which provides its own language, WhyML, to specify a program and bindings to multiple different SMT solvers for the formal verification. The solver selection was done via decision trees which predicted the runtime needed for each solver constructing a ranking from fastest to slowest. The fastest solver is then proposed for verification of a given proof obligation.

In contrast to the works of Goller or Bridge, this article concerns itself with the higher-level language B. Besides first order logic with equality (c.f. Bridge's work) B also captures multiple different theories as is briefly outlined in the upcoming Sect. 3, including functions, sets, quantifiers, and non-deterministic assignments.

In contrast to Healy, this article concerns itself with a classification problem rather than a regression task. Further, *unknown* is used as its own class to capture instances neither of the involved backends is able to provide an answer for. Although an unknown solvability of a given proof obligation is implicitly detected in Healy's work (predicted runtime for all backends is greater than the timeout the data was generated for), having an actual probability of how likely a backend would return no answer for a given constraint might be more expressive. For instance, one might intervene early rather than sequentially querying each solver in the ranked list, depending on a probability threshold. Further, the calculated probability distribution also provides an implicit ranking ordering the backends by descending probabilities.

3   Primer on B and PROB

B [1] is a formal verification language for specifying, designing, and coding software systems as well as for performing formal proof of their properties. It follows the correct-by-construction approach and is based on first-order-logic and the Zermelo-Fraenkel set theory with the axiom of choice [14,15]. Further, it makes use of general substitution for state modifications, and of refinement calculus [2,3] to describe models at different levels of abstraction [8].

B machines consist of variable and type definitions as well as possible initial states. By defining machine operations, one is able to specify transitions between states. These transitions consist of substitutions, which may be non-deterministic depending on the level of abstraction. An operation can have a precondition enabling or disabling execution based on the current state. To ensure certain behaviour, the user can define machine invariants, i.e. safety properties that have to hold in every reachable state. The correctness of a formal model hence refers to the preservation of the specified properties in each reachable state.

For instance, consider the invariant $\forall x \in S \cdot (\exists n \cdot x = 2^n)$ for a manually assembled set S, and an operation with parameter n which adds 2^n to the set if not yet present: `op(n) = PRE n:NAT & 2**n/:S THEN S:=S\/{2**n} END`. The invariant now poses a constraint onto S which has to be satisfied in each reachable state including the states transitioned into by executing `op`.

Using Atelier B [11] or PROB [29–31] one can verify a B model and analyse its state space. In particular, PROB allows the user to animate formal models, providing a model checker and constraint solver. PROB's kernel [29] is implemented in SICStus Prolog [10], using the CLP(FD) finite domain library [9]. Alternatively, the backend can be substituted with a binding to a different solver. For one, a constraint solving backend based on Kodkod [41] is available [34]. Furthermore, an integration with the SMT solver Z3 [12] (connected to PROB as outlined in [24]) can be used to solve constraints.

The different backends have their own strengths and weaknesses. As the name suggests, CLP(FD) is particularly strong when dealing with variables having finite domains. On unrestricted problems, CLP(FD) can fail even on trivial problems such as $X < Y \wedge Y < X$, whereas it easily detects unsatisfiability if we restrict the domains of X and Y.

The Kodkod backend performs well on problems involving relations between different sets. However, it does not support the full range of constructs available in B. Consequently, PROB includes a fallback to the CLP(FD) backend for untranslatable parts.

In contrast to CLP(FD), the SMT-based backend performs well on unrestricted problems. Its particular strength is detecting unsatisfiability, while it does not perform as well for model finding, i.e. for finding variable valuations for satisfiable constraints. Again, the backend can be used on its own, i.e. with Z3 as the only solver involved. Comparable to Kodkod, Z3 can also be used together with the CLP(FD) backend in an integrated solving procedure as described by Krings et al. [24]. As we wanted to understand what influences the performance of the different backends, we used the standalone backend in the following.

4   Machine Learning on B Constraints

In this article, we consider three different classification problems:

Singular PROB Classification Given a single constraint p, is it possible to classify whether PROB's default backend will be able to determine whether p has a solution?

PROB+Kodkod Classification Given a single constraint p, is it possible to classify whether the default backend or the one based on Kodkod can determine satisfiability of p faster than the other, or if both will answer with unknown?

PROB+Z3 Classification Given a single constraint p, is it possible to classify whether the default backend or the one based on Z3 can determine satisfiability of p faster than the other, or if both will answer with unknown?

Initially, we aimed at creating an expert system able to propose a suitable backend for a given task or constraint. However, soon we realised that we lack deeper understanding of why a solver performs better on certain tasks than another. Further, the assembly of an expert system of this magnitude of complexity requires an unreasonable amount of pure programming work presumably consisting of myriads of edge-cases.

Hence, we opted for machine learning techniques. We supposed a machine learning algorithm might be capable of capturing any characteristics necessary for selecting the most suited backend for a given constraint in a fast and automated way.

4.1   Brief Introduction to Deep Learning

A deep neural network (DNN) [36,37] aims to approximate a function $y = f^\star(x)$ by learning a function $\hat{y} = f(x; W)$. Hereby, W is a matrix of parameters to be learned, whereas $\hat{y}$ is the prediction. During a training phase, the difference between the prediction $\hat{y}$ and the corresponding ground truth y is calculated and minimised by adjustments to the parameters in W. This process is called backpropagation (c.f. [38]). Internally, a neural network conducts a matrix multiplication $\hat{y} = f(x; W) = g(W^\mathsf{T}x)$ with a chosen activation function $g : \mathbb{R} \longrightarrow \mathbb{R}$. This matrix application can be layered by alternating parameters and activation functions, resulting in multiple parameter matrices $W_1, \ldots, W_n$. Such a neural network is said to have n layers, with $n-1$ *hidden layers*. For $n > 1$, a neural network is said to be a deep neural network. Besides parameters to be learned, a neural network further depends on a selection of hyperparameters, which are manually selected configurations referring to a network's architecture that are not adjusted during training, e.g. the amount of layers n is a hyperparameter.

DNNs work over numeric vectors of fixed length d as input. Constraints however are neither vectors nor of fixed length. Hence, a translation from a given B constraint into a vector $x \in \mathbb{R}^d$ is necessary. For this, d characterizing features $x_1, \ldots, x_d$ are collected per constraint, resulting in a vector $(x_1, \ldots, x_d)^\mathsf{T} \in \mathbb{R}^d$.

Such features should be descriptive enough to characterise the sample they were collected from sufficiently for the problem at hand. As an example for classification purposes: it is easy to distinguish between cats and elephants by size, and it is impossible to do so by number of legs.

We present two different translations from constraints as they would be presented to our backends into vectors, one based on 17, the other based on 185 features. All features are manually selected characteristics incorporating knowledge of the problem domain. Note that these features are not invariant under rewriting that preserves logical equivalence, i.e. two constraints that are logically equivalent possibly result in two different feature vectors. For instance, the expressions x+x+x and 3*x have different features but equivalent semantics.

Additionally, we followed an alternative approach relying on convolutional neural networks (CNNs). A CNN is a specialised kind of neural network, which processes data with a grid-like topology, most notably images [18,27]. For this, we translate B constraints into images of a predetermined size of $n \times n$ pixels. As this translation requires no prior domain knowledge, it serves as a comparison metric for the aforementioned hand-crafted features. Internally, a set of image processing filters are learned during training, suitable to the very problem at hand. Thus, one might say that a CNN learns necessary features itself.

4.2 The Initial Set of 17 Features

The initial set of features consists of 17 values mainly consisting of the absolute numbers of certain operators used in a constraint. These features capture the usages over the different theories supported in B mainly on an operator level. For instance, the features include the number of arithmetic operators used in the constraint, the number of set operations such as set memberships, as well as the number of universal and existential quantifiers. Further, they aim to capture some properties of the contained identifiers, e.g. the amount of unique identifiers used, or the amount of identifiers with finite or infinite domains.

4.3 The Set of 185 Features

The second set of features grew bigger as we aimed to cover most of the operators and theories used in the B method more precisely than the 17 features did. This led to 185 distinct features. One of the main differences to the first set of features is that the features formulate a ratio per operator over the corresponding theory or the number of top-level conjuncts in the given constraint.

For instance, for a given theory T (such as integer arithmetic) for which B implements n operators $op_1, \ldots op_n$ (e.g. $+, \times, \div, mod, succ, pred$), some features are: The amount of occurrences of an operator op_i divided by the number of top-level conjuncts in the respective constraint; The amount of operator occurrences divided by the sum of all operators belonging to the theory T; The sum of all of T's operators divided by the sum of top-level conjuncts.

4.4   A Convolution Approach

Constraints are of dynamic size, i.e. their string representation can be arbitrarily long. Furthermore, they do not inherit an obvious grid-like topology. Thus, CNNs cannot be used for classification without appropriate preprocessing. However, Loreggia et al. [33] proposed a promising approach of translating SAT, CSP, or MIP problems into images, visualised by an example in Fig. 1.

The translation process makes use of the fact that ASCII character codes range from 0 to 255. This makes the constraints conveniently mappable into grey scale pixels by an identity mapping. A given constraint of length N is fit into an $M \times M$ matrix with $M = \lceil \sqrt{N} \rceil$. The missing entries are filled with the value 32 (ASCII value for the space character). This matrix is a lossless mapping from the original constraint with each entry being interpretable as a grey scale pixel. The image now is scaled to an arbitrary target size of $n \times n$ pixels.

Choosing the space character as a filler is arbitrary, as it could have also been the line feed character (10) or even a null byte (0). However, the space character already has a natural occurrence in the ASCII version of a B constraint, as it may separate variables from operators and such alike. Meanwhile, neither the line feed nor the null byte occur in any of those constraints.

Although potential downscaling results in the translation no longer being lossless, Loreggia et al. express the strong believe that structure and self-similarity exposed by the instances remain throughout the scaling step: "While scaling the images incurs a high loss in information it seems to be the case that the retained structure is sufficient to address decision problems [. . .]" [33].

For this article, the resulting images are scaled to the sizes of 32×32 and 64×64 pixels, which hold up to 1024 and 4096 ASCII characters respectively. As the constraints have no theoretical upper limit on their size, it is not possible to find an image size that can contain any constraint losslessly (i.e. the resulting image does not need to be down-scaled). However, of the training data gathered for this article, around 64.6% of constraints fit into 1024 ASCII characters, and even 92.0% of them fit into 4096 characters. Thus, the chosen sizes compromise between fitting most of the data losslessly and having a part of the data being downscaled to decrease computational complexity.

5   Methodology

For the training of the DNNs, the training data was randomly split into three subsets. These are the training set, the validation, and the test set, consisting of 64%, 14%, and 20% of the training constraints respectively, and being pairwise distinct.

During training, the training set is fed through the model multiple times, referred to as epochs, in order to enable the model to learn to generalise over it. The performance is then measured on the validation set. Usually, the performance drops from training set to validation set, as the model has already adapted to the training data. If the performance on the validation set can keep up, this suggests that the model actually learned to generalise. Otherwise, the model is

Constraint:

$$\mathbf{coins} \in \mathbb{N} \wedge \mathbf{soda} \in \mathbb{N} \Rightarrow \mathbf{coins} > 0 \wedge \mathbf{soda} > 0 \wedge \mathbf{coins} - 1 \in \mathbb{N} \wedge \mathbf{soda} - 1 \in \mathbb{N}$$

Classical B syntax:

```
coins:NATURAL & soda:NATURAL => coins>0 & soda>0 & coins-1:NAT...
```

ASCII codes:

$\langle 99, 111, 105, 110, 115, 58, 78, 65, 84, 85, 82, 65, 76, 32, 38, 32, 115, 111, 100, 97, 58, 78, 65, 84, 85, 82, 65, \dots \rangle$

$M \times M$ Matrix:

$$\begin{bmatrix} 99 & 111 & 105 & 110 & 115 & 58 & 78 & 65 & 84 & 85 \\ 82 & 65 & 76 & 32 & 38 & 32 & 115 & 111 & 100 & 97 \\ 58 & 78 & 65 & 84 & 85 & 82 & 65 & 76 & 32 & 61 \\ 62 & 32 & 99 & 111 & 105 & 110 & 115 & 62 & 48 & 32 \\ 38 & 32 & 115 & 111 & 100 & 97 & 62 & 48 & 32 & 38 \\ 32 & 99 & 111 & 105 & 110 & 115 & 45 & 49 & 58 & 78 \\ 65 & 84 & 85 & 82 & 65 & 76 & 32 & 38 & 32 & 115 \\ 111 & 100 & 97 & 45 & 49 & 58 & 78 & 65 & 84 & 85 \\ 82 & 65 & 76 & 32 & 32 & 32 & 32 & 32 & 32 & 32 \\ 32 & 32 & 32 & 32 & 32 & 32 & 32 & 32 & 32 & 32 \end{bmatrix}$$

$M = \lceil \sqrt{83} \rceil = 10$, fill with spaces

ASCII values as pixels, scale to 64×64 image size

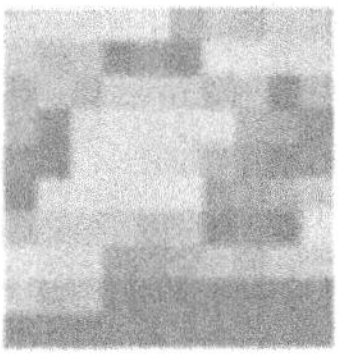

Fig. 1. The translation of constraints into images. A given constraint is interpreted as a sequence of characters. Those characters are then fit into a grid with each character's ASCII value being interpreted as a pixel value generating an image of size $M \times M$. The image is scaled to a fixed size, here 64×64 pixels.

adjusted to increase performance on the validation set after a new training step. At no point in time, the model is trained on any sample of the validation set. The test set serves as a final sanity-check for performance. Training multiple models, their performances on the validation set are implicitly dependent on the choice of hyperparameters. Testing the performance of the most promising models one can see whether the models generalise over the data, or only fit the validation set. Samples from the test set are never used for training or validation of the model. To find suitable architectures for the neural networks employed, we used a random search approach. That is, we set up ranges of possible values for any hyperparameters, and created new models by randomly choosing values from those given ranges. This was done to get a good intuition about what hyperparameters work best for the problem at hand. Found architectures were not reused for other experiments. We assumed it sensible to keep the architectures between the different experimental settings independent from each other. As they all shared the same search space, similar models should be found were suitable. To reduce the time needed for the random search, the training process for a model was terminated if it could not increase its performance for a set number of training epochs.

6   Training Data

To obtain the necessary training set, the first step was to acquire a sufficient amount of constraints. For this, we extracted invariants, preconditions of each operation, properties, and more data from 3638 B machines[1]. These were gathered from the chair of *Software Engineering and Programming Languages* at the University of Düsseldorf stemming from different application areas and thus varying in size and complexity.

These gathered constraints were then used to construct more complex ones. This served two purposes. Firstly, the amount of examples at hand was increased. Secondly, it ensured the presence of constraints which are harder to solve. In total, the generation yielded 321,742 constraints. Measured on number of characters in their ASCII representation, the average constraint length is 1,377.66 characters, with a minimum of 5 and a maximum of 15,383. The length distribution throughout the constraints is shown in Fig. 2.

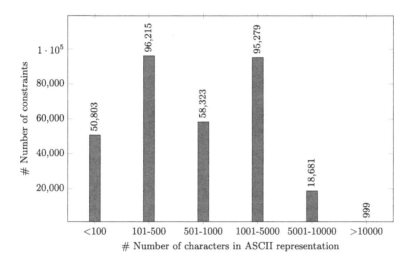

Fig. 2. Length distribution of the constraints in the training data.

Each constraint is annotated with the information of which backend is able to find a solution or show unsatisfiability. For this, we measured the average run time needed in three runs per backend. As timeout, ProB's default setting of 2.5 s per constraint was used. The resulting dataset can be found on GitHub[2]. From a classification point of view, constraints for which a backend can determine whether they are satisfiable or unsatisfiable belong to the class of this backend's *positive samples*, while those for which a backend is unable to determine satisfiability, for example, due to a timeout or unsupported constructs, belong to the class of its *negative samples*.

---

[1] www3.hhu.de/stups/downloads/prob/source/ProB_public_examples.tgz.
[2] https://github.com/hhu-stups/prob-examples-metadata.

Analysing the generated training data reveals that the data poses the class imbalance problem as shown in Fig. 3. The class imbalance problem [22,26] occurs in a training set for classification with a significant disproportion of class representation. Ideally, the classes are equally distributed. Otherwise, one runs at risk to train a dummy-classifier predicting only the stronger presented classes but classifying poorly elsewise [26,32].

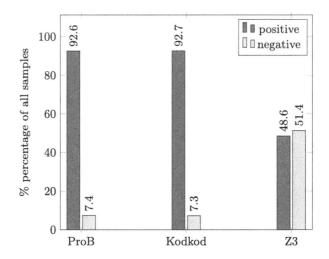

Fig. 3. Distribution of positive and negative samples throughout the training data.

Note, that the positive and negative samples may differ between two backends. For instance, the 92.6% of positive samples for PROB might not necessarily all be positive for Kodkod as well.

As a look at the intersatisfiability shows, there are indeed positive samples for each backend, that are negative samples for another one:

	PROB	Kodkod	Z3
PROB	–	99.80%	49.78%
Kodkod	99.60%	–	49.74%
Z3	94.76%	94.90%	–

Each row states the percentages of positive samples of the solver on the left, which also belong to the positive samples of the solver on the top. Omitted were the trivial 100% entries where a solver is compared to itself.

The class distribution is unequal, except of Z3 where it is roughly equal. To overcome this problem, Japkowicz et al. [22] proposed the method of *random under-sampling*, where samples from the training data are randomly deleted from the overrepresented classes, until all classes pose an equal distribution in the data set. Following this approach, an individual training set was generated by random under-sampling for each of the three aforementioned classification problems. For the singular PROB classification the resulting training set consisted of 47,850 remaining constraints, 49.9% of which PROB could determine satisfiability for and with the satisfiability of the other 50.1% being unknown to PROB. The training data for the PROB+Kodkod classification still contained 68,201 constraints, where both backends returned the result unknown for 33.4% of the data, PROB determining satisfiability faster than KodKod for 33.4%, and for the remaining 33.2% Kodkod being faster. The data of the PROB+Z3 classification consisted of 47,248 samples split into the classes unknown, PROB, and Z3 to 33.4%, 33.2%, and 33.4% respectively.

7   Results

Before discussing the results of the training phase, a quick note about how the performance of the resulting neural networks was measured. As in classification each sample belongs to one class, the aim is to measure correctly and incorrectly predicted classes. For each class, a sample constraint x in the training data can be labelled with $l \in \{+, -\}$, where $+$ indicates the belonging of x to the positive class, and $-$ indicates the belonging to the negative class respectively. Another such labelling $z \in \{+, -\}$ can be given to the prediction $\hat{y}(x)$, indicating whether x was predicted to belong to the class in question or not. From said labels one can now build a confusion matrix [19] consisting of the number of *true positives* (TP), *true negatives* (TN), *false positives* (FP), and *false negatives* (FN) as entries:

	$z = +$	$z = -$
$l = +$	TP	FN
$l = -$	FP	TN

Using the confusion matrix, we can apply the common definitions of the performance measurements precision, recall, and F_1-score [19,40]:

$$p = \frac{TP}{TP + FP} \qquad \text{(precision)}$$

$$r = \frac{TP}{TP + FN} \qquad \text{(recall)}$$

$$F_1 = \frac{2pr}{p + r}. \qquad \text{(F}_1\text{-score)}$$

Precision represents the predictive value of a label [40] and high precision for a class indicates that predicting said class usually is correct. Recall represents effectiveness for a single class [40] and high recall indicates that most of the samples belonging to said class are predicted as such as well. Now, the F_1-score is defined as the harmonic mean of precision and recall. As we ultimately aim for a predictor that achieves both, a high precision and recall, we will use the F_1-score as measure of performance.

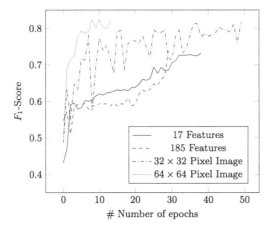

Features	F_1-score
17 Features	0.732
185 Features	0.738
32 × 32 Pixels	0.815
64 × 64 Pixels	0.823

Fig. 4. Best performing models for singular PROB classification. Learning curves over the validation set are shown on the left, the table on the right summarises the best performances achieved.

7.1   Results for Singular PROB Classification

For the singular PROB classification, the results appear to be promising. The best performing models' performances on the validation set are plotted against the respective training epochs in Fig. 4.

In conclusion, the 185 B-features do not appear to be much more expressive as the initial 17 already were, as can be seen by both models achieving an almost identical performance on the validation set: **0.732** and **0.738** respectively. As in the experiments the number and size of the hidden layers was chosen randomly, the model for 17 happened to have more hidden layers of a larger size (namely 7 layers with 48 units each) than the one for 185 features (2 layers with 4 units each). As hidden layers can be interpreted as more abstract features themselves, the smaller architecture might suggest that a small and precise set of features is sufficient for training a well-performing predictor.

For us, the most notable surprise was the performance of the image based approach. With an F_1-score of **0.823**, the best performing CNN model topped those models for hand-crafted features by a notable margin. This result can be interpreted in two manners. Firstly, it appears that the structure of a constraint observable in the ASCII representation is sufficient for classification. In consequence, it may be that a hand-crafted feature set does not need to include features which are counting nodes in the constraint's syntax tree. Secondly, as the CNNs could not rely on any domain knowledge and still outperformed the models trained on specifically designed features, it may be that the crafted features themselves still lack the crucial characteristics needed to properly classify the constraints. On the other hand, it is possible that the CNN's advantage lies simply in the amount of parameters learned. The top CNN model learned 162,348 parameters, whereas the top FNN models only employed 14,736 parameters for 17 B-features, and 766 parameters for 185 B-features.

Overall, the reached F_1-score of 0.823 appears to be a promising result, indicating that this approach is indeed feasible. Verifying the performance on the test set still yielded an F_1-score of 0.819.

7.2   Results for PROB+Kodkod Classification

For the PROB+Kodkod classification, there exist three distinct classes as mentioned in Sect. 4. Thus, the base performance of a respective classifier has to be greater than 0.333 to outperform uninformed guessing. The training performances on the corresponding validation set are shown in Fig. 5.

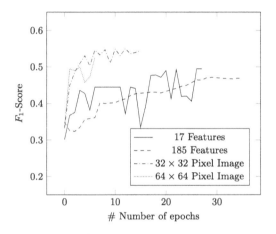

Features	F_1-score
17 Features	0.495
185 Features	0.472
32 × 32 Pixels	0.550
64 × 64 Pixels	0.524

Fig. 5. Best performing models for the PROB+Kodkod classification. Learning curves over the validation set are shown on the left, the table on the right summarises the best performances achieved.

Top performances for the 17 and 185 feature sets were **0.495** and **0.472** respectively. Again, the CNN approach takes the first place with an F_1-score of **0.550** on the validation set. It even performed a bit better on the corresponding test set achieving an F_1-score of **0.562**. Table 1 shows the corresponding test set precision and recall performances for each class.

As can be seen, the average precision and recall are fairly close. On a per-class basis, the model seems to predict unknown instances right most of the time (precision of 0.768), whereas PROB appears to be a class that the model struggles to recognise in the first place (recall of 0.369), tending to generally predict in favour of Kodkod (high recall but moderate precision). While the Kodkod selection models performed better than guessing, having a model which is only correct in every other case appears not to be practical in the context of backend selection. Under the assumption that one backend will be chosen eventually, the model does not perform notably better than picking a backend at random. The high precision on unknown constraints however may still help to detect problematic constraints beforehand.

Table 1. Precision and recall for the PROB+Kodkod classification on the test set.

Class	Precision	Recall
Unknown	0.768	0.591
PROB	0.516	0.369
Kodkod	0.447	0.683
Average	0.577	0.548

7.3   Results for PROB+Z3 Classification

For the PROB+Z3 classification, the results outperformed the respective ones from the Kodkod experiments notably. Although tackling a comparable problem, the better performances might reside in the fact that PROB and Z3 excel on more divergent problem classes than PROB and Kodkod do. Again, the image based approach is the best, reaching an F_1-score of **0.658** on the validation set, and still one of **0.652** on the test set. Figure 6 summarises the learning curves and validation set performances of the top models for each feature set, whereas Table 2 displays the best model's precision and recall on the test set.

Like in the PROB+Kodkod classification, the precision and recall values for unknown instances are quite high compared to those of PROB or Z3. However, this time the model appears to predict in favour of PROB, contrary to the results in the PROB+Kodkod classification. While an F_1-score of 0.652 is not a satisfying rate of success, it notably outperforms uninformed guessing and, contrary to the respective Kodkod variant, could already improve the selection step. Further, a corresponding uninformed workflow could consist of defaulting to one backend, then switching to the second one for instances where the first one failed to provide a definite answer, rather than guessing. Considering the high precision of the Z3 class, a workflow that defaults to PROB could already be improved in overall-performance by using Z3 over PROB for instances where the model predicts to do so.

Table 2. Precision and recall for the PROB+Z3 classification on the test set.

Class	Precision	Recall
Unknown	0.845	0.668
PROB	0.490	0.789
Z3	0.714	0.416
Average	0.683	0.624

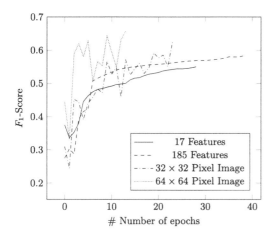

Features	F_1-score
17 Features	0.550
185 Features	0.582
32 × 32 Pixels	0.624
64 × 64 Pixels	0.658

Fig. 6. Best performing models for the PROB+Z3 classification. Learning curves over the validation set are shown on the left, the table on the right summarises the best performances achieved.

8   Conclusion and Future Work

In summary, we conducted a broad random search over different deep learning models for the classification problems stated in Sect. 4. For this, we gathered a training set consisting of various constraints, and crafted two feature sets, one of 17 and one of 185 features respectively, which incorporated domain knowledge of the B language and method.

As an alternative approach to compare with, the constraints were translated into images to train convolutional neural networks, as outlined in Sect. 4.4. To our surprise, the image based approach outperformed the domain-specific features notably. These results might suggest that our hand-crafted features are still too domain-unspecific. This underlines the initial motivation to use machine learning instead of an expert system, as we apparently do not understand the problem domain well enough to precisely formulate meaningful characteristics as of why a certain backend might outperform another.

We assume that a concise and domain-specific set of features should be able to yield a better performance than the image based approach. Ideally, the learned correlations between constraints and suitable backends can be extracted from trained models. This could lead to a more sophisticated understanding of the problem domain which allows to formulate more precise feature sets. Thus, it might be sensible to change the machine learning algorithm to a more transparent one, Refining the feature sets with the help of decision trees [6,35] and random forests [5] is subject to future work.

Be that as it may, one of the main take-aways is that approaches which require no domain knowledge can be preferred for initial performance probing and kickstarting results. Regarding deep learning, such techniques include an image based approach, as presented in this article, or a sequence based approach with recurrent neural networks (RNNs). Comparing performances achieved by an RNN to those of our CNNs would be quite interesting.

The performances of the best models lead us to the belief, that our approach is feasible after all. Putting more work into fine-grained training of the top-performing models should lead to even better results allowing to assemble a portfolio of different backends from which the most suitable is selected automatically on a per-instance base.

The classification problems which were concerned with selecting between *unknown* and two backends tend to favour one of the backends over the other. This is fine, as in such a case the corresponding uninformed workflow would presumably consist of defaulting to one backend, then switching to the second one for instances where the first one failed to provide a definite answer. As already discussed for the PROB+Z3 classifier, the overall computation time could be decreased for this workflow by only partially following the predictions (e.g. for predictions with a high precision).

The performances for detecting instances for which both backends could not return any answer were consistently the highest in the respective classification problem, which falls also in line with the notably better performances achieved for the singular PROB classification. In fact, if we revisit the best performing model for PROB+Z3 classification and interpret it as a binary classifier between the classes *unknown* and *either* PROB *or Z3*, it achieves an F_1-score of 0.827 which is quite comparable to the singular PROB classifier.

Comparing the presented approach again with the regression approach of Healy [20,21] it stands out that the latter is more extensible. Adding another backend would consist of adding a new regression model for said backend's runtime under Healy's approach, whereas in our approach we are not able to add Kodkod easily to the PROB+Z3 model, since we would have to train a new neural network instead which classifies between the three backends and the class of *unknown* samples. This is a huge drawback, rooted in the fact that the backends' runtimes are pairwise independent, but determining the fastest in the mix directly depends on the performances of all.

As the prediction of *unknown* samples per backend appeared to work well as stated above, implementing two models per backend might combine the best of both worlds. On the one hand, a runtime regression model per backend would easily allow for ranking the individual backends as in Healy's work. On the other hand, a singular classifier like the one presented for PROB in Sect. 7.1 can give an *independently computed* estimation over the backend's capability of finding an answer. For instance, given a ranking of PROB $\succ$ Z3 $\succ$ Kodkod with success probabilities of 62%, 51%, and 97% respectively, it might actually be more feasible to directly run Kodkod instead of risking two timeouts by running PROB and Z3 first. In fact the computed probability can be used for a weighted and more informed ranking.

References

1. Abrial, J.R.: The B-Book: Assigning Programs to Meanings. Cambridge University Press, Cambridge (1996)
2. Back, R.J., Wright, J.: Refinement Calculus: A Systematic Introduction. Springer (2012)
3. Back, R.: On correct refinement of programs. J. Comput. Syst. Sci. **23**(1), 49–68 (1981)
4. Bobot, F., Filliâtre, J.C., Marché, C., Paskevich, A.: Why3: shepherd your herd of provers. In: Boogie 2011: First International Workshop on Intermediate Verification Languages, Wrocław, pp. 53–64, August 2011. https://hal.inria.fr/hal-00790310
5. Breiman, L.: Random forests. Mach. Learn. **45**(1), 5–32 (2001)
6. Breiman, L., Friedman, J.H., Olshen, R.A., Stone, C.J.: Classification and regression trees (1984)
7. Bridge, J.P.: Machine learning and automated theorem proving. Technical report, University of Cambridge, Computer Laboratory (2010)
8. Cansell, D., Méry, D.: Foundations of the B method. Comput. Inform. **22**(3–4), 221–256 (2012)
9. Carlsson, M., Ottosson, G., Carlson, B.: An open-ended finite domain constraint solver. In: Glaser, H., Hartel, P., Kuchen, H. (eds.) PLILP 1997. LNCS, vol. 1292, pp. 191–206. Springer, Heidelberg (1997). https://doi.org/10.1007/BFb0033845
10. Carlsson, M., et al.: SICStus Prolog User's Manual, vol. 3. Swedish Institute of Computer Science Kista, Sweden (1988)
11. ClearSy: Atelier B, user and reference manuals. Aix-en-Provence, France (2016). http://www.atelierb.eu/
12. de Moura, L., Bjørner, N.: Z3: an efficient SMT solver. In: Ramakrishnan, C.R., Rehof, J. (eds.) TACAS 2008. LNCS, vol. 4963, pp. 337–340. Springer, Heidelberg (2008). https://doi.org/10.1007/978-3-540-78800-3_24
13. Filliâtre, J.-C., Paskevich, A.: Why3—where programs meet provers. In: Felleisen, M., Gardner, P. (eds.) ESOP 2013. LNCS, vol. 7792, pp. 125–128. Springer, Heidelberg (2013). https://doi.org/10.1007/978-3-642-37036-6_8
14. Fraenkel, A.A., Bar-Hillel, Y., Levy, A.: Foundations of Set Theory, vol. 67. Elsevier, Burlington (1973)
15. Fraenkel, A.: Zu den Grundlagen der Cantor-Zermeloschen Mengenlehre. Mathematische Annalen **86**(3), 230–237 (1922)
16. Goller, C.: Learning search-control heuristics for automated deduction systems with folding architecture networks. In: ESANN, pp. 45–50 (1999)
17. Goller, C., Kuchler, A.: Learning task-dependent distributed representations by backpropagation through structure. In: Proceedings of International Conference on Neural Networks (ICNN 1996), vol. 1, pp. 347–352. IEEE (1996)
18. Goodfellow, I., Bengio, Y., Courville, A.: Deep Learning. MIT Press, Cambridge (2016). http://www.deeplearningbook.org
19. Goutte, C., Gaussier, E.: A probabilistic interpretation of precision, recall and F-score, with implication for evaluation. In: Losada, D.E., Fernández-Luna, J.M. (eds.) ECIR 2005. LNCS, vol. 3408, pp. 345–359. Springer, Heidelberg (2005). https://doi.org/10.1007/978-3-540-31865-1_25
20. Healy, A.: Predicting SMT solver performance for software verification. Master's thesis, National University of Ireland Maynooth (2016)

21. Healy, A., Monahan, R., Power, J.F.: Evaluating the use of a general-purpose benchmark suite for domain-specific SMT-solving. In: Proceedings of the 31st Annual ACM Symposium on Applied Computing, SAC 2016, pp. 1558–1561. ACM, New York (2016)
22. Japkowicz, N.: The class imbalance problem: Significance and strategies. In: Proceedings of the International Conference on Artificial Intelligence (2000)
23. Krings, S., Bendisposto, J., Leuschel, M.: From failure to proof: the ProB disprover for B and Event-B. In: Calinescu, R., Rumpe, B. (eds.) SEFM 2015. LNCS, vol. 9276, pp. 199–214. Springer, Cham (2015). https://doi.org/10.1007/978-3-319-22969-0_15
24. Krings, S., Leuschel, M.: SMT solvers for validation of B and Event-B models. In: Ábrahám, E., Huisman, M. (eds.) IFM 2016. LNCS, vol. 9681, pp. 361–375. Springer, Cham (2016). https://doi.org/10.1007/978-3-319-33693-0_23
25. Krings, S., Schmidt, J., Brings, C., Frappier, M., Leuschel, M.: A translation from alloy to B. In: Butler, M., Raschke, A., Hoang, T.S., Reichl, K. (eds.) ABZ 2018. LNCS, vol. 10817, pp. 71–86. Springer, Cham (2018). https://doi.org/10.1007/978-3-319-91271-4_6
26. Kubat, M., Matwin, S., et al.: Addressing the curse of imbalanced training sets: one-sided selection. In: ICML, Nashville, USA, vol. 97, pp. 179–186 (1997)
27. LeCun, Y., Kavukcuoglu, K., Farabet, C.: Convolutional networks and applications in vision. In: Proceedings of 2010 IEEE International Symposium on Circuits and Systems (ISCAS), pp. 253–256. IEEE (2010)
28. Letz, R., Schumann, J., Bayerl, S., Bibel, W.: Setheo: a high-performance theorem prover. J. Autom. Reasoning **8**(2), 183–212 (1992)
29. Leuschel, M., Bendisposto, J., Dobrikov, I., Krings, S., Plagge, D.: From animation to data validation: the ProB constraint solver 10 years on. In: Boulanger, J.L. (ed.) Formal Methods Applied to Complex Systems: Implementation of the B Method, pp. 427–446. Wiley ISTE, Hoboken (2014). Chapter 14
30. Leuschel, M., Butler, M.: ProB: an automated analysis toolset for the B method. Int. J. Softw. Tools Technol. Transfer **10**(2), 185–203 (2008)
31. Leuschel, M., Butler, M.: ProB: a model checker for B. In: Araki, K., Gnesi, S., Mandrioli, D. (eds.) FME 2003. LNCS, vol. 2805, pp. 855–874. Springer, Heidelberg (2003). https://doi.org/10.1007/978-3-540-45236-2_46
32. Lewis, D.D., Catlett, J.: Heterogeneous uncertainty sampling for supervised learning. In: Proceedings of the Eleventh International Conference on Machine Learning, pp. 148–156 (1994)
33. Loreggia, A., Malitsky, Y., Samulowitz, H., Saraswat, V.A.: Deep Learning for Algorithm Portfolios. In: AAAI, pp. 1280–1286 (2016)
34. Plagge, D., Leuschel, M.: Validating B,Z and TLA$^+$ Using ProB and Kodkod. In: Giannakopoulou, D., Méry, D. (eds.) FM 2012. LNCS, vol. 7436, pp. 372–386. Springer, Heidelberg (2012). https://doi.org/10.1007/978-3-642-32759-9_31
35. Quinlan, J.R.: Induction of decision trees. Mach. Learn. **1**(1), 81–106 (1986)
36. Rosenblatt, F.: The perceptron: a probabilistic model for information storage and organization in the brain. Psychol. Rev. **65**(6), 386 (1958)
37. Rosenblatt, F.: Principles of neurodynamics. perceptrons and the theory of brain mechanisms. Technical report, Cornell Aeronautical Lab, Inc., Buffalo, NY (1961)
38. Rumelhart, D., Hinton, G., Williams, R.: Learning representations by backpropagating errors. Nature **323**(6088), 533–538 (1986)
39. Schulz, S.: E-A Brainiac theorem prover. AI Commun. **15**(2, 3), 111–126 (2002)

40. Sokolova, M., Japkowicz, N., Szpakowicz, S.: Beyond accuracy, F-score and ROC: a family of discriminant measures for performance evaluation. In: Sattar, A., Kang, B. (eds.) AI 2006. LNCS (LNAI), vol. 4304, pp. 1015–1021. Springer, Heidelberg (2006). https://doi.org/10.1007/11941439_114

41. Torlak, E., Jackson, D.: Kodkod: a relational model finder. In: Grumberg, O., Huth, M. (eds.) TACAS 2007. LNCS, vol. 4424, pp. 632–647. Springer, Heidelberg (2007). https://doi.org/10.1007/978-3-540-71209-1_49

42. Wolpert, D.H., Macready, W.G.: No free lunch theorems for optimization. IEEE Trans. Evol. Comput. **1**(1), 67–82 (1997)

43. Wolpert, D.H., Macready, W.G., et al.: No free lunch theorems for search. Technical Report SFI-TR-95-02-010, Santa Fe Institute (1995)

Optimizing a Verified SAT Solver

Mathias Fleury[1,2(✉)] (iD)

[1] Max-Planck-Institut für Informatik,
Saarland Informatics Campus, Saarbrücken, Germany
`mathias.fleury@mpi-inf.mpg.de`
[2] Saarbrücken Graduate School of Computer Science,
Saarland Informatics Campus, Saarbrücken, Germany

Abstract. In previous work, I verified a SAT solver with dedicated imperative data structures, including the two-watched-literal scheme. In this paper, I extend this formalization with four additional optimizations. The approach is still based on refining an abstract calculus to a deterministic program. In turn, an imperative version is synthesized from the latter, which is then exported to Standard ML. The first optimization is the extension with blocking literals. Then, the memory management is improved in order to implement the heuristics necessary to implement search restart and forget, which were subsequently implemented. This required changes to the abstract calculus. Finally, the solver uses machine words until they overflow before switching to unbounded integers. Performance has improved and is now closer to MiniSAT without preprocessing.

1 Introduction

SAT solvers are highly optimized programs full of tricks. This makes them an interesting case study for verification, both for the calculi and the data structures involved. Since SAT solvers are a prototypical example of highly optimized programs, it is interesting to see to what extent verification is feasible.

A common approach to increasing the trustworthiness of SAT solvers is to make them return independently verifiable *proofs* that certify the correctness of their answers. Such proofs were successfully produced by tools that solved long-standing open problems such as the *Pythagorean Triples Problem* [20] or *Schur Number Five* [19]. However, the production of proofs does not provide total correctness guarantees: Although a correct proof guarantees that a solver produced a correct result, it is not guaranteed that the solver will be able to produce a proof in the first place. Moreover, proof checkers and SAT solvers share similar techniques and data structures. They, thus, face similar efficiency challenges, and the techniques presented here are applicable to checkers too.

In previous work with Blanchette, Lammich, and Weidenbach, I developed a SAT solver, called IsaSAT [9], which I verified in Isabelle [34]. The first functional implementation, IsaSAT-0, could not solve any problem on a collection of problems from the SAT competitions. To improve performance, I extended

© Springer Nature Switzerland AG 2019
J. M. Badger and K. Y. Rozier (Eds.): NFM 2019, LNCS 11460, pp. 148–165, 2019.
https://doi.org/10.1007/978-3-030-20652-9_10

IsaSAT with *watched literals* [15]. The resulting version, IsaSAT-17, could solve 390 problems. Watched literals are a well-known optimization [24] but there is more to a modern SAT solver. In this article, I present four additional optimizations.

IsaSAT is specified using stepwise refinement, starting from a non-deterministic transition system [9] that is refined [15] in several steps using the *Isabelle Refinement Framework* [27–29]. Each layer refines and restricts the possible behavior until the program is fully deterministic. After that, *Sepref* [28] synthesizes an imperative version of the functions which can be exported to Haskell, OCaml, Scala, or Standard ML by Isabelle's code generator. Each layer also inherits properties from previous layers; for example, termination of the executable solver is derived from the termination of the initial transition system (Sect. 3).

Because some idioms made the proofs hard to maintain and slow to process, I first refactored the Isabelle formalization (Sect. 4). The first optimization is the use of *blocking literals* [12] to improve Boolean constraint propagation (Sect. 5). The idea is to cache a literal for each clause—if the literal is true in the current partial model of the solver, the clause can be ignored (saving a likely cache miss by not accessing the clause).

To avoid focusing on hard parts of the search space, the search of a SAT solver is heuristically restarted and the search direction changed. Clauses that are deemed useless are also forgotten. However, the standard heuristics rely on the presence of meta-information in clauses that can be efficiently accessed. To make this possible, I redesigned the clause representation, which also allowed me to implement the *position saving* [16] heuristic (Sect. 6). Extending the SAT solver with *restart* and *forget* required the extension of the calculus with watched literals: Both behaviors were already present in my abstract calculus but were not implemented in the next refinement step. Heuristics are critical and easy to verify, but hard to implement in a way that improves performance (Sect. 7).

Using machine integers instead of unbounded integers is another useful optimization. The new IsaSAT thus uses machine integers until the numbers don't fit in them anymore, in which case unbounded integers are used to maintain completeness (theoretically, IsaSAT could have to learn more than 2^{64} clauses before reaching the conclusion, which would overflow clause counters). The code is duplicated in the solver but specified only once (Sect. 8).

I analyze the importance of the different features and compare IsaSAT with state-of-the-art solvers (Sect. 9). Even though the new features improve IsaSAT significantly, much more work is required to match the best unverified solvers. The formalization is available online[1] and is part of the *Isabelle Formalization of Logic* (IsaFoL) effort [3]. The results presented here were briefly mentioned in Blanchette's invited talk at CPP 2019 [7, Section 3].

---

[1] https://bitbucket.org/isafol/isafol/src/master/Weidenbach_Book/.

2   The Isabelle Refinement Framework

The Isabelle Refinement Framework is at the center of my approach. Several refinement layers are used and each layer inherits properties from previous steps. Each step can change data structures and restrict the behavior of the program.

The framework allows me to express programs in a non-determinism monad. A program can either fail if any execution fails (FAIL); otherwise, it returns a set of all possible results (RES X where any element of X is a possible outcome). RETURN x is a special case that returns the single value x; i.e., RES $\{x\}$. The bind function bind $m\,f$ applies f to every outcome of m and is most of the time written with the Haskell-style 'do' notation do $\{a \leftarrow m;\ fa\}$. Then higher-level constructs are defined such as 'while' loops.

The framework provides a way to express refinement relations between two programs. First, a program can restrict the behavior of another program. The framework provides a partial order $\leq$ such that RES $X \leq$ RES Y if and only if $X \subseteq Y$ and FAIL is the top element (for all programs r, $r \leq$ FAIL). Second, data structures can also be refined. Given a relation R, $g \leq \Downarrow_R f$ means that every outcome of g is also an outcome of f up to conversion by R. To reason on program refinement, the framework provides tactics that heuristically map or *align* one instruction of the refined program to one instruction of the refining one; for example, they can align RETURN x and RES X, yielding the goal $x \in X$.

Finally, the framework provides the Sepref tool [28], which can synthesize a deterministic program with imperative data structures in Imperative HOL [10] from a non-deterministic program. For example, it can refine lists to arrays if all accesses are proven valid. Once synthesized, Isabelle's code generator [18] can be used to export the code to Haskell, OCaml, Scala, and Standard ML.

Code generation in Isabelle is built around a mapping from Imperative HOL operations to concrete code in the target language. This mapping is composed of *code equations* translating code and the correctness of the mapping cannot be verified in Isabelle. For example, accessing the n-th element of an Imperative HOL array is mapped to accessing the n-th element of the target language (e.g., `Array.sub` in Standard ML). These equations are the *trusted code base*.

3   IsaSAT

The IsaSAT solver, which this work extends, is organized in several refinement layers. Each one restricts the behavior or refines the data structures.

The most abstract layer [9], called CDCL, describes a conflict-driven clause learning (CDCL) transition system with dedicated transitions for restarts and forget. CDCL builds a candidate model, called the *trail* or M. Each time a clause is not satisfied by the trail, CDCL analyzes the clause to adapt the trail.

The second layer is a non-determinism transition system, called TWL, for two watched literals, and is expressed using an inductive predicate. It is connected to the previous calculus but restricts the behavior by forbidding restarts and forgets. Each clause has two literals called *watched*; the others are *unwatched*.

The calculus operates on states $(M, N, U, D, NP, UP, WS, Q)$, where M is the trail; N and U are the set of clauses of length greater than one; D is the conflict that is analyzed or $\top$; NP and UP are sets of clauses of length one; WS is a multiset of pairs (L, C) in the clause $C \in N + U$ such that L is a literal watched; Q is a multiset of literals. The SAT solver must visit each clause once after one of its watched literal has been set, i.e. the clause C in (L, C) of WS. Each visit results in either a change of one watched literal in order to maintain the two-watched-literal invariant or no change. The Ignore rule describes the latter:

Ignore $(M, N, U, \top, NP, UP, \{(L, C)\} \uplus WS, Q) \implies_{\mathsf{TWL}} (M, N, U, \top, NP, UP,$
   $WS, Q)$ if $L' \in$ watched C and $L' \in M$.

Informally, if the other watched literal L' is true, then no change of the watched literals of the clause C is required.

The third layer, called Algo, is expressed using the non-determinism monad of the Refinement Framework. Compared with TWL, the non-deterministic program fixes the order of rules, restricting its behavior.

In the first three layers, clauses are represented by multisets. In the fourth layer, called List, clauses become lists that are accessed by indices. This layer mostly features invariants stating that accesses using indices are in bounds. In the fifth layer, called WList, watch lists are added. They keep a mapping from a literal to all the clauses that are watching it. This mapping is critical for performance (recalculating them when required is too costly), but it is easier to introduce watch lists separately. In previous refinement steps, the mapping was recalculated when required. In a sixth layer, we add some additional invariants.

All heuristics are defined in the seventh and last layer, called Heur, leading to fully deterministic functions. Sepref is used to synthesize an imperative version of the code. Following the DIMACS format used in the SAT Competition, the generated code uses 32-bit machine words for the literals. Finally, Isabelle's code generator is used to export code in Standard ML, where it is combined with a trusted parser to get an executable program. IsaSAT is correct:

Theorem 1 (End-to-End Correctness). *If the literals in the input clauses fit in 32-bits and the input clauses do no contain duplicate literals, then IsaSAT returns a model if its input is satisfiable, or none if it is unsatisfiable.*

4   Refactoring IsaSAT

The optimizations require changes in the proofs and in the code. My first step is a refactoring to simplify maintenance and writing of proofs.

Proof Style. The original and most low-level proof style is the apply script: It is a forward style and each tactic creates subgoals. It is ideal for proof exploration and simple proofs. It is, however, hard to maintain. A more readable style states explicit statements of properties in Isar [42]. The styles can be combined:

definition PCUI_{Algo} where
   PCUI_{Algo} LC S = do {
      let $(L, C) = LC$;
      $L' \leftarrow$ RES (watched $C - \{L\}$);
      if $L' \in$ trail_{List} S then
         RETURN S
      else ...
   }

definition PCUI_{WList} where
   PCUI_{List} LC S = do {
      let $(L, C) = LC$;
      $L' \leftarrow$ RES (watched $C - \{L\}$);
      if $L' \in$ trail_{List} S then
         RETURN S
      else ...
   }

(a) Ignore rule after refactoring   (b) Ignore rule after refactoring

Fig. 1. Comparison of the code of Ignore rule in Algo before and after refactoring

each intermediate step can be recursively justified by apply scripts or Isar. For robustness, I use Isar where possible.

The tactics aligning goals are inherently apply style, but I prefer Isar. I will show the difference on the example of the refinement of PCUI_{Algo} (Fig. 1a) by PCUI_{List} (Fig. 1b). Assume the arguments of the function are related by the relation $((LC, S), (LC', S')) \in R_{state}$. The first two goals stemming from aligning PCUI_{Algo} with PCUI_{List} are

$$\forall L'\, L\, C\, C'.\ ((LC, S), (LC', S')) \in R_{state} \wedge LC = (L, C) \wedge LC' = (L', C') \rightarrow$$
$$(LC, LC') \in R_{watched} \tag{1}$$
$$\forall L'\, L\, C\, C'.\ ((LC, S), (LC', S')) \in R_{state} \wedge LC = (L, C) \wedge LC' = (L', C')$$
$$\wedge\ (LC, LC') \in R_{watched} \rightarrow$$
$$\text{RES (watched } C - \{L\}) \leq\Downarrow R_{\text{other watched}}(\text{RES (watched } C' - \{L'\})) \tag{2}$$

where Eq. (1) relates the two lets, Eq. (2) the two RES, and the relations $R_{watched}$ and $R_{\text{other watched}}$ are two schematic variables that have to be instantiated during the proof (e.g., by the identity). Although I strive to use sensible variable names, they are lost when aligning the programs, making the goals harder to understand.

A slightly modified version of Haftmann's explore tool [17] transforms the goals into Isar statements. The workflow to use it is the following. First, use Sepref's tactic to align two programs. Then, explore prints the structured statements. Finally, those statements can be inserted in the theory, before the goal. Figure 2a shows the output: Eqs. (1) and (2) corresponds to the two **have** statements, where **have** $R\,x$ **if** $P\,x$ **and** $Q\,x$ for x stands for the unstructured goal $\forall x.\, (P\,x \wedge Q\,x \longrightarrow R\,x)$. Each goal can be named and used to solve one proof obligations arising from the alignment of the two programs.

explore does not change the goals and hence, variables and assumptions are not shared between proof steps, leading to duplication across goals. I later expanded the explore to preprocess the goals before printing them: It uses **context**s (Fig. 2b) that introduces blocks sharing variables and assumptions. These proofs are now faster to check and write and minor changes are easier to do. There is no formal link between the statements and the goal obligations: If the goal obligations changes, the Isar statements have to be updated by hand. After big changes in the refined functions, it can be easier to regenerate the new statements, re-add them to the theory, and reprove them than to adapt the old one. Thankfully, this only happens a few times, usually when significantly changing the function anyway, which also significantly changes the proof.

have $(LC, LC') \in R_{\text{watched}}$
  if $LC = (L, C)$ **and** $LC' = (L', C')$
    and $((LC, S), (LC', S')) \in R_{\text{state}}$
  for $L'\ L\ C\ C'$
  sorry
have RES (watched $C - \{L\}$)
  $\leq\!\Downarrow R_{\text{other watched}}$
    (RES (watched $C' - \{L'\}$)
  if $(LC, LC') \in R_{\text{watched}}$ **and**
    $LC = (L, C)$ **and** $LC' = (L', C')$
    and $((LC, S), (LS', S')) \in R_{\text{state}}$
  for $L'\ L\ C\ C'\ C\ C'$
  sorry

context
  fixes $L'\ L\ C\ C'\ C\ C'$
  assumes $((LC, S), (LC', S')) \in R_{\text{state}}$
    and $LC = (L, C)$ **and**
    $LC' = (L', C')$
begin
lemma $(LC, LC') \in R_{\text{watched}}$
  sorry
lemma RES (watched $C - \{L\}$)
  $\leq\!\Downarrow R_{\text{other watched}}$
    (RES (watched $C' - \{L'\}$))
  sorry
end

(a) Proof as generated by `explore`: no sharing of assumptions and variables

(b) Proof with contexts as generated `explore_context`, with sharing.

Fig. 2. Different ways of writing the proof that PCUI$_{\text{List}}$ from Fig. 1a refines PCUI$_{\text{Algo}}$

Heuristics and Data Structures. At first, the implementation of heuristics and optimized data structures was carried out in three steps:

1. use specification and abstract data structure in Heur (e.g., the conflict clause is an optional multiset);
2. map the operations on abstract to concrete functions (e.g., the function converting a clause to a conflict clause is refined to a specific function converting a clause to a lookup table);
3. discharge the preconditions from step 2 with Sepref (e.g., no duplicate literal).

In principle, if step 2 is changed, Sepref can synthesize a new version of the code without other changes, making it easy to generate several versions to compare heuristics and data structures. However, in practice, this never happens because optimizing code further always requires stronger invariants, requiring to change the proofs for step 3. Moreover, Sepref's failures to discharge preconditions are tedious to debug. To address this, I switched to a different approach:

1'. introduce the heuristics and data structures in Heur (e.g., the conflict is a lookup table);
2'. add assertions for preconditions on code generation to Heur.

The theorems used to prove steps 2 are now used during the refinement to Heur. Sepref is also faster since the proofs of 2' are now trivial. In one extreme case,

Sepref took 24 min before failing with the old approach. After identifying the error, the solution was to add another theorem, recall Sepref, and wait. Thanks to this simpler approach and the entire-state based refinement, Sepref now takes only 16 s to synthesize the code (or fail).

5   Adding Blocking Literals

Blocking literals [12] are an extension of the two-watched-literal scheme and are composed of two parts: a relaxed invariant and the caching of a literal. Most SAT solvers implement both aspects. Blocking literals reduce the number of memory accesses (and, therefore, of cache misses).

```
definition PCUI_Algo where
    PCUI_Algo LC S = do {
        let (L, C) = LC;
        L' ← RES {L' | L' ∈ C};
        if L' ∈ trail S then
            RETURN S
        else do {
            L'' ← RES (watched C − {L});
            if L'' ∈ trail S then
                RETURN S
            else ...
        }
    }
```

```
definition PCUI_WList where
    PCUI_WList L i S − do {
        let (L', C) = watch_list_at S L i;
        let L' = L';
        if L' ∈ trail S then
            RETURN S
        else do {
            L'' ← RES (watched C − {L});
            if L'' ∈ trail S then
                RETURN S
            else ...
        }
    }
```

(a) Ignore part of the PCUI_Algo in Algo with blocking literals   (b) Ignore in WList with watch lists and blocking literals

Fig. 3. Refinement of the rule Ignore with blocking literals from Algo to WList

Invariant. IsaSAT-17's version of the two-watched-literal scheme is inspired by MiniSAT 1.13. The key invariant is the following [15]:

> A watched literal can be false only if *the other watched literal* is true or all the unwatched literals are false.

I now relax the condition by replacing "the other watched literal" by "any other literal". This weaker version means that there are fewer changes to the watched literals to do: If there is a true literal, no change is required. Accordingly, the side conditions of the Ignore rule of TWL can be relaxed from $L' \in$ watched C to $L' \in C$. Adapting the proof of correctness was relatively easy. The proofs are easy to fix (after adding some key lemmas) thanks to Sledgehammer [8], a tool that uses automatic theorem provers to find proofs.

The generalized Ignore rule is refined to the non-determinism monad (Fig. 3a). Since the calculus has only been generalized, no change in the refinement would have been necessary. In the code, the rule can be applied in three different ways:

Either L', the other watched literal L'', or another literal from the clause is true (the last case is not shown in Fig. 3). Any literal (even the false watched literal L) can be chosen for L'.

Caching of a Literal. Most SAT solvers contain an second part: When visiting a clause, it is often sufficient to visit a single literal [37]. Therefore, to avoid a likely cache miss, a literal per clause, called *blocking literal*, is cached in the watch lists. If it is true, no additional work is required; otherwise, the clause is visited: If a true literal is found, this literal is elected as new blocking literal, requiring no update of the watch lists.

In the refinement step WList, the choice is fixed to the cached literal from the watch list (Fig. 3b). The identity "let $L' = L'$;" helps the tactics of the Refinement Framework to recognize L' as the choice for RES $\{L' \mid L' \in C\}$, i.e. yielding the goal obligation $L' \in$ RES $\{L' \mid L' \in C\}$.

IsaSAT's invariant on the blocking literal forces the blocking literal to be *different* from the associated watch literal (corresponding to the condition $L \neq L'$ in Fig. 3). This is not necessary for correctness but offers better performance (since L is always false) and enables special handling of binary clauses: No memory access is necessary to know the content of the clause. IsaSAT's watched lists contain an additional Boolean indicating whether the clause is binary.

6   Improving Memory Management

The representation of clauses and their metadata used for heuristics is crucial for the performance of SAT solvers. Most solvers use two ideas: First, they keep the metadata and clauses together. For example, MiniSAT puts the metadata before the clause. The second idea is that memory allocation puts clauses one after the other in memory to improve locality.

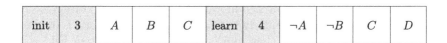

Fig. 4. Example of arena module with two clauses $A \vee B \vee C$ (initial clause, 'init') and $\neg A \vee \neg B \vee C \vee D$ (learned clause, 'learn')

However, none of these two tricks can be directly obtained by refinement and Isabelle offers no control over the memory allocator. Therefore, I implemented both optimizations at once, similarly to the implementation in CaDiCaL [4]. The implementation uses a large array, the *arena*, to allocate each clause one after the other, with the metadata before the clauses (Fig. 4): The lengths (here 3 and 4) precede the clause. Whereas the specifications allow the representation to contain holes between clauses, the concrete implementation avoids it.

In IsaSAT-17, the clauses were a list of clauses, each one being a list of literals (both list being refined to arrays). This representation could not be refined to an arena. Moreover, it was not compatible with removing clauses without shifting the positions. For example, if the first clause was removed from the list $[A \vee B \vee C; \neg A \vee \neg B \vee C \vee D]$, then the position of the second clause changed. This was a problem as the indices are used in the trail. Therefore, I first changed the representation from a list of lists to a mapping from natural numbers to clauses. Then, every element of the domain was mapped to a clause in the arena with the same index (for example, in Fig. 4, the clause 2 is $A \vee B \vee C$; 7 is $\neg A \vee \neg B \vee C \vee D$; there are no other clauses).

Introducing arenas requires some subtle changes to the existing code base. First, the arena contains natural numbers (clause length) and literals (clause content). Therefore, I use a datatype (as a tagged union) that contains either a literal or a natural number. Both types are refined to the same type, a 32-bits word and the datatype is removed when synthesizing code. An invariant on the whole arena describes its content. Moreover, because literals are refined to 32-bit machine words, the length has to fit in 32 bits. However, as the input problems can contain at most 2^{16} different atoms and duplicate-free tautologies, the maximum length of a clause is 2^{32}. To make it possible to represent all clauses including those of size 2^{32}, the arena actually keeps the number of unwatched literals (i.e., the length minus 2), unlike Fig. 4.

While introducing the arena, I also optimized parts of the formalization. I replaced loops on a clause starting at position C in the arena (i.e., iterations on $C+i$ for i in $[0, \text{length } C]$) by loops on the arena fragment (i.e., iteration on i for i in $[C, C+\text{length } C]$). This makes it impossible to compare IsaSAT-30 with and without the memory module without changes in the formalization. The impact of the arena was small (improvement of 2%, and a few more problems could be solved), but arenas make it possible to add metadata for heuristics.

Position Saving. I implemented a heuristic called *position saving* [16], which requires an additional metadata. It considers a clause as a circular buffer: When looking for a new literal, the search starts from the last searched position instead of starting from the first non-watched literal of the clause. The position is saved as a metadata of the clause. Similarly to CaDiCaL [4], the heuristic is only used for long clauses (length larger than four). Otherwise, the position field is not allocated in the arena (i.e., the size of the metadata depends on the clause size). Incorporating the heuristic was easy thanks to non-determinism. For example, to apply the Ignore rule, finding a true literal is sufficient, *how* it is found is not specified. This makes it easy to verify a different search algorithm.

Although there exist some benchmarks showing that this technique improve the performance of solvers [5], only CaDiCaL and Lingeling [4] implement it and I did not know if it would improve IsaSAT: The generated code is hardly readable and hard to change in order to test such techniques. However, it was easy to add and it improves performance on most problems (see Sect. 9).

7   Implementing Restarts and Forgets

CDCL-based SAT solvers have a tendency to get stuck in a fruitless area of the search space and to clutter their memory with too many learned clauses. Most modern SAT solvers offer two countermeasures. Restarts try to avoid focusing on a hard part of the search space. Forgets limit the number of clauses because too many of them slow down the solver.

```
to_skip ← RES {n. True};
WHILE(λ(to_skip, i, S). ⟨there is a clause to update or to_skip > 0⟩))
   (λ(to_skip, i, S). do {
      skip_element ← RES {b | b → to_skip > 0}
      if skip_element then RETURN(to_skip − 1, i, S)          (∗ do nothing ∗)
      else do{
         LC ← ⟨some literal and clause to update⟩;
         PCUI_Algo LC S }
   })
```

Fig. 5. Skipping deleted clauses during iteration over the watch list

Completeness is not guaranteed anymore if restart and forget are applied too often. To keep completeness, I delay them more and more. TWL does not propagate clauses of length 1, because they do not fit in the two-watched-literal scheme. These clauses are propagated during the initialization are cannot be removed from the trail. However, such clauses will always be repropagated by CDCL. Therefore, a TWL restart corresponds to a CDCL restart and some propagations. If decisions are also kept, then IsaSAT can reuse parts of the trail [36]. This technique avoids redoing some work after a restart. The trail could even be entirely reused if the decision heuristics would do the same decisions.

When forgetting several clauses at once, called one *reduction step*, IsaSAT uses the LBD [1] (least block distance) to sort the clauses by importance, and then keeps only linearly many (linear in the number restarts). All other learned clauses are deleted. I have not yet implemented garbage collection for the arena, so deleted clauses currently remain in memory forever.

After clauses have been marked as deleted, the watch lists are not garbage collected. Instead, before accessing a clause, IsaSAT tests if the clause has been deleted or not. However, this is an implementation-specific detail I don't want to mirror in Algo. To address this, I changed Algo in a less intrusive way. Before Algo was iterating over WS. After the change, a finite number of no-ops is added to the while loop (Fig. 5). When aligning the two programs, an iteration over a deleted clause is mapped to a no-op. More precisely, there are two tests: whether the blocking literal is true and whether the clause is marked as deleted. If the blocking literal is true, the state does not change (whether the clause is deleted or not). Otherwise, the clause has to be accessed. If the clause is deleted, it is removed from the watch list.

IsaSAT uses the EMA-14 heuristic [6], which is based on two exponential moving averages of scores, implemented using fixed-points numbers: a "slow" average measuring the long-term tendency of the scores and a "fast" one for the local tendency. If the fast average is worse than the slow one, the heuristic is triggered. Then, depending on the number of clauses, either restart or reduce is triggered. The heuristic follows the unpublished implementation of CaDiCaL [4], with fixed-point calculations. This is easier to implement than Glucose's queue for scores. Due to programming errors, it took several iterations to get EMA-14 right: The first version never restarted while the second did as soon as possible. Although both versions were complete, the last version performed better.

8   Using Machine Integers

When I started to work on IsaSAT, it was natural to use unbounded integers to index clauses in the arena (refined from Isabelle's natural numbers). First, they are the only way to write lists accesses in Isabelle (further refined to array accesses). Second, they are also required for completeness to index the clauses and there was also no code-generation setup for array accesses with machine words. Finally, the Standard ML compiler I use, MLton [41], efficiently implements numbers first as machine words and then as unbounded GMP integers. However, profiling showed that subtractions and additions took among them around 10% of the time.

I decided to switch to machine words. Instead of failing upon overflow or restarting the search from scratch with unbounded integers, IsaSAT switches in the middle of the search:

while $\neg \, done \wedge \neg \, overflow$ do
    ⟨invoke the 64-bit version of the solver's body⟩;
if $\neg \, done$ then
    ⟨convert the state from 64-bit to unbounded integers⟩;
    while $\neg \, done$ do
        ⟨invoke the unbounded version of the solver's body⟩

The switch is done pessimistically. When the length of the arena is longer than $2^{64} - 2^{16} - 5$ (maximum size of a non-tautological clause without duplicate literals is 2^{16} and 5 is the maximal number of header fields), the solver switches to unbounded integers, regardless of the size of the next clause. This bound is large enough to make a switch unlikely in practice. In Isabelle, the two versions of the solver's body are just two instances of the same function where Sepref has refined Isabelle's natural numbers differently during the synthesis. To synthesize machine words, Sepref must prove that numbers cannot overflow. For example, if i is refined to the 64-bit machine word w, then the machine-word addition $w+1$ refines $i+1$ if the addition does not overflow, i.e., $i+1 < 2^{64}$. The code for data structures like resizable arrays (used for watch lists) has not been changed and, therefore, still uses unbounded integers. However, some code was changed to limit manipulation on the length of resizable arrays.

IsaSAT uses 64-bit machine words instead of 32-bit machine words. They are used in the trail but mostly in the watch lists. Using 32-bits words would be more cache friendlier for the trail. However, this would not make any difference for watch lists. Each element in a watch list contains a clause index, a 32-bit literal, and a Boolean. Due to padding, there is not size difference for 32 and 64-bit words. Moreover, the SAT Competition contains problems that require more memory than fits in 32 bits: After hitting the limit, IsaSAT would switch to the slower unbounded version of the solver, whereas no switch is necessary for 64-bit indices.

9 Evaluation

I evaluated IsaSAT-30 on preprocessed problems from the SAT Competitions 2009 to 2017 and from the SAT Race 2015 using a timeout of 1800s. The hardware was an Intel Xeon E5620, 2.40 GHz, 4 cores, 8 threads. Each instance was limited to 10 GB of RAM. The problems were preprocessed by Crypto-MiniSat [38]. The motivation behind this is that preprocessing can significantly simplify the problem. Detailed results can be found on the companion web page[2].

SAT solver	Default options		No simplification	
	Solved	Average time (s)	Solved	Average time (s)
CryptoMiniSat	1774	349	1637	349
Glucose	1703	320	1696	303
CaDiCaL	1677	361	1602	346
MiniSAT	1388	326	1373	317
MicroSAT	1018	310	N/A	
IsaSAT-30 fixed heuristic	801	359	N/A	
IsaSAT-30 without the four optimizations	433	301	N/A	
IsaSAT-17	393	220	N/A	
versat	368	224	N/A	

Fig. 6. Performance of some SAT solvers (N/A if no simplification is done by default)

State-of-the-art solvers solve more problems than IsaSAT with the default options (Fig. 6). Since the instances have already been preprocessed, the difference comes from a combination of simplifications (pre- and inprocessing), better heuristics, and a better implementation. To assess the difference, I have also benchmarked the solvers without simplification (third column of Fig. 6). Heule's MicroSAT [21] aims at being very short (240 lines of code including comments). Compared with IsaSAT, it has neither position saving nor blocking literals but is highly optimized and its heuristics work well together. The version without

---
[2] https://people.mpi-inf.mpg.de/~mfleury/paper/results-NFM/results.html.

Reduction	Restarts	Position saving	Machine words	Solved	Average time (s)	memory (GB)
				520	294	2.1
			✓	551	291	2.3
		✓		526	281	2.1
		✓	✓	547	289	2.3
	✓			666	292	2.2
	✓		✓	713	312	2.5
	✓	✓		712	294	2.4
	✓	✓	✓	**753**	306	2.7
✓				433	213	1.6
✓			✓	448	207	1.7
✓		✓		446	212	1.6
✓		✓	✓	456	204	1.7
✓	✓			677	336	2.8
✓	✓		✓	738	339	3.1
✓	✓	✓		705	324	2.9
✓	✓	✓	✓	749	338	3.2

Fig. 7. Benchmarks of variants of IsaSAT-30 before fixing the forget heuristic

the four presented optimizations differs from IsaSAT-17 by various minor optimizations. IsaSAT performs better than the only other verified SAT solver with efficient data structures I know of, versat [35].

I compared the impact of reduction, restart, position saving, and machine words (Fig. 7). Since Standard ML is garbage-collected, the peak memory usage depends on the system's available memory. The results show that restarts and machine words have a significant impact on the number of solved problems. The results are less clear for the other features. Position saving mostly has a positive impact. The negative influence of reduction hints at a bad heuristic: I later tuned the heuristic by keeping clauses involved in the conflict analysis and the results improved from 749 to 801 problems. The fact that garbage collection of the arena is not implemented could also have an impact, as memory is wasted.

10   Discussion and Related Work

Extracting Efficient Code. When refining the code, it is generally not clear which invariants will be needed later. However, I noticed that improvements on data structures also require stronger properties. Therefore, proving them early can help further refinement but also makes the proofs more complicated. Another issue is that the generated code is not readable, which makes it extremely hard to change in order to test if a data structure or a heuristic improves speed.

Profiling is crucial to obtain good performance. First, it shows if there are some obvious gains. However, profiling Standard ML code is not easy. MLton has a profiler which only gives the total amount of time spent in the function (not including the function calls in its body) and not the time per path in the call graph. So performance bugs in functions that don't dominate run time are impossible to identify. One striking example was the insertion sort used to sort the clauses during reduction. It was the comparison function that was dominating the run time, not the sort itself, which I changed to quicksort.

Continuous testing also turned out to be important. It can catch performance regression before any change in the search behavior is done, allowing me to debug them. One extreme example was the special handling of binary clauses: A Boolean was added to every element of the watch list, changing the type from `word64 * word32` to `word64 * (word32 * bool)`. This change in the critical spot of any SAT solver caused a performance loss of around 20% due to 3.5 times as many cache misses. Since the search behavior had not changed, I took a single problem and tried to understand where the regression came from. First, `word64 * (word32 * bool)` is less efficient than `word64 * word32 * bool` as it requires a pointer for `word32 * bool`. This can be alleviated by using a single constructor datatype (the code generator generates the later version and the single constructor is optimized away). However, there is a second issue: The tuple uses three 64-bit words, whereas only two would be used in the equivalent C structure. I added code equations to merge the `word32 * bool` into a single `word64` (with 31 unused bits), solving the regression. Developers of non-verified SAT solvers face similar issues[3] but they are more tools for C and C++.

While working on the SAT solver, I added several code equations to the trusted code base. The additional code equations are either trying to avoid conversions to unbounded integers (`IntInf`) and back (as would happen by default when accessing arrays) or related to printing statistics during the execution. Whether or not the equations are safe is not always obvious. For example, the code equations to access arrays *without* converting the numbers to unbounded integers and back[4] are safe as long as the array bounds are checked.

However, IsaSAT is compiled with an option that deactivates array-access bound checks. When accessing elements outside of an array, the behavior is undefined. As long as I am using Sepref and the assumptions of Theorem 1 hold, validity of the memory accesses is proved. Without the custom code equations and with bound checks, only 536 problems are solved, instead of 749.

Equivalent C code would be more efficient. First, as already mentioned, there are differences in the memory guarantees. Standard ML does not provide information on the alignment. A second issue are spurious reallocations. A simple example is the function `fun (propa, s) => (propa + 1, s)`. This simple function (counting the number of propagations) is responsible for 1.7% of all allocations although I would expect no extra allocation. A third issue is that the generated code is written in a functional style with many unit arguments `fun () => ...` to ensure that side effects are done in the right order. Not every compiler supports optimizing these additional constructs away.

---

[3] E.g., https://www.msoos.org/2016/03/memory-layout-of-clauses-in-minisat/.
[4] Although the Standard ML specification encourages compilers to optimize such code.

All the optimizations have an impact on the length of the formalization. The whole formalization is around 31 000 lines of proof for refinement from TWL to the last layer Heur, 35 000 lines (Heur and code generation), and 9000 lines for libraries. The entiree generated Standard ML code is 8100 lines long.

Related Work. This work is related to other verification attempts of fast code, like Lammich's GRAT toolchain [26,30]. One of the differences is that he uses a C++ program to preprocess the certificates in order to be able to check them more efficiently later. However, like a SAT solver, a checker uses many arrays and therefore would likely benefit from machine words.

Unlike the top-down approach used here, the verification of the seL4 micro-kernel [25] relies on abstracting the program to verify. An abstract specification in Isabelle is refined to an Haskell program. Then, a C program is abstracted and connected to the Haskell program. Unbounded integers are not supported in C and therefore achieving completeness of a SAT solver would not be possible. Other techniques to abstract programs exist, like Chargueraud's characteristic formulas [11]. Another option is Why3 [14] or a similar verification condition generator like Dafny [31]. Some meta-arguments in Why3 (for example, incrementing a 64-bit machine integer initialized with 0 will not overflow in a reasonable amount of time; therefore, machine integers are safe [13]) would simplify the generation of efficient code. In any case, refinement helps to verify a large program.

Isabelle's code generator does not formally connect the generated code to the original function. On the one hand, Hupel's verified compiler [23] from Isabelle to the semantics of the verified Standard ML compiler CakeML could bridge the gap. However, code export from Imperative HOL is not yet supported. On the other hand, HOL4 in conjunction with CakeML makes it possible to bridge this gap and also to reason about input and output like parsing the input file and printing the answer [22]. There is, however, no way to eliminate the array-access checks. Moreover, CakeML uses boxed machine words unlike MLton, which probably leads to a significant slowdown.

Marić has developed another verified SAT solver [33] in Isabelle without refinement, making his formalization impossible to extend. Moreover, a different version of watched literals, no efficient data structures (only lists), nor heuristics are used. Oe et al. use a different verification approach without refinement for versat. The Guru proof assistant [39] is used to generate C code. Termination or correctness of the generated model is not proven. Similarly to IsaSAT, versat uses machine words—it relies on int to be 32 bits, which is not guaranteed in C—but cannot solve larger instances. The SAT competition includes such problems which usually can be solved easily if the decision heuristic initially makes literals false. There is no bound checking for arrays. versat features a different flavor of watched literals but neither blocking literals nor restart or forget.

Among SAT solvers, there are two main lines of research: Solvers derived from MiniSAT, like Glucose [2] and MapleSAT [32], focus on improving CDCL (and especially the heuristics) whereas solvers like CaDiCaL [4], CryptoMiniSat [38] and Lingeling [4] also feature inprocessing.

11   Conclusion

I have extended a verified SAT solver, IsaSAT, with four additional optimizations to improve performance and I have verified those extensions. Even if the refinement approach is helpful, adding these optimizations is a significant effort. Lammich is currently working on generating LLVM code which could give more control on the generated code (e.g., the tuples representation is more efficient).

I now plan to extend my calculus to be able to represent $CDCL(\mathcal{T})$, the calculus behind SMT solvers. The theory of linear arithmetic has already been implemented by Thiemann [40].

Acknowledgment. Jasmin Blanchette discussed several earlier drafts with me. This work would not have been possible without Christoph Weidenbach and Peter Lammich. Marijn Heule, Benjamin Kiesl, Peter Lammich, Hans-Jörg Schurr, Petar Vukmirović, and the anonymous reviewers suggested many textual improvements.

References

1. Audemard, G., Simon, L.: Predicting learnt clauses quality in modern SAT solvers. In: Boutilier, C. (ed.) IJCAI 2009, pp. 399–404. Morgan Kaufmann Publishers Inc. (2009). http://ijcai.org/Proceedings/09/Papers/074.pdf
2. Audemard, G., Simon, L.: Glucose 2.1: aggressive–but reactive–clause database management, dynamic restarts. In: Workshop on the Pragmatics of SAT 2012 (2012)
3. Becker, H., Bentkamp, A., Blanchette, J.C., Fleury, M., From, A.H., Jensen, A.B., Lammich, P., Larsen, J.B., Michaelis, J., Nipkow, T., Peltier, N., Popescu, A., Robillard, S., Schlichtkrull, A., Tourret, S., Traytel, D., Villadsen, J., Petar, V.: IsaFoL: Isabelle Formalization of Logic. https://bitbucket.org/isafol/isafol/
4. Biere, A.: CaDiCaL, Lingeling, Plingeling, Treengeling, YalSAT entering the SAT competition 2017. In: Balyo, T., Heule, M., Järvisalo, M. (eds.) SAT Competition 2017: Solver and Benchmark Descriptions, pp. 14–15. University of Helsinki (2017)
5. Biere, A.: Deep bound hardware model checking instances, quadratic propagations benchmarks and reencoded factorization problems. In: Balyo, T., Heule, M., Järvisalo, M. (eds.) SAT Competition 2017: Solver and Benchmark Descriptions, pp. 37–38. University of Helsinki (2017)
6. Biere, A., Fröhlich, A.: Evaluating CDCL restart schemes. In: Proceedings POS-15. Sixth Pragmatics of SAT Workshop (2015)
7. Blanchette, J.C.: Formalizing the meta theory of logical calculi and automatic provers in Isabelle/HOL (invited talk). In: Mahboubi, A., Myreen, M.O. (eds.) CPP 2019. pp. 1–13. ACM (2019). https://doi.org/10.1145/3293880.3294087
8. Blanchette, J.C., Böhme, S., Fleury, M., Smolka, S.J., Steckermeier, A.: Semi-intelligible ISAR proofs from machine-generated proofs. J. Autom. Reasoning **56**(2), 155–200 (2016). https://doi.org/10.1007/s10817-015-9335-3
9. Blanchette, J.C., Fleury, M., Weidenbach, C.: A verified SAT solver framework with learn, forget, restart, and incrementality. In: Olivetti, N., Tiwari, A. (eds.) IJCAR 2016. LNCS (LNAI), vol. 9706, pp. 25–44. Springer, Cham (2016). https://doi.org/10.1007/978-3-319-40229-1_4

10. Bulwahn, L., Krauss, A., Haftmann, F., Erkök, L., Matthews, J.: Imperative functional programming with Isabelle/HOL. In: Mohamed, O.A., Muñoz, C., Tahar, S. (eds.) TPHOLs 2008. LNCS, vol. 5170, pp. 134–149. Springer, Heidelberg (2008). https://doi.org/10.1007/978-3-540-71067-7_14

11. Charguéraud, A.: Characteristic formulae for the verification of imperative programs. In: ICFP, pp. 418–430. ACM (2011). https://doi.org/10.1145/2034773.2034828

12. Chu, G., Harwood, A., Stuckey, P.J.: Cache conscious data structures for Boolean satisfiability solvers. JSAT **6**(1–3), 99–120 (2009)

13. Clochard, M., Filliâtre, J.-C., Paskevich, A.: How to avoid proving the absence of integer overflows. In: Gurfinkel, A., Seshia, S.A. (eds.) VSTTE 2015. LNCS, vol. 9593, pp. 94–109. Springer, Cham (2016). https://doi.org/10.1007/978-3-319-29613-5_6

14. Filliâtre, J.-C., Paskevich, A.: Why3—Where programs meet provers. In: Felleisen, M., Gardner, P. (eds.) ESOP 2013. LNCS, vol. 7792, pp. 125–128. Springer, Heidelberg (2013). https://doi.org/10.1007/978-3-642-37036-6_8

15. Fleury, M., Blanchette, J.C., Lammich, P.: A verified SAT solver with watched literals using Imperative HOL. In: CPP, pp. 158–171. ACM (2018). https://doi.org/10.1145/3167080

16. Gent, I.P.: Optimal implementation of watched literals and more general techniques. J. Artif. Intell. Res. **48**, 231–251 (2013). https://doi.org/10.1613/jair.4016

17. Haftmann, F.: Draft toy for proof exploration, August 2013. www.mail-archive.com/isabelle-dev@mailbroy.informatik.tu-muenchen.de/msg04443.html

18. Haftmann, F., Nipkow, T.: Code Generation via Higher-Order Rewrite Systems. In: Blume, M., Kobayashi, N., Vidal, G. (eds.) FLOPS 2010. LNCS, vol. 6009, pp. 103–117. Springer, Heidelberg (2010). https://doi.org/10.1007/978-3-642-12251-4_9

19. Heule, M.J.H.: Schur Number Five. In: McIlraith, S.A., Weinberger, K.Q. (eds.) Proceedings of AAAI 2018, pp. 6598–6606. AAAI Press (2018). https://www.aaai.org/ocs/index.php/AAAI/AAAI18/paper/view/16952

20. Heule, M.J.H., Kullmann, O., Marek, V.W.: Solving and verifying the Boolean Pythagorean triples problem via cube-and-conquer. In: Creignou, N., Le Berre, D. (eds.) SAT 2016. LNCS, vol. 9710, pp. 228–245. Springer, Cham (2016). https://doi.org/10.1007/978-3-319-40970-2_15

21. Heule, M.: microsat (2014). https://github.com/marijnheule/microsat

22. Ho, S., Abrahamsson, O., Kumar, R., Myreen, M.O., Tan, Y.K., Norrish, M.: Proof-producing synthesis of CakeML with I/O and local state from monadic HOL functions. In: Galmiche, D., Schulz, S., Sebastiani, R. (eds.) IJCAR 2018. LNCS (LNAI), vol. 10900, pp. 646–662. Springer, Cham (2018). https://doi.org/10.1007/978-3-319-94205-6_42

23. Hupel, L., Nipkow, T.: A verified compiler from Isabelle/HOL to CakeML. In: Ahmed, A. (ed.) ESOP 2018. LNCS, vol. 10801, pp. 999–1026. Springer, Cham (2018). https://doi.org/10.1007/978-3-319-89884-1_35

24. Katebi, H., Sakallah, K.A., Marques-Silva, J.P.: Empirical study of the anatomy of modern sat solvers. In: Sakallah, K.A., Simon, L. (eds.) SAT 2011. LNCS, vol. 6695, pp. 343–356. Springer, Heidelberg (2011). https://doi.org/10.1007/978-3-642-21581-0_27

25. Klein, G., et al.: seL4: formal verification of an operating-system kernel. Commun. ACM **53**(6), 107–115 (2010). https://doi.org/10.1145/1743546.1743574

26. Lammich, P.: GRAT–efficient formally verified SAT solver certification toolchain. http://www21.in.tum.de/~lammich/grat/

27. Lammich, P.: Automatic data refinement. In: Blazy, S., Paulin-Mohring, C., Pichardie, D. (eds.) ITP 2013. LNCS, vol. 7998, pp. 84–99. Springer, Heidelberg (2013). https://doi.org/10.1007/978-3-642-39634-2_9

28. Lammich, P.: Refinement to Imperative/HOL. In: Urban, C., Zhang, X. (eds.) ITP 2015. LNCS, vol. 9236, pp. 253–269. Springer, Cham (2015). https://doi.org/10.1007/978-3-319-22102-1_17

29. Lammich, P.: Refinement based verification of imperative data structures. In: Avigad, J., Chlipala, A. (eds.) CPP 2016, pp. 27–36. ACM (2016). https://doi.org/10.1145/2854065.2854067

30. Lammich, P.: Efficient verified (UN)SAT certificate checking. In: de Moura, L. (ed.) CADE 2017. LNCS (LNAI), vol. 10395, pp. 237–254. Springer, Cham (2017). https://doi.org/10.1007/978-3-319-63046-5_15

31. Leino, K.R.M.: Dafny: an automatic program verifier for functional correctness. In: Clarke, E.M., Voronkov, A. (eds.) LPAR 2010. LNCS (LNAI), vol. 6355, pp. 348–370. Springer, Heidelberg (2010). https://doi.org/10.1007/978-3-642-17511-4_20

32. Liang, J.H., Ganesh, V., Poupart, P., Czarnecki, K.: Learning rate based branching heuristic for SAT solvers. In: Creignou, N., Le Berre, D. (eds.) SAT 2016. LNCS, vol. 9710, pp. 123–140. Springer, Cham (2016). https://doi.org/10.1007/978-3-319-40970-2_9

33. Marić, F.: Formal verification of a modern SAT solver by shallow embedding into Isabelle/HOL. Theor. Comput. Sci. **411**(50), 4333–4356 (2010). https://doi.org/10.1016/j.tcs.2010.09.014

34. Nipkow, T., Paulson, L.C., Wenzel, M.: Isabelle/HOL: A Proof Assistant for Higher-Order Logic. LNCS, vol. 2283. Springer, Heidelberg (2002). https://doi.org/10.1007/3-540-45949-9

35. Oe, D., Stump, A., Oliver, C., Clancy, K.: `versat`: a verified modern SAT solver. In: Kuncak, V., Rybalchenko, A. (eds.) VMCAI 2012, vol. 7148, pp. 363–378. Springer, Heidelberg (2012). https://doi.org/10.1007/978-3-642-27940-9_24

36. Ramos, A., van der Tak, P., Heule, M.J.H.: Between restarts and backjumps. In: Sakallah, K.A., Simon, L. (eds.) SAT 2011. LNCS, vol. 6695, pp. 216–229. Springer, Heidelberg (2011). https://doi.org/10.1007/978-3-642-21581-0_18

37. Ryan, L.: Efficient algorithms for clause-learning SAT solvers. Master's thesis, Simon Fraser University (2004)

38. Soos, M., Nohl, K., Castelluccia, C.: Extending SAT solvers to cryptographic problems. In: Kullmann, O. (ed.) SAT 2009. LNCS, vol. 5584, pp. 244–257. Springer, Heidelberg (2009). https://doi.org/10.1007/978-3-642-02777-2_24

39. Stump, A., Deters, M., Petcher, A., Schiller, T., Simpson, T.W.: Verified programming in Guru. In: Altenkirch, T., Millstein, T.D. (eds.) PLPV 2009, pp. 49–58. ACM (2009). https://doi.org/10.1145/1481848.1481856

40. Thiemann, R.: Extending a verified simplex algorithm. In: Barthe, G., Korovin, K., Schulz, S., Suda, M., Sutcliffe, G., Veanes, M. (eds.) LPAR-22 Workshop and Short Paper Proceedings. Kalpa Publications in Computing, vol. 9, pp. 37–48. EasyChair (2018). https://easychair.org/publications/paper/6JF3

41. Weeks, S.: Whole-program compilation in MLton. In: ML, p. 1. ACM (2006). https://doi.org/10.1145/1159876.1159877

42. Wenzel, M.: Isabelle/Isar–A generic framework for human-readable proof documents. In: Matuszewski, R., Zalewska, A. (eds.) From Insight to Proof: Festschrift in Honour of Andrzej Trybulec, Studies in Logic, Grammar, and Rhetoric, vol. 10(23). University of Białystok (2007)

Model Checking of Verilog RTL Using IC3 with Syntax-Guided Abstraction

Aman Goel$^{(\boxtimes)}$ and Karem Sakallah

University of Michigan, Ann Arbor, USA
{amangoel,karem}@umich.edu

Abstract. While bit-level IC3-based algorithms for hardware model checking represent a major advance over prior approaches, their reliance on propositional clause learning poses scalability issues for RTL designs with wide datapaths and complex word-level operations. In this paper we present a novel technique that combines IC3 with *syntax-guided abstraction* (SA) to allow scalable word-level model checking using SMT solvers. SA defines the abstraction implicitly from the syntax of the input problem, has high granularity and an abstract state-space size completely independent of the bit widths of the design's registers. We show how to efficiently integrate IC3 with SA, and demonstrate its effectiveness on a suite of open-source and industrial Verilog RTL designs. Additionally, SA aligns easily with data abstraction using uninterpreted functions. We demonstrate how IC3+SA with data abstraction allows reasoning that is completely independent of the bit width of variables, and becomes scalable irrespective of the state-space size or complexity of operations.

1 Introduction

IC3 [13] (also known as PDR [25]) is arguably the most successful technique for hardware model checking. Bit-level engines using IC3 (e.g. ABC [8], IIMC [14], PDTRAV [16], AVY [49]) have shown exceptional performance in hardware model checking competitions (HWMCC) [10]. As the size and complexity of the problem increases, the bit-level IC3 algorithm suffers from two main scalability issues: poor SAT solver performance, and learning too many weak propositional frame restrictions. Several techniques have been proposed to address these challenges (e.g. [20,31–33,40,48,50]), including different ways of adding a layer of *abstraction refinement* [22,37] to reduce the burden on reasoning engines. Approaches like [20,40] suggest raising IC3 to the word level by exploiting high-level information missing at the bit level. These techniques replace bit-level reasoning using SAT solvers with word-level clause learning in *first order logic* (FOL) using SMT [7] solvers.

The Averroes system [39,40] demonstrated how EUF abstraction [4,5,15] can be exploited to perform word-level IC3 on control-centric Verilog RTL designs. The technique performed backward reachability using a weakest precondition algorithm, effectively causing an *implicit* unrolling of the transition relation

© Springer Nature Switzerland AG 2019
J. M. Badger and K. Y. Rozier (Eds.): NFM 2019, LNCS 11460, pp. 166–185, 2019.
https://doi.org/10.1007/978-3-030-20652-9_11

which leads to poor performance and possible non-termination in some situations. This typically happens when the property being checked is strongly dependent on data operations, for which EUF abstraction is ill-suited, and leads to an excessive number of *data* refinement iterations to repair the abstraction.

In this paper we address these issues by extending the Averroes approach beyond control-centric problems using *syntax-guided abstraction* (SA). Inspired by EUF abstraction, SA implicitly creates an abstraction using the terms present in the syntax of the problem yielding an abstract domain whose size is completely independent of the bit widths of the registers or the *sequential depth* [43] of the design. SA offers high granularity and captures *all equality* relations among the terms present in the syntax of the problem, while also interpreting data operations. Any *spurious* behavior is eliminated by adding new terms that were missing in the original problem. We show how to efficiently combine IC3 with SA (IC3+SA), and extend IC3+SA with data abstraction using uninterpreted functions (UF). IC3+SA with data abstraction allows for abstract reasoning that is completely independent of the design's bit widths and offers scalability irrespective of the problem size or complexity of operations.

Our main contributions are as follows:

- We present syntax-guided abstraction to implicitly capture the most relevant details from the syntax of the system with negligible computation cost.
- We present an efficient syntax-guided cube generalization procedure for word-level IC3 that is quantifier-free, doesn't require any solver calls, and does not perform any implicit or explicit unrolling of the transition relation.
- We suggest a fully incremental procedure to refine SA and eliminate any spurious behavior in the abstract domain.
- We show how IC3+SA can be easily extended with data abstraction using UF for complete and scalable model checking on control-intensive problems.

The paper is organized as follows: Sect. 2 presents the relevant background to describe the detailed SA approach in Sect. 3. Section 4 shows how SA is integrated within the IC3 framework, and the correctness of this method is proved in Sect. 5. Section 6 covers implementation details and presents an experimental evaluation on a diverse set of RTL benchmarks. The paper concludes with a brief survey of related work in Sect. 7, and a discussion of future directions in Sect. 8.

2   Background

2.1   Notation

Our setting is standard first-order logic with the notions of *sort, universe, signature*, and *structure* defined in the usual way [7]. A *term* is a constant symbol, or an n-ary function symbol applied to n terms. An *atom* is $\top$, $\bot$ or an n-ary predicate symbol applied to n terms. A *literal* is an atom or its negation, a *cube* is a conjunction of literals, and a *clause* is a negation of a cube, i.e., a disjunction of literals. A quantifier-free *formula* is a literal or the application of logical connectives to formulas.

We will refer to all terms with a non-boolean range as *words*, and refer to words with 0-arity as *ground* words. A *partition assignment* for a formula φ is defined as a boolean assignment to each predicate in φ, and a set of partitions (one for each sort) dividing the words in φ into equivalence classes. An interpretation $\mathcal{I}$ assigns a meaning to terms by means of a uniquely determined (total) mapping ($[\![\_]\!]^{\mathcal{I}}$) of such terms into the universe of its structure. A model of a formula φ for an interpretation $\mathcal{I}$ is a structure that satisfies φ (i.e. $[\![\varphi]\!]^{\mathcal{I}} = \top$). For example, the interpretation for the theory of free sort and function symbols (call it $\mathcal{I}_P$) maps terms into the universe of partition assignments. The interpretation for the theory of bitvectors (call it $\mathcal{I}_B$) maps terms into a universe composed of bitvector assignments.

Given a transition system, we will use primes to represent a variable after a single transition step. Given a set of variables X, X' is the set obtained by replacing each variable in X with its primed version. We will use φ (resp. φ') as a shorthand for a formula $\varphi(X)$ (resp. $\varphi(X')$).

2.2   Model Checking

A model checking problem $\mathcal{P}$ can be described by a 4-tuple $\langle X, I, T, P \rangle$, where X denotes the set of present state variables, $I(X)$ is a formula representing the initial states, $T(X, X')$ is a formula for the transition relation, and $P(X)$ is a formula for a given *safety* property. Given $\mathcal{P}$, the model checking problem can be stated as follows: either prove that $P(X)$ holds for any sequence of executions starting from a state in $I(X)$, or disprove $P(X)$ by producing a counterexample.

We assume that T is expressed as a conjunction of equalities that express next-state variables as functions of present-state variables. Input variables are conveniently modeled as state variables whose corresponding next states are completely unconstrained. Our focus is on verifying Verilog RTL designs which we encode as *finite* transition systems that are naturally expressed in the QF_BV theory of SMT-LIB.

3   Syntax-Guided Abstraction

Predicate abstraction (PA) [28] encodes the abstract state space using a set of predicates whose boolean assignments encode the abstract states. In contrast, syntax-guided abstraction (SA) encodes the abstract state space using the set of terms present in the word-level syntax of the problem. Abstract states in SA correspond to partition assignments that capture the equality relations among the problem's terms. The relevant parts of the abstract transition relation in both *implicit* PA [20,21] and SA are constructed incrementally, as needed, during the reachability search using bitvector queries. We will use $\mathcal{P}$ to denote the original *concrete* problem and $\hat{\mathcal{P}}$ to denote its *syntactically-abstracted* version. Models in $\mathcal{P}$ use the interpretation $\mathcal{I}_B$, i.e. exact bitvector assignments, whereas models in $\hat{\mathcal{P}}$ use the $\mathcal{I}_P$ interpretation, i.e. partition assignments. Effectively, SA hides away irrelevant bit-level details and is able to infer higher-level equality relations among the words in the problem description.

Example 1: Let $\mathcal{P} = \langle \{u, v\}, (u = 1) \wedge (v = 1), (u' = ite(u < v, u + v, v + 1)) \wedge (v' = v + 1), ((u + v) \neq 1) \rangle$, where u, v are k-bit wide. $\mathcal{P}$ has 1 predicate $(u < v)$ and 5 words $(1, u, v, u + v, v + 1)$. Consider a concrete state $s := (u, v) = (1, 2)$. Its corresponding abstract state is obtained by evaluating the problem's predicates and terms using the concrete state assignment and creating a partition assignment based on these evaluations. In this example, the abstract state is easily seen to be $\hat{s} := (u < v) \wedge \{\, 1, u \mid v \mid u + v, v + 1\,\}^1$.

The biggest advantage of SA is that the abstract state-space size is completely independent of the bit-width of variables while still accounting for all relations among terms in the original problem. Given $\mathcal{P}$ with, say, m total state bits, the concrete system has 2^m states. On the other hand, the total number of abstract states is bounded by $2^p \times B_n$, where p is the number of predicates in $\hat{\mathcal{P}}$, n is the number of words in $\hat{\mathcal{P}}$, and B_n is the nth Bell number [46] (the number of unique partitions on n terms). For example, let $k = 16$ in Example 1. The size of the concrete state space is $2^{2 \times 16}$ i.e. $\sim$4.2 billion, while the number of abstract states is $2^1 \times B_5 = 104$, completely independent of k.

Given a formula φ, we use concrete theory reasoning (i.e. QF_BV) for abstract SMT solving (similar to [20,21]) with the modification that the solution (i.e. model) of φ in the abstract domain is expressed as a partition assignment on terms in φ, i.e. for a partition assignment $\hat{s}$, $\hat{s} \models \varphi$ iff there exists a bitvector assignment s such that $s \models \varphi$ and $\hat{s} = \alpha(\varphi, s)$, where α is the abstraction function that converts a bitvector assignment s to a partition assignment on terms in φ. We perform a simple evaluation of each term in the formula to construct a partition assignment based on the bitvector assignment.

Example 2: Consider $\mathcal{P}$ from Example 1. Let $k = 2$. Consider the formula $\varphi = P \wedge T \wedge \neg P'$ and a satisfying concrete solution $s := (u, v, u', v') = (0, 2, 2, 3)$. Terms in φ evaluate as $(u < v, u + v, v + 1, u' + v') = (\top, 2, 3, 1)$ under s, resulting in the abstract solution to be $\hat{s} := (u < v) \wedge \{\, u \mid 1, u' + v' \mid v, u + v, u' \mid v + 1, v'\,\}$.

We can always construct a *unique* abstract solution $\hat{s}$ given a formula φ and its concrete solution s. Modern SMT solvers (e.g. [23,24]) have support to give the bitvector assignment for each term in the formula without any extra cost. Words with the same assigned value go in the same equivalence class of a partition, while different assignments mean different classes.

An abstract solution is *complete* if it contains all the terms in $\mathcal{P}$. The abstract state space is defined by the universe of complete abstract solutions. An abstract solution can be *projected* on any subset of symbols (a *projection set*) by *co-factoring* the solution to eliminate all terms with any symbol outside the projection set, i.e. by simply dropping terms from the partition assignment that contain symbol(s) outside the projection set. An abstract solution can be converted to an equivalent cube by adding all constraints needed to *cover* the solution.

---

[1] In this notation, vertical bars separate the equivalence classes of the partition. Thus $\{a, b | c\}$ should be interpreted to mean $\{\{a, b\}, \{c\}\}$ in the standard notation for partitions.

Example 3: Consider $\hat{s}$ from Example 2. $\hat{s}$ can be projected on the projection set $\sigma = \{+, 1, u', v'\}$ to get a *partial* abstract solution representing the destination states as $\hat{s}|_\sigma := \{\, 1, u' + v' \mid u' \mid v' \,\}$. The corresponding cube representation is $cube(\hat{s}|_\sigma) = ((u' + v') = 1) \wedge (u' \neq 1) \wedge (v' \neq 1) \wedge (u' \neq v')$.

The SA abstract state space induces a partition on the concrete state space such that each concrete state is mapped to a single abstract state. An abstract state, thus, corresponds to a (possibly empty) set of concrete states causing the abstract transition relation to be *non-deterministic*. This abstraction is *sound* but may lead to *spurious* behavior.

Example 4: Consider the following abstract path from $\mathcal{P}$ in Example 2:

$$\hat{s}_1 := \neg(u < v) \wedge \{\, 1, u, v \mid u + v, v + 1 \,\}$$
$$\hat{s}_2 := \neg(u < v) \wedge \{\, 1 \mid u, v \mid u + v \mid v + 1 \,\}$$
$$\hat{s}_3 := \neg(u < v) \wedge \{\, 1, v + 1 \mid u, v, u + v \,\}$$

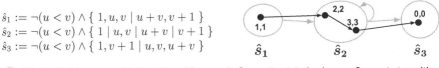

⭕ **Abstract state** ⟶ **Abstract transition** ● **Concrete state (u,v)** ⟶ **Concrete transition**

$\hat{s}_1$ has a concrete transition to $\hat{s}_2$, $\hat{s}_2$ can concretely transition to $\hat{s}_3$, though there isn't a continuous 2-step concrete path from $\hat{s}_1$ to $\hat{s}_3$ via $\hat{s}_2$. SA can be refined by adding new terms. For example, we can add the constant term 2 (or 3) to eliminate the spurious behavior of Example 4.

To better understand how SA compares to PA, consider $\mathcal{P}$ from Example 2. There are 16 concrete states in $\mathcal{P}$. The four predicates in $\mathcal{P}$, i.e. p_1: $(u = 1)$, p_2: $(v = 1)$, p_3: $((u + v) = 1)$ and p_4: $(u < v)$ are a natural choice as initial predicates for PA. Table 1 compares the abstract domain for SA and PA against the concrete state space. PA with p_{1-4} as predicates partitions the concrete states into 9 *feasible* abstract states. SA on the other hand offers higher expressiveness and partitions the concrete states into 13 feasible abstract states.

Syntax-guided abstraction has the following advantages over PA:

– Unlike predicate abstraction or its variants [6,28], SA is *implicitly* defined by the original syntax and does not require a user-specified set of initial predicates or solver queries to generate the abstract state space.
– By construction, SA accounts for all equality relations among terms in the syntax and offers higher granularity and expressiveness than implicit predicate abstraction [20,21], resulting in less spurious behavior.
– SA is refined by adding new terms that are absent in the original problem syntax, while PA relies on adding new predicates for refinement. Furthermore, equality propagation, which is at the heart of SA, allows all equality relations involving a newly-introduced term to be automatically detected; in PA such relations are discovered one by one in multiple refinement iterations.

SA + UF: SA uses bit-precise QF_BV queries and may not scale for large problems with complex operations. Since SA requires only a partition assignment on terms

Table 1. Mapping of abstract states on concrete states for SA and PA

Index	SA: partition assignment on $\{u < v, 1, u, v, u + v, v + 1\}$	Concrete states: (u, v)	PA: $p_1 p_2 p_3 p_4$
1	$\neg(u < v) \wedge \{\, 1, v + 1 \mid u, v, u + v \,\}$	$(0, 0)$	0000
2	$\neg(u < v) \wedge \{\, 1, v + 1 \mid u, u + v \mid v \,\}$	$(2, 0), (3, 0)$	
3	$\neg(u < v) \wedge \{\, 1 \mid u, v \mid u + v \mid v + 1 \,\}$	$(2, 2), (3, 3)$	
4	$(u < v) \wedge \{\, 1 \mid u \mid v, u + v \mid v + 1 \,\}$	$(0, 2)$	0001
5	$(u < v) \wedge \{\, 1 \mid u, v + 1 \mid v, u + v \,\}$	$(0, 3)$	
6	$\neg(u < v) \wedge \{\, 1, u + v \mid u, v + 1 \mid v \,\}$	$(3, 2)$	0010
7	$(u < v) \wedge \{\, 1, u + v \mid u \mid v \mid v + 1 \,\}$	$(2, 3)$	0011
8	$\neg(u < v) \wedge \{\, 1, v \mid u, v + 1 \mid u + v \,\}$	$(2, 1)$	0100
9	$\neg(u < v) \wedge \{\, 1, v \mid u \mid u + v \mid v + 1 \,\}$	$(3, 1)$	
10	$(u < v) \wedge \{\, 1, v, u + v \mid u \mid v + 1 \,\}$	$(0, 1)$	0111
11	$(u < v) \wedge \{\, 1, u \mid v \mid u + v, v + 1 \,\}$	$(1, 2), (1, 3)$	1001
12	$\neg(u < v) \wedge \{\, 1, u, u + v, v + 1 \mid v \,\}$	$(1, 0)$	1010
13	$\neg(u < v) \wedge \{\, 1, u, v \mid u + v, v + 1 \,\}$	$(1, 1)$	1100
	Others: $(2^1 \times B_5 - 13 = 91)$	Infeasible	Others: $(2^4 - 9 = 7)$

and not exact bitvector assignments, it aligns perfectly with data abstraction where data operations (like arithmetic, shift, etc.) are treated as uninterpreted functions [4,5,15,40]. SA+UF is most appropriate for control-centric properties where correctness is largely independent of data state. IC3 with SA+UF extends [40] and allows for efficient reasoning using QF_UF queries regardless of the bit-width of variables or complexity of data operations.

Example 5: Consider $\mathcal{P}$ from Example 1. Using SA+UF, the abstract problem becomes $\bar{\mathcal{P}} = \langle \bar{X}, \bar{I}, \bar{T}, \bar{P} \rangle$:

$$\bar{X} = \{\, \bar{u}, \bar{v} \,\} \qquad \bar{I} = (\bar{u} = \bar{1}) \wedge (\bar{v} = \bar{1}) \qquad \bar{P} = (ADD(\bar{u}, \bar{v}) \neq \bar{1})$$
$$\bar{T} = (\bar{u}' = ite(LT(\bar{u}, \bar{v}), ADD(\bar{u}, \bar{v}), ADD(\bar{v}, \bar{1}))) \wedge (\bar{v}' = ADD(\bar{v}, \bar{1}))$$

SA+UF uses uninterpreted sorts instead of bitvectors (indicated by ⁻), and converts data operations (e.g. $<$, $+$) to UFs (e.g. LT, ADD) and ground terms to UFs with 0-arity.

4   IC3 with Syntax-Guided Abstraction (IC3+SA)

IC3+SA uses SMT solving to raise reasoning from propositional to FOL, similar in spirit to [19–21,34,40]. The IC3+SA algorithm performs the core IC3 procedure in the syntactically-abstracted state space and tightens the abstraction using a typical CEGAR loop [22,37]. There are 2 key differences between IC3+SA and bit-level IC3.

- How to **generalize a satisfiable query** from a particular solver solution?
- How to **refine** spurious counterexamples?

Most other concepts in IC3 remain identical to the bit level and can be equivalently applied in IC3+SA using word-level clauses and SMT solvers (as elaborated in [11,19,40]).

4.1   Generalization of a Satisfiable Query

Consider a 1-step reachability query from frame m to a destination cube c (i.e. $SAT\ ?\ [F_m \wedge T \wedge c']$). If the query is satisfiable, it is essential for performance to *generalize* the particular solution returned by the solver into a generalized cube c_m (as indicated in [11,13,25]). For the propositional case, the authors of [25] suggest *ternary simulation* to generalize the particular solution into a cube. This generalization (as well as cube generalization suggested in the original IC3 algorithm [13]) ensures *strict continuity*.

Definition 1 *(Strict Continuity).*   *Given a destination cube c, every state in the generalized cube c_m should have a transition under T to the destination cube c, i.e. $\forall_s\ SAT\ ?\ [s \wedge T \wedge c']$ is satisfiable, where $\{s \in c_m \mid s$ is a state $\}$.*

Strict continuity is not necessary for IC3, though it is sufficient to guarantee "relaxed" *continuity*.

Definition 2 *(Continuity).*   *Given a sequence of cubes $\mathcal{C} = \langle c_m, \ldots, c_n \rangle$ with $c_n = \neg P$, there exists a path $\pi = \langle s_m, \ldots, s_n \rangle$ such that $\{s_i \in c_i \mid s_i$ is a state $\}$ for all $i \in \{m, \ldots, n\}$.*

For correctness, the necessary condition for any cube generalization procedure is to ensure *continuity* (Definition 2), i.e. there should exist a path from the generalized cube c_m to $\neg P$. After all, any cube with a continuous path to a bad state (i.e. a state satisfying $\neg P$) needs to be checked for reachability from the initial states.

It is unclear how to extend ternary simulation to word-level semantics, since ternary simulation inherently relies on modeling the system as a boolean circuit. Instead, we use a *syntax-guided* generalization technique that exploits the word-level structure of the problem to *cheaply* generalize a particular abstract solution. The procedure exploits structural *cone-of-influence* (COI) and model-based justification to identify *relevant* portions that are sufficient to *justify* the particular solution (similar to justification in test pattern generation [47]), and creates a projection set with relevant symbols. The particular solution is projected on these relevant symbols to get the generalized cube.

Algorithm 1 presents the syntax-guided generalization procedure using COI with model-based justification. Given the particular abstract solution $\hat{s}$ and the destination cube c', the procedure traverses the *concrete* structural COI of c' and collects symbols encountered in the process (line 3, 7–25). The key idea is that during the traversal we can syntactically prune away portions that are

Algorithm 1. Syntax-guided Generalization

1. **procedure** GENERALIZE($\hat{s}$, c')▷ $\hat{s}$ is a particular abstract solution. c' is a destination cube
2. $\quad \sigma \leftarrow \sigma_{refine}$ ▷ initialize projection set (initially $\sigma_{refine} = \emptyset$)
3. $\quad$ JustifyCOI($\hat{s}$, c', σ) ▷ build projection set σ
4. $\quad \sigma \leftarrow \sigma - X'$ ▷ get rid of next state symbols
5. $\quad \hat{s}|_\sigma \leftarrow$ Project($\hat{s}$, σ) ▷ project $\hat{s}$ on σ
6. $\quad$ **return** $cube(\hat{s}|_\sigma)$ ▷ convert to a cube and return

7. **procedure** JUSTIFYCOI($\hat{s}$, φ, σ) ▷ φ is a FOL expression, σ is passed by reference
8. $\quad$ **if** φ is a conditional operation **then** ▷ if φ is an if-then-else expression
9. $\quad\quad \langle cond, v_\top, v_\bot \rangle \leftarrow$ BreakCondition(φ) ▷ get condition and arguments
10. $\quad\quad$ JustifyCOI($\hat{s}$, $cond$, σ)
11. $\quad\quad val \leftarrow$ Evaluate($cond$, $\hat{s}$) ▷ evaluate $cond$ under $\hat{s}$
12. $\quad\quad$ JustifyCOI($\hat{s}$, ($val = \top$) ? $v_\top$: $v_\bot$, σ) ▷ recurse only on the relevant branch
13. $\quad$ **else if** φ is a logical operation **then**
14. $\quad\quad val \leftarrow$ Evaluate(φ, $\hat{s}$) ▷ evaluate φ under $\hat{s}$
15. $\quad\quad$ **if** IsControlling(val, φ) **then** ▷ if assigned a controlling value ($\bot$ for $\wedge$, $\top$ for $\vee$)
16. $\quad\quad\quad$ JustifyCOI($\hat{s}$, GetControlling(φ, $\hat{s}$), σ) ▷ recurse only on controlling arg.
17. $\quad\quad$ **else**
18. $\quad\quad\quad$ **for each** $a \in$ Argument(φ) **do**
19. $\quad\quad\quad\quad$ JustifyCOI($\hat{s}$, a, σ)
20. $\quad$ **else**
21. $\quad\quad$ **for each** $a \in$ Argument(φ) **do**
22. $\quad\quad\quad$ JustifyCOI($\hat{s}$, a, σ)
23. $\quad$ **if** φ is a next state variable **then**
24. $\quad\quad$ JustifyCOI($\hat{s}$, GetRelation(φ), σ) ▷ get the next state relation for φ from T
25. $\quad$ Add symbol(φ) to σ ▷ add symbol of φ to the projection set

not important under the given particular solution (lines 12, 16) and only visit portions that justify leading to the destination. Once the relevant symbols are collected, the algorithm projects $\hat{s}$ on these symbols to get the generalized cube (lines 5–6).

Algorithm 1 guarantees abstract continuity (Definition 2), with the generalized cube always having an abstract path to $\neg P$ in $\hat{\mathcal{P}}$. The algorithm however does not guarantee strict continuity (Definition 1), as evident from the following example:

Example 6: Let $\mathcal{P} = \langle \{u, v, w\}, (u = 1) \wedge (v = 1) \wedge (w = 1), (u' = ite((u < v) \vee (v < w), u + v, v + 1)) \wedge (v' = v + 1) \wedge (w' = w + 1), ((u + v) \neq 1)) \rangle$, with u, v, w being 3-bit wide. Consider the following query and its particular solution:

$$F_1 = P \qquad\qquad \varphi = F_1 \wedge T \wedge \neg P'$$

$$Q_1 := SAT \ ? \ [\varphi] \text{ gives SAT with solution } s$$

$$s = (u, v, w, u', v', w') = (0, 4, 2, 4, 5, 3) \qquad \hat{s} = \alpha(\varphi, s)$$

$$\hat{s} = (u < v) \wedge \neg(v < w) \wedge \{ \ u \mid 1, u' + v' \mid w \mid w + 1 \mid v, u + v, u' \mid v + 1, v' \ \}$$

Generalize($\hat{s}$, $\neg P'$) creates the generalized cube c_1 as follows:

$$\sigma = \{ \ +, u', v', 1, <, u, v \ \} - \{ \ u', v', w' \ \}$$
$$= \{ \ +, <, u, v, 1 \ \}$$
$$c_1 = cube(\hat{s}|_\sigma) = (u < v) \wedge \{ \ u \mid 1 \mid v, u + v \mid v + 1 \ \}$$

On careful analysis one can see that not all abstract states in c_1 have an abstract transition to the destination $(\neg P')$. For example, consider the abstract state $\hat{a}_1 = (u < v) \wedge \neg(v < w) \wedge \{\, u \mid 1, w \mid v, u + v, w + 1 \mid v + 1 \,\}$. $\hat{a}_1$ is an abstract state in the cube c_1, but it does not have a transition under T to any destination state, i.e. $SAT\ ?\ [cube(\hat{a}_1) \wedge T \wedge \neg P']$ is UNSAT.

We believe *non-determinism* in the word-level abstract domain is the reason why Algorithm 1 does not follow strict continuity. Even though Definition 1 is violated, Algorithm 1 still guarantees continuity (Definition 2) in the abstract domain. This is because the `Generalize` algorithm ensures that all terms in $\hat{\mathcal{P}}$ that are required to lead to the destination c' under the particular abstract solution $\hat{s}$ are retained in the generalized cube $cube(\hat{s}|_\sigma)$ as is from $\hat{s}$. As a result, even though $cube(\hat{s}|_\sigma)$ has abstract states that do not have an abstract transition to the destination c', this cannot result in an abstract path discontinuity while still limiting to terms in $\hat{\mathcal{P}}$. The `Generalize` procedure acts as a quick sweeper that removes irrelevant terms that will never get involved with any query that satisfies $cube(\hat{s}|_\sigma) \wedge T \wedge c'$, and encodes the sufficient information using the relevant symbols in $cube(\hat{s}|_\sigma)$.

The proposed generalization procedure has the following advantages:

- In contrast to solver-based methods suggested in [11,18,34], syntax-based generalization is inexpensive since it does not required any solver query.
- Since the generalization is driven from the syntactic cone of the destination, the procedure only captures the relevant information leading to a bad state.
- The technique guarantees continuity with no need for *lifting refinement* [11].
- Unlike [39,40], the technique does not use weakest preconditions (WP) for generalization, which can be regarded as implicitly unrolling the transition relation. WP-based techniques generate new terms through function compositions, which complicates the abstract state space and can often cascade to cause incompleteness and poor SMT solving.

Syntax-based generalization offers an inexpensive and effective procedure to expand a single solver solution to a set of solutions for word-level IC3. An identical generalization procedure can be used for SA+UF and possibly even for PA.

4.2   Refinement

Running IC3 in the abstract domain either generates an inductive invariant that proves the property to be true, or produces an abstract counterexample evidence $\mathcal{C}$. An abstract counterexample $\mathcal{C}$ of length $n + 1$ is represented by a sequence of $n + 1$ abstract cubes $\langle c_0, c_1, c_2, \ldots, c_n \rangle$, where $c_n = \neg P$.

We concretize $\mathcal{C}$ by restoring the interpretation to $\mathcal{I}_B$, i.e. exact bitvector assignments. $\mathcal{C}$ can be spurious when the terms in the original problem are insufficient to express the bit-precise nature of the concrete problem.

One way to identify spurious behavior in $\mathcal{C}$ is by checking the satisfiability of a single concrete path query along $\mathcal{C}$ with explicit unrolling, i.e. $SAT\ ?$

$[I \wedge (\bigwedge_{i=0}^{n-1} c_i^i \wedge T^i) \wedge c_n^n]$ (where φ^i denotes the formula φ at i^{th} transition step) using QF_BV SMT solving. Checking satisfiability of such a query with multiple copies of T is not scalable in practice as the length of C increases. We instead perform *incremental* refinement *along the counterexample* (Algorithm 2) which uses 1-step queries to perform *forward image computation* [29] along C. We formulate at most n queries $Q_i := SAT ? [p_{i-1} \wedge c_{i-1} \wedge T \wedge c_i']$ $(1 \leq i \leq n)$ such that $p_0 = I$, and p_i equals the *symbolic post image* [29,42] of $p_{i-1} \wedge c_{i-1}$ under the solution of the query Q_i. To compute p_i after a satisfiable query Q_i (say with solution s), we use fresh symbolic constants to replace unconstrained variables at that step and *syntactically* evaluate T under s to get the symbolic post image of $p_{i-1} \wedge c_{i-1}$ for the next step (line 6). This generates new terms and results in an *implicit* unrolling of T, which in practice is simpler compared to explicit unrolling. We check for the satisfiability of Q_i in increasing order (from $i = 1$ to n) and stop as soon as a query is found unsatisfiable (lines 3–14). From the unsatisfiable query, we extract a minimal unsatisfiable subset [41,45] (MUS) m and get rid of any symbolic constant in m using substitution or rarely instantiation using last solver assigned value if substitution is not possible (lines 8–9). Since the unsatisfiability is due to a concrete *path infeasiblity*, m necessarily contains constraints from the forward image computation that include new terms generated from substitution. These new terms are important to eliminate the spurious counterexample. We add these newly discovered terms to the abstract domain by deriving a *refinement (path) axiom* by negating m (line 10). We refine the abstract problem $\hat{\mathcal{P}}$ by conjoining the refinement axiom to the transition relation T (line 11).

Algorithm 2. Refinement of SA

---
1. **procedure** REFINE(C)
2. $p_0 \leftarrow I$
3.   **for** $i = 1$ to n **do**
4. $\psi_i \leftarrow p_{i-1} \wedge c_{i-1} \wedge T \wedge c_i'$
5.   **if** SAT ? $[\psi_i]$: solution s **then**
6. $p_i \leftarrow$ PostImage($p_{i-1} \wedge c_{i-1}, s$)   ▷ compute image($p_{i-1} \wedge c_{i-1}$) under s
7.   **else**   ▷ i.e. C is spurious
8. $m \leftarrow$ MUS(ψ_i)   ▷ find MUS for the UNSAT query
9. $m \leftarrow$ Substitute(m)   ▷ eliminate symbolic constants
10. $\Phi \leftarrow \neg m$
11. $T \leftarrow T \wedge \Phi$ ▷ conjoin axiom to $\hat{T}$
12. $\sigma_{new} \leftarrow$ symbols(NewTerms(Φ))   ▷ find symbols in new terms
13. $\sigma_{refine} \leftarrow \sigma_{refine} \cup \sigma_{new}$ ▷ add permanent symbols
14.   **return** $\emptyset$
15.   **return** C ▷ i.e. C is a true counterexample

New terms created are crucial to eliminate spurious counterexamples. They were absent in the original problem and hence the abstract domain wasn't expressive enough to capture infeasibilities involving them. Adding the refinement axiom with these new terms automatically augments the abstract problem and makes them part of future iterations of IC3+SA. We add the symbols in the new terms as permanent members of all projection sets computed using Algorithm 1 so as to ensure that future iterations of Generalize doesn't ambitiously generalize them away (lines 12–13). This is essential since these new terms are not part of the original problem syntax but are required to eliminate spurious counterexamples.

If all queries Q_i are satisfiable, it means that $\mathcal{C}$ is indeed including true counterexample(s) that disprove the property. One instance of a true counterexample can be easily retrieved by keeping tracking of solutions to the queries Q_i.

After learning a refinement axiom, IC3+SA *incrementally* resumes the abstract IC3 procedure from the last top frame. Since the abstraction refinement procedure is completely *monotonic* with each iteration making the abstract domain more precise and finer by adding new terms, we can reuse all of the reachability information and abstract clauses from previous iterations.

The refinement procedure provides the following advantages:

- All concrete queries involve a single instance of the transition relation and avoids explicit unrolling.
- There is no path explosion since the refinement is constrained to the paths along the abstract counterexample.
- Symbolic constants for unconstrained variables allow avoiding enumerative simulation on exact variable assignments returned by the solver.
- The procedure is completely incremental and allows reuse of all previous abstract clause learning.

SA + UF: Data abstraction using UF can introduce additional spurious behavior with inconsistencies resulting from the usage of UF instead of concrete data operations. Given $\mathcal{C} = \langle c_0, \ldots, c_n \rangle$, we can check for such inconsistencies using at most n concrete queries $Q_i := SAT\ ?\ [c_{i-1} \wedge T \wedge c_i']\ (0 < i \leq n)$ in any order (similar to [40]). In the case any query returns UNSAT, we can learn a *refinement (data) axiom* to constrain T. Data axioms will never add any new term and therefore will never increase the size of the abstract state space. They eliminate spurious abstract states/transitions that got introduced due to data abstraction, while path axioms add more granularity.

5   Proof of Correctness

Inspired from [13, 20, 25], we list the properties on frames preserved by IC3+SA.

(p1) $F_0 = I$ (p2) $F_i \rightarrow P$
(p3) The clauses F_{i+1} is a subset of F_i for $i > 0$ (p4) $F_i \rightarrow F_{i+1}$
(p5) F_{i+1} is an over-approximation of the image of F_i

(p1-5) are true and preserved by the IC3 algorithm [13, 25]. After a refinement iteration, all frame clauses remain valid since the refinement procedure (Algorithm 2) is monotonic with respect to the terms describing the abstract state space. After each refinement iteration $T_{new} \models T$, implying $F_{new} \models F$, preserving (p1-5).

Lemma 1 *(Correctness).* *If IC3+SA($\mathcal{P}$) returns an invariant Φ, then Φ is inductive and $\Phi \rightarrow P$ under $\mathcal{P}$.*

Proof. From the IC3 algorithm, let F_{conv} be the frame that reached the fixed point (i.e. $F_{conv} = F_{conv+1}$). Let $\Phi = F_{conv}$. Due to (p5) and (p2), Φ is inductive and $\Phi \rightarrow P$.

Lemma 2 *(Correctness).* *If IC3+SA($\mathcal{P}$) returns a counterexample $\mathcal{C}$, then $\mathcal{C}$ has a path under T starting from I and violating P.*

Proof. Let $\mathcal{C} = \langle c_0, \ldots, c_n \rangle$. By construction, $c_n = \neg P$. From Sect. 4.1, $\mathcal{C}$ is abstractly continuous. The refinement procedure (Algorithm 2) will return $\mathcal{C}$ iff $(I \wedge \left(\bigwedge_{i=0}^{n-1} c_i^i \wedge T^i \right) \wedge c_n^n)$ is satisfiable, implying $\mathcal{C}$ is concretely continuous and a true counterexample.

Lemma 3 *(Termination).* *IC3+SA($\mathcal{P}$) will eventually terminate.*

Proof. For a given abstract problem $\hat{\mathcal{P}}$, the IC3 algorithm will eventually terminate since all abstract queries are decidable, the number of abstract states is finite, and the maximum number of frames is bounded by the number of abstract states (due to (p2-5)). Each refinement iteration introduces new term(s) making the abstract state space more precise with respect to the concrete state space. The number of new terms that can be added is limited by the sequential depth of the concrete problem $\mathcal{P}$ (which is finite), making the number of refinement iterations finite. Hence, IC3+SA will eventually terminate.

Theorem 1. *IC3+SA($\mathcal{P}$) is sound and complete.*

Proof. From Lemmas 1, 2 and 3, IC3+SA is sound and complete.

6 Implementation and Evaluation

We implemented IC3+SA in C++ in the Averroes system [40]. We made a complete rewrite to the frontend and backend of Averroes, with a primary focus on model checking of Verilog RTL. The new version [26] (Averroes 2, or *avr* in short) uses *yosys* [51] as the preprocessor frontend to allow direct translation of Verilog RTL and SystemVerilog assertions (SVA) into a word-level model checking problem. *yosys* parses the Verilog RTL, removes any hierarchy, and exports the flat word-level design to *avr* in the .ilang format[2]. *avr* uses Yices 2 [24] (version 2.6) for solving abstract SMT queries and Z3 [23] (version 2.5) for concrete SMT queries.

---

[2] .ilang is a format for textual representation of the *yosys*'s design.

Setup: We analyzed a total of 535 invariant checking problems (Verilog RTL files with SVA) that can be classified as follows:

- *opensource*: a set of 141 problems collected from benchmark suites accompanying tools *vcegar* [36] (#23), *v2c* [44] (#32) and *verilog2smv* [35] (#86). Problems include cores from picoJava, USB 1.1, CRC generation, Huffman coding, mutual exclusion algorithms, simple microprocessor, etc.
- *industry*: a set of 370 problems collected from industrial collaborators[3]. Of these, 124 were categorized as *easy* (code sizes between 155 and 761 lines; # of flip-flops between 514 and 931), and 235 as *challenging* (code sizes between 109 and 22065 lines; # of flip-flops between 6 and 7249). The remaining 11 problems involved sequential equivalence checking on a multiplier design before and after clock gating optimization.
- *crafted*: a set of 24 simple problems synthetically created for calibration (includes both control- and data-centric problems).

We compared the following techniques:
From ABC version 1.01 [8]:

- *pdr:* *pdr* is one of the best implementations of the bit-level IC3 algorithm.
- *dprove:* *dprove* employs a preprocessing stage using a portfolio of techniques (BMC [9], retiming, fraiging, simulation, interpolation, etc.) with carefully-tuned heuristics to quickly solve/reduce the problem. If the problem remains unsolved, *dprove* invokes *pdr* on the reduced problem.
- *pdr-nct:* the -nct flags configure *pdr* to use better generalization [30] and enable *localization* abstraction [33].

From nuXmv version 1.1.1 [17]:

- *nuxmv-ic3ia*: a word-level IC3 implementation in nuXmv using implicit predicate abstraction [20].

From *Averroes* version 2.0 [26]:

- *avr-ic3sa*: IC3+SA i.e. IC3 with syntax-guided abstraction.
- *avr-ic3sa-uf*: IC3+SA+UF i.e. IC3+SA with data abstraction using UF.

For comparison against bit-level IC3, we chose implementations from ABC since these have shown exceptional performance in HWMCC [10]. We also considered including other abstraction based IC3 techniques like *L-IC3* [48], *UFAR* [31] and *PDR-WLA* [32]. However, *PDR-WLA* was not able to process the designs due to input format issues, while *L-IC3* and *UFAR* do not have, to the best of our knowledge, a publicly available implementation. Techniques like [11,12,34,38] do not have implementations that can handle hardware designs.

We used *yosys* [51] as the common frontend. The Verilog designs and SVA were parsed by *yosys*, which removes any hierarchy and produces flat RTL

---

[3] We obtained these designs under non-disclosure agreements and, unfortunately, cannot make them publicly available.

Verilog. For *nuxmv-ic3ia* and *avr-**, the flat word-level format is syntactically exported by *yosys* into the equivalent word-level input formats used by these tools. Since ABC based tools cannot exploit word-level information and operate at the bit level, we used *yosys* to *synthesize* the flat RTL to an And-Inverter Graph (AIG) and exported to ABC in .blif format. All experiments were conducted on a cluster of 163 2.5 GHz Intel Xeon E5-2680v3 processors (cores) running 64-bit Linux. Each verification run was given exclusive access to a single core, with a memory limit of 16 GB and a time limit of 5 h.

6.1   Results

Even though experimental evaluations are necessarily biased by the suite of problems used, we nonetheless believe that useful insights can still be gained from a careful analysis of the results. The raw data along with detailed benchmark statistics and plots along with *opensource* and *crafted* benchmarks can be retrieved from a publicly-accessible repository [1]. The three tool packages used ABC, nuXmv and Averroes 2 are publicly available from [2,3] and [26] respectively.

The reader is referred to [27] for a summary on the performance of *avr-ic3sa-uf*, which demonstrates the effectiveness of IC3+SA with data abstraction. Here, we provide an in-depth analysis compared to *avr-ic3sa* to better understand the strengths and weaknesses of SA and SA+UF.

Aggregate Results: Table 2 and Fig. 1 provide an overview on the performance of each tool. Overall, techniques from ABC, nuXmv and Averroes 2 solved 480,

Table 2. Number of problems solved. TO: timed out, MO: out of memory, Unique: solved uniquely (not solved by others), IN: *industry*, OS: *opensource*, CR: *crafted*

Tool	Solved (535)	TO	MO	Error	Unique	IN (370)	OS (141)	CR (24)
pdr	466	69	**0**	**0**	1	308	137	21
dprove	477	57	**0**	1	3	315	**138**	**24**
pdr-nct	466	68	1	**0**	1	308	137	21
nuxmv-ic3ia	389	92	46	8	0	232	133	**24**
avr-ic3sa	461	69	5	**0**	0	302	135	**24**
avr-ic3sa-uf	**526**	**0**	9	**0**	**52**	**368**	134	**24**

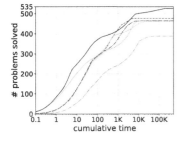
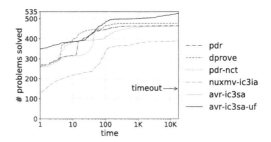

Fig. 1. Survival plot comparing the number of problems solved versus time

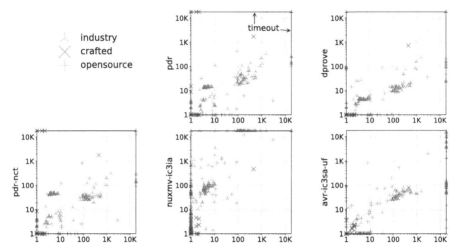

Fig. 2. *avr-ic3sa* runtime comparisons. *avr-ic3sa*'s times are better (resp. worse) above (resp. below) the diagonal.

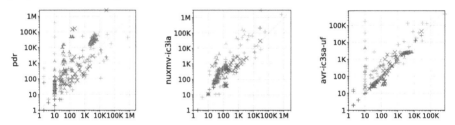

Fig. 3. Number of solver calls (SAT solver calls for *pdr*, SMT solver calls for others)

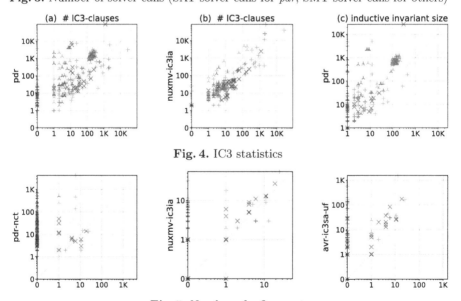

Fig. 4. IC3 statistics

Fig. 5. Number of refinements

avr-ic3sa is always on x-axis. All plots exclude runs in which a tool reported an error or ran out of memory, and all runtime refer to CPU time in seconds.

389 and 527 problems respectively in total. IC3+SA with data abstraction (*avr-ic3sa-uf*) performed the best, particularly in the *industry* category. The performance of *avr-ic3sa* is competitive to ABC tools even though ABC tools have a highly tuned and efficient implementation developed over years of innovation.

Runtime Comparison: Figure 2 compares *avr-ic3sa*'s runtime against other tools. ABC tools marginally dominated *avr-ic3sa*, though there is a significant number where *avr-ic3sa* performed better. Bit-level techniques enjoy the advancements in hardware synthesis that can significantly reduce the complexity in the synthesized design, though they loose this advantage for larger and complex designs. Compared to *nuxmv-ic3ia*, *avr-ic3sa* shows good benefits and demonstrates the benefits of SA over implicit predicate abstraction [20]. Data abstraction helps *avr-ic3sa-uf* to outperform *avr-ic3sa* in the *industry* category (where the property is control intensive), while *avr-ic3sa* is better in the data-dependent *opensource* category.

Solver Calls: Figure 3 shows the comparison of the total number of solver calls. Bit-level IC3 (represented by *pdr*) makes orders-of-magnitude more SAT solver calls compared to the number of SMT calls made by word-level tools. Even with many more solver calls, bit-level techniques are competitive to word-level techniques w.r.t. runtime (Fig. 2), indicating the advancement gap between SAT versus SMT solving. Structural cube generalization and syntax-guided abstraction allows *avr-ic3sa* to require fewer solver calls than *nuxmv-ic3ia*. The large number of solver calls made by *avr-ic3sa-uf* compared to *avr-ic3sa* in the *opensource* category reflects the importance of correct abstraction procedure and suggests possible benefits from a hybrid abstraction on a subset of data operations that can tune automatically based on the nature of the property.

Clause Learning: Figure 4a–b compares the number of frame clauses derived by *avr-ic3sa* versus *pdr* and *nuxmv-ic3ia*. *avr-ic3sa* requires orders-of-magnitude fewer clauses compared to *pdr*, showing the benefits of word-level clause learning as against weak propositional learning. Fewer frame clauses derived by *avr-ic3sa* as compared to *nuxmv-ic3ia* reflects that SA is better in capturing the important details of the problem compared to implicit predicate abstraction.

Number of Refinements: Figure 5 shows the comparison of the number of refinements required for the techniques that use an abstraction refinement procedure (*pdr-nct, nuxmv-ic3sa, avr-***). The number of refinements required by *avr-ic3sa* is the least compared to all others, demonstrating the effectiveness of syntax-guided abstraction. As expected, *avr-ic3sa-uf* has to undergo several refinement iterations for the data-dependent *opensource* category.

Invariant Size: Model checking on Verilog RTL instead of post-synthesis netlist has the additional benefit of producing human-readable word-level inductive invariants. *avr-ic3sa* produces a concise and informative word-level inductive invariant with much fewer clauses than one produced by *pdr* (Fig. 4c).

7   Related Work

Several approaches from different domains have been suggested to extend the bit-level IC3 procedure. From the hardware domain, the authors of [48] suggest *lazy abstraction* using "visible variables". The authors of [31] use UF to abstract away expensive data operations, followed by bit-blasting. The authors of [32] use unconstrained new primary inputs to abstract away parts of the system. The authors of [33] suggest using *localization abstraction* to cut away irrelevant logic. All these approaches [31–33,48] use bit-level IC3 as the core engine and suffer with the same scalability issues as with bit-level IC3.

Certain approaches propose performing word-level IC3 using SMT solvers. The authors in [50] generalize IC3 to the theory of bitvectors by using *polytopes* and interval simulation. The authors of [39,40] suggest performing word-level IC3 with data abstraction using uninterpreted functions.

Beyond hardware, different approaches propose to lift the IC3 procedure to richer logics and infinite state systems [11,12,19,34,38]. Our approach differ significantly from these techniques as IC3+SA does not rely on theory specific under-approximation of the pre-image, quantifier elimination, weakest preconditions or interpolation. The authors of [20,21] suggest using *implicit predicate abstraction* that performs a word-level IC3 procedure (IC3IA), and refines the abstraction by adding new predicates. Our approach is partly similar to IC3IA, but with better granularity and expressiveness resulting in fewer occurrences of spurious behavior. We also suggest an inexpensive syntax-driven cube generalization procedure for word-level IC3, along with a fully incremental refinement procedure without using multiple copies of the transition relation. Unlike CTI-GAR [11], our cube generalization technique does not require any *lifting* solver query to eliminate non-essential symbols and still guarantees continuity.

Data abstraction using UF has been applied for both hardware [4,15,39,40] and software [5]. IC3+SA allows for an easy and scalable extension to data abstraction, and unlike [39,40], it does not face non-termination issues.

8   Conclusions and Future Work

Syntax-guided abstraction suggests an alternative way to raise bit-level IC3 procedure to the word level. SA is implicitly defined by the terms in the syntax of the problem and offers high granularity. We demonstrate how to integrate IC3 with SA efficiently, and propose a word-level structural cube generalization procedure without any need for additional solver queries or unrolling. We show the correctness of the technique and evaluate the effectiveness of the approach on a suite of open-source and industrial hardware problems.

Future work include extending SA to theories beyond bitvector, adding hybrid data abstraction on a subset of data operations, and performing a rigorous analysis against other model checking tools including techniques beyond IC3.

Acknowledgement. We would like to thank the reviewers for their valuable comments. The authors thank developers of Yosys [51], Yices 2 [24] and Z3 [23] for making their tools openly available. The authors thank Alberto Griggio for providing a custom version of nuXmv with detailed statistics output.

References

1. https://github.com/aman-goel/nfm2019exp
2. ABC: System for Sequential Logic Synthesis and Formal Verification. https://github.com/berkeley-abc/abc
3. The nuXmv model checker. https://nuxmv.fbk.eu
4. Andraus, Z.S., Liffiton, M.H., Sakallah, K.A.: Reveal: a formal verification tool for Verilog designs. In: Cervesato, I., Veith, H., Voronkov, A. (eds.) LPAR 2008. LNCS (LNAI), vol. 5330, pp. 343–352. Springer, Heidelberg (2008). https://doi.org/10.1007/978-3-540-89439-1_25
5. Babić, D., Hu, A.J.: Structural abstraction of software verification conditions. In: Damm, W., Hermanns, H. (eds.) CAV 2007. LNCS, vol. 4590, pp. 366–378. Springer, Heidelberg (2007). https://doi.org/10.1007/978-3-540-73368-3_41
6. Ball, T., Podelski, A., Rajamani, S.K.: Boolean and cartesian abstraction for model checking C programs. In: Margaria, T., Yi, W. (eds.) TACAS 2001. LNCS, vol. 2031, pp. 268–283. Springer, Heidelberg (2001). https://doi.org/10.1007/3-540-45319-9_19
7. Barrett, C., Fontaine, P., Tinelli, C.: The Satisfiability Modulo Theories Library (SMT-LIB) (2016). www.SMT-LIB.org
8. Berkeley Logic Synthesis and Verification Group: ABC: A system for sequential synthesis and verification (2017). http://www.eecs.berkeley.edu/~alanmi/abc/
9. Biere, A., Cimatti, A., Clarke, E.M., Strichman, O., Zhu, Y., et al.: Bounded model checking. Adv. Comput. **58**(11), 117–148 (2003)
10. Biere, A., van Dijk, T., Heljanko, K.: Hardware model checking competition 2017. In: FMCAD, p. 9 (2017)
11. Birgmeier, J., Bradley, A.R., Weissenbacher, G.: Counterexample to induction-guided abstraction-refinement (CTIGAR). In: Biere, A., Bloem, R. (eds.) CAV 2014. LNCS, vol. 8559, pp. 831–848. Springer, Cham (2014). https://doi.org/10.1007/978-3-319-08867-9_55
12. Bjørner, N., Gurfinkel, A.: Property directed polyhedral abstraction. In: D'Souza, D., Lal, A., Larsen, K.G. (eds.) VMCAI 2015. LNCS, vol. 8931, pp. 263–281. Springer, Heidelberg (2015). https://doi.org/10.1007/978-3-662-46081-8_15
13. Bradley, A.R.: SAT-based model checking without unrolling. In: Jhala, R., Schmidt, D. (eds.) VMCAI 2011. LNCS, vol. 6538, pp. 70–87. Springer, Heidelberg (2011). https://doi.org/10.1007/978-3-642-18275-4_7
14. Bradley, A.R., Somenzi, F., Hassan, Z.: IIMC: incremental inductive model checker. http://www.github.com/mgudemann/iimc
15. Burch, J.R., Dill, D.L.: Automatic verification of pipelined microprocessor control. In: Dill, D.L. (ed.) CAV 1994. LNCS, vol. 818, pp. 68–80. Springer, Heidelberg (1994). https://doi.org/10.1007/3-540-58179-0_44
16. Cabodi, G., Nocco, S., Quer, S.: The PdTRAV tool. http://fmgroup.polito.it/index.php/download/viewcategory/3-pdtrav-package
17. Cavada, R., et al.: The NUXMV symbolic model checker. In: Biere, A., Bloem, R. (eds.) CAV 2014. LNCS, vol. 8559, pp. 334–342. Springer, Cham (2014). https://doi.org/10.1007/978-3-319-08867-9_22

18. Chockler, H., Ivrii, A., Matsliah, A., Moran, S., Nevo, Z.: Incremental formal verification of hardware. In: Proceedings of the International Conference on Formal Methods in Computer-Aided Design, pp. 135–143. FMCAD Inc. (2011)
19. Cimatti, A., Griggio, A.: Software model checking via IC3. In: Madhusudan, P., Seshia, S.A. (eds.) CAV 2012. LNCS, vol. 7358, pp. 277–293. Springer, Heidelberg (2012). https://doi.org/10.1007/978-3-642-31424-7_23
20. Cimatti, A., Griggio, A., Mover, S., Tonetta, S.: IC3 modulo theories via implicit predicate abstraction. In: Ábrahám, E., Havelund, K. (eds.) TACAS 2014. LNCS, vol. 8413, pp. 46–61. Springer, Heidelberg (2014). https://doi.org/10.1007/978-3-642-54862-8_4
21. Cimatti, A., Griggio, A., Mover, S., Tonetta, S.: Infinite-state invariant checking with IC3 and predicate abstraction. Formal Methods Syst. Des. **49**(3), 190–218 (2016)
22. Clarke, E., Grumberg, O., Jha, S., Lu, Y., Veith, H.: Counterexample-guided abstraction refinement. In: Emerson, E.A., Sistla, A.P. (eds.) CAV 2000. LNCS, vol. 1855, pp. 154–169. Springer, Heidelberg (2000). https://doi.org/10.1007/10722167_15
23. de Moura, L., Bjørner, N.: Z3: an efficient SMT solver. In: Ramakrishnan, C.R., Rehof, J. (eds.) TACAS 2008. LNCS, vol. 4963, pp. 337–340. Springer, Heidelberg (2008). https://doi.org/10.1007/978-3-540-78800-3_24
24. Dutertre, B.: Yices 2.2. In: Biere, A., Bloem, R. (eds.) CAV 2014. LNCS, vol. 8559, pp. 737–744. Springer, Cham (2014). https://doi.org/10.1007/978-3-319-08867-9_49
25. Een, N., Mishchenko, A., Brayton, R.: Efficient implementation of property directed reachability. In: FMCAD, pp. 125–134 (2011)
26. Goel, A., Sakallah, K.: Averroes 2. http://www.github.com/aman-goel/avr
27. Goel, A., Sakallah, K.: Empirical evaluation of IC3-based model checking techniques on Verilog RTL designs. In: Proceedings of the Conference on Design, Automation and Test in Europe. EDA Consortium (2019)
28. Graf, S., Saïdi, H.: Construction of abstract state graphs with PVS. In: Grumberg, O. (ed.) CAV 1997. LNCS, vol. 1254, pp. 72–83. Springer, Heidelberg (1997). https://doi.org/10.1007/3-540-63166-6_10
29. Gupta, A., Yang, Z., Ashar, P., Gupta, A.: SAT-based image computation with application in reachability analysis. In: Hunt, W.A., Johnson, S.D. (eds.) FMCAD 2000. LNCS, vol. 1954, pp. 391–408. Springer, Heidelberg (2000). https://doi.org/10.1007/3-540-40922-X_22
30. Hassan, Z., Bradley, A.R., Somenzi, F.: Better generalization in IC3. In: FMCAD, pp. 157–164 (2013)
31. Ho, Y.S., Chauhan, P., Roy, P., Mishchenko, A., Brayton, R.: Efficient uninterpreted function abstraction and refinement for word-level model checking. In: FMCAD, pp. 65–72 (2016)
32. Ho, Y.S., Mishchenko, A., Brayton, R.: Property directed reachability with word-level abstraction. In: FMCAD, pp. 132–139 (2017)
33. Ho, Y.S., Mishchenko, A., Brayton, R., Eén, N.: Enhancing PDR/IC3 with localization abstraction (2017)
34. Hoder, K., Bjørner, N.: Generalized property directed reachability. In: Cimatti, A., Sebastiani, R. (eds.) SAT 2012. LNCS, vol. 7317, pp. 157–171. Springer, Heidelberg (2012). https://doi.org/10.1007/978-3-642-31612-8_13
35. Irfan, A., Cimatti, A., Griggio, A., Roveri, M., Sebastiani, R.: Verilog2SMV: a tool for word-level verification. In: Proceedings of the 2016 Conference on Design, Automation & Test in Europe, pp. 1156–1159. EDA Consortium (2016)

36. Jain, H., Kroening, D., Sharygina, N., Clarke, E.: VCEGAR: Verilog CounterEx-ample guided abstraction refinement. In: Grumberg, O., Huth, M. (eds.) TACAS 2007. LNCS, vol. 4424, pp. 583–586. Springer, Heidelberg (2007). https://doi.org/10.1007/978-3-540-71209-1_45
37. Kurshan, R.P.: Computer-aided verification of coordinating processes. Princeton series in computer science (1994)
38. Lange, T., Neuhäußer, M.R., Noll, T.: IC3 software model checking on control flow automata. In: Proceedings of the 15th Conference on Formal Methods in Computer-Aided Design, pp. 97–104. FMCAD Inc. (2015)
39. Lee, S.: Unbounded scalable hardware verification (2016)
40. Lee, S., Sakallah, K.A.: Unbounded scalable verification based on approximate property-directed reachability and datapath abstraction. In: CAV, pp. 849–865 (2014)
41. Liffiton, M.H., Sakallah, K.A.: Algorithms for computing minimal unsatisfiable subsets of constraints. J. Automated Reasoning **40**(1), 1–33 (2008)
42. McMillan, K.L.: Applications of craig interpolants in model checking. In: Halbwachs, N., Zuck, L.D. (eds.) TACAS 2005. LNCS, vol. 3440, pp. 1–12. Springer, Heidelberg (2005). https://doi.org/10.1007/978-3-540-31980-1_1
43. Mneimneh, M., Sakallah, K.: Sat-based sequential depth computation. In: Proceedings of the 2003 Asia and South Pacific Design Automation Conference, pp. 87–92. ACM (2003)
44. Mukherjee, R., Tautschnig, M., Kroening, D.: v2c – a Verilog to C translator. In: Chechik, M., Raskin, J.-F. (eds.) TACAS 2016. LNCS, vol. 9636, pp. 580–586. Springer, Heidelberg (2016). https://doi.org/10.1007/978-3-662-49674-9_38
45. Oh, Y., Mneimneh, M.N., Andraus, Z.S., Sakallah, K.A., Markov, I.L.: Amuse: a minimally-unsatisfiable subformula extractor. In: Proceedings of the 41st Annual Design Automation Conference, pp. 518–523. ACM (2004)
46. Rota, G.C.: The number of partitions of a set. Am. Math. Monthly **71**(5), 498–504 (1964)
47. Tafertshofer, P., Ganz, A.: Sat based ATPG using fast justification and propagation in the implication graph. In: Proceedings of the 1999 IEEE/ACM International Conference on Computer-Aided Design, pp. 139–146. IEEE Press (1999)
48. Vizel, Y., Grumberg, O., Shoham, S.: Lazy abstraction and sat-based reachability in hardware model checking. In: FMCAD, pp. 173–181 (2012)
49. Vizel, Y., Gurfinkel, A.: Interpolating property directed reachability. In: CAV, pp. 260–276 (2014)
50. Welp, T., Kuehlmann, A.: QF BV model checking with property directed reachability. In: Proceedings of the Conference on Design, Automation and Test in Europe, pp. 791–796. EDA Consortium (2013)
51. Wolf, C.: Yosys open synthesis suite. http://www.clifford.at/yosys/

Towards a Two-Layer Framework for Verifying Autonomous Vehicles

Rong Gu[✉], Raluca Marinescu, Cristina Seceleanu, and Kristina Lundqvist

Mälardalen University, Västerås, Sweden
{rong.gu,raluca.marinescu,cristina.seceleanu,kristina.lundqvist}@mdh.se

Abstract. Autonomous vehicles rely heavily on intelligent algorithms for path planning and collision avoidance, and their functionality and dependability can be ensured through formal verification. To facilitate the verification, it is beneficial to decouple the static high-level planning from the dynamic functions like collision avoidance. In this paper, we propose a conceptual two-layer framework for verifying autonomous vehicles, which consists of a static layer and a dynamic layer. We focus concretely on modeling and verifying the dynamic layer using hybrid automata and UPPAAL SMC, where a continuous movement of the vehicle as well as collision avoidance via a dipole flow field algorithm are considered. In our framework, decoupling is achieved by separating the verification of the vehicle's autonomous path planning from that of the vehicle autonomous operation in its continuous dynamic environment. To simplify the modeling process, we propose a pattern-based design method, where patterns are expressed as hybrid automata. We demonstrate the applicability of the dynamic layer of our framework on an industrial prototype of an autonomous wheel loader.

1 Introduction

Autonomous vehicles such as driverless construction equipment bear the promise of increased safety and industrial productivity by automating repetitive tasks and reducing labor costs. These systems are being used in safety- or mission-critical scenarios, which require thorough analysis and verification. Traditional approaches such as simulation and prototype testing are limited in their scope of verifying a system that interacts autonomously with an unpredictable environment that assumes the presence of humans and varying site conditions. These techniques are either applied later in the system's development cycle (testing), or they simply cannot prove, exhaustively or statistically, the satisfaction of properties related to autonomous behaviors such as path planning, path following, and collision avoidance (simulation). Formal verification is usually adopted to compensate such shortage, yet verifying such a complex system in a continuous and dynamic environment is still considered a big challenge [1,4].

In this paper, we approach this challenge by proposing a two-layer framework consisting of a *static* and a *dynamic* layer, which facilitates verifying autonomous vehicles. The structure of the framework separates the static high-level path

© Springer Nature Switzerland AG 2019
J. M. Badger and K. Y. Rozier (Eds.): NFM 2019, LNCS 11460, pp. 186–203, 2019.
https://doi.org/10.1007/978-3-030-20652-9_12

planning that assumes an environment with a predefined sequence of milestones that need to be reached, as well as static obstacles, from the dynamic functions like collision avoidance, thus providing a separation of concerns for the system's design, modeling, and verification. To improve on existing formal models of vehicle movement [17,26], in the dynamic layer, we propose a continuous model of the vehicle's motion, together with a model of the environment, where moving obstacles are either predefined or dynamically generated. The resulting models are hybrid automata, as accepted by the input language of UPPAAL Statistical Model Checker (SMC). The vehicle's dynamics is modeled as ordinary differential equations assigned to locations in the hybrid automata. In this paper, the hybrid automata only have non-deterministic time-bounded delays that are encoded based on the default uniform distributions assigned by UPPAAL SMC. We also consider the embedded control system of the autonomous vehicle including the involved processes, as well as the scheduling and communication among them. The path planning is following the Theta* algorithm [6], and the collision avoidance relies on the dipole flow field one [29]. Both algorithms are encoded as C-code functions in UPPAAL SMC, within the dynamic layer of our framework. Once this is accomplished, we can statistically model check the resulting network of hybrid automata, against probabilistic invariance properties expressed in weighted metric temporal logic [5]. To simplify the modeling process, we propose a pattern-based design method to provide reusable templates for various components of the framework. We demonstrate the applicability of our approach for modeling and analyzing the dynamic layer on an industrial autonomous wheel loader prototype that should meet certain safety-critical requirements.

This paper is organized as follows. In Sect. 2, we overview hybrid automata and UPPAAL SMC, as well as the Theta* algorithm for path planning, and the dipole flow field algorithm for collision avoidance. Section 3 describes the function of the autonomous wheel loader and its architecture. In Sect. 4, we present the conceptual two-layer framework, and in Sect. 5 we propose the pattern-based modeling of the components (of the dynamic layer) and their formal encoding. Next, we demonstrate the applicability of the framework on the autonomous wheel loader, and we present the verification results in Sect. 6. We compare to related work in Sect. 7, before concluding and outlining future lines of research in Sect. 8.

2   Preliminaries

In this section, we overview the background information needed for the rest of the paper, that is, hybrid automata and UPPAAL SMC, as well as the Theta* and dipole flow field algorithms.

2.1   Hybrid Automata and UPPAAL SMC

UPPAAL SMC [7] is an extension of the tool UPPAAL [21], which supports statistical model checking of hybrid automata (HA). A HA is defined as the following tuple:

$$HA = < L, l_0, X, \Sigma, E, F, I >, \tag{1}$$

where: L is a finite set of *locations*, $l_0 \in L$ is the *initial location*, X is a finite set of continuous variables, $\Sigma = \Sigma_i \uplus \Sigma_o$ is a finite set of actions that are partitioned into inputs (Σ_i) and outputs (Σ_o), E is a finite set of edges of the form (l, g, a, φ, l'), where l and l' are locations, g is a predicate on $\mathbb{R}^X$, $a \in \Sigma$ is an action label, and φ is a binary relation on $\mathbb{R}^X$, $F(l)$ is a delay function for the location $l \in L$, and I assigns an invariant predicate $I(l)$ in/of L, which bounds the delay time in the respective location. In UPPAAL SMC, locations are marked as *urgent* (denoted by encircled u) or *committed* (denoted by encircled c), indicating that time cannot progress in such locations. Committed locations are more restrictive, requiring that the next edge to be traversed needs to start from a committed location. The delay function $F(l)$ for a simple clock variable x, which is used in (priced) timed automata, is encoded as the linear differential equation $x' = 1$ or $x' = e$ appearing in the invariant of l.

The semantics of the HA is defined over a timed transition system, whose states are pairs $(l, u) \in L \times \mathbb{R}^X$, with $u \vDash I(l)$, and transitions defined as: (i) delay transitions $(< l, u > \xrightarrow{d} < l, u + d >$ if $u \vDash I(l)$ and $(u + d') \vDash I(l)$, for $0 \leq d' \leq d)$, and (ii) discrete transitions $(< l, u > \xrightarrow{a} < l', u' >$ if edge $l \xrightarrow{g,a,r} l'$ exists such that $a \in \Sigma, u \vDash g$, clock valuation u' in the target state (l', u') is derived from u by resetting all clocks in the reset set r of the edge, such that $u' \vDash I(l'))$.

In UPPAAL SMC, the automata have a stochastic interpretation based on: (i) the probabilistic choices between multiple enabled transitions, and (ii) the non-deterministic time delays that can be refined based on probability distributions, either uniform distributions for time-bounded delays or user-defined exponential distributions for unbounded delays. In this paper, only the default uniform distributions for time-bounded delays are used. Moreover, the UPPAAL SMC model is a network of HA that communicate via broadcast channels and global variables. Only broadcast channels are allowed for a clean semantics of purely non-blocking automata, since the participating HA repeatedly race against each other, that is, they independently and stochastically decide on their own how much to delay before delivering the output, with the "winner" being the automaton that chooses the minimum delay.

UPPAAL SMC supports an extension of *weighted metric temporal logic* for probability estimation, whose queries are formulated as follows: Pr[bound] (ap), where bound is the simulation time, ap is the statement that supports two temporal operators: *"Eventually"* ($\Diamond$) and *"Always"* ($\Box$). Such queries estimate the probability that ap is satisfied within the simulation time bound. Hypothesis testing (Pr[bound] (ψ) $\geq p_0$) and probability comparison (Pr[bound] (ψ_1) $\geq$ Pr[bound] (ψ_2)) are also supported.

2.2 Theta* Algorithm

In this paper, we employ the Theta* algorithm to generate an initial path for our autonomous wheel loader. The Theta* algorithm has been firstly proposed by

Nash et al. [6] to generate smooth paths with few turns, from the starting position to the destination, for a group of autonomous agents. Similar to the A* algorithm that we have used in our previous study [17], the Theta* algorithm explores the map and calculates the cost of nodes by the function $f(n) = g(n) + h(n)$, where n is the current node being explored, $g(n)$ is the Euclidean distance from the starting node to n, and $h(n)$ is the estimated cheapest cost from n to the destination. In this paper, we use Manhattan distance [2] for $h(n)$. In each search iteration, the node with the lowest cost among the nodes that have been explored is selected, and its reachable neighbors are also explored by calculating their costs. The iteration is eventually ended if the destination is found or all reachable nodes have been explored. As an optimized version of A*, Theta* determines the preceding node of a node to be any node in the searching space instead of only neighbor nodes. In addition, Theta* adds a line-of-sight (LOS) detection to each search iteration to find an any-angle path that is less zigzagged than those generated by A* and its variants. For the detailed description of the algorithm, we refer the reader to the literature [6].

2.3   Dipole Flow Field for Collision Avoidance

Searching for a path from the starting point to the goal point, assuming a large map, is not an easy task and it is usually computationally intensive. Hence, some studies have adopted methods to generate a small deviation from the initial path, which is much easier to compute than an entirely new path, while being able to avoid obstacles. To avoid collisions, Trinh et al. [29] propose an approach to calculate the *static flow field* for all objects, and the *dynamic dipole field* for the moving objects in the map. In the theory of dynamic dipole field, every object is assumed to be a source of magnetic dipole field, in which the magnetic moment is aligned with the moving direction, and the magnitude of the magnetic moment is proportional to the velocity. In this approach, the static flow field is created within the neighborhood of the initial path generated by the Theta* algorithm. The flow field force is a combination of the attractive force drawing the autonomous wheel loader to the initial path, and the repulsive force pushing it away from obstacles. Unlike the dipole field force, the flow field force always exists, regardless of whether the vehicle is moving or not. As soon as the vehicle equipped with this algorithm gets close enough to a moving obstacle, the magnetic moment around the objects keeps them away from each other. The combination of the static flow field and the dynamic dipole field ensures that the vehicle moves safely by avoiding all kinds of obstacles and that it eventually reaches the destination, as long as a safe path exists. Compared with other methods [16,30], this algorithm provides a novel method for path planning of mobile agents, in the shared working environment of humans and agents, which suits our requirements well. For details, we refer the reader to the literature [29].

3   Use Case: Autonomous Wheel Loader

In this section, we introduce our use case, which is an industrial prototype of an autonomous wheel loader (AWL) that is used in construction sites to perform operations without human intervention [17]. On one hand, like other autonomous vehicles, autonomous wheel loaders need to be equipped with path-planning and collision-avoidance capabilities. On the other hand, they also ought to accomplish several special missions, e.g., autonomous digging, loading and unloading, often in a predefined sequence. Furthermore, autonomous wheel loaders usually work in unpredictable environments – dust and various sunlight conditions (from dim to extremely bright) that might cause inaccuracy or even errors in image recognition and obstacle detection. Moving entities, e.g., humans, animals, and other machines, might also behave unpredictably, for there are no traffic lights and lanes. Despite such disadvantages, the AWL's movements are less restricted if compared to, for instance, self-driving cars, as there are only a few traffic rules in sites. They can also stop and wait as long as they need without influencing the vehicles behind them. All these characteristics make our path-planning (Theta*) and collision-avoidance (Dipole Flow Field) algorithms applicable.

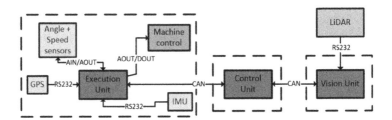

Fig. 1. The architecture of the AWL's embedded control system

   The architecture of the AWL's control system, presented in Fig. 1, consists of three main units: a vision unit, a control unit, and an execution unit, which are connected by CAN buses. In this paper, we mainly focus on the control unit that consists of three parallel processes, namely `ReadSensor`, `Main`, and `CalculateNewPath`, as depicted in Fig. 2. These three processes are executed in parallel on independent cores. The process `ReadSensor` acquires data from sensors (e.g., LIDAR, GPS, angle and speed sensors, etc.) and sends them to the shared memory before they are accessed by process `Main` that runs the path-planning algorithm and invokes a function called `Execution Function`, in which three sub-functions are called. The function `AdjustAngle` adjusts the moving angle of the AWL, based on its own and the obstacles' positions. Function `Turn` judges if the AWL arrives at one of the milestones on its initial path calculated by the path-planning algorithm, and changes its direction based on the result. Function `Arrive` judges if the AWL reaches the destination and sends the corresponding commands. Basically, the processes `Main` and `ReadSensor` are

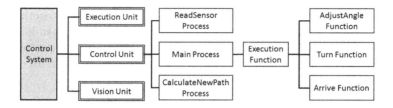

Fig. 2. Process allocation in the control system

responsible for the AWL's regular routine. However, when an unforeseen obstacle suddenly appears in its vision, the process `Main` sends a request to process `CalculateNewPath`, in which the collision-avoidance algorithm is executed and a new and safe path segment is generated if it exists. Note that, although the AWL has more functionality, e.g., digging and loading, we focus only on the path planning and collision avoidance in this paper.

The loader's architecture (Figs. 1, 2), including the parallel processes and functions, is hierarchical. Moreover, the distributed nature of the AWL's components, and the dynamic nature of its movement (including collision avoidance) call for a separation of concerns along the static and the dynamic dimensions of the system. Hence, in the following, we propose a two-layer framework to model and verify autonomous vehicles on different levels.

4   A Two-Level Framework for Planning and Verifying Autonomous Vehicles

As it is shown in Fig. 3, our two-level framework consists of a static layer and a dynamic layer, between which data is exchanged according to a defined/chosen communication protocol. The *static layer* is responsible for path and mission planning for the AWL, according to possibly incomplete information of the

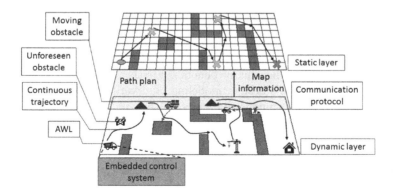

Fig. 3. Two-layer framework for planning and verifying autonomous vehicles

environment. In this layer, known static obstacles are assumed, together with milestones representing points of operation of the loader. The *dynamic layer* is dedicated to simulating and verifying the system following the reference path given by the static layer, while considering continuous dynamics in an environment containing moving and unforeseen obstacles.

Static Layer. The static layer is defined as a tuple $< E_s, S_s, M_s >$, where E_s denotes a discrete environment, S_s is a set of known static obstacles, and M_s is a set of milestones associated to missions (e.g., digging, loading, unloading, charging), including the order of execution, and timing requirements. As the path found by the path-planning algorithm is a connection of several straight-line segments on the map, realistic trajectories and continuous dynamics do not need to be considered in this layer. Hence, the environment is modeled as a discrete Cartesian grid whose resolution is defined appropriately to present various sizes of static obstacles, e.g., holes, rocks, signs, etc. Even if not entirely faithful to reality, the Cartesian grid provides a proper abstraction of the map for path and mission planning. As the static layer is still at the conceptual stage currently, we propose several possible options for modeling and verification of this layer. DRONA [10] is a programming framework for building safe robotics systems. which has been applied in collision-free mission planning for drones. Rebeca is a generic tool for actor-based modeling and has been proven to be applicable for motion planning for robots [18]. Mission Management Tool (MMT) is a tool allowing a human operator an intuitive way of creating complex missions for robots with non-overlapping abilities [25].

Dynamic Layer. The dynamic layer is defined as a tuple $< E_d, T_s, S_d, M_d, D_d >$, where E_d is a continuous environment, T_s is the trajectory plan input by the static layer, S_d is a set of static obstacles, M_d is a set of moving obstacles that are predefined, D_d is a set of unforeseen moving obstacles that are dynamically generated. The speed and direction of a moving obstacle $m_0 \in M_d$ are predefined as constant values in our model. The dynamically generated moving obstacle $d_0 \in D_d$ is instantiated during the verification when its initial location, moving speed and angle are randomly determined. Collision-avoidance algorithms are executed in this layer if the vehicle meets moving obstacles or unforeseen static obstacles. Ordinary differential equations (ODEs) are adopted to model the continuous dynamics of moving objects (e.g., vehicle, human, etc.), and the embedded control system of the autonomous vehicle is modeled in this layer.

This two-layer design has many benefits. Firstly, it provides a separation of concerns for the system's design, modeling, and verification. As a path plan does not concern the continuous dynamics of the vehicle, the discrete model in the static layer is a proper abstraction, which sacrifices some unnecessary realistic elements but preserves the possibility of exhaustive verification. The dynamic layer, which concerns the actual trajectories of moving objects, consists of hybrid models that contain relatively more realistic details of the system and environment, which enhance the truthfulness of the model. However, as a tradeoff, only probabilistic verification is supported in this layer. In addition, modification of algorithms or design is only restricted within the corresponding layer, so potential errors will not propagate in the entire system. Secondly, the two-layer framework is open for extension. It provides a possibility to add layers for new functions, such as artificial intelligence or centralized control.

5   Pattern-Based Modeling of the Dynamic Layer

A classic control system consists of four components: a plant containing the physical process that is to be controlled, the environment where the plant operates, the sensors that measure some variables of the plant and the environment, and the controller that determines the system state and outputs timed-based signals to the plant [22]. In our case, as shown in Fig. 1, the execution unit is the "plant" that describes the continuous dynamics of the AWL. The "sensors" are divided into two classes: vision sensors (LiDAR) connecting to the vision unit, and motion sensors (GPS, IMU, Angle and Speed sensors) connecting to the execution unit.

5.1   Patterns for the Execution Unit

Currently, the vision unit and vision sensors have no computation ability, so they are simply modeled as data structures. The execution unit is modeled in terms of hybrid automata, in which the motion of the AWL is given by a system of three ordinary differential equations:

$$\dot{x}(t) = v(t)cos\theta(t) \quad \dot{y}(t) = v(t)sin\theta(t) \tag{2}$$

$$\dot{\theta}(t) = \omega(t), \tag{3}$$

where, $\dot{x}(t)$ and $\dot{y}(t)$ are the projections of the linear velocity on x and y axes, $\omega(t)$ is the angular velocity, and $v(t)$ is the linear velocity, which follows the Newton's Law of Motion: $v(t) = \frac{F-k \times M}{M}$, where F is the force acting on the AWL, k is the friction coefficient, and M is the mass of the AWL.

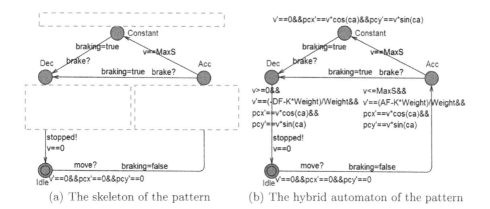

(a) The skeleton of the pattern   (b) The hybrid automaton of the pattern

Fig. 4. The pattern of the linear motion component in the execution unit

The pattern of the execution unit is a hybrid model consisting of two hybrid automata, namely linear motion and rotation. Here we use the linear motion component as an example to present the idea. As depicted in Fig. 4(a), there are four locations indicating four moving states of the AWL, that is, stop at `Idle`, acceleration at `Acc`, moving at a constant speed at `Constant`, and deceleration at `Dec`. Therefore, the derivatives of the position (pcx', pcy') and the velocity (v') are assigned to zero at `Idle` for the stop state. According to different moving states, variations of Eq. 2 should be encoded in the refinement of each location in the blank boxes in Fig. 4(a). Figure 4(b) is an instance of the pattern, where v' is set to a positive value $(v' == (AF - k * m)/m)$ at location `Acc` to present acceleration. Once the velocity reaches the maximum value $(maxS)$ or the automaton receives a brake signal (denoted as a channel $brake$), it goes to location `Constant` or `Dec`, where the ODEs are changed to make the AWL move at a constant speed or decelerate.

5.2   Patterns for the Control Unit

As a part of an embedded system, the control unit model has three basic components: a scheduler, a piece of memory, and a set of processes. Currently, the memory is modeled as a set of global variables, hence the scheduler pattern and the processes patterns are the essence. Due to its safety-critical nature, the control unit is assumed to be a multi-core system and the processes are scheduled in a parallel, predictable, and non-preemptive fashion. This scheduling policy is inspired by *Timed Multitasking* [22], which tackles the real-time programming problem using an event-driven approach. However, instead of the preemptive scheduling, we apply a non-preemptive strategy. To illustrate this scheduling strategy, we use the three processes in the control unit (Fig. 2) as an example. The process `ReadSensor` is firstly triggered at the moment $Trigger_1$ when the process reads data from sensors and runs its function as illustrated in Fig. 5. Regardless of the exact execution time of a process, the inputs are consumed and the outputs are produced at well-defined time instances, namely trigger and deadline. As the input of `Main` is the output of `ReadSensor`, the former is triggered after the latter finishes. At same the moment, `CalculateNewPath` finishes its execution immediately as no input comes. This is actually reasonable, since

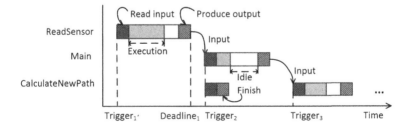

Fig. 5. Process scheduling

process `CalculateNewPath` does not need to be executed every round, as it is responsible for generating a new path segment only when the AWL encounters an obstacle. For the benefits brought by the explicit execution time and deadline, we refer the interested readers to the literature [22] for detail.

The pattern of a process consists of two parts: a state module and an operation module. Similar to the state machine function-block and modal function-block in related work [19], the state module describes the mode transition structure of the processes, and the operation module describes the procedure or computation of the process. Because of their definition, the state modules are modeled as discrete automata, and the operation modules are modeled as discrete automata or computation formulas according to their specific functionality. Figure 6 shows the inputs of the process coming to the state module in which the state of the process transfers according to the inputs. Some state transitions of the state module are detailed by the functions in the operation module in the sense that the former invokes the latter for concrete computation. Specifically, functions in the operation module could be modeled as discrete automata when they involve logic, or executable code when they are purely about computation. After executing the corresponding functions in the operation module, some results are sent out of the process as output, and some are sent back to the state module for state transitions, which might also produce output. The designs of the state module and operation module for different processes have both similarities and differences. They all need to be scheduled, to receive input, produce output, etc., but their specific functionality is different. To make our patterns reusable, we design fixed skeletons of the process patterns, which are presented as hybrid automata.

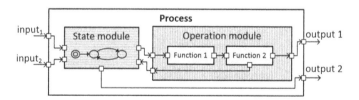

Fig. 6. A process model example

5.3   Encoding the Control Unit Patterns as Hybrid Automata

Scheduler. To model the scheduler as a hybrid automaton in UPPAAL SMC, we first discretize the continuous time as a set of basic time units to mimic the clock in an embedded system. As depicted in Fig. 7, we use an invariant at location `Init` (clock $xd \leq UNIT$), and a guard on its outgoing edge ($xd ==$ $UNIT$) to capture the coming basic time unit. We also declare a data structure representing processes, as follows:

```
typedef struct{
    int id; //process id
    bool running; // whether the process is being executed
    int period; //counter for the period of the process
    int executionTime; //counter for the execution time of the
        process
}PROCESS;
```

When a basic time unit comes, the scheduler transfers to location Updating. In the function update(), the period counters of all processes are decreased by one, and so are the execution time counters if the variable running in the process structure is true. When the period of a process equals zero, its id is inserted into a queue called ready and the variable readyLen indicating the length of the queue is increased by one. Similarly, when the executionTime equals zero, the process's id is inserted into a queue called done. The fact that the queue done is not empty (doneLen > 0) implies that the execution times of some processes have elapsed, so the scheduler changes from Updating to Finishing to generate the outputs of those processes. The self loop at location Finishing indicates that the outputs of all the processes in queue done are generated orderly by the synchronization between the scheduler and the corresponding process automaton via the channel output. If the queue ready is not empty (readyLen > 0), similarly, the scheduler moves to location Execution to trigger the top process in ready via the channel execute, and waits there until the process finishes, when the scheduler is then synchronized again with the process via channel finish. Note that the process finishes its function instantaneously and stores its output in the local variables, which will only be transferred to the other processes via global variables when the execution time passes.

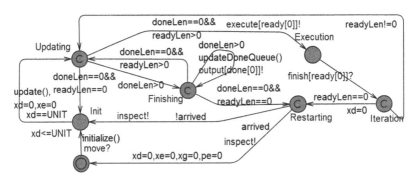

Fig. 7. The pattern of the scheduler

Process. A typical state module of a process consists of four states: being triggered, doing its own function, idle, and output. A typical pattern for it is shown in Fig. 8(a). Except locations Start and Idle, all locations are urgent because the execution is instantaneous, and the output is generated when the execution time is finished. From location Start to 01, the process is being triggered by the scheduler by synchronizing on channel execute[id], in which id is the process's ID. If the input is valid (input == true), the process starts to execute by leaving O1 to the next location, otherwise, it finishes its execution immediately by going back to Start without any output generated, just as the description of the scheduling policy in Sect. 5.2. The blank box indicates the process's own function that is created in an ad-hoc fashion, so it is not part of the fixed skeleton of the pattern. After executing its own function, the process synchronizes again with the scheduler on channel finish[id], when the process finishes and gives control back to the scheduler. The output is generated from location Idle to Notification. The broadcast channel notify[id] is for notifying other processes waiting for the output of the current process. Based on this idea, we give an example instantiated from this pattern in Fig. 8(b). The automaton goes from O2 to O3 through two possible edges based on data1, which is the outcome of function ownJob1(). The concrete computation is encoded in functions ownJob2() and ownJob3(), which are the counterparts of the functions in the operation module of Fig. 6. If the specific function of the process is more complex than in this example, or it includes function invocation, this blank box can be extended with synchronizations with other automata. We will elaborate this by revisiting our use case in the next section.

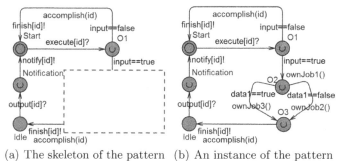

(a) The skeleton of the pattern   (b) An instance of the pattern

Fig. 8. The pattern of a generic process

6   Use Case Revisited: Applying Our Method on AWL

As the patterns of linear motion and rotation components and the scheduler are totally applicable in the use case, they are simply transplanted in the model of the AWL with parameter configuration. Hence, in this section, we mainly demonstrate how the processes in AWL's control unit are modeled using the proposed patterns, and present the verification results.

6.1   Formal Model of the Control Unit

The control unit contains three parallel processes (Fig. 2). ReadSensor and CalculateNewPath are relatively simple because they do not invoke other functions, while Main calls function Execution, which calls other three functions:

AdjustAngle, Turn, and Arrive. Therefore, The state modules of ReadSensor and CalculateNewPath are modeled as single automata and the operation modules are the functions at edges encoding the computation of their functionality. Differently, the state module of Main is a mutation of the process pattern extended with a preprocessing step calculating an initial path by running Theta* algorithm. Figure 9 depicts the automaton of the state module of Main, in which another automaton representing the function Execution is invoked via channel invoke[0], where 0 is the ID of the function Execution. Note that the transition from the location Init to Moving is the preprocessing step and Theta* algorithm is implemented in the function main, which will be moved to the static layer eventually after the entire framework is accomplished. As the process Main invokes other functions, its operation module is a network of automata containing the function Execution, AdjustAngle, Turn, and Arrive, which are called by using synchronizations between the state module automata and operation module automata (channels invoke, respond, finish). After calling other functions, Main goes to the location Idle via three edges based on the return values of the invoked functions and waits to generate output there.

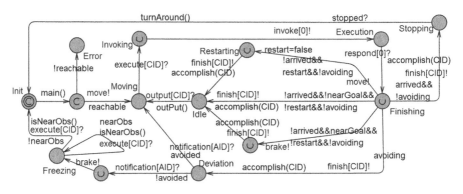

Fig. 9. The automaton of the state module of the process Main

6.2   Statistical Model Checking of the AWL Formal Model

Environment Configuration. In the following we consider a continuous map with the size 55×55, where five static obstacles and two moving obstacles are predefined, and another moving obstacle is dynamically generated during the verification. In order to achieve this, we leverage the spawning command of UPPAAL SMC to instantiate new time automata instance of the moving obstacle that "appears" in the map whenever it is generated by the automaton called generator and "disappears" from the map when its existence time terminates. The speed of the moving obstacles is a constant value indicating that they move one unit distance per second and their moving directions are either opposite or the same as it of the AWL. The parameters of the AWL are the weight of it, acceleration and deceleration force, friction coefficient and maximum speed, which are defined as constant values in UPPAAL SMC.

Path Generation and Following. Given a start and a goal and a set of milestones, the AWL must be able to calculate a safe path passing through them orderly avoiding static obstacles if the path exists and follow it. To verify this requirement, we first simulate the model in UPPAAL SMC using the command:

$$simulate\ 1[<=110]\ \{pcx, pcy\} \tag{4}$$

where pcx and pcy are the real-valued coordinate of the AWL. Figure 10(a) shows the result of the simulation, and the result data is exported into Excel to depict the moving trajectory of the AWL shown in Fig. 10(b). The AWL perfectly follows the generated path that avoids all the static obstacles. But the simulation only runs one possible execution trace of the AWL model. Hence, we further verify the model with a query:

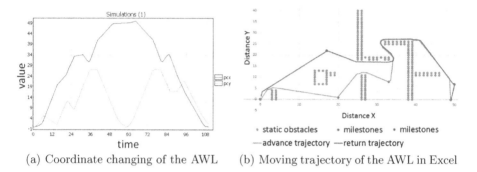

(a) Coordinate changing of the AWL   (b) Moving trajectory of the AWL in Excel

Fig. 10. Moving trajectory of the AWL generated by the command {simulate 1[<=110] pcx,pcy} in UPPAAL SMC and exported in Excel

$$Pr[<=70](<>\ arrived\ \&\&\ counter <=60) \tag{5}$$

$$Pr[<=110]([]\ followedPath) \tag{6}$$

where arrived and counter in query 5 are a Boolean variable and a clock that reflect if the AWL arrives at the destination and what the minimum time does it take, followedPath in query 6 is a Boolean variable indicating if the AWL has reached the destination and come back to the start by visiting all the milestones orderly. To update the value of followedPath timely and periodically during the verification, we create an independent automaton called monitor that checks the index of the model. The monitor is triggered by the scheduler every time unit that is small enough to ensure the position of the AWL does not change much during this time interval. The probability interval of satisfying these queries is [0.902606, 1] with 95% confidence obtained from 36 runs.

Collision Avoidance. By the nature of the Theta* algorithm, AWL is able to avoid the static obstacles as long as it sticks to the initial path. When it meets an unforeseen static obstacle or a moving obstacle, the AWL must run the dipole flow field algorithm timely to avoid it. Two queries are designed to get the simulated moving trajectory and estimate the probability of satisfaction:

$$simulate\ 1[<=110]\ \{pcx, pcy, ocx[0], ocy[0], ocx[1], ocy[1], ocx[3], ocy[3]\} \quad (7)$$

$$Pr[<=110]([]\ !collided) \quad (8)$$

Arrays ocx and ocy in query 7 represent the positions of moving obstacles at x and y axes. The trajectories got from query 7 is shown in Fig. 11, where "A" and "B" are two predefined moving obstacles and "C" is a dynamically generated obstacle that moves "recklessly" towards the AWL, so the latter turns around to avoid the obstacle. The overlap of two trajectories at "C" does not imply a collision because the AWL and the moving obstacle are not at the same position at the same moment. To prove this, query 8 is designed, where collided is a Boolean variable indicating if the AWL has collided with any static or moving obstacles during the verification time. Similar to the verification of path generation and following, the automaton monitor is extended to update this variable periodically by checking if the current coordinate of the AWL is close to any obstacle in the map, and the threshold of the distance is 0.8 in this case. The probability interval of satisfying this query is [0.902606,1] with 95% confidence obtained from 36 runs.

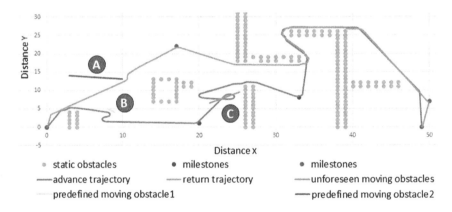

Fig. 11. The trajectory of the AWL in a map with three moving obstacles

7   Related Work

Automata-based methods [12,20,26,28] have been used for path or motion planning. Different from our work, these studies aim to solve the vehicle-routing problem by using temporal logic. These studies accomplish many typical autonomous tasks like searching for an object, avoiding an obstacle, and missions sequencing. However, as they focus on achieving collision avoidance in design, uncertainties in the real deployment like transmission time of sensors data in the embedded system and unforeseen obstacles have not been considered.

Runtime verification that monitors the behavior of autonomous systems complements this shortage to some extend [11,15,23,24]. This technique extracts information from a running system, based on which the behavior of the system is verified. Runtime overhead caused by the monitor is the most common problem introduced by this method.

Agent-based method is another widely studied approach for autonomous systems [3,8,11,13,14]. As the predominant form of rational agent architecture is that provided through the Beliefs, Desires, and Intentions (BDI) approach, these studies aim to translate the agent-based language to a formal language to verify the behavior of the agent. But this method usually does not concern the detail of the embedded control system and continuous dynamics of the vehicle.

There are also some studies providing a framework for verification of autonomous vehicles or robots. In [27], the authors captured the behavior of an unmanned aerial vehicle performing cooperative search mission into a Kripke model to verify it against the temporal properties expressed in Computation Tree Logic (CTL). Their model contains a decision making layer and a path planing layer. In [9], the authors propose an approach combining model checking with runtime verification to bridge the gap between software verification (discrete) and the actual execution of the software on a real robotic platform in the physical world. The software stack of a robotics system providing different verification capability focusing on different functionality has inspired our work. However, our framework provides an ability to encode the collision avoidance algorithm in the model and verifying it in a continuous environment.

8 Conclusions and Future Work

We have proposed a conceptual two-layer framework for formally verifying autonomous vehicles that decouples the high-level static planning from dynamic functions like collision avoidance, etc. The framework provides a separation of concerns for the complex modeling and verification of autonomous vehicles. The static layer focuses on making the optimal plan for the vehicle to accomplish a sequence of missions based on the incomplete information of the environment. While the dynamic layer concerns the execution of the plan with vehicle dynamics in a continuous environment model where unforeseen moving obstacles appear randomly. Hence, a collision avoidance algorithm relying on dipole flow field is implemented in the model of the embedded control system in this layer. We are currently engaged in modeling the dynamic layer using hybrid automata and UPPAAL SMC, and designing a pattern-based method to simplify the modeling process and increase reusability. The dynamic layer has been applied to model and verify a prototype of an autonomous wheel loader and the verification result shows the capability and applicability of statistical model checking adopted in autonomous vehicles. We expect to report our research of the static layer and the combination of these two layers in the years to come.

Acknowledgement. The research leading to the presented results has been performed within the research profile DPAC - Dependable Platform for Autonomous Systems and Control project, funded by grant 20150022 of the Swedish Knowledge Foundation that is gratefully acknowledged.

References

1. Bhatia, A., Maly, M.R., Kavraki, L.E., Vardi, M.Y.: Motion planning with complex goals. IEEE Rob. Autom. Mag. **18**(3), 55–64 (2011)
2. Black, P.E.: Manhattan distance. Dictionary Algorithms Data Struct. **18**, 2012 (2006)
3. Bordini, R.H., Fisher, M., Visser, W., Wooldridge, M.: Verifying multi-agent programs by model checking. Auton. Agent. Multi-Agent Syst. **12**(2), 239–256 (2006)
4. Branicky, M.S., Borkar, V.S., Mitter, S.K.: A unified framework for hybrid control: model and optimal control theory. IEEE Trans. Autom. Control **43**(1), 31–45 (1998)
5. Bulychev, P., et al.: Monitor-based statistical model checking for weighted metric temporal logic. In: Bjørner, N., Voronkov, A. (eds.) LPAR 2012. LNCS, vol. 7180, pp. 168–182. Springer, Heidelberg (2012). https://doi.org/10.1007/978-3-642-28717-6_15
6. Daniel, K., Nash, A., Koenig, S., Felner, A.: Theta*: any-angle path planning on grids. J. Artif. Intell. Res. **39**, 533–579 (2010)
7. David, A., et al.: Statistical model checking for stochastic hybrid systems. arXiv preprint arXiv:1208.3856 (2012)
8. Dennis, L.A., Fisher, M., Webster, M.P., Bordini, R.H.: Model checking agent programming languages. Autom. Softw. Eng. **19**(1), 5–63 (2012)
9. Desai, A., Dreossi, T., Seshia, S.A.: Combining model checking and runtime verification for safe robotics. In: Lahiri, S., Reger, G. (eds.) RV 2017. LNCS, vol. 10548, pp. 172–189. Springer, Cham (2017). https://doi.org/10.1007/978-3-319-67531-2_11
10. Desai, A., Saha, I., Yang, J., Qadeer, S., Seshia, S.A.: DRONA: a framework for safe distributed mobile robotics. In: Proceedings of the 8th International Conference on Cyber-Physical Systems, pp. 239–248. ACM (2017)
11. Doherty, P., Kvarnström, J., Heintz, F.: A temporal logic-based planning and execution monitoring framework for unmanned aircraft systems. Auton. Agent. Multi-Agent Syst. **19**(3), 332–377 (2009)
12. Fainekos, G.E., Kress-Gazit, H., Pappas, G.J.: Temporal logic motion planning for mobile robots. In: Proceedings of the 2005 IEEE International Conference on Robotics and Automation, ICRA 2005, pp. 2020–2025. IEEE (2005)
13. Fisher, M., Bordini, R.H., Hirsch, B., Torroni, P.: Computational logics and agents: a road map of current technologies and future trends. Comput. Intell. **23**(1), 61–91 (2007)
14. Fisher, M., Dennis, L., Webster, M.: Verifying autonomous systems. Commun. ACM **56**(9), 84–93 (2013)
15. Gat, E., Slack, M.G., Miller, D.P., Firby, R.J.: Path planning and execution monitoring for a planetary rover. In: Proceedings of the IEEE International Conference on Robotics and Automation, pp. 20–25 (1990)
16. Golan, Y., Edelman, S., Shapiro, A., Rimon, E.: Online robot navigation using continuously updated artificial temperature gradients. IEEE Rob. Autom. Lett. **2**(3), 1280–1287 (2017)

17. Gu, R., Marinescu, R., Seceleanu, C., Lundqvist, K.: Formal verification of an autonomous wheel loader by model checking. In: Proceedings of the 6th Conference on Formal Methods in Software Engineering, pp. 74–83. ACM (2018)
18. Jafari, A., Nair, J.J.S., Baumgart, S., Sirjani, M.: Safe and efficient fleet operation for autonomous machines: an actor-based approach. In: Proceedings of the 33rd Annual ACM Symposium on Applied Computing, pp. 423–426. ACM (2018)
19. Ke, X., Sierszecki, K., Angelov, C.: COMDES-II: a component-based framework for generative development of distributed real-time control systems. In: 13th IEEE International Conference on Embedded and Real-Time Computing Systems and Applications, pp. 199–208. IEEE (2007)
20. Kloetzer, M., Mahulea, C.: A petri net based approach for multi-robot path planning. Discrete Event Dyn. Syst. **24**(4), 417–445 (2014)
21. Larsen, K.G., Pettersson, P., Yi, W.: Uppaal in a nutshell. Int. J. Softw. Tools Technol. Transf. **1**(1–2), 134–152 (1997)
22. Lee, E.A., Seshia, S.A.: Introduction to Embedded Systems: A Cyber-Physical Systems Approach. MIT Press, Cambridge (2016)
23. Lotz, A., Steck, A., Schlegel, C.: Runtime monitoring of robotics software components: increasing robustness of service robotic systems. In: 2011 15th International Conference on Advanced Robotics (ICAR), pp. 285–290. IEEE (2011)
24. Luo, C., et al.: Runtime verification of robots collision avoidance case study. In: 2018 IEEE 42nd Annual Computer Software and Applications Conference (COMPSAC), pp. 204–212. IEEE (2018)
25. Miloradović, B., Cürüklü, B., Ekström, M., Papadopoulos, A.: Extended colored traveling salesperson for modeling multi-agent mission planning problems. In: Proceedings of the 8th International Conference on Operations Research and Enterprise Systems - Volume 1, ICORES, pp. 237–244, INSTICC. SciTePress (2019). https://doi.org/10.5220/0007309002370244
26. Quottrup, M.M., Bak, T., Zamanabadi, R.: Multi-robot planning: a timed automata approach. In: 2004 IEEE International Conference on Robotics and Automation, Proceedings, ICRA 2004, vol. 5, pp. 4417–4422. IEEE (2004)
27. Sirigineedi, G., Tsourdos, A., White, B.A., Zbikowski, R.: Modelling and verification of multiple UAV mission using SMV. arXiv preprint arXiv:1003.0381 (2010)
28. Smith, S.L., Tumova, J., Belta, C., Rus, D.: Optimal path planning for surveillance with temporal-logic constraints. Int. J. Rob. Res. **30**(14), 1695–1708 (2011)
29. Trinh, L.A., Ekström, M., Cürüklü, B.: Toward shared working space of human and robotic agents through dipole flow field for dependable path planning. Front. Neurorob. **12** (2018)
30. Valbuena, L., Tanner, H.G.: Hybrid potential field based control of differential drive mobile robots. J. Intell. Rob. Syst. **68**(3–4), 307–322 (2012)

Clausal Proofs of Mutilated Chessboards

Marijn J. H. Heule[1], Benjamin Kiesl[2,3], and Armin Biere[4($\boxtimes$)]

[1] Department of Computer Science, The University of Texas, Austin, USA
[2] Institute of Logic and Computation, TU Wien, Vienna, Austria
[3] CISPA Helmholtz Center for Information Security, Saarbrücken, Germany
[4] Institute for Formal Models and Verification, JKU Linz, Linz, Austria
armin.biere@gmail.com

Abstract. Mutilated chessboard problems have been called a "tough nut to crack" for automated reasoning. They are, for instance, hard for resolution, resulting in exponential runtime of current SAT solvers. Although there exists a well-known short argument for solving mutilated chessboard problems, this argument is based on an abstraction that is challenging to discover by automated-reasoning techniques. In this paper, we present another short argument that is much easier to compute and that can be expressed within the recent (clausal) PR proof system for propositional logic. We construct short clausal proofs of mutilated chessboard problems using this new argument and validate them using a formally-verified proof checker.

1 Introduction

The success of automated reasoning presents us with an interesting peculiarity: While modern solving tools can routinely handle gigantic real-world instances, they often fail miserably on supposedly easy problems. Their poor performance is frequently caused by the weakness of their underlying proof systems, which only allow them to derive facts that are logically implied. A recently proposed proof system, called PR [6], overcomes this issue by allowing the derivation of facts that are not necessarily implied but whose addition preserves satisfiability.

A well-known family of problems on which traditional reasoning approaches fail are the *mutilated chessboard problems*. Given a chessboard of size $n \times n$ from which two opposite corner squares have been removed (see Fig. 1), a mutilated chessboard problem asks if the remaining squares can be fully covered with dominos (i.e., with stones that cover exactly two squares). The answer is *no*, based on a simple argument: Assume to the contrary that a mutilated chessboard can be fully covered with dominos. Then, since every domino covers exactly one black square and one white square, the number of covered black squares must equal the number of covered white squares. But the number of black squares on a mutilated chessboard is different from the number of white squares since opposite corner squares (of which two were removed) are of the same color.

Supported by NSF under grant CCF-1813993, by AFRL Award FA8750-15-2-0096, Austrian Science Fund (FWF) under projects W1255-N23 and S11409-N23 (RiSE) and the LIT Secure and Correct Systems Lab funded by the State of Upper Austria.

J. M. Badger and K. Y. Rozier (Eds.): NFM 2019, LNCS 11460, pp. 204–210, 2019.
https://doi.org/10.1007/978-3-030-20652-9_13

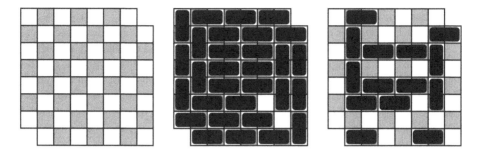

Fig. 1. An empty (left), almost full (middle), and reduced (right) mutilated chessboard.

Automated-reasoning methods on various representations have severe difficulties finding this argument because they do not have colored squares, so they need to come up with this abstraction themselves in order to use a similar argument. John McCarthy has called the mutilated chessboard problems a "tough nut to crack" for automated reasoning [10], and it has been shown that these problems admit only proofs of exponential size within the propositional resolution proof system, which forms the basis of many SAT solvers [1,3].

In this paper, we show that the recently introduced PR proof system facilitates a completely different but equally short argument for solving mutilated chessboard problems. The new argument rules out possible patterns for the dominos by generalizing—*without loss of generality*—from certain specific patterns that are similar to them. Moreover, the argument also seems to be well suited for automated reasoning since we discovered it when analyzing PR proofs that were found by one of our tools [7]. We argue that the key to automatically solving the mutilated chessboard problems and many other hard problems is not to simulate human thinking but to equip computers with capabilities to find their own short arguments. Moreover, our example demonstrates that automated-reasoning tools cannot only provide us with simple yes/no answers but that they can also help us gain further insights into the nature of a problem.

2   Representation

A successful approach to solving hard combinatorial problems is to encode them into propositional logic and to solve the resulting propositional formulas with a SAT solver. Mutilated chessboard problems can be naturally encoded in propositional logic: We consider only propositional formulas in conjunctive normal form (CNF). Such formulas are conjunctions of clauses where each clause is a disjunction of literals and each literal is either a variable or the negation of a variable. We use a distinct Boolean variable for each possible placement of a domino on the chessboard. On each square (apart from some border squares), a domino can be placed either horizontally or vertically, having the square either left or top. Intuitively, a variable should be true if and only if a domino is placed on the corresponding location in the corresponding way (horizontally or vertically). The number of variables is thus roughly twice the number of squares.

Only one constraint needs to be encoded for mutilated chessboard problems: Each square must be covered by exactly one domino. This constraint can be easily expressed in propositional logic, resulting in two clauses for corner squares, four clauses for border squares, and seven clauses for center squares: One clause (consisting only of positive literals) expresses that the square is covered by *at least one* domino whereas the other clauses (each containing exactly two negative literals) express that the square is covered by *at most one* domino.

Mutilated chessboard problems using this encoding were part of the SAT Competition 2018 (in the *main, parallel,* and *no-limits* tracks). The problems used in the competition encoded mutilated chessboards of size $n \times n$, with $n \in \{15, 16, 17, 18, 19, 20\}$. None of the solvers were able to solve the two largest instances within the time limit of 5000 seconds. In this paper, we consider significantly larger mutilated chessboards with $n \in \{20, 30, 40, 50\}$.

Notice that the problem encoding does not include any information regarding the colors of squares as in the illustrations. It would be possible to include this information using only a subset of the clauses, allowing at most one domino for white squares and requiring at least one domino for black squares (assuming that the removed corner squares are black). These formulas would still be hard for resolution (using a subset of the clauses cannot yield shorter resolution proofs) but they would become easy for cutting-plane reasoning [8].

3   Clausal Proofs

Informally, a clausal proof system allows us to show the unsatisfiability of a CNF formula by continuously deriving more and more clauses until we obtain the empty clause. Thereby, the addition of a derived clause to the formula and all previously derived clauses must preserve satisfiability. As the empty clause is trivially unsatisfiable, a clausal proof shows the unsatisfiability of the original formula. Moreover, it must be checkable in polynomial time that each derivation step does preserve satisfiability. This requirement ensures that the correctness of proofs can be efficiently verified. In practice, this is achieved by allowing only the derivation of specific clauses that fulfill some efficiently checkable criterion.

Formally, clausal proof systems are based on the notion of *clause redundancy*. A clause C is *redundant* with respect to a formula F if F and $F \wedge C$ are equisatisfiable (i.e., they are either both satisfiable or both unsatisfiable). Given a formula $F = C_1 \wedge \cdots \wedge C_m$, a *clausal proof* of F is a sequence $(C_{m+1}, \omega_{m+1}), \ldots, (C_n, \omega_n)$ of pairs where each C_i is a clause, each ω_i (called the *witness*) is a string, and C_n is the empty clause [6]. Such a sequence gives rise to formulas $F_m, F_{m+1}, \ldots, F_n$, where $F_i = C_1 \wedge \cdots \wedge C_i$. A clausal proof is *correct* if every clause C_i $(i > m)$ is redundant with respect to F_{i-1}, and if this redundancy can be checked in polynomial time (with respect to the size of the proof) using the witness ω_i.

An example for a clausal proof system is the resolution proof system, which only allows the derivation of resolvents (with no/empty witnesses). Moreover,

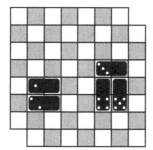 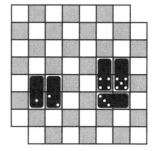

Fig. 2. Two equivalent placements of five dominos on a mutilated chessboard.

the recently introduced proof system PR [6] is a clausal proof system that allows to derive a clause C_i if that clause is *propagation redundant* with respect to F_{i-1}. For the details of propagation redundancy, we refer to the original paper [6]. Here, we just note that (1) propagation-redundant clauses are clauses for which it can be checked efficiently that their addition preserves satisfiability, and (2) every resolvent is a propagation-redundant clause but not vice versa.

The key to constructing short clausal proofs is to aim for deriving short clauses to quickly obtain the empty clause. One approach to achieve this is the *clause learning* technique based on *first unique implication points* [9] used in modern SAT solvers. Starting from a falsifying assignment (found by the solver), this technique derives a redundant clause by computing a subassignment of the falsifying assignment. The derived clause is then the maximal clause that is falsified by that subassignment, thereby ruling out the subassignment and all its extensions. Thus, if the subassignment makes x true and y false, then the derived clause is $\overline{x} \vee y$. When the empty clause is eventually derived, all possible assignments are ruled out, implying that the formula is unsatisfiable.

On mutilated chessboards, clauses intuitively rule out possible placements of dominos. For instance, if a SAT solver arrives at the falsifying placement of the 30 dominos shown on the middle of Fig. 1, it is able to derive the clause that rules out the placement of 14 dominos on the right of Fig. 1, resulting in a 14 literal redundant clause. Deriving this clause rules out all placements that extend the smaller placement, including the falsifying placement of 30 dominos.

Can we immediately learn way shorter clauses, ruling out way more placements? Yes, but not within the resolution proof system. Within the PR proof system, however, much shorter clauses—consisting of only two literals—can be derived. Placements that are represented by such clauses will be discussed below.

4 Without Loss of Satisfaction

Consider the placements of dominos in Fig. 2. Although the placement on the left is different from the one on the right, they are equivalent in the sense that both cover exactly the same squares. A common way in mathematics to deal with such similar cases is to argue *without loss of generality*, thereby generalizing a specific case to other similar cases. Within the PR proof system, we can formalize such arguments by deriving clauses that rule out cases that are similar to others.

For mutilated chessboard problems, PR allows us to derive clauses that rule out placements where two horizontal dominos are placed below each other (like the left two dominos on the left mutilated chessboard of Fig. 2). The reasoning is as follows: If it were possible to extend such a placement to a valid placement that covers the whole board, then this would also be possible for the similar placement where two vertical dominos are placed next to each other (such as the left pattern on the right chessboard of Fig. 2). We thus argue *without loss of satisfaction*: If there was a satisfying assignment before ruling out a placement, then there will be a satisfying assignment afterwards. Ruling out all the placements where two horizontal dominos are placed below each other shrinks the number of possible placements aggressively, thus leading to short proofs.

We observed that this pattern and others can be ruled out within the PR proof system when we analyzed automatically generated PR proofs produced by a modified version of the SAT solver LINGELING. This modified version of LIN-GELING is based on our recently introduced *satisfaction-driven clause learning* (SDCL) paradigm [7]. In the proofs, derived clauses represent the ruled out assignments while the witnesses represent the equivalent placements. Our modified LINGELING is not particularly strong on the mutilated chessboard problems but these binary clauses stood out since they are so short. We thus believe that the solver might be able to solve large mutilated chessboard problems efficiently if we can equip it with the right decision heuristics.

Another pattern that can be ruled out in the PR proof system is the placement of a horizontal domino on top of two vertical dominos as in the right pattern on the left mutilated chessboard of Fig. 2. Such a pattern can be replaced by moving the two vertical dominos one square up and the horizontal domino two squares down as in the right pattern on the right mutilated chessboard of Fig. 2.

Deriving clauses to rule out both patterns—no two horizontal dominos and no horizontal domino on top of two vertical dominos—on all positions of the mutilated chessboard exponentially reduces the number of placements that a solver explores. We require $\mathcal{O}(n^3)$ PR clauses to rule out these patterns for a $n \times n$ mutilated chessboard. The resulting formula can be easily solved using a usual SAT solver. The observed runtime and number of conflicts is also $\mathcal{O}(n^3)$.

5   Proof Production and Validation

We constructed and validated PR proofs of reasonably large mutilated chessboard problems. Both the problem encodings and the proofs are available at https://github.com/marijnheule/mchess. The proofs consist of a first part that eliminates the earlier mentioned patterns by deriving PR clauses and a second part that refutes the remaining cases using resolution. We generated the first part of the proofs with a dedicated tool that enumerates the required PR clauses. For the second part, we used a SAT solver. Both proof parts are roughly equal in size. The largest problem instance for which we produced a proof is a 50×50

Table 1. Overview of the proof validation results. The second and third column show the numbers of variables and clauses in the encodings of mutilated chessboard problems. The fourth and fifth column show the numbers of clause addition steps in the PR and DRAT proofs, respectively. The last four columns show the runtimes (in CPU seconds, 2.9 GHz Intel Core i7) of non-verified PR proof checking, PR to DRAT conversion, DRAT proof optimization, and verified DRAT proof checking (certification), respectively.

size	#var	#cls	#PR	#DRAT	check	convert	optimize	certify
20×20	760	2 552	7 598	501 766	0.71	0.99	7.06	10.78
30×30	1 740	5 932	22 879	2 489 657	5.74	11.11	85.38	99.45
40×40	3 120	10 712	48 967	7 776 380	32.77	62.57	488.40	518.38
50×50	4 900	16 892	91 665	18 845 988	134.24	252.01	1 862.03	1 702.61

chessboard. Proof production took only a second. Recall that not even the 20×20 mutilated chessboard problem could be solved in the SAT Competition 2018.

To increase the confidence in the correctness of the proofs, we converted the PR proofs into DRAT proofs for which formally-verified checkers exist. We used the tool pr2drat [4] for the conversion, optimized the DRAT proofs using the drat-trim tool [12] and validated the optimized proofs using the formally-verified tool ACL2check [5]. Table 1 provides an overview of the results. Notice that there is a significant gap between verified and non-verified proof checking. This gap is mainly caused by the blowup of the proofs during the conversion.

6   Conclusion and Challenges

We constructed and validated short propositional proofs of mutilated chessboard problems in the PR proof system. Our proofs show the unsatisfiability of problem instances that are much larger than the largest instances that can be solved by state-of-the-art SAT solvers. The proofs are based on an argument we found when analyzing automatically generated PR proofs. This argument allows us to rule out two small patterns, which exponentially reduces the number of placements that need to be explored. There is an enormous gap between the size of the proofs generated by the modified LINGELING solver and the ones we constructed manually. We believe that an SDCL solver should be able to produce proofs that are close in size to our manual proofs when using the right heuristics and restart strategy, which we consider an important challenge for future research.

Even though the usage of PR clauses in mutilated chessboard problems goes beyond plain symmetry reasoning—existing symmetry-breaking techniques, both static [2] and dynamic [11], are not effective on these formulas—the general argument has a symmetry-reasoning flavor. To further illustrate the power of the PR proof system, we are seeking examples where PR clauses give an exponential benefit without this kind of global and semantic symmetry argument.

Acknowledgements. The authors thank Alexey Porkhunov for contributing the mutilated chessboard formulas to the 2018 SAT Competition and for his suggestion to study these formulas in the context of the PR proof system, and also thank Jasmin Blanchette for his comments on an earlier version of this paper.

References

1. Alekhnovich, M.: Mutilated chessboard problem is exponentially hard for resolution. Theoret. Comput. Sci. **310**(1–3), 513–525 (2004)
2. Aloul, F.A., Markov, I.L., Sakallah, K.A.: Shatter: efficient symmetry-breaking for Boolean satisfiability. In: Proceedings of the 40th Annual Design Automation Conference, DAC 2003, pp. 836–839. ACM (2003)
3. Dantchev, S.S., Riis, S.: "Planar" tautologies hard for resolution. In: Proceedings of the 42nd Annual Symposium on Foundations of Computer Science (FOCS 2001), pp. 220–229. IEEE Computer Society (2001)
4. Heule, M.J.H., Biere, A.: What a difference a variable makes. In: Beyer, D., Huisman, M. (eds.) TACAS 2018. LNCS, vol. 10806, pp. 75–92. Springer, Cham (2018)
5. Heule, M.J.H., Hunt Jr., W.A., Kaufmann, M., Wetzler, N.D.: Efficient, verified checking of propositional proofs. In: Ayala-Rincón, M., Muñoz, C.A. (eds.) ITP 2017. LNCS, vol. 10499, pp. 269–284. Springer, Cham (2017)
6. Heule, M.J.H., Kiesl, B., Biere, A.: Short proofs without new variables. In: de Moura, L. (ed.) CADE 2017. LNCS (LNAI), vol. 10395, pp. 130–147. Springer, Cham (2017)
7. Heule, M.J.H., Kiesl, B., Seidl, M., Biere, A.: PRuning through satisfaction. In: Strichman, O., Tzoref-Brill, R. (eds.) HVC 2017. LNCS, vol. 10629, pp. 179–194. Springer, Cham (2017)
8. de Klerk, E., van Maaren, H., Warners, J.P.: Relaxations of the satisfiability problem using semidefinite programming. J. Autom. Reason. **24**(1), 37–65 (2000)
9. Marques-Silva, J.P., Sakallah, K.A.: GRASP: a search algorithm for propositional satisfiability. IEEE Trans. Comput. **48**(5), 506–521 (1999)
10. McCarthy, J.: A tough nut for proof procedures. Stanford Artificial Intelligence Project Memo 16 (1964)
11. Metin, H., Baarir, S., Colange, M., Kordon, F.: CDCLSym: introducing effective symmetry breaking in SAT solving. In: Beyer, D., Huisman, M. (eds.) TACAS 2018. LNCS, vol. 10805, pp. 99–114. Springer, Cham (2018)
12. Wetzler, N.D., Heule, M.J.H., Hunt Jr., W.A.: DRAT-trim: efficient checking and trimming using expressive clausal proofs. In: Sinz, C., Egly, U. (eds.) SAT 2014. LNCS, vol. 8561, pp. 422–429. Springer, Cham (2014)

Practical Causal Models
for Cyber-Physical Systems

Amjad Ibrahim[1]([⊠]), Severin Kacianka[1], Alexander Pretschner[1],
Charles Hartsell[2], and Gabor Karsai[2]

[1] Technical University of Munich, Munich, Germany
{amjad.ibrahim,severin.kacianka,alexander.pretschner}@tum.de
[2] Vanderbilt University, Nashville, TN, USA
{charles.a.hartsell,gabor.karsai}@vanderbilt.edu

Abstract. Unlike faults in classical systems, faults in Cyber-Physical Systems will often be caused by the system's interaction with its physical environment and social context, rendering these faults harder to diagnose. To complicate matters further, knowledge about the behavior and failure modes of a system are often collected in different models. We show how three of those models, namely attack trees, fault trees, and timed failure propagation graphs can be converted into Halpern-Pearl causal models, combined into a single holistic causal model, and analyzed with actual causality reasoning to detect and explain unwanted events. Halpern-Pearl models have several advantages over their source models, particularly that they allow for modeling preemption, consider the non-occurrence of events, and can incorporate additional domain knowledge. Furthermore, such holistic models allow for analysis across model boundaries, enabling detection and explanation of events that are beyond a single model. Our contribution here delineates a semi-automatic process to (1) convert different models into Halpern-Pearl causal models, (2) combine these models into a single holistic model, and (3) reason about system failures. We illustrate our approach with the help of an Unmanned Aerial Vehicle case study.

Keywords: Causal reasoning · Halpern-Pearl Causality ·
Timed Failure Propagation Graphs · Cyber-Physical Systems

1   Introduction

When Cyber-Physical Systems (CPS) are causally involved in accidents or unwanted events, rapid diagnosis of the underlying fault is paramount. On the one hand, this builds public trust in those systems, and on the other hand, this is necessary to prevent similar accidents with identically constructed systems.

This work was supported by the Deutsche Forschungsgemeinschaft (DFG) under grant no. PR1266/3-1, Design Paradigms for Societal-Scale Cyber-Physical Systems. Amjad Ibrahim and Severin Kacianka contributed equally to this paper.

© Springer Nature Switzerland AG 2019
J. M. Badger and K. Y. Rozier (Eds.): NFM 2019, LNCS 11460, pp. 211–227, 2019.
https://doi.org/10.1007/978-3-030-20652-9_14

However, the analysis of faults and the attribution of accountability in CPS [15] is especially hard, because these systems interact with their physical environment, have no clear boundaries, and the necessary knowledge is often spread across different models. An example is an Unmanned Aerial Vehicle (UAV) that violates a no-fly zone (NFZ). NFZs are areas in which a UAV is not permitted to fly, and are typically enforced around sensitive sites such as nuclear facilities, prisons, or airports. Airspace regulators like the FAA [8] in the United States and Eurocontrol [7] in Europe publish maps of NFZs, and manufacturers embed instructions in the operating systems of their UAVs to ensure these vehicles do not violate NFZs (e.g., [5]). Thus, if a UAV enters an NFZ despite these technical precautions, it is always an unwanted event and often also a security and safety-critical event. Rapid identification of the reasons for such events is crucial, given the likelihood that the same error will affect all identically constructed systems. For example, if the cause is a programming mistake, it will affect all UAVs running the same code, if it is a mistake in the map data, many other UAVs will use the same faulty data; and if a security vulnerability is abused by a third party, it is likely that the same vulnerability affects all UAVs controlled by the same software. Insights into these errors can be gained from models of the systems, such as fault trees, attack trees, Timed Failure Propagation Graphs (TFPGs), or information external to the system, e.g., eye-witness reports. Thus, to determine the ultimate cause of an unwanted event, experts currently need to scrutinize different system models, incorporate external information, propose a likely causal model and argue, usually in natural language, for its verisimilitude.

In this paper, we investigate the *problem* of automatically creating a holistic causal model of a system that allows us to (1) incorporate additional domain knowledge and (2) formally reason about causes for events. As a *solution*, we propose to convert three system models, namely attack trees, fault trees, and TFPGs, into Halpern-Pearl [11] causal models, then combine them into a single, holistic model and use causal reasoning to explain events. To this end, our primary *contribution* is a semi-automatic process to convert these three models into HP models. Additionally, we show under which circumstances models can be automatically combined, how they can be enriched with domain knowledge, and how causal reasoning can be automated.

2   Background and Related Work

TFPGs [1,2] are directed acyclical graphs which model the failure propagation routes for typical systems, taking into account modal and temporal constraints. Nodes within TFPGs represent either *failure modes* (i.e., root causes that are not directly observable) or *discrepancies* (i.e., off-nominal effects resulting from failure modes which may be observable). Discrepancies that can be detected at run-time (e.g., with a dedicated sensor) are associated with an *alarm* node. *Edges* in TFPGs represent the cause-effect relationships in failure propagation, are directional, and may be parameterized with activation conditions based on the current system *mode* and propagation time limits. Figure 1a depicts an example

TFPG constructed in the Systems Engineering and Assurance Modeling toolset[1] and Fig. 1b shows a more detailed TFPG for the GPS sensor.

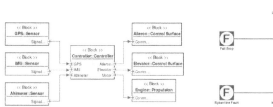 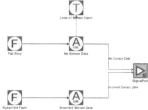

(a) System architecture view.

(b) The detailed view of the UAV's GPS module. **F** - Failure Mode, **A** - Anomaly/Discrepancy, **T** - Test/Alarm.

Fig. 1. An example of a UAV's timed failure propagation graph.

Simon et al. presented a model-based, fault-adaptive control architecture which combined multiple fault-modeling paradigms to diagnose and mitigate faults in complex dynamic systems [28]. Their architecture uses TFPGs for discrete diagnosis alongside temporal causal graphs for fault diagnosis via transient-effect analysis. This approach fuses domain knowledge from multiple models for more effective fault identification and mitigation. Similarly, Dubey et al. introduced a software health management system which combines TFPGs for reasoning at the system-level with finite state machines at the component-level [6]. However, in both approaches, each type of model was evaluated independently instead of being combined into a single common language. Additionally, the models do not provide a concept for incorporating additional information which may become available in an offline, post-mortem analysis of the system.

Because of TFPGs' run-time nature, the faults in these models focus on functional failures of the system's hardware and software components. In practical applications, failure modes are usually abstracted to the lowest level that can be uniquely identified using information available to run-time diagnosis engines. For example, a Byzantine fault (as in Fig. 1b) is a common failure mode in each software component. Typically, it cannot be determined at run-time if a Byzantine fault is the result of a latent fault in the software, a radiation-induced single-event upset, a malicious attacker, etc., so this additional information is omitted from the TFPG model. Additionally, faults which are not related to a specific component failure often have a broad impact on the system which complicates the disambiguation of faults at run-time. For these reasons non-functional faults, such as process or operator errors, are modeled using an appropriate domain-specific modeling language.

Fault trees are an essential top-down artifact in the domain of safety, reliability, and risk assessment methodology [16]. The quantitative (e.g., calculating

---

[1] Accessible at http://modelbasedassurance.org.

the probabilities of failure), and qualitative (e.g., determining the minimal cut sets) analysis of fault trees investigates the system resilience to faults at design time [25]. Moreover, fault trees have been used to monitor systems at run-time and detect failures [21]. Narayanan and Viswanadham [20] have used fault trees to represent and reason about knowledge of system failures. In contrast to the approach presented later in this paper, the authors use rule-oriented reasoning, akin to that used by human experts. In contrast, our approach enables reasoning about actual causality in a way that matches human intuition [10], without explicitly stating all the rules.

A fault tree [30] is the (often graphical) representation of possible component faults leading to system failures, and their relationship to each other. There are two general elements within a fault tree: events and gates. Events represent happenings (faults) that can possibly result in an undesired event in the root of the fault tree, e.g., a system failure. In [30], the authors distinguish between *basic*, *conditioning*, *undeveloped*, *external*, and *intermediate* events. Gates allow for connecting two or more events or other gates to express particular relationships between events. For instance, it may be the case that two events must occur together to cause a third event. This would be expressed using an *AND* gate. Additionally, [30] defines *OR*, *EXCLUSIVE OR*, *PRIORITY AND*, and *INHIBIT* gates. A different symbol is used for different types of gates and events. Figure 2a depicts an example fault tree for a UAV.

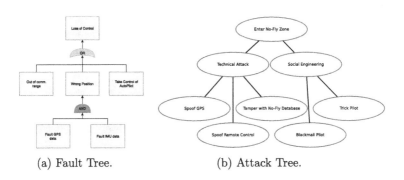

(a) Fault Tree.   (b) Attack Tree.

Fig. 2. Part of the UAV's fault and attack tree.

Attack trees [26,27] model and describe potential security threats within a system and the steps necessary to successfully perform an attack. Attack trees are mainly used to represent and assess security scenarios in a system at design time [16]. However, Poolsapassit and Ray [24] used attack trees in a way similar to our approach. They do not convert it to another model, but rather combine it with an attacker's intent to predict malicious activity. In [23] they used attack trees to investigate logs. These two papers are related to our goal but differ in the approach of converting attack trees to causal models and combining them for after the fact analysis.

Similar to fault trees, a hierarchical tree representation is used in attack trees. The root node contains the ultimate goal of an attack tree (e.g., violate the NFZ) and sub-nodes describe activities that are necessary to accomplish the respective parent activity/goal (e.g., spoof GPS). The relationship between a parent node and its children can be either *OR* or *AND*, i.e., either any child activity/goal will fulfill the parent activity, or all child activities/goals together are required. Figure 2b shows an example attack tree for a UAV.

Causal Models, specifically Halpern and Pearl (HP for short) models of causality, [10–12,22], model the world using a set of variables which are characterized as *endogenous* or *exogenous*, and a set of *structural equations*. The value of the exogenous variables is determined by factors outside the model. In a sense, they are the state of the world and the input to the causal model. The endogenous variables model our understanding of the causal relations, and their value is ultimately determined by the exogenous variables. Additionally, a causal model incorporates equations that model the influence of all these variables upon one another. The causality conditions provided in [10] define under which circumstances one or more (endogenous) variables within a causal model need to be considered as causes for a specific state of other variables. The specific state of the variables is called a *context* and, essentially, is a setting of their values.

Formally, Definition 1 describes a binary causal model. A causal model is visualized as a *causal network* where a variable is presented as a graph node, and dependency among variables from the structural equations is presented as an edge (see Sect. 4 for examples).

Definition 1. *Binary Causal Model* [10]
A binary causal model M is a tuple $M = ((\mathcal{U}, \mathcal{V}, \mathcal{R}), \mathcal{F})$, where

- *$\mathcal{U}$ is a set of exogenous variables,*
- *$\mathcal{V}$ is a set of endogenous variables,*
- *$\mathcal{R}$: associates every variable with a value $\in \{true, false\}$,*
- *$\mathcal{F}$ associates with each variable $X \in \mathcal{V}$ a function that determines the value of X (from the set of possible values $\mathcal{R}(X)$) given the values of all other variables $F_X : (\times_{U \in \mathcal{U}} \mathcal{R}(U)) \times (\times_{Y \in \mathcal{V} - \{X\}} \mathcal{R}(Y)) \to \mathcal{R}(X)$.*

We present the required notations to define the *Actual Cause* according to HP. A *primitive event*, given $(\mathcal{U}, \mathcal{V}, \mathcal{R})$, is a formula of the form $X = x$ for $X \in \mathcal{V}$ and $x \in \mathcal{R}(X)$. A *causal formula* is of the form $[Y_1 \leftarrow y_1, \dots, Y_k \leftarrow y_k]\varphi$, where φ is a Boolean combination of primitive events. $Y_1, \dots, Y_k$ (abbreviated $\overrightarrow{Y}$) are distinct variables in $\mathcal{V}$, and $y_i \in \mathcal{R}(Y_i)$. Intuitively, this notation says that φ would hold if Y_i were set to y_i for each i. $(M, \overrightarrow{u}) \models X = x$ if the variable X has value x in the unique solution to the equations in M in context $\overrightarrow{u}$ (i.e., the specific values of the variables). An intervention on a model is expressed either by setting the values of $\overrightarrow{X}$ to $\overrightarrow{x}$, written as $[X_1 \leftarrow x_1, .., X_k \leftarrow x_k]$, or by fixing the values of $\overrightarrow{X}$ in the model, written as $M_{\overrightarrow{X} \leftarrow \overrightarrow{x}}$. So, $(M, \overrightarrow{u}) \models [\overrightarrow{Y} \leftarrow \overrightarrow{y}]\varphi$ is identical to $(M_{\overrightarrow{Y} \leftarrow \overrightarrow{y}}, \overrightarrow{u}) \models \varphi$.

Definition 2. **Actual Cause** *(latest/modified version* [10]*)*
$\vec{X} = \vec{x}$ *is an actual cause of φ in $(M, \vec{u})$ if the following three conditions hold:*
AC1. *$(M, \vec{u}) \models (\vec{X} = \vec{x})$ and $(M, \vec{u}) \models \varphi$.*
AC2. *There is a set $\vec{W}$ of variables in $\mathcal{V}$ and a setting $\vec{x}'$ of the variables in $\vec{X}$ such that if $(M, \vec{u}) \models \vec{W} = \vec{w}$, then $(M, \vec{u}) \models [\vec{X} \leftarrow \vec{x}', \vec{W} \leftarrow \vec{w}] \neg \varphi$.*
AC3. *$\vec{X}$ is minimal, i.e., no subset of $\vec{X}$ fulfills AC1 and AC2.*

This definition and its theoretical foundation enable us to handle the main challenges faced by causality definitions [17]: With causal models, we have the advantage of choosing what to count as a possible cause (*endogenous*) and what not to (*exogenous*), enabling the **irrelevance** of causal factors to be judged. This enables us to limit our attribution or explanation based on the goal of the analysis. If we are interested in legal liability, we include possible human actors. If we are looking for an explanation for a technical failure, we include components as endogenous variables.

In complex systems, one cause can frequently preempt others. An example is an empty battery of a UAV will preclude any emergency maneuvers. In contrast to the HP definition, simple counter-factual definitions cannot identify the actual cause for such cases of **preemption** (examples by Lewis [18]).

Using the HP definition, we can also identify the **non-occurrence** of one or more events (i.e., the value of $V_i = 0$) as a cause for another event. For example, we can infer that an operator failing to add the coordinates for an NFZ is a cause. HP is able to specify an actual cause or effect as a **conjunction and disjunction** of events. This is a crucial aspect in our approach since we reason about factors that originated from different models, like a sensor failure in a fault tree and a malicious action in an attack tree. For example, a UAV may violate a no-fly zone because the GPS sensor was disabled and the remote-control pilot was deliberately steering it into the NFZ.

Finally, in complex modern systems like UAVs, we often have to deal with uncertain situations using partial knowledge. **Uncertainty** is embedded in HP at two levels [10]. First, the model that represents our understanding of the causal relations (Definition 1), and second, the context ($\vec{u}$) that represents a specific scenario defining the environment of a model. Uncertainty in the model reflects the cases where there is incomplete understanding of the causal relations between events, and uncertainty in the context reflects situations where there is incomplete understanding of the exact situation.

3   Methodology

A causal model (as described in Definition 1) is required to enable reasoning about actual causality. While there has been work on learning causal models from data [29], in this paper, we aim to combine different threat and hazard models into a single, holistic causal model. Our approach is motivated by the fact that we often have different models for describing the cause and effect relations that lead

Table 1. Comparison of formats.

	Fault tree	Attack tree	TFPG	Causal model
Inner element or gate	Describes a failure which occurs as a consequence of other failures connected by an operator	Describes an attack/subgoal achieved by executing its child-attacks	Describes off-nominal conditions resulting from a set of failure modes being present	An endogenous variable which is defined by other endogenous variables composed to a formula
Leaf elements	Describes a basic failure which is not a consequence of other failures	Describes a basic attack which does not rely on others and can be executed as is	Describes failure modes of a component at the lowest level of abstraction which is useful at run-time	An endogenous variable defined by an exogenous variable. Describes whether or not a specific event occurred
Operators	OR, AND, XOR, PRIORITY_AND, PRIORITY_OR, INHIBIT, ORMORE, ORLESS	Conjunctive (i.e., AND), disjunctive (i.e., OR)		AND, OR, NOT, XOR, IFF, NAND, NOR, ATLEAST(min), CARDINAL-ITY(min,max)

to unwanted behavior. Although such models are generally used for risk assessment and mitigation during system design or run-time, we use the knowledge gleaned from these models to explain behavior in the post-mortem analysis of a failure. Commonly, attack trees, fault trees, and TFPGs model causal relations, represent binary events, allow for combining events using propositional logic relations like *AND* and *OR*, and are acyclic (see Table 1 for a comparison). These properties make the transformation of these models to causal models, based on Definition 1, rather straightforward. However, such transformations entail assigning new, possibly different, semantics to those utilized within the source models. Hence, showing the equivalence of these semantics is required to prove the correctness of the mapping. However, our methodology does not examine specific semantic details, but rather shows that the idea works in general. As such, we consider the equivalence proof to be beyond the scope of this paper, but believe that this fact does not detract from our conclusions. Here we focus on incorporating these transformations as explicit parts of our methodology, to create a holistic causal model that incorporates different design-time models focusing on different aspects, and possibly created by different teams.

Figure 3 shows the three steps of our methodology, together with their corresponding input and output. In the transformation step, we show how to create a causal model from each input model. Next, we use notions of causal model compatibility defined by Alrajeh et al. [3], and Friedenberg and Halpern [9] to combine those models into a single model. Finally, domain experts can edit the combined model to include additional factors from other system models, specific un-formalized knowledge, or the social context.

Ultimately, this methodology generates a holistic causal model that is derived from several source models. Such a model can then be used by investigators to reason about the actual causes of an observed behavior in hindsight. To incorporate additional domain knowledge, an investigator can edit, update, and rephrase these assumptions to incorporate additional knowledge at any point in the process.

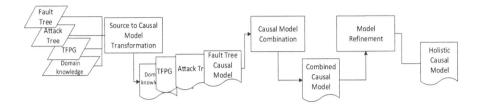

Fig. 3. Process diagram of the methodology.

3.1   Transforming Trees into Causal Models

Although fault and attack trees emerged from different domains to address different purposes, their syntax are similar. Thus, we present a common definition for both fault and attack trees. Definition 3 follows from Mauw and Oostdijk's [19] formalization of attack trees. However, we do not use their multi-set semantics for the trees. Instead, Bruns and Anderson [4] introduced a propositional semantics for fault trees and Hansen et al. [13] proposed a similar semantics that uses duration calculus to express leaves. We follow the propositional semantics because it matches the semantics of binary structural equations used in causal models. Therefore, each non-leaf node in the tree is expressed with a propositional formula of its parents, e.g., $out = in_1 \wedge in_2$.

Definition 3. *Attack/Fault Tree*
$A(F)T$ *is a 3-tuple* $A(F)T = (\mathcal{N}, \rightarrow, n_0)$ *where* $\mathcal{N}$ *is a finite set of nodes,* $n_0 \in \mathcal{N}$ *is the root node and* $\rightarrow \subseteq \mathcal{N} \times \mathcal{N}$ *is a finite set of acyclic relations.*

Definition 4 now shows how to map Definition 3 to Definition 1. We want to consider each node as a possible cause, hence we consider each node within these trees as an *endogenous variable* that defines whether or not a specific failure occurred (fault trees) or an attack has been conducted (attack trees). In this paper, we only consider Boolean variables, but plan to generalize our approach in the future. Since the nodes are connected with different operators, we can reuse them to construct necessary structural equations and therefore express relationships between the variables.

In fault and attack trees, leaf nodes represent a failure event or an atomic attack activity that is not refined further [26]. However, when transferring such nodes into variables of a causal model, we have to respect the requirement that, according to HP [11], each endogenous variable needs to be defined by other endogenous or exogenous variables. Therefore, for each endogenous variable created from a leaf node, we define an exogenous variable (having the same name, but with an _exo suffix appended) that will supply the value for the former. Because they are now endogenous variables, we can identify leaf nodes (or a combination of leaf nodes) as a cause of an event. It is also important to note that in both tree types, the same element can occur multiple times (e.g., same failure event in a different situation). However, in our causal model, exactly one instance of each variable exists.

Definition 4. *Attack/Fault Tree To Causal Model*
$T = (\mathcal{N}, \rightarrow, n_0)$ *is mapped to a* $M = ((\mathcal{U}, \mathcal{V}, \mathcal{R}), \mathcal{F})$, *i.e.,* $T \rightarrow M$ *as follows*

- $\mathcal{U} = E(T, \_exo)$, *where* $E(T, suffix)$ *returns a renamed copy of the leaf nodes of a tree* T *with a suffix* _ *"exo".*
- $\mathcal{V} = N$.
- $\mathcal{R} = \{true, false\}$.
- $\mathcal{F}$ *associates with each* $X \in V - E(T)$ *a propositional formula based on the tree gates; and with each* $X \in E(T)$ *a formula of the form* $X = X \_exo$.

3.2 TFPG

TFPGs are represented as a tuple (F, D, E, M, ET, EM, DE), where F is a non-empty set of failure modes which are always root nodes, meaning that these modes cannot be the destination of an edge. This makes these modes equivalent to $\mathcal{U}$, the exogenous variables. However, since we would like to include the failure modes as possible causes which may be refined further by other models (described in Sect. 3.3), we include F within endogenous variables. We use a similar technique as with fault and attack trees, i.e., we copy the set F and rename the items with the suffix $\_exo$. D is a non-empty set of discrepancy nodes, which cannot be root nodes and must be the successor for either a failure mode of another discrepancy node. This equates them to the endogenous variables, $\mathcal{V}$, in the HP model. $E \subseteq V \times V$ is the set of all edges; $V = F \cup D$. M is a non-empty set of system modes; at each time instance t the system can only be in one mode. While HP models usually do not model time, it can be modeled using time-index variables. We can enforce the restriction of system modes in the valid set of exogenous variables in this case.

$ET : E \rightarrow I$ associates every edge with a time interval $[t_1, t_2] \in I$ and $EM : E \rightarrow \mathcal{P}(M)$ associates every edge with a system mode. In HP, we can model these with the structural equations. $DC : D \rightarrow \{AND, OR\}$ maps each discrepancy to an AND or an OR node. $DS : D \rightarrow \{A, I\}$ defines the monitoring status of a discrepancy as either active or inactive. These last two functions can be expressed in a binary causal model.

Definition 5. *TFPG To Causal Model*
$TFPG = (F, D, E, M, ET, EM, DE)$ *is mapped to a* $M = (\mathcal{U}, \mathcal{V}, \mathcal{R}, \mathcal{F})$ *i.e.,* $TFPG \rightarrow M$ *as follows:* $\mathcal{U} = rename(F, \_exo)$, $\mathcal{V} = F \cup D$, $\mathcal{R} = \{true, false\}$, $\mathcal{F}$ *associates with each* $X \in \mathcal{V}$ *a propositional formula based on DC which maps a* $D \rightarrow \{AND, OR\}$; *and with each* $X \in F$ *a formula of the form* $X = X\_exo$.

3.3 Combining Causal Models

In safety and security, among other domains, we need models for two distinct purposes: to *detect* abnormal behavior and to *explain* any course of events.

Detection works by comparing the actual behavior of a system to some ideal behavior model of the system. In this paper, we consider two models for detection: TFPGs model the system and help developers place *alarms* that detect deviations from the expected behavior. The second model we implicitly consider is the mental model of the users or any observers: such observers will expect a particular occurrence, and, if it does not occur, they will attempt to garner an explanation. Unfortunately, this second model is difficult to formalize ahead of time. The advantage of HP causal models is they are very good at capturing the expectations and any deviation from them a posteriori. This ad-hoc formalization can then be combined with existing causal models in fault or attack trees to furnish an explanation for observed deviations from expected chains of events.

Explanations can be given by dissecting the system and then building a mental model of how it should work. Fault and attack trees simplify this process by capturing expected failure patterns in easy-to-navigate trees. TFPGs also serve as a causal model that can give explanations for expected faults. Their analysis, however, may not yield an explanation of sufficient detail, but instead, end in generic nodes like "Byzantine fault". Since faults in CPS often transcend the system boundary, we require additional models to find a satisfactory explanation for a fault. For example, a TFPG model might tell us that the GPS is faulty; however, only an attack tree can explain to us that this may be because of a spoofing attack. This emphasizes further the strength of HP causal models: they allow us to reason about the absence of evidence and show us where we need to look for additional evidence.

(a) Refine.

(b) Extend.

Fig. 4. Merging causal models.

Cross-model Explanations are required when no single model has all the details to explain an event. However, since we are using different models that may describe the same incident from different perspectives, the models from the previous step may overlap, and, hence, can be combined to provide an explanation. In this case, one causal model can either *refine* or *extend* another one. A refinement means that the two models share a common node, but that one model has more details about that node (see Fig. 4a). An example is the TFPG can point to a faulty GPS, and the fault tree can then point to an error in setting up the antenna. Conversely, an extension, happens when two models share a node (which may only be the top-level node), and adding those two models gives us an alternative explanation (see Fig. 4b). Such explanations may be in some preemption-relation: an example would be that we know that the UAV's propellers stopped spinning mid-flight, and that an explanation from the fault tree could be that the battery ran out, while an alternative explanation from the attack tree could be that an attacker switched them off. In this case, an empty battery would preempt any action from an attacker. For the model refinement step, we borrow the notions of model *dominance, compatibility,* and *combination* from the domain of decision-making described by Alrajeh et al. [3], allowing us to combine models where the modelers agree on the causal relationships among the common variables but use different levels of detail to describe how the variables are affected by other variables.

Informally, the work by Alrajeh et al. provides conditions for the *compatibility* of causal models as a prerequisite for *combining* them. To that end, they introduce the notion of a *dominant* relation, essentially comparing the information expressiveness of two models about a variable C. One model, M_1, *dominates* another, M_2 in expressing variable C, denoted as $M_1 \succeq_C M_2$, if they agree on the causal dependence of C, but M_1 provides a more detailed picture. For each common variable, if the two models have a dominance relation (regardless of which model is dominating the other), the models are *compatible*. Only compatible models can then be combined, denoted as $M_1 \oplus M_2$.

Definition 6. *Domination relation* [3]. *Let* $M_1 = ((U_1, V_1, R_1), F_1)$ *and* $M_2 = ((U_2, V_2, R_2), F_2)$. *Let* $Par_M(C)$ *denote the variables that are parents of* C *in* M. *M_1 strongly dominates M_2 with respect to C, denoted $M_1 \succeq_C M_2$, if the following conditions hold:*

$MI1_{M_1,M_2,C}$ The parents of C in M_2 are the immediate M_2-ancestors of C in M_1.

$MI2_{M_1,M_2,C}$ every path from an exogenous variable to C in M_1 goes through a variable in $Par_{M_2}(C)$.

$MI3_{M_1,M_2,C}$ Let $X = ((U_1 \cup V_1) \cap (U_2 \cup V_2)) - \{C\}$ then for all settings x of the variables in X, all values c of C, all contexts u_1 for M_1, and all contexts u_2 for M_2 $(M_1, \overrightarrow{u_1}) \models [\overrightarrow{X} \leftarrow \overrightarrow{x}](C = c)$ iff $(M_2, \overrightarrow{u_2}) \models [\overrightarrow{X} \leftarrow \overrightarrow{x}](C = c).$[2]

The idea of refinement as shown in Fig. 4a can be considered as a special case of the combination step. We limit our work to *refining* causal models on the leaf nodes. That is, we only consider a detailed model M_1 to be appended to a more abstract model M_2 if the root, or the root of a sub-tree, of M_1 is identical to one of the leaf-nodes of M_2 (of the causal graph with exogenous variables omitted). In this specific case, according to the *strong domination* definition in [3] (Definition 6), the two causal models are always compatible. Hence, they can be combined resulting in a new model M as defined in Definition 7.

Definition 7. *Combination* [3]. *If* $M_1 = ((U_1, V_1, R_1), F_1)$ *and* $M_2 = ((U_2, V_2, R_2), F_2)$, *then M_1 and M_2 are compatible if (1) for all variables $C \in ((U_1 \cup V_1) \cap (U_2 \cup V_2))$, we have $R_1(C) = R_2(C)$ and (2) for all variables $C \in (V_1 \cap V_2)$, either $M_1 \preceq_C M_2$ or $M_2 \preceq_C M_1$. If M_1 and M_2 are compatible, then $M_1 \oplus M_2$ is the causal model $((U, V, R), F)$, where $U = U_1 - U_2 - (V_1 \cup V_2)$; $V = V_1 \cup V_2$; if $C \in U_1 \cup V_1$, then $R(C) = R_1(C)$, and iff $C \in U_2 \cup V_2$, then $R(C) = R_2(C)$ if $C \in V_1 - V_2$ or if both $C \in V_1 \cap V_2$ and $M_1 \preceq_C M_2$ then $F(C) = F_1(C)$; if $C \in V_2 - V_1$ or if both $C \in V_1 \cap V_2$ and $M_2 \preceq_C M_1$, then $F(C) = F_2(C)$.*

Combining Extensions (Fig. 4b) is, unfortunately, more complex than merging refinements. In general, extensions will be *incompatible* and cannot be merged automatically. If two models disagree on the variables and their causal relationships, we have to defer the merging decision to an expert. To illustrate this

---

[2] For more details on the notations see Sect. 2.

using an example, we can think of two models that explain why a UAV enters a
NFZ. One model blames a broken GPS receiver, and the other model blames an
attacker for spoofing the GPS signal. Without more information, it is impossible
to decide which model is correct. The same applies when merging FTs, ATs, and
TFPGs: often we will need an expert's input to merge the models and decide
upon preemption relations and the overall causal structure.

For some specific models, Friedenberg and Halpern [9] provide an automatic
way of joining the models. Such FH-compatible models are causal models that
are extended with a focus function $\mathcal{G} : \mathcal{U} \cup \mathcal{V} \to 2^{(\mathcal{U} \cup \mathcal{V})}$ that, given a variable
C, provides the set of variables that the modeler considered as having an effect
on C. Using this additional information, if one model "can explain and has
everything considered by" some other model, these two models can be merged.
The intuition is that if both models consider the same variable C, they consider
the same parents of a variable C, and, thus one model can explain all of the other
model's observations, they are compatible in a similar sense as Alrajeh et al. [3]
consider a model to be compatible. If one of the two models provides additional
information, this information can be merged into a joint model. As an example,
if a TFPG model explains that a power loss caused an engine failure and a fault
tree shows that power loss can cause a loss of control, these two models can be
merged into one.

4   Example

In this paper, we introduced four sources of knowledge to analyze CPS: domain
knowledge, fault trees, attack trees, and TFPGs. We convert them all into HP
causal models and then combine them using the rules presented in Sect. 3. While
merging the models is not commutative, any order of combination will yield a
valid causal model. We found that we get the most "natural" results by starting
with the domain knowledge, continuing with the TFPG, and then using the
attack tree and fault tree to refine cover areas where the TFPG ends in Byzantine
faults.

In Fig. 5 we provide highly simplified causal models for our example. Models (a)–(d) were created from the corresponding source models and model (e) is
the combined model. In real applications, such models will be significantly larger
and more detailed. While this complicates the merging process, we have shown
in previous work that, as long as the causal models are binary, reasoning can be
performed in a fast and efficient manner, even for very large models [14].

The combination process can now follow our semi-automatic methodology.
First, we use the domain model to initialize the combined model: this models
the knowledge that the UAV can either be human-controlled or fly on autopilot.
If there is human control, the human can preempt the autopilot; however, even
if a human is in control, they might not intervene. Next, the TFPG is added:
this models the fact that a GPS fault can be caused by no GPS data, which we
can detect and go into a fail-stop state, or by incorrect data, which we cannot
detect at run-time, and leads to a Byzantine fault. Adding the TFPG to the

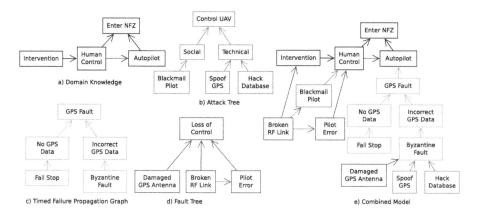

Fig. 5. All causal models color coded by their source model. Dashed edges represent preemption relations, and solid edges are normal causal relations. (Color figure online)

Autopilot can be done automatically because we can link the *Controller* node in the TFPG (see Fig. 1a) directly to the *Autopilot* in the causal model. To combine those two models, we can use a simple *refine* operation. The attack tree is slightly more complicated and models two main attack vectors: social engineering and technical attacks. In our example, we restrict ourselves to the blackmailing of the pilot and either spoofing the GPS signal or hacking the GPS database. Joining the attack tree can be done semi-automatically: the connection between the nodes *Human Control* and *Social* can be made automatically, but mapping the *Technical* attacks to the *Byzantine Fault* requires an expert's intervention. The fault tree, finally, provides reasons why a loss of control may happen. The GPS antenna may fail and yield erratic values, the pilot may make an error, or the RF link may break. A broken link also preempts a pilot error, because it prevents all actions by the pilot. Combining the fault tree is also the most complex operation: first, we require expert knowledge to join the *Damaged GPS antenna* to the *Byzantine Fault*. It is also an *extend* operation and, thus, requires us to check that it does not contradict the attack tree nodes. If the respective *focus sets* are given, this process can be automated, otherwise we need an expert's judgment. Adding *Broken RF Link* also requires an expert's intervention. For one, because it is another *extension* operation, but also because a *Broken RF Link* will preempt *Blackmail Pilot*. So even if pilots were blackmailed, they could not carry out any orders, because the broken link would prevent them from doing so. This means that the blackmail would not be a cause for the violation of the NFZ. Additionally *Broken RF Link* will influence *Intervention*, in the sense that a broken RF link would make any intervention impossible.

To evaluate the effectiveness of our generated causal model, we briefly show its usage to explain the violation of the NFZ in three different scenarios. The scenarios are represented by different contexts (see Fig. 6 for graphical representations and Fig. 7 for the equations). A context is a specific setting (true or false values) of the exogenous variables. Usually, these settings are collected from

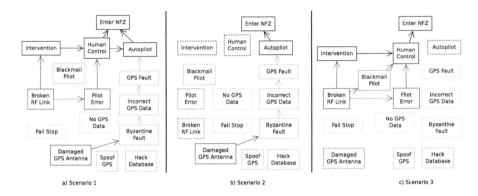

a) Scenario 1   b) Scenario 2   c) Scenario 3

Fig. 6. Graphical representation of the three scenarios.

monitors, logs, or eyewitness reports. For this example, the contexts are simplified and contrived. All reasoning, however, is automated with the tool-support described in our previous work [14]. The tool answers causal queries of the form *is* $\overrightarrow{X} = \overrightarrow{x}$ *an actual cause (based on Definition2) of* $\overrightarrow{Y} = \overrightarrow{y}$, *given a context* $\overrightarrow{U} = \overrightarrow{u}$? The output of the tool, if the answer is *yes*, is a 3-tuple$(\overrightarrow{X}, \overrightarrow{x'}, \overrightarrow{W})$, corresponding to the elements defined in the definition.

Scenario 1. In this context the variables that are set to true, i.e., were observed, are *Broken RF Link_exo*, *Pilot Error_exo*, and *Damaged GPS antenna_exo*. We then used the HP definition to check which endogenous variable (corresponding to the mentioned exogenous variables) is the cause of *Enter NFZ= true*. Although we have a *Damaged GPS antenna*, this is not the actual cause, because this damage is preempted by the *Human control*, since the domain knowledge specifies that the commands from the

- $EnterNFZ = HumanControl \lor Autopilot$
- $HumanControl = PilotError \lor BlackmailPilot \lor \neg Intervention$
- $PilotError = PilotError\_exo \land \boxed{\neg BrokenRFLink}$
- $\boxed{BlackmailPilot} = BlackmailPilot\_exo \land \boxed{\neg BrokenRFLink}$
- $Intervention = \neg BrokenRFLink$
- $BrokenRFLink = BrokenRFLink\_exo$
- $Autopilot = GPSFault \land \boxed{\neg HumanControl}$
- $GPSFault = NoGPSData \lor IncorrectGPSdata$
- $NoGPSData = FailStop$
- $IncorrectGPSdata = ByzantineFault$
- $ByzantineFault = DamagedGPSantenna \lor HackDatabase \lor SpoofGPS$

Fig. 7. The equations for the scenarios. Dashed Boxes highlight preemption relations.

remote have a higher priority than the autopilot. However, we found that the actual cause is the *Broken RF Link* because it precludes any command from reaching the UAV, and, thus, also any *Pilot Error*. This scenario represents cases of *preemption* between factors coming from different sources. The causal queries were executed in a total of 3 ms (performed on Ubuntu 16.04

LTS machine equipped with an Intel® Core™ i7-3740QM CPU and 8 GB RAM), the result for *Broken RF Link* query was yes with the 3-tuple($\vec{X}$ = $\{BrokenRFLink\}$, $\vec{x'}$ = $\{false\}$, $\vec{W}$ = $\{Autopilot, Piloterror\}$).

Scenario 2. Here, the only variable set to true is *Damaged GPS antenna_exo*. We then check if *Damaged GPS antenna* is the cause for *Enter NFZ=true*, and the answer is *yes* with the 3-tuple($\vec{X}$ = $\{DamagedGPSantenna\}$, $\vec{x'}$ = $\{false\}$, $\vec{W}$ = $\emptyset$). In the same context, the causal model of the TFPG (Fig. 5(d)) is only able to explain the scenario with a *Byzantine Fault*. This scenario represents cases where the refinement, which we did as part of the methodology, is beneficial. The causal query was executed in ≤ 1 ms.

Scenario 3. In this context only *Broken RF Link_exo* is set to true. We then use the HP definition to check if the absence of human intervention, *Intervention=false*, is the cause for *Enter NFZ=true*, and the answer is *yes* with the 3-tuple($\vec{X}$ = $\{Intervention\}$, $\vec{x'}$ = $\{true\}$, $\vec{W}$ = $\emptyset$). This scenario represents cases where the non-occurrence of events is attributed as the actual cause. The causal query was also executed in ≤ 1 ms.

5   Conclusion

In this paper, we presented an approach to convert Timed Failure Propagation Graphs, Attack Trees and Fault Trees into Halpern-Pearl causal models, combine these into a single holistic causal model, and then enrich this holistic model with additional domain knowledge. Besides making the expert's knowledge explicit, the causal model enables us to use automated tools to reason about causes of violations even in cases of *preemption, non-occurrence of events*, or *cross-model refinements*. Using HP causal models has the unique advantage that we can use a machine to reason about causality as a human would. Halpern and Pearl have shown that their approach can solve even complex philosophical problems in a way that is congruent with human intuition as detailed in the literature. We expect our semi-automatic approach not only to reduce the workload for modelers, but also to provide a systematic process to create models that can then be enriched with domain knowledge. Nonetheless, modeling is still an art and very subjective, meaning that the models will be biased and their answers model-relative. Furthermore, we have no measure for the quality or completeness of a model. Another area requiring future research is finding and describing heuristics to merge models. While refinements are easy to merge, extensions are notoriously difficult and often require manual intervention. Incorporating information on the socio-technical context will allow us to improve the merging process, develop more sophisticated heuristics and improve our understanding of vaguely defined "expert interventions".

References

1. Abdelwahed, S., Dubey, A., Karsai, G., Mahadevan, N.: Model-based tools and techniques for real-time system and software health management. In: Srivastava, A., Han, J. (eds.) Machine Learning and Knowledge Discovery for Engineering Systems Health Management. Chapman and Hall/CRC, London (2011). Chapter 9

2. Abdelwahed, S., Karsai, G., Biswas, G.: A consistency-based robust diagnosis approach for temporal causal systems. In: The 16th International Workshop on Principles of Diagnosis, pp. 73–79 (2005)

3. Alrajeh, D., Chockler, H., Halpern, J.Y.: Combining experts' causal judgments. In: Thirty-Second AAAI Conference on Artificial Intelligence (AAAI-2018) (2018)

4. Bruns, G., Anderson, S.: Validating safety models with fault trees. In: Górski, J. (ed.) SAFECOMP 1993, pp. 21–30. Springer, London (1993). https://doi.org/10.1007/978-1-4471-2061-2_3

5. DJI: Fly safe - geo zone map (2018). https://www.dji.com/en/flysafe/geo-map. Accessed 03 Dec 2018

6. Dubey, A., Karsai, G., Mahadevan, N.: Model-based software health management for real-time systems. In: 2011 Aerospace Conference, pp. 1–18, March 2011. https://doi.org/10.1109/AERO.2011.5747559

7. Eurocontrol: Useful information on UAS no-fly areas (2018). https://www.eurocontrol.int/articles/useful-information-uas-no-fly-areas. Accessed 03 Dec 2018

8. FAA: Airspace restrictions (2018). https://www.faa.gov/uas/where_to_fly/airspace_restrictions/. Accessed 03 Dec 2018

9. Friedenberg, M., Halpern, J.Y.: Combining the causal judgments of experts with possibly different focus areas (2018). http://www.cs.cornell.edu/home/halpern/papers/focus.pdf

10. Halpern, J.Y.: A modification of the Halpern-Pearl definition of causality. In: International Joint Conference on Artificial Intelligence, pp. 3022–3033 (2015). https://www.aaai.org/ocs/index.php/IJCAI/IJCAI15/paper/view/11058/11085

11. Halpern, J.Y., Pearl, J.: Causes and explanations: a structural-model approach. Part I: causes. Br. J. Philos. Sci. **56**(4), 843–887 (2005). https://doi.org/10.1093/bjps/axi147

12. Halpern, J.Y., Pearl, J.: Causes and explanations: a structural-model approach. Part II: explanations. Br. J. Philos. Sci. **56**(4), 889–911 (2005). https://doi.org/10.1093/bjps/axi148

13. Hansen, K.M., Ravn, A.P., Stavridou, V.: From safety analysis to software requirements. IEEE Trans. Software Eng. **24**, 573–584 (1998). https://doi.org/10.1109/32.708570. doi.ieeecomputersociety.org/10.1109/32.708570

14. Ibrahim, A., Rehwald, S., Pretschner, A.: Efficiently checking actual causality with sat solving. In: Dependable Software Systems Engineering (2019, to appear)

15. Kacianka, S., Pretschner, A.: Understanding and formalizing accountability for cyber-physical systems. In: IEEE International Conference on Systems, Man, and Cybernetics (SMC), October 2018. https://arxiv.org/abs/1810.09704

16. Kordy, B., Piètre-Cambacédès, L., Schweitzer, P.: DAG-based attack and defense modeling: don't miss the forest for the attack trees. Comput. Sci. Rev. **13**, 1–38 (2014)

17. Leitner-Fischer, F., Leue, S.: Causality checking for complex system models. In: Giacobbazzi, R., Berdine, J., Mastroeni, I. (eds.) VMCAI 2013. LNCS, vol. 7737, pp. 248–267. Springer, Heidelberg (2013). https://doi.org/10.1007/978-3-642-35873-9_16

18. Lewis, D.: Causation. J. Philos. **70**(17), 556–567 (1973). https://doi.org/10.2307/2025310
19. Mauw, S., Oostdijk, M.: Foundations of attack trees. In: Won, D.H., Kim, S. (eds.) ICISC 2005. LNCS, vol. 3935, pp. 186–198. Springer, Heidelberg (2006). https://doi.org/10.1007/11734727_17
20. Narayanan, N.H., Viswanadham, N.: A methodology for knowledge acquisition and reasoning in failure analysis of systems. IEEE Trans. Syst. Man Cybern. **17**(2), 274–288 (1987)
21. Papadopoulos, Y.: Model-based system monitoring and diagnosis of failures using statecharts and fault trees. Reliab. Eng. Syst. Saf. **81**(3), 325–341 (2003)
22. Pearl, J., Mackenzie, D.: The Book of Why. Basic Books, New York (2018)
23. Poolsapassit, N., Ray, I.: Investigating computer attacks using attack trees. In: Craiger, P., Shenoi, S. (eds.) DigitalForensics 2007. ITIFIP, vol. 242, pp. 331–343. Springer, New York (2007). https://doi.org/10.1007/978-0-387-73742-3_23
24. Ray, I., Poolsapassit, N.: Using attack trees to identify malicious attacks from authorized insiders. In: di Vimercati, S.C., Syverson, P., Gollmann, D. (eds.) ESORICS 2005. LNCS, vol. 3679, pp. 231–246. Springer, Heidelberg (2005). https://doi.org/10.1007/11555827_14
25. Ruijters, E., Stoelinga, M.: Fault tree analysis: a survey of the state-of-the-art in modeling, analysis and tools. Comput. Sci. Rev. **15**, 29–62 (2015)
26. Schneier, B.: Attack trees - modeling security threats. DR DOBBS J. (1999). http://www.schneier.com/paper-attacktrees-ddj-ft.html
27. Schneier, B.: Secrets and Lies - Digital Security in a Networked World: With New Information About Post-9/11 Security. Wiley, Indianapolis (2004)
28. Simon, G., et al.: Model-based fault-adaptive control of complex dynamic systems. In: Proceedings of the 20th IEEE Instrumentation Technology Conference (Cat. No. 03CH37412), vol. 1, pp. 176–181, May 2003. https://doi.org/10.1109/IMTC.2003.1208147
29. Triantafillou, S., Tsamardinos, I.: Constraint-based causal discovery from multiple interventions over overlapping variable sets. J. Mach. Learn. Res. **16**, 2147–2205 (2015)
30. Vesely, W., Goldberg, F., Roberts, N., Haasl, D.: Fault tree handbook (1981)

Extracting and Optimizing Formally Verified Code for Systems Programming

Eleftherios Ioannidis$^{(\boxtimes)}$, Frans Kaashoek, and Nickolai Zeldovich

Massachusetts Institute of Technology, Cambridge, UK
`elefthei@mit.edu`

Abstract. MCQC is a compiler for extracting verified systems programs to low-level assembly, with no runtime or garbage collection requirements and an emphasis on performance. MCQC targets the Gallina functional language used in the Coq proof assistant. MCQC translates pure and recursive functions into C++17, while compiling monadic effectful functions to imperative C++ system calls. With a few memory and performance optimizations, MCQC combines verifiability with memory and runtime performance. By handling effectful and pure functions separately MCQC can generate executable verified code directly from Gallina, reducing the effort of implementing and executing verified systems.

Keywords: Formal verification · Functional compiler · Extraction · Systems

1 Introduction

The formal verification of computer systems has been a continuous subject of research over the last decade, with verified file systems [1,5], kernels [10,14], distributed systems [23] and cryptographic algorithms [4,9]. Formal proofs about programs are developed in a dependently-typed language [24], inside a mechanized proof-assistant, like Coq [3,24]. Coq has its own programming language, Gallina which together with the proof-language Ltac enable the development of formally verified algorithms. The compilation and execution of formally verified software written in Gallina, for systems programming with side-effects and an emphasis on performance, is the focus of this paper.

1.1 The Problem of Code Generation

The functional, dependent nature of Gallina makes it difficult to execute outside Coq. There are a few roadblocks to generating performant, effectful code from Gallina, which must be addressed:

1. Coq relies on a runtime system (RTS) and garbage collection (GC) for memory management, which makes it hard to execute verified code on bare hardware (OS, embedded systems, firmware etc).

© Springer Nature Switzerland AG 2019
J. M. Badger and K. Y. Rozier (Eds.): NFM 2019, LNCS 11460, pp. 228–236, 2019.
https://doi.org/10.1007/978-3-030-20652-9_15

2. Integral and bitfield types are inductively defined in Coq and they do not fit into CPU registers, making the performance overhead of executing Gallina prohibitive.
3. Gallina is completely pure and it cannot generate any observable effects.
4. The performance of dynamic memory datastructures such as lists, maps and trees, suffers during extraction. Coq passes arguments by value, which leads to excessive copying and a dependence on GC.

There are currently two approaches to generating formally verified, executable code and they each address a subset of the issues stated above; by verified compilation of deep embeddings and by extraction of shallow embeddings [2, 17]. The first method requires advanced knowledge of programming language theory and involves defining, proving and compiling an embedded Domain Specific Language (eDSL) inside Coq, with varying degrees of proof automation available.

This paper focuses on the second approach of shallow embeddings and introduces the Monadic Coq Compiler (MCQC), a compiler for Gallina by means of extraction using C++17 as an intermediate representation. C++17 is a suitable intermediate language as it offers parametric polymorphism through templates, algebraic datatypes (ADTs) through variants and GC through smart pointers. The output C++17 can be compiled by any modern C compiler with no external dependencies. We chose the clang C compiler [15] for MCQC.

1.2 Previous Work

The CertiCoq compiler [2] implements Coq's language inside the Coq proof-assistant, allowing for the verified compilation of Gallina. However, CertiCoq depends on a runtime GC and cannot generate static, stand-alone assembly. The Œuf verified extractor [20] reifies Gallina into an abstract syntax tree (AST) that it then translates to CompCert's intermediate representation [16] but does not target full Gallina, only a small subset of it relevant to reactive systems. The Fiat compiler does verified compilation of an eDSL down to static C but is only applicable to the domain of cryptographic algorithms [9].

1.3 Contributions

MCQC is a compiler, a library of native bitfield types and an IO library for interacting with the real world. The MCQC native library is modeled after the Coq standard library and obeys the same semantics, while offering fast, native computations. MCQC supports pure functional programming and effectful monadic IO operations, similar to the Haskell IO monad. Although side-effects cannot be executed inside Coq, they are compiled to real system calls by MCQC and executed by the underlying OS.

Using MCQC we have successfully compiled multiple types and functions from Coq's standard library. We have also written a proof-of-concept web application for online payments, with the web server written in Gallina and compiled to C++17 and the client written in Gallina and compiled to Webassembly. In both cases, a minimal amount of boilerplate code and proofs was required, while MCQC made it possible to write and test verified client and server code without leaving the Coq proof-assistant.

MCQC has some limitations compared to Gallina executed inside Coq. MCQC cannot generate code for Gallina typeclass instances, as typeclasses offer a model for ad-hoc polmorphism more general than C++ templates [22]. MCQC has limited multi-threading support. As part of `Proc` MCQC implements $spawn : \forall T, (T \rightarrow unit) \rightarrow T \rightarrow proc\ unit$ which can execute functions with no return values in parallel via `std::future`. To support parallel execution with return types, a promises interface would be more effective [18] in the future. Finally, the library of base types in C++17 is not formally verified. To ensure correctness with respect to the Coq standard library, a property-based testing suite is used [6].

2   Design

This section covers the most interesting part of the design; the full design is described in a master thesis [11]. MCQC is a compiler and a library of base types and system calls in C++17. The compiler is written in Haskell and accepts as input Gallina abstract syntax trees (AST) in a JSON format, extracted by the Coq JSON extraction plugin (Coq-8.5.1). MCQC compiles the Gallina AST to C++17 which then clang compiles to assembly [15] and links with the library, as shown in Fig. 1.

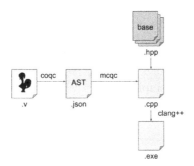

Fig. 1. MCQC block diagram. Coq files are the input, MCQC generates C++17 code and clang compiles it and links with the base type library to produce an executable. The white box is the input Gallina program, green boxes show imported libraries and yellow boxes show auto-generated files. (Color figure online)

The input Gallina AST is described by an input grammar which is defined in the MCQC thesis [11] and is the starting point for MCQC. The top level structure is a `Module`, which contains multiple top-level `Declarations`. Gallina declarations can be either inductive types, type aliases, named fixpoints or named expressions. MCQC breaks the compilation process into five stages; type inference, base semantics, algebraic datatypes, monadic effects and pretty-printing C++17.

2.1 Type Inference

Coq extraction transforms dependently typed Gallina to a simpler Hindley-Milner (HM) language similar to ML [8]. Type inference starts at each function declaration, which is always guaranteed to be well-typed by Coq prior to extraction. Each binder is added to the local context as a constraint and those constraints are solved while traversing the AST by standard HM type inference [8].

The C++17 type system does not have support for function types. MCQC preserves function types until the pretty-printing stage, when they are transformed to C++ templates. We chose function templates over `std::function` as clang will inline functional arguments when they are passed as templates, offering better performance for higher-order functions. In addition, MCQC adds a type annotation in the return type with the `std::invoke_result_t` template function, to help clang type resolution [13].

2.2 Base Semantics

Using Coq's standard library of base types can have a significant performance overhead as Coq defines base types inductively. MCQC substitutes slow Coq base types with their corresponding C++17 native, safe types. More details on safety of the base type library can be found in the MCQC thesis [11]. Base types are always passed by value in MCQC and conversely, ADTs are always passed by smart pointer.

Pattern matching in Coq corresponds to the polymorphic high-order function `match` in C++17, which is implemented differently for each type as seen in Fig. 2. As native types are susceptible to weak typing MCQC strengthens the C++17 type system with template metaprogramming (TMP) as seen is Fig. 2. A substitution failure at `std::enable_if_t` means the function will quietly disappear at clang compile-time without errors, a pattern known in C++ as SFINAE (Substitution Failure Is Not An Error) [13].

2.3 Algebraic Data Types (ADTs)

MCQC transforms Coq ADT definitions, like lists, trees etc, to a reference-counted, pointer datastructure in C++17. Sum types are transformed to tagged-unions implemented by `std::variant` [7] and product types are implemented by C structs. The combination of sums and products allows MCQC to define any algebraic data type in C++17 [19]. Finally, pattern-matching for those types is auto-generated as the polymorphic, high-order `match` function. ADTs are passed by smart pointer, a reference counted pointer that requires no GC, implemented

```
Inductive nat : Set :=        // Nat type alias for bitvector type
  | 0 : nat                   using nat = unsigned int;
  | S : nat -> nat.
                              // Pattern matching on nat
                              template<typename F0, typename FS,
                                typename = enable_if_t<CallableWith<F0>>,
                                typename = enable_if_t<CallableWith<FS, nat>>>
                              constexpr auto match(nat a, F0 f, FS g) {
                                switch(a) {
                                case 0:  return f();    // Call 0 clause
                                default: return g(a-1); // Call S clause
                                }
                              }
```

```
Fixpoint fib(n: nat) :=       nat fib(nat n) {
  match n with                  return match(n,
    | 0 => 1                      [=]() { return 1; },
    | S sm =>                     [=](nat sm) { return match(sm,
    match sm with                   [=]() { return 1; },
      | 0 => 1                      [=](nat m) {
      | S m =>                        return add(fib(m), fib(sm));
      (fib m) + (fib sm)            });
    end                         });
end.                          }
```

Fig. 2. Compiling the `fibonacci` function on the left in C++17, on the right. The shaded box surrounds Coq and C++17 boilerplate code for natural numbers. The definitions are almost isomorphic, except for overflow exceptions in native types which are safely detected and propagated to the caller.

via `std::shared_ptr`. An example of generating a pointer list from the ADT list definition in Coq can be seen in Fig. 3 and more details on ADT generation can be found in the MCQC thesis [11].

2.4   Monadic Effects (`Proc`)

Coq is so pure it has no way of interacting with the underlying OS in an effectful way. MCQC offers an interface for effectful computations by means of monadic composition with the `Proc` monad, similar to the Haskell `IO` monad [12]. Effectful monads in Gallina elaborate to imperative-style C++ statements, as shown in Fig. 4. An example of generating an implementation for the `cat` utility is shown in Fig. 4.

2.5   Pretty-Print C++17

In order to apply transformations and finally pretty-print C++17, MCQC transforms the input Coq AST to an intermediate representation closer to C++17. Going from that representation to a `.cpp` file is a matter of implementing a Wadler/Leijen prettyprinter [21].

```
Inductive list (T:Type) : Type :=     template<class T>
 | nil : list T                        struct Coq_nil {};
 | cons : T -> list T -> list T.       // Forward declarations
                                       template<class T>
                                       struct Coq_cons;
                                       template<class T>
                                       // Reference counted tagged-union
                                       using list = std::shared_ptr<
                                            std::variant<Coq_nil<T>, Coq_cons<T>>>;

                                       template<class T>
                                       struct Coq_cons {
                                         T a;
                                         list<T> b;
                                       };

                                       // Pattern match
                                       template<class T, class U, class V>
                                       auto match(list<T> self, U f, V g) {
                                         return std::visit(*self, overloaded {
                                           [=](Coq_nil<T> _) { return f(); },
                                           [=](Coq_cons<T> _) { return g(_.a, _.b); }
                                         });
                                       }
```

Fig. 3. Polymorphic list definition in Coq, MCQC generates the pointer data structure on the right, as well as `match` to deconstruct it.

```
(** Filedescriptor type *)          // Filedescriptor type
Definition fd := nat.               using fd = nat;

(** Effect composition *)           static proc<fd> open(string s) {
Inductive proc: Type -> Type :=       if (int o = sys::open(FWD(s).c_str(), O_RDWR) {
 | open : string -> proc fd            return static_cast<fd>(o);
 | read: fd -> proc string           }
 | close : fd -> proc unit           throw IOException("File not found");
 | print : string -> proc unit      }
(** Monad *)                        static proc<string> read(fd f, nat size) {
 | ret: forall T, T -> proc T         auto dp = string(size, '\0' );
 | bind: forall T T',                 sys::read(f, &(dp[0]), sizeof(char)*size);
   proc T                             return dp;
   -> (T -> proc T')                }
   -> proc T'.                       static proc<void> close(fd f) {
                                       if(sys::close(f)) {
Notation "p1 >>= p2" :=                 throw IOException("Could not close file");
  (bind p1 p2).                        }
                                     }
                                     static proc<void> print(string s) {
                                       std::cout << s << std::endl;
                                     }
```

```
Definition cat (path fn: string):=  proc<void> cat(string path, string fn) {
 open (path ++ "/" ++ fn) >>=         fd f = open(append(path, append("/", fn)));
  (fun f => read f >>=                string data = read(f);
   (fun data => close f >>=           close(f);
    (fun _ => print data >>=          print(data);
     (fun _ => ret unit)))).        }
```

Fig. 4. The `cat` UNIX utility that displays a text file. Instances of `proc` are translated to imperative C++ system calls. The shaded box surrounds Coq and C++17 boilerplate code, part of the MCQC library.

3   Implementation and Evaluation

In this section we present the runtime properties and performance of programs compiled with MCQC. The three questions we try to answer are; can we link verified and unverified code to create end-to-end applications, can we get better memory performance than extracted Haskell and can we get runtime performance comparable to Haskell compiled with GHC.

MCQC is open source under an MIT license and can be found here https://github.com/mit-pdos/mcqc. MCQC is implemented in 1800 lines of Haskell and 600 lines of C++17 code for the base type and `proc` library.

3.1   Linking Verified Applications

In order to demonstrate MCQC's capabilities we have developed a demo web application for payments, the verified *Zoobar* server. The *Zoobar* server demonstrates the ease of linking code compiled with MCQC, as both the server and client were built and proven in Coq and extracted to C++17 before linking with the HTTP libraries. The proof effort required for proving the transaction logic is minimal and focuses on the code that is most important. With the *Zoobar* demo we demonstrate a hybrid approach to verification, by combining verified logic with unverified trusted code. The design and implementation details of the *Zoobar* server are presented in full detail in the mcqc thesis [11].

3.2   Benchmarks

MCQC compares fairly well against GHC in terms of run-time performance and total memory used. The execution time of MCQC programs is on average 14.8% faster than GHC programs, as seen in Fig. 5a. MCQC reduces the memory footprint of executing verified programs by 66.25% on average compared to GHC, as seen in Fig. 5b.

We compare the performance of C++17 code generated with MCQC against Haskell code extracted from Coq with native types to ensure the comparison is fair. The clang-7.0 compiler compiles generated C++17 and `GHC-8.4.4` compiles extracted Haskell. More details on the hardware and profiling tools used can be found in the MCQC thesis [11].

The results in Fig. 5 show MCQC extracted code performs with considerably less memory compared to Haskell and at comparable run-time. Tail-call optimization is supported in clang so it is supported in MCQC, even across pattern matching. For `fact`, we see no heap or stack usage which confirms TCO has optimized recursion away. Finally, in algorithms that rely on GC we show that MCQC uses less memory compared to Haskell and in most cases, MCQC is faster.

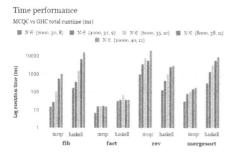

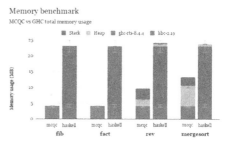

(a) Run-time in logarithmic scale.

(b) Memory; shared libraries, heap and stack.

Fig. 5. Performance and memory benchmarks for four Coq programs compiled with MCQC versus GHC. Increasing values for N were used for calculating Fig. 5a and only the highest value N was used for memory benchmarks.

4 Conclusion

We have presented the MCQC compiler, a novel approach to generating executable formally verified code directly from the Gallina functional specification. Code compiled with MCQC has a TCB comparable to standard Coq extraction mechanisms [17]. The MCQC TCB includes the clang compiler and MCQC itself, as well as the base types library. Coq extraction to Haskell and Ocaml includes the compiler and runtime in the TCB, which MCQC does not. We hope to see MCQC used as part of the Coq ecosystem, for the execution of formally verified code without scraping the full stack.

References

1. Amani, S., et al.: Cogent: verifying high-assurance file system implementations. ACM SIGOPS Oper. Syst. Rev. **50**(2), 175–188 (2016)
2. Anand, A., et al.: Certicoq: a verified compiler for coq. In: The Third International Workshop on Coq for Programming Languages (CoqPL) (2017)
3. Barras, B., et al.: The Coq proof assistant reference manual: Version 6.1. Ph.D. thesis, Inria (1997)
4. Bhargavan, K., et al.: Everest: towards a verified, drop-in replacement of https. In: LIPIcs-Leibniz International Proceedings in Informatics, vol. 71. Schloss Dagstuhl-Leibniz-Zentrum fuer Informatik (2017)
5. Chen, H., Ziegler, D., Chajed, T., Chlipala, A., Kaashoek, M.F., Zeldovich, N.: Using crash hoare logic for certifying the FSCQ file system. In: Proceedings of the 25th Symposium on Operating Systems Principles, pp. 18–37. ACM (2015)
6. Claessen, K., Hughes, J.: Quickcheck: a lightweight tool for random testing of haskell programs. ACM SIGPLAN Not. **46**(4), 53–64 (2011)
7. Cock, D.: Bitfields and tagged unions in C: verification through automatic generation. VERIFY **8**, 44–55 (2008)
8. Damas, L., Milner, R.: Principal type-schemes for functional programs. In: Proceedings of the 9th ACM SIGPLAN-SIGACT Symposium on Principles of Programming Languages, pp. 207–212. ACM (1982)

9. Erbsen, A., Philipoom, J., Gross, J., Sloan, R., Chlipala, A.: Simple high-level code for cryptographic arithmetic-with proofs, without compromises. In: Simple High-Level Code for Cryptographic Arithmetic-With Proofs, Without Compromises, p. 0. IEEE

10. Gu, L., Vaynberg, A., Ford, B., Shao, Z., Costanzo, D.: Certikos: a certified kernel for secure cloud computing. In: Proceedings of the Second Asia-Pacific Workshop on Systems, p. 3. ACM (2011)

11. Ioannidis, E.: Extracting and optimizing low-level bytecode from high-level verified coq (2019)

12. Jones, S.P., Hall, C., Hammond, K., Partain, W., Wadler, P.: The glasgow haskell compiler: a technical overview. In: Proceedings of the UK Joint Framework for Information Technology (JFIT) Technical Conference, vol. 93 (1993)

13. Josuttis, N.M.: C++ Templates: The Complete Guide. Addison-Wesley Professional, Boston (2003)

14. Klein, G., et al.: sel4: formal verification of an OS kernel. In: Proceedings of the ACM SIGOPS 22nd Symposium on Operating Systems Principles, pp. 207–220. ACM (2009)

15. Lattner, C.: LLVM and clang: Next generation compiler technology. In: The BSD Conference, pp. 1–2 (2008)

16. Leroy, X., et al.: The compcert verified compiler. Documentation and user's manual, INRIA Paris-Rocquencourt (2012)

17. Letouzey, P.: Extraction in Coq: an overview. In: Beckmann, A., Dimitracopoulos, C., Löwe, B. (eds.) CiE 2008. LNCS, vol. 5028, pp. 359–369. Springer, Heidelberg (2008). https://doi.org/10.1007/978-3-540-69407-6_39

18. Liskov, B., Shrira, L.: Promises: linguistic support for efficient asynchronous procedure calls in distributed systems, vol. 23. ACM (1988)

19. Magalhães, J.P., Dijkstra, A., Jeuring, J., Löh, A.: A generic deriving mechanism for haskell. ACM SIGPLAN Not. **45**(11), 37–48 (2010)

20. Mullen, E., Pernsteiner, S., Wilcox, J.R., Tatlock, Z., Grossman, D.: Œuf: minimizing the coq extraction TCB. In: Proceedings of the 7th ACM SIGPLAN International Conference on Certified Programs and Proofs, pp. 172–185. ACM (2018)

21. Wadler, P.: A prettier printer. In: The Fun of Programming, Cornerstones of Computing, pp. 223–243 (2003)

22. Wadler, P., Blott, S.: How to make ad-hoc polymorphism less ad hoc. In: Proceedings of the 16th ACM SIGPLAN-SIGACT Symposium on Principles of Programming Languages, pp. 60–76. ACM (1989)

23. Wilcox, J.R., et al.: Verdi: a framework for implementing and formally verifying distributed systems. In: ACM SIGPLAN Notices, vol. 50, pp. 357–368. ACM (2015)

24. Xi, H., Pfenning, F.: Dependent types in practical programming. In: Proceedings of the 26th ACM SIGPLAN-SIGACT symposium on Principles of Programming Languages, pp. 214–227. ACM (1999)

Structured Synthesis for Probabilistic Systems

Nils Jansen[1]($\boxtimes$), Laura Humphrey[2], Jana Tumova[3], and Ufuk Topcu[4]

[1] Radboud University, Nijmegen, The Netherlands
nilsjansen123@gmail.com
[2] Air Force Research Laboratory, Dayton, USA
[3] KTH Royal Institute of Technology, Stockholm, Sweden
[4] University of Texas at Austin, Austin, USA

Abstract. We introduce the concept of structured synthesis for Markov decision processes. A structure is induced from finitely many pre-specified options for a system configuration. We define the structured synthesis problem as a nonlinear programming problem (NLP) with integer variables. As solving NLPs is not feasible in general, we present an alternative approach. A transformation of models specified in the PRISM probabilistic programming language creates models that account for all possible system configurations by nondeterministic choices. Together with a control module that ensures consistent configurations throughout a run of the system, this transformation enables the use of optimized tools for model checking in a black-box fashion. While this transformation increases the size of a model, experiments with standard benchmarks show that the method provides a feasible approach for structured synthesis. We motivate and demonstrate the usefulness of the approach along a realistic case study involving surveillance by unmanned aerial vehicles in a shipping facility.

1 Introduction

The problem introduced in this paper is motivated by the following scenario stemming from the area of physical security. Consider a shipping facility equipped with a number of ground sensors to discover potential intruders. The facility operates unmanned aerial vehicles (UAVs) to perform surveillance and maintenance tasks. Intruders appear randomly, there are uncertainties in sensor performance, and the operation of the UAVs is driven by scheduling choices and the activation of sensors. Suitable models to capture such randomization, uncertainty, and scheduling choices are *Markov decision processes* (MDPs), where measures such as "the probability to encounter dangerous states of the system" or "the expected cost to achieve a certain goal" are directly assessable.

System designers may have to choose among a pre-specified family of possibly interdependent options for the system configuration, such as different sensors or

---

U. Topcu—Partially supported by AFRL FA8650-15-C-2546 and Sandia National Lab 801KOB.

J. M. Badger and K. Y. Rozier (Eds.): NFM 2019, LNCS 11460, pp. 237–254, 2019.
https://doi.org/10.1007/978-3-030-20652-9_16

the operating altitude of UAVs. Each of these options triggers different system behavior, such as different failure probabilities and acquisition cost. We call such possible design choices an underlying *structure of the system*; all concrete instantiations of the system adhere to this structure. For instance, imagine a structure describing the option of installing one of two types of sensors. The cheaper sensor induces a smaller expected cost, while the more expensive sensor induces a higher probability of discovering intruders. The changes in the instantiations of the system are necessarily according to the structure, i.e., the replacement of one sensor type with the other. A question of interest is then which instantiation yields the lowest cost while it guarantees to adhere to a target specification regarding the desired probability.

We introduce *multiple–instance MDPs* (MIMDPs) as underlying semantic model for structured synthesis. Arbitrary expressions over system parameters capture a structure that describes dependencies between uncertain behavior and system cost. Each parameter has an associated finite set of values out of which it can be instantiated. Thereby, a MIMDP induces a finite family of MDPs. MIMDPs are inspired by *parametric MDPs* [2,24,27,33] (pMDPs), whose transition probabilities are defined by functions over yet-to-be-specified parameters. However, the existing definitions of pMDPs only allow restrictions on parameter valuations in the form of continuous intervals. State-of-the-art methods as implemented in the tools PARAM [9], PRISM [10], or PROPhESY [19] do not support the definition of discrete sets of valuations. Consequently, to the best of our knowledge, these techniques cannot directly handle the scenarios we consider.

Another related approach to modeling structured systems is *feature-based modeling* [29], which allows to specify families of stochastic systems. Although feature-based modeling supports discrete parametrization, it does not directly offer parametrization of probabilities. Furthermore, it analyses a family in an all-in-one fashion as opposed to focusing on individual instantiations.

The formal problem considered in this paper is to compute an optimal instantiation of parameters and a control strategy for a given MIMDP subject to reachability specifications and cost minimization. We define this problem naturally as a *non–linear integer optimization problem* (NLIP). As a computationally tractable alternative, we present a transformation of an MIMDP to an MDP where all possible parameter instantiations are relayed to *nondeterministic choices*. The common language used for model specification in all available tools is the probabilistic programming language [17] originally developed for PRISM. We define the transformation of the MIMDP as a *program transformation*. By adding control variables to the transformed program, we keep track of all instantiations, ensuring system executions that are in accordance with the given structure. Computing a solution to the original problem is thereby reduced to *MDP model checking*, which is equivalent to solving a linear program (LP). From a practical viewpoint, the transformation enables the use of all capabilities of model checkers such as PRISM [10], Storm [28], or IscasMC [18].

We illustrate the feasibility of the proposed approach on several basic case studies from the PRISM benchmark suite [12]. We also report promising results for a more realistic case study based on the shipping facility example. In our experiments, we observe that the transformation from a MIMDP to an MDP involves an increase in the number of states or transitions of up to two orders of magnitude. However, using an efficient model checker, we are able to demonstrate the applicability of our approach in examples with millions of states.

In summary, the contribution of this paper is threefold: (i) We define a parametric model supporting discrete valuation sets and formalize the structured synthesis problem. (ii) We develop a transformation of the parametric model to the PRISM language allowing us to practically address the structured synthesis problem. (iii) We present a detailed, realistic case study of a shipping facility as well as experimental evaluation on standard benchmarks.

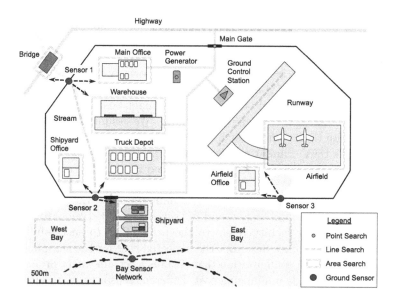

Fig. 1. A shipping facility that uses UAVs to perform surveillance tasks.

2   Case Study

In this section we introduce the case study that originally motivated the problem and the proposed approach. Several technical details are available in [31].

Scenario. Consider a shipping facility which uses one or more UAVs equipped with electro-optical (EO) sensors to perform surveillance tasks over various facility assets as shown in Fig. 1. These assets include an *Airfield* with a *Runway* and *Airfield Office*, a *Truck Depot*, a *Warehouse*, a *Main Office*, a *Shipyard* with a *Shipyard Office*, and a small bay that is partitioned into *West Bay*, *East Bay*, and *Shipyard* areas. An external *Highway* connects to the *Main Gate*, and a nearby *Bridge* crosses a *Stream* that cuts through the facility and empties into the bay. The facility is surrounded by a fence, but points where waterways run under the fence might allow intruders to enter. These points and the bay are monitored by *Sensor 1, Sensor 2, Sensor 3,* and a *Bay Sensor Network.* All of these *ground sensors* can detect intruders with a certain false alarm rate.

UAVs take off and land from an area near the *Ground Control Station* (GCS). For each of the facility assets, a UAV can be tasked to perform a point, line, or area search as indicated in Fig. 1. Each of these search tasks requires the UAV to fly a certain distance to get to the task location, carry out the task, and fly back to the GCS. For point searches, simply flying to the point and back is enough. For line searches, the UAV must fly to one end, follow the line, and fly back from the other end. For area searches, the UAV must fly to one corner of the area, perform sequential parallel passes over it until the entire area has been covered by the UAV's sensor footprint, then fly back from the terminating corner. Note that the sensor footprint size increases with altitude, so more passes are needed to cover an area as a UAV's altitude decreases.

If a ground sensor reports that an intruder has been detected, a UAV may be tasked to fly to the respective area and perform a search; otherwise, the UAV can return to the GCS and continue on to another task. Probabilities for which areas intruders are likely to head toward might be estimated over time or assumed to be uniform if data are not available. We assume surveillance occurs frequently enough that at most one intruder will pass by a ground sensor before it is queried by a UAV. Similar problems involving UAVs searching for intruders based on ground sensor information are discussed in, e.g., [15] and [22].

System Configuration, Safety, and Cost. A configuration of the shipyard facility refers to the types of ground sensors and EO sensors installed onboard the UAVs. *Safety* of the shipping facility refers to the probability to successfully detect intruders, and *performance* describes the expected cost for the shipping facility.

Our goal is to find a configuration that ensures a certain safety probability on detecting intruders while minimizing cost. Different sensor types result in safety and performance tradeoffs for several reasons. First, each sensor type has a different one-time purchase cost. In turn, each sensor type has tunable parameters that result in a tradeoff between the probability of detecting an intruder and cost in terms of UAV flight time, with sensors that have a higher purchase cost providing a better tradeoff. The tradeoff between intruder detection and UAV flight time is also affected by the adjustable UAV operating altitude.

This tradeoff can be understood using two factors. The first is *ground sample distance* (GSD) [25], i. e., the number of meters per pixel of images sent back by a UAV, which depends on UAV altitude and EO sensor resolution. The second is the ground sensor *receiver operating characteristic* (ROC) [7], i. e., the tunable true positive versus false positive rate. Both true and false positives result in a UAV performing an area search for intruders. We now describe how probabilistic parameters relating to GSD and ROC can be adjusted by acquiring different types of sensors, tuning sensor parameters, or changing UAV operating altitude.

Basic Task Costs. For tasks that do not involve intruder detection, cost is driven mainly by manpower, logistics, and maintenance requirements, which roughly corresponds to cost per flight second c_f. Suppose the UAVs in this scenario all fly at some standard operating ground speed v_g measured in meters per second. The cost $c(t) = d(t)c_f/v_g$ for a task t that does not involve intruder detection depends in a straightforward way on the distance $d(t)$ that a UAV must fly.

Image GSD. An important consideration for UAV surveillance tasks is the amount of visual detail a human operator needs to analyze, depending on the number of pixels comprising objects of interest in the images. GSD can be decreased by *decreasing altitude* or *increasing horizontal resolution* of the EO sensor. For this scenario, we consider three common EO sensor resolution options (480p, 720p, 1080p), with hypothetical purchase prices ($15k, $30k, $45k).

We use GSD in conjunction with the Johnson criteria [1] to estimate the probability that a human operator successfully analyzes an object. For each type of task and a corresponding digital image, a quantity n_{50} defines the number of pairs of pixel lines across the "critical" or smaller dimension of an object needed for a 50% probability of task success. For instance, $n_{50} = 1$ for object detection.

Given n_{50} and the number of pixels pairs n across the critical dimension of an object (which depends on the size of the object and GSD), the probability for analysis success p_d given sufficient time to analyze the image is estimated as

$$p_d = \frac{(n/n_{50})^{x_0}}{1 + (n/n_{50})^{x_0}} \quad \text{where} \quad x_0 = 2.7 + 0.7(n/n_{50}). \tag{1}$$

Ground Sensor ROC. The ROC curve of a sensor performing binary classification describes the tradeoff between the sensor's true positive rate/probability versus false positive rate/probability as the sensor's discrimination threshold is varied. Consider the three solid curves in Fig. 2. These represent hypothetical "low", "mid", and "high" cost ground sensors, with one-time purchase costs of $15k, $30k, and $45k, respectively. For each such ground sensor, the discrimination threshold can be varied to achieve an operating point on the corresponding curve. In order to reliably detect intruders, we need true positive rates to be fairly high. As the curves show, a high cost ground sensor provides the best tradeoff, since for each false positive rate, it provides a higher true positive rate. In our approach, we use quadratic approximations of the curves.

To help understand the effect ground sensors have on system costs and probabilistic parameters, suppose we choose to purchase a high cost sensor for Sensor 1. Clearly the purchase cost is higher than if we had chosen a mid or low cost sensor. However, each time the ground sensor generates a false positive, a UAV has to perform an unnecessary area search, which incurs additional system operational cost. To counteract this, we could decrease the ground sensor's false positive rate, but this would also decrease its true positive rate, resulting in a higher false negative rate. When a false negative occurs, the sensor fails to detect the presence of an intruder. A high cost sensor then mitigates operational cost by providing a lower false positive rate. Given these tradeoffs between purchase

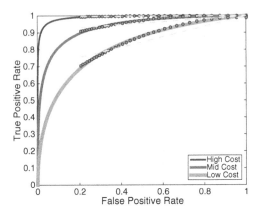

Fig. 2. ROC curves for different cost ground sensors. Linear and quadratic approximations are shown as green dashed lines and traces of black dots, respectively.

cost, operational cost, and probability of intruder detection, it is not clear which sensor minimizes cost while meeting safety specifications on intruder detection.

3   Preliminaries

A *probability distribution* over a finite set X is a function $\mu\colon X \to [0,1] \subseteq \mathbb{R}$ with $\sum_{x \in X} \mu(x) = \mu(X) = 1$. The set of all distributions on X is $Distr(X)$.

Definition 1 (MDP). *A* Markov decision process (MDP) *$\mathcal{M} = (S, s_I, A, \mathcal{P})$ consists of a finite set of states S, a unique initial state $s_I \in S$, a finite set A of actions, and a probabilistic transition function $\mathcal{P}\colon S \times A \times S \to [0,1] \subseteq \mathbb{R}$ with $\sum_{s' \in S} \mathcal{P}(s, \alpha, s') = 1$ for all $s \in S, \alpha \in A$.*

The *enabled* actions at state $s \in S$ are $A(s) = \{\alpha \in A \mid \exists s' \in S. \mathcal{P}(s, \alpha, s') > 0\}$. A *cost function* $\mathcal{C}\colon S \to \mathbb{R}_{\geq 0}$ for an MDP $\mathcal{M}$ adds cost to a *state*. If $|A(s)| = 1$ for all $s \in S$, all actions can be disregarded and the MDP $\mathcal{M}$ reduces to a *discrete-time Markov chain (MC)*, also denoted by $\mathcal{D}$. To define a probability measure and expected cost on MDPs, the nondeterministic choices of actions are resolved by *strategies*. We restrict ourselves to *memoryless* strategies, see [34] for details.

Definition 2 (Strategy). *A randomized strategy[1] for an MDP $\mathcal{M}$ is a function $\sigma\colon S \to Distr(A)$ such that $\sigma(s)(a) > 0$ implies $a \in A(s)$. A strategy with $\sigma(s)(a) = 1$ for $a \in A$ and $\sigma(b) = 0$ for all $b \in A \setminus \{a\}$ is called* deterministic. *The set of all strategies over $\mathcal{M}$ is denoted by $Str^{\mathcal{M}}$.*

Applying strategy $\sigma \in Str^{\mathcal{M}}$ to MDP $\mathcal{M}$ yields an *induced Markov chain* $\mathcal{M}^{\sigma}$.

---

[1] If needed, we extend the state space of the original MDP to account for memory.

Definition 3 (Induced MC). *Let MDP* $\mathcal{M} = (S, s_I, A, \mathcal{P})$ *and strategy* $\sigma \in Str^{\mathcal{M}}$. *The MC induced by* $\mathcal{M}$ *and* σ *is* $\mathcal{M}^{\sigma} = (S, s_I, \mathcal{P}^{\sigma})$ *where*

$$\mathcal{P}^{\sigma}(s, s') = \sum_{a \in A(s)} \sigma(s)(a) \cdot \mathcal{P}(s, a, s') \quad \textit{for all } s, s' \in S \ .$$

PRISM's Guarded Command Language. We briefly introduce the probabilistic programming language used to specify probabilistic models in PRISM. For a finite set Var of integer variables, let $\mathcal{V}(\text{Var})$ denote the set of all variable valuations.

Definition 4 (Probabilistic program). *A probabilistic program* $(\text{Var}, s_I, \mathfrak{M})$ *consists of* Var, *an initial variable valuation* $s_I \in \mathcal{V}(\text{Var})$, *and a finite set of modules* $\mathfrak{M} = \{M_1, \dots, M_k\}$. *A module* $M_i = (\text{Var}_i, A_i, C_i)$ *consists of* $\text{Var}_i \subseteq$ Var *such that* $\text{Var}_i \cap \text{Var}_j = \emptyset$ *for* $i \neq j$, *a finite set* A_i *of (synchronizing) actions, and a finite set* C_i *of commands.*

A command has the form $[\alpha] \ g \rightarrow p_1 \colon f_1 + \dots + p_n \colon f_n$ *with* $\alpha \in A_i$, g *a Boolean guard over the variables in* Var, $p_j \in [0, 1] \subseteq \mathbb{R}$ *with* $\sum_{j=1}^{n} p_j = 1$, *and* $f_j \colon \mathcal{V}(\text{Var}) \rightarrow \mathcal{V}(\text{Var}_i)$ *a variable update function.*

A model with several modules is equivalent to a single module, obtained by the *parallel composition* using synchronizing actions. For details we refer to [21].

Specifications. For threshold $\lambda \in [0, 1]$ and MC $\mathcal{D}$, a *reachability specification* $\varphi = \mathbb{P}_{\leq \lambda}(\Diamond T)$ asserts that a set of target states $T \subseteq S$ is to be reached with probability at most λ. The expected cost of reaching a set of goal states G is denoted by $\text{EC}^{\mathcal{D}}(\Diamond G)$. Using recent results from [30], we also consider the probability $\text{Pr}^{\mathcal{D}}(\Diamond T \wedge C < n)$, where the total cost C, i. e., the sum of the costs of all paths satisfying $\Diamond T$, is bounded by n. For MDPs, one needs to compute minimizing/maximizing strategies. Formal definitions are given in e.g., [34].

4   Structured Synthesis

We first introduce *multiple–instance Markov decision process* (MIMDP) over a finite set $V = \{p_1, \dots, p_n\}$ of parameters. Each parameter $p \in V$ has a finite range of values $Val(p) = \{v_1, \dots, v_m\} \subseteq \mathbb{R}$. A *valuation* is a function $u \colon V \rightarrow \bigcup_{p \in V} Val(p)$ that respects the parameter ranges, meaning that for a parameter p, $u(p) = v \in Val(p)$. Let $U(V)$ denote the (finite) set of valuations on V.

Let $Expr(V)$ denote the set of *expressions* over V and $p \in l$ state that parameter p occurs in expression $l \in Expr(V)$. $Val(l)$ denotes the (finite) set of possible values for $l \in Expr(V)$ according to the parameters $p \in l$ and their value ranges $Val(p)$. With a slight abuse of notation, we lift valuation functions from $U(V)$ to expressions: $u \colon Expr(V) \rightarrow \bigcup_{l \in Expr(V)} Val(l)$. In particular, $u(l) = v \in Val(l)$ is the valuation of l obtained by the instantiation of each $p \in l$ with $u(p)$.

Remark 1. A valuation of two expressions l, l' in $Expr(V)$ does not guarantee consistent parameter valuations. A parameter valuation $u(p)$ that results in expression valuation $u(l)$ might be different than a $u'(p)$ that results in $u(l')$.

Example 1. For $V = \{p, q\}$, $Val(p) = \{0.1, 0.2\}$, $Val(q) = \{0.3, 0.4\}$, and $Expr(V) = \{p + q, p + 2 \cdot q\}$, the ranges of values for the expressions are $Val(p + q) = \{0.4, 0.5, 0.6\}$, and $Val(p + 2 \cdot q) = \{0.7, 0.8, 0.9, 1\}$. For parameter valuation $u(p) = 0.1, u(q) = 0.3$, the associated valuation on expressions is $u(p+q) = 0.4$, $u(p+2 \cdot q) = 0.7$. For a valuation on the expressions $v(p+q) = 0.4$, $v(p + 2 \cdot q) = 1$, there is no consistent parameter valuation: the first is consistent with $u(p) = 0.1$ and $u(q) = 0.3$, the second with $u(p) = 0.2$ and $u(q) = 0.4$.

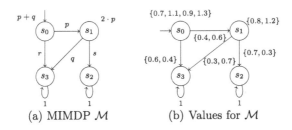

(a) MIMDP $\mathcal{M}$ (b) Values for $\mathcal{M}$

Fig. 3. An example MIMDP and its possible valuations.

Definition 5 (MIMDP). *A multiple-instance MDP $\mathcal{M} = (S, V, s_I, A, \mathcal{P})$ has a finite set S of states, a finite set V of parameters with associated finite sets of valuations from $Val(V)$, a unique initial state $s_I \in S$, a finite set A of actions, and a transition function $\mathcal{P}: S \times A \times S \to Expr(V)$.*

A *cost function* $\mathcal{C}: S \to Expr(V)$ associates (parametric) cost to states. For each valuation $u \in Val(V)$ of parameters, the *instantiated MIMDP* is $\mathcal{M}[u]$. We denote the set of all expressions occurring in the MIMDP by $\mathcal{L}_{\mathcal{M}}$.

Remark 2. An MIMDP is a special kind of parametric MDP (pMDP) [9, 26] in the sense that each parametric cost and probabilities can only take a finite number of values, i.e., there are multiple but finite instantiations of a MIMDP. The state–of–the–art tools such as PARAM [9], PRISM [10], or PROPhESY [19], however, only allow for defining continuous intervals to restrict parameter valuations.

Example 2. Figure 3(a) shows a MIMDP $\mathcal{M}$ with parametric transition probabilities p, q, r and s. Costs are $p + q$ and $2 \cdot p$. The valuations of parameters are $Val(p) = \{0.4, 0.6\}$, $Val(q) = \{0.3, 0.7\}$, $Val(s) = \{0.7, 0.3\}$, $Val(r) = \{0.6, 0.4\}$, $Val(p + q) = \{0.7, 1.1, 0.9, 1.3\}$, and $Val(2 \cdot p) = \{0.8, 1.2\}$. The sets of valuations are depicted in Fig. 3(b) to show all instantiations of the MIMDP. E.g., a valuation u with $u(p) = 0.4$ and $u(r) = 0.4$ is *not well–defined* as it induces no probability distribution, thereby not yielding an MDP.

Formal Problem Statement. For a MIMDP $\mathcal{M}$, a specification $\varphi = \mathbb{P}_{\leq \lambda}(\Diamond T)$, and a set of goal states G, the structured synthesis problem is to determine a valuation $u \in U(V)$ and a strategy σ for the MDP $\mathcal{M}[u]$ such that $\mathcal{M}[u]^{\sigma} \models \varphi$, and the expected cost $EC^{\mathcal{M}[u]^{\sigma}}(\Diamond G)$ is minimal.

5   An Integer Programming Approach

We first observe that the synthesis problem is in fact a multi-objective verification problem that requires randomized strategies as in Definition 2 [8,11,14]. We formulate the corresponding optimization problem using the following variables:

- $c_s \in \mathbb{R}_{\geq 0}$ for each $s \in S$ represents the expected cost to reach $G \subseteq S$ from s.
- $p_s \in [0,1]$ for each $s \in S$ represents the probability to reach $T \subseteq S$ from s.
- $\sigma_s^\alpha \in [0,1]$ for each $s \in S$ and $\alpha \in A$ represents the probability to choose action $\alpha \in A(s)$ at state s.

We also introduce a characteristic variable $x_u \in \{0,1\}$ for each valuation $u \in U(V)$. If x_u is set to 1, all parameters and expressions are evaluated using u.

$$\text{minimize } c_{s_I} \tag{2}$$
$$\text{subject to}$$

$$p_{s_I} \leq \lambda \tag{3}$$

$$\forall s \in T.\ p_s = 1 \tag{4}$$

$$\forall s \in G.\ c_s = 0 \tag{5}$$

$$\forall s \in S.\ \sum_{\alpha \in A} \sigma_s^\alpha = 1 \tag{6}$$

$$\sum_{u \in U(V)} x_u = 1 \tag{7}$$

$$\forall s \in S.\ p_s = \sum_{\alpha \in A(s)} \sigma_s^\alpha \cdot \left(\sum_{s' \in S} \sum_{u \in U(V)} x_u \cdot u(\mathcal{P}(s,\alpha,s')) \cdot p_{s'} \right) \tag{8}$$

$$\forall s \in S.\ c_s = \sum_{\alpha \in A(s)} \sigma_s^\alpha \cdot \left(\sum_{s' \in S} \sum_{u \in U(V)} x_u \cdot (u(\mathcal{C}(s)) + u(\mathcal{P}(s,\alpha,s')) \cdot c_{s'}) \right) \tag{9}$$

$$\forall s \in S, \alpha \in A(s).\ \sum_{s' \in S} \sum_{u \in U(V)} x_u \cdot u(\mathcal{P}(s,\alpha,s')) = 1 \tag{10}$$

Theorem 1 (Soundness and completeness). *The optimization problem* (2)–(10) *is sound in the sense that each minimizing assignment induces a solution to the synthesis problem. It is complete in the sense that for each solution to the problem there is a minimizing assignment for* (2)–(10).

Proof Sketch. The first two equations induce satisfaction of the specifications: (2) minimizes the expected cost to reach goal states $G \subseteq S$ at s_I; (3) ensures that the probability to reach the target states $T \subseteq S$ from s_I is not higher than the threshold. (4) and (5) set the probability and the expected cost at target and goal states to 1 and 0, respectively. (6) ensures well-defined strategies, and (7) ensures for all possibles values $u \in U(V)$ that exactly one characteristic variable x_u is set to 1. In (8), p_s is assigned the probability of reaching T from s by multiplying the probability to reach successor s' with the probability of reaching T from s', depending on the scheduler variables σ^{α_s}. Variables c_s are analogously assigned the expected cost in (9). (10) ensures that the concrete instantiations chosen at each transition form well–defined probability distributions.

Any satisfying assignment yields a well-defined randomized strategy and a well-defined assignment of parameters. Moreover, such an assignment necessarily satisfies the safety specification $\varphi = \mathbb{P}_{\leq\lambda}(\Diamond T)$, as the probability to reach T is ensured to be smaller than or equal to λ. Likewise, the expected cost to reach G from the initial state is minimized while at each state the c_s variables are assigned the exact expected cost. We need to assume that the probability to reach G is one under all strategies. If this assumption is not true, additional constraints can enforce that property for each solution of the optimization problem. Thus, a satisfying assignment induces a solution to the synthesis problem. *Completeness* is given by construction, as the optimization problem encodes each instantiation of the problem.

Complexity of the Optimization Problem. Consider constraint (8), where an integer variable x_v is multiplied with the real–valued variable $p_{s'}$ and the strategy variable σ_s^α. Such constraints render this program a *non–linear integer optimization problem*. The number of constraints is governed by the number of state and action pairs and the number of possible instantiations of expressions i. e., the *size of the problem* is in $\mathcal{O}(|S_r| \cdot |A| \cdot |Val(\mathcal{L}_\mathcal{M})|^2)$. The problem is, that already solving nonlinear problems without integer variables is NP-hard [4,35]. Summarized, despite the compact problem representation in form of a MIMDP, the problem is hard.

6   Transformation of PRISM Programs

As a feasible—yet not optimal—solution to the synthesis problem, we present a transformation of MIMDPs specified as probabilistic programs in the PRISM language as in Definition 4. Similar to [26], we see the possible choices of parameter values as nondeterminism. Say, a parameter $p \in V$ has valuations $Val(p) = \{v_1, v_2\}$ and state s has cost $\mathcal{C}(s) = 2 \cdot p$. First, the MIMDP is transformed in the following way. From state s, a nondeterministic choice between actions α_{v_1} and α_{v_1} replaces the original transitions. Each action leads with probability one to a fresh state having cost $2 \cdot v_1$ or $2 \cdot v_2$, respectively. From these states, the original transitions of state s emanate. Minimal or maximal expected cost in this transformed MDP correspond to upper and lower bounds to the optimal solution of the synthesis problem. Intuitively, we *relax dependencies between parameters*. That is, if at one place p is assigned its value v_1, it is not necessarily assigned the same everywhere in the MIMDP, leading to inconsistent valuations. To tighten these bounds, a further program transformation ensures parameter dependencies for each execution of the model. Intuitively, in the resulting MDP each nondeterministic choice corresponding to a parameter value leads to a (sub-)MDP where the assignment of that value is fixed.

Remark 3 (Nondeterminism and continuous parameters). If the original MIMDP has nondeterministic choices, we introduce a new level of nondeterminism. We then assume that both types of nondeterminism minimize the expected cost for our problem. Alternatively, one can generate and evaluate a stochastic game [13].

If the original problem has continuous parameters in addition, we gain a parametric MIMDP. In that case, mature tools for pMDPS like PARAM [9] or PROPhESY [19] may be employed following the program transformation.

Program Transformation 1—Parametric Cost. Intuitively, for each state satisfying a certain guard, transitions with the same guard are added. Each of the transitions leads to new states with an instantiated rewards. From these states, the transitions of the original system emanate. Assume a PRISM program $M = (\text{Var}, A, C)$ as in Definition 4, and a parametric reward structure of the form:

---

rewards
$\quad g_1 : l$
end rewards

---

with g_1 the guard and $l \in Expr(\text{Var})$. Let $Val(l) = \{\bar{v}_1, \ldots, \bar{v}_m\}$ be the finite set of instantiations of l with $\bar{v}_i \in \mathbb{R}$ for $1 \leq i \leq m$. We introduce a fresh (characteristic) variable x_l with $\text{dom}(x_l) = \{0, \ldots, m\}$. Intuitively, there is a unique variable value for x_l for each valuation from $Val(l)$. Consider now all commands $c \in C$ of the form

---

$[\alpha]\ g \to p_1 : f_1 + \ldots + p_n : f_n;$

---

with $g \models g_1$, i.e., the guard of the command satisfies the guard of the reward structure. Replace each such commands c by the following set of commands:

$[]\ g \to 1 : x_l' = 1;$

$\quad \vdots$

$[]\ g \to 1 : x_l' = m;$
$[\alpha]\ \bigvee_{1 \leq i \leq m} x_l = i \to p_1 : f_1 + \ldots + p_n : f_n;$

---

and replace the reward structure for each command c by

---

rewards
$\quad x_l = 1 : v_1;$

$\quad \vdots$

$\quad x_l = m : v_m;$
end rewards

This transformation corresponds to a nondeterministic choice between the concrete reward values.

Program Transformation 2—Parametric Transitions. For all parameters values, transitions with concrete probabilities are introduced. As all transitions satisfy the same guard, we have again a nondeterministic choice between these transitions. For program $M = (\text{Var}, A, C)$, consider a command $c \in C$ of the form

$$[\alpha]\ g \to p_1 \colon f_1 + \ldots + p_n \colon f_n$$

with $p_1, \ldots, p_n \in Expr(\text{Var})$. Let $Val(p_1, \ldots, p_n) = \{v_1^n, \ldots, v_m^n\}$ with $v_i^n = (v_{i1}, \ldots, v_{in})$ for $1 \leq i \leq n$ and $v_{ij} \in \mathbb{R}$ for $1 \leq j \leq m$.

Replace each such command c by the following set of commands:

$$[\alpha]\ g \to v_{11} \colon f_1 + \ldots + v_{1n} \colon f_n;$$
$$\vdots$$
$$[\alpha]\ g \to v_{m1} \colon f_1 + \ldots + v_{mn} \colon f_n;$$

For a program M, we denote the program after Transformation 1 and Transformation 2 by M'. The induced MIMDP of M is denoted by $\mathcal{M}_M$ and the induced MDP of M' by $\mathcal{M}_{M'}$.

Program Transformation 3—Parameter Dependencies. We finally propose a transformation of the transformed MDP $\mathcal{M}_{M'}$ which enforces that once a parameter is assigned a specific value, this assignment is always used throughout a system execution. Therefore, we add a *control module* to the PRISM formulation.

In the transformed MDP, taking actions α_{v_1} or α_{v_2} induces that parameter p is assigned its value v_1 or v_2. In the PRISM encoding, the corresponding commands are of the form

$$[\alpha_{v_1}]\ g_1 \to \ldots;$$
$$[\alpha_{v_2}]\ g_2 \to \ldots;$$

where g_1 and g_2 are arbitrary guards. Now, for each of these actions α_{v_1} and α_{v_2}, we use control variables q_{v_1} and q_{v_2} and build a control module of the form:

module *control*
   q_{v_1}: **bool init** 0;
   q_{v_2}: **bool init** 0;
   $[\alpha_{v_1}]\ \neg q_{v_1} \to (q'_{v_1} = \textbf{true});$
   $[\alpha_{v_1}]\ q_{v_1} \to (q'_{v_1} = \textbf{true});$
   $[\alpha_{v_2}]\ \neg q_{v_2} \to (q'_{v_2} = \textbf{true});$
   $[\alpha_{v_2}]\ q_{v_2} \to (q'_{v_2} = \textbf{true});$
endmodule

If this module is included in the parallel composition, a control variable is set to **true** once the corresponding action is taken in the MDP. We can now guard the commands such that only non–conflicting assignments are possible. The original commands are transformed in the following way:

$$[\alpha_{v_1}]\ g_1 \wedge \neg q_{v_2} \to \ldots;$$
$$[\alpha_{v_2}]\ g_2 \wedge \neg q_{v_1} \to \ldots;$$

With the control module, consistent choices are enforced for any execution of the system, while there may be inconsistencies in parameter valuations at states or transitions that are not visited by the same run of the system. In these (rare) cases, the resulting strategy does not offer any guarantees. Specifically, an optimal strategy does not necessarily induce consistent parameter assignments, which is an NP-hard problem and handled in [32].

Technically, we transform an integer nonlinear optimization problem to a linear program at the cost of increasing the size of the underlying MDP. We exploit highly optimized model checking tools. Aggressive state space reduction techniques together with a preprocessing that removes inconsistent combinations of parameter values beforehand render the MIMDP synthesis problem feasible.

7   Experiments

We first report on results for the case study from Sect. 2. We created a PRISM program for the MIMDP underlying all aspects of the shipyard example with 430 lines of code. We use the program to generate an explicit Markov chain (MC) model where the parameter instantiations are fixed. That explicit model has 1 728 states and 5 145 transitions. From the MIMDP model, we generate the MDP according to the transformations in Sect. 6. The underlying (extended) PRISM program has 720 lines of code. The explicit MDP generated from the transformed program has 2 912 states and 64 048 transitions. For our case study, the size of the transformed MDP is reasonable: From the MIMDP to the MDP, states increase by a factor of 1.8, transitions by a factor of 12.5. We performed all experiments on a MacBook Pro with a 2.3 GHz Intel Core i5 CPU and 8 GB of RAM with the standard configuration of the Storm model checker.

Results Case Study. The experiments show several (partially unforeseeable) intricacies of the case study. We have the following structure for the MIMDP defined by parameters and their valuation sets. For details see Sect. 2.

- EO sensor for the UAV: $V_{EO} = \{480p, 720p, 1080p\}$.
- Deviation from the UAV operational altitude: $V_{Alt} = \{-60, -30, 0, 30, 60\}$.
- ROC ground sensors (Sensor 1, Sensor 2, Sensor 3, Bay Area Network): $V_{ROC} = \{\text{low}, \text{med}, \text{high}\}$.
- False positive rates for each ROC ground sensor: $V_{fp} = \{0.2, 0.3, \ldots, 1.0\}$.

This structure induces 1 440 possible system configurations. However, as we restrict ground sensors to have the same quality, we have only 360 possibilities. We implemented benchmark scripts using the Python interface of Storm. For the results presented below, we iteratively try all possible combinations for measures of interest, and compare the time to compute an optimal value obtained from the transformed MDP to these cumulated model checking times.

Probability of Recognition Error. First, we investigate the probability of not recognizing an intruder—after a ground sensor was triggered—in dependence of the number of missions an UAV flies. The curves shown in Fig. 4(a) depend on the deviation from the standard UAV operational altitude and on the type of EO sensor. The cheap 480p EO sensor has the lowest probability for a recognition error at a low altitude. For all other sensors and altitudes, the probability quickly approaches one. The cumulated model checking time was 78.13 s, computing the optimal result on the transformed MDP took 2.3 s.

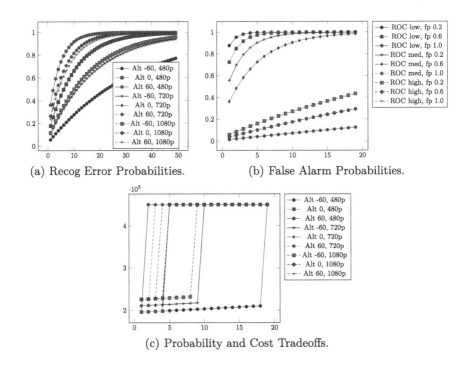

(a) Recog Error Probabilities.   (b) False Alarm Probabilities.

(c) Probability and Cost Tradeoffs.

Fig. 4. Safety and performance measures per number of missions.

Probability of False Alarms. For the ROC sensors, we measured the probability for a false alarm, depending again on the number of missions. The curves in Fig. 4(b) depend on the quality of the ROC sensor and on the false positive rates. The high-quality sensor is the only one with relatively low false alarm probabilities. The cumulated model checking time was 52.13 s, computing the optimal result on the transformed MDP took less than one second.

Probability and Cost Tradeoffs. Finally, we show the expected cost in dependence of the number of missions in Fig. 4(c). Additionally, for each data point, the probability for a recognition error needs to be below 50%. The violation of this property is indicated by the maximum value $4.5 \cdot 10^{-5}$. The results show that for this kind of property indeed the low-resolution (480p) sensor at lowest altitude is the best choice, as it has relatively low initial cost. While the task cost at low altitude is slightly larger than at higher altitudes, with this sensor, the UAV is able to maintain the probability threshold of safely recognizing an intruder. The cumulated model checking time was 59.1 s, computing the optimal result on the transformed MDP took 1.2 s.

Table 1. Parametric benchmarks

Model	Type	States	Transitions	MC (s)	SE (s)
Die	parametric	13	20	—	0.04
	transformed	13	48	0.04	—
	controlled	37	60	0.02	—
Zeroconf1	parametric	1 004	2 005	—	60.3
	transformed	1 004	6 009	0.18	—
	controlled	9 046	18 075	0.19	—
Zeroconf2	parametric	100 004	200 005	—	TO
	transformed	100 004	600 009	0.90	—
	controlled	900 046	1 800 075	7.36	—
Crowds1	parametric	7 421	12 881	—	5.80
	transformed	7 421	20 161	0.08	—
	controlled	66 826	116 148	0.42	—
Crowds2	parametric	572 153	1 698 233	—	18.81
	transformed	572 153	2 261 273	4.39	—
	controlled	5 149 474	15 284 736	33.70	—
Crowds3	parametric	2 018 094	7 224 834	—	TO
	transformed	2 018 094	9 208 354	17.15	—
	controlled	18 162 973	65 024 355	137.71	—

Further Benchmarks. We additionally assessed our approach on well-known parametric Markov chain examples from the PARAM-website [20], that originally stem from the PRISM benchmark suite [12]. We tested a parametric version of the Knuth-Yao Die (Die), several instances of the Zeroconf protocol [5], and the Crowds protocol [3]. For all benchmarks, we introduced three discrete values as domain for each parameter. Table 1 shows the results, where we list the number of states and transitions as well as the model checking times (MC): "transformed" refers to the MDP after Transformation 1 and 2, "controlled" refers to the MDP after Transformations 1–3. For the original parametric Markov chains, we tested the time to perform state elimination (SE), which is the standard model checking method for such models [6,9]. We used a timeout (TO) of 600 s.

We draw the following conclusions: (1) The first two program transformations only increase the number of transitions with respect to the MIMDP model, the third transformation increases the states and transitions by up to one order of magnitude. (2) Except for the Crowds2 instance, model checking the transformed and controlled MDP is superior to performing state elimination. (3) For these benchmarks, we are able to handle instances with millions of states.

8   Conclusion and Future Work

We introduced structured synthesis for MDPs. Driven by a concrete case study from the area of physical security, we defined MIMDPs and demonstrated the hardness of the corresponding synthesis problem. As a feasible solution, we presented a transformation to an MDP where nondeterministic choices represented the underlying structure of the MIMDP. Our experiments showed that we are able to analyze meaningful measures for such problems. In the future, we will investigate further intricacies of the case study regarding continuous state spaces. Moreover, we will extend our approaches to account for so-called high-level counterexamples, that provide insight on errors in the system on the level of the PRISM language [16,23].

Acknowledgements. We want to thank Sebastian Junges for providing us with valuable insights on the correctness of our approaches.

References

1. Johnson, J., Analysis of image forming systems. In: Image Intensifer Symposium, pp. 249–273 (1958)
2. Satia, J.K., Lave Jr., R.E.: Markovian decision processes with uncertain transition probabilities. Oper. Res. **21**(3), 728–740 (1973)
3. Reiter, M.K., Rubin, A.D.: Crowds: anonymity for web transactions. ACM Trans. Inf. Syst. Secur. **1**(1), 66–92 (1998)
4. Lasserre, J.B.: Global optimization with polynomials and the problem of moments. SIAM J. Optim. **11**(3), 796–817 (2001)
5. Bohnenkamp, H., Van Der Stok, P., Hermanns, H., Vaandrager, F.: Cost-optimization of the IPv4 zeroconf protocol. In: DSN, pp. 531–540. IEEE CS (2003)
6. Daws, C.: Symbolic and parametric model checking of discrete-time markov chains. In: Liu, Z., Araki, K. (eds.) ICTAC 2004. LNCS, vol. 3407, pp. 280–294. Springer, Heidelberg (2005). https://doi.org/10.1007/978-3-540-31862-0_21
7. Fawcett, T.: An introduction to ROC analysis. Pattern Recogn. Lett. **27**(8), 861–874 (2006)
8. Etessami, K., Kwiatkowska, M.Z., Vardi, M.Y., Yannakakis, M.: Multi-objective model checking of Markov decision processes. Logical Meth. Comput. Sci. **4**(4), 1–21 (2008)
9. Hahn, E.M., Hermanns, H., Zhang, L.: Probabilistic reachability for parametric Markov models. Softw. Tools Technol. Transfer **13**(1), 3–19 (2010)

10. Kwiatkowska, M., Norman, G., Parker, D.: PRISM 4.0: verification of probabilistic real-time systems. In: Gopalakrishnan, G., Qadeer, S. (eds.) CAV 2011. LNCS, vol. 6806, pp. 585–591. Springer, Heidelberg (2011). https://doi.org/10.1007/978-3-642-22110-1_47
11. Forejt, V., Kwiatkowska, M., Parker, D.: Pareto curves for probabilistic model checking. In: Chakraborty, S., Mukund, M. (eds.) ATVA 2012. LNCS, pp. 317–332. Springer, Heidelberg (2012). https://doi.org/10.1007/978-3-642-33386-6_25
12. Kwiatkowska, M., Norman, G., Parker, D.: The PRISM benchmark suite. In: QEST, pp. 203–204. IEEE CS (2012)
13. Chen, T., Forejt, V., Kwiatkowska, M., Parker, D., Simaitis, A.: PRISM-games: a model checker for stochastic multi-player games. In: Piterman, N., Smolka, S.A. (eds.) TACAS 2013. LNCS, vol. 7795, pp. 185–191. Springer, Heidelberg (2013). https://doi.org/10.1007/978-3-642-36742-7_13
14. Baier, C., Dubslaff, C., Klüppelholz, S.: Trade-off analysis meets probabilistic model checking. In: CSL-LICS, pp. 1:1–1:10. ACM (2014)
15. Chen, H., Kalyanam, K., Zhang, W., Casbeer, D.: Continuous-time intruder isolation using Unattended Ground Sensors on graphsround sensors on graphs. In: ACC (2014)
16. Dehnert, C., Jansen, N., Wimmer, R., Ábrahám, E., Katoen, J.-P.: Fast debugging of PRISM models. In: Cassez, F., Raskin, J.-F. (eds.) ATVA 2014. LNCS, vol. 8837, pp. 146–162. Springer, Cham (2014). https://doi.org/10.1007/978-3-319-11936-6_11
17. Gordon, A.D., Henzinger, T.A., Nori, A.V., Rajamani, S.K.: Probabilistic programming. In: Future of Software Engineering (FOSE), pp. 167–181. ACM Press (2014)
18. Hahn, E.M., Li, Y., Schewe, S., Turrini, A., Zhang, L.: iscasMc: a web-based probabilistic model checker. In: Jones, C., Pihlajasaari, P., Sun, J. (eds.) FM 2014. LNCS, vol. 8442, pp. 312–317. Springer, Cham (2014). https://doi.org/10.1007/978-3-319-06410-9_22
19. Dehnert, C., et al.: PROPhESY: a probabilistic parameter synthesis tool. In: Kroening, D., Păsăreanu, C.S. (eds.) CAV 2015. LNCS, vol. 9206, pp. 214–231. Springer, Cham (2015). https://doi.org/10.1007/978-3-319-21690-4_13
20. PARAM Website (2015). http://depend.cs.uni-sb.de/tools/param/
21. PRISM Website (2015). http://prismmodelchecker.org
22. Rasmussen, S., Kingston, D.: Development and flight test of an area monitoring system using unmanned aerial vehicles and unattended ground sensors. In: International Conference on Unmanned Aircraft Systems, pp. 1215–1224 (2015)
23. Wimmer, R., Jansen, N., Vorpahl, A., Ábrahám, E., Katoen, J.-P., Becker, B.: High-level counterexamples for probabilistic automata. Logical Meth. Comput. Sci. 11(1), 1 (2015)
24. Delgado, K.V., de Barros, L.N., Dias, D.B., Sanner, S.: Real-time dynamic programming for markov decision processes with imprecise probabilities. Artif. Intell. 230, 192–223 (2016)
25. Kingston, D., Rasmussen, S., Humphrey, L.: Automated UAV tasks for search and surveillance. In: CCA, pp. 1–8. IEEE (2016)
26. Quatmann, T., Dehnert, C., Jansen, N., Junges, S., Katoen, J.-P.: Parameter synthesis for Markov models: faster than ever. In: Artho, C., Legay, A., Peled, D. (eds.) ATVA 2016. LNCS, vol. 9938, pp. 50–67. Springer, Cham (2016). https://doi.org/10.1007/978-3-319-46520-3_4

27. Cubuktepe, M., et al.: Sequential convex programming for the efficient verification of parametric MDPs. In: Legay, A., Margaria, T. (eds.) TACAS 2017. LNCS, vol. 10206, pp. 133–150. Springer, Heidelberg (2017). https://doi.org/10.1007/978-3-662-54580-5_8

28. Dehnert, C., Junges, S., Katoen, J.-P., Volk, M.: A storm is coming: a modern probabilistic model checker. In: Majumdar, R., Kunčak, V. (eds.) CAV 2017. LNCS, vol. 10427, pp. 592–600. Springer, Cham (2017). https://doi.org/10.1007/978-3-319-63390-9_31

29. Chrszon, P., Dubslaff, C., Klüppelholz, S., Baier, C.: Profeat: feature-oriented engineering for family-based probabilistic model checking. Formal Asp. Comput. **30**(1), 45–75 (2018)

30. Hartmanns, A., Junges, S., Katoen, J.-P., Quatmann, T.: Multi-cost bounded reachability in MDP. In: Beyer, D., Huisman, M. (eds.) TACAS 2018. LNCS, vol. 10806, pp. 320–339. Springer, Cham (2018). https://doi.org/10.1007/978-3-319-89963-3_19

31. Jansen, N., Humphrey, L.R., Tumova, J., Topcu, U.: Structured synthesis for probabilistic systems. CoRR, abs/1807.06106 (2018)

32. Ceska, M., Jansen, N., Junges, S., Katoen, J.-P.: Shepherding hordes of Markov chains. CoRR, abs/1902.05727 (2019)

33. Junges, S., et al.: Parameter synthesis for Markov models. arXiv preprint arXiv:1903.07993 (2019)

34. Baier, C., Katoen, J.-P.: Principles of Model Checking. The MIT Press, Cambridge (2008)

35. Bertsekas, D.P.: Nonlinear Programming. Athena Scientific, Belmont (1999)

Design and Runtime Verification Side-by-Side in eTrice

Sudeep Kanav[1]([⊠]), Levi Lúcio[1], Christian Hilden[2], and Thomas Schuetz[2]

[1] fortiss GmbH, Munich, Germany
{kanav,lucio}@fortiss.org
[2] PROTOS Software GmbH, Munich, Germany
{christian.hilden,thomas.schuetz}@protos.de

Abstract. eTrice is a mature open-source model-based software engineering tool, based on the ROOM methodology. It is currently used in the industry for the development of solutions for domains such as health, heavy machinery and the automotive. eTrice natively incorporates mechanisms for runtime verification. At the request of the developers of eTrice, we have incorporated model checking in their tool chain, by partly reusing the existing runtime verification architecture. We report on the implementation of the tool, experiments that we conducted, and lessons learned regarding the synergies between the two verification techniques.

1 Introduction

Protos GmbH is a company that develops model-based software solutions for a range of domains, such as health, heavy machinery and the automotive. Since 2003, Protos has continuously been developing their own open-source model-based development environment named eTrice [2]. eTrice is used to model component based event-driven systems where components communicate by message passing.

eTrice implements the ROOM (Real-Time Object-Oriented Modeling) methodology [12,13] and relies technically on the Eclipse Modeling Framework (EMF). It is an open source tool mainly developed and used by Protos GmbH.

A large number of Protos' solutions aim at improving the reliability of existing systems, or, to a lesser extent, at developing new systems that are intrinsically reliable. Examples of concretely implemented solutions are: to protect human or machine interfaces in the medical domain from unforeseen and potentially dangerous interactions; to prevent undesired messages, resulting from poor system integration, from being passed between components of heavy machinery; to generate model-based test cases for automotive and industrial ECUs.

Being that reliability is high priority for Protos, eTrice uses runtime verification (Rv) as a means to log, debug and even protect behaviors of the system. Rv has repeatedly proven itself at Protos as a verification technique that is efficient, robust and easy to implement and operate.

J. M. Badger and K. Y. Rozier (Eds.): NFM 2019, LNCS 11460, pp. 255–262, 2019.
https://doi.org/10.1007/978-3-030-20652-9_17

Runtime monitors are currently specified at the level of eTrice models as contracts, which are used to generate the Rv code. Rv then allows reacting to contract violations in the form of raising alarms, shutting down the system, or moving it to a failsafe state. Moreover, Rv provides Protos with precise logging of the events leading to a contract violation, from which message sequence charts (MSCs) can be automatically generated for debugging purposes. Other uses of Rv at Protos include: protecting components at runtime against unreliable communication coming from third party components; pruning the input space when generating test cases by filtering out messages not pertaining to the expected protocol; detecting contract violations while executing test cases.

The work we present in this paper investigates the application of design-time formal verification to eTrice, as a means to complement and enhance Rv at Protos[1]. Given that the solutions developed for eTrice are model-based, the use of model checking (Mc) follows naturally. Protos is keen on experimenting with the use of design-time verification (Mc) in practice, as they believe the technique will allow deeper verification that will find seldom-occurring errors (e.g. race conditions), earlier in the software development process. The work presented in this paper reports our findings while building Mc into eTrice.

The paper is organized as follows: Sect. 2 describes the background for this work; Sect. 3 explains our solution for integrating Mc in eTrice; Sect. 4 describes a case study for our approach; Sect. 5 considers related work; and finally Sect. 6 discusses our findings and concludes.

2   Background

In this section we provide a brief introduction to eTrice and then go on to explain how contracts are specified and verified at runtime in eTrice. This existing framework provided the starting point for our work on design-time verification.

eTrice: eTrice is an open source model based development tool for embedded systems, based on the ROOM [12] methodology. It aims at reducing the structural and behavioral complexity of a system by using (de)composition, layering and inheritance – the main concepts supported by ROOM. The tool itself uses a set of *domain specific languages* (DSLs) to describe ROOM models. eTrice supports both graphical and textual editors with features such as validation, highlighting and code completion. It also supports code generation and includes runtime environments for Java, C++ and C.

For our work on design-time verification we restrict eTrice models to using finite types: enumerations, words, and booleans. As well, we use linear arithmetic as the expression language for declaring transition guards and action code.

---

[1] The models and generated artifacts can be found at: https://github.com/skanav/rv_mc_etrice_artifacts.

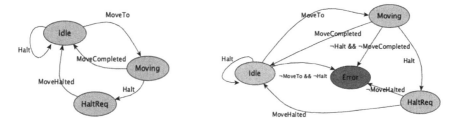

Fig. 1. An example PSM

Fig. 2. PSM with the *Error* state (Color figure online)

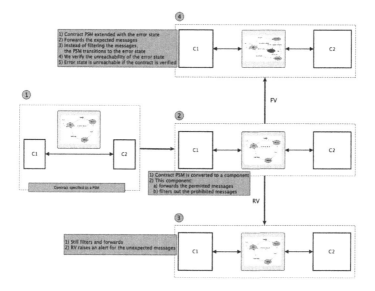

Fig. 3. Fv and Rv of a PSM contract defined in eTrice

Contract Specification: Protos uses contracts specified in eTrice to allow for Rv. A contract is specified on a communication channel in the form of a *protocol state machine* (PSM) (Fig. 1) – a simplified form of statecharts. (① in Fig. 3).

Rv: As a first step to allow for Rv, a model transformation is used to convert the contract PSM into an eTrice component. This new component is interjected between the two eTrice components whose communication is being verified (② in Fig. 3). This allows reading, forwarding, and filtering the messages being passed. The new component (a) reads the messages being communicated; (b) forwards an expected message, i.e., one for which a transition is defined in the PSM; and (c) filters out the unexpected messages, i.e., a message for which no transition in the PSM can be triggered. At runtime each message being communicated is logged and an alert is raised when an unexpected message is encountered (③ in Fig. 3).

This interpretation of the PSM contract can be seen as a way to avoid hazardous situations by monitoring and sanitizing the inputs to a component – the contract provides an *benign* environment for a component to operate. The adopted contract semantics allows only the communication patterns described in the contract, rejecting the others. Protos highlights several advantages in the usage of Rv: only expected states of the system are reached; state explosion is much reduced in systems that are protected by the runtime monitors generated from contracts; the analysis and debugging of contract violations using MSCs to display executions is of great practical value.

3   Solution

In this section first we explain how we convert a PSM into a formal specification for the model checker. We then briefly describe the transformation of the eTrice specification to NuSMV [7] and the lifting of the results of Mc back to eTrice.

Contract Interpretation: Rv allows the system to keep on executing when an unexpected message is encountered, whereas for Mc we are interested in finding out if the messaging protocol between two components does not respect the contract. With Mc, we do not filter the unexpected messages as Rv does – we rather transform the PSM contract to a state machine (Fig. 2) such that it transitions to an *error* state (colored red in Fig. 2) on receiving an unexpected message. We can then formally verify the reachability of the *error* state; the contract is satisfied if this state is not reachable, meaning that the communication between the components always respects the protocol defined in the PSM.

Verification Domain Specific Language (DSL): We have defined an EMF [1] core based DSL for the input language of NuSMV to ease integration with eTrice via model transformations. This allows further using the model-to-text transformation to generate the textual specification to be consumed by the model checker. Our verification DSL enables us to describe a system consisting of components communicating over typed channels. We have created this DSL instead of developing a direct transformation from eTrice to NuSMV. In the future we plan on generalizing our approach to other model-based software development environments.

Integration with NuSMV: We have designed the eTrice-to-NuSMV transformation as a composition of several small step transformations. For this we reused the Java based transformation composition framework described in [10], used to allow formal verification of AutoFOCUS3 [3] specifications. Additionally, we have reused the underlying machinery we developed for [10] which calls the NuSMV model checker and parses its output.

Lifting the Results: In case of a runtime failure, eTrice displays the information to the user in the form of a MSC. This MSC is generated based on the messages logged during runtime. We lift the trace from the model checker to the

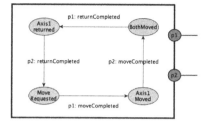

Fig. 4. The controller model in eTrice

Fig. 5. The counterexample lifted to eTrice

MSC and then reuse the machinery built in eTrice to view the results. Again, similarly to the transformation into NuSMV, for lifting also we have reused the concept for counterexample interpretation and lifting mechanism in [10].

4   Real-World Case Study

Protos often encounters in practice a control pattern where a central controller issues commands to subcomponents dealing with the physical world. Specific instances of this pattern might be for instance to move a certain machine part by a certain distance or change the temperature of a machine part by certain amount. The concrete example we will use to illustrate the use of Mc in practice consists of a main controller and two *axes* controllers for an industrial front loader. In production, to achieve moving the loader's bucket to the expected position, the controller dispatches a command to each of the axis controllers which responds back with success or failure of the move. Because of the real-world variability of the parts and of the environment in which the loader operates, the two commands can be completed in any sequence. As such, the controller must be implemented to accommodate such behaviors. The complexity of the controller increases quickly with the number of subcomponents (Fig. 5).

Liveness Check: The controller in Fig. 4 is a reactive system, meaning it is supposed to run in an infinite loop. As such, it should be possible to visit all states of the controller infinitely often. This translates into a liveness analysis of the states of the controller, when the controller specification is composed with the contracts on the communication channels with the axes controllers. Note that during model-checking the contracts act as the environment for the controller. In particular, the liveness check fails for the controller in Fig. 4 as the controller stagnates when the acknowledgments from the axes controllers arrive in a different order than expected.

Reachability Check: We have used the mechanism described in Fig. 2 to check that the communication protocol between the controller and the axes controllers is always respected. Here we have equally found an error, reported in the native MSC viewer in eTrice. The error happens because of duplicate message sending code occurring in the entry action and incoming transition of the state *MoveRequested*. According to Protos, this is a typical and hard-to-catch copy/paste mistake that often happens during development.

5   Related Work

To the best of our knowledge there exists, at the time of the writing of this paper, no modeling tool which can simultaneously perform runtime and design-time verification. The idea of combining Mc and Rv has been discussed in the literature [9] and explored mostly at the programming level [5, 6, 11]. The key idea of such research is to apply static analyses to the code (including Mc) and to use the results thereof to optimize the runtime verification. Both [5] and [11] use such techniques to reduce the required instrumentation, thereby reducing the runtime overhead. In our work we use Mc to find bugs at the design time, and keep the Rv intact – as intended by Protos due to business considerations. The Clara framework [5] performs static typestate checks [14] on Java programs and tries to find out the *safe* locations of those programs. Events triggered from a safe location do not cause a property to fail – thus a *safe* location does not need to be monitored. The Rv is optimized to monitor only unsafe locations, thus reducing overhead. The work in [11] uses static analysis (information flow analysis and model checking) to find the security vulnerabilities in web applications. As in Clara, the results of the static checks are then used to optimize the dynamic checks by reducing the required instrumentation for Rv, thereby decreasing the runtime overhead. In [4, 6] a model checker is used to generate the inputs for the test case and Rv is partly as an oracle during the test case execution. Desai et al. [8] discuss using explicit state model checking for verifying properties under certain assumptions and using Rv to guarantee those assumptions in a robotic application, whereas we use symbolic model checking for our work.

6   Discussion and Conclusion

Despite its success in the academia, design-time verification using model checking is not yet in use in the practical day-by-day of software development. The reasons for this state of affairs are outside of the scope of this paper (we refer the interested reader to e.g. [9]), but it is commonly understood that the formality of the logical input specification languages for model checkers play an important role in the lack of practical adoption. In this paper we have described our integration of the NuSMV model checker in eTrice. In order to do so, we have made heavy reuse of the existing Rv infrastructure already in place: on the one hand we have used the existing contract language as a means to have input specifications for the model checker; on the other hand we have leveraged the MSC viewer for the existing eTrice Rv mechanism in order to output counterexample traces. Because we have also reused some of our previous model transformation work for verifying AutoFOCUS3 specifications, the integration of Mc in eTrice was accomplished in a short time span of a couple of weeks. The experience of integrating Mc in a model-based software development tool such as eTrice has emboldened us to think that such integration (also having in mind contracts has properties to be checked) might be extended to other IDEs in an affordable fashion.

Our results are very promising for Protos and its business. It has been often highlighted during our discussions how theoretically simple checks such as the ones described in Sect. 4 can be of high impact in practice. We have shown with a real-world example that liveness and reachability properties can be checked on eTrice specifications while not intruding whatsoever in the currently existing specification language. Due to our work, liveness properties that could not be proved with Rv can now be checked in eTrice specifications. Additionally, while violations of the protocol stated in the contract PSMs can indeed eventually be caught by Rv, model checking allows doing so efficiently, at design time and covering corner cases that might occur very sparsely in practice. Although Rv is currently used by Protos in production, this naturally incurs in decreased efficiency at runtime and does not prevent faults from occurring in practice.

Our next steps are to make design-time verification an intrinsic part of Protos' software development cycle. This implies on the one hand bringing the technical integration with NuSMV up-to-speed to the professional software development requirements of Protos, while on the other hand further investigating the scalability of our approach. In this paper we have provided hints on how model-checking could be used in the software development lifecycle at Protos, but clearly the methodological aspects of such usage by software developers would also need to be understood and fine-tuned to achieve increased productivity in practice.

References

1. Eclipse modeling project. http://www.eclipse.org/modeling/emf/
2. eTrice (2012–2017). http://www.eclipse.org/etrice//
3. Aravantinos, V., Voss, S., Teufl, S., Hölzl, F., Schätz, B.: AutoFOCUS 3: tooling concepts for seamless, model-based development of embedded systems. In: ACES-MB&WUCOR@ MoDELS, pp. 19–26 (2015)
4. Artho, C., et al.: Combining test case generation and runtime verification. Theoret. Comput. Sci. **336**(2–3), 209–234 (2005)
5. Bodden, E., Lam, P., Hendren, L.: Clara: a framework for partially evaluating finite-state runtime monitors ahead of time. In: Barringer, H., et al. (eds.) RV 2010. LNCS, vol. 6418, pp. 183–197. Springer, Heidelberg (2010). https://doi.org/10.1007/978-3-642-16612-9_15
6. Cadar, C., Ganesh, V., Pawlowski, P.M., Dill, D.L., Engler, D.R.: Exe: automatically generating inputs of death. ACM Trans. Inf. Syst. Secur. (TISSEC) **12**(2), 10 (2008)
7. Cimatti, A., Clarke, E., Giunchiglia, F., Roveri, M.: NuSMV: a new symbolic model verifier. In: Halbwachs, N., Peled, D. (eds.) CAV 1999. LNCS, vol. 1633, pp. 495–499. Springer, Heidelberg (1999). https://doi.org/10.1007/3-540-48683-6_44
8. Desai, A., Dreossi, T., Seshia, S.A.: Combining model checking and runtime verification for safe robotics. In: Lahiri, S., Reger, G. (eds.) RV 2017. LNCS, vol. 10548, pp. 172–189. Springer, Cham (2017). https://doi.org/10.1007/978-3-319-67531-2_11

9. Hinrichs, T.L., Sistla, A.P., Zuck, L.D.: Model check what you can, runtime verify the rest. In: HOWARD-60, pp. 234–244 (2014)
10. Kanav, S., Aravantinos, V.: Modular transformation from AF3 to nuXmv. MoDeVVa @ MoDELS (2017)
11. Lam, M.S., Martin, M., Livshits, B., Whaley, J.: Securing web applications with static and dynamic information flow tracking. In: Proceedings of the 2008 ACM SIGPLAN Symposium on Partial Evaluation and Semantics-Based Program Manipulation, pp. 3–12. ACM (2008)
12. Selic, B., Gullekson, G., Ward, P.: Real-time object oriented modeling and design (1994)
13. Selic, B., et al.: Real-time object-oriented modeling (ROOM). In: RTAS, p. 214. IEEE (1996)
14. Strom, R.E., Yemini, S.: Typestate: a programming language concept for enhancing software reliability. IEEE Trans. Softw. Eng. 1, 157–171 (1986)

Data Independence for Software Transactional Memory

Jürgen König$^{(\boxtimes)}$ and Heike Wehrheim

Department of Computer Science, Paderborn University, Paderborn, Germany
jkoenig@mail.upb.de

Abstract. Software Transactional Memory (STM) algorithms provide programmers with a synchronisation mechanism for concurrent access to shared variables. Basically, programmers can specify *transactions* (reading from and writing to shared state) which then execute in a "seeming" atomicity. This property is captured in a correctness criterion called *opacity*. For model checking the opacity of an STM algorithm, we – in principle – need to check opacity for all possible combinations of transactions with all possible values to be written. This leads to several sources of infinity during model checking: infinitely many data values, infinitely many possible accesses in transactions, and unboundedly many transactions being executed.

In this paper, we propose a technique for avoiding the first source of infinity: infinitely many different data values. To this end, we employ a notion of *data independence* and provide two results. First, we prove that opacity as a correctness criterion is data independent. Second, we develop conditions for checking data independence of STM algorithms and show their soundness. Together, these results allow to reduce model checking (of data independent STMs) to transactions with a single choice for values written.

1 Introduction

Today, multi-core processors are widely utilized since their usage yields a large increase in computing power. This additional computing power can best be used in concurrent programs. When writing programs with concurrent threads accessing shared state, programmers – however – have to provide appropriate synchronisation among threads as to avoid access to inconsistent memory values. Software Transactional Memory (STM) (as proposed by Shavit and Touitou [17]) aims at providing programmers with an easy to use synchronisation technique for such an access to shared state.

STMs allow programmers to define software *transactions*, much alike database transactions. A transaction consists of a number of read and write operations to the shared state, and the STM algorithm should guarantee these operations to take place "seemingly atomic", while ideally also allowing transactions to run concurrently. This seeming atomicity is formalized in a correctness criterion called *opacity* [12]. As the consequences of incorrect behaviour may be severe, it is necessary to show all proposals for STM algorithms to be opaque.

© Springer Nature Switzerland AG 2019
J. M. Badger and K. Y. Rozier (Eds.): NFM 2019, LNCS 11460, pp. 263–279, 2019.
https://doi.org/10.1007/978-3-030-20652-9_18

Current approaches for proving opacity of STMs are either deductive verification or model checking. The typical approach for deductive verification (e.g. [7,8]) is showing a refinement relationship to exist between the actual algorithm and an intermediate specification called TMS2 [9]. As TMS2 has been shown to be opaque, the actual STM algorithm is then opaque as well. A different approach by Lesani et al. uses a decomposition of opacity into several properties called *markability* which can be shown to hold via deductive verification [15]. For model checking STMs, there are less approaches. Guerraoui et al. [10,11] propose to carry out model checking on two variables (in the shared state) and two transactions only, and justify this restriction by a reduction theorem. A similar approach is taken by Abdulla et al. [1] for a hybrid TM, i.e., a combination of hardware and software transactional memory. However, both their correctness conditions are not exactly opacity as they ignore the values written and read by transactions. A model checking approach for opacity is proposed in [3]. However, in this approach checking is only carried out for a *fixed* STM instantiation (i.e., a fixed number of transactions executing a fixed number of reads and writes with fixed values).

In general, all techniques using some form of automatic state space exploration like model checking for proving opacity of STM algorithms have to tackle the problem of (in principle) needing to show infinitely many STM instantiations to be opaque. This infinity has three sources: we have (a) unboundedly many possibilities for threads using the STM, (b) transactions with unboundedly many options for reading and writing shared state and (c) infinitely many different values to be written in these transactions.

In this paper we address the latter source of infinity. We tackle the problem of unboundedly many different possible values to be written by employing the notion of data independence (first introduced by Wolper et al. [19]). When a program is data independent – roughly speaking – its inputs do not influence its control flow. For STMs that means that specific values written by any transaction do not determine the outcome of itself or other transactions. Similarly, a correctness property is data independent if the fulfillment of the property does not dependent on specific values.

Here, we define data independence in our context and prove opacity to be a data independent property. We furthermore provide conditions on STM algorithms which ensure an algorithm to be data independent. Together, this allows for model checking STMs *without* needing to check all possible values for inputs to write operations.

2   Foundations

We start with giving an example of an STM algorithm which we use throughout this paper. Afterwards we present the basic definitions of data independence.

Transactional Mutex Lock. Figure 1 gives a simple example of an STM algorithm. It is the Transactional Mutex Lock (TML) of Dalessandro et al. [6].

```
Init: glb = 0

Begin:                        Commit:
B1   do loc := glb            E1   if (loc & 1)
B2   while (loc & 1);         E2     glb++;
B3   return ok;               E3   return commit;

Read(addr):                   Write(addr,val):
R1   tmp := *addr;            W1 if (loc & 0)
R2   if (glb = loc)           W2   if (!CAS(&glb,loc,loc+1))
R3     return tmp;            W3       return abort;
R4   else return abort;       W4 else loc++;
W5 *addr := val;
W6 return ok;
```

Fig. 1. The Transactional Mutex Lock (TML)

Like other STM algorithms, TML provides four operations to the programmer: Begin to start a transaction, Read to read from and Write to write to some shared location and Commit to commit it. For achieving the necessary synchronisation, TML uses a global counter glb (initially 0) and local variables loc (storing a copy of glb) and tmp (temporarily storing the value read from a location). These variables are sometimes also called *meta data* because they are used for synchronisation only. The shared state to be concurrently accessed are the values of parameters addr of Read and Write. The operation CAS (compare-and-swap) atomically executes a comparison and an assignment: $CAS(var, v_1, v_2)$ compares the value of var to v_1 and sets var to v_2 in case that these are equal, and does not change var else. It returns the result of the comparison.

TML allows for transactions to be executed concurrently as long as no write operation has been called. The variable glb records whether there is a live writing transaction. Namely, glb is odd if there is a writing transaction and even otherwise. The first execution of Write in a writing transaction attempts to increment glb by using a CAS. If the CAS attempt fails, a write by another transaction must have occured, and hence, the current transaction aborts. If the CAS succeeds, glb becomes odd, which prevents other transactions from starting, and causes all concurrent live transactions still wanting to read or write to abort.

In the following, we assume that programmers use transactions correctly, i.e., a transaction is always started with a call to Begin, then a number of calls to Read and Write follow ending with a call to Commit (unless some previous operation has aborted). We furthermore assume w.l.o.g. that transactions only write *once* to each location. During an execution of a program, method calls give rise to *invocation* and *response* events. We say that invocations and responses of the same call *match*. In the following, we let *Loc* be the set of all locations which transactions want to access and *Val* be the values these locations can take. We always assume $loc \in Loc$ and $val \in Val$. We furthermore use a set

T of thread identifiers and let $t \in T$. For simplicity we assume every thread $t \in T$ to execute a single transaction only and thus identify a transaction by the executing thread. Table 1 lists the events arising in executions of transactions. We see that operations can also return with *abort*. In TML, the `Begin` operation never aborts.

Table 1. Events of STM algorithms

Invocations	Possible matching responses
$Inv(\text{BEGIN}())_t$	$Resp(\text{BEGIN}(ok))_t, Resp(\text{BEGIN}(abort))_t$
$Inv(\text{READ}(loc))_t$	$Resp(\text{READ}(loc, val, ok))_t, Resp(\text{READ}(abort))_t$
$Inv(\text{WRITE}(loc, val))_t$	$Resp(\text{WRITE}(loc, ok))_t, Resp(\text{WRITE}(abort))_t$
$Inv(\text{COMMIT}())_t$	$Resp(\text{COMMIT}(ok))_t, Resp(\text{COMMIT}(abort))_t$

The purpose of model checking is now to check whether an STM algorithm actually ensures the desired "seeming atomicity" of transactions. This requires running different transactions with different numbers of reads and writes, and different values being written (i.e., passed as argument to `Write`). In order to avoid having to check "atomicity" for all possible data values, we apply a data independence argument.

Data Independence. We build on the definition of data independence as given by Abdulla et al. [2] which itself builds on that of Wolper [19]. Data independence is defined on traces which are sequences of events.

An *event* $m(v_1, \ldots, v_k, d_1, \ldots, d_n)$, $k, n \in \mathbb{N}$ consists of an *identifier* m, a number of *non-data values*[1] v_j (out of an arbitrary domain) and a number of *data values* d_i from some domain $\mathbb{D}$. In our setting of STMs, the identifiers will denote the invocations or responses of operations like `Begin` or `Write` together with the thread identifiers. The non-data values are the addresses of shared locations Loc and the data values the values to be written, i.e. $\mathbb{D} = Val$.

The number of data values in an event is fixed per identifier m and we denote it by $dpar(m)$. We let M be the set of all identifiers and Σ the set of traces over events. A correctness property is then simply a subset of traces, namely the ones satisfying the property.

Definition 1. *A correctness property is a set $P \subseteq \Sigma$.*

A program *satisfies* a correctness property P if all traces arising from executing the program are in P.

---

[1] This is the main difference to [2]: Abdulla et al. only have data values as they consider operations on concurrent data structures where the data structure is fixed and thus need not be a parameter to the method.

Events describe executions of methods in which the d_i values are concrete actual parameters or return values. We denote $v_1, \ldots, v_n$ by $\overline{v}$ and $d_1, \ldots, d_n$ by $\overline{d}$. If $m(\overline{v}, \overline{d})$ is occurring in a trace σ, we also write $m(\overline{v}, \overline{d}) \in \sigma$.

For the definition of data independence, we need to distinguish between data values in events which are *inputs* and those which are *outputs*. For instance, the value in a `Write` is an input whereas in a `Read` it is an output. As an example (for brevity without invocation and response events and using w/r instead of WRITE/READ) we will consider the domain $\mathbb{D} = \mathbb{Z}$ with events $w(v, d)$ (write) and $r(v, d)$ (read), v being a non-data value and $d \in \mathbb{D}$ a data value.

Definition 2. *An* input function *is a mapping* $I : M \to 2^{\mathbb{N}}$ *such that* $I(m) \subseteq \{1, \ldots, dpar(m)\}$ *for all* $m \in M$.

In the example, I is defined as follows: $I(w) = \{1\}^2$ and $I(r) = \emptyset$. The second argument of w is the value to be written and the read has no inputs.

With input functions at hand, we can define the notion of *differentiated* trace, meaning that all the inputs in a trace take different values.

Definition 3. *A trace* $\sigma = m_1(\overline{v}, \overline{d_1}) \ldots m_k(\overline{v}, \overline{d_k})$ *is differentiated w.r.t. an input function* I *if the following holds:*

$$\forall i, i', 1 \le i, i' \le k, i \ne i' : \forall j \in I(m_i), j' \in I(m_{i'}) : d_{i,j} \ne d_{i',j'}$$

Let Σ_I be the set of traces differentiated w.r.t. I. For example, the trace $\sigma_{ex} = w(x, 1)w(x, 0)r(x, 1)$ is differentiated. Note that the value in r does not matter since it is not an input value.

A *renaming* (of data values) is a function $f : \mathbb{D} \to \mathbb{D}$ and we let F be the set of all renamings. We apply renamings to events by letting $f(m(v_1, \ldots, v_m, d_1, \ldots, d_n))$ be $m(v_1, \ldots, v_m, f(d_1), \ldots, f(d_n))$ (i.e., the renaming is applied on data values only) and also lift this to entire traces. For example, for $f_{ex}(x) = x + 1$ the renaming of our example trace by f_{ex} would be $f_{ex}(\sigma_{ex}) = w(x, 2)w(x, 1)r(x, 2)$, which is also a differentiated trace. This lets us define data independence.

Definition 4. *A set of traces* $X \subseteq \Sigma$ *is* data independent *w.r.t. an input function* I *iff the following holds for all* $\sigma \in X$:

- $\forall f \in F : f(\sigma) \in X$,
- $\exists f \in F, \exists \sigma_d \in X \cap \Sigma_I : f(\sigma_d) = \sigma$.

In our example, let X be $\{w(x, a)w(x, b)r(x, a) \mid a, b \in \mathbb{Z}\}$. This set is data independent. For every $\sigma \in X$ each renaming of it is still in X since the identical values for the first w and the r will be preserved by the fact that renamings are functions. Furthermore, all traces $\sigma = w(x, a)w(x, b)r(x, a)$ can be obtained as renamings of σ_{ex} by setting $f(1) = a$ and $f(0) = b$.

Next we define the key correctness property for STMs which is *opacity* and investigate data independence of opacity.

---

[2] Note that non-data values are not counted here.

3   Opacity

The traces we consider in this paper are *histories* generated by software transactional memory executions consisting of the events defined in Table 1. In STMs, the data domain consists of values *Val* read from or written to the shared state. In our setting, we furthermore have a single input parameter, namely the value to be written by a write event. The input function I_{STM} thus returns $\{1\}$ (first data value) for $Inv(\text{WRITE})_t$ and the empty set for all other identifiers.

In the following, we will refer to traces over this set of events as *histories*. We will use the histories h_1, h_2, h_3 in Fig. 2 as running examples. To save space BEGIN_t represents the consecutive invoke and ok response of the BEGIN method of t, similarly for COMMIT_t.

$$h_1 = \text{BEGIN}_{t_1} Inv(\text{WRITE}(x,1))_{t_1} Resp(\text{WRITE}(x,ok))_{t_1} \text{COMMIT}_{t_1}$$
$$h_2 = \text{BEGIN}_{t_2} Inv(\text{READ}(x))_{t_2} Resp(\text{READ}(x,1,ok))_{t_2} \text{COMMIT}_{t_2}$$
$$h_3 = \text{BEGIN}_{t_1} Inv(\text{WRITE}(x,1))_{t_1} Resp(\text{WRITE}(x,ok))_{t_1} \text{BEGIN}_{t_2} \text{COMMIT}_{t_1}$$
$$\quad Inv(\text{READ}(x))_{t_2} Resp(\text{READ}(x,2,ok))_{t_2} Inv(\text{COMMIT}())_{t_2}$$

Fig. 2. Example histories

For a history h, the *transaction view* of a transaction $t \in T$, $h|t$, is the sequence of all events indexed with t. Opacity studies well formed histories only.

Definition 5. *A history h is* well formed *iff for each transaction $t \in T$, $h|t$ satisfies the following requirements:*

- *It starts with $Inv(\text{BEGIN}())_t$,*
- *every response event is directly preceded by a matching invocation,*
- *when a commit response or a response returning abort exists, it is the last element of the sequence $h|t$.*

For example the history $Inv(\text{BEGIN}())_t Resp(\text{WRITE}(x,ok))_t$ is not well formed since it contains a response before a matching invoke event but histories h_1, h_2 and h_3 are. We will only consider well formed histories from now on.

A transaction t is *commit pending* in a history, if a commit invocation of that transaction exists but there is no commit response afterwards; t is *committed* if a successful commit response of t exists; t is *aborted* if a response of t returning *abort* exists. If a BEGIN invocation exists in t and none of the previous terms apply, the transaction is *live*. In h_3, t_2 is commit pending. Adding an abort response would make it aborted. Removing the COMMIT invoke would make it live. In h_1, t_1 is committed.

A given history may thus be *incomplete*: it might contain pending invocations without matching responses. The history h_3 is incomplete for example. For the definition of opacity, we first need to make it complete. To this end, we add for all live transactions t – to the end of h – events $Resp(\text{COMMIT}(ok))_t$ or $Resp(\text{COMMIT}(abort))_t$ if t is commit pending, the corresponding returning $abort$ if t has another pending operation, or the sequence $Inv(\text{COMMIT}())_t$ $Resp(\text{COMMIT}(abort))_t$ in all other cases. The set of all such completions is denoted $complete(h)$. For example, h_3 can be completed by adding $Resp(\text{COMMIT}(ok))_{t_2}$, since it is commit pending.

Opacity is defined by reordering transactions in a history into a sequential history. This reordering has to keep certain orders among transactions. Transactions t, t' are *real time ordered* in a history $h = ev_0 \ldots ev_n$, denoted $t <_h t'$, if

$$\exists i, j \in \mathbb{N}, i < j < n : (ev_i \in \{Resp(\text{COMMIT}(ok))_t, Resp(\text{COMMIT}(abort))_t,$$
$$Resp(\text{WRITE}(abort))_t, Resp(\text{READ}(abort))_t\})$$
$$\wedge \, ev_j = Inv(\text{BEGIN}())_{t'}$$

In the concatenation $h_1 h_2$, $t_1 <_{h_1 h_2} t_2$ holds. A history h is *sequential* if all transactions t, t' which are executed in h (i.e., for which $h|t \neq \epsilon \wedge h|t' \neq \epsilon$) are real time ordered in one or the other way: $t <_h t'$ or $t' <_h t$. For opacity, we need to ensure that read operations only read valid writes. To this end, we need to determine the last write to a variable.

Definition 6. *In a sequential history $h = ev_0 \ldots ev_n$ for an event ev_i, $0 \leq i \leq n$, of a transaction t, the event $ev_j = Inv(\text{WRITE}(loc, val))_{t'}$, $0 \leq j < i$, is the* last write *on loc before ev_i if either*

- $t = t'$[3], *or*
- t' *is committed and there is no $j', val', t'', j < j' < i$ such that $ev_{j'} = Inv(\text{WRITE}(loc, val'))_{t''}$ and t'' is committed or $t'' = t$.*

The second condition implicitly includes the existence of a write response, since it is implied by the existence of a write invocation in a committed transaction.

In a sequential history h, a read response $ev_i = Resp(\text{READ}(loc, val, ok))_t$ is *legal* if the last write on val before ev_i is $ev_j = Inv(\text{WRITE}(loc, val))_{t'}$. The existence of a read response implies the existence of a matching invocation in a well formed sequential history. We say a history is *legal* if all its read responses are legal. A history h is furthermore *equivalent* to another history h' ($h \equiv h'$) if all of their transaction views are identical. With this at hand, we can finally define the correctness property opacity [12].

Definition 7. *A history h is* opaque *if there exists a sequential legal history h_s and a history $h' \in complete(h)$ such that $h_s \equiv h'$ and $<_{h'} \subseteq <_{hs}$.*

For any pair h, h_s as occurring in this definition we say h_s *witnesses* the opacity of h. History h_3 is opaque because the completion $h_4 = h_3 Resp(\text{COMMIT}(ok))_{t_2}$ is equivalent to the sequential legal history $h_1 h_2$. For history $h_2 h_1$ one may think

---

[3] Note that a transaction writes at most once to a location.

that $h_1 h_2$ (the only possible sequential equivalent history) can be used as proof of opacity. But their real time orders are different: $<_{h_2 h_1} \not\subseteq <_{h_1 h_2}$. Thus it is not opaque.

Key to a model checking technique not needing to check all possible inputs to writes is now the following theorem.

Theorem 1. *The set of all opaque histories is data independent w.r.t. the input function I_{STM}.*

Due to lack of space the proof is omitted here.

4   Modelling STMs

Besides knowing that our correctness property opacity is data independent, we also need to be able to check when the STM algorithm is data independent. To this end, we next introduce a simple programming language allowing for the description of STMs. We first describe the syntax of the language and then its semantics.

We allow for variables of two types: integers (i.e., *Val* is the set of integers) and pointers. They are further grouped into local and global variables. For each combination of visibility and type a set of (pairwise disjoint) variables is defined:

- GV are global integer variables (i.e., shared among threads),
- LV are local integer variables (i.e., every thread has its own version) and
- GPV and LPV are global and local pointer variables, respectively.

Note that the set GV both contains the locations the threads write to and read from via the STM operations as well as the meta data of the STM. We let $PV = GPV \cup LPV$ be the set of pointer variables and $Var = PV \cup LV \cup GV$ the set of all variables. In TML the variable glb is in GV, addr in LPV and tmp in LV.

To allow for methods to receive arguments and return values we require that input variables and one output variable are part of the local variables. The variables representing the inputs to methods will be called in_j (for some index j) and are elements of $LV \cup LPV$, and the output variable is $out \in LV$. For example addr would correspond to in_0.

Variables may occur inside expressions. We distinguish arithmetic and boolean expressions. The set of *arithmetic expressions AExp* contains all (in the arithmetic sense) well formed combinations of variables, integers and $+, -, \cdot, *$, *mod* and all expressions consisting of a single $\&v$ with $v \in GV$. Here $\&$ is the *reference* operator while $*$ is the *dereference* operator. The set of *boolean expressions BExp* is the set of well formed boolean terms containing the operators $\wedge, \vee, \neg, \leq, <, >, \geq, =, \neq$ and $*$. Additionally the following set of terms are in $BExp$:

$$\{\&v' == \&v \mid v, v' \in GV\} \text{ and}$$
$$\{CAS(x, a, a'), \neg CAS(x, a, a') \mid (x \in PV \vee x \in \{\&v' \mid v' \in GV\}), a, a' \in AExp\}$$

If a boolean condition b occurs in one of the CAS instructions, we write $b \in CAS$.

Next we define (sequential) *programs*. In this, we assume the set of all method names is MID. We use these names to call methods.

Definition 8. *A* single-threaded *program Prog is defined by the following grammar (in BNF) where ϵ is the empty program and $v \in Var, v_0, \ldots, v_n \in GV \cup GPV, a \in AExp, b \in BExp, m \in MID$:*

$$
\begin{array}{llll}
Prog:: = \epsilon & \mid v := a & \mid {}^*p := a & \mid \\
\quad m(v_0, \ldots, v_n) & \mid \textbf{return } (v \mid ok \mid abort) & \mid Prog; Prog & \mid \\
\quad \textbf{while}(b)\{Prog\} & \mid \textbf{if}(b)\{Prog\} \textbf{ else } \{Prog\} &&
\end{array}
$$

We use brackets {and} to define blocks. For simplicity we assume that there are no nested method calls.

A software transactional memory algorithm defines a program for every method it provides. More generally, a *library* is a function $lib : MID \to Prog$, assigning a program to every method identifier. Additionally there is a function $arg : MID \to (LPV \cup LV)^*$ assigning to each method an ordered sequence of pairwise different local variables, the formal parameters of the method. Since lib is always clear from the context, we do not use it in notation to avoid obfuscation.

For the semantics, we first of all need to define the *states* of programs. Program states consist of two elements: A mapping of threads to programs and a memory function mapping variables to values. The set $T = \{0, \ldots, n\}$ with n fixed contains all thread identifiers. Since we have different sorts of variables (local and global, integers and pointers), we need memory functions with different domains and ranges. In the following definition, we thus overload the name mem.

Definition 9. *A* memory function *is a function mem with one of the following signatures:*

- $mem : GV \to \mathbb{Z}$ or $mem : GPV \to GV \cup \{null\}$ *(for global variables) or*
- $mem : LV \times T \to \mathbb{Z}$ or $mem : LPV \times T \to GV \cup \{null\}$ *(for local variables).*

Note that pointers only have a non-pointer global variable as their value, other cases are excluded for simplicity. The *memory view* of thread t on variable $v \in Var$ is denoted $mem_t(v)$ which either is $mem(v)$, if $v \in GV \cup GPV$, or $mem(t, v)$, if $v \in LV \cup LPV$. To evaluate expressions we overload the memory function further by adding arithmetic and boolean expressions to its domain. For this we first define the memory view of thread t on a dereference call on $v \in PV$: $mem_t({}^*v)$, which either equals $= mem(mem_t(v))$ if $mem_t(v) \in GV$ and returns an error symbol otherwise.

The term $mem_t(a)$ with $a \in AExp, t \in T$ in case of a being a standard arithmetic term returns the evaluation of a to an integer (where each variable and dereference is replaced by its memory view) or when $a = \&v, v \in GV$, returns v. Then $mem_t(b)$ denotes the evaluation to 1 or 0 of $b \in BExp$, where each arithmetic term a occurring in b is replaced by the value of $mem_t(a)$ and the remaining part of the expression is evaluated as standard for boolean expressions.

A $CAS(x, a, a')$ instruction evaluates to true iff $mem_t(x) == mem_t(v)$. Given this memory function we can define a program state.

Definition 10. *A program state is a pair $ps = (tf, mem)$, where $tf : T \to Prog$ is the thread function and mem is a memory function.*

We use dot notation like $ps.tf(t)$ to refer to the elements of such pairs. A program execution is defined by an initial program state, called *start state*, the set of actions AC, the set of all program states PS and the transition relation $\delta \subseteq PS \times AC \times PS$. We give the semantics of actions in the style of IO-automata (see e.g. [13]) defining a *precondition* and an *effect* for all actions. An action is called *enabled* in a program state when its precondition is met. A definition of all actions and their transitions can be found in Fig. 3. This figure does not include the negated CAS actions which are defined analogously to the non negated CASs.

The semantics uses the symbol **ret** which marks the end of a method, making it possible to define a jump to the end of a method when a response statement is executed. For simplicity we assume each instruction to contain well formed arguments, which includes that any variable having *null* as its value is never read or used in expressions in any way and that pointers are not assigned to integer variables and vice versa. If there is a transition with action ac enabled in a state ps_0 and its effect results in state ps_1, we write $ps_0 \xrightarrow{ac} ps_1$. The start state has all variables initialized.

Definition 11. *A start state is a program state ps with the following properties:*

- $\forall v \in LV, \forall t \in T : ps.mem_t(v) = 0$,
- $\forall v \in LPV, \forall t \in T : ps.mem_t(v) = null$,
- $\forall v \in GV : ps.mem(v) = 0$ *and* $\forall v \in GPV : ps.mem(v) = null$.

A program state is called *terminated* if $tf(t) = \epsilon$ for all $t \in T$. A program *run* is a sequence of program states $ps_0 \ldots ps_n$ starting in a start state ps_0, ending in a terminated program state ps_n, and where each following state is derived by executing an enabled transition on the previous state, i.e., $\forall 0 \leq i < n, \exists ac \in AC : ps_i \xrightarrow{ac} ps_{i+1}$. The program *trace* for a run $ps_0 \ldots ps_n$ is the sequence $tr = ac_0 \ldots ac_{n-1}$ such that $ps_i \xrightarrow{ac_i} ps_{i+1}$, for all $i, 0 \leq i < n - 2$.

In case of STMs, the library and the programs using it take the following shape:

- The method identifiers are "BEGIN, WRITE, READ, COMMIT",
- Methods BEGIN and COMMIT have no formal parameters, i.e., $arg(\text{BEGIN}) = arg(\text{COMMIT}) = \epsilon$, method WRITE takes two and READ one argument: $arg(\text{WRITE}) = var_0 var_1$, $var_0 \in LPV$, $var_1 \in LV$, $arg(\text{READ}) = var_0'$, $var_0' \in LPV$,
- the start state for each thread is a well formed transaction,
- for a start state ps the program of a thread t is either empty or a well-formed transaction.

State variables: $ps : PS, tf = ps.tf, mem = ps.mem$
Auxiliary variables: $Prog, Prog'$: arbitrary programs
Transition relation:

$m(v_0, \ldots, v_n)_t$
Pre: $tf(t) = m(iv_0, \ldots, iv_n); Prog$
  $\forall i, 0 \le i \le n :$
  $mem_t(arg(m, i)) = v_i$
Eff: $tf(t) = lib(m)$ ret; $Prog$
  $\forall i, 0 \le i \le n :$
  $mem_t(arg(m, i)) = mem_t(iv_i)$

$v := n_t$
Pre: $tf(t) = {}^*v' := a; Prog$
  $n = mem_t(a)$
  $v = mem_t(v')$
Eff: $tf(t) = Prog$
  $mem_t(mem_t(v)) = mem_t(a)$

$v := n_t$
Pre: $tf(t) = v := a; Prog$
  $n = mem_t(a)$
Eff: $tf(t) = Prog$
  $mem_t(v) = mem_t(a)$

while$_t$, $true$
Pre: $tf(t) =$ **while**(b)
  $\{Prog\}; Prog'$
  $mem_t(b) = 1$
  $b \ne CAS(v, a, a')$
Eff: $tf(t) = Prog;$
  while$(b) \{Prog\}; Prog'$

while$_t$, $false$
Pre: $tf(t) =$ **while**$(b) \{Prog\}; Prog'$
  $mem_t(b) = 0$
Eff: $tf(t) = Prog'$

if$_t$, $true$
Pre: $tf(t) =$ **if**$(b)\{Prog\}$
  else$\{Prog'\}; Prog''$
  $mem_t(b) = 1$
  $b \ne CAS(v, a, a')$
Eff: $tf(t) = Prog; Prog''$

if$_t$, $false$
Pre: $tf(t) =$ **if**$(b)\{Prog\}$
  else$\{Prog'\}; Prog''$
  $mem_t(b) = 0$
Eff: $tf(t) = Prog'; Prog''$

return n_t
Pre: $tf(t) =$ **return** $(v);$
  $Prog$ ret; $Prog'$
  $n = mem_t(v)$
Eff: $tf(t) = Prog'$
  $mem_t(out) = v$

return $(ok)_t$
Pre: $tf(t) =$ **return** $(ok); Prog$ ret;
  $Prog'$
Eff: $tf(t) = Prog'$

return $(abort)_t$
Pre: $tf(t) =$ **return** $(abort);$
  $Prog$ ret; $Prog'$
Eff: $tf(t) = \epsilon$

$CAS(v, n, n')_t$
Pre: $tf(t) =$ **if**$(CAS(v', a, a'))\{Prog\}$
  else $\{Prog'\}; Prog''$
  $mem_t(mem_t(v')) = mem_t(a)_t$
  $v = mem_t(v')$
  $n = mem_t(a), n' = mem_t(a')$
Eff: $tf(t) = Prog; Prog''$
  $mem_t(mem(v)) = mem_t(a'')$

$CAS(v, n, n')_t$
Pre: $tf(t) =$ **while**$(CAS(v, a, a'))$
  $\{Prog\}; Prog'$
  $mem_t(mem_t(v')) = mem_t(a')$
  $v = mem_t(v')$
  $n = mem_t(a), n' = mem_t(a')$
Eff: $tf(t) =$ **while**$(CAS(v, a, a'))$
  $\{Prog\}; Prog'$
  $mem_t(mem_t(v)) = mem_t(a')$

Fig. 3. The semantics of instructions

Table 2. Corresponding history event for each action

$$
ev_i := \begin{cases}
Inv(\text{BEGIN}())_t & \text{if } ac_i = Begin()_t \\
Inv(\text{READ}(loc))_t & \text{if } ac_i = Read(loc)_t \\
Inv(\text{WRITE}(loc, val))_t & \text{if } ac_i = Write(loc, val)_t \\
Inv(\text{COMMIT}())_t & \text{if } ac_i = Commit(v)_t \\
Resp(\text{READ}(loc, val, ok))_t & \text{if } ac_i = \textbf{return } (val)_t \in Read(loc) \\
Resp(\text{WRITE}(loc, ok))_t & \text{if } ac_i = \textbf{return } (ok)_t \in Write(loc, val) \\
Resp(\text{COMMIT}(ok))_t & \text{if } ac_i = \textbf{return } (ok)_t \in Commit() \\
Resp(\text{BEGIN}(ok))_t & \text{if } ac_i = \textbf{return } (ok)_t \in Begin() \\
Resp(\text{WRITE}(abort))_t & \text{if } ac_i = \textbf{return } (abort)_t \in Write() \\
Resp(\text{READ}(abort))_t & \text{if } ac_i = \textbf{return } (abort)_t \in Read() \\
Resp(\text{COMMIT}(abort))_t & \text{if } ac_i = \textbf{return } (abort)_t \in Commit() \\
\epsilon & else
\end{cases}
$$

To be able to uniquely reason about the inputs to methods and executions being independent of this input data, we give the arguments a unique name: the first argument will always be called in_0, the second in_1 and so on. Instead of using the formal parameters as stated in the algorithm (like **addr** for write), we thus use $in_0, in_1, \ldots$.

A well formed transaction is a program $p_0; \ldots; p_n$ such that $p_0 = \text{BEGIN}()$, $p_n = \text{COMMIT}()$, and $\forall 0 < i < n : p_i \in \{\text{READ}(loc), \text{WRITE}(loc, val)) \mid loc \in GV, val \in \mathbb{Z} \setminus \{0\}, loc$ does not occur in any method$\}$[4]. We exclude 0 so that it is recognizable if a variable has been written to by a transactional write or not.

Finally, to extract histories from the traces of concurrent programs calling transactional methods we need to relate calls to invocation events and returns to response events. We say that $\textbf{return } (v)_t \in m(iv_0, \ldots, iv_n)$ if it is a return from method m called by t with arguments $iv_0, \ldots, iv_n$. This can be determined for any program trace by searching for the last method call before the return.

Definition 12. *The history of a given program trace $tr = ac_0 \ldots ac_n$ is a sequence $h = ev_0 \ldots ev_n$ where for all i s.t. $0 \le i \le n$ ev_i is given in Table 2.*

The ϵ events are elided at the end.

5   Data Independence of STMs

With a definition of the semantics of STM libraries in place, we can study when a particular STM algorithm is data independent. Basically, we would like to ensure that (1) the input values to writes do not influence the control flow of

---

[4] Meta data cannot be accessed via TM operations.

the program (in particular, do not influence whether the transaction aborts or commits), and (2) a change in the input values of writes results in a corresponding change in the output of reads reading from that write.

Next, we formalize some *static* conditions on STMs (i.e., conditions on the library) which are sufficient to ensure these two requirements and thereby guarantee data independence. To formalize the conditions we need to introduce a few more definitions. We denote that a term t is occurring somewhere in an arithmetic expression $a \in AExp$ by $t \in a$, analogously for $b \in BExp$. When a boolean expression b or arithmetic expression a occurs in an instruction p we denote it as $a \in p$ or $b \in p$ respectively.

First, we define a dependency relationship between variables. A variable v depends on another variable v' in a specific statement whenever v' is directly or indirectly assigned to v. Note that assignments to pointer variables set a dependency in both directions, since modifications to either one can influence the other one.

Definition 13. *We say $v \in Var$ potentially depends on $v' \in Var$ (in a library lib) iff there exists $m \in MID$, $lib(m) = Prog$ and Prog contains a statement p such that*

1. *p is $v := a$, and either $v' \in a$ or $*v' \in a$,*
2. *p is $*v := a$ and either $v' \in a$ or $*v' \in a$,*
3. *p is $v := \&v'$ or $p = v' := \&v$,*
4. *$b \in p$ and $b = CAS(v, a, a') \lor b = \neg CAS(v, a, a')$ and $v' \in a'$,*
5. *or $p = \mathbf{resp}(v')$ and $v = out$.*

For the last case, note that in our semantics return statements write their return values to the variable *out*. In TML (Fig. 1) `loc` potentially depends on `glb`.

Using these definitions we can next define the *closure* of a variable, which is the set of variables which the variable directly or indirectly depends on. We are interested in closures of input variables only.

Definition 14. *The* closure *of an input variable $in \in Var$ in a library lib is defined as the smallest set $cl(in)$ such that*

- *$in \in cl(in)$ and*
- *when v potentially depends on v' and $v' \in cl(in)$, then $v \in cl(in)$.*

We will give the closure for TML. Note that $out = $ `tmp`, $in_0 = $ `addr` and $in_1 = $ `val`. Then $cl(\mathtt{val})$ is $\{\mathtt{val}, \mathtt{addr}, \mathtt{tmp}\}$.

Using this we can formalize our conditions on an STM. Conditions 1 and 2 below ensure that no boolean condition is influenced by an input value, while conditions 3, 4 and 5 ensure that only unmodified input values can be returned by a read. Recall that the input function I_{STM} returns 1 for writes and the first data input to writes is stored in variable in_1.

Theorem 2. *An STM library is data independent w.r.t. input function I_{STM} if the following holds for all methods $m \in MID$, statements $p \in lib(m)$ and arithmetic and boolean expressions $a \in AExp, b \in BExp$ and all variables $v \in Var$:*

1. *If $b \in p, b \notin CAS$, then $v \in b$ implies $v \notin cl(in_1)$,*
2. *if $b \in p$, $b = CAS(x, a, a') \vee b = \neg CAS(x, a, a')$, then $v \in a \vee v \in a' \vee x = v$ implies $v \notin cl(in_1)$,*
3. *if $a \in p$, then $v \in a \wedge v \in cl(in_1)$ implies $a = v \vee a = \&v \vee a = {}^*v$,*
4. *if $v \in cl(in_1)$, p is not any assignment of a variable $v' \notin cl(in_1)$ to v,*
5. *$out \in cl(in_1)$.*

Due to lack of space the proof is omitted here. These requirements were chosen to ensure data independence on the level of program execution, e.g. that if a program is correct (opaque) for a set of inputs, it is also correct for another set of inputs. We will illustrate the requirements of Theorem 2 on TML.

1. If Line R2 (`if (glb = loc)`), would be changed to `glb = tmp`, then the success or abortion of the read function could depend on `val`.
2. Analogous for CAS conditions, e.g. if W2 would instead compare `&glb` to `val` the control flow would depend on the input to the write value.
3. For requirement 3 assume R1 `tmp:=*addr` (fulfilling the requirement) would be changed to `tmp:=(*addr * 2)-1`. Thus a read may not return a value corresponding to an input value, e.g. if `*addr` is 2.
4. Analogous to the above: if e.g. R1 would be `tmp := glb` an output event may not have a corresponding input event.
5. If `tmp` is not in the closure then the returned value of the read would not be influenced by the inputs at all which could result in events not corresponding to each other.

From the previous theorem we will derive a corollary stating that for data independent STMs whenever for a given start state with differentiated inputs (all writes contain pairwise different second arguments) each possible trace results in an opaque history, then for any renaming of that start state the histories of all possible traces are also opaque.

We first have to formally define what a renaming of a start state for a given function f is. For a transaction program *Prog*, its renaming by f (denoted as $f(Prog)$) is the replacement of every occurrence of $write(v, x)$ where $v \in GV$ and $x \in \mathbb{Z} \setminus \{0\}$ by $write(v, f(x))$. For a thread function $ps.tf$, a renaming by f is denoted as $f(ps).tf$ and is defined as $f(ps).tf(t) = f(ps.tf(t))$. The renaming of a start state ps_0 is then denoted as $f(ps_0) = (f(ps_0).tf, ps_0.mem)$.

Corollary 1. *Let lib be an STM library that fulfils the requirements of Theorem 2. Let ps_0 be a start state with differentiated inputs. If the history of every trace starting in ps_0 is opaque, then for every renaming f the history of every trace starting in $f(ps_0)$ is also opaque.*

Thus when model checking a transactional memory it is sufficient for each workload (the set of all start states executing the same set of transactions, only differing the second argument of WRITE invokes) to only check one set of pairwise different values which results in a large reduction of the state space that needs to be generated for each workload.

6 Related Work

In Sect. 1 a overview over works concerning STM verification can be found. There is a large body of work concerning utilizing data independence for validating software (e.g. [2,4,5,18]). There is to the best of our knowledge no approach combining STMs and data independence. Here we will only focus on the works closest to our approach.

Guerraoui et al. present a state space reduction approach for a variation of opacity [11]. It is data independent in a literal way, as it does not contain any values at all. We have proven this variation to be different from opacity even under limiting assumptions [14]. They have shown that – under certain conditions for STMs – proving the STM conflict opaque can be reduced to proofs for 2 threads and 2 variables. However, no explicit approach for checking these conditions is given. The conditions and proofs are not easily, if at all, applicable to the value based definition of opacity.

In the related literature Shacham et al. come closest to our approach verifying another atomicity correctness criterion, namely linearisability for composed operations on maps [16]. They divide these operations into three types which all have different degrees of data independence. The first class where one key and one value can be input and be used to invoke PUT, GET and REMOVE comes closest to our approach. They state syntactical requirements for such an operation to be data independent. As in this work they require that their inputs cannot be changed or reassigned, and – except for one exception – cannot be (transitively) used in boolean conditions. The exception allows - contrary to our requirement - to check whether an input value has been written to. Additionally they have map specific requirements which have no equivalent in our case. Then they apply a state space reduction theorem for more efficient model checking. While they focus on the model checking itself, we focus more on the formal groundwork a model checking approach can be based on.

An approach similar to the previous one is used in [5] for the linearisability verification of priority queues, although they completely focus on checking the property and already assume the checked queues to be data independent.

7 Conclusion

In our paper, we have adapted the notion of data independence to STMs and their correctness condition. Our main result is that when checking opacity of data independent STMs, it is sufficient to look at one set of input values for each workload. To achieve this, we have proven that opacity is a data independent correctness criterion, have given a specification language for STMs and then have formalized statically checkable conditions which imply data independence of an STM algorithm. This work is one step towards reducing the state space to be inspected during model checking STMs.

Future work regarding this specific approach will involve implementing a model checking approach to evaluate how well these results improve performance. The checker should include an automatic test if an STM is data independent and then should use the results of this paper to conduct efficient model checking of opacity. One example of using the results could be to abstract from the actual values of input variables and only save actual values for meta data variables.

References

1. Abdulla, P.A., Dwarkadas, S., Rezine, A., Shriraman, A., Zhu, Y.: Verifying safety and liveness for the FlexTM hybrid transactional memory. In: DATE 2013, pp. 785–790 (2013)
2. Abdulla, P.A., Haziza, F., Holík, L., Jonsson, B., Rezine, A.: An integrated specification and verification technique for highly concurrent data structures. In: Piterman, N., Smolka, S.A. (eds.) TACAS 2013. LNCS, vol. 7795, pp. 324–338. Springer, Heidelberg (2013). https://doi.org/10.1007/978-3-642-36742-7_23
3. Baek, W., Bronson, N.G., Kozyrakis, C., Olukotun, K.: Implementing and evaluating a model checker for transactional memory systems. In: ICECCS 2010, pp. 117–126 (2010)
4. Bouajjani, A., Enea, C., Guerraoui, R., Hamza, J.: On verifying causal consistency. SIGPLAN Not. **52**(1), 626–638 (2017)
5. Bouajjani, A., Enea, C., Wang, C.: Checking linearizability of concurrent priority queues. In: CONCUR 2017. Schloss Dagstuhl-Leibniz-Zentrum fuer Informatik (2017)
6. Dalessandro, L., Dice, D., Scott, M., Shavit, N., Spear, M.: Transactional mutex locks. In: D'Ambra, P., Guarracino, M., Talia, D. (eds.) Euro-Par 2010. LNCS, vol. 6272, pp. 2–13. Springer, Heidelberg (2010). https://doi.org/10.1007/978-3-642-15291-7_2
7. Derrick, J., Dongol, B., Schellhorn, G., Travkin, O., Wehrheim, H.: Verifying opacity of a transactional mutex lock. In: Bjørner, N., de Boer, F. (eds.) FM 2015. LNCS, vol. 9109, pp. 161–177. Springer, Cham (2015). https://doi.org/10.1007/978-3-319-19249-9_11
8. Doherty, S., Dongol, B., Derrick, J., Schellhorn, G., Wehrheim, H.: Proving opacity of a pessimistic STM. In: OPODIS 2016. LIPIcs, vol. 70, pp. 35:1–35:17. Schloss Dagstuhl-Leibniz-Zentrum fuer Informatik (2017)
9. Doherty, S., Groves, L., Luchangco, V., Moir, M.: Towards formally specifying and verifying transactional memory. Formal Aspects Comput. **25**(5), 769–799 (2013)
10. Guerraoui, R., Henzinger, T.A., Singh, V.: Completeness and nondeterminism in model checking transactional memories. In: van Breugel, F., Chechik, M. (eds.) CONCUR 2008. LNCS, vol. 5201, pp. 21–35. Springer, Heidelberg (2008). https://doi.org/10.1007/978-3-540-85361-9_6
11. Guerraoui, R., Henzinger, T.A., Singh, V.: Model checking transactional memories. Distrib. Comput. **22**(3), 129–145 (2010)

12. Guerraoui, R., Kapalka, M.: On the correctness of transactional memory. In: Proceedings of the 13th ACM SIGPLAN Symposium on Principles and Practice of Parallel Programming, PPoPP 2008, pp. 175–184 (2008)
13. Kaynar, D.K., Lynch, N.A., Segala, R., Vaandrager, F.W.: The Theory of Timed I/O Automata. Synthesis Lectures on Distributed Computing Theory, 2nd edn. Morgan & Claypool Publishers, San Rafael (2010)
14. König, J., Wehrheim, H.: Value-based or conflict-based? Opacity definitions for STMs. In: Hung, D., Kapur, D. (eds.) ICTAC 2017. LNCS, vol. 10580, pp. 118–135. Springer, Cham (2017). https://doi.org/10.1007/978-3-319-67729-3_8
15. Lesani, M., Palsberg, J.: Decomposing opacity. In: Kuhn, F. (ed.) DISC 2014. LNCS, vol. 8784, pp. 391–405. Springer, Heidelberg (2014). https://doi.org/10.1007/978-3-662-45174-8_27
16. Shacham, O., et al.: Verifying atomicity via data independence. In: Proceedings of the 2014 International Symposium on Software Testing and Analysis, pp. 26–36. ACM (2014)
17. Shavit, N., Touitou, D.: Software transactional memory. Distrib. Comput. **10**(2), 99–116 (1997)
18. Wang, C., Lv, Y., Wu, P.: Decomposable relaxation for concurrent data structures. In: Steffen, B., Baier, C., van den Brand, M., Eder, J., Hinchey, M., Margaria, T. (eds.) SOFSEM 2017. LNCS, vol. 10139, pp. 188–202. Springer, Cham (2017). https://doi.org/10.1007/978-3-319-51963-0_15
19. Wolper, P.: Expressing interesting properties of programs in propositional temporal logic. In: POPL, pp. 184–193 (1986)

Transaction Protocol Verification with Labeled Synchronization Logic

Mohsen Lesani$^{(\boxtimes)}$

University of California, Riverside, USA
lesani@cs.ucr.edu

Abstract. Synchronization algorithms that provide the transaction interface are intricate. We present an algorithm description language that explicitly captures the type of the used synchronization objects and associates labels to method calls to explicitly capture their intra-thread order. We use the language to capture architecture independent representations of transactional memory (TM) algorithms. We present a novel logic that enables reasoning about synchronization algorithms that are described in the language. The logic quantifies over program labels and provides specific predicates and intuitive inference rules to reason about the inter-thread execution and linearization orders of labeled method calls. In particular, the logic assertions can directly capture orders that are fundamental to the correctness of transactions. We present a denotational semantics for the language and prove the soundness of the logic. We have formalized the logic in the PVS proof assistant and mechanically constructed the challenging correctness proof of the TL2 TM algorithm.

1 Introduction

Synchronization algorithms such as mutual exclusion, concurrent data structures and transactional memory are subtle. Designing a synchronization algorithm involves choosing *synchronization objects* and programming the coordination logic using them. There is a trade-off in the choice between consistency and efficiency of a synchronization object. For example, although an atomic register maintains consistency in every concurrent execution, it is less efficient than a basic register that does not provide any guarantee in the presence of race. In addition, algorithm designers have to decide and properly program the *order* of method calls in each thread. These orders are crucial to the correctness of the algorithm in every possible interleaving. Intra-thread orders are usually specified using architecture-dependent fence instructions. As a result, a synchronization algorithm is complicated, low-level and prone to bugs. Engineering reliable software stacks built on top of these algorithms requires their precise description and rigorous verification. In this paper, we present a *description language* for synchronization algorithms, a novel *logic* to reason about synchronization algorithm descriptions and apply the logic to *mechanize* the verification of TM algorithms.

Dekker Example in the Description Language. The language explicitly captures the type of the base synchronization objects and the intra-thread order

© Springer Nature Switzerland AG 2019
J. M. Badger and K. Y. Rozier (Eds.): NFM 2019, LNCS 11460, pp. 280–297, 2019.
https://doi.org/10.1007/978-3-030-20652-9_19

(a)

$T:$ f_1, f_2 : **AtomicRegister**		
$\mathcal{D}:$		

def $init()$
$W_{01} \triangleright f_1.write(0),$
$W_{02} \triangleright f_2.write(0),$
	def $tryLock_1()$
	$W_1 \triangleright f_1.write(1),$
	$R_2 \triangleright x_2 = f_2.read(),$
	    if $(x_2 = 0),$
	$C_{1t} \triangleright$ **return** $true$
	    else
	$C_{1f} \triangleright$ **return** $false,$
	$\{W_1 \rightarrow R_2\},$
		def $tryLock_2()$
		$W_2 \triangleright f_2.write(1),$
		$R_1 \triangleright x_1 = f_1.read(),$
		    if $(x_1 = 0)$
		$C_{2t} \triangleright$ **return** $true$
		    else
		$C_{2f} \triangleright$ **return** $false,$
		$\{W_2 \rightarrow R_1\},$

$\mathcal{P}:$ $L_0 \triangleright$ $init(),$ $L_1 \triangleright$ $l_1 = tryLock_1()$ $\parallel$ $L_2 \triangleright$ $l_2 = tryLock_2()$		

X2L

$$\frac{\mathcal{T}(o) \in LT \qquad \pi, \Gamma \vdash obj(l) = obj(l') = o \qquad \pi, \Gamma \vdash l \prec l'}{\pi, \Gamma \vdash l \prec_o l'}$$

P2X

$$\frac{c_1 \rightarrow_\pi c_2 \qquad \pi, \Gamma \vdash exec(\varsigma'c_1) \qquad \pi, \Gamma \vdash exec(\varsigma'c_2)}{\pi, \Gamma \vdash \varsigma'c_1 \prec \varsigma'c_2}$$

(b)

Fig. 1. (a) Dekker description $\pi_D = (\mathcal{T}, \mathcal{D}, \mathcal{P})$. (b) Example inference rules.

of method calls on them. As an example, consider the description of the Dekker mutual exclusion algorithm [10] in Fig. 1(a). The description comprises three sections. The first section, typing $\mathcal{T}$, describes the base synchronization objects that the algorithm uses. Dekker uses two atomic registers as flags. Using basic registers as flags can lead to a race and violation of mutual exclusion. The second section, definitions $\mathcal{D}$, describes the definition of methods. The initialization method initializes the two flags to zero. In the two try-lock methods, each thread first writes to its own flag and then reads from the flag of the other thread. Each try-lock method allows entry to the critical region only if it finds the flag of the other thread unset. Every method call in the description is uniquely marked with a *label*. The order of writing the flag of the current thread and then reading the flag of the other thread is crucial to the correctness. Reordering these two method calls can violate mutual exclusion. The required orders for the body of each method definition are declared after the body. For example, the order $W_1 \rightarrow R_2$ requires the methods call W_1 to be executed before the method call R_2. The third section, program $\mathcal{P}$, represents the concurrent client program for the defined methods. First, the initialization method is called and then two concurrent threads are executed, each calling one of the try-lock methods.

Reasoning and Orders. The mutual exclusion property states that at most one of the two threads can enter the critical section. More precisely, if either of the two methods calls labeled L_1 and L_2 returns *true*, the other one returns *false*. An intuitive classical proof for the mutual exclusion property of the Dekker algorithm is as follows. We directly reason about execution and linearization orders across threads and use the properties of linearizable registers such as the totality of the linearization order. In particular, we use the real-time-preservation property [19] of linearizability that states that if a method call is executed before another on a linearizable object, then the former is linearized before the latter as well. Assume that L_1 returns true, we prove that L_2 does not return true. If L_1 has returned true, it should have been by C_{1t}. Therefore, the condition of the if statement is satisfied (that is $x_2 = 0$). Therefore, the read operation R_2 from the flag f_2 returns 0. There are two write method calls W_{02} and W_2 on f_2. The initialization method call W_{02} is executed before both R_2 and W_2; therefore, by the real-time preservation property, is linearized before them. Now, W_2 can either linearize before or after R_2. The first case is not possible because otherwise, W_2 would be the last write to f_2 before R_2. Therefore, R_2 would return the value that W_2 writes. However, W_2 writes 1, and R_2 has returned 0.

In the second case, the method call R_2 linearizes before W_2. Therefore, (1) R_2 is executed before or concurrent to W_2. (This holds because otherwise, R_2 would be executed after W_2. Thus, by the real-time-preservation property, R_2 would be linearized before W_2 as well that contradicts the assumption of this case.) According to the explicit program orders, (2) W_1 is executed before R_2 and (3) W_2 is executed before R_1. From the transitivity of the execution order on the three orders 2, 1, and 3 above, we have that W_1 is executed before R_1. Therefore, W_1 linearizes before R_1 as well. The initialization method call W_{01} is executed before R_1 and W_1 and is therefore linearized before the two. Therefore, W_1 is the last write to f_1 before R_1. Therefore, R_1 returns the value that W_1 writes that is 1. Therefore, $x_1 = 1$. Therefore, as the condition of the if statement is not satisfied, C_{2f} is executed. Therefore, L_2 returns false.

Labeled Synchronization Logic. Can we build a rigorous foundation for this intuitive style of reasoning? Is it possible to construct formal proofs in this style? We present a novel first-order logic called *labeled synchronization logic (LSL)* that enables reasoning about synchronization algorithms based on the *execution and linearization orders* of method calls on the base synchronization objects. It quantifies over program labels and provides specific predicates for execution order, execution overlap and linearization orders of labeled method calls across threads. These assertions capture critical orders between concurrent operations. In addition, LSL provides simple-to-use *inference rules* to reason about these orders and deduce algorithm correctness. For example, we applied LSL to stated and prove the mutual exclusion property of the Dekker algorithm. The following theorem states that for the Dekker description (π_D) with no prior assumptions ($\cdot$), it can be inferred that if L_1 returns true, then L_2 returns false. If the first thread can enter the critical section, then the second cannot. The symmetric property can be state and proved similarly.

Theorem 1. $\pi_D, \cdot \vdash (retv(L_1) = true) \Rightarrow (retv(L_2) = false)$.

The full proof is available in the appendix [27] §10 and the mechanised proof is available at [26]. We show two inference rules of LSL as examples in Fig. 1(b). LSL uses dynamic labels l to uniquely identify method call instances. For example, the label $L_2'W_2$ is a call string that refers to the instance of the method call labeled W_2 (in the definitions section $\mathcal{D}$) that is executed in the body of the caller method labeled L_2 (in the program section $\mathcal{P}$).

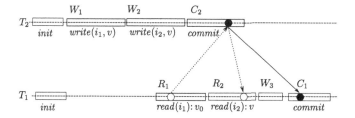

Fig. 2. Illustration of read-preservation

The rule X2L states the real-time-preservation property of linearizability [19]: the execution order $\prec$ of method calls on an object o of a linearizable type LT is preserved in the linearization order $\prec_o$ of the object o. If a method call is executed before another on a linearizable object, then the former is linearized before the latter as well. Using the rule X2L, a step that we saw in the informal proof of the Dekker algorithm can be formalized as follows. From the fact that method call $L_0'W_{02}$ is executed before $\prec$ the method call $L_2'W_2$ and that both are on the atomic register f_2,

$$\pi_D, \Gamma \vdash obj(L_0'W_{02}) = obj(L_2'W_2) = f_2 \ \wedge \ L_0'W_{02} \prec L_2'W_2$$

we can deduce that $L_0'W_{02}$ is before $L_2'W_2$ in the linearization order $\prec_{f_2}$ of the atomic register f_2

$$\pi_D, \Gamma \vdash L_0'W_{02} \prec_{f_2} L_2'W_2$$

In the sequent, Γ is any set of assumption assertions.

The rule P2X states the *program-order-preservation* property: the program order is preserved in the execution order. (The prefix label variable is denoted by ς.) For example, the Dekker description π_D declares the method call W_1 to be ordered before the method call R_2 i.e. $W_1 \to_\pi R_2$. Using the rule P2X, from the declared order and that both $L_1'W_1$ and $L_1'R_2$ are executed

$$\pi_D, \Gamma \vdash exec(L_1'W_1) \ \wedge \ exec(L_1'R_2)$$

we can deduce that $L_1'W_1$ is executed before $L_1'R_2$

$$\pi_D, \Gamma \vdash L_1'W_1 \prec L_1'R_2$$

Correctness of Transactional Memory. Execution and linearization orders of method calls on the base synchronization objects play a critical role in the reasoning about the correctness of transactional memory algorithms. In a previous work [30], we represented a decomposition called *markability* of the TM correctness condition opacity [14]. Markability decomposes opacity to separate intuitive invariants that can be separately verified. An execution history is markable if there is a specific ordering relation on the set of transactions and their read operations called marking such that three invariants are satisfied.

A marking of a transaction history is a relation on the union of the *transactions* and the *read operations* in the history. We can think of the marking as the union of a collection of orders: The *effect order*: The effect order is a total order of the transactions. It represents the order in which the transactions appear to take effect. The *access orders*: Let us refer to the committed transactions that have write operation(s) to location i as *writers of i*. Consider an unaborted read operation R on a location i. For each such R, the access order is an antisymmetric relation that orders R and every writer of i. The access order of R represents where R has read i between the writers of i.

For example, Fig. 2 presents the sketch of a transaction history with two transactions T_1 and T_2. The horizontal lines from left to right show the time for the two threads executing T_1 and T_2, and the boxes show execution of method calls on the transactional interface. These method calls may call multiple methods on the base synchronization objects. The dark circles show the effect points of the two transactions and the solid arrow shows the effect order. The transaction T_2 takes effect before T_1. The transaction T_2 is a writer of both i_1 and i_2. The white circles show the access points for the two reads R_1 and R_2. The read R_1 reads i_1 before T_2 writes to it. Similarly, the read R_2 reads i_2 after T_2 writes to it. The relation is called marking as these points can be usually marked as particular *method calls on the base synchronization objects* in the algorithm and the orders are defined as execution and linearization orders on these calls.

As an example, the second invariant of markability called *read-preservation* requires that the location read by a read operation is not overwritten between the two points that the read takes place and the transaction takes effect. Consider an unaborted read operation R from a location i by a transaction T. Intuitively, read-preservation requires that no writer of i comes between R and T in the marking relation. The read-preservation property is violated in Fig. 2. The read R_1 is an unaborted read from i_1 in T_1. The transaction T_2 is a writer of i_1. The read R_1 is before T_2 in the access order and T_2 is before T_1 in the effect order. The value that R_1 reads is overwritten by T_2 before T_1 is committed. The transaction T_2 writes a new value to both i_1 and i_2. The read R_1 reads the old value of i_1 and R_2 reads the new value of i_2 that can be inconsistent. Read-preservation is usually simply verified by the validations checks in the commit and read operations.

In this project, we have used LSL to construct a new mechanized proof of TL2 [9], in the PVS proof assistant. Specifically, we have *expressed markability* in the assertion language and then applied LSL inference rules to deduce the markability assertion. This result shows that LSL is scalable to complicated transactional memory algorithms. We have proved the *soundness* of LSL: If an assertion is deduced using valid assumptions, then the deduced assertion is valid as well. An assertion is valid if it evaluates to true in every execution.

The Structure of the Paper. In Sects. 2 and 3, we present the description language and LSL, and In Sect. 4, we state a marking for TL2 and prove the markability of TL2 in LSL. We present the related works in Sect. 5 before conclusion.

2   Description Language

We now present the language that we describe concurrent algorithms in. An algorithm description π is a triple $(\mathcal{T}, \mathcal{D}, \mathcal{P})$ where $\mathcal{T}$ is the *type declarations* for the used synchronization objects, $\mathcal{D}$ is *the method definitions*, and $\mathcal{P}$ is a concurrent *client program* that calls the defined methods. The set of descriptions Π is defined as follows:

$$
\begin{aligned}
\pi \in \Pi &::= (\mathcal{T}, \mathcal{D}, \mathcal{P}) \\
\mathcal{T} &::= (\phi : ot)^* \\
\mathcal{D} &::= d^* \\
d &::= \mathbf{def}\ n_t(x^*)\ s, r \\
s &::= s, s \quad | \quad \mathbf{if}\ (b)\ s\ \mathbf{else}\ s \quad | \quad q \quad | \quad c \triangleright \mathbf{foreach}\ (i \in set)\ s \\
q &::= c \triangleright\ x = o.n_\tau(u^*) \quad | \quad c \triangleright \mathbf{return}\ u \\
b &::= \neg b \quad | \quad b \wedge b \quad | \quad u = u \quad | \quad u = u + u \quad | \quad u < u \\
r &::= `\{'\ (c \rightarrow c)^*\ `\}' \\
\mathcal{P} &::= p_0, (p_1 \| p_2 \| ... \| p_n) \\
p &::= p; p \quad | \quad \mathbf{if}\ (b)\ p\ \mathbf{else}\ p \quad | \quad c \triangleright\ x = n_\tau(u^*)
\end{aligned}
$$

The description of the Dekker algorithm is presented in Fig. 1(a) as an example. We look at each section in turn.

A typing $\mathcal{T}$ is a mapping from object names ϕ to object types ot. We use x^* to denote a finite sequence of x's. An object type ot is either a scalar or an array type. A scalar type is either a basic type BT such as BasicRegister, BasicSet, or BasicMap, or a linearizable type LT such as AtomicRegister, AtomicCASRegister, Lock, TryLock, or strong counter SCounter. As an example, in the Dekker description of Fig. 1(a), both flags f_1 and f_2 are declared to be atomic registers. Using basic registers can lead to a race and violation of mutual exclusion. We will revisit synchronization object types when we present their specific inference rules. An array type of a scalar type st is of the form $st[]$. A thread-local type is an array type and the well-formedness conditions enforce that a thread-local object is only indexed by the identifier of the calling thread.

The definitions $\mathcal{D}$ is a sequence of method definitions d. We denote a method name by n, a value by v, a variable by x, a value or variable by u, a thread value by T, a thread variable by t, and a thread value or variable by τ. The method definition $\mathbf{def}\ n_t(x^*)\ s, r$ defines a method named n with thread parameter t and data parameters x^* with the body s and the declared order r. The Dekker description of Fig. 1(a) defines three methods: $init$, $tryLock_1$ and $tryLock_2$. A statement s is either a sequence, a conditional, a method call or a return statement. A condition b is a boolean expression on variables and values. In a method call $c \triangleright\ x = o.n_\tau(u^*)$, c is the label, x is the return variable, o is the receiving object, n is the method name, τ is the current thread argument, and u^* are the data arguments. The labels of statements are unique in π. Every variable is uniquely bound. An object o is either a single object ϕ or an element of an array $\phi[u]$. In a return statement $c \triangleright \mathbf{return}\ u$, c is the label and u is the returned value or variable. In the appendix [27] §7, we define the **foreach** iteration statement on sets and maps as a syntactic sugar. As we will see, the semantics of the language supports out-of-order or *relaxed* execution. Any two labels that are left unordered by the description may be reordered in the execution. Data and control dependencies in the method body s impose order between statements. However, the programmer can explicitly require additional orders. The declared program order r of a method definition is a binary relation on the set of labels in the body s. For example, the Dekker description of Fig. 1(a) declares the orders $W_1 \rightarrow R_2$ and $W_2 \rightarrow R_1$ that are crucial to the correctness. Programming fences is complicated and error-prone. This platform-independent description of the required orders can be used by compilers to optimize fence insertion [4] for different target architectures. The declared order facilitates architecture-independent verification. Further, if the order of two statements that is unnecessary for correctness is changed, the proof stays unchanged.

The client program section $\mathcal{P}$ is of the form $p_0, (p_1 \| p_2 \| ... \| p_n)$ where p_0 is the initialization program, and p_1, p_2, ..., and p_n are the parallel programs. For example, the program section of the Dekker description in Fig. 1(a) has two parallel programs that each call one of the two defined try-lock methods. A sequential program p is either a sequence, a conditional or a method call. In a method call $c \triangleright x = n_\tau(u^*)$, n is name of a method that is defined in the method definitions section $\mathcal{D}$. The object **this** is the default receiver object and is therefore elided in the client calls. We use θ to denote a synchronization object o or the **this** object.

Let $\rightarrow_n$ denote the irreflexive transitive closure of the data and control dependencies and the declared order of method n. Let the program order $\rightarrow_\pi$ be the irreflexive partial order on $Labels(\pi)$ defined as the union of the following: (1) the initialization order (that orders the labels of p_0 before the labels of parallel programs), (2) the sequential order of the sequential programs p_i, and (3) For each method definition n, the order $\rightarrow_n$.

LSL uses the following functions that are directly derived from the program description. The names of methods defined in a description are unique. Thus, we define the functions $par1_\pi$ and $par2_\pi$ that map method names to their first and second parameters. Similarly, $tpar_\pi$ maps method names to their thread parameter. As the labels in a description are unique, we define the function obj_π that maps the label of a method call to its receiver object. Similarly, the functions $index_\pi$, $name_\pi$, $thread_\pi$, $arg1_\pi$, $arg2_\pi$ and $retv_\pi$ map the label of a call to the array index of the receiver object, the name of the method, the thread identifier, first and second arguments and the return variable of the method call. For a return statement, we let $name_\pi$ and $arg1_\pi$ map to the name $return$ and the argument of the return statement respectively.

We call the conjunction of all the enclosing if (and else) conditions of a statement, its *enclosing condition*. Let the function $cond_\pi$ map statement labels to their enclosing conditions. Let $Labels_\pi(n)$ denote the set of labels in the body of the method n. Let $Returns_\pi(n)$ denote the set of labels of return statements in the body of n. Let $PreReturns_\pi(c)$ denote the set of labels of the return statements before the statement labeled c in π.

3   Labeled Synchronization Logic

Now, we present our first-order logic to reason about synchronization algorithm descriptions.

XASYM

$$\frac{\pi, \Gamma \vdash l \prec l'}{\pi, \Gamma \vdash \neg(l' \prec l) \wedge \neg(l' \sim l) \wedge \neg(l' = l)}$$

X2L

$$\frac{\mathcal{T}(o) \in LT \qquad \pi, \Gamma \vdash obj(l) = obj(l') = o \qquad \pi, \Gamma \vdash l \prec l'}{\pi, \Gamma \vdash l \prec_o l'}$$

XTRANS

$$\frac{\pi, \Gamma \vdash l \prec l' \qquad \pi, \Gamma \vdash l' \prec l''}{\pi, \Gamma \vdash l \prec l''}$$

LASYM

$$\frac{\pi, \Gamma \vdash l \prec_o l'}{\pi, \Gamma \vdash \neg(l' \prec_o l) \wedge \neg(l = l')}$$

X2TRANS

$$\frac{\pi, \Gamma \vdash l_1 \prec l_2 \qquad \pi, \Gamma \vdash l_2 \sim l_3 \qquad \pi, \Gamma \vdash l_3 \prec l_4}{\pi, \Gamma \vdash l_1 \prec l_4}$$

LTRANS

$$\frac{\pi, \Gamma \vdash l \prec_o l' \qquad \pi, \Gamma \vdash l' \prec_o l''}{\pi, \Gamma \vdash l \prec_o l''}$$

XTOTAL

$$\frac{\pi, \Gamma \vdash exec(l) \wedge exec(l')}{\pi, \Gamma \vdash (l \prec l') \vee (l' \prec l) \vee (l \sim l') \vee (l = l')}$$

(a)

LTOTAL

$$\frac{\mathcal{T}(o) \in LT \qquad \pi, \Gamma \vdash exec(l) \wedge exec(l')}{\pi, \Gamma \vdash obj(l) = obj(l') = o}{\pi, \Gamma \vdash (l \prec_o l') \vee (l' \prec_o l) \vee (l = l')}$$

(b)

X2X

$$\frac{\pi, \Gamma \vdash l \prec l'}{\pi, \Gamma \vdash exec(l) \wedge exec(l')}$$

L2X

$$\frac{\pi, \Gamma \vdash l \prec_o l'}{\pi, \Gamma \vdash exec(l) \wedge exec(l') \wedge \; obj(l) = obj(l') = o}$$

(c)

Fig. 3. The Basic Inference Rules. (a) properties of execution orders, (b) linearization orders, and (c) derived rules.

Assertions. We first define the set of dynamic labels that uniquely identify method call instances. As an example, in execution histories for the Dekker algorithm (Fig. 1(a)), we have the two labels L_1 and $L_1'W_1$. The label L_1 refers to a call site in the program section $\mathcal{P}$. On the other hand, the label $L_1'W_1$ is a call string that refers to the instance of the method call labeled W_1 (in the definitions section $\mathcal{D}$) that is executed in the body of the client method call labeled L_1. Thus, a dynamic label l is of the form $\varsigma'c$ where the pre-label ς is either a static label c or no label ϵ. The symbol ϵ is the left identity element of the prefixing operator.

A method can be called several times in the program. To have unique local variable names, every variable (including the parameters) of the method is prefixed by the caller label. The labeled variable $c'x$ denotes the instance of the local variable x in the body of the method call labeled with c. Similarly, the prefixing operator is lifted to expressions over variables. The assertions language of LSL is described by the following grammar.

$$
\begin{aligned}
e ::= \ & obj(\ell) \ \mid \ name(\ell) \ \mid \ thread(\ell) \ \mid & \text{Expression} \\
& arg1(\ell) \ \mid \ arg2(\ell) \ \mid \ retv(\ell) \ \mid \\
& initOf(\tau) \ \mid \ commitOf(\tau) \ \mid \\
& o \ \mid \ n \ \mid \ \varsigma`x \ \mid \ v \ \mid \ \varsigma`t \ \mid \ T \\
\mathcal{R} ::= \ & e = e \ \mid \ e < e \ \mid \ \ell = \ell' \ \mid \ c = c \ \mid & \text{Proposition} \\
& exec(\ell) \ \mid \ \ell \prec \ell' \ \mid \ \ell \sim \ell' \ \mid \ \ell \prec_o \ell' \ \mid \ \tau \lll \tau' \\
\mathcal{A} ::= \ & \mathcal{R} \ \mid \ \neg \mathcal{A} \ \mid \ \mathcal{A} \wedge \mathcal{A} \ \mid \ \forall \ell : \mathcal{A} \ \mid \ \forall t : \mathcal{A} & \text{Assertion}
\end{aligned}
$$

Here, c is a program label (such as C_{1t} in the Dekker description of Fig. 1(a)), l is a constant label (such as the dynamic labels L_1 and $L_1`C_{1t}$ for the Dekker description), ℓ is a label variable, T is a thread (or transaction) identifier value, t is a thread identifier variable, τ is a thread value or variable, x is a variable, v is a value, o is an object name, and n is a method name. Expressions use six function symbols. The functions $obj, name, thread, arg1, arg2$ and $retv$ map a label of the program to its object, method name, thread name, first and second argument, and return value. The function $initOf$ maps each transaction to the label of its $init$ method call. The function $commitOf$ maps each committed transaction to the label of its $commit$ method call. Propositions use seven predicates. The first two are equality ($=$) and integer comparison ($<$). The proposition $exec(\ell)$ states that the method call labeled ℓ is *executed*. The proposition $\ell \prec \ell'$ asserts that ℓ is *executed before* ℓ'. The proposition $\ell \sim \ell'$ asserts that ℓ is *executed concurrent* to ℓ'. For a linearizable object o, the proposition $\ell_1 \prec_o \ell_2$ states that ℓ_1 is *linearized before* ℓ_2 in the linearization order of o. (As we will describe in the semantics section, any concurrent execution on a linearizable object is equivalent to a correct sequential execution. The total order of method calls in that sequential execution is called the linearization order.) The proposition $\tau \lll \tau'$ asserts that all the labels of thread τ are executed before all the labels of thread τ'. This assertion is used to state that a transaction is executed before another.

An assertion is either a proposition, negation of an assertion, conjunction of two assertions, or existential quantification over labels or transactions. As usual, we can define, disjunction $\vee$, universal quantification $\forall$, less than or equal $\leq$, executes before or equal $\preceq$, linearized before or equal $\preceq_o$, thread executed before or equal $\preccurlyeq$ as syntactic sugar.

For an algorithm description π, a judgement is of the form $\pi, \Gamma \vdash \mathcal{A}$, where Γ is the context, that is, a list of assertions, and $\mathcal{A}$ is a closed assertion. The judgement is read as for every execution of the program π, if the assertions in Γ hold, then the assertion $\mathcal{A}$ holds. For example, $\pi, \Gamma \vdash l \prec l'$ says that in every execution of π where Γ holds, the statement labeled l is executed before the statement labeled l'.

Algorithms can be verified modularly. The client program section $\mathcal{P}$ of an algorithm description π can specify general clients. For example a lock algorithm description π (such as Dekker) can be verified separately. Then, the lock object (with its abstracted implementation) can be used to implement a TM. Verification of the description π' of the TM is restricted to the labels of π' and does not involve π.

$$\text{AREG} \quad \frac{\mathcal{T}(r) = AtomicRegister \qquad \pi, \Gamma \vdash isRead_r(l_R)}{\pi, \Gamma \vdash \exists \ell_W : isWriter_r(\ell_W, l_R) \wedge retv(l_R) = arg1(\ell_W)}$$

$$\text{BREG} \quad \frac{\mathcal{T}(r) = BasicRegister \qquad \pi, \Gamma \vdash isSingleWriter(r) \qquad \pi, \Gamma \vdash isRead_r(l_R) \qquad \pi, \Gamma \vdash isRaceFree_r(l_R)}{\pi, \Gamma \vdash \exists \ell_W : isEWriter_r(\ell_W, l_R) \wedge retv(l_R) = arg1(\ell_W)}$$

$$\text{LOCKUNLOCKPAIR} \quad \frac{\mathcal{T}(o) = Lock \qquad \pi, \Gamma \vdash isOwnerRespect(o) \qquad \pi, \Gamma \vdash isLock_o(l_{a_1}) \qquad \pi, \Gamma \vdash isUnlock_o(l_{r_2}) \qquad \pi, \Gamma \vdash l_{a_1} \prec_o l_{r_2}}{\pi, \Gamma \vdash \exists l_{r_1}, l_{a_2} : isUnlock_o(l_{r_1}) \wedge thread(l_{r_1}) = thread(l_{a_1}) \wedge isLock_o(l_{a_2}) \wedge thread(l_{a_2}) = thread(l_{r_2}) \wedge l_{r_1} \prec_o l_{a_2}}$$

$$\text{COUNTSEQ} \quad \frac{\mathcal{T}(o) = SCounter \qquad \pi, \Gamma \vdash exec(l_1) \wedge obj(l_1) = o \wedge name(l_1) = iaf \qquad \pi, \Gamma \vdash exec(l_2) \wedge obj(l_2) = o \qquad \pi, \Gamma \vdash retv(l_1) < retv(l_2)}{\pi, \Gamma \vdash l_1 \prec_o l_2}$$

$$isRead_r(\ell_R) \Leftrightarrow exec(\ell_R) \wedge obj(\ell_R) = r \wedge name(\ell_R) = read$$

$$isWrite_r(\ell_W) \Leftrightarrow exec(\ell_W) \wedge obj(\ell_W) = r \wedge name(\ell_W) = write$$

$$isWriter_r(\ell_W, \ell_R) \Leftrightarrow isWrite_r(\ell_W) \wedge \ell_W \prec_r \ell_R \wedge \forall \ell'_W : isWrite_r(\ell'_W) \Rightarrow (\ell'_W \preceq_r \ell_W \vee \ell_R \prec_r \ell'_W)$$

$$isEWriter_r(\ell_W, \ell_R) \Leftrightarrow isWrite_r(\ell_W) \wedge \ell_W \prec \ell_R \wedge \forall \ell'_W : isWrite_r(\ell'_W) \Rightarrow (\ell'_W \preceq \ell_W \vee \ell_R \prec \ell'_W)$$

$$isRaceFree_r(\ell) \Leftrightarrow \forall \ell_W : isWrite_r(\ell_W) \Rightarrow (\ell_W \prec \ell \vee \ell \prec \ell_W)$$

$$isSingleWriter(r) \Leftrightarrow \forall \ell_w : isWrite_r(\ell_w) \Rightarrow isRaceFree_r(\ell_w)$$

$$isLock_o(l) \Leftrightarrow exec(l) \wedge obj(l) = o \wedge name(l) = lock$$

$$isUnlock_o(l) \Leftrightarrow exec(l) \wedge obj(l) = o \wedge name(l) = unlock$$

$$isOwnerRespect(o) \Leftrightarrow \forall \ell : isUnlock_o(\ell) \Rightarrow \exists \ell' : isLock_o(\ell') \wedge thread(\ell') = thread(\ell) \wedge \ell' \prec \ell \wedge \forall \ell'' : (isUnLock_o(\ell'') \wedge thread(\ell'') = thread(\ell)) \Rightarrow \ell'' \prec \ell' \vee \ell \preceq \ell''$$

Fig. 4. Synchronization object inference rules. Four of the rules for atomic and basic registers, lock and strong counter.

Inference Rules. We now present the inference rules of LSL. The inference rules can be conceptually divided into four groups. First, the first-order logic rules (which are standard and omitted here). Second, the basic rules that axiomatize the properties of execution and linearization orders and their interdependence (Fig. 3). Third, the synchronization object rules that axiomatize the properties of common synchronization object types (Fig. 4). Fourth, the inference rules that axiomatize the relation of the algorithm description and the execution. We showcase a few rules. The full set of rules for the common synchronization objects is available in the appendix [27] §9.

Figure 3 represents the set of basic inference rules that intuitively capture the properties of execution and linearization orders and their relation. The rule XASYM states the asymmetry property of the execution order. If a method call is executed before another method call, then the latter is not executed before the former and they are not executed concurrently. The rule XTRANS states the transitivity property of the execution order. The rule X2TRANS states the transitivity of the sequence of precedence, concurrency and precedence execution relations. If l_1 is executed before l_2, l_2 is executed concurrent to l_3 and l_3 is executed before l_4, then l_1 is executed before l_4. The rule XTOTAL states the totality property of the precedence and concurrency execution relations. Every pair of executed method calls either execute in order or concurrently. The rule X2L states the *real-time-preservation* property of linearization orders: The execution order of two method calls on a linearizable object (specified by $\mathcal{T}(o) \in LT$) is preserved in the linearization order. The rule LASYM states the asymmetry property of linearization orders. If a method call is linearized before another one, then the latter is not linearized before the former. The rule LTRANS states the transitivity property of linearization orders. The rule LTOTAL states the totality property of linearization orders. Every two executed method calls on a linearizable object are ordered in its linearization order. The two derived rules X2X and L2X can be established by an inductive reasoning on the length of the proof of $l \prec_o l'$. The rule X2X states that if a method call is executed before another one, then clearly both are executed. The rule L2X states that if a method call is linearized before another one, then clearly both are executed.

Now let us look at a few synchronization object rules in Fig. 4. First, the rule AREG states that for every read method call l_R on an atomic register, there is a write method call ℓ_W on it that writes the same value that l_R reads and ℓ_W is the last write method call that is linearized before l_R. Second, the rule BREG states that if a basic register r is single-writer, for every race-free read method call l_R on r, there is a write method call ℓ_W on r that writes the same value that l_R reads and ℓ_W is the last write method call that is executed before l_R. A register r is single-writer if and only if every pair of write method calls on it are ordered in the execution order or in other words, every write method call on it is race-free. A method call r is race-free if an only if there is no *write* method call on r that executes concurrent to it. The rules AREG and BREG model Lamport's notion of atomic and safe registers [25]. Third, the rule LOCKUNLOCKPAIR states the *lock-unlock-pair* property: if ownership of a lock object o is respected and a *lock* method call on o by a thread τ_1 is linearized before an *unlock* method call on o by a thread τ_2, then an *unlock* method call on o by τ_1 is linearized before a *lock* method call on o by τ_2. The rule is derived from the fact that if the ownership of a lock is respected, its linearization order is a sequence of matching pairs of *lock* and *unlock* method calls. Intuitively, ownership for a lock o is respected, if and only if every thread unlocks o only if it has already locked o and has not unlocked o since then. Fourth, the rule COUNTSEQ states the *count-sequence* property: for a strong counter object co, if the return value of an *iaf* (inc-and-fetch) method call on co is less than the return value of another method call on co, then the former is linearized before the latter. The rule is derived from the fact that the return values of method calls in the linearization order of a strong counter is non-decreasing.

P2X
$$\frac{c_1 \to_\pi c_2 \qquad \pi, \Gamma \vdash exec(\varsigma'c_1) \qquad \pi, \Gamma \vdash exec(\varsigma'c_2)}{\pi, \Gamma \vdash \varsigma'c_1 \prec \varsigma'c_2}$$

CALLEE
$$\frac{c' \in Labels_\pi(n) \qquad tpar_\pi(n) = t \qquad par1_\pi(n) = x \qquad \pi, \Gamma \vdash exec(\varsigma'c')}{\pi, \Gamma \vdash \neg(\varsigma = \epsilon) \wedge exec(\varsigma) \wedge}$$
$$obj(\varsigma) = \mathbf{this} \wedge name(\varsigma) = n \wedge thread(\varsigma) = \varsigma't \wedge arg(\varsigma) = \varsigma'x$$

The rules presented above refer to the algorithm description. The rule P2X states the *program-order-preservation* property: the program order is preserved in the execution order. If the algorithm description requires a method call l_1 to be ordered before another method call l_2, the order is preserved in the execution of them from any call site ς. That is if $\varsigma' l_1$ and $\varsigma' l_2$ are executed, then $\varsigma' l_1$ is executed before $\varsigma' l_2$. The rule CALLEE states that if a method call c' in the body of the caller method call ς is executed, then the later is also executed, is a *this* method call and its parameters and arguments are equal.

We define the semantics $[\![\pi]\!]$ of a description π as a set of execution histories $\mathcal{X}$. A specification π models an assertion $\mathcal{A}$, written as $\pi \models \mathcal{A}$, iff every execution $\mathcal{X}$ of π models $\mathcal{A}$ written as $\mathcal{X} \models \mathcal{A}$. The soundness theorem states that if LSL deduces an assertion $\mathcal{A}$ for a description π using valid assumptions for π, then the deduced assertion $\mathcal{A}$ is valid for π as well. Formally, $\forall \pi, \mathcal{A}: (\pi, \Gamma \vdash \mathcal{A} \land \pi \models \Gamma) \Rightarrow (\pi \models \mathcal{A})$. The semantics and soundness of LSL is available in the appendix [27] §8 & 11.

4   TM Verification

We now state the correctness of TM algorithms as an LSL assertion and apply LSL to prove the correctness of the TL2 [9] algorithm. The challenge is to verify that any concurrent execution of any set of well-formed transactions on TL2 is opaque. Markability factors out a large part of the proof, allows specification of the critical points of the algorithm and reduces verification to separate proof obligations about the order of these points. LSL inference rules can be easily used to prove the obligations based on the validation checks in the algorithm.

Transactional Memory. A TM object encapsulates a set of locations and provides four methods $init_t()$, $read_t(i)$, $write_t(i, v)$, and $commit_t()$. A well-formed transaction first calls $init_t()$ and then calls a sequence of $read_t(i)$ and $write_t(i, v)$ methods, and finally calls $commit_t()$. The method $commit_t()$ tries to commit transaction t and returns $\mathbb{C}$ (if it is successful). A TM object should detect if an inconsistency is about to happen between two concurrent transactions and should at least abort one of them. All methods may return abort $\mathbb{A}$ and terminate the transaction.

Correctness Assertion. We presented a decomposition called *markability* [30] of the correctness condition *opacity* [14]. Markability restates opacity in terms of three intuitive invariants. We *state Markability as an assertion in LSL*. The markability assertion $isMarking(\sqsubseteq)$ is parametric with the marking relation $\sqsubseteq$. The marking assertion is available in the appendix [27] §13. We briefly explain markability. A TM algorithm is markable iff there exists a *marking* relation for it that is *write-observant, read-preserving,* and *real-time-preserving.*

A marking is a relation on the union of the transactions and the read method calls. We can think of the marking relation as the union of a collection of orders: (1) The *effect order*: The effect order is a total order of the transactions. The effect order represents the order in which the transactions appear to take effect, that is, the order that justifies the correctness of the execution. (2) The *access orders*: Let writers of location i be the committed transactions that have write method call(s) to i. Consider a read method call l_R that reads from a location i and doesn't abort. For each such l_R, the access order is an antisymmetric relation that orders l_R and every writer of i. The access order represents where l_R's access to location i has happened between the accesses by the writers of i.

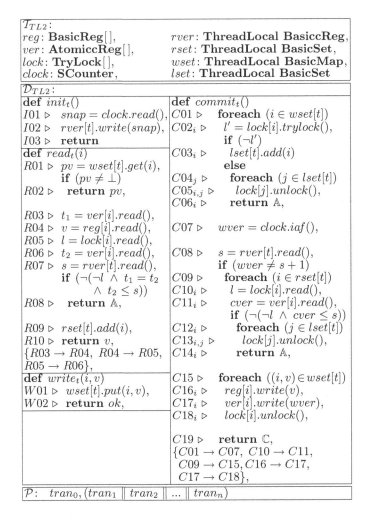

$\mathcal{T}_{TL2}$:

reg: **BasicReg**[ ],	$rver$: **ThreadLocal BasiccReg**,
ver: **AtomiccReg**[ ],	$rset$: **ThreadLocal BasicSet**,
$lock$: **TryLock**[ ],	$wset$: **ThreadLocal BasicMap**,
$clock$: **SCounter**,	$lset$: **ThreadLocal BasicSet**

$\mathcal{D}_{TL2}$:

def $init_t()$	**def** $commit_t()$
$I01 \triangleright \quad snap = clock.read(),$	$C01 \triangleright \quad$ **foreach** $(i \in wset[t])$
$I02 \triangleright \quad rver[t].write(snap),$	$C02_i \triangleright \quad l' = lock[i].trylock(),$
$I03 \triangleright \quad$ **return**	$\qquad$ **if** $(\neg l')$
def $read_t(i)$	$C03_i \triangleright \quad lset[t].add(i)$
$R01 \triangleright \quad pv = wset[t].get(i),$	$\qquad$ **else**
$\qquad$ **if** $(pv \neq \bot)$	$C04_j \triangleright \quad$ **foreach** $(j \in lset[t])$
$R02 \triangleright \quad$ **return** $pv,$	$C05_{i,j} \triangleright \quad lock[j].unlock(),$
	$C06_i \triangleright \quad$ **return** $\mathbb{A},$
$R03 \triangleright \quad t_1 = ver[i].read(),$	
$R04 \triangleright \quad v = reg[i].read(),$	$C07 \triangleright \quad wver = clock.iaf(),$
$R05 \triangleright \quad l = lock[i].read(),$	
$R06 \triangleright \quad t_2 = ver[i].read(),$	$C08 \triangleright \quad s = rver[t].read(),$
$R07 \triangleright \quad s = rver[t].read(),$	$\qquad$ **if** $(wver \neq s + 1)$
$\qquad$ **if** $(\neg(\neg l \wedge t_1 = t_2$	$C09 \triangleright \quad$ **foreach** $(i \in rset[t])$
$\qquad\qquad\qquad \wedge t_2 \leq s))$	$C10_i \triangleright \quad l = lock[i].read(),$
$R08 \triangleright \quad$ **return** $\mathbb{A},$	$C11_i \triangleright \quad cver = ver[i].read(),$
	$\qquad$ **if** $(\neg(\neg l \wedge cver \leq s))$
$R09 \triangleright \quad rset[t].add(i),$	$C12_i \triangleright \quad$ **foreach** $(j \in lset[t])$
$R10 \triangleright \quad$ **return** $v,$	$C13_{i,j} \triangleright \quad lock[j].unlock(),$
$\{R03 \to R04,\ R04 \to R05,$	$C14_i \triangleright \quad$ **return** $\mathbb{A},$
$R05 \to R06\},$	
def $write_t(i, v)$	$C15 \triangleright \quad$ **foreach** $((i, v) \in wset[t])$
$W01 \triangleright \quad wset[t].put(i, v),$	$C16_i \triangleright \quad reg[i].write(v),$
$W02 \triangleright \quad$ **return** $ok,$	$C17_i \triangleright \quad ver[i].write(wver),$
	$C18_i \triangleright \quad lock[i].unlock(),$
	$C19 \triangleright \quad$ **return** $\mathbb{C},$
	$\{C01 \to C07,\ C10 \to C11,$
	$C09 \to C15, C16 \to C17,$
	$C17 \to C18\},$

$\mathcal{P}$: $tran_0, (tran_1 \parallel tran_2 \parallel \dots \parallel tran_n)$

Fig. 5. TL2 algorithm description $\pi_{TL2} = (\mathcal{T}_{TL2}, \mathcal{D}_{TL2}, \mathcal{P})$

Write-observation requires that each read method call should read the most current value. Read-preservation requires that the location read by a read method call is not overwritten between the read accesses the location and the transaction takes effect. The real-time-preservation condition requires that the marking relation preserves the real-time order of transactions.

Algorithm Description. We have represented the TL2 algorithm [9] in our description language in Fig. 5. The description π_{TL2} provides implementations of the four TM methods $init_t()$, $read_t(i)$, $write_t(i,v)$, and $commit_t()$ in the definitions section $\mathcal{D}$. The program in section $\mathcal{P}$ represents well-formed general client transactions. A client program first runs $tran_0$ to initialize the shared variables and then concurrently runs n well-formed transactions $tran_1, .., tran_n$. A well-formed transaction t executes $init_t()$, then a sequence of $read_t(i)$ and $write_t(i,v)$ calls and finally a $commit_t()$; it finishes if any call returns $\mathbb{A}$.

TL2 is a subtle algorithm. We briefly review how it works. TL2 uses the basic register $reg[i]$ to store the value of a location i. The algorithm reads $reg[i]$ at $R04$ and writes to $reg[i]$ at $C16$. Additionally, TL2 uses synchronization objects to help abort executions that would violate consistency. The idea is to give the value written in $reg[i]$ a *version number* that is stored in the $ver[i]$ register. TL2 uses a strong counter $clock$, whose value increases monotonically, to create such version numbers. Specifically, TL2 takes snapshots of $clock$ both at $I01$ when a transaction starts and at $C07$ (with an increment-and-fetch operation, abbreviated iaf) during commit. TL2 validates the versions of read values before completing both the read and commit methods.

Verification. We state the marking relation for the TL2 algorithm as an assertion in LSL as follows:

The marking $\sqsubseteq$ is the reflexive closure of $\sqsubset$. The relation $\sqsubset$ is defined as follows:
$\forall t, t': \quad t \sqsubset t' \Leftrightarrow Eff(t) \prec_{clock} Eff(t')$
$\forall \ell_R, t: isTRead(\ell_R) \land isTWriter_i(t) \Rightarrow$
    Let $i = arg1(\ell_R)$:
    $t \sqsubset \ell_R \Leftrightarrow writeAcc_i(t) \precsim readAcc(\ell_R)$
    $\ell_R \sqsubset t \Leftrightarrow readAcc(\ell_R) \prec writeAcc_i(t)$
where
$$Eff(\tau) = \begin{cases} initOf(\tau)'I01 & \text{if } isAborted(\tau) \\ commitOf(\tau)'C07 & \text{if } isCommitted(\tau) \end{cases}$$
$readAcc(\ell_R) = \ell_R'R04$
$writeAcc_i(\tau) = commitOf(\tau)'C16_i$

Intuitively, the effect order of transactions is the linearization order of their calls to $clock$ at $I01$ and $C07$. The access order of read operations and writer transactions to location i is the execution order of their access to the $reg[i]$ register at $R04$ and $C16$. The following theorem states that the relation $\sqsubseteq$ defined above is a marking relation for TL2. The assertions Γ_0 are the properties of well-formed client transactions. We have mechanically checked the proof in PVS. The PVS theories for TL2 and Dekker are available [26].

Theorem 2 (TL2 Correctness). $\pi_{TL2}, \Gamma_0 \vdash isMarking(\sqsubseteq)$.

5   Related Works and Conclusion

Manovit et al. [35] applied random testing to the TCC TM system. Lourenco et al. [32] reported several bugs during the porting of the TL2 algorithm. Given a TM algorithm and a bug pattern, our previous work [29] constructs a bug trace if the algorithm is prone to the bug pattern. It showed the incorrectness of algorithms that were deemed verified.

Although testing can find bugs, it does not prove their absence. To verify the correctness of TM algorithms, researchers have employed model checking and theorem proving. Model checkers from Cohen et al. [5,6], and Guerraoui et al. [15–17] are the pioneering approach to verification of TM. Subsequently, the same approach was taken by O'Leary et al. [39] and Baek et al. [3]. Model checking can automate the verification process but it has been dependent on assuming properties about the TM algorithm and only scalable to a finite number of threads and locations or simplified algorithms. Later, Emmi et al. [12] tried to infer algorithm invariants from small number of threads and memory locations. However, it worked on simplified algorithms due to scalability issues.

Attiya et al. [2] proved that opacity is sufficient for observational refinement of high-level atomic block semantics. Our previous work [30] showed the equivalence of opacity and markability and an informal proof of correctness for TL2. Koskinen and Parkinson presented a semantic model of serializability based on pulls from and pushes to an abstract shared log. Khyzha et al. [24] extended opacity to account for non-transactional accesses. In contrast to the current work, these works consider the correctness criteria, include only informal or non-mechanized proofs and do not include a logic and its soundness.

Singh [40] developed a runtime verification tool for TM algorithms. Although the tool is optimized with sound approximation techniques, the runtime overhead is still not negligible. Our previous work [28] presented a machine-checked theorem proving framework based on simulation between specifications and implementations [18,33] represented as IOA [34] and verified the NORec algorithm [7]. Doherty et al. [11] adopted the same approach and proved the correctness of a pessimistic TM algorithm [36]. In follow-up works, Derrick et al. and Armstrong et al. [1,8] simplified their simulation proofs by first model checking or proving the linearizability of the TM algorithm. In contrast to LSL that can reason about the algorithm description, these works require the algorithm to be translated to a transition system. In addition, they do not feature a logic.

To the best of our knowledge, LSL is the first logic that is applied to verification of transaction algorithms. In particular, it provides assertions for inter-thread execution and linearization orders that can directly capture the marking relation and the markability condition. Leveraging the proof of sufficiency of markability for opacity, verification of opacity is reduced to separate markability conditions that can be proved by the logic based on the validation checks in the algorithm. Logics based on concurrent separation logic [20,38] and rely-guarantee reasoning [21] such as RGSep [42], LRG [13,31], FCSL [37], GPS [41] and Iris [22,23] require the specification of inter-thread relations as complicated global rely and guarantee conditions. Further, they need auxiliary variables even for the simple Dekker algorithm which may obscure the underlying design intuitions of the algorithms.

Conclusion. We presented a logic that supports syntactic reasoning about synchronization algorithm descriptions and features novel assertions and inference rules for execution and linearization orders. These assertions enable capturing critical orders between concurrent operations and in particular markability orders between transactions. We proved the soundness of the logic and used it to machine-check a significant proof of TL2.

References

1. Armstrong, A., Dongol, B., Doherty, S.: Proving opacity via linearizability: a sound and complete method. In: Bouajjani, A., Silva, A. (eds.) FORTE 2017. LNCS, vol. 10321, pp. 50–66. Springer, Cham (2017). https://doi.org/10.1007/978-3-319-60225-7_4
2. Attiya, H., Gotsman, A., Hans, S., Rinetzky, N.: A programming language perspective on transactional memory consistency. In: Proceedings of the 2013 ACM Symposium on Principles of Distributed Computing, PODC 2013, pp. 309–318. ACM, New York (2013)
3. Baek, W., Bronson, N., Kozyrakis, C., Olukotun, K.: Implementing and evaluating a model checker for transactional memory systems. In: 2010 15th IEEE International Conference on Engineering of Complex Computer Systems (ICECCS), pp. 117–126 (2010)
4. Bender, J., Lesani, M., Palsberg, J.: Declarative fence insertion. In: OOPSLA 2015, pp. 367–385 (2015)
5. Cohen, A., O'Leary, J.W., Pnueli, A., Tuttle, M.R., Zuck, L.D.: Verifying correctness of transactional memories. In: FMCAD (2007)
6. Cohen, A., Pnueli, A., Zuck, L.D.: Mechanical verification of transactional memories with non-transactional memory accesses. In: Gupta, A., Malik, S. (eds.) CAV 2008. LNCS, vol. 5123, pp. 121–134. Springer, Heidelberg (2008). https://doi.org/10.1007/978-3-540-70545-1_13
7. Dalessandro, L., Spear, M.F., Scott, M.L.: NOrec: streamlining STM by abolishing ownership records. In: PPoPP (2010)
8. Derrick, J., Dongol, B., Schellhorn, G., Travkin, O., Wehrheim, H.: Verifying opacity of a transactional mutex lock. In: Bjørner, N., de Boer, F. (eds.) FM 2015. LNCS, vol. 9109, pp. 161–177. Springer, Cham (2015). https://doi.org/10.1007/978-3-319-19249-9_11
9. Dice, D., Shalev, O., Shavit, N.: Transactional locking II. In: Dolev, S. (ed.) DISC 2006. LNCS, vol. 4167, pp. 194–208. Springer, Heidelberg (2006). https://doi.org/10.1007/11864219_14
10. Dijkstra, E.W.: Cooperating sequential processes, technical report EWD-123 (1965)
11. Doherty, S., Dongol, B., Derrick, J., Schellhorn, G., Wehrheim, H.: Proving opacity of a pessimistic STM. Leibniz International Proceedings in Informatics, vol. 70, pp. 35:1–35:17. Dagstuhl Publishing (2017)
12. Emmi, M., Majumdar, R., Manevich, R.: Parameterized verification of transactional memories. In: PLDI (2010)
13. Feng, X.: Local rely-guarantee reasoning. In: POPL 2009 (2009)
14. Guerraoui, R., Kapalka, M.: On the correctness of transactional memory. In: PPOPP (2008)

15. Guerraoui, R., Henzinger, T.A., Jobstmann, B., Singh, V.: Model checking transactional memories. In: ACM SIGPLAN Conference on Programming Languages Design and Implementation, pp. 372–382 (2008)
16. Guerraoui, R., Henzinger, T.A., Singh, V.: Software transactional memory on relaxed memory models. In: Bouajjani, A., Maler, O. (eds.) CAV 2009. LNCS, vol. 5643, pp. 321–336. Springer, Heidelberg (2009). https://doi.org/10.1007/978-3-642-02658-4_26
17. Guerraoui, R., Henzinger, T.A., Singh, V.: Model checking transactional memories. Distrib. Comput. **22**, 129–145 (2010)
18. Hawblitzel, C., Petrank, E., Qadeer, S., Tasiran, S.: Automated and modular refinement reasoning for concurrent programs. In: Kroening, D., Păsăreanu, C.S. (eds.) CAV 2015, Part II. LNCS, vol. 9207, pp. 449–465. Springer, Cham (2015). https://doi.org/10.1007/978-3-319-21668-3_26
19. Herlihy, M.P., Wing, J.M.: Linearizability: a correctness condition for concurrent objects. TOPLAS **12**(3), 463–492 (1990)
20. Hobor, A., Appel, A.W., Nardelli, F.Z.: Oracle semantics for concurrent separation logic. In: Drossopoulou, S. (ed.) ESOP 2008. LNCS, vol. 4960, pp. 353–367. Springer, Heidelberg (2008). https://doi.org/10.1007/978-3-540-78739-6_27
21. Jones, C.B.: Specification and design of (parallel) programs. In: Information Processing 83, vol. 9, pp. 321–332 (1983)
22. Jung, R., Krebbers, R., Birkedal, L., Dreyer, D.: Higher-order ghost state. In: Proceedings of the 21st ACM SIGPLAN International Conference on Functional Programming, ICFP 2016, pp. 256–269. ACM, New York (2016)
23. Jung, R., et al.: Iris: monoids and invariants as an orthogonal basis for concurrent reasoning. In: POPL 2015 (2015)
24. Khyzha, A., Attiya, H., Gotsman, A., Rinetzky, N.: Safe privatization in transactional memory. In: Proceedings of the 23rd ACM SIGPLAN Symposium on Principles and Practice of Parallel Programming, pp. 233–245. ACM (2018)
25. Lamport, L.: On interprocess communication. Part I: basic formalism. Distrib. Comput. **1**(2), 77–85 (1986)
26. Lesani, M.: PVS Proof Theories (2018). http://www.cs.ucr.edu/%7Elesani/companion/nfm19/PVSTheories.tar.gz
27. Lesani, M.: Submission appendix (2018). http://www.cs.ucr.edu/%7Elesani/companion/nfm19/Appendix.pdf
28. Lesani, M., Luchangco, V., Moir, M.: A framework for formally verifying software transactional memory algorithms. In: Koutny, M., Ulidowski, I. (eds.) CONCUR 2012. LNCS, vol. 7454, pp. 516–530. Springer, Heidelberg (2012). https://doi.org/10.1007/978-3-642-32940-1_36
29. Lesani, M., Palsberg, J.: Proving non-opacity. In: Afek, Y. (ed.) DISC 2013. LNCS, vol. 8205, pp. 106–120. Springer, Heidelberg (2013). https://doi.org/10.1007/978-3-642-41527-2_8
30. Lesani, M., Palsberg, J.: Decomposing opacity. In: Kuhn, F. (ed.) DISC 2014. LNCS, vol. 8784, pp. 391–405. Springer, Heidelberg (2014). https://doi.org/10.1007/978-3-662-45174-8_27
31. Liang, H., Feng, X.: Modular verification of linearizability with non-fixed linearization points. In: PLDI 2013, pp. 459–470 (2013)
32. Lourenço, J., Cunha, G.: Testing patterns for software transactional memory engines. In: Proceedings of the 2007 ACM Workshop on Parallel and Distributed Systems: Testing and Debugging, PADTAD 2007, pp. 36–42. ACM, New York (2007)

33. Lynch, N., Vaandrager, F.: Forward and backward simulations for timing-based systems. In: de Bakker, J.W., Huizing, C., de Roever, W.P., Rozenberg, G. (eds.) REX 1991. LNCS, vol. 600, pp. 397–446. Springer, Heidelberg (1992). https://doi.org/10.1007/BFb0032002
34. Lynch, N.A., Tuttle, M.R.: An introduction to input/output automata. CWI Q. **2**, 219–246 (1989)
35. Manovit, C., Hangal, S., Chafi, H., McDonald, A., Kozyrakis, C., Olukotun, K.: Testing implementations of transactional memory. In: Proceedings of the 15th International Conference on Parallel Architectures and Compilation Techniques, PACT 2006, pp. 134–143. ACM, New York (2006)
36. Matveev, A., Shavit, N.: Towards a fully pessimistic STM model (2012)
37. Nanevski, A., Ley-Wild, R., Sergey, I., Delbianco, G.A.: Communicating state transition systems for fine-grained concurrent resources. In: Shao, Z. (ed.) ESOP 2014. LNCS, vol. 8410, pp. 290–310. Springer, Heidelberg (2014). https://doi.org/10.1007/978-3-642-54833-8_16
38. O'Hearn, P.W.: Resources, concurrency, and local reasoning. Theor. Comput. Sci. **375**(1–3), 271–307 (2007)
39. O'Leary, J., Saha, B., Tuttle, M.R.: Model checking transactional memory with spin. In: 29th IEEE International Conference on Distributed Computing Systems, ICDCS 2009, pp. 335–342 (2009)
40. Singh, V.: Runtime verification for software transactional memories. In: Barringer, H., et al. (eds.) RV 2010. LNCS, vol. 6418, pp. 421–435. Springer, Heidelberg (2010). https://doi.org/10.1007/978-3-642-16612-9_32
41. Turon, A., Vafeiadis, V., Dreyer, D.: GPS: navigating weak memory with ghosts, protocols, and separation. In: Proceedings of the 2014 ACM International Conference on Object Oriented Programming Systems Languages & Applications, OOPSLA 2014, pp. 691–707. ACM, New York (2014)
42. Vafeiadis, V., Parkinson, M.: A marriage of rely/guarantee and separation logic. In: Caires, L., Vasconcelos, V.T. (eds.) CONCUR 2007. LNCS, vol. 4703, pp. 256–271. Springer, Heidelberg (2007). https://doi.org/10.1007/978-3-540-74407-8_18

Symbolic Model Checking of Weighted PCTL Using Dependency Graphs

Mathias Claus Jensen, Anders Mariegaard$^{(\boxtimes)}$, and Kim Guldstrand Larsen

Department of Computer Science, Aalborg University,
Selma Lagerlöfs Vej 300, 9220 Aalborg, Denmark
{mcje,am,kgl}@cs.aau.dk

Abstract. We present a global and local algorithm for model checking a weighted variant of PCTL with upper-bound weight constraints, on probabilistic weighted Kripke structures where the weights are vectors with non-zero magnitude. Both algorithms under- and over approximate a fixed-point over a symbolic dependency graph, until sufficient evidence to prove or disprove the given formula is found. Fixed-point computations are carried out in the domain of (multidimensional) probabilistic step functions, encoded as interval decision diagrams. The global algorithm works similarly to classic value iteration for PCTL in that it evaluates all nodes of the dependency graph iteratively, while the local algorithm performs a search-like evaluation of the given dependency graph in an attempt to find enough evidence locally to prove/disprove a given formula, without having to evaluate all nodes. Both algorithms are evaluated on several experiments and we show that the local algorithm generally outperforms the global algorithm.

Keywords: Model checking · PCTL · Fixed-point computation

1 Introduction

The ubiquity of embedded systems in modern-day society calls for robust and efficient methodologies for the design, production and implementation of more and more complex systems. These systems usually interact with the physical world, as well as the Internet, as a so called cyber-physical system. In this area, model-driven development is gaining popularity as a way to deal with early design-space exploration and automatic verification. Especially important in this context is the incorporation of non-functional aspects, such as resource consumption, timing constraints and probabilistic behavior. This has lead to a large variety of mathematical models having been created for the purpose of modeling these quantitative systems. In conjunction with these models, an assorted landscape of logics have also been proposed for the sake of specifying desired properties regarding the aforementioned models. Within the model-checking community this has lead to tools such as UPPAAL [16], PRISM [14], MRMC [12] and STORM [7], for analysis of systems involving continuous time,

© Springer Nature Switzerland AG 2019
J. M. Badger and K. Y. Rozier (Eds.): NFM 2019, LNCS 11460, pp. 298–315, 2019.
https://doi.org/10.1007/978-3-030-20652-9_20

stochastic behavior and various types of resources, in an efficient manner. At the heart of such tools are algorithms that verify user given properties on specified models.

Our Contribution. We present two algorithms for model-checking a weighted subset of probabilistic CTL (PCTL) [8] with upper-bound weight constraints, on probabilistic weighted Kripke structures.

We allow for the weights of both the model and formula to be multidimensional, i.e. vectors. This allows for the modeling of consumption/production of resources in multiple dimensions. E.g. for cyber-physical systems we might be interested in both the time and energy it takes to perform some action.

Both algorithms approximate a fixed point on a *symbolic dependency graph* by repeated computation of under- and over-approximations. Termination is guaranteed as the transition weight vectors are required to have non-zero magnitude, in addition to path-formulae having upper-bound weight-constraints. Our symbolic dependency graphs extend the dependency graphs introduced by Liu and Smolka [17] to cope with the multidimensional probabilistic domain. The first algorithm, the global algorithm, is, with minor modifications, an instance of the approach presented in our previous work in [18] which in turn is an extension of the global algorithm by Liu and Smolka. The second algorithm, the local algorithm, was not a part of [18] and is our novel extension of the local algorithm presented by Liu and Smolka.

Both algorithms have been implemented in a prototype tool written in Python, using Interval Decision Diagrams [19] as the back-end data-structure for symbolic computations. For experimental evaluation, we present results on two case-studies based on PRISM [14] models and show that the local approach is, also in this domain, generally more efficient than the global approach, especially in cases where complete exploration of the underlying dependency graph is not needed to prove/disprove a property of the model. An extended version of the paper, with proofs, can be found online at http://people.cs.aau.dk/~am/nfm19/ext.pdf.

Related Work. The framework of fixed point computations introduced by Liu and Smolka has recently been extended in different ways. A distributed version of the local algorithm, that also deals with negation has been developed in [6]. The framework has also been extended to a weighted domain in [11] for model-checking weighted CTL on weighted Kripke structures where a symbolic graph encoding ensures an efficient local algorithm. An extension for Timed Games has been developed in [4]. In [5] the global algorithm was extended for parametric model-checking, used in [2] for model-checking on models with real-valued random variables as weights. Our global algorithm is reminiscent of the PCTL model-checking algorithm on which PRISM is based [13], in the sense that we consider the parse-tree of the formula and recursively compute the satisfaction of sub-formulae in an iterative manner. For MRMC, the algorithms based on *path graph generation* presented in [1] are used to solver similar model-checking problems, based on a local unfolding of the model as our local approach.

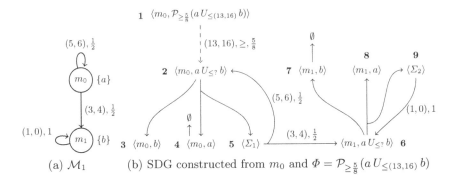

Fig. 1. A simple PWKS with 2-dimensional weights and its associated SDG

Each node in a path graph represents a certain reward, associated with a number of finite path fragments and their probabilities, in contrast to our approach where nodes encode probabilities associated with the satisfaction of a given formulae in a state.

2   Models and Properties

For any set X, X^n is the set of all n-dimensional vectors with elements from X. For $x \in X$ we let x^n denote the n-dimensional vector with all elements being x. Hence $\mathbb{N}^n$ is the set of all n-dimensional vectors of natural numbers and $\mathbb{N}_+^n = \mathbb{N}^n \setminus 0^n$ restricts $\mathbb{N}^n$ to vectors with strictly positive magnitude. For the remainder of the paper we assume a fixed dimensionality n, with $n > 0$. Any vector is written in boldface e.g. $\boldsymbol{x} = (x_1, \ldots, x_n), \boldsymbol{y} = (y_1, \ldots, y_n)$ are vectors. Finally, we assume a fixed finite set of labels AP.

Definition 1 (Probabilistic Weighted Kripke Structure). *A* Probabilistic Weighted Kripke Structure *(PWKS) is a structure* $\mathcal{M} = (M, \rightarrow, \ell)$ *where M is a finite set of states,* $\rightarrow \subseteq M \times \mathbb{N}_+^n \times (0, 1] \times M$ *is the finite weighted probabilistic transition relation such that for all $m \in M$,* $\sum_{(m, w_i, p_i, m_i) \in \rightarrow} p_i = 1$ *and* $\ell \colon M \rightarrow 2^{AP}$ *is the labeling function, assigning to each state a set of atomic propositions.*

Whenever $(m, \boldsymbol{w}, p, m') \in \rightarrow$ we write $m \xrightarrow{\boldsymbol{w}, p} m'$. A *path* from a state m_0 is an infinite sequence of transitions $\pi = (m_0, \boldsymbol{w_0}, p_0, m_1), (m_1, \boldsymbol{w_1}, p_1, m_2), \ldots$ with $m_i \xrightarrow{w_i, p_i} m_{i+1}$ for any $i \in \mathbb{N}$. We denote by $\pi[j]$ the j'th state of π, m_j and by $\mathcal{W}(\pi)(j)$ the accumulated weight along path π up until m_j. Hence $\mathcal{W}(\pi)(0) = 0$ and $\mathcal{W}(\pi)(j) = \sum_{i=0}^{j-1} \boldsymbol{w_i}$ for $j > 0$. See Fig. 1a for an example PWKS with two states and weights from $\mathbb{N}^2$.

As specification language we define the logic Probabilistic Weighted CTL (PWCTL), extending a subset of Probabilistic CTL (PCTL), with weight-vectors.

Definition 2 (PWCTL). *The set of PWCTL state formulae, $\mathcal{L}$, is given by the following grammar:*

$$\mathcal{L}: \quad \Phi ::= a \mid \neg a \mid \Phi_1 \wedge \Phi_2 \mid \Phi_1 \vee \Phi_2 \mid \mathcal{P}_{\rhd \lambda}(\Psi)$$

where $a \in AP, \lambda \in [0,1]$ and $\rhd = \{>, \geq\}$. The path formulae *are given by the following grammar, with $\boldsymbol{k} \in \mathbb{N}^n$:*

$$\Psi ::= X_{\leq \boldsymbol{k}}\Phi \mid \Phi_1 U_{\leq \boldsymbol{k}}\Phi_2 \ .$$

We also define a set of symbolic unbounded until-formulae for later use, namely $\mathcal{S} = \{\Phi_1 U_{\leq ?}\Phi_2 \mid \Phi_1, \Phi_2 \in \mathcal{L}\} \cup \{X_{\geq ?}\Phi \mid \Phi \in \mathcal{L}\}$.

For the probabilistic modality $\mathcal{P}_{\rhd \lambda}(\Psi)$, the satisfaction is dependent on the probability of picking a path satisfying the path-formulae Ψ, from some state m. To this end we employ the standard cylinder-set construction (see [3, Chapter 10]) to obtain a unique probability measure $\mathbb{P}$, assigning probabilities to sets of paths sharing a common prefix (a cylinder).

Definition 3 (PWCTL Semantics). *For a PWKS $\mathcal{M} = (M, \rightarrow, \ell)$ with state $m \in M$, the satisfiability relation $\models$ is inductively defined by:*

$$
\begin{array}{lll}
\mathcal{M}, m \models a & \text{iff} & a \in \ell(m) \\
\mathcal{M}, m \models \neg a & \text{iff} & a \notin \ell(m) \\
\mathcal{M}, m \models \Phi_1 \wedge \Phi_2 & \text{iff} & \mathcal{M}, m \models \Phi_1 \text{ and } \mathcal{M}, m \models \Phi_2 \\
\mathcal{M}, m \models \Phi_1 \vee \Phi_2 & \text{iff} & \mathcal{M}, m \models \Phi_1 \text{ or } \mathcal{M}, m \models \Phi_2 \\
\mathcal{M}, m \models \mathcal{P}_{\rhd \lambda}(\Psi) & \text{iff} & \mathbb{P}(\pi \mid \pi[0] = m, \mathcal{M}, \pi \models \Psi) \rhd \lambda
\end{array}
$$

where, for any path π:

$$
\begin{array}{lll}
\mathcal{M}, \pi \models X_{\leq \boldsymbol{k}}\Phi & \text{iff} & \pi[0] \xrightarrow{w,p} \pi[1], \mathcal{M}, \pi[1] \models \Phi, \text{ and } \boldsymbol{w} \leq \boldsymbol{k} \\
\mathcal{M}, \pi \models \Phi_1 U_{\leq \boldsymbol{k}}\Phi_2 & \text{iff} & \text{there exists a } j \text{ such that } \mathcal{M}, \pi[j] \models \Phi_2, \\
& & \mathcal{M}, \pi[i] \models \Phi_1 \text{ for all } i < j \text{ and } \mathcal{W}(\pi)(j) \leq \boldsymbol{k}.
\end{array}
$$

If $\mathcal{M}$ is clearly implied by the context, we simply write $m \models \Phi$ if the state m of PWKS $\mathcal{M}$ satisfies the formula Φ and similarly $\pi \models \Psi$ if π is a path in $\mathcal{M}$.

Example 1. For the PWKS $\mathcal{M}_1$ in Fig. 1a, we have that $m_0 \models \mathcal{P}_{\geq \lambda}(a\, U_{\leq \boldsymbol{k}}\, b)$ with $\boldsymbol{k} = (8, 10)$ and $\lambda = \frac{5}{8}$ as $\mathbb{P}(\pi \mid \pi[0] = m_0, \pi \models a\, U_{\leq (8,10)}\, b) = \frac{1}{2} + \frac{1}{2} \cdot \frac{1}{2} = \frac{6}{8}$. In fact, this is the case for any $\boldsymbol{k} \geq (8, 10)$. Finally, if $\lambda \leq \frac{1}{2}$, considering only the path $m_0 \xrightarrow{(3,4),\frac{1}{2}} m_1 \cdots$ instead of the entire set of paths, would be sufficient.

3 Symbolic Dependency Graphs

As the semantics of PWCTL is given by induction in the structure of the formula, a solution to the model-checking problem $m \models \Phi$ is *dependent* on the solution to related model-checking problems involving sub-formulae of Φ and the reachable states of m. We encode these dependencies as edges between nodes in a *Symbolic Dependency Graph* and reduce the model-checking problem to fixed-point computations on these graphs.

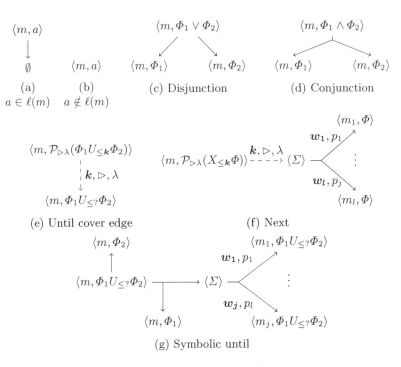

Fig. 2. SDG construction rules for state m where $m \xrightarrow{w_i, p_i} m_i$ for all i with $1 \leq i \leq j$.

Definition 4 (Symbolic Dependency Graph). *For a PWKS $\mathcal{M} = (M, \rightarrow, \ell)$, a symbolic dependency graph (SDG) is a tuple, $G = (C, E_H, E_C, E_\Sigma)$, where*

- *$C \subseteq M \times \mathcal{L} \cup M \times \mathcal{S} \cup \{\Sigma\} \times M \times \mathcal{S}$ is a finite set of configurations (nodes),*
- *$E_H \subseteq C \times 2^C$ is a finite set of hyper-edges,*
- *$E_C \subseteq C \times \mathbb{N}^n \times \triangleright \times [0,1] \times C$ is a finite set of cover-edges, and*
- *$E_\Sigma \subseteq C \times 2^{\mathbb{N}^n_+ \times [0,1] \times C}$ is a finite set of sum-edges.*

We will refer to elements of: $M \times \mathcal{L}$ as concrete-, $M \times \mathcal{S}$ as symbolic-, and $\{\Sigma\} \times M \times \mathcal{S}$ as sum-configurations. For brevity, we will often write $\langle \Sigma \rangle$ for sum-configurations when the state and symbolic formula is clear from context. If a configuration $s \in C$ can transition to another configuration $t \in C$ using any type of edge, we write $s \rightsquigarrow t$. Given a state m and formula Φ, one can construct the SDG rooted in $\langle m, \Phi \rangle$ by recursively applying the rules of Fig. 2. Singular *hyper-edges* are used to encode conjunction (Fig. 2d) and multiple *hyper-edges* encode disjunction (Fig. 2c). *Cover-edges* are used to abstract away concrete bounds on probabilities and weights and introduces symbolic configurations (Fig. 2e and f). Lastly, *sum-edges* encode the probabilistic weighted transitions of the underlying model (Fig. 2g and f).

Example 2. Consider again the PWKS $\mathcal{M}_1$ of Fig. 1a and the formula $\Phi = \mathcal{P}_{\geq \frac{5}{8}}(a\,U_{\leq(13,16)}\,b)$. The SDG obtained by applying the construction rules in Fig. 2 can be seen in Fig. 1b.

For the rest of this section we assume a fixed model, $\mathcal{M} = (M, \rightarrow, \ell)$, with $m \in M$ and a fixed PWCTL-formula, Φ. Let $G = (C, E_H, E_C, E_\Sigma)$ be the SDG constructed using the rules given in Fig. 2 with root $s_0 = \langle m, \Phi \rangle$. The semantics of configurations is given by assignments, encoding the probability of satisfaction, given a cost-bound (weight).

Definition 5 (Assignments). *An* assignment *is a function,* $a : \mathbb{N}^n \rightarrow [0, 1]$, *assigning to each vector a probability.*

We use $\mathcal{A}$ *to denote the set of assignments.*

For any $a_1, a_2 \in \mathcal{A}$, $a_1 \sqsubseteq a_2$ *iff* $\forall \boldsymbol{w} \in \mathbb{N}^n . a_1(\boldsymbol{w}) \leq a_2(\boldsymbol{w})$.

Assignments naturally extends to SDGs.

Definition 6 (Assignment Mapping). *An* assignment mapping *on G is a function,* $A : C \rightarrow \mathcal{A}$, *mapping each configuration to an assignment.*

We use $\mathcal{C}_G$ *to denote the set of assignment mappings over G.*

For any $A_1, A_2 \in \mathcal{C}_G$, $A_1 \sqsubseteq_G A_2$ *iff* $\forall s \in C . A_1(s) \sqsubseteq A_2(s)$.

We define $\mathbb{0}, \mathbb{1} \in \mathcal{A}$ to be the assignments that map any vector to the probabilities 0 and 1, respectively. We will refer to these assignments as Boolean assignments. Similarly, we define $A^\mathbb{0}, A^\mathbb{1}$ to be the assignment mappings that map any configuration to the Boolean assignments $\mathbb{0}$ and $\mathbb{1}$, respectively. Generally, concrete configurations will receive Boolean assignments. For symbolic configurations, e.g. $\langle m, \Phi_1 U_{\leq ?} \Phi_2 \rangle$, assignments will be used to compute probabilities associated with the sets of paths satisfying any concrete instance of the formula induced by replacing ? with a cost-bound $\boldsymbol{k} \in \mathbb{N}^n$.

Clearly, $(\mathcal{A}, \sqsubseteq)$ and $(\mathcal{C}_G, \sqsubseteq_G)$ are complete lattices with $\mathbb{0}$, $\mathbb{1}$ and $A^\mathbb{0}$, $A^\mathbb{1}$, as their respective bottom and top elements. We will use $\bigsqcup X$ and $\bigsqcap X$ to denote the supremum and infimum of any subset $X \subseteq \mathcal{A}$. As usual we let $\bigsqcup \emptyset = \mathbb{0}$ and $\bigsqcap \emptyset = \mathbb{1}$. The supremum of X can be realised as the assignment defined, for arbitrary $\boldsymbol{w} \in \mathbb{N}^n$, as $(\bigsqcup X)(\boldsymbol{w}) = \sup\{p \in [0, 1] \mid a \in X, a(\boldsymbol{w}) = p\}$. The infimum can be realised in a similar fashion. For $a_1, a_2 \in \mathcal{A}$, we define $(a_1 + a_2)$ to be the assignment given, for arbitrary $\boldsymbol{w} \in \mathbb{N}^n$ as, $(a_1 + a_2)(\boldsymbol{w}) = a_1(\boldsymbol{w}) + a_2(\boldsymbol{w})$. Another useful operation on assignments as that of *shifting*:

Definition 7 (Shifting). *For* $\boldsymbol{w} \in \mathbb{N}^n$, *and* $p, q \in [0, 1]$, $\texttt{shift}_{\boldsymbol{w}, p, q} : \mathcal{A} \rightarrow \mathcal{A}$ *is a function that, given an assignment* $a \in \mathcal{A}$, *produces a shifted assignment* $\texttt{shift}_{\boldsymbol{w}, p, q}(a) \in \mathcal{A}$, *defined for any* $\boldsymbol{v} \in \mathbb{N}^n$ *as,*

$$\texttt{shift}_{\boldsymbol{w}, p, q}(a)(\boldsymbol{v}) = \begin{cases} a(\boldsymbol{v} - \boldsymbol{w}) \cdot p & \text{if } \boldsymbol{w} \leq \boldsymbol{v} \\ q & \text{otherwise} \end{cases}$$

Shifting an assignment increases the cost of satisfaction, represented by the assignment, by an amount $\boldsymbol{w}$ while adjusting the degree of satisfaction by p and setting the probabilities to q if the cost is below $\boldsymbol{w}$.

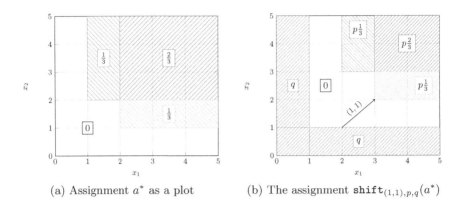

(a) Assignment a^* as a plot   (b) The assignment $\texttt{shift}_{(1,1),p,q}(a^*)$

Fig. 3. Assignment shifting

Example 3. Suppose $m \xrightarrow{(1,1),\frac{1}{2}} m_1$ and $m \xrightarrow{(2,2),\frac{1}{2}} m_2$. Let the assignment in Fig. 3a be a^* with the property $a^*(\boldsymbol{w}) = \mathbb{P}(\pi \mid \pi[0] = m_1, m_1 \models X_{\leq w}\,\varPhi) = \mathbb{P}(\pi \mid \pi[0] = m_2, m_2 \models X_{\leq w}\varPsi)$ for all $\boldsymbol{w} \in \mathbb{N}^n$ and some state-formula $\varPhi$. a^* thus encodes the exact probability of paths starting in m_1 (or m_2) that satisfy $X_{\leq w}\,\varPhi$, for all $\boldsymbol{w}$. By applying the shift operator, and addition on assignments, we get $a_m = \texttt{Shift}_{(1,1),\frac{1}{2},0}(a^*) + \texttt{Shift}_{(2,2),\frac{1}{2},0}(a^*)$. a_m has the desired property that $a_m(\boldsymbol{w}) = \mathbb{P}(\pi \mid \pi[0] = m, m \models X_{\leq w}\,\varPhi)$ for any $\boldsymbol{w}$. Figure 3b shows the result of the first term ($q = 0, p = \frac{1}{2}$).

We now introduce the fixed-point operator from our previous work in [18].

Definition 8. *For a SDG* $G = (C, E_H, E_C, E_\Sigma)$, $F \colon \mathcal{C}_G \to \mathcal{C}_G$ *is a function that, given an assignment mapping A on G, produces a new updated assignment mapping, $F(A)$. F is given for any node $s \in C$ as follows,*

$$F(A)(s) = \begin{cases} \begin{cases} \mathbb{1} & \text{if } A(t)(\boldsymbol{k}) \rhd \lambda \\ \mathbb{0} & \text{otherwise} \end{cases} & \text{if } (s, \boldsymbol{k}, \rhd, \lambda, t) \in E_C \\ \displaystyle\sum_{(\boldsymbol{w},p,t)\in T} \texttt{shift}_{\boldsymbol{w},p,0}\,(A(t)) & \text{if } (s,T) \in E_\Sigma \\ \displaystyle\bigsqcup_{(s,T)\in E_H} \bigsqcap_{t\in T} A(t) & \text{otherwise} \end{cases}$$

F is well-defined as all configuration have at most one type of outgoing edge. For cover-edges we simply check the cover-condition. For sum-edges we compute a sum over all assignments to targets, shifted by the corresponding weight and probability as exemplified in Example 3. Lastly, for configurations with outgoing hyper-edges or no outgoing edges we compute a supremum over all hyper-edges and for each hyper-edge an infimum.

As F is monotonic (see [18]) on a complete lattice, we get, by Tarski's fixed point theorem [20], that F must have a unique least fixed point, $A_{\min}$. The following theorem states that our construction of a SDG from a pair $\langle m, \varPhi \rangle$ along with its associated least fixed point, $A_{\min}$, as given by F, is indeed sound.

Theorem 1 (Soundness). $m \models \Phi$ iff $A_{\min}(\langle m, \Phi \rangle) = \mathbb{1}$.

Corollary 1. $\mathbb{P}(\pi \mid \pi[0] = m, \pi \models \Phi_1 U_{\leq k} \Phi_2) = A_{\min}(\langle m, \Phi_1 U \Phi_2 \rangle)(\boldsymbol{k})$.

For any concrete configuration, i.e. on the form $\langle m, \Phi \rangle$, we have that any assignment mapping generated by F will be assigned either $\mathbb{0}$ or $\mathbb{1}$. Thus, we have the following corollary.

Corollary 2. $m \not\models \Phi$ iff $A_{\min}(\langle m, \Phi \rangle) = \mathbb{0}$.

As $(\mathcal{C}_G, \sqsubseteq_G)$ can be a lattice of infinite size, it is not given that we can construct $A_{\min}$ through repeated applications of F on the bottom element $\mathbb{0}$. The following theorem however states that F can be used to sufficiently approximate $A_{\min}$, from above and below, in a finite number of iterations, so that we may answer our model checking query.

Theorem 2 (Realisability). *There exists an $i \in \mathbb{N}$ such that,*

$$m \models \Phi \iff F^i(A^{\mathbb{0}})(\langle m, \Phi \rangle) = \mathbb{1} \ and \ m \not\models \Phi \iff F^i(A^{\mathbb{1}})(\langle m, \Phi \rangle) = \mathbb{0}.$$

This theorem follows in part from our SDGs being finite. If the SDG is acyclic then it is trivial to show. If not, then the only cycles that occur, occur within the sub-tree of a node of type $\langle \mathcal{P}_{\triangleright \lambda}(\Phi_1 U_{\leq k} \Phi_2) \rangle$, which is directly dependent on $\langle m, \Phi_1 U_{\leq ?} \Phi_2 \rangle$. Since the weights of transitions are of positive magnitude, there is only a finite number of ways to concretely unfold the symbolic node $\langle m, \Phi_1 U_{\leq ?} \Phi_2 \rangle$ and its dependencies for any given $\boldsymbol{k} \in \mathbb{N}^n$. As such, there exists a $j \in \mathbb{N}$, such that $F^j(A^{\mathbb{0}})(\langle m, \Phi_1 U_{\leq ?} \Phi_2 \rangle)(\boldsymbol{k}) = F^j(A^{\mathbb{1}})(\langle m, \Phi_1 U_{\leq ?} \Phi_2 \rangle)(\boldsymbol{k}) = A_{\min}(\boldsymbol{k})$.

3.1 Global Algorithm

We now introduce an algorithm based on the function in Definition 8. This algorithm will be referred to as the global algorithm as it updates the entire assignment mapping of a given SDG each iteration, therefore in a sense, globally applying the iterator. The algorithm is as follows: repeatedly apply F on all configurations $s \in C$ until $F^i(0)(s_0) = \mathbb{1}$ or $F^j(1)(s_0) = \mathbb{0}$ for some $i, j \in \mathbb{N}$, where s_0 is the root of the SDG. Termination and correctness is guaranteed by Theorems 1 and 2.

Example 4. Consider the repeated application of F on the root of the SDG from Fig. 1b, starting from $\mathbb{0}$. Table 1 shows the results, with configurations in bold and one row per iteration. Only configurations that change value from $\mathbb{0}$ are listed. Assignments are written as pairs of weights and probabilities e.g. $\{((3,4), \frac{1}{2}), ((8,10), \frac{3}{4})\}$ is the assignment a s.t $a(\boldsymbol{w}) = 0$ for $\boldsymbol{w} < (3,4)$, $a(\boldsymbol{w}) = \frac{1}{2}$ for $(3,4) \leq \boldsymbol{w} < (8,10)$ and $a(\boldsymbol{w}) = \frac{3}{4}$ for $\boldsymbol{w} \geq (8,10)$. As seen, F^7 assigns $\mathbb{1}$ to $\mathbb{1}$ i.e $m_0 \models \mathcal{P}_{\geq \frac{5}{8}}(a \, U_{\leq(8,10)} \, b)$ as expected.

Table 1. Lower bound assignments for Fig. 1b

	1	2	4	5	6	7	9
1	-	-	$\mathbb{1}$	-	-	$\mathbb{1}$	-
2	-	-	-	-	$\mathbb{1}$	-	-
3	-	-	-	$\{((3,4),\frac{1}{2})\}$	-	-	$\{((1,0),1)\}$
4	-	$\{((3,4),\frac{1}{2})\}$	-	-	-	-	-
5	-	-	-	$\{((3,4),\frac{1}{2}),((8,10),\frac{3}{4})\}$	-	-	-
6	-	$\{((3,4),\frac{1}{2}),((8,10),\frac{3}{4})\}$	-	-	-	-	-
7	$\mathbb{1}$	-	-	-	-	-	-

In practice, we need a finite representation of assignments. To this end we use Interval Decision Diagrams (IDDs) [19], a generalization of Binary Decision Diagrams (BDDs). IDDs, like BDDs, test on variables but now the values of variables are partitioned into disjoint intervals that must be independent, in the sense that any two values within the same interval must produce the same function value.

Recall that all assignments are of the form $\alpha : \mathbb{N}^n \to [0,1]$ i.e. functions that, given a vector of natural numbers, yields some probability. The simplest assignments, $\mathbb{0}$ and $\mathbb{1}$ are encoded directly as IDD terminals. In the general case, we have n variables, where n is the dimension of the weight-vectors. As all assignments of interest are built from $\mathbb{0}$ and $\mathbb{1}$ by applying operations $\texttt{shift}_{w,p,q}(a)$, $\bigsqcup\{a,b\}$, $\bigsqcap\{a,b\}$, and $a + b$, where $a, b \in \mathcal{A}$, we only need that IDDs are closed under these operations. For the binary operations, this is a straight-forward extension of the procedure for BDDs and it is easy to show that IDDs are closed under shifting.

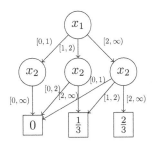

Fig. 4. Example IDD

Example 5. As an example of an IDD encoding a non-trivial assignment, see Fig. 4, here encoding the assignment $a*$ of Fig. 3a. a_* can be generated by the assignment $\texttt{shift}_{(1,2),\frac{1}{3},0}(\mathbb{1}) + \texttt{shift}_{(2,1),\frac{1}{3},0}(\mathbb{1})$.

4 Local Algorithm

As an alternative to globally updating the assignment to all nodes in each iteration, we propose a *local* algorithm. The pseudocode for the local algorithm can be seen in Algorithm 1. It takes as input a SDG $G = (C, E_H, E_C, E_\Sigma)$ and a configuration $s_0 = \langle m, \Phi \rangle$ and outputs $A_{\min}(s_0)$. The fixed-point computation is done in the while loop (lines 15–17) by calling $\texttt{nextlower}$ and $\texttt{nextupper}$ to compute the next lower and upper bound of $A_{\min}$, respectively. To this end, single edges are processed locally according to the type of the edge. Assignments to configurations are now from the domain $\mathcal{A} \cup \{\bot, \top\}$, $\bot(\top)$ being the smallest (largest) assignment w.r.t $\sqsubseteq$. The SDG G is assumed to be constructed according to the rules in Fig. 2 for a model-checking problem $m \models \Phi$. For termination, we define a required precision $\boldsymbol{k} = \sup K(\Phi)$ on assignments, as the supremum of all the weight-bounds found in Φ. Given $\boldsymbol{k}$, we are only interested in assignment with this precision. We therefore introduce a $\boldsymbol{k}$-ordering of assignments.

Definition 9 ($\boldsymbol{k}$-ordering). *For a given $\boldsymbol{k} \in \mathbb{N}^n$, we define the binary relation $\sqsubseteq_{\boldsymbol{k}}$ on assignments by $a_1 \sqsubseteq_{\boldsymbol{k}} a_2$ iff $\forall \boldsymbol{w} \leq \boldsymbol{k} . a_1(\boldsymbol{w}) \leq a_2(\boldsymbol{w})$, where $a_1, a_2 \in \mathcal{A}$ and let $a_1 =_{\boldsymbol{k}} a_2$ if $a_1 \sqsubseteq_{\boldsymbol{k}} a_2$ and $a_2 \sqsubseteq_{\boldsymbol{k}} a_1$. For a given SDG $G = (C, E_H, E_C, E_\Sigma)$, we extend the relation to assignment mappings by $A_1 \sqsubseteq_{\boldsymbol{k}} A_2$ iff $\forall s \in C . A_1(s) \sqsubseteq_{\boldsymbol{k}} A_2(s)$, where $A_1, A_2 \in \mathcal{C}_G$.*

Algorithm 1. Symbolic Local Algorithm

---

    input : SDG $G = (C, E_H, E_C, E_\Sigma)$ and configuration $s_0 = \langle m, \Phi \rangle \in C$
    output : $A_{\min}(s_0)$
1 $k = \sup K(\Phi)$;
2 **foreach** $v \in \{L, U\}$ **do**
3   **foreach** $s \in C$ **do** $R^v(s) = \emptyset$;
4   **foreach** $(s, T) \in E_\Sigma$ **do**
5   **foreach** $(\boldsymbol{w}, p, t) \in T$ **do** $\Sigma_\Delta^v(s)(t) = \mathbb{0}$;

6 **foreach** $s \in C$ **do**
7     $A^L(s) = \bot$;
8     $A^U(s) = \top$;
9 $A^L(s_0) = a_{def}^L = a_{max}^U = \mathbb{0}$;
10 $A^U(s_0) = a_{def}^U = a_{max}^L = \mathbb{1}$;
11 $W_L^\downarrow = W_U^\downarrow = \texttt{succ}(s_0)$;
12 $W_L^\uparrow = W_U^\uparrow = \emptyset$;
13 **while** $(W_L^\downarrow \cup W_L^\uparrow) \neq \emptyset \wedge (W_U^\downarrow \cup W_U^\uparrow) \neq \emptyset$ **do**
14     $\texttt{nextlower}()$;
15     $\texttt{nextupper}()$;
16 **if** $(W_L^\downarrow \cup W_L^\uparrow) = \emptyset$ **then return** $A^L(s_0)$;
17 **else return** $A^U(s_0)$;

Given $\boldsymbol{k}$, termination and correctness does not rely on computing both the upper and lower bound and as the two functions are almost identical, we only show pseudo-code responsible for computing lower bounds. In practice, computing upper bounds can be beneficial in cases where the query is unsatisfied. The pseudo-code for **nextlower** can be seen in Algorithm 2, with edge processing functions in Algorithm 4.

Functions `nextlower` and `nextupper` utilize different data-structures to process edges of the graph. Let $\alpha \in \{L, U\}$. Then the data-structures are: $Crt: C \rightharpoonup \mathcal{A}, A^L: C \rightarrow \mathcal{A} \cup \{\bot\}, A^U: C \rightarrow \mathcal{A} \cup \{\top\}, W_\alpha^\downarrow, W_\alpha^\uparrow \subseteq 2^E, \Sigma_\Delta^\alpha: C \rightarrow (C \rightarrow \mathcal{A}), R^\alpha: C \rightarrow 2^C$ and $a_{def}^\alpha, a_{max}^\alpha \in \mathcal{A}$.

All data-structures with $\alpha = L$ ($\alpha = U$) are only used in `nextlower` (`nextupper`) Crt is a partial function with $Crt(s) = a$ if s has received its fixed-point assignment a. Crt is used to skip the processing edges for which the source configuration has already received its fixed point assignment. A^L and A^U contain the cur-

---

Algorithm 2. `nextlower`

1 **function** nextlower():
2   Pop e from $W_L^\downarrow$ or $W_L^\uparrow$;
3     $s = \mathsf{source}(e)$;
4   **if** $Crt(s) = a$ **then**
5         $A^L(s) = a$;
6         $W_L^\uparrow = W_L^\uparrow \cup \mathsf{D}(s)$;
7   **else if** $e \in E_H$ **then**
8   HyperEdgeLower(e);
9   **else if** $e \in E_\Sigma$ **then**
10   SumEdgeLower(e);
11   **else if** $e \in E_C$ **then**
12   CoverEdgeLower(e);

---

rent approximations of the fixed point. If $A^L(s) = \bot$ ($A^U(s) = \top$) then configuration s has no under-approximation (over-approximation) yet. $W_\alpha^\downarrow$ and $W_\alpha^\uparrow$ are sets containing all edges to be processed for exploration and back-propagation, respectively. For a sum-edge (s, T) with $T = \{(\boldsymbol{w}_1, p_1, t_1), \ldots (\boldsymbol{w}_j, p_j, t_j)\}$, $\Sigma_\Delta^\alpha(s)(t_i)$ contains the contribution from the partial sum-edge $(s, \boldsymbol{w}_i, p_i, t_i)$ to the assignment of s. For two configuration $s, t \in C$, $s \in R^\alpha(t)$ indicates that the assignment to s, $A^\alpha(s)$ is dependent on the assignment to t, $A^\alpha(t)$ and that $A^\alpha(t)$ was changed since the last update to $A^\alpha(s)$. When processing an edge e with s as the source ($\mathsf{source}(e) = s$), we can thus safely skip any $t \in \mathsf{targets}(e)$ for which $s \notin R^\alpha(t)$, when updating $A^\alpha(s)$. We will refer to $R^\alpha(t)$ as the *read list* of t. a_{def}^α is the default assignment given to newly discovered configurations and a_{max}^α is the maximal possible assignment any configuration can get. All data structures are initialized in Algorithm 1 and are used throughout Algorithms 1–3. For any edge e, we let $\mathsf{source}(e)$ be its source configuration and $\mathsf{targets}(e) = \{t \mid \mathsf{source}(e) \leadsto t\}$ be its set of targets. For any configuration s we let $\mathsf{succ}(s) = \{(s, T) \in E_H \cup E_\Sigma\} \cup \{(s, \boldsymbol{w}, \triangleright, p, t) \in E_C\}$ be the set of edge-successors of s and $\mathsf{D}(s) = \{e \mid e \in E_H \cup E_\Sigma \cup E_C \wedge s \in \mathsf{targets}(e)\}$ the set of edges dependent on the assignment to s. Informally, if the assignment to s is changed, edges from $\mathsf{D}(s)$ should be processed.

For edge processing, we utilize helper functions. Algorithm 3 shows the pseudo-code. We use InitLower(t) when a new target t is discovered. The assignment of t is set to the specified default value a_{def}^L and a forward exploration is prepared from t by adding all successors of t to $W_L^\downarrow$. Finally, t is added to all relevant read lists. BackPropLower(s, a_{new}) is used when updating assignment $A^L(s)$ to a_{new}. If it cannot be further improved, $Crt(s) = a_{new}$. Back-propagation is prepared by adding all dependent edges, $D(s)$, to $W_L^\uparrow$. If the source of any such edge has not been discovered and therefore has assignment $\perp$, it is

---

Algorithm 3. Helper functions

```
1 function InitLower(s):
2       A^L(s) = a_def^L;
3       W_L^↓ = W_L^↓ ∪ succ(s);
4       foreach e ∈ succ(s) do
5           foreach t ∈ targets(e) do
6               if A^L(t) ≠ ⊥ then
7                   R^L(t) = R^L(t) ∪ {s};

8 function BackPropLower(s, a_new):
9       foreach e ∈ D(s) do
10          if A^L(source(e)) = ⊥ then
11              InitLower(source(e));
12          R^L(s) = R^L(s) ∪ {source(e)};
13          W_L^↑ = W_L^↑ ∪ {e};
14      if a_new = a_max^L then
15          Crt(s) = a_max^L;
```

---

initialized. Finally, for any edge in $D(s)$, the newly updated assignment should be read. Hence the read list of s, $R^L(s)$ is updated to include the sources of all such edges.

We now present our termination and correctness theorems, saying that the while loop in Algorithm 1 terminates and that the computed assignments for explored nodes are equal to the assignment given by the minimal fixed-point $A_{\min}$, within the given precision $\boldsymbol{k}$.

Lemma 1 (Termination). *The local algorithm (Algorithm 1) terminates with*

$$(W_L^\downarrow \cup W_L^\uparrow) = \emptyset \ or \ (W_U^\downarrow \cup W_U^\uparrow) = \emptyset.$$

Theorem 3 (Correctness). *Upon termination, the local algorithm has computed assignments A^L, A^U, such that for any $s \in C$,*

- *If $(W_L^\downarrow \cup W_L^\uparrow) = \emptyset$ then $A^L(s) \neq \perp \implies A^L(s) =_k A_{\min}(s)$.*
- *If $(W_U^\downarrow \cup W_U^\uparrow) = \emptyset$ then $A^U(s) \neq \top \implies A^U(s) =_k A_{\min}(s)$.*

5   Experiments

Both the local and global algorithm have been implemented in a prototype tool written in Python. For both algorithms, we use two separate processes to compute the under- and over-approximations in parallel. For the local algorithm, successors of configurations are generated on-the-fly. Both algorithms terminate when the root configuration is fixed. For the local algorithm we may also terminate when the waiting lists of either the under- or over-approximator are empty.

Algorithm 4. Processing functions for `nextlower`

---

1 **function** HyperEdgeLower($e = (s, T)$):
2   **if** $\exists t \in T.A^L(t) = \mathbb{0}$ **then return** ;
3   **else if** $\exists t \in T.A(t)^L = \bot$ **then** InitLower(t) ;
4   **else**
5        $a = \bigsqcup\{\bigsqcap\{A^L(t) \mid t \in T\}, A^L(s)\}$;
6   **if** $a \sqsupseteq_k A^L(s)$ **then**
7   BackPropLower(s, a);
8        $A^L(s) = a$;
9 **function** SumEdgeLower($e = (s, T)$):
10    $a = A^L(s)$;
11   **foreach** $(w, p, t) \in T$ **do**
12   **if** $A^L(t) \neq \bot \wedge s \in R^L(t)$ **then**
13          $R^L(t) = R^L(t) \setminus \{s\}$;
14          $\Delta^{new} = \text{shift}_{w,p,0}(A^L(t))$;
15          $\Delta^{old} = \Sigma^L_\Delta(s)(t)$;
16   **if** $\Delta^{new} \neq_k \Delta^{old}$ **then**
17             $a = a + (\Delta^{new} - \Delta^{old})$;
18             $\Sigma^L_\Delta(s)(t) = \Delta^{new}$;
19   **if** $a \sqsupseteq_k A^L(s)$ **then**
20   BackPropLower(s, a);
21    $A^L(s) = a$;
22   **if** $\exists(w, p, t) \in T.A^L(t) = \bot$ **then** InitLower(t) ;
23   **if** $\exists(w, p, t) \in T.A^L(t) = \bot$ **then** $W^\downarrow_L = W^\downarrow_L \cup \{e\}$;
24 **function** CoverEdgeLower($e = (s, k, \rhd, \lambda, t)$):
25   **if** $A^L(t) = \bot$ **then** InitLower(t) ;
26   **if** $A^L(t)(k) \rhd \lambda$ and $A^L(s) \neq \mathbb{1}$ **then**
27   BackPropLower($s, \mathbb{1}$);
28       $A^L(s) = \mathbb{1}$;

For experimental evaluation, our prototype tool supports DTMC models (with transition rewards/costs), written in the PRISM language [14]. PRISM cannot directly handle our models with weights from $\mathbb{N}^n$ with $n > 1$. To this end, we interpret multiple reward structures as defining a vector in n dimensions, with n being the number of reward structures. Hence one can define a proper PWKS in the PRISM language and use it as input to our tool.

We run both the global and local algorithm on two PRISM models (synchronous leader election [10] and the bounded retransmission protocol [9]), derived from DTMC models of the PRISM benchmark suite [15]. All models can be found online at http://people.cs.aau.dk/~am/nfm19/code/prism_ex/.

For all models, the model-checking query is an instance of cost-bounded probabilistic reachability: $m \models \mathcal{P}_{\triangleright\lambda}(tt\, U_{\leq k}\, prop)$, where m is the initial state of the underlying DTMC and $prop$ is a label assigned to all states satisfying the property of interest. Our tool invokes PRISM on a given model and exports the underlying DTMC (with transition rewards), which our tool then parses to construct a PWKS. For each instantiation of a PRISM model we run four queries with a fixed cost-bound $\boldsymbol{k} \in \mathbb{N}^n$ where n is the arity. These four queries differ in the comparison of probabilities in the formula. For comparator and probability we use the following four configurations: $> p + \frac{1-p}{10}$, $> p - \frac{p}{10}$, > 0, and ≥ 1; where p is the exact probability of picking a path from state m, that satisfies the given until-formula. The expressions > 0 and ≥ 1 encode existential and universal quantification, respectively.

5.1   Results

We evaluate different hyper-parameters on the case-studies consisting of data-structures for the waiting lists and the weights associated with preferring forward exploration to back-propagation. For waiting lists we experimented with *queues* (Q), *stacks* (S), and *counters* (C), where a counter is a priority queue with priority given by the number of times an element is added. We weigh the decision of either forward exploring or back-propagating with integers weights in $[1,5]$.

For what follows, we present only the results of experiments involving the global algorithm and the local algorithm with the best hyper-parameters. We will use weighted tuples of data-structures to indicate the hyper-parameters of the local algorithm, e.g. (Q1,S3) would indicate that we used the local algorithm with a *queue* for forward exploration, a *stack* for backwards propagation, and that when given the choice, we are 3 times more likely to back-propagate than forward explore. Additionally, we will use GMC to indicate the use of the global algorithm. All experiments were run using 2 cores of an AMD Opteron 6376 processor allowing for parallelism.

Synchronous Leader Election. Table 2 shows our results for synchronous leader election protocol. The data is an average over the run times using 1-, 2-, and 3-dimensional weights. We find that the local algorithm outperforms the global one, with average speedups of around 6 when answering the non-existential or - universal queries. For the existential and universal queries we find that the local algorithm is on average 400 times faster. In Table 3 we compare the relative speedup across 1-, 2-, and 3-dimensional weights.

Table 2. Results for synchronous leader election.

Leader election, N = number of processes, K = number of probabilistic choices								
N	K	$> p + \frac{1-p}{10}$		$> p - \frac{p}{10}$		> 0		≥ 1	
		GMC	Q5,Q1	GMC	C5,Q1	GMC	Q1,C3	GMC	Q1,C3
4	3	10.59	1.71	12.41	2.32	6.01	0.09	1.60	0.11
	4	39.98	9.49	47.96	6.33	17.51	0.13	42.22	0.23
	5	45.25	11.70	101.87	13.95	46.96	0.13	104.22	0.15
	6	102.77	20.40	264.65	46.69	118.33	0.29	275.88	0.28
	8	259.07	121.42	657.20	200.43	354.57	0.94	752.16	0.83
5	2	7.80	0.91	9.60	0.93	3.92	0.09	10.53	0.17
	3	44.56	9.13	57.28	9.59	22.89	0.13	60.59	0.16
	4	227.02	25.64	265.09	34.36	117.54	0.35	264.75	0.36
	5	385.77	110.85	958.42	179.50	394.71	0.67	93.05	0.67
	6	921.52	395.49	2040.88	433.37	1182.46	1.71	283.81	1.91
6	2	21.45	2.29	29.47	2.68	10.31	0.08	30.68	0.17
	3	199.64	73.93	247.00	71.63	100.63	0.30	23.18	0.36
	4	1670.63	315.67	1742.46	346.03	724.10	0.89	2008.89	0.88

Table 3. Average relative speedup for synchronous leader election per arity.

Leader election				
Arity	GMC/(Q5,Q1)		GMC/(Q1,C3)	
	$> p + \frac{1-p}{10}$	$> p - \frac{p}{10}$	> 0	≥ 1
1	4.65	6.34	112.71	144.92
2	5.40	7.69	230.29	343.69
3	6.09	9.21	364.82	503.89

Bounded Retransmission Protocol. Table 4 shows our results for the bounded retransmission protocol. All data is for 1-dimensional weights. Again, we find that the local algorithm outperforms the global. In the unsatisfied and satisfied case we see speedups averaging around 25 and 30, respectively. For the existential queries we find the local algorithm to be, on average, 850 times faster than the global. In the universal case we see only a speedup of about 30.

Table 4. Results for the bounded retransmission protocol.

\multicolumn{2}{}{BRP, M = max number of retransmissions, N = number of chunks}								
N	M	$> p + \frac{1-p}{10}$		$> p - \frac{p}{10}$		> 0		≥ 1	
		GMC	S1,S3	GMC	S1,S3	GMC	S1,Q5	GMC	S1,S3
16	2	191.20	11.93	229.28	6.94	8.02	0.03	227.62	6.75
	3	253.99	16.80	313.45	9.65	13.15	0.03	315.30	9.64
	4	327.73	20.65	395.51	11.37	18.78	0.03	396.06	11.34
	5	503.98	23.59	621.86	13.72	33.50	0.04	593.56	13.57
32	2	420.88	27.26	507.14	14.71	16.92	0.03	506.48	14.58
	3	522.58	37.05	650.74	19.59	26.10	0.03	649.89	19.32
	4	864.38	49.78	660.95	24.41	49.91	0.04	669.76	24.26
	5	810.14	52.34	959.49	28.76	52.58	0.05	958.92	28.87
62	2	797.97	54.61	961.92	28.87	31.13	0.04	961.50	28.67
	3	1051.64	75.64	1319.02	38.43	51.60	0.05	n/a	37.96
	4	1339.32	92.68	1631.08	47.91	75.77	0.05	n/a	47.50
	5	1610.09	108.73	1923.06	57.34	102.77	0.06	n/a	57.18

6   Conclusion

We have presented two approaches for model-checking a variant of PCTL, interpreted over probabilistic weighted Kripke structures. We introduce a reduction to fixed-point computations on symbolic dependency graphs where nodes represent model-checking problems and edges explicitly encode dependencies among said problems. The first approach, the global algorithm, is a minor extension of the algorithm presented in [18] which iteratively computes an update to each node of the entire graph. The second approach, the local algorithm, is a novel adaptation of existing dependency graph algorithms, to our probabilistic weighted domain. The algorithm performs a local search-like exploration of the graph and lends itself to an on-the-fly unfolding. Both algorithms were implemented in a prototype tool, using Interval Decision Diagrams (IDDs) as the back-end data-structure. It is shown that the local algorithm generally outperforms the global algorithm, especially in cases where a complete exploration of the model is not needed to prove or disprove a property of the model. Our work could be extended to incorporate negation in the logic as shown in [6].

Future work includes investigating clever memoization schemes to deal with the expensive IDD operations, as has been previously done for BDDs. Preliminary experiments by the authors with a naïve caching mechanism has shown that it provides a significant speed-up, especially for the global algorithm. A process calculus is another direction that could be promising as our local approach lends itself to a local-unfolding of the model, instead of an up-front construction of the entire state-space. Lastly, more research is required to develop better search strategies such that the local algorithm more robustly can efficiently solve most queries.

References

1. Andova, S., Hermanns, H., Katoen, J.-P.: Discrete-time rewards model-checked. In: Larsen, K.G., Niebert, P. (eds.) FORMATS 2003. LNCS, vol. 2791, pp. 88–104. Springer, Heidelberg (2004). https://doi.org/10.1007/978-3-540-40903-8_8

2. Bacci, G., Hansen, M., Larsen, K.G.: On the verification of weighted kripke structures under uncertainty. In: McIver, A., Horvath, A. (eds.) QEST 2018. LNCS, vol. 11024, pp. 71–86. Springer, Cham (2018). https://doi.org/10.1007/978-3-319-99154-2_5

3. Baier, C., Katoen, J.: Principles of Model Checking. MIT Press, Cambridge (2008)

4. Cassez, F., David, A., Fleury, E., Larsen, K.G., Lime, D.: Efficient on-the-fly algorithms for the analysis of timed games. In: Abadi, M., de Alfaro, L. (eds.) CONCUR 2005. LNCS, vol. 3653, pp. 66–80. Springer, Heidelberg (2005). https://doi.org/10.1007/11539452_9

5. Christoffersen, P., Hansen, M., Mariegaard, A., Ringsmose, J.T., Larsen, K.G., Mardare, R.: Parametric verification of weighted systems. In: 2nd International Workshop on Synthesis of Complex Parameters, SynCoP 2015, London, United Kingdom, 11 April 2015, pp. 77–90 (2015). https://doi.org/10.4230/OASIcs.SynCoP.2015.77

6. Dalsgaard, A.E., et al.: A distributed fixed-point algorithm for extended dependency graphs. Fundam. Inform. **161**(4), 351–381 (2018). https://doi.org/10.3233/FI-2018-1707

7. Dehnert, C., Junges, S., Katoen, J.-P., Volk, M.: A STORM is coming: a modern probabilistic model checker. In: Majumdar, R., Kunčak, V. (eds.) CAV 2017, Part II. LNCS, vol. 10427, pp. 592–600. Springer, Cham (2017). https://doi.org/10.1007/978-3-319-63390-9_31

8. Hansson, H., Jonsson, B.: A logic for reasoning about time and reliability. Formal Asp. Comput. **6**(5), 512–535 (1994). https://doi.org/10.1007/BF01211866

9. Helmink, L., Sellink, M.P.A., Vaandrager, F.W.: Proof-checking a data link protocol. In: Barendregt, H., Nipkow, T. (eds.) TYPES 1993. LNCS, vol. 806, pp. 127–165. Springer, Heidelberg (1994). https://doi.org/10.1007/3-540-58085-9_75

10. Itai, A., Rodeh, M.: Symmetry breaking in distributed networks. Inf. Comput. **88**(1), 60–87 (1990). https://doi.org/10.1016/0890-5401(90)90004-2

11. Jensen, J.F., Larsen, K.G., Srba, J., Oestergaard, L.K.: Efficient model-checking of weighted CTL with upper-bound constraints. STTT **18**(4), 409–426 (2016). https://doi.org/10.1007/s10009-014-0359-5

12. Katoen, J., Khattri, M., Zapreev, I.S.: A Markov reward model checker. In: Second International Conference on the Quantitative Evaluaiton of Systems (QEST 2005), Torino, Italy, 19–22 September 2005, pp. 243–244 (2005). https://doi.org/10.1109/QEST.2005.2

13. Kwiatkowska, M., Norman, G., Parker, D.: Stochastic model checking. In: Bernardo, M., Hillston, J. (eds.) SFM 2007. LNCS, vol. 4486, pp. 220–270. Springer, Heidelberg (2007). https://doi.org/10.1007/978-3-540-72522-0_6

14. Kwiatkowska, M., Norman, G., Parker, D.: PRISM 4.0: verification of probabilistic real-time systems. In: Gopalakrishnan, G., Qadeer, S. (eds.) CAV 2011. LNCS, vol. 6806, pp. 585–591. Springer, Heidelberg (2011). https://doi.org/10.1007/978-3-642-22110-1_47

15. Kwiatkowska, M.Z., Norman, G., Parker, D.: The PRISM benchmark suite. In: Ninth International Conference on Quantitative Evaluation of Systems, QEST 2012, London, United Kingdom, 17–20 September 2012, pp. 203–204 (2012). https://doi.org/10.1109/QEST.2012.14

16. Larsen, K.G., Pettersson, P., Yi, W.: UPPAAL in a nutshell. STTT **1**(1–2), 134–152 (1997). https://doi.org/10.1007/s100090050010
17. Liu, X., Smolka, S.A.: Simple linear-time algorithms for minimal fixed points. In: Larsen, K.G., Skyum, S., Winskel, G. (eds.) ICALP 1998. LNCS, vol. 1443, pp. 53–66. Springer, Heidelberg (1998). https://doi.org/10.1007/BFb0055040
18. Mariegaard, A., Larsen, K.G.: Symbolic dependency graphs for PCTL$_{\leq}^{\geq}$ model-checking. In: Abate, A., Geeraerts, G. (eds.) FORMATS 2017. LNCS, vol. 10419, pp. 153–169. Springer, Cham (2017). https://doi.org/10.1007/978-3-319-65765-3_9
19. Strehl, K., Thiele, L.: Symbolic model checking of process networks using interval diagram techniques. In: Proceedings of the 1998 IEEE/ACM International Conference on Computer-Aided Design, ICCAD 1998, San Jose, CA, USA, 8–12 November 1998, pp. 686–692 (1998). https://doi.org/10.1145/288548.289117
20. Tarski, A., et al.: A lattice-theoretical fixpoint theorem and its applications. Pac. J. Math. **5**(2), 285–309 (1955)

Composing Symmetry Propagation and Effective Symmetry Breaking for SAT Solving

Hakan Metin[1]([✉]), Souheib Baarir[1,2], and Fabrice Kordon[1]

[1] Sorbonne Université, CNRS UMR 7606 LIP6, 75005 Paris, France
{hakan.metin,souheib.baarir,fabrice.kordon}@lip6.fr
[2] Université Paris Nanterre, Nanterre, France

Abstract. SAT solving is an active research area aiming at finding solutions to a large variety of problems. Propositional Satisfiability problems often exhibit symmetry properties, and exploiting them extends the class of problems that state-of-the-art solvers can handle.

Two classes of approaches have been developed to take benefit of these symmetries: Static and Dynamic Symmetry Breaking based approaches. They bring benefits for complementary classes of problems. However, and to the best of our knowledge, no tentative has been made to combine them.

In this paper, we study the theoretical and practical aspects of the composition of two of these approaches, namely Symmetry Propagation and Effective Symmetry Breaking. Extensive experiments conducted on symmetric problems extracted from the last seven editions of the SAT contest show the effectiveness of such a composition on many symmetrical problems.

Keywords: Dynamic symmetry breaking · Symmetry propagation · Effective Symmetry Breaking Predicates · Boolean satisfiability

1 Introduction

Context. Nowadays, Boolean satisfiability (SAT) is an active research area finding its applications in many contexts such as planning decision [13], hardware and software verification [3], cryptology [17], computational biology [15], etc. Hence, the development of approaches that could treat increasingly challenging SAT problems has become a focus.

State-of-the-art complete SAT solvers rely on the well-known *Conflict Driven Clause Learning (CDCL)* algorithm [16], itself inspired from the Davis–PutnamLogemann–Loveland algorithm [5]. These are backtracking based search algorithms that can be associated to numerous heuristics/optimisations pruning parts of the explored search tree. In this paper, we are interested in exploiting the symmetry properties of SAT problems to perform such pruning.

© Springer Nature Switzerland AG 2019
J. M. Badger and K. Y. Rozier (Eds.): NFM 2019, LNCS 11460, pp. 316–332, 2019.
https://doi.org/10.1007/978-3-030-20652-9_21

The Problem. SAT problems often exhibit symmetries[1], and not taking them into account forces solvers to needlessly explore isomorphic parts of the search space.

For example, the "pigeonhole problem" (where n pigeons are put into $n-1$ holes, with the constraint that each pigeon must be in a different hole) is a highly symmetric problem. Indeed, all the pigeons (resp. holes) are swappable without changing the initial problem. Trying to solve it with a standard SAT solver, like MiniSAT [9], turns out to be very time consuming (and even impossible, in reasonable time, for high values of n). Here, such a standard solver ignores the symmetries of the problem, and then potentially tries all variable combinations. This eventually leads to a combinatorial explosion.

Symmetries of a SAT problem are classically obtained through a reduction to an equivalent graph automorphism problem. Technically, the SAT problem is converted to a colored graph, then it is passed to a tool, like saucy3 [12] or bliss [11], to compute its automorphism group.

A common approach to exploit such symmetries is to pre-compute and enrich the original SAT problem with *symmetry breaking predicates (sbp)*. These added predicates will prevent the solver from visiting equivalent (isomorphic) parts that eventually yield the same results [1,4]. This technique, called *static symmetry breaking*, has been implemented first in the state-of-the-art tool SHATTER [2] and then improved in BREAKID [7]. However, while giving excellent results on numerous symmetric problems, these approaches still fail to solve some classes of symmetric problems.

Another class of approaches exists, known as *dynamic symmetry breaking* techniques. They operate during the exploration of the search tree. It concerns, to mention but a few, the injection of symmetric versions of *learned clauses* [6,20], particular classes of symmetries [19], or speeding up the search by inferring symmetric facts [8]. These approaches succeeded in treating particular and hand crafted problems but, to the best of our knowledge, none of them is competitive face to the *static symmetry breaking* methods.

Goal. Recently, we developed an approach that reuses the principles of the static approaches, but operates dynamically (namely, the effective symmetry breaking approach [18]): the symmetries are broken during the search process without any pre-generation of the *sbp*. The main advantage of this technique is to cope with the heavy (and potentially blocking) pre-generation phase of the static-based approaches. It also gives more flexibility for adjusting some parameters on the fly. The evaluation of our approach on the symmetric formulas of six SAT contests shows that it outperforms the state-of-the-art techniques in terms of the number of solved instances.

Nevertheless, we also observed that many formulas easily solved by the pure dynamic approaches remained unsolvable by our approach and vice-versa. This is particularly true with the *symmetry propagation* technique developed by Devriendt et al. [8].

---

[1] Roughly speaking, a SAT problem exhibits symmetries when it is possible to swap some variables while keeping the original problem unchanged.

Hence, our goal is to explore the composition of our algorithm with the *symmetry propagation* technique in a new approach that would mix the advantages of the two classes of techniques while alleviating their drawbacks. At first sight, the two approaches appear to be orthogonal, and hence could be mixed easily. However, as we show in the rest of the paper, this is not completely true: both theoretical and practical issues have to be analysed and solved to get a running complementarity. The resulting algorithm provides better performances on the 1400 symmetric formulas extracted from the last seven editions of the SAT contest.

Content of the Paper. Section 2 presents the state of the art and definitions. Section 3 introduces the key notion of *local symmetries*, that is a prerequisite to the definition of a combo algorithm. Section 4 discusses the implementation and evaluation of our proposition before a conclusion in Sect. 5.

2   State of the Art and Definitions

This section introduces some definitions. First, we define the problem of Boolean satisfiability. Then, we recall our approach [18] and the one of Devriendt et al. [8]. Finally, we state the assumptions on which we base our composed solution.

2.1   Basics on Boolean Satisfiability

A *Boolean variable*, or *propositional variable*, is a variable that has two possible values: true or false (noted $\top$ or $\bot$, respectively). A *literal* l is a propositional variable or its negation. For a given variable x, the positive literal is represented by x and the negative one by $\neg x$. A *clause* ω is a finite disjunction of literals represented equivalently by $\omega = \bigvee_{i=1}^{k} l_i$ or the set of its literals $\omega = \{l_i\}_{i \in [\![1,k]\!]}$. A clause with a single literal is called *unit clause*. A *conjunctive normal form (CNF) formula* φ is a finite conjunction of clauses. A CNF can be either noted $\varphi = \bigwedge_{i=1}^{k} \omega_i$ or $\varphi = \{\omega_i\}_{i \in [\![1,k]\!]}$. We denote $\mathcal{V}_\varphi$ ($\mathcal{L}_\varphi$) the set of variables (literals) used in φ (the index in $\mathcal{V}_\varphi$ and $\mathcal{L}_\varphi$ is usually omitted when clear from context).

For a given formula φ, an *assignment* of the variables of φ is a function $\alpha : \mathcal{V} \mapsto \{\top, \bot\}$. As usual, α is *total*, or *complete*, when all elements of $\mathcal{V}$ have an image by α, otherwise it is *partial*. By abuse of notation, an assignment is often represented by the set of its true literals. The set of all (possibly partial) assignments of $\mathcal{V}$ is noted $Ass(\mathcal{V})$.

The assignment α *satisfies* the clause ω, denoted $\alpha \models \omega$, if $\alpha \cap \omega \neq \emptyset$. The assignment α satisfies the propositional formula φ, denoted $\alpha \models \varphi$, if α satisfies all the clauses of φ. Note that a formula may be satisfied by a partial assignment. A formula is said to be *satisfiable* (SAT) if there is at least one assignment that satisfies it; otherwise the formula is *unsatisfiable* (UNSAT).

When ω is satisfied in all satisfying assignments of φ, we say that ω is a *logical consequence* of φ, and we denote this by $\varphi \vdash \omega$.

Example. Let $\varphi = \{\omega_1 = \{x_1, x_2, x_3\}, \omega_2 = \{x_1, \neg x_2\}, \omega_3 = \{\neg x_1, \neg x_2\}\}$ be a formula. Naturally, $\varphi \vdash \omega_i, \forall i \in [\![1, 3]\!]$. φ is satisfied under the assignment $\alpha = \{x_1, \neg x_2\}$ (meaning $\alpha(x_1) = \top$ and $\alpha(x_2) = \bot$) and is reported to be SAT. Note that the assignment α, making φ SAT, does not need to be complete because x_3 is a *don't care variable* with respect to α.

2.2   Symmetry Group of a Formula

The group of permutations of $\mathcal{V}$ (i.e., bijections from $\mathcal{V}$ to $\mathcal{V}$) is noted $\mathfrak{S}(\mathcal{V})$. The group $\mathfrak{S}(\mathcal{V})$ naturally acts on the set of literals: for $g \in \mathfrak{S}(\mathcal{V})$ and a literal $\ell \in \mathcal{L}$, $g.\ell = g(\ell)$ if ℓ is a positive literal, $g.\ell = \neg g(\neg \ell)$ if ℓ is a negative literal.

The group $\mathfrak{S}(\mathcal{V})$ also acts on (partial) assignments of $\mathcal{V}$ as follows: for $g \in \mathfrak{S}(\mathcal{V})$, $\alpha \in Ass(\mathcal{V})$, $g.\alpha = \{g.\ell \mid \ell \in \alpha\}$. Let φ be a formula, and $g \in \mathfrak{S}(\mathcal{V})$.

We say that $g \in \mathfrak{S}(\mathcal{V})$ is a symmetry of φ if for every *complete* assignment α, $\alpha \models \varphi$ if and only if $g.\alpha \models \varphi$. The set of symmetries of φ is noted $S(\varphi) \subseteq \mathfrak{S}(\mathcal{V})$.

Let G be a subgroup of $\mathfrak{S}(\mathcal{V})$. The *orbit of α under G* (or simply the *orbit of α* when G is clear from the context) is the set $[\alpha]_G = \{g.\alpha \mid g \in G\}$.

Given a total order, noted $\prec$, on the set $\mathcal{V}$ (naturally extended on the total assignments of $Ass(\mathcal{V})$), the lexicographic leader (*lex-leader* for short) of an orbit $[\alpha]_G$ is the minimal/maximal element of $[\alpha]_G$ w.r.t. $\prec$.

2.3   Approach Based on Effective Symmetry Breaking

When using the approach based on symmetry breaking predicates to optimise the solving of a symmetric SAT problem, the main idea is to limit the search tree exploration to only one assignment per orbit (e.g., each *lex-leader*). However, finding the *lex-leader* of an orbit is computationally hard [14]. Instead, a best effort approach is commonly used [2,7].

The one we developed in [18], which relies on esbp (*Effective Symmetry Breaking Predicate*), deals with the notions of *reducer*, *inactive* and *active* permutation with respect to an assignment α. These notions keep track of the status of a permutation, during the solving, to detect non *lex-leader* assignments as soon as possible.

This approach is then opportunistic and thus avoids the pre-generation of sbp that could have a dramatical effects of the overall performances of the classical static symmetry breaking approaches.

Definition 1. *A permutation g is a* reducer *of an assignment α if $g.\alpha \prec \alpha$ (hence α cannot be the lex-leader of its orbit because g reduces α and all its extensions). g is* inactive *on α when $\alpha \prec g.\alpha$ (so, g cannot reduce α and all its extensions). A symmetry is said to be* active *with respect to α when it is neither inactive nor a reducer of α.*

When g is a *reducer* of α we can define a predicate contradicting α yet preserves the satisfiability of the formula. Such a predicate will be used to discard α, and all its extensions, from a further visit, thus pruning the search tree.

Proposition 1. *Let $\alpha \in Ass(\mathcal{V})$, and $g \in \mathfrak{S}(\mathcal{V})$. We say that the formula ψ is an effective symmetry breaking predicate (esbp for short) for α under g if:*

$$\alpha \not\models \psi \text{ and for all } \beta \in Ass(\mathcal{V}), \beta \not\models \psi \Rightarrow g.\beta \prec \beta$$

The following theorem states the equi-satisfiability of the original formula φ with the one augmented with esbps.

Theorem 1. *Let φ be a formula and ψ an ebsp for some assignment α under $g \in S(\varphi)$. Then, φ and $\varphi \cup \psi$ are equi-satisfiable.*

On the fly efficient algorithms tracking the status of a permutation (reducer, active and inactive) and the generation of esbps along with the correctness proofs are given in [18].

The extensive experiments we conducted state that this approach solves many hard symmetrical problems. Moreover it outperformed the state-of-the-art, dynamic and static, symmetry breaking techniques when considering the total number of solved instances.

However, we observed it fails to solve some problems that have been trivially concluded by other dynamic symmetry breaking techniques such as the one developed in [8]. We give an overview of this one in the following section.

2.4   Approach Based on Symmetry Propagation

Unlike the approaches based on static symmetry breaking, the technique developed in [8] does not operate any explicit search tree pruning. It tries to accelerate the tree traversal by "transforming some guessing to deductions". Indeed, knowing that the processed problem presents symmetries makes it possible to deduce some values for the variables that would be guessed if those symmetries were ignored. These deductions will reduce the overall tree traversal depth and hence eventually accelerate the solving process.

Let us recall here the definitions that are important for the rest of this work.

Proposition 2. *Let φ be a formula, α an assignment and l a literal. If g is a symmetry (permutation) of $\varphi \cup \alpha$ and $\varphi \cup \alpha \vdash \{l\}$, then $\varphi \cup \alpha \vdash g.\{l\}$ is also true.*

In other words, if we can deduce a fact (here, the unitary clause $\{l\}$) using $\varphi \cup \alpha$ then the symmetrical of this fact is also true (the unitary clause $\{g.l\}$).

The critical point here is to detect the permutations that are actually symmetries of $\varphi \cup \alpha$. Authors of this approach developed an efficient algorithm that detects such symmetries. It relies on the following proposition.

Proposition 3. *Let φ be a formula, α an assignment. If there exists a subset $\delta \subseteq \alpha$ and a symmetry g of φ such that $g.\delta \subseteq \alpha$ and $\varphi \cup \delta \vdash \varphi \cup \alpha$, then g is also a symmetry of $\varphi \cup \alpha$.*

In other words, we can detect with a minimal effort, the symmetries of $\varphi \cup \alpha$ by keeping track of the set of variables δ. Technically, in a state-of-the-art complete SAT solving algorithms, δ is the set of decision variables.

The experimental results show that this technique behaves very well on many highly symmetrical problems.

2.5   Summary

The two presented techniques operate dynamically, by injecting some breaking predicates for the one and deducing symmetrical facts for the other. They perform well on different classes of symmetrical SAT problems.

So, one can raise the following questions: (1) is it possible to combine them? (2) If it is the case, how does the combo behave? In the rest of this paper, we try to answer these questions.

3   A Composed Technique

Since the approach based on symmetry propagation (later called SPA) focuses on accelerating the tree traversal and the approach based on effective symmetry breaking (later called ESBA) targets to prune the tree traversal, the question of combining these approaches, to solve a formula φ, can be reformulated as: *is it possible to accelerate the traversal while pruning the tree?* More precisely, *is there room to apply Propositions 2 and 3 in the presence of espbs?*

3.1   Theoretical Foundations

To answer the previous questions, we analyse the evolution of φ during its solving. In ESBA, φ evolves, incrementally, to an equi-satisfiable formula of the form $\varphi \equiv \varphi \cup \varphi_e \cup \varphi_d$, where φ_e is a set of injected esbps and φ_d is a set of deduced clauses (logical consequences). Both sets are modified continuously during the solving. Hence, to be able to compose ESBA with SPA, we have to study Propositions 2 and 3, when replacing φ by $\varphi' = \varphi \cup \varphi_e \cup \varphi_d$. We thus have to consider in these propositions, the symmetries of φ' as allowed permutations in place of those of φ.

A first naive solution could be to recompute, dynamically, the set $S(\varphi \cup \varphi_e \cup \varphi_d)$ for each new $\varphi_e \cup \varphi_d$, but this would be an intractable solution generating a huge complexity.

A computationally less expensive solution would be to keep track of all globally unbroken symmetries as the clauses of φ_e are injected during the solving process: considering formula φ and a set of esbps φ_e then the set of global unbroken symmetries is $GUS = \bigcap_{w_e \in \varphi_e} Stab(w_e) \cap S(\varphi)$ where $Stab(w_e) = \{g \in \mathfrak{S}(V) \mid$

$\omega_e = g.\omega_e\}$ is the stabilizer set of ω_e and $S(\varphi)$ is the set of symmetries of φ. Since $\varphi \cup \varphi_e \vdash \varphi_d$, then GUS is a valid set of symmetries for $\varphi \cup \varphi_e \cup \varphi_d$. Then, (1) each time a new set of esbp clauses is added, its stabilizer will be used to reduce GUS; (2) conversely, when a set of esbp clauses is reduced[2], GUS cannot be enlarged by the recovered broken symmetries because of the retrieved set: *at that point, we do not know which symmetries become valid!*

As a consequence, the set of globally unbroken symmetries will converge very quickly to the empty set. At this point, SPA will be blocked for the rest of the solving process without any chance to recover. Therefore, this solution is of limited interest in practice.

We propose here to improve aforementioned solution by alleviating the issue cited in point (2). We first present the intuition, then we will detail and formalize it.

Consider formula φ' as before. It can be rewritten as: $\varphi' = \varphi \bigcup_i (\varphi_e^i \cup \varphi_d^i)$ such that $\varphi_e \cup \varphi_d = \bigcup_i (\varphi_e^i \cup \varphi_d^i)$ and $\varphi \cup \varphi_e^i \vdash \varphi_d^i$ for all i. So, $GUS_i = \bigcap_{\omega_e \in \varphi_e^i} Stab(\omega_e) \cap S(\varphi)$ is a valid set of symmetries for the sub-formula $\varphi \cup \varphi_e^i \cup \varphi_d^i$, and GUS can be obtained by $GUS = \bigcap_i GUS_i$. If some esbp clauses are added to φ', then the new GUS is computed as described in (1). The novelty here comes with the retrieval of some set of clauses: by keeping track of the symmetries associated to each sub-formula (GUS_i), it is now easy to recompute a valid set of symmetries for φ' when some set $\varphi_e^k \cup \varphi_d^k$ is retrieved. It suffices to operate the intersection on the valid symmetries of the rest of the sub-formulas: $GUS = \bigcap_{i \neq k} GUS_i$.

Just say your approach keeps track of a set of particular symmetries for each clause. For a deduced clause, this set of symmetries captures which esbp's were involved in a deduced clause's derivation. The intersection of these sets is a superset of the globally unbroken symmetries, and a strict superset after clause deletion.

The general and formal framework that embodies the above idea is given by the following. It first relies on the notion of *local symmetries* that we introduce in Definition 2.

Definition 2. *Let φ be a formula. We define $L_{\omega,\varphi}$, the set of local symmetries for a clause ω, and with respect to a formula φ, as follows:*

$$L_{\omega,\varphi} = \{g \in \mathfrak{S}(\mathcal{V}) \mid \varphi \vdash g.\omega\}$$

$L_{\omega,\varphi}$ is local since the set of permutations applies locally to ω. It is then straightforward to deduce the next proposition that gives us a practical framework to compute, incrementally, a set of symmetries for a formula (by using the intersection of all local symmetries).

Proposition 4. *Let φ be a formula. Then, $\bigcap_{\omega \in \varphi} L_{\omega,\varphi} \subseteq S(\varphi)$.*

---

[2] In classical CDCL algorithm, this can be due to a back-jump or a restart.

Proof. Let φ be a formula. Then, $\forall \omega \in \varphi, \forall g \in L_{\omega,\varphi}, \varphi \vdash g.\varphi$. So, $\forall g \in \bigcap_{\omega \in \varphi} L_{\omega,\varphi}, \varphi \vdash g.\varphi$. This is combined with the fact that the number of satisfying assignments for a formula is not changed by permuting the variables of the formula, we have $g.\varphi \vdash \varphi$. Hence $\varphi \equiv g.\varphi$, and $g \in S(\varphi)$ (by definition).

Using this proposition, it becomes easy to reconsider the symmetries on-the-fly: each time a new clause ω is added to the formula φ, we can just operate an intersection between $L_{\omega,\varphi}$ and $\bigcap_{\omega' \in \varphi} L_{\omega',\varphi}$ to get a new set of valid symmetries for $\varphi \cup \{\omega\}$.

Proposition 5 establishes the relationship between the local symmetries of a deduced clause and those of the set of clauses that allow its derivation.

Proposition 5. *Let φ_1 and φ_2 be two formulas, with $\varphi_2 \subseteq \varphi_1$. Let ω be a clause such that $\varphi_2 \vdash \omega$. Then, $(\bigcap_{\omega' \in \varphi_2} L_{\omega',\varphi_1}) \cup Stab(\omega) \subseteq L_{\omega,\varphi_1}$;*

Proof. Let us consider a clause ω and a permutation $g \in (\bigcap_{\omega' \in \varphi_2} L_{\omega',\varphi_1}) \cup Stab(\omega)$. Since, $\varphi_2 \vdash \omega$, then $g.\varphi_2 \vdash g.\omega$. Since $\varphi_1 \vdash \varphi_2 (\varphi_2 \subseteq \varphi_1)$, and $g \in (\bigcap_{\omega' \in \varphi_2} L_{\omega',\varphi_1}) \cup Stab(\omega)$, then we have $\varphi_1 \vdash g.\varphi_2$ (from Definition 2). Hence, $\varphi_1 \vdash g.\varphi_2 \vdash g.\omega$, and then, $g \in L_{\omega,\varphi_1}$ (by definition).

3.2 Practical Considerations

As full $L_{\omega,\varphi}$ sets are hard to compute in general, we give here practical frameworks to their approximation.

Let us come back to the statement, where the formula is $\varphi' = \varphi \cup \varphi_e \cup \varphi_d$, and the symmetries of (the original formula) φ are already known (namely $S(\varphi)$). Hence, the local symmetries of each clause ω can be approximated depending on the belonging of ω to each of three sets φ, φ_e, and φ_d:

1. if $\omega \in \varphi$, this is a clause of the original formula, then we know that $S(\varphi) \subseteq L_{\omega,\varphi'}$ (by definition). So, we can take $S(\varphi)$ as a representative for $L_{\omega,\varphi'}$.
2. if $\omega \in \varphi_e$, this is an esbp clause, and the only local symmetries that we can consider (without any correctness issue) for such a clause is the stabilizing symmetries: $Stab(\omega) = \{g \in \mathfrak{S}(V) \mid \omega = g.\omega\} \subseteq L_{\omega,\varphi'}$;
3. if $\omega \in \varphi_d$, this is a deduced clause, and the set of local symmetries that we propose here can be approximated by $(\bigcap_{\omega' \in \varphi_1} L_{\omega',\varphi'}) \cup Stab(\omega_d)$ (according to Proposition 5), where φ_1 is the set of clauses that derives ω_d.

3.3 Algorithm

This section shows how to integrate the propositions developed in Sect. 3.1 as the basis of our combo approach in a concrete Conflict-Driven Clause Learning (CDCL)-like solver.

We first recall the basics of the CDCL algorithm. Then, we make an overview on the CDCLSym and CDCLSp algorithms that implement, respectively, ESBA and SPA. Finally, we present our combo algorithm.

```
1  function CDCL(φ: CNF formula)
2      returns ⊤ if φ is SAT and ⊥ otherwise
3      dl ← 0 ;                                    // Current decision level
4      while not all variables are assigned do
5          isConflict ← unitPropagation();
6          if isConflict then
7              if dl = 0 then
8                  return ⊥;                       // φ is UNSAT
9              ω ← anlConflict();
10             dl ← bckjmpAndRstrtPolicies();
11             φ ← φ ∪ {ω} ;
12         else
13             assignDecisionLiteral();
14             dl ← dl + 1;
15     return ⊤;                                   // φ is SAT
```

Algorithm 1. The CDCL algorithm.

CDCL (see Algorithm 1) walks a binary search tree. It first applies unit propagation to the formula φ for the current assignment α (line 5). A conflict at level 0 indicates that the formula is not satisfiable, and the algorithm reports it (lines 7–8). If a conflict is detected, it is analysed, which provides a *conflict clause* explaining the reason for the conflict (line 9). This clause is learnt (line 11), as it does not change the satisfiability of φ, and avoids encountering a conflict with the same causes in the future. The analysis is completed by the computation of a backjump point to which the algorithm backtracks (line 10). Finally, if no conflict appears, the algorithm chooses a new decision literal (lines 13–14). The above steps are repeated until the satisfiability status of the formula is determined. Detailing the existing variations for the conflict analysis and for the decision heuristic is out of the scope of this paper.

CDCLSym (see Algorithm 2) implements ESBA and borrows its main structure from CDCL. All symmetry-based actions are operated by the symmetry controller component (symCtrl) passed as a parameter. It controls all partial assignments (crtAss) and detects non lex-leading ones as soon as possible (lines 6–7). If it is the case, it generates an esbp clause (line 14) to be injected as an (ordinary) learnt clause (line 16). When a back-jump is performed (line 15), the controller updates its internal state accordingly (line 17).

```
 1  function CDCLSym(φ: CNF formula, symCtrl: symmetry controller)
 2      returns ⊤ if φ is SAT and ⊥ otherwise
 3  |   dl ← 0 ;                                  // Current decision level
 4  |   while not all variables are assigned do
 5  |   |   isConflict ← unitPropagation();
 6  |   |   symCtrl.updateAssign(crtAss());
 7  |   |   isReduced ← symCtrl.isNotLexLeader(crtAss());
 8  |   |   if isConflict ∨ isReduced then
 9  |   |   |   if dl = 0 then
10  |   |   |   |   return ⊥;                      // φ is UNSAT
11  |   |   |   if isConflict then
12  |   |   |   |   ω ← anlConflict();
13  |   |   |   else
14  |   |   |   |   ω ← symCtrl.genEsbp(crtAss());
15  |   |   |   dl ← bckjmpAndRstrtPolicies();
16  |   |   |   φ ← φ ∪ {ω} ;
17  |   |   |   symCtrl.updateCancel(crtAss());
18  |   |   else
19  |   |   |   assignDecisionLiteral();
20  |   |   |   dl ← dl + 1;
21  |   return ⊤;                                 // φ is SAT
```

Algorithm 2. The CDCLSym algorithm. Blue (or grey) parts denote additions to CDCL.

```
 1  function CDCLSp(φ: CNF formula, spCtrl: symmetry propagation controller)
 2      returns ⊤ if φ is SAT and ⊥ otherwise
 3  |   dl ← 0 ;                                  // Current decision level
 4  |   while not all variables are assigned do
 5  |   |   isConflict ← unitPropagation() ∧ spCtrl.symPropagation();
 6  |   |   if isConflict then
 7  |   |   |   if dl = 0 then
 8  |   |   |   |   return ⊥;                      // φ is UNSAT
 9  |   |   |   ω ← anlConflict();
10  |   |   |   dl ← bckjmpAndRstrtPolicies();
11  |   |   |   φ ← φ ∪ {ω} ;
12  |   |   |   spCtrl.cancelActSymmetries();
13  |   |   else
14  |   |   |   assignDecisionLiteral();
15  |   |   |   dl ← dl + 1;
16  |   |   |   spCtrl.updateActSymmetries();
17  |   return ⊤;                                 // φ is SAT
```

Algorithm 3. The CDCLSp algorithm. Red (or grey) parts denote additions to CDCL.

CDCLSp (see Algorithm 3) implements SPA, and also has a structure similar to the one of CDCL. In this algorithm, the symmetry propagation actions are executed by the controller component (spCtrl) through a call to the function symPropagation (line 5). This propagation is allowed only if the conditions of Proposition 3 are met. Such conditions are evaluated by tracking on-the-fly the status of the symmetries. This is implemented by functions updateSymmetries (line 12) and cancelSymmetries (line 16).

```
1  function CDCLSymSp(φ: CNF formula, symCtrl: symmetry controller,
     spCtrl: symmetry propagation controller)
2      returns ⊤ if φ is SAT and ⊥ otherwise
3      dl ← 0 ;                                    // Current decision level
4      while not all variables are assigned do
5          isConflict ← unitPropagation() ∧ spCtrl.symPropagation();
6          symCtrl.updateAssign(crtAssignment());
7          isReduced ← symCtrl.isNotLexLeader(crtAssignment());
8          if isConflict ∨ isReduced then
9              if dl = 0 then
10                 └ return ⊥;                      // φ is UNSAT
11             if isConflict then
12                 ⟨ω, L = ⋂_{ω'∈φ₁} L_{ω',φ₁} ∪ Stab(ω)⟩ ← anlConflictSymSp();
13             else
14                 ⟨ω, L = Stab(ω)⟩ ← symCtrl.genEsbpSp(crtAssignment());
15             dl ← backjumpAndRestartPolicies();
16             φ ← φ ∪ {ω} ;
17             symCtrl.updateCancel(crtAssignment());
18             spCtrl.cancelActSymmetriesSym() ;
19             spCtrl.updateLocSymmetries(L);
20         else
21             assignDecisionLiteral();
22             dl ← dl + 1;
23             spCtrl.updateActSymmetriesSym() ;
24     return ⊤;                                    // φ is SAT
```

Algorithm 4. The CDCLSymSP algorithm. Additions derived from CDCLSym and CDCLSp are reported in blue and red (or grey). Additions due to the composition of the two algorithms are reported with a gray background.

The algorithm we propose for the composed approach is presented in Algorithm 4. Lines 3–10, 15–17 and 20–22 correspond to the exact union of CDCLSym and CDCLSp. Let us detail the critical points.

- Lines 11–14: when a conflict is detected, then the analysing procedure is triggered. According to Proposition 5, the generated conflicting clause ω, should be associated with the computation of its set of local symmetries. Thus, we update the classical `anlConflict` procedure to `anlConflictSymSp` that produces such a set: φ_1 contains all the clauses that are used to derive ω[3]. So, at the end of the conflict analysis we operate the intersection of a local symmetries of these clauses to get the set of local symmetries of ω. We can thus complete this set with the stabilizer set (see as Proposition 5).
  In Algorithm 2, when a non lex-leader assignment is detected (line 13–14), then the esbp generation function, `genEsbp`, is called. In the new algorithm this function is replaced by a new one called `genEsbpSp`. In addition to compute the esbp clause ω, it produces the stabilizer set of ω[4].
- Line 18: `cancelActSymmetriesSym` extends function `cancelActSymmetries` of Algorithm 3 with the additional reactivation of the symmetries that have been broken (deactivated) by ESBPA. Technically speaking, each time a deduced literal is unassigned, all symmetries that became inactive because of its assignment (see `updateLocSymmetries` and `updateActSymmetriesSym` functions below) are *reactivated*.
- Line 19: `updateLocSymmetries` is a new function of `spCtrl`. It is responsible of updating the status of the manipulated symmetries so that only those respecting Proposition 4 are active each time the `symPropagation` function is called. Technically speaking, each symmetry of the complement set (to $S(\varphi)$) of the set L is marked *inactive* (it is a broken symmetry), if it is not already marked so. Here, the asserting literal of clause ω becomes responsible of this deactivation.
- Line 23: `updateActSymmetriesSym` extends function `updateActSymmetries` of Algorithm 3. The reason clause, ω_l, of each propagated literal, l, by the `unitPropagation` function is analysed. Each symmetry of the complement set (to $S(\varphi)$) of the set local symmetries of ω_r is marked *inactive*, if it is not already marked so. l becomes responsible of this deactivation.

4   Implementation and Evaluation

In this section, we first highlight some details on our implementation. Then, we experimentally compare the performance of the combo against ESBA and SPA.

4.1   Implementation

We have implemented our combo on top of the `minisat-SPFS`[5] solver, developed by the authors of SPA.

---

[3] These are clauses of the *conflict side* of the implication graph when applying the classical conflict analysis algorithm.

[4] The only allowed local symmetries in case of an esbp, according to point 2 of Sect. 3.2.

[5] https://github.com/JoD/minisat-SPFS.

This choice has been influenced by two points: (1) take advantage of the expertise used to implement the original SPA method; (2) the easiness of integrating our implementation of ESBA to any CDCL-like solver because it is an off-the-shelf library[6].

However, this choice has the drawback of doubling the representation of symmetries. This can be a hard limit to treat certain big problems from the memory point of view.

The implemented combo solver can be found at: https://github.com/lip6/minisat-SymSp.

4.2 Evaluation

This section compares our combo approach against ESBA and SPA. All experiments have been performed with a modified version of the well-known MiniSAT solver [9]: minisat-Sp, for SPA; minisat-Sym, for ESBA; and minisat-SymSP, for the combo. Symmetries of the SAT problems have been computed by bliss [11].

We selected from the last seven editions of the SAT contest [10], the CNF problems for which bliss finds some symmetries that could be computed in at most 1000 s of CPU time. We obtained a total of 1400 SAT problems (discarding repetitions) out of the 4000 proposed by the seven editions of the contest.

Table 1. Comparison of the number of SAT problems solved by each approach.

Benchmark	minisat-Sp	minisat-Sym	minisat-SymSP
generators 0-20 (704)	194	197	**198**
generators 20-40 (136)	33	**34**	**34**
generators 40-60 (141)	28	28	**29**
generators 60-80 (168)	**65**	64	**65**
generators 80-100 (51)	28	**34**	**34**
generators >100 (200)	58	59	**60**
TOTAL no dup (1400)	406	416	**420**

Table 2. Comparison of the number of UNSAT problems solved by each approach.

Benchmark	minisat-Sp	minisat-Sym	minisat-SymSP
generators 0-20 (704)	**233**	220	226
generators 20-40 (136)	50	**54**	**54**
generators 40-60 (141)	75	**83**	**83**
generators 60-80 (168)	**11**	**11**	10
generators 80-100 (51)	**11**	**11**	**11**
generators >100 (200)	90	**109**	107
TOTAL no dup (1400)	470	488	**491**

[6] This library is released under GPL v3 license, see https://github.com/lip6/cosy.

All experiments have been conducted using the following settings: each solver has been run once on each problem, with a time-out of 7200 s (including the execution time of symmetries generation) and limited to 64 GB of memory. Experiments were executed on a computer with an Intel(R) Xeon(R) Gold 6148 CPU @ 2.40 GHz featuring 80 cores and 1500 GB of memory, running a Linux 4.17.18, along with g++ compiler version 8.2.

Tables 1 and 2 present the obtained results for SAT and UNSAT problems respectively. The first column of each table lists the classes of problems on which we operated our experiments: we classify the problems according to the number of symmetries they admit. A line noted "generators X-Y (Z)" groups the Z problems having between X and Y generators (i.e., symmetries). Other columns show the number of solved problems for each approach.

Globally, we observe that the combo approach can be effective in many classes of symmetric problems. For SAT problems, the combo has better results than the two other approaches (4 more SAT problems when compared to the best of the two others) and this is despite the significant cost paid for the tracking of the symmetries' status. When looking at the UNSAT problems, things are more mitigated. Although, the total number of solver problems is greater than the best of the two others, we believe that the cost for tracking the symmetries' status has an impact on the performances. This can be observed on the first and last lines of Table 2: when the number of generators is small (first line), the ESBA benefits greatly from the SPA. When the number of generators is high (last line), we see a small loose of the combo with respect to ESBA. It is also worth noting that the combo approach solved **8** problems that could not be handled by ESBA nor SPA.

Table 3. Comparison of PAR-2 and CTI times (in seconds) of the global solving.

Solvers	PAR2 (1400)	CTI (825)
minisat-SymSp	5653089	614856
minisat-Sym	5682892	584868
minisat-Sp	6026840	612638

Table 3 compares the different techniques with respect to the PAR-2 and the CTI time measures. PAR-2 is the official ranking measure used in the yearly SAT contests [10]. CTI measures the Cumulative solving Time of the problem Intersection (i.e., 825 problems solved by all solvers). While PAR-2 value gives a global indication on the effectiveness of an approach, CTI is a good mean to evaluate its speed compared to other approaches.

Hence, we observe that the combo has a better PAR-2 score, and this shows its effectiveness. However, it is the least fast when coming to solved intersection. This is clearly due the double cost paid for tracking the symmetries' status (one for ESBA and the other for SPA). Having a unified management of symmetries tracking would probably reduce this cost.

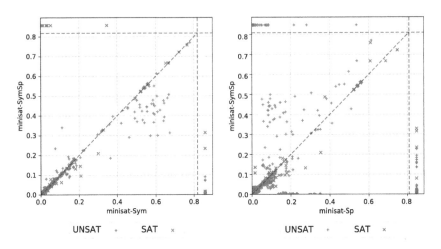

Fig. 1. Comparison of the ratio between the number of decisions and the number of propagations for the comb w.r.t. ESBA and SPA.

To go further in our analyse, we also compare the ratio between the number of decisions and the number of propagations. This is a fair measure to assess the quality of a SAT solving approach: if the ratio is small, then this means that the developed algorithm is producing more deduced facts than making guesses, which is the best way to conclude quickly on a problem!

The scatter plots of Fig. 1 show a comparison between the aforementioned ratios. When comparing `minisat-Sp` to `minisat-SymSp` (right hand side scatter plot), we observe that the ratio goes in favour of `minisat-Sp` for the problems solved by both approaches. This is an expected result since the main objective of SPA is to minimise the number of decisions while augmenting the number of propagations. What is important to underline here is highlighted on the left hand side scatter plot: on a large majority of UNSAT problems, the ratio goes in favour of `minisat-SymSp` w.r.t. `minisat-Sym`. This confirms the positive impact of SPA when applied in conjunction with ESBA.

5   Conclusion

This paper proposed a way to combine two approaches – Symmetry propagation (SPA) and effective symmetry breaking (ESBA) – to increase efficiency of SAT Solving by exploiting the symmetry properties of propositional problems.

Despite the fact that these approaches appear to be orthogonal, the composition is far from being trivial since the way one exploits symmetries ruins the way the other does. To achieve this composition, we had to introduce the notion of local symmetries in the context of SAT solving.

Both SPA and ESBA are efficient of different classes of problem. Extensive experiments conducted on symmetric problems extracted from the last seven editions of the SAT contest show that our combo approach roughly cumulate the advantages of SPA and ESBA.

The current implementation remains at a prototype stage and could be improved (especially on the way symmetries are managed). So, improvement can be expected.

Another research direction could be to use the notion of local symmetries to process problems that exhibit no global symmetries.

References

1. Aloul, F., Ramani, A., Markov, I., Sakallah, K.: Solving difficult instances of boolean satisfiability in the presence of symmetry. IEEE Trans. CAD Integr. Circ. Syst. **22**(9), 1117–1137 (2003)
2. Aloul, F., Sakallah, K., Markov, I.: Efficient symmetry breaking for boolean satisfiability. IEEE Trans. Comput. **55**(5), 549–558 (2006)
3. Biere, A., Cimatti, A., Clarke, E., Zhu, Y.: Symbolic model checking without BDDs. In: Cleaveland, W.R. (ed.) TACAS 1999. LNCS, vol. 1579, pp. 193–207. Springer, Heidelberg (1999). https://doi.org/10.1007/3-540-49059-0_14
4. Crawford, J., Ginsberg, M., Luks, E., Roy, A.: Symmetry-Breaking Predicates for Search Problems, pp. 148–159. Morgan Kaufmann, San Francisco (1996)
5. Davis, M., Logemann, G., Loveland, D.: A machine program for theorem-proving. Commun. ACM **5**(7), 394–397 (1962)
6. Devriendt, J., Bogaerts, B., Bruynooghe, M.: Symmetric explanation learning: effective dynamic symmetry handling for SAT. In: Gaspers, S., Walsh, T. (eds.) SAT 2017. LNCS, vol. 10491, pp. 83–100. Springer, Cham (2017). https://doi.org/10.1007/978-3-319-66263-3_6
7. Devriendt, J., Bogaerts, B., Bruynooghe, M., Denecker, M.: Improved static symmetry breaking for SAT. In: Creignou, N., Le Berre, D. (eds.) SAT 2016. LNCS, vol. 9710, pp. 104–122. Springer, Cham (2016). https://doi.org/10.1007/978-3-319-40970-2_8
8. Devriendt, J., Bogaerts, B., de Cat, B., Denecker, M., Mears, C.: Symmetry propagation: improved dynamic symmetry breaking in SAT. In: IEEE 24th International Conference on Tools with Artificial Intelligence, ICTAI 2012, Athens, Greece, 7–9 November 2012, pp. 49–56 (2012)
9. Eén, N., Sörensson, N.: An extensible SAT-solver. In: Giunchiglia, E., Tacchella, A. (eds.) SAT 2003. LNCS, vol. 2919, pp. 502–518. Springer, Heidelberg (2004). https://doi.org/10.1007/978-3-540-24605-3_37
10. Järvisalo, M., Le Berre, D., Roussel, O., Simon, L.: The international SAT solver competitions. AI Mag. **33**(1), 89–92 (2012)
11. Junttila, T., Kaski, P.: Engineering an efficient canonical labeling tool for large and sparse graphs. In: Applegate, D., Brodal, G.S., Panario, D., Sedgewick, R. (eds.) Proceedings of the Ninth Workshop on Algorithm Engineering and Experiments and the Fourth Workshop on Analytic Algorithms and Combinatorics, pp. 135–149. SIAM (2007)
12. Katebi, H., Sakallah, K.A., Markov, I.L.: Symmetry and satisfiability: an update. In: Strichman, O., Szeider, S. (eds.) SAT 2010. LNCS, vol. 6175, pp. 113–127. Springer, Heidelberg (2010). https://doi.org/10.1007/978-3-642-14186-7_11
13. Kautz, H.A., Selman, B., et al.: Planning as satisfiability. In: ECAI, vol. 92, pp. 359–363 (1992)

14. Luks, E.M., Roy, A.: The complexity of symmetry-breaking formulas. Ann. Math. Artif. Intell. **41**(1), 19–45 (2004). https://doi.org/10.1023/B:AMAI.0000018578. 92398.10

15. Lynce, I., Marques-Silva, J.: SAT in bioinformatics: making the case with haplotype inference. In: Biere, A., Gomes, C.P. (eds.) SAT 2006. LNCS, vol. 4121, pp. 136–141. Springer, Heidelberg (2006). https://doi.org/10.1007/11814948_16

16. Marques-Silva, J.P., Sakallah, K., et al.: Grasp: a search algorithm for propositional satisfiability. IEEE Trans. Comput. **48**(5), 506–521 (1999)

17. Massacci, F., Marraro, L.: Logical cryptanalysis as a SAT problem. J. Autom. Reason. **24**(1), 165–203 (2000)

18. Metin, H., Baarir, S., Colange, M., Kordon, F.: CDCLSym: introducing effective symmetry breaking in SAT solving. In: Beyer, D., Huisman, M. (eds.) TACAS 2018. LNCS, vol. 10805, pp. 99–114. Springer, Cham (2018). https://doi.org/10. 1007/978-3-319-89960-2_6

19. Sabharwal, A.: SymChaff: exploiting symmetry in a structure-aware satisfiability solver. Constraints **14**(4), 478–505 (2009)

20. Schaafsma, B., Heule, M.J.H., van Maaren, H.: Dynamic symmetry breaking by simulating Zykov contraction. In: Kullmann, O. (ed.) SAT 2009. LNCS, vol. 5584, pp. 223–236. Springer, Heidelberg (2009). https://doi.org/10.1007/978-3-642-02777-2_22

Formal Methods Assisted Training of Safe Reinforcement Learning Agents

Anitha Murugesan[1]([⊠]), Mohammad Moghadamfalahi[1],
and Arunabh Chattopadhyay[2]

[1] Honeywell International Inc., Plymouth, USA
{anitha.murugesan,mohammad.moghadamfalahi}@honeywell.com
[2] Swift Navigation, San Francisco, USA
arun@swift-nav.com

Abstract. *Reinforcement learning* (RL) is emerging as a powerful machine learning paradigm to develop autonomous safety critical systems; RL enables the systems to learn optimal control strategies by interacting with the environment. However, there is also widespread apprehension to deploying such systems in the real world since rigorously ensuring if they had learned safe strategies by interacting with an environment that is representative of the real world remains a challenge. Hence, there is a surge of interest to establish safety-focused RL techniques.

In this paper, we present a safety-assured training approach that augments standard RL with formal analysis and simulation technology. The benefits of coupling these techniques is three-fold: the formal analysis tools (SMT solvers) guide the system to learn strategies that rigorously uphold specified safety properties; the sophisticated simulators provide a wide-range of quantifiable, realistic learning environments; the adequacy of the safety properties can be assessed as agent explores complex environments. We illustrate this approach using a Flappy Bird game.

Keywords: Reinforcement learning · Assurance · Formal methods

1 Introduction

Recently, there is a tremendous surge of interest to use Machine Learning (ML) techniques to the develop smart, autonomous systems. In particular, *Reinforcement learning (RL)* (a ML technique) is emerging as a powerful paradigm since it allows systems to self-learn their functions through exploration and feedback from the environment, without any expert supervision [14]. However, in the safety critical domain where safety assurance is of utmost importance, there is apprehension to deploying RL-based systems in the real-world since they pose unique challenges to upholding safety similar to traditional systems [16].

Fundamentally, RL is an inductive process; it makes broad generalizations from trained observations and feedback from environment. RL-based systems

© Springer Nature Switzerland AG 2019
J. M. Badger and K. Y. Rozier (Eds.): NFM 2019, LNCS 11460, pp. 333–340, 2019.
https://doi.org/10.1007/978-3-030-20652-9_22

learn their behaviors by randomly exploring the environment and exploiting learned knowledge within its learning environment. While this randomness helps optimize behaviors, it is not necessarily guaranteed to be safe, especially as behavioral, computational and structural complexity evolve over time and the system makes generalizations based on past observations. Also, in comparison to the complex environments these systems can be exposed in practice, it is hard to ensure that a representative subset of environment has been chosen for learning. All this complicates the task of making behavioral predictions and safety assertions based on current RL-based training inadequate. Hence, enhancements to RL techniques that are supportive of safety-assurance is warranted in the safety-critical domain.

To that end, we present an approach to augment standard RL with advanced simulators to provide a wide range of realistic learning environments and formal method-based tools such as SMT solvers [5] to rigorously restrict the learning to uphold the specified safety properties. This combination of approaches rigorously guides the system to discover optimal actions within the pre-defined safety zone in training environments that can be quantified with respect to the real operational environment of the system. Further, our approach helps systematically discover, refine and assess the adequacy of the specified safety properties as the agent trains in complex environments. In this paper, we illustrate the implementation of our approach [1] over an existing Flappy bird game [2].

1.1 Reinforcement Learning Overview

In a nutshell, RL is a framework that allows entities – *agents* – to learn control strategies by interacting with the environment. In standard RL, shown in Fig. 1, an agent iteratively performs *actions* on the environment and, in response it receives the description of the environment (called *state*) and feedback (called *reward*) that indicates the impact of

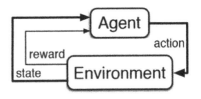

Fig. 1. Reinforcement learning

the action on the environment. Based on the reward, the agent learns an optimal strategy or *policy* for choosing its next action that would receive higher reward in an iterative manner.

RL techniques can be broadly divided into two types: *model-based* in which the agent relies on a complete environment model to learn the policy and choose actions; and, *model-free* where the agent learns based on a limited observation of the environment at every iteration. The latter is preferred for training critical agents since the real world is often very complex to represent.

2   Safety-Focused Reinforcement Training

Figure 2 shows our approach to model-free safety-assured RL. We augment standard RL with a hi-fidelity simulator to provide a wide range of realistic training scenarios, and an SMT solver to restrict the agent from perform actions that violate the specified safety properties.

Advanced simulators have the capability to provide a wide range of realistic, continuous training data for RL-agents. For instance, commercially-rated simulators such as X-Plane [3] have rich models of flight dynamics, weather patterns, etc. that serve as a suitable training environments for agents to interact and learn. Further, such simulators provide detailed reports that help quantify the training environment with respect to real operational environments.

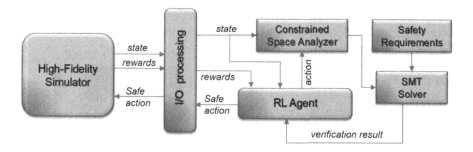

Fig. 2. Safety-focused Reinforcement learning

To interface simulators with RL-agents, a custom *input/output (I/O) processor* is typically warranted. The primary function of the I/O processor is to forward the state and reward from the simulation environment to the RL-agent, and return the agent's action at every step.

The state and reward information is used by the RL-agent to update its policy in a model-free manner; i.e. the policy update depends only on the observation of the agent at each time and not on the entire dynamics of simulation. We use Q-learning [18], an algorithm for model-free RL, to train the agent. The algorithm returns a list of possible actions and their expected future reward.

To check if the action with highest expected reward is indeed safe in the given state of the environment, we employ formal verification tool, namely a Satisfiability Modulo Theories (SMT) solver. Typically, environmental observations from simulators are rich with large state spaces that affect SMT solver performance. Hence, we first use a constrained state analyzer to restrict the state space to a size that is relevant for safety analysis. Similar to the I/O processor, the constrained state analyzer depends on the application domain and the safety properties in consideration.

We formulate the problem of checking whether the action in the given environment meets/violates the safety properties as a propositional logic formula and use the SMT solver to verify it. If the verification passes, the agent receives a positive reward and the action is sent back to the simulator. Otherwise, the agent receives a high negative reward indicating that the action was unsafe and the action with the next-highest expected reward is sent for SMT analysis. This is performed iteratively for each step of training to rigorously guide the agent to learn the actions that meet the safety properties. As per our proposal, such a trained agent would mitigate safety violations more often than a traditionally (non-SMT solver assisted) trained agent post deployment.

3   Case Studies

To illustrate our approach, we use a Flappy Bird game, shown in Fig. 3. The aim of this game is to train an agent (a bird) to fly between sets of pipes with dynamically varying heights without colliding on those pipes, ceiling or floor. This game serves as an abstract example to understand and draw conclusions on the application of our approach to real safety-critical systems.

Firstly, the game is an exemplar for model-free learning. The action of the bird depending upon the current game state with random pipe heights is analogous to a real agent's decision based on its current state and non-deterministic environmental inputs. Secondly, the flap up and flap down actions of the bird is comparable to real control commands such as pitch up and down. Thirdly, the safety consideration in the game such as maximum height and collision avoidance with pipes are similar to typical safety properties of real systems such as range limits and obstacle avoidance. Finally, the configurable parameters of the game that allows training the bird in varying environments helps abstractly formulate training of real agents in wide-ranging environments and dynamics.

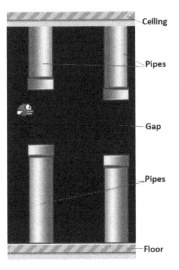

Fig. 3. Flappy Bird game

3.1   Implementation Details

We implemented our approach over an existing Flappy Bird game developed using Python 3, TensorFlow 0.7, Keras and pygame [2]. We used a Windows 7 OS with an Intel I-5 Core processor and 8 GB RAM for this experiment.

At each step of the game, the agent receives the game state as an array of raw pixel values of the visible screen (512×280 pixels). The I/O pre-processor re-sizes the image (80×80 pixels) and removes details from the image such as background colors and patterns that are irrelevant for the agent's decision. Based on this pre-processed game state, the Q-learning agent computes the expected reward for the next possible actions of the bird (flap up and flap down).

To check if taking the optimal action (with highest reward) in the given state meets/violates the set of specified safety properties, we used Z3, an efficient SMT solver [7]. Prior to SMT analysis, the constrained state analyzer further crops the state to a size that is sufficient to analyze safety properties to scale down the state space for SMT analysis. For instance, if a requirement necessitated looking ahead for x next states of the bird, the constrained state analyzer dynamically crops the image based on the knowledge of the bird dynamics.

To interface with the solver and formulate the propositional logic formula consisting of constrained state, action and safety properties for verification we used PySMT [10] – a Python API for SMT. Depending upon the result of verification, the agent receives a positive reward and performs the action or receives a negative reward and next optimal action is analyzed. Hence, at each step, the agent only learns most optimal and safe actions.

Further, to train the agent in wide ranging environmental conditions, we systematically increased the randomness at which the height of the pipes appear in the game screen and changed the velocity of the bird.

3.2 Safety Analysis

We considered two safety properties for this training. The first property is: *the flap-up action is safe if (1) the vertical distance between the bird and ceiling is more than a certain threshold; and, (2) there is at-least one obstacle-free path (x steps look ahead) after taking the flap-up action.* To formulate the second requirement that looks ahead for x steps, the flap-up acceleration and bird dynamics were taken into account. As visually shown in Fig. 4, the look ahead is nothing but the states that the bird could possibly go after it takes the flap-up action in the current state and any further actions. SMT checks if the look-ahead states for that action violates the safety properties or not. Similar to the first property, the second one checks for safety of flap-down action.

Prior to safety checks, the bird trivially collided with the pipes, ceiling and floor several times in a row before it learns to avoid them. However, with our safety-guided approach, right from the first step of training, the bird was able to successfully navigate through the pipes without colliding most of the time. In fact, it collided only in situations that were not constrained by the safety-properties. The rate of collision was approximately once in 200 simulation steps. Hence, our approach guides the agent to avoid the known failure scenarios; rather, it allows the agent to learn optimal actions within the zone of safety.

Fig. 4. Flap-up action

From a performance perspective, we found that the SMT solving time was negligible for properties that look for collision free movement of the bird for 6 subsequent time steps. However, when we increased the time steps to 10, SMT took about 1 to 2 s per step. We plan to improve this performance with better computing infrastructures and optimization techniques in the future.

3.3   Property Discovery

To train the agent in wide-ranging environment, as we increased the randomness of the pipe height, in some states all the possible actions are determined unsafe by the SMT solver. This lead to discovery of new safety properties.

When we analyzed one of the violations, we found that at the beginning of the game when there no pipes in its vicinity, the bird tends to flap up and stay close to the ceiling. In that scenario, when the pipes start appearing with gaps closer to the floor, as shown in Fig. 5, the bird collides with the pipes despite the safety checks. This is because, the bird's dynamics does not allow it to rapidly fly down and pass through the pipes. On analyzing the game, this was due the lack of properties to encourage the bird to stay in the middle when there are no pipes in its vicinity. Once we added that safety property, it mitigated that failure.

Fig. 5. Case 1

In another scenario, though the bird successfully navigates through the gap between pipes, it collides with the pipe as it exits the gap. On examining the root cause, we found that the safety property formulation did not account for the bird's width and height. Hence, when the bird leaves the gap while being closer to the upper/lower pipe, its rear end collides with the pipe corner, as shown in Fig. 6. In addition to the inadequacy in the existing property to account for bird size, we also added a property that specified a safe minimum distance between the top/bottom end of the bird and the nearest pipe. Hence, analyzing such violations during training helped improve the safety properties.

Fig. 6. Case 2

4   Discussion

We presented an approach that integrates RL with formal analysis and simulation technology to provide design-time safety assurance of RL-based agents. Though we illustrated our approach using a Flappy Bird example (available at [1]), the benefits of training real safety-critical RL-agents using this approach is manifold: it is guaranteed to learn safe actions; the attributes of the training environment and its divergence from actual operating environments can be captured from the simulators and this coverage can be presented for safety-assurance; by examining the violations during the training, the sufficiency of the safety properties can be quantified. Hence, an agent trained using our approach would need minimal run-time safety mitigation (based on the coverage).

Safe-RL has been researched in several directions [9]. Among those that have explored the use of formal methods, most are predominately model-based [8,12,13,15] that are not practicable for most real safety critical systems.

Some promising approaches based on Bayesian optimization [6], Gaussian process sampling [17] and optimization [11] have not been evaluated with practical deep neural networks. A closely related work uses linear temporal logic for safety assurance of deep Q-learning agents [4]; while it works on continuous input and output domains (regression), it is not suitable for image-based inputs, that are mostly used in practice. On the contrary, our approach leverages simulation technology to provide training environments that provide image inputs in a model-free learning that is suitable to train deep neural networks for real world application. While the use of high-fidelity simulators have been previously tried with RL [14], by integrating formal methods our approach assures safety.

The use of formal analysis in the loop makes design-time safety assurance straightforward since the safety properties can be validated by domain experts and presented for assurance; Alternatively, if one chooses to code those safety rules as a complex reward function, it becomes a part of the nebulous machine learning component that is hard to characterize and thoroughly verify. Further, our approach is modular; depending upon the system in consideration, the formal tool, simulator or learning algorithm can be easily interchanged, customized and/or further optimized.

References

1. Flappy bird safe RL git. https://github.com/sinamf/SafeRL. Accessed 3 Aug 2019
2. Using keras and deep q-network to play flappy bird. https://yanpanlau.github.io/2016/07/10/FlappyBird-Keras.html. Accessed 3 Aug 2019
3. X-plane. https://www.x-plane.com. Accessed 3 Aug 2019
4. Alshiekh, M., Bloem, R., Ehlers, R., Könighofer, B., Niekum, S., Topcu, U.: Safe reinforcement learning via shielding. In: Thirty-Second AAAI Conference on Artificial Intelligence (2018)
5. Barrett, C., Tinelli, C.: Satisfiability modulo theories. In: Clarke, E., Henzinger, T., Veith, H., Bloem, R. (eds.) Handbook of Model Checking, pp. 305–343. Springer, Cham (2018). https://doi.org/10.1007/978-3-319-10575-8_11
6. Berkenkamp, F., Krause, A., Schoellig, A.P.: Bayesian optimization with safety constraints: safe and automatic parameter tuning in robotics (2016). arXiv preprint: arXiv:1602.04450
7. de Moura, L., Bjørner, N.: Z3: an efficient SMT solver. In: Ramakrishnan, C.R., Rehof, J. (eds.) TACAS 2008. LNCS, vol. 4963, pp. 337–340. Springer, Heidelberg (2008). https://doi.org/10.1007/978-3-540-78800-3_24
8. Fulton, N., Platzer, A.: Safe reinforcement learning via formal methods: toward safe control through proof and learning. In: Thirty-Second AAAI Conference on Artificial Intelligence (2018)
9. Garcıa, J., Fernández, F.: A comprehensive survey on safe reinforcement learning. J. Mach. Learn. Res. 16(1), 1437–1480 (2015)
10. Gario, M., Micheli, A.: PySMT: a solver-agnostic library for fast prototyping of SMT-based algorithms. In: Proceedings of the 13th International Workshop on Satisfiability Modulo Theories (SMT), pp. 373–384 (2015)
11. Hahn, E.M., Perez, M., Schewe, S., Somenzi, F., Trivedi, A., Wojtczak, D.: Omega-regular objectives in model-free reinforcement learning (2018). arXiv preprint: arXiv:1810.00950

12. Jansen, N., Könighofer, B., Junges, S., Bloem, R.: Shielded decision-making in MDPS (2018). arXiv preprint: arXiv:1807.06096
13. Junges, S., Jansen, N., Dehnert, C., Topcu, U., Katoen, J.-P.: Safety-constrained reinforcement learning for MDPs. In: Chechik, M., Raskin, J.-F. (eds.) TACAS 2016. LNCS, vol. 9636, pp. 130–146. Springer, Heidelberg (2016). https://doi.org/10.1007/978-3-662-49674-9_8
14. Jin Kim, H., Jordan, M.I., Sastry, S., Ng, A.Y.: Autonomous helicopter flight via reinforcement learning. In: Advances in Neural Information Processing Systems, pp. 799–806 (2004)
15. Mason, G.R., Calinescu, R.C., Kudenko, D., Banks, A.: Assured reinforcement learning for safety-critical applications. In: Doctoral Consortium at the 10th International Conference on Agents and Artificial Intelligence. SciTePress (2017)
16. Moldovan, T.M., Abbeel, P., Jordan, M., Borrelli, F.: Safety, Risk Awareness and Exploration in Reinforcement Learning. Ph.D. thesis, University of California, Berkeley, USA (2014)
17. Schreiter, J., Nguyen-Tuong, D., Eberts, M., Bischoff, B., Markert, H., Toussaint, M.: Safe exploration for active learning with gaussian processes. In: Bifet, A., May, M., Zadrozny, B., Gavalda, R., Pedreschi, D., Bonchi, F., Cardoso, J., Spiliopoulou, M. (eds.) ECML PKDD 2015. LNCS (LNAI), vol. 9286, pp. 133–149. Springer, Cham (2015). https://doi.org/10.1007/978-3-319-23461-8_9
18. Watkins, C.J.C.H., Dayan, P.: Q-learning. Mach. Learn. 8(3), 279–292 (1992)

Formalizing CNF SAT Symmetry Breaking in PVS

David E. Narváez[(✉)] [iD]

Golisano College of Computing and Information Sciences,
Rochester Institute of Technology, Rochester, NY 14623, USA
den9562@rit.edu

Abstract. The Boolean satisfiability problem (SAT) remains a central
problem to theoretical as well as practical computer science. Recently, the
need to trust the results obtained by SAT solvers has led to research in
formalizing these. Nevertheless, tools in the ecosystem of SAT problems
(such as preprocessors, model counters, etc.) would need to be verified
as well in order for the results to be trusted. In this paper we explore a
step towards a formalized symmetry breaking tool for SAT: formalizing
SAT symmetry breaking for formulas in conjunctive normal form (CNF)
using the Prototype Verification System (PVS).

Keywords: SAT · PVS · Symmetry breaking

1 Motivation

The Boolean satisfiability problem (SAT) and its variants have played an important role in the development of all parts of computer science. From the theoretical
perspective, it plays a fundamental role in the theory of NP-completeness [4].
From the practical point of view, it has found several applications in fields like
model checking [16] and combinatorial search [10]. The applications SAT has
found in industry have brought along interesting consequences. On the one hand,
it has spurred the development of an entire ecosystem of related software, from
preprocessors to software to verify proofs of unsatisfiability. On the other hand,
it has increased the complexity of SAT solvers themselves as they are used
to tackle larger instances with intricate structures. The fact that SAT solvers
are becoming more complex while at the same time being used in more mission-
critical scenarios has sparked interest in the verification of SAT solvers [3,11,15].
Nevertheless, industrial applications usually depend not only on the SAT solver
employed to find satisfying assignments (models) of the generated instances but
also on preprocessing and postprocessing tools. For instance, most SAT solvers
available accept the input formula in DIMACS format[1], which assumes the input
is in conjunctive normal form (CNF), so depending on the application, a CNF
transformation may be needed as a preprocessing step, introducing a new trust
issue.

---

[1] https://www.satcompetition.org/2009/format-benchmarks2009.html.

© Springer Nature Switzerland AG 2019
J. M. Badger and K. Y. Rozier (Eds.): NFM 2019, LNCS 11460, pp. 341–354, 2019.
https://doi.org/10.1007/978-3-030-20652-9_23

The particular type of preprocessing tool we focus on in this paper is symmetry breaking tools. Symmetry breaking has been identified as a crucial step towards using SAT solvers successfully in combinatorial search [9]. Symmetries in a given instance of the SAT problem may arise from several sources, some of them domain-specific and some of them at the syntactic level. The seminal work by Crawford [5,6] addressed syntactic symmetry in CNF formulas by interpreting these as graphs and using the automorphism group of such graphs to identify syntactic symmetry. These symmetries are broken by appending symmetry breaking clauses to the input formula. Aloul et al. [1] later improved the original construction to be able to detect phase-shifts symmetries (symmetries that map a literal to its negation). Aloul et al. [2] exploited the recursive nature of the symmetry breaking predicates formulated in this technique to reduce the size of the symmetry breaking clauses added to the input formula and made their work available as the widely successful tool `Shatter`. More recently, Devriendt et al. [7] improved the symmetry breaking clauses added by `Shatter` and added another technique for symmetry breaking detection, namely row interchangeability, making these available in the `BreakID` tool. The idea of detecting syntactic symmetries through a graph representation of the input formula has also found its way into the related paradigms of Answer Set Programming (ASP) and model expansion [8]. This brief overview, although by no means thorough, is enough to make the argument that by using today's tools in syntactic symmetry breaking we are leveraging decades of work. At the heart of this work is the concept introduced by Crawford [5,6], still present in modern tools: the representation of a Boolean formula as a graph whose automorphisms correspond to syntactic symmetries in the input formula. Thus formalizing this idea would be a step towards formalizing state-of-the-art tools.

In this paper we explore the formalization in the Prototype Verification System (PVS) [13] of the graph construction by Crawford [5,6] and the verification of the fundamental property linking the automorphisms of this graph with symmetric assignments of the variables. Our formalization is based on the `graph` theory from NASA's PVS library[2]. We believe this formalization is an interesting undertaking because it requires us to go beyond the mere formalization of CNF formulas and transformations at the formula level. We need to jump out of the realm of CNF formulas into the language of graphs and then back to CNF formulas.

The rest of this paper is organized as follows. Crawford's symmetry breaking method is defined in detail in Sect. 2. Section 3 then delves into the details of our formalization and some of the proof techniques used to verify the main theorems of Crawford's approach to syntactic symmetry breaking. We discuss some directions for future research and conclude in Sect. 4.

2   Main Theorem

In this section we lay out the fundamentals of Crawford's approach to syntactic symmetry breaking, which we then formalize in Sect. 3. The first concept we define is that of a CNF formula:

---

[2] https://shemesh.larc.nasa.gov/fm/ftp/larc/PVS-library/pvslib.html.

Definition 1 (CNF Formula). *A CNF Clause is a set of literals (variables and their negations). A CNF Formula is a set of CNF clauses.*

For simplicity, we identify variables with natural numbers. Thus an assignment of variables can be defined as a function from the natural numbers to the Boolean domain. Alternatively, one could define an assignment as a function from the set of variables in a formula to the Boolean domain, but this has interesting implications which we discuss briefly in Sect. 4. Regardless of the choice of representation of assignments, these can naturally be extended to an assignment of literals in the obvious way.

Definition 2. *An assignment σ models a formula F if for every clause $C \in F$ there exists a literal $l \in C$ such that σ assigns True to l.*

Definition 3 (Graph Representation). *The graph representation of a CNF formula F is a vertex-colored undirected graph G_F whose set of vertices is the union of the clauses of F in one color and the literals of F in another color. The set of edges is defined as: (a) the set of edges between a literal l and its negation $\bar{l}$ and (b) the set of edges between a clause C and the literals $l \in C$.*

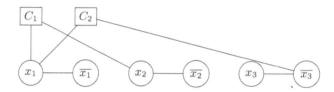

Fig. 1. The graph corresponding to the CNF formula $(x_1 \vee x_2) \wedge (x_1 \vee \overline{x_3})$. Vertex colors are represented by different node shapes.

Figure 1 shows what the graph G_F would be for a formula $F = (x_1 \vee x_2) \wedge (x_1 \vee \overline{x_3})$. Recall that the automorphisms of a graph are the vertex permutations that preserve the set of edges. In our particular case, since we deal with vertex-colored graphs, we only consider color-preserving automorphisms (i.e., automorphisms that map vertices to vertices of the same color). Since literal vertices will be mapped to literal vertices, the automorphisms of G_F naturally induce a permutation of the literals of F. The main theorem behind Crawford's method for syntactic symmetry breaking is the following.

Theorem 1. *Given a formula F and a color-preserving automorphism ϕ of G_F, an assignment σ models a formula F if and only if the assignment $\sigma \circ \phi$ models F.*

Notice that Theorem 1 can be easily stated if we allow for an abuse of notation and consider ϕ both a permutation of the vertices of G_F *and* a permutation of literals. In fact, a closer look at the composition $\sigma \circ \phi$ reveals that we are both recasting σ as an assignment of literals (as explained above) and ϕ as a permutation of literals. This will prove somewhat problematic in Sect. 3, since PVS will require us to make these casts explicit, thus increasing the complexity of the proofs.

Theorem 1 in itself does not break symmetries in CNF formulas. In order to use Theorem 1 for symmetry breaking, one can look at lexicographical orderings of assignments. Fix an ordering of the literals of F (say, $l_1, l_2, \ldots, l_n$) and let π be a permutation of these. We define the symmetry breaking predicate $P(\pi)$ as follows: $P_1(\pi) = l_1 \leq \pi(l_1)$, $P_i(\pi) = \left(\bigwedge_{j=1}^{i-1} l_j \equiv \pi(l_j) \right) \rightarrow (l_i \leq \pi(l_i))$ for $i > 1$,

and $P(\pi) = \bigwedge_{i=1}^{n} P_i(\pi)$. Predicate $P(\pi)$ imposes a lexicographical order between two assignments since only one of them will satisfy $P(\pi)$. Since, by Theorem 1, it is true that for any satisfying assignment σ and any automorphism ϕ both σ and $\sigma \circ \phi$ satisfy F, $P(\phi)$ allows us to prefer σ over $\sigma \circ \phi$ if σ is less or equal to $\sigma \circ \phi$ in lexicographical order. If F is satisfiable, such an assignment exists because $P(\pi)$ is a total order over the satisfying assignments of F. By adding symmetry breaking predicates we are able to reduce the number of satisfying assignments to search for while preserving satisfiability.

Theorem 2. *Given a formula F and a color-preserving automorphism ϕ of G_F, F is satisfiable if and only if $(F) \wedge P(\phi)$ is satisfiable.*

One can in fact add symmetry breaking predicates for any number of automorphisms while preserving satisfiability: observe that the lexicographical minimum of the set of models of F is by definition less or equal to all of its permutations, thus it satisfies all possible symmetry breaking predicates. This version of Theorem 2 is the one we formalize in the next section.

3   Formalizing Crawford's Symmetry Breaking

We begin our formalization by defining a new datatype for literals with constructors for positive and negative literals. The type CNFClause is then defined as an alias for a finite set of literals, and the type CNFFormula is in turn defined as a finite set of clauses.

```
lit: DATATYPE
BEGIN
 poslit(n: nat): poslit?
 neglit(n: nat): neglit?
END lit

CNFClause: TYPE = finite_set[lit]

CNFFormula: TYPE = finite_set[CNFClause]
```

We define some natural operations over literals and assignments, namely the **neg** function which returns the negation of a literal, and the `litval` function which takes a literal l and an assignment a and returns the Boolean value assigned to l under a. We omit the definition of these for the sake of space. We define the **models** predicate indicating an assignment models a formula and the **SAT** predicate indicating a satisfying assignment exists for the input formula.

```
models(F: CNFFormula, assignment: [nat -> bool]): bool =
FORALL (c: (F)): EXISTS (l: (c)): litval(assignment, l) = True

SAT(F: CNFFormula): bool =
EXISTS (assignment: [nat -> bool]): models(F, assignment)
```

Next, we define the **vertex** datatype, the type of the vertices of our graph. A vertex can be a literal vertex or a clause vertex so our datatype has a constructor for each.

```
vertex: DATATYPE
BEGIN
 litvertex (l: lit): litvertex?
 clausevertex (C: CNFClause): clausevertex?
END vertex
```

We are now prepared to define the functions that will extract the vertices that are used to build the graph of a formula. These are essentially `formula_lits` which collects all the literals that appear in a formula, `lit_vertices` which maps a set of literals to a set of literal vertices, and `clause_vertices` which maps CNF formulas to sets of clause vertices.

```
formula_lits(F: CNFFormula): finite_set[lit] =
lits_for_vars(formula_vars(F))

lit_vertices(L: finite_set[lit]): finite_set[vertex] =
image(litvertex, L)

clause_vertices(F: CNFFormula): finite_set[vertex] =
image(clausevertex, F)
```

We also define functions to generate the edges of the graph G_F. We take a similar approach as with the vertices of G_F, defining functions that output different sets of edges. The function `connect_lits` takes a set of natural numbers (variables, in our domain) and generates a set of edges connecting the positive and negative literals of those variables. The `connect_clauses` function connects the clauses of a CNF formula to the literals they contain. From Definition 3 it follows that the set of edges of G_F is the union of the output of these functions.

```
connect_lits(V: finite_set[nat]): finite_set[doubleton[vertex]] =
image(
  (LAMBDA (v: nat): dbl(litvertex(poslit(v)), litvertex(neglit(v)))), V)

connect_clause_internal(C: CNFClause, D: CNFClause):
finite_set[doubleton[vertex]] =
image((LAMBDA (l: lit): dbl(clausevertex(C), litvertex(l))), D)

connect_clause(C: CNFClause): finite_set[doubleton[vertex]] =
connect_clause_internal(C, C)

connect_clauses(F: CNFFormula): finite_set[doubleton[vertex]] =
IUnion[(F),doubleton[vertex]](connect_clause)
```

With the definitions above we are finally ready to define what the graph of a formula F is and prove a *type-correctness condition (TCC)* generated by PVS. The TCC generated asks us to prove that if an edge is in the union of the sets connect_lits(formula_vars(F)) and connect_clauses(F), then both of the members of the edge are in the union of lit_vertices(formula_lits(F)) and clause_vertices(F).

```
formula_graph(F: CNFFormula): graph[vertex] =
  (# vert := union(lit_vertices(formula_lits(F)), clause_vertices(F)),
  edges:= union(connect_lits(formula_vars(F)), connect_clauses(F)) #)
```

A fundamental property of this graph is that a literal l is a member of a clause C of a formula F if and only if the edge $\{C, l\}$ is in the set of edges of the graph. We prove this property as a separate lemma.

```
graph_clause_lit: LEMMA
FORALL (F: CNFFormula, C: CNFClause, l: lit):
  (member(C, F) AND member(l, C)) IFF
  member(dbl(clausevertex(C), litvertex(l)), edges(formula_graph(F)))
```

The next concept we need to formalize is that of automorphisms. In particular, for our application we need to define color-preserving automorphisms. Notice that our definition of a vertex does not explicitly allow for us to specify a color, but the separate constructors naturally induce a coloring on the vertex datatype. We leverage the induced coloring of vertices by using the ord function in PVS [14]. An overload of this function which assigns a natural number to each constructor of an abstract datatype is automatically generated by PVS when a new abstract datatype is defined. We start by defining the concept of a (color-preserving) vertex permutation, which is a nonempty type dependent on a graph. We define them as bijective functions from the set of vertices to itself such that vertices of the graph are mapped to vertices of the graph and the color of the vertex is preserved.

```
vertex_permutation(G: graph[vertex]): TYPE+ =
{pi: [vertex -> vertex] | bijective?(pi) AND
  (FORALL (v: vertex): member(v, vert(G))
    IMPLIES member(pi(v), vert(G))) AND
  FORALL (v: vertex): ord(v) = ord(pi(v))}
CONTAINING id
```

We now define an operation **permute_edges** on graphs which generates a new set of edges using a vertex permutation of the graph. It will then allow us to define automorphisms as the nonempty type of vertex permutations for which this operation preserves the set of edges.

```
permute_edges(G: graph[vertex], pi: vertex_permutation(G)):
finite_set[doubleton[vertex]] =
{ e: doubleton[vertex] |
  EXISTS (x: vertex, y: vertex):
    member(x, vert(G)) AND member(y, vert(G)) AND x /= y AND
    member(dbl(x, y), edges(G)) AND e = dbl(pi(x), pi(y)) }

automorphism(G: graph[vertex]): TYPE+ =
{ pi: vertex_permutation(G) | permute_edges(G, pi) = edges(G) }
CONTAINING id
```

A fundamental property that follows from the structure of G_F and the fact that automorphisms preserve the set of edges is the following:

Lemma 1. *If ϕ is an automorphism of G_F, then for any literal l in F, ϕ maps $\bar{l}$ to $\overline{\phi(l)}$.*

Proof. $\phi(l)$ is a literal from the formula, so $\{\phi(l), \overline{\phi(l)}\}$ is an edge of G_F and there must exist vertices x, y in G_F such that $\{\phi(l), \overline{\phi(l)}\} = \{\phi(x), \phi(y)\}$. One of x or y, say x, must be l because ϕ is injective, and that forces y to be $\bar{l}$ since ϕ is color preserving and the only edges connecting literals to literals connect every literal to its negation.   ■

We show the formalization of Lemma 1 below, where we can see how the abuse of notation throughout our informal proof of the lemma (using ϕ as both a permutation of the vertices of G_F as well as a permutation of literals) is made explicit and causes some clutter. Nevertheless, it is worth noting it could be worse: since **phi** is of type **[vertex->vertex]**, the expression **phi(litvertex(1))** could in principle be a **clausevertex**, in which case we would not be able to use the **1** accessor. Instead of flagging this as an issue, PVS will formulate a type-correctness condition (TCC) asking to prove that **phi(litvertex(1))** is a **litvertex**, which is easy to show from the fact that **phi** is color-preserving. We include the generated TCC below. An important issue to point out is that, despite the fact that Lemma 1 is fairly straightforward, proving the **mapped_lit_neg** lemma required laborious case analysis.

```
mapped_lit(F: CNFFormula, l: (formula_lits(F)),
           phi: automorphism(formula_graph(F))) : lit =
l(phi(litvertex(l)))


mapped_lit_TCC1: OBLIGATION
  FORALL (F: CNFFormula, l: (formula_lits(F)),
          phi: automorphism(formula_graph(F))):
    litvertex?(phi(litvertex(l)));


mapped_lit_neg: LEMMA
FORALL (F: CNFFormula, l: lit):
 member(l, formula_lits(F)) IMPLIES
  (FORALL (phi: automorphism(formula_graph(F))):
   mapped_lit(F, l, phi) = neg(mapped_lit(F, neg(l), phi)))
```

The last piece we need to formalize before stating and proving Theorem 1 is the notion of permuting an assignment. The crucial property of this operation is that, if l is a literal of a formula F, the value of $\phi(l)$ under an assignment σ is the value of l under the assignment $\sigma \circ \phi$. We have intentionally given a provocatively simple description of this property which seems to go without saying. In reality, the description is making use of some notation overloading that we cannot obviate when formalizing this property in PVS: ϕ is a vertex permutation, so a composition of ϕ with σ is impossible—not even if we consider σ as an assignment of literals, which is another overloading we employ in our description. Because of all the overloading that is needed to express this property, we state it as a lemma whose proof actually requires rather heavy case analysis.

```
permute_assignment(F: CNFFormula, a: [nat->bool],
                   phi: automorphism(formula_graph(F))): [nat->bool] =
LAMBDA (n: nat): litval(a, mapped_lit(F, poslit(n), phi))


permute_assignment_preserves: LEMMA
FORALL (F: CNFFormula, a: [nat->bool], l: lit,
        phi: automorphism(formula_graph(F))):
 member(l, formula_lits(F)) IMPLIES
  litval(a, mapped_lit(F, l, phi)) =
  litval(permute_assignment(F, phi, a), l)
```

We are finally ready to state and prove Theorem 1. We can in fact state a weaker version of this theorem: that if σ models F and ϕ is an automorphism of G_F, then $a \circ \phi$ models F. We can then use that theorem and the fact that ϕ^{-1} is an automorphism of G_F as well to prove Theorem 1. As mentioned before, the proof relies heavily on the graph_clause_lit lemma. It also uses the permute_assignment_preserves lemma and the fact that, since an automorphism is injective and maps the set of vertices of G_F to itself, its inverse also maps the set of vertices of G_F to itself.

```
Crawford_imp: THEOREM
FORALL (F: CNFFormula, a: [nat->bool],
        phi: automorphism(formula_graph(F))):
models(F, a) IMPLIES models(F, permute_assignment(F, phi, a))

Crawford: THEOREM
FORALL (F: CNFFormula, a: [nat->bool],
        phi: automorphism(formula_graph(F))):
models(F, a) IFF models(F, permute_assignment(F, phi, a))
```

We now focus on defining a total order over the assignments of a formula. This proved to be tricky given our choice of defining assignments as functions from the natural numbers to the Boolean domain. We define a relation `assignment_leq` between two assignments σ_1 and σ_2 which depends on a list of variables. This relation essentially says that σ_1 is lexicographical less or equal to σ_2 over the given list of variables. Notice that the list of variables induces an order over the variables. There are a number of ways to define this relation, we chose to define it in a recursive fashion which will facilitate proofs by induction.

```
assignment_leq (vars: list[nat])(a1: [nat->bool], a2: [nat->bool]):
RECURSIVE [bool] =
CASES vars OF
  null: TRUE,
  cons(v, rest_vars):
  IF a1(v) THEN
    IF a2(v) THEN assignment_leq(rest_vars)(a1, a2) ELSE FALSE ENDIF
  ELSE
    IF a2(v) THEN TRUE ELSE assignment_leq(rest_vars)(a1, a2) ENDIF
  ENDIF
ENDCASES
MEASURE vars by <<
```

On the other hand, it will sometimes be helpful to work with an explicit definition of what this recursive function means. This will be particularly helpful later on to prove that there is a lexicographical minimum model for any satisfiable formula. In order to work with this alternative formulation, we define a predicate over natural numbers `assignments_differ` which depends on two assignments σ_1 and σ_2 stating that these two assignments differ on a given number. We then prove an equivalence between the recursive definition of `assignment_leq` and the property that if the two assignments σ_1 and σ_2 differ over a list of variables and σ_1 is less or equal to σ_2, then σ_1 assigns *False* to the first variable where they both differ.

```
assignments_differ(a1, a2: [nat->bool])(n: nat): bool =
a1(n) /= a2(n)

assignment_leq_alt: LEMMA
FORALL (vars: list[nat], a1: [nat->bool], a2: [nat->bool]):
assignment_leq(vars)(a1, a2) IFF
  (some(assignments_differ(a1, a2))(vars) IMPLIES
  NOT a1(nth(vars, find_first(vars, assignments_differ(a1, a2)))))
```

Notice that `assignment_leq` as defined is not a total order over assignments. In order to use this definition as a total order, we need to consider a restricted version `assignment_leq_restricted` which also depends on a list of variables but is defined over functions that assign specifically those variables in the list. This definition uses the `extend` function in PVS to extend the assignments over a list of variables to assignments of natural numbers in order to define this restricted predicate in terms of `assignment_leq`.

```
assignment_leq_restricted(D: list[nat])
(a1, a2: [(set_as_list.list2set(D))->bool]): bool =
assignment_leq(D)(
  extend[nat,(set_as_list.list2set(D)),bool,TRUE](a1),
  extend[nat,(set_as_list.list2set(D)),bool,TRUE](a2))

assignment_leq_iff_restricted: LEMMA
FORALL (D: list[nat], S: finite_set[nat], a1, a2: [nat->bool]):
set_as_list.list2set(D) = S IMPLIES
  (assignment_leq(D)(a1, a2) IFF
    assignment_leq_restricted(D)(
      restrict[nat,(S),bool](a1),
      restrict[nat,(S),bool](a2)))

assignment_leq_restricted_total_order: LEMMA
FORALL (D: list[nat], S: set[nat]):
set_as_list.list2set(D) = S IMPLIES
  total_order?[[(S)->bool]](assignment_leq_restricted(reverse(D)))
```

We mention in passing that the `assignment_leq_restricted_total_order` lemma was the most challenging lemma to prove in the entire specification.

We now need a way to encode the symmetry breaking predicate $P(\pi)$ described in Sect. 2 as a CNF formula. The standard way to do this is to use auxiliary variables $e_i \equiv (l_i = \pi(l_i))$ which would lead to an encoding of the predicates that is quadratic in the number of variables in the formula. While implementing this in a procedural fashion is straightforward, implementing it in a functional fashion in a way that lends itself to proving properties about the encoding is more involved. We opted for an alternative approach: expressing the $P(\pi)$ predicate entirely in terms of the variables of F without employing auxiliary variables.

A way to do this is to notice that predicates of the type $\left(\bigwedge_{j=1}^{i-1} (l_{i-1} \equiv \phi(l_{i-1})) \right) \rightarrow$

$(l_i \rightarrow \pi(l_i))$ are equivalent to $\left(\bigvee_{j=1}^{i-1} ((\overline{l_i} \wedge \pi(l_i)) \vee (l_i \wedge \overline{\pi(l_i)})) \right) \vee (l_i \rightarrow \pi(l_i))$ and

$\bigvee_{j=1}^{i-1} ((\overline{l_i} \wedge \pi(l_i)) \vee (l_i \wedge \overline{\pi(l_i)}))$ is in *disjunctive normal form* (DNF). Then we can
employ a brute-force transformation from DNF to CNF which, although adding a
number of clauses that is exponential in the number of variables in the formula, is
theoretically simple enough to fit our purposes. We implement this transformation
in a recursive function add_symbreaking_predicates_dnf_helper but we omit
its definition here for the sake of clarity. We do, however, present the lemma formalizing the main property of this function, namely, that an assignment models
the formula output by the add_symbreaking_predicates_dnf_helper if and only
if there is a literal i in the list of variables for which a assigns different values to l_i
and $\phi(l_i)$.

```
add_symbreaking_predicates_dnf_helper_neq: LEMMA
FORALL (F: CNFFormula, vars: finite_set[nat],
        phi: automorphism(formula_graph(F)), a: [nat->bool]):
models(add_symbreaking_predicates_dnf_helper(F, vars, phi), a) IFF
(EXISTS (v: (vars)):
  litval(a, poslit(v)) /= litval(a, mapped_lit(F, poslit(v), phi)))
```

In order to build the predicate $P(\pi)$ we process the list of variables as follows:
Let the head of the list be the variable v, and let l_v be the positive literal of
v. We take the output of add_symbreaking_predicates_dnf_helper applied to
the rest of the list and add $\overline{l_v}$ and $\phi(l_v)$ to each clause, then repeat the same
procedure for the rest of the list.

```
add_symbreaking_predicates_helper(F: CNFFormula, vars: list[nat],
  phi: automorphism(formula_graph(F))): RECURSIVE CNFFormula =
CASES vars OF
  null: emptyset[CNFClause],
  cons(v, rest_vars):
  union(
    add_lit_to_clauses(
      add_lit_to_clauses(
        add_symbreaking_predicates_dnf_helper(F, list2set(rest_vars), phi),
        mapped_lit(F, poslit(v), phi)),
      neglit(v)),
    add_symbreaking_predicates_helper(F, rest_vars, phi))
ENDCASES
MEASURE vars BY <<
```

Notice the procedure above imposes a lexicographical order of the variables
in the list using the *reverse* of the order induced by the list, as stated in the
following lemma.

```
models_add_symbreaking_predicates_helper_leq: THEOREM
FORALL (F: CNFFormula, phi: automorphism(formula_graph(F)),
        a: [nat->bool], vars: list[nat]):
models(add_symbreaking_predicates_helper(F, vars, phi), a) IFF
assignment_leq(reverse(vars))(a, permute_assignment(F, phi, a))
```

We define another function that takes a list of automorphisms of the formula graph of F and adds symmetry breaking predicates for all of them. We also prove a simple lemma stating a model σ of the formula output by such function will be less or equal to $\sigma \circ \phi$ for every automorphism ϕ in the list.

```
add_symbreaking_predicates(F: CNFFormula,
  phis: list[automorphism(formula_graph(F))]): CNFFormula =
reduce(F,
 LAMBDA (phi: automorphism(formula_graph(F)), G: CNFFormula):
  union(
   add_symbreaking_predicates_helper(F, set2list(formula_vars(F)), phi),
   G))(phis)

add_symbreaking_predicates_models: LEMMA
FORALL (F: CNFFormula, phis: list[automorphism(formula_graph(F))],
        a: [nat->bool]):
models(add_symbreaking_predicates(F, phis), a) IFF
(models(F, a) AND
  FORALL (phi: automorphism(formula_graph(F))):
  member(phi, phis) IMPLIES
    assignment_leq(reverse(set2list(formula_vars(F))))(
      a, permute_assignment(F, phi, a)))
```

Finally, we prove (a list version of) Theorem 2. The fact that F is satisfiable if the formula together with the symmetry breaking predicates is satisfiable follows easily from the fact that F is a subset of that formula (see the base case of the **reduce** function call above). The interesting part of this proof is providing a model that will satisfy all the symmetry breaking predicates given that F is satisfiable. We provide the extension of the lexicographical minimum of the set of satisfying assignments of the variables of the formula as a witness. In order to do this, PVS will ask us to prove (a) that the set of satisfying assignments of the variables of F is non-empty, (b) that `assignment_leq_restricted` is in fact a total order over assignments of the variables of F, and (c) that the lexicographical minimum satisfies all the symmetry breaking predicates appended to F. Part (a) is true because the restriction of the witness to the satisfiability of F belongs to the set, part (b) is true by lemma `assignment_leq_restricted_total_order`, and part (c) follows from Theorem 1.

```
symbreaking: THEOREM
FORALL (F: CNFFormula, phis: list[automorphism(formula_graph(F))]):
SAT(F) IFF SAT(add_symbreaking_predicates(F, phis))
```

This concludes our formalization of symmetry breaking for Boolean formulas in CNF. The complete development of our formalization, which consists of 61 formulas at the time of this writing, is available online[3].

4   Conclusion and Future Work

We presented the formalization in PVS of the syntactic symmetry breaking technique for Boolean formulas in conjunctive normal form (CNF) introduced by Crawford [5,6]. We discussed the main components of our formalization and the challenges we faced formulating and proving them.

There are several directions for future work that could stem from this work. One relatively simple improvement would be to specify and prove properties for an encoding of the symmetry breaking predicate $P(\pi)$ that uses auxiliary variables and adds a number of clauses that is polynomial in the number of variables of the formula. Our choice of representing assignments as functions from natural numbers to the Boolean domain would allow for using auxiliary variables without affecting the proof of `symbreaking`. This would bring our formalization closer to the actual implementations available in tools like `shatter` [2].

Related to the extension discussed above, an interesting direction for future work would be to obtain executable code out of this formalization and compare it to the performance of tools like `shatter` [2] and `BreakID` [7]. PVSio[4] [12] could in principle help in this task, yet one big roadblock in using it for our purpose is that basic functions related to finite sets (like adding elements to the set and calculating set unions) are, to the best of our knowledge, not supported by default. Adding support for these would be a major improvement towards being able to run our specification and compare it to the CNF symmetry breaking tools available in the industry.

Acknowledgments. The author would like to thank Dr. Edith Hemaspaandra, Dr. Matthew Fluet, and the anonymous reviewers of NFM 2019 for their valuable comments and suggestions.

References

1. Aloul, F.A., Ramani, A., Markov, I.L., Sakallah, K.A.: Solving difficult instances of Boolean satisfiability in the presence of symmetry. IEEE Trans. CAD Integr. Circ. Syst. **22**(9), 1117–1137 (2003). https://doi.org/10.1109/TCAD.2003.816218
2. Aloul, F.A., Sakallah, K.A., Markov, I.L.: Efficient symmetry breaking for Boolean satisfiability. IEEE Trans. Comput. **55**(5), 549–558 (2006). https://doi.org/10.1109/TC.2006.75
3. Blanchette, J.C., Fleury, M., Lammich, P., Weidenbach, C.: A verified SAT solver framework with learn, forget, restart, and incrementality. J. Autom. Reason. **61**(1–4), 333–365 (2018). https://doi.org/10.1007/s10817-018-9455-7

---

[3] https://doi.org/10.5281/zenodo.2597138.
[4] https://shemesh.larc.nasa.gov/people/cam/PVSio/.

4. Cook, S.A.: The complexity of theorem-proving procedures. In: 3rd Annual ACM Symposium on Theory of Computing, pp. 151–158. ACM (1971). https://doi.org/10.1145/800157.805047

5. Crawford, J.: A theoretical analysis of reasoning by symmetry in first-order logic. In: AAAI Workshop on Tractable Reasoning, pp. 17–22 (1992)

6. Crawford, J.M., Ginsberg, M.L., Luks, E.M., Roy, A.: Symmetry-breaking predicates for search problems. In: Aiello, L.C., Doyle, J., Shapiro, S.C. (eds.) Knowledge Representation and Reasoning, pp. 148–159. Morgan Kaufmann, Burlington (1996)

7. Devriendt, J., Bogaerts, B., Bruynooghe, M., Denecker, M.: Improved static symmetry breaking for SAT. In: Creignou, N., Le Berre, D. (eds.) SAT 2016. LNCS, vol. 9710, pp. 104–122. Springer, Cham (2016). https://doi.org/10.1007/978-3-319-40970-2_8

8. Devriendt, J., Bogaerts, B., Bruynooghe, M., Denecker, M.: On local domain symmetry for model expansion. Theory Pract. Logic Program. **16**(5–6), 636–652 (2016)

9. Heule, M.: The quest for perfect and compact symmetry breaking for graph problems. In: Davenport, J.H., et al. (eds.) 18th International Symposium on Symbolic and Numeric Algorithms for Scientific Computing, pp. 149–156. IEEE Computer Society (2016). https://doi.org/10.1109/SYNASC.2016.034

10. Heule, M., Kullmann, O.: The science of brute force. Commun. ACM **60**(8), 70–79 (2017). https://doi.org/10.1145/3107239

11. Marić, F.: Formal verification of a modern SAT solver by shallow embedding into Isabelle/HOL. Theor. Comput. Sci. **411**(50), 4333–4356 (2010). https://doi.org/10.1016/j.tcs.2010.09.014

12. Muñoz, C.: Rapid prototyping in PVS. Contractor Report NASA/CR-2003-212418, NASA, Langley Research Center, Hampton VA 23681–2199, USA, May 2003

13. Owre, S., Rushby, J.M., Shankar, N.: PVS: a prototype verification system. In: Kapur, D. (ed.) CADE 1992. LNCS, vol. 607, pp. 748–752. Springer, Heidelberg (1992). https://doi.org/10.1007/3-540-55602-8_217

14. Owre, S., Shankar, N.: Abstract datatypes in PVS. Technical report SRI-CSL-93-9R, Computer Science Laboratory, SRI International, Menlo Park, CA, December 1993. Extensively revised June 1997; Also available as NASA Contractor Report CR-97-206264

15. Shankar, N., Vaucher, M.: The mechanical verification of a DPLL-based satisfiability solver. Electron. Notes Theor. Comput. Sci. **269**, 3–17 (2011). https://doi.org/10.1016/j.entcs.2011.03.002

16. Yu, Y., Subramanyan, P., Tsiskaridze, N., Malik, S.: All-SAT using minimal blocking clauses. In: 27th International Conference on VLSI Design and 13th International Conference on Embedded Systems, pp. 86–91 (2014). https://doi.org/10.1109/VLSID.2014.22

Fly-by-Logic: A Tool for Unmanned Aircraft System Fleet Planning Using Temporal Logic

Yash Vardhan Pant[1(✉)], Rhudii A. Quaye[1], Houssam Abbas[2], Akarsh Varre[1], and Rahul Mangharam[1]

[1] Department of Electrical and Systems Engineering,
University of Pennsylvania, Philadelphia, PA 19104, USA
{yashpant,quayerhu,akarshv,rahulm}@seas.upenn.edu
[2] Department of Electrical Engineering and Computer Science,
Oregon State University, Corvallis, OR 97330, USA
houssam.abbas@oregonstate.edu

Abstract. Safe planning for fleets of Unmaned Aircraft Systems (UAS) performing complex missions in urban environments has typically been a challenging problem. In the United States of America, the National Aeronautics and Space Administration (NASA) and the Federal Aviation Administration (FAA) have been studying the regulation of the airspace when multiple such fleets of autonomous UAS share the same airspace, outlined in the Concept of Operations document (ConOps). While the focus is on the infrastructure and management of the airspace, the Unmanned Aircraft System (UAS) Traffic Management (UTM) ConOps also outline a potential airspace reservation based system for operation where operators reserve a volume of the airspace for a given time interval to operate in, but it makes clear that the safety (separation from other aircraft, terrain, and other hazards) is a responsibility of the drone fleet operators. In this work, we present a tool that allows an operator to plan out missions for fleets of multi-rotor UAS, performing complex time-bound missions. The tool builds upon a correct-by-construction planning method by translating missions to Signal Temporal Logic (STL). Along with a simple user interface, it also has fast and scalable mission planning abilities. We demonstrate our tool for one such mission.

Keywords: UAS mission planning · Signal Temporal Logic · Correct-by-construction planning · Multi-rotor UAS

1 Introduction

It is inevitable that autonomous UAS will be operating in urban airspaces [1]. In the near future, operators will increasingly rely on fleets of multiple UAS to

---

Y. V. Pant and R. A. Quaye—Are contributed equally.

© Springer Nature Switzerland AG 2019
J. M. Badger and K. Y. Rozier (Eds.): NFM 2019, LNCS 11460, pp. 355–362, 2019.
https://doi.org/10.1007/978-3-030-20652-9_24

perform a wide variety of complicated missions which could consist of a combination of: (1) spatial objectives, e.g. geofenced no fly zones, or delivery zones, (2) temporal objectives, e.g. a time window to deliver a package, (3) reactive objectives, e.g. action when battery is low.

In this paper, we present a tool[1] that allows an operator to specify such requirements over a fleet of UAS operating in a bounded workspace and generates trajectories for all UAS such that they all satisfy their given mission in a safe manner. In order to generate these flights paths, or trajectories, our tool relies on interpreting the mission objectives as Signal Temporal Logic (STL) specifications [2]. We then formulate the problem of mission satisfaction as that of maximizing a notion of *robustness* of STL specifications [3]. Using the approach of [4], we generate trajectories for all the UAS involved such that they satisfy the given mission objectives.

1.1 Related Work

Existing mission planner software for autonomous drone operations like ArduPilot mission planner [5] and QGroundControl [6] offer UAS enthusiasts the ability to quickly plan out autonomous UAS flights by sequencing multiple simple operations (like take-off, hover, go to a way-point, land) together. However these planners either cannot handle missions involving multiple UAS and complicated requirements like co-ordination between UAS or completing tasks within given time intervals, or require hand-crafted sequences of maneuvers to meet the requirements in a safe manner. We propose a tool that can inherently deal with multi-agent missions as well as timing constraints on completion of tasks while guaranteeing that planned flight paths are safe. As opposed to existing mission planning software, our tool does not require the user to explicitly plan out maneuvers for the drones to execute to follow out a mission, e.g. in the case where two UAS have to enter the same region during the same time interval, our method generates trajectories that ensure the two UAS do so without crashing into each other without any user based scheduling of which drones enters first.

The tool presented here relies on interpreting a mission as a STL specification and generating trajectories that satisfy it. While there are multiple methods and tools that aim to solve such a problem, e.g. Mixed Integer Programming-based [7] and based on stochastic heuristics [8], we use an underlying method [4] that is tailored for generating trajectories for multi-rotor UAS, including those that allow hovering, to satisfy STL specifications in continuous-time. A detailed comparison can be found in [4,9].

1.2 Contributions

With this proposed tool we aim to bridge the gap between the ease-of-use of the UAS mission planning software popular among amateur drone enthusiasts,

---

[1] https://github.com/yashpant/FlyByLogic.

and the capabilities of academic tools [7,8] for control/planning with STL specifications. By doing this, we generate trajectories for multi UAS fleets that can satisfy complicated mission requirements while providing strong guarantees on mission satisfaction as well as the ability of the multi-rotor UAS to follow out their planned trajectories [4]. The main contributions of our tool are:

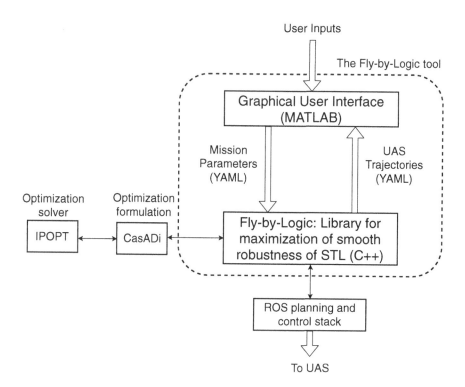

Fig. 1. The Fly-by-Logic tool-chain. Through a MATLAB-based graphical interface (Fig. 2), the user defines the workspace and the multi UAS mission. This mission is interpreted as an STL specification (of the form in Eq. 1), the parameters of which are passed from the interface to the Fly-by-Logic C++ library. Through interfacing with off-the-shelf optimization tools, trajectories that satisfy the mission are generated for each UAS and visualized through the user interface. The way-points that generate these trajectories can also be sent to a Robot Operating Systems (ROS) implementation of trajectory following control to be deployed on board actual robots (e.g. bit.ly/varvel8).

1. An easy to use graphical interface to specify mission requirements for multi-rotor UAS fleets,
2. The ability to interpreting these as missions as STL specifications and automatically generate an optimization to maximize a notion of robustness of this STL specification,

3. By interfacing to an off-the-shelf optimization solver, generation of trajectories that satisfy the mission requirements, are optimal with respect to minimizing jerk [10], and respect (potentially different) kinematic constraints for all UAS.
4. Does not require the UAS fleet operator to know how to write specifications in STL, but through an object-oriented C++ library allows the advanced user to generate custom missions specifications with even more flexibility than the graphical interface.

2   Fly-by-Logic: The Tool

2.1   Architecture and Outline

Figure 1 shows the architecture of the Fly-by-Logic tool. Through the user interface in MATLAB, the user defines the missions (more details in Sect. 2.2). The mission specific spatial and temporal parameters are then read in by the Fly-by-Logic C++ back-end. Here, these parameters are used to generate a function for the continuously differentially approximation of the robustness of the STL specification associated with the mission. An optimization to maximize this function [4] value is then formulated in Casadi [11]. Solving this optimization via IPOPT [12] results in a sequence of way-points for every UAS (uniformly apart in time). Also taken into account in the formulation is the motion to connect these way-points, which is via jerk-minimizing splines [10] and results in trajectories for each UAS. Through the Fly-by-Logic library, the (original non-smooth) robustness of these trajectories is evaluated for the mission STL specification and displayed back to the user via the MATLAB interface. A positive value of this robustness implies that the generated trajectories satisfy the mission and can be flown out, while a negative value (or 0) implies that the trajectories do not satisfy the mission [13] and either some additional parameters need to be tweaked (e.g. allowable velocity and acceleration bounds for the UAS, time intervals to visit regions, or a constant for the smooth robustness computation) or that the solver is incapable of solving this particular mission from the given initial positions of the UAS.

2.2   The Mission Template

Through the interface, the user starts by defining the number of way-points N (same number for each drone), as well as the (fixed) time, T that the UAS take to travel from one way-point to the next. These way-points are the variables that the tool optimizes over, and the overall duration of the mission is then $H = NT$ seconds. Next, the user defines regions in a bounded 3-dimensional workspace (see Fig. 2). These regions are axis-aligned hyper-rectangles and can be either *Unsafe* no-fly zones (in red), or *Goal* regions that the UAS can fly to. For each UAS, the user specifies their starting position in the workspace, as well as the velocity and acceleration bounds that their respective trajectories should respect. Finally, the user also specifies the time intervals within which the UAS need to visit some goal sets.

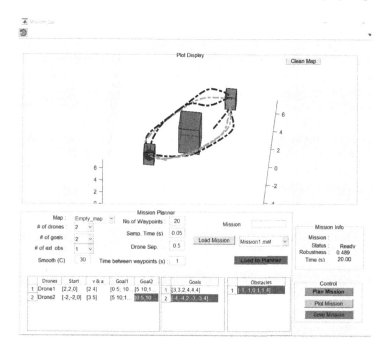

Fig. 2. The user interface and the planned trajectories for a two UAS patrolling mission (see Example 1). Real-time playback can be seen at http://bit.ly/fblguiexmpl (Color figure online)

Through the user interface, the user-defined missions result in specifications corresponding to the following fragment of STL:

$$\varphi = \wedge_{u=1}^{U} \wedge_{d=1}^{D} (\Box_I \neg (p_d \in \text{Unsafe}_u)) \wedge \wedge_{d \neq d'} (\Box_I (||p_d - p_{d'}||_2 \geq d_{\min})) \wedge$$
$$\wedge_{g=1}^{G} \wedge_{d=1}^{D} (\Diamond_{I_{g,d}^1} (p_d \in \text{Goal}_g) \wedge \ldots \wedge \Diamond_{I_{g,d}^c} (p_d \in \text{Goal}_g)) \tag{1}$$

Here, D, U, G are the number of UAS, *Unsafe* sets and *Goal* sets in the mission respectively. $I = [0, NT]$ is an interval that covers the entire mission duration, while $I_{g,d}^i \subseteq I, \forall i = 1, \ldots, c$ is the ith interval in which UAS d must visit *Goal* g. $\neg$ is the boolean negation operator. p_d is the position of UAS d.

The symbol $\Box_I \phi$ corresponds to the *Always* operator of STL and encodes the requirement that a boolean formula ϕ should be *true* through the time interval I. We use this operator to enforce that the UAS never enter the *Unsafe* zones or get closer than $d_{\min}$ meters of each other. Similarly, $\Diamond_I \phi$ corresponds to the *Eventually* operator which encodes the requirement that ϕ should be true at some point in time in the interval I. We use this to capture the requirement that the a UAS visits a *Goal* region within the user defined interval I. More details on STL and its grammar can be found in [14].

**Example 1. *Two UAS patrolling mission.* ** *Two UAS, starting off at positions* $[2,2,0]$ *and* $[-2,-2,0]$, *are tasked with patrolling two sets (in green), while making sure not to enter the set in red, and also maintaining a minimum distance of* 0.5 m *from each other. For a mission of time* 20 s, *we set the number of way-points to* 20, *and the time between them to be* 1 s. *The timing constraints on the patrolling are as follows: UAS 1 has to visit the first set in green in an interval of time* $[0, 5]$ *seconds from the missions starting time, has to visit the other green set in the interval* $[5, 10]$ *seconds, re-visit the first set in the interval* $[10, 15]$, *and the second set again in the interval* $[15, 20]$. *UAS 2 has a similar mission, visiting the first set in the intervals the UAS 1 has to visit the second set and so on. Figure 2 shows the trajectories generated by our method, and http://bit.ly/fblguiexmpl shows a real-time playback of the planned trajectories visualized through the user interface.*

For the mission of Example 1, the temporal logic specification is:

$$\varphi = \wedge_{u=1}^2 \wedge_{d=1}^2 (\square_{[0,20]} \neg(p_d \in \text{Unsafe}_u)) \wedge \square_{[0,20]}(||p_1 - p_2||_2 \geq 0.5) \wedge$$
$$\Diamond_{[0,5]}(p_1 \in Goal_1) \wedge \Diamond_{[5,10]}(p_1 \in Goal_2) \wedge \Diamond_{[10,15]}(p_1 \in Goal_1) \wedge$$
$$\Diamond_{[15,20]}(p_1 \in Goal_2) \wedge \Diamond_{[0,5]}(p_2 \in Goal_2) \wedge \Diamond_{[5,10]}(p_2 \in Goal_1) \wedge$$
$$\Diamond_{[10,15]}(p_2 \in Goal_2) \wedge \Diamond_{[15,20]}(p_2 \in Goal_1)$$

(2)

The tool comes pre-loaded with some example missions, and offers the user the ability to save new missions, as well save and load workspaces as text files. More details on the usage of the tool are in [15].

Note: Through the C++ library that forms the back-end for the tool, specifications involving the nested operators $\square_{I_1} \Diamond_{I_2}$ and $\Diamond_{I_1} \square_{I_2}$ can be used in conjunction with the template of Eq. 1. This functionality will be added to the user interface at a later time.

2.3   Behind-the-Scenes: Generating the Trajectories

In order to generate the trajectories that satisfy the mission specification, an optimization is solved (in the C++ back-end) to maximize, over N way-points for each drone, the smooth robustness of the mission STL specification evaluated for the UAS trajectories of NT seconds in duration. The constraints in the optimization ensure that the resulting trajectories are such that the resulting trajectories have velocity and accelerations within the user-defined bounds for each UAS, i.e. are kinematically feasible for the UAS to fly. See [4] for details.

3   Conclusions and Ongoing Work

In this paper we presented Fly-by-Logic, a tool for planning for multi-rotor UAS missions. By interpreting the missions as STL specifications, the underlying method generates kinematically feasible trajectories to satisfy missions with complicated spatial and temporal requirements while ensuring safety. Through an example, we introduce the kind of missions that can be specified in the tool. At the time of writing this paper, the tool is suitable only for offline trajectory generation for UAS missions. In [4] the underlying method has been shown to work in an online manner as well (see `bit.ly/varvel2`), and current work on the tool is focused on wrapping the Fly-by-Logic C++ library as a ROS package to seamlessly integrate with off-the-shelf planning and control implementations. Also planned is a method to import 3-d maps for actual geographical locations with *Unsafe* zones covering landmarks.

References

1. Federal Aviation Administration. Concept of operations v1.0 (2018). https://utm. arc.nasa.gov/docs/2018-UTM-ConOps-v1.0.pdf. Accessed 19 Nov 2018
2. Maler, O., Nickovic, D.: Monitoring temporal properties of continuous signals. In: Lakhnech, Y., Yovine, S. (eds.) FORMATS/FTRTFT -2004. LNCS, vol. 3253, pp. 152–166. Springer, Heidelberg (2004). https://doi.org/10.1007/978-3-540-30206-3_12
3. Fainekos, G.: Robustness of temporal logic specifications. Ph.D. dissertation, University of Pennsylvania (2008). http://www.public.asu.edu/~gfaineko/pub/fainekos_thesis.pdf
4. Pant, Y.V., Abbas, H., Quaye, R.A., Mangharam, R.: Fly-by-logic: control of multi-drone fleets with temporal logic objectives. In: Proceedings of the 9th ACM/IEEE International Conference on Cyber-Physical Systems, pp. 186–197. IEEE Press (2018)
5. Ardupilot Mission Planner. ardupilot.org/planner/. Accessed 15 Dec 2018
6. QGROUNDCONTROL. Intuitive and powerful ground control station for PX4 and ArduPilot UAVs. qgroundcontrol.com. Accessed 15 Dec 2018
7. Raman, V., Donze, A., Maasoumy, M., Murray, R.M., Sangiovanni-Vincentelli, A., Seshia, S.A.: Model predictive control with signal temporal logic specifications. In: 53rd IEEE Conference on Decision and Control, pp. 81–87, December 2014
8. Annpureddy, Y., Liu, C., Fainekos, G., Sankaranarayanan, S.: S-TaLiRo: a tool for temporal logic falsification for hybrid systems. In: Abdulla, P.A., Leino, K.R.M. (eds.) TACAS 2011. LNCS, vol. 6605, pp. 254–257. Springer, Heidelberg (2011). https://doi.org/10.1007/978-3-642-19835-9_21. http://dl.acm.org/citation.cfm?id=1987389.1987416
9. Pant, Y.V., Abbas, H., Mangharam, R.: Smooth operator: control using the smooth robustness of temporal logic. In: 2017 IEEE Conference on Control Technology and Applications (CCTA), pp. 1235–1240. IEEE (2017)
10. Mueller, M.W., Hehn, M., DÁndrea, R.: A computationally efficient motion primitive for Quadrocopter trajectory generation. IEEE Trans. Robot. **31**, 1294–1310 (2015)
11. Andersson, J.: A general-purpose software framework for dynamic optimization. Ph.D. thesis, Arenberg Doctoral School, KU Leuven (2013)
12. Wächter, A., Biegler, L.T.: On the implementation of an interior-point filter line-search algorithm for large-scale nonlinear programming. Math. Program. **106**, 25–57 (2006)
13. Fainekos, G., Pappas, G.: Robustness of temporal logic specifications for continuous-time signals. Theor. Comput. Sci. **410**, 4262–4291 (2009)

14. Donzé, A., Maler, O.: Robust satisfaction of temporal logic over real-valued signals. In: Chatterjee, K., Henzinger, T.A. (eds.) FORMATS 2010. LNCS, vol. 6246, pp. 92–106. Springer, Heidelberg (2010). https://doi.org/10.1007/978-3-642-15297-9_9
15. Fly-by-Logic: User documentation. https://github.com/yashpant/FlyByLogic. Accessed 15 Dec 2018

A Mixed Real and Floating-Point Solver

Rocco Salvia[1], Laura Titolo[2(✉)], Marco A. Feliú[2], Mariano M. Moscato[2],
César A. Muñoz[3], and Zvonimir Rakamarić[1]

[1] University of Utah, Salt Lake City, USA
{rocco,zvonimir}@cs.utah.edu
[2] National Institute of Aerospace, Hampton, USA
{laura.titolo,marco.feliu,mariano.moscato}@nianet.org
[3] NASA Langley Research Center, Hampton, USA
cesar.a.munoz@nasa.gov

Abstract. Reasoning about mixed real and floating-point constraints is essential for developing accurate analysis tools for floating-point programs. This paper presents FPRoCK, a prototype tool for solving mixed real and floating-point formulas. FPRoCK transforms a mixed formula into an equisatisfiable one over the reals. This formula is then solved using an off-the-shelf SMT solver. FPRoCK is also integrated with the PRECiSA static analyzer, which computes a sound estimation of the round-off error of a floating-point program. It is used to detect infeasible computational paths, thereby improving the accuracy of PRECiSA.

1 Introduction

Floating-point numbers are frequently used as an approximation of real numbers in computer programs. A round-off error originates from the difference between a real number and its floating-point representation, and accumulates throughout a computation. The resulting error may affect both the computed value of arithmetic expressions as well as the control flow of the program. To reason about floating-point computations with possibly diverging control flows, it is essential to solve mixed real and floating-point arithmetic constraints. This is known to be a difficult problem. In fact, constraints that are unsatisfiable over the reals may hold over the floats and vice-versa. In addition, combining the theories is not trivial since floating-point and real arithmetic do not enjoy the same properties.

Modern *Satisfiability Modulo Theories* (SMT) solvers, such as Mathsat [3] and Z3 [11], encode floating-point numbers with bit-vectors. This technique is usually inefficient due to the size of the binary representation of floating-point numbers. For this reason, several abstraction techniques have been proposed to approximate floating-point formulas and to solve them in the theory of real numbers. Approaches based on the *counterexample-guided abstraction refinement*

Partially supported by NSF awards CCF 1346756 and CCF 1704715.
Research by the first four authors was supported by the National Aeronautics and Space Administration under NASA/NIA Cooperative Agreement NNL09AA00A.

J. M. Badger and K. Y. Rozier (Eds.): NFM 2019, LNCS 11460, pp. 363–370, 2019.
https://doi.org/10.1007/978-3-030-20652-9_25

364 R. Salvia et al.

(CEGAR) framework [2,14,18] simplify a floating-point formula and solve it in a proxy theory that is more efficient than the original one. If a model is found for the simplified formula, a check on whether this is also a model for the original formula is performed. If it is, the model is returned, otherwise, the proxy theory is refined. Realizer [9] is a framework built on the top of Z3 to solve floating-point formulas by translating them into equivalent ones in real arithmetic. Molly [14] implements a CEGAR loop where floating-point constraints are lifted in the proxy theory of mixed real and floating-point arithmetics. To achieve this, it uses an extension of Realizer that supports mixed real and floating-point constraints. However, this extension is embedded in Molly and cannot be used as a standalone tool. The Colibri [10] solver handles the combination of real and floating-point constraints by using disjoint floating-point intervals and difference constraints. Unfortunately, the publicly available version of Colibri does not support all the rounding modalities and the negation of Boolean formulas. JConstraints [7] is a library for constraint solving that includes support for floating-points by encoding them into reals.

This paper presents a prototype solver for mixed real and floating-point constraints called FPRoCK.[1] It extends the transformation defined in Realizer [9] to mixed real/floating-point constraints. Given a mixed real-float formula, FPRoCK generates an equisatisfiable real arithmetic formula that can be solved by an external SMT solver. In contrast to Realizer, FPRoCK supports mixed-precision floating-point expressions and different ranges for the input variables. FPRoCK is also employed to improve the accuracy of the static analyzer PRECiSA [16]. In particular, it identifies spurious execution traces whose path conditions are unsatisfiable, which allows PRECiSA to discard them.

2 Solving Mixed Real/Floating-Point Formulas

A *floating-point number* [8], or simply a *float*, can be represented by a tuple (s, m, exp) where s is a sign bit, m is an integer called the *significand* (or *mantissa*), and exp is an integer *exponent*. A float (s, m, exp) encodes the real number $(-1)^s \cdot m \cdot 2^{exp}$. Henceforth, $\mathbb{F}$ represents the set of floating-point numbers. Let $\tilde{v}$ be a floating-point number that represents a real number r. The difference $|\tilde{v} - r|$ is called the *round-off error* (or *rounding error*) of $\tilde{v}$ with respect to r. Each floating-point number has a format f that specifies its dimensions and precision, such as single or double. The expression $F_f(r)$ denotes the floating-point number in format f *closest* to r assuming a given rounding mode.

Let $\mathbb{V}$ and $\widetilde{\mathbb{V}}$ be two disjoint sets of variables representing real and floating-point values respectively. The set $\mathbb{A}$ of mixed arithmetic expressions is defined by the grammar

$$A ::= d \mid x \mid \tilde{d} \mid \tilde{x} \mid A \odot A \mid A \widetilde{\odot} A \mid F_f(A),$$

where $d \in \mathbb{R}$, $x \in \mathbb{V}$, $\odot \in \{+, -, *, /, |\cdot|\}$ (the set of basic real number arithmetic operators), $\tilde{d} \in \mathbb{F}$, $\tilde{x} \in \widetilde{\mathbb{V}}$, $\widetilde{\odot} \in \{\tilde{+}_f, \tilde{-}_f, \tilde{*}_f, \tilde{/}_f\}$ (the set of basic floating-point

---

[1] The FPRoCK distribution is available at https://github.com/nasa/FPRoCK.

arithmetic operators) and $f \in \{single, double\}$ denotes the desired precision for the result. The rounding operator F_f is naturally extended to arithmetic expressions. According to the IEEE-754 standard [8], each floating-point operation is computed in exact real arithmetic and then rounded to the nearest float, i.e., $A \widetilde{\odot}_f A = F_f(A \odot A)$. Since floats can be exactly represented as real numbers, an explicit transformation is not necessary. The set of mixed real-float Boolean expressions $\mathbb{B}$ is defined by the grammar

$$B ::= true \mid false \mid B \wedge B \mid B \vee B \mid \neg B \mid A < A \mid A = A,$$

where $A \in \mathbb{A}$.

The input to FPRoCK is a formula $\tilde{\phi} \in \mathbb{B}$ that may contain both real and floating-point variables and arithmetic operators. Each variable is associated with a type (real, single or double precision floating-point) and range that can be either bounded, e.g., $[1, 10]$, or unbounded, e.g., $[-\infty, +\infty]$. The precision of a mixed-precision floating-point arithmetic operation is automatically detected and set to the maximum precision of its arguments. Given a mixed formula $\tilde{\phi} \in \mathbb{B}$, FPRoCK generates a formula ϕ over the reals such that $\tilde{\phi}$ and ϕ are equisatisfiable. Floating-point expressions are transformed into equivalent real-valued expressions using the approach presented in [9], while the real variables and operators are left unchanged. It is possible to define $x \widetilde{\odot} y$ as

$$x \widetilde{\odot} y = \left(\frac{\rho(\frac{x \odot y}{2^{exp}} \cdot 2^p)}{2^p} \right) \cdot 2^{exp}, \tag{2.1}$$

where p is the precision of the format, $exp = max\{i \in \mathbb{Z} \mid 2^i \leq |x \odot y|\}$, and $\rho : \mathbb{R} \to Int$ is a function implementing the rounding modality [9]. Therefore, given a floating-point formula $\tilde{\phi}$, an equisatisfiable formula without floating-point operators is obtained by replacing every occurrence of $x \widetilde{\odot} y$ using Equation (2.1). This is equivalent to replacing the occurrences of $x \widetilde{\odot} y$ with a new fresh real-valued variable v and imposing $v = x \widetilde{\odot} y$. From Equation (2.1) it follows that $v \cdot 2^{p-exp} = \rho((x \odot y) \cdot 2^{p-exp})$. Thus, the final formula ϕ is

$$\phi :- \tilde{\phi}[v/x \widetilde{\odot} y] \wedge v \cdot 2^{p-exp} = \rho((x \odot y) \cdot 2^{p-exp}), \tag{2.2}$$

where $\tilde{\phi}[v/x \widetilde{\odot} y]$ denotes the Boolean formula $\tilde{\phi}$ where all the occurrences of $x \widetilde{\odot} y$ are replaced by v. The precision p is a constant that depends on the chosen floating-point format, while exp is an integer representing the exponent of the binary representation of $x \widetilde{\odot} y$.

To find an assignment for the exponent exp, FPRoCK performs in parallel a sequential and binary search over the dimension of $x \widetilde{\odot} y$, as opposed to the simple sequential search implemented in Realizer. The implementation of the function ρ depends on the selected rounding mode and can be defined using floor and ceiling operators (see [9] for details). Therefore, the transformed formula ϕ does not contain any floating-point operators, and hence it can be solved by any SMT solver that supports the fragment of real/integer arithmetics including floor and ceiling operators. FPRoCK uses three off-the-shelf SMT solvers as back-end procedures to solve the transformed formula: Mathsat [3], Z3 [11], and CVC4 [1]. Optionally, the constraint solver Colibri [10] is also available for use within FPRoCK. FPRoCK provides the option to relax the restriction on the minimum exponent to handle subnormal floats. This solution is sound in the sense that it preserves the unsatisfiability of the original formula. However, if this option is used, it is possible that FPRoCK finds an assignment to a float that is not representable in the chosen precision, and therefore is not a solution for the original formula. Furthermore, FPRoCK currently does not support special floating-point values such as *NaN* and *Infinity*.

3   Integrating FPRoCK in PRECiSA

PRECiSA[2] (Program Round-off Error Certifier via Static Analysis) [16] is a static analyzer based on abstract interpretation [4]. PRECiSA accepts as input a floating-point program and automatically generates a sound over-approximation of the floating-point round-off error and a proof certificate in the Prototype Verification System (PVS) [13] ensuring its correctness. For every possible combination of real and floating-point execution paths, PRECiSA computes a *conditional error bound* of the form $\langle \eta, \widetilde{\eta} \rangle \twoheadrightarrow (r, e)$, where η is a symbolic path condition over the reals, $\widetilde{\eta}$ is a symbolic path condition over the floats, and r, e are symbolic arithmetic expressions over the reals. Intuitively, $\langle \eta, \widetilde{\eta} \rangle \twoheadrightarrow (r, e)$ indicates that if the conditions η and $\widetilde{\eta}$ are satisfied, the output of the program using exact real number arithmetic is r and the round-off error of the floating-point implementation is bounded by e.

PRECiSA initially computes round-off error estimations in symbolic form so that the analysis is modular. Given the initial ranges for the input variables, PRECiSA uses the Kodiak global optimizer [12] to maximize the symbolic error expression e. Since the analysis collects information about real and floating-point execution paths, it is possible to consider the error of taking the incorrect branch compared to the ideal execution using real arithmetic. This happens when the guard of a conditional statement contains a floating-point expression whose round-off error makes the actual Boolean value of the guard differ from the value that would be obtained assuming real arithmetic. When the floating-point computation diverges from the real one, it is said to be *unstable*.

For example, consider the function $sign(\tilde{x}) = if\ \tilde{x} \geq 0\ then\ 1\ else\ -1$. PRECiSA computes a set of four different conditional error bounds: $\{\langle \chi_r(\tilde{x}) \geq 0, \tilde{x} \geq 0 \rangle \twoheadrightarrow (r = 1, e = 0), \langle \chi_r(\tilde{x}) < 0, \tilde{x} < 0 \rangle \twoheadrightarrow (r = -1, e = 0), \langle \chi_r(\tilde{x}) \geq 0, \tilde{x} < 0 \rangle \twoheadrightarrow (r = -1, e = 2), \langle \chi_r(\tilde{x}) < 0, \tilde{x} \geq 0 \rangle \twoheadrightarrow (r = 1, e = 2)\}$. The function $\chi_r : \widetilde{\mathbb{V}} \to \mathbb{V}$ associates with the floating-point variable $\tilde{x}$ a variable $x \in \mathbb{V}$ representing the real value of $\tilde{x}$. The first two elements correspond to the cases where real and floating-point computational flows coincide. In these cases, the error is 0 since the output is an integer number with no rounding error. The other two elements model the unstable paths. In these cases, the error is 2, which corresponds

---

[2] The PRECiSA distribution is available at https://github.com/nasa/PRECiSA.

to the difference between the output of the two branches. PRECiSA may produce conditional error bounds with unsatisfiable symbolic conditions (usually unstable), which correspond to execution paths that cannot take place. The presence of these spurious elements affects the accuracy of the computed error bound. For instance, in the previous example, if $|\chi_r(\tilde{x}) - \tilde{x}| \leq 0$ both unstable cases can be removed, and the overall error would be 0 instead of 2.

Real and floating-point conditions can be checked separately using SMT solvers that support real and/or floating-point arithmetic. However, the inconsistency often follows from the combination of the real and floating-point conditions. In fact, the floating-point expressions occurring in the conditions are implicitly related to their real arithmetic counterparts by their rounding error. Therefore, besides checking the two conditions separately, it is necessary to check them in conjunction with a set of constraints relating each arithmetic expression $\widetilde{expr}$ occurring in the conditions with its real number counterpart $R_{\mathbb{A}}(\widetilde{expr})$. $R_{\mathbb{A}}(\widetilde{expr})$ is defined by simply replacing in $\widetilde{expr}$ each floating-point operation with the corresponding real one and by applying χ_r to floating-point variables.

FPRoCK is suitable for solving such constraints thanks to its ability to reason about mixed real and floating-point formulas. Given a set ι of ranges for the input variables, for each conditional error bound $c = \langle \eta, \widetilde{\eta} \rangle \twoheadrightarrow (r, e)$ computed by PRECiSA, the following formula ψ modeling the information contained in the path conditions is checked using FPRoCK:

$$\psi :- \eta \wedge \widetilde{\eta} \wedge \bigwedge \{ |\widetilde{expr} - R_{\mathbb{A}}(\widetilde{expr})| \leq \epsilon \mid \widetilde{expr} \text{ occurs in } \widetilde{\eta},$$

$$\widetilde{expr} \notin \widetilde{\mathbb{V}}, \widetilde{expr} \notin \mathbb{F}, \epsilon = max(e)|_\iota \}$$
(3.1)

The value $max(e)|_\iota$ is the round-off error of $\widetilde{expr}$ assuming the input ranges in ι, and it is obtained by maximizing the symbolic error expression e with the Kodiak global optimizer. If ψ is unsatisfiable, then c is dropped from the solutions computed by PRECiSA. Otherwise, a counterexample is generated that may help to discover cases for which the computation is diverging or unsound.

Since FPRoCK currently supports only the basic arithmetic operators, while PRECiSA supports a broader variety of operators including transcendental functions, a sound approximation is needed for converting PRECiSA conditions into a valid input for FPRoCK. The proposed approach replaces in ψ each floating-point (respectively real) arithmetic expression with a fresh floating-point (respectively real) variable. This is sound but not complete, meaning it preserves just the unsatisfiability of the original formula. In other words, if $\psi[v_i/\widetilde{expr}_i]_{i=1}^n$ is unsatisfiable it follows that ψ is unsatisfiable, but if a solution is found for $\psi[v_i/\widetilde{expr}_i]_{i=1}^n$ there is no guarantee that an assignment satisfying ψ exists. This is enough for the purpose of eliminating spurious conditional bounds since it assures that no feasible condition gets eliminated. In practice, it is accurate enough to detect spurious unstable paths. When a path condition is deemed unsatisfiable by FPRoCK, PRECiSA states such unsatisfiability in the PVS formal certificate. For simple path conditions, this property can be automatically checked by PVS. Unfortunately, there are cases where human intervention is required to verify this part of the certificates.

Table 1 compares the original version of PRECiSA with the enhanced version that uses FPRoCK to detect the unsatisfiable conditions, along with the analysis tool Rosa [6] which also computes an over-approximation of the round-off error of a program. All the benchmarks are obtained by applying the transformation defined in [17] to code fragments from avionics software and the FPBench library [5]. A transformed program is guaranteed to return either the result of the original floating-point program, when it can be assured that both its real and floating-point flows agree, or a warning when these flows may diverge. The results show that FPRoCK helps PRECiSA improving the computed round-off error in 8 out of 11 benchmarks total. FPRoCK runs all search encoding (linear, binary) plus solver (MathSAT5, CVC4, Z3) combinations in parallel. It waits for all solvers to finish and performs a check on the consistency of the solutions.

Table 1. Experimental results showing absolute round-off error bounds and execution time in seconds (best results in bold).

Benchmark	PRECiSA		PRECiSA+FPRoCK		Rosa	
	Error	Time(s)	Error	Time(s)	Error	Time(s)
cubicSpline	2.70E+01	**0.07**	2.70E+01	97.8	**2.50E − 01**	24.1
eps_line	2.00E+00	**0.02**	**1.00E+00**	48.8	2.00E+00	15.5
jetApprox	1.51E+01	**12.79**	8.11E+00	263.3	**4.97E+00**	924.8
linearFit	1.08E+00	**0.06**	5.42E − 01	259.7	**3.19E − 01**	12.4
los	2.00E+00	**0.02**	**1.00E+00**	46.2	Not supported	n/a
quadraticFit	3.68E+00	**0.90**	3.68E+00	259.8	**1.27E − 01**	82.4
sign	2.00E+00	**0.02**	**1.00E+00**	32.1	2.00E+00	4.7
simpleInterpolator	2.25E+02	**0.03**	1.16E+02	93.8	**3.33E+01**	6.3
smartRoot	**1.75E+00**	0.32	**1.75E+00**	0.6	Not supported	n/a
styblinski	9.35E+01	**1.06**	6.66E+01	260.1	**6.55E+00**	77.0
tau	8.40E+06	**0.03**	**8.00E+06**	101.8	8.40E+06	20.7

4   Conclusions

This paper presents FPRoCK, a prototype tool for solving mixed real and floating-point formulas. FPRoCK extends the technique used in Realizer by adding support for such mixed formulas. FPRoCK is integrated into PRECiSA to improve its precision. Similarly, it could be integrated into other static analyzers, such as FPTaylor [15]. The current version of FPRoCK has some limitations in terms of expressivity and efficiency. Support for a vast range of operators, including transcendental functions, is contingent on the expressive power of the underlying SMT solvers. The performance of FPRoCK can be improved by returning a solution as soon as the first solver finalizes its search. However, finding an assignment for the exponent of each floating-point variable is still the major bottleneck of the analysis. The use of a branch-and-bound search to divide the state-space may help to mitigate this problem.

References

1. Barrett, C., et al.: CVC4. In: Gopalakrishnan, G., Qadeer, S. (eds.) CAV 2011. LNCS, vol. 6806, pp. 171–177. Springer, Heidelberg (2011). https://doi.org/10.1007/978-3-642-22110-1_14
2. Brillout, A., Kroening, D., Wahl, T.: Mixed abstractions for floating-point arithmetic. In: Proceedings of the 9th International Conference on Formal Methods in Computer-Aided Design (FMCAD), pp. 69–76. IEEE (2009)
3. Cimatti, A., Griggio, A., Schaafsma, B.J., Sebastiani, R.: The MathSAT5 SMT solver. In: Piterman, N., Smolka, S.A. (eds.) TACAS 2013. LNCS, vol. 7795, pp. 93–107. Springer, Heidelberg (2013). https://doi.org/10.1007/978-3-642-36742-7_7
4. Cousot, P., Cousot, R.: Abstract interpretation: a unified lattice model for static analysis of programs by construction or approximation of fixpoints. In: Proceedings of the 4th ACM SIGPLAN-SIGACT Symposium on Principles of Programming Languages (POPL), pp. 238–252. ACM (1977)
5. Damouche, N., Martel, M., Panchekha, P., Qiu, C., Sanchez-Stern, A., Tatlock, Z.: Toward a standard benchmark format and suite for floating-point analysis. In: Bogomolov, S., Martel, M., Prabhakar, P. (eds.) NSV 2016. LNCS, vol. 10152, pp. 63–77. Springer, Cham (2017). https://doi.org/10.1007/978-3-319-54292-8_6
6. Darulova, E., Kuncak, V.: Sound compilation of reals. In: Proceedings of the 41st Annual ACM SIGPLAN-SIGACT Symposium on Principles of Programming Languages (POPL), pp. 235–248. ACM (2014)
7. Howar, F., Jabbour, F., Mues, M.: JConstraints: a library for working with logic expressions in Java. In: Essays Dedicated to Bernhard Steffen on the Occasion of His 60th Birthday (2019, to appear)
8. IEEE: IEEE standard for binary floating-point arithmetic. Technical report, Institute of Electrical and Electronics Engineers (2008)
9. Leeser, M., Mukherjee, S., Ramachandran, J., Wahl, T.: Make it real: effective floating-point reasoning via exact arithmetic. In: Proceedings of the 17th Design, Automation and Test in Europe Conference and Exhibition (DATE), pp. 1–4. IEEE (2014)
10. Marre, B., Bobot, F., Chihani, Z.: Real behavior of floating point numbers. In: Proceedings of the 15th International Workshop on Satisfiability Modulo Theories (SMT) (2017)
11. de Moura, L., Bjørner, N.: Z3: an efficient SMT solver. In: Ramakrishnan, C.R., Rehof, J. (eds.) TACAS 2008. LNCS, vol. 4963, pp. 337–340. Springer, Heidelberg (2008). https://doi.org/10.1007/978-3-540-78800-3_24
12. Narkawicz, A., Muñoz, C.: A formally verified generic branching algorithm for global optimization. In: Cohen, E., Rybalchenko, A. (eds.) VSTTE 2013. LNCS, vol. 8164, pp. 326–343. Springer, Heidelberg (2014). https://doi.org/10.1007/978-3-642-54108-7_17
13. Owre, S., Rushby, J.M., Shankar, N.: PVS: a prototype verification system. In: Kapur, D. (ed.) CADE 1992. LNCS, vol. 607, pp. 748–752. Springer, Heidelberg (1992). https://doi.org/10.1007/3-540-55602-8_217
14. Ramachandran, J., Wahl, T.: Integrating proxy theories and numeric model lifting for floating-point arithmetic. In: Proceedings of the 16th International Conference on Formal Methods in Computer-Aided Design, (FMCAD), pp. 153–160. FMCAD Inc (2016)

15. Solovyev, A., Jacobsen, C., Rakamarić, Z., Gopalakrishnan, G.: Rigorous estimation of floating-point round-off errors with symbolic taylor expansions. In: Bjørner, N., de Boer, F. (eds.) FM 2015. LNCS, vol. 9109, pp. 532–550. Springer, Cham (2015). https://doi.org/10.1007/978-3-319-19249-9_33
16. Titolo, L., Feliú, M.A., Moscato, M., Muñoz, C.A.: An abstract interpretation framework for the round-off error analysis of floating-point programs. In: Dillig, I., Palsberg, J. (eds.) Verification, Model Checking, and Abstract Interpretation. LNCS, vol. 10747, pp. 516–537. Springer, Cham (2018). https://doi.org/10.1007/978-3-319-73721-8_24
17. Titolo, L., Muñoz, C.A., Feliú, M.A., Moscato, M.M.: Eliminating unstable tests in floating-point programs. In: Mesnard, F., Stuckey, P.J. (eds.) LOPSTR 2018. LNCS, vol. 11408, pp. 169–183. Springer, Cham (2019). https://doi.org/10.1007/978-3-030-13838-7_10
18. Zeljić, A., Backeman, P., Wintersteiger, C.M., Rümmer, P.: Exploring approximations for floating-point arithmetic using UppSAT. In: Galmiche, D., Schulz, S., Sebastiani, R. (eds.) IJCAR 2018. LNCS (LNAI), vol. 10900, pp. 246–262. Springer, Cham (2018). https://doi.org/10.1007/978-3-319-94205-6_17

Online Parametric Timed Pattern Matching with Automata-Based Skipping

Masaki Waga[1,2,3]($\boxtimes$) (ID) and Étienne André[1,4,5] (ID)

[1] National Institute of Informatics, Tokyo, Japan
mwaga@nii.ac.jp
[2] Sokendai (The Graduate University for Advanced Studies),
Kanagawa, Japan
[3] JSPS Research Fellow, Tokyo, Japan
[4] Université Paris 13, LIPN, CNRS, UMR 7030, 93430 Villetaneuse, France
[5] JFLI, CNRS, Tokyo, Japan

Abstract. Timed pattern matching has strong connections with *monitoring* real-time systems. Given a log and a specification containing timing parameters (that can capture uncertain or unknown constants), *parametric* timed pattern matching aims at exhibiting for which start and end dates, as well as which parameter valuations, a specification holds on that log. This problem is notably close to robustness. We propose here a new framework for parametric timed pattern matching. Not only we dramatically improve the efficiency when compared to a previous method based on parametric timed model checking, but we further propose optimizations based on skipping. Our algorithm is suitable for online monitoring, and experiments show that it is fast enough to be applied at runtime.

Keywords: Monitoring · Real-time systems ·
Parametric timed automata

1 Introduction

Monitoring real-time systems consists in deciding whether a log satisfies a specification. A problem of interest is to determine *for which segment* of the log the specification is satisfied or violated. This problem can be related to string matching and pattern matching. The *timed pattern matching problem* was formulated in [33], with subsequent works varying the setting and improving the technique (e.g., [8,34,35,37]). The problem takes as input a log and a specification, and decides where in the log the specification is satisfied or violated. In [35,37], we introduced a solution to the timed pattern matching problem where the log is given in the form of a timed word (a sequence of events with their associated

This work is partially supported by JST ERATO HASUO Metamathematics for Systems Design Project (No. JPMJER1603), by JSPS Grants-in-Aid No. 15KT0012 & 18J22498 and by the ANR national research program PACS (ANR-14-CE28-0002).

J. M. Badger and K. Y. Rozier (Eds.): NFM 2019, LNCS 11460, pp. 371–389, 2019.
https://doi.org/10.1007/978-3-030-20652-9_26

timestamps), and the specification in the form of a timed automaton (TA), an
extension of finite-state automata with clocks [1].

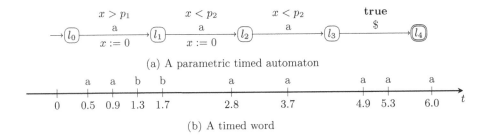

(a) A parametric timed automaton

(b) A timed word

Fig. 1. An example of parametric timed pattern matching [37]

Example 1. Consider the automaton in Fig. 1a, and fix $p_1 = 1$ and $p_2 = 1$—
which gives a timed automaton [1]. Here $ is a special terminal character. For
this timed automaton (say $\mathcal{A}$) and the target timed word w in Fig. 1b, the
output of the timed pattern matching problem is the set of matching intervals
$\{(t, t') \mid w|_{(t,t')} \in \mathcal{L}(\mathcal{A})\} = \{(t, t') \mid t \in [3.7, 3.9), t' \in (6.0, \infty)\}$.

While the log is by definition concrete, it may happen that the specification is
subject to uncertainty. For example, we may want to detect *cyclic patterns* with
a period d, without knowing the value of d with full certainty. Therefore, the
more abstract problem of *parametric timed pattern matching* becomes of interest:
**given a (concrete) timed log and an incomplete specification where
some of the timing constants may be known with limited precision or
completely unknown, what are the intervals and the valuations of the
parameters for which the specification holds?**

Coming back to Fig. 1, the question becomes to exhibit values for t, t', p_1, p_2
for which the specification holds on the log, i.e., $\{(t, t', v) \mid w|_{(t,t')} \in \mathcal{L}(v(\mathcal{A}))\}$,
where v denotes a valuation of p_1, p_2 and $v(\mathcal{A})$ denotes the replacement of p_1, p_2
in $\mathcal{A}$ with their respective valuation in v. In [5], we showed that this problem is
decidable (mainly due to the finiteness of the logs), and we proposed an approach
based on parametric timed model checking using timed words and parametric
timed automata [2], implemented in the IMITATOR model checker [4].

Contribution. Our contribution is threefold. First, we propose a new *ad-hoc*
technique for performing efficient parametric timed pattern matching. Second,
we propose optimizations based on *skipping*, in the line of [37]. Third, we implement our framework in a prototypical tool ParamMONAA, we perform a set of
experiments on a set of automotive benchmarks, and show that we increase the
efficiency compared to the state-of-the-art [5] by an order of magnitude. Our
algorithm is suitable for online monitoring, as it does not need the whole run
to be executed, and experiments show that it is fast enough to be applied at
runtime.

Related Work. Several algorithms have been proposed for online monitoring of real-time temporal logic specifications. Online monitoring consists in monitoring on-the-fly at runtime, while offline monitoring is performed after the execution is completed, with less hard constraints on the monitoring algorithm performance. An online monitoring algorithm for ptMTL (a past time fragment of MTL [29]) was proposed in [30] and an algorithm for MTL[U, S] (a variant of MTL with both forward and backward temporal modalities) was proposed in [22]. In addition, a case study on an autonomous research vehicle monitoring [27] shows such procedures can be performed in an actual vehicle.

The approaches most related to ours are [32–34]. In that series of works, logs are encoded by *signals*, i.e., values that vary over time. This can be seen as a *state-based* view, while our timed words are *event-based*. The formalism used for specification in [33,34] is timed regular expressions (TREs). An offline monitoring algorithm is presented in [33] and an online one is in [34]. These algorithms are implemented in the tool *Montre* [32]. In [12], the setting is signals matched against a temporal pattern; the construction is automata-based as in [35,37].

We described our previous work [5] as an *offline* algorithm. In fact, it is essentially *online* in the sense that it can potentially run with only a portion of the log: it relies on parallel composition of a specification automaton and a log automaton, and this parallel composition can be achieved on-the-fly. However, as mentioned in [13], "a good online monitoring algorithm must: (1) be able to generate intermediate estimates of property satisfaction based on partial signals, (2) use minimal amount of data storage, and (3) be able to run fast enough in a real-time setting." So, at least for point (3), the algorithm in [5] cannot really run in a real-time setting. In contrast, we claim our contribution here to be fast enough to run in a real-time setting, with runs of dozens of thousands of events being analyzable in less than a second.

Some algorithms have also been proposed for parameter identification of a temporal logic specification with uncertainty over a log. In the discrete time setting, an algorithm for an extension of LTL is proposed in [20]; and in the real-time setting, algorithms for parametric signal temporal logic (PSTL) are proposed in [7,10]. Although these works are related to our approach, previous approaches do not focus on segments of a log but on a whole log. In contrast, we exhibit intervals together with their associated parameter valuations, in a fully symbolic fashion. We believe our matching-based setting is advantageous in many usage scenarios e.g., from hours of a log of a car, extracting timing constraints of a certain actions to cause slipping. Also, our setting allows the patterns with complex timing constraints (see the pattern in Fig. 3c for example).

In [11], the robust pattern matching problem is considered over signal regular expressions, consisting in computing the *quantitative* (robust) semantics of a signal relative to an expression. For piecewise-constant and piecewise-linear signals, the problem can be effectively solved using a finite union of zones.

Further works attempted to quantify the distance between a specification and a signal temporal logic (STL) specification (e.g., [15,18,25]). The main difference with our work is that these works compute a distance w.r.t. to a whole log, while we aim at exhibiting where in the log is the property satisfied; our notion of parameters can also be seen as a relative time distance. However, our work is closer to the robust satisfaction of guards rather than signal values; in that sense, our contribution is more related to the time robustness in [19] or the distance in [6].

Finally, while our work is related to parameter synthesis, in the sense that we identify parameter valuations in the property such that it holds (or not), the term "parameter synthesis" is also used in monitoring with a slightly different meaning: given a *model* with parameters, the goal is to find parameters that maximize the robustness of the specification, i.e., satisfying behaviors for a range of parameters for which the model robustly satisfies the property. A notable tool achieving this is BREACH [17].

A summary of various matching problems is recalled in Table 1.

Table 1. Matching problems

	Log, target	Specification, pattern	Output
String matching	A word $w \in \Sigma^*$	A word $pat \in \Sigma^*$	$\{(i,j) \in (\mathbb{N}_{>0})^2 \mid w(i,j) = pat\}$
Pattern matching (PM)	A word $w \in \Sigma^*$	An NFA $\mathcal{A}$	$\{(i,j) \in (\mathbb{N}_{>0})^2 \mid w(i,j) \in \mathcal{L}(\mathcal{A})\}$
Timed PM	A timed word $w \in (\Sigma \times \mathbb{R}_{>0})^*$	A TA $\mathcal{A}$	$\{(t,t') \in (\mathbb{R}_{>0})^2 \mid w|_{(t,t')} \in \mathcal{L}(\mathcal{A})\}$
Parametric timed PM	A timed word $w \in (\Sigma \times \mathbb{R}_{>0})^*$	A PTA $\mathcal{A}$	$\{(t,t',v) \mid w|_{(t,t')} \in \mathcal{L}(v(\mathcal{A}))\}$

Outline. We introduce the necessary definitions and state our main objective in Sect. 2. We introduce an online algorithm for parametric timed pattern matching in Sect. 3, and enhance it with skipping in Sect. 4. We evaluate our algorithms in Sect. 5 and conclude in Sect. 6.

2 Preliminaries and Objective

Our target strings are *timed words* [1], that are time-stamped words over an alphabet Σ. Our patterns are given by parametric timed automata [2].

For an alphabet Σ, a *timed word* is a sequence w of pairs $(a_i, \tau_i) \in (\Sigma \times \mathbb{R}_{>0})$ satisfying $\tau_i < \tau_{i+1}$ for any $i \in [1, |w| - 1]$. We require $\tau_0 = 0$. For an alphabet Σ, we denote the set of the timed words on Σ by $\mathcal{T}(\Sigma)$. For an alphabet Σ and $n \in \mathbb{N}_{>0}$, we denote the set of the timed words of length n on Σ by $\mathcal{T}^n(\Sigma)$. Given a timed word w, we often denote it by $(\overline{a}, \overline{\tau})$, where $\overline{a}$ is the sequence $(a_1, a_2, \cdots)$ and $\overline{\tau}$ is the sequence $(\tau_1, \tau_2, \cdots)$. Let $w = (\overline{a}, \overline{\tau})$ be a timed word. We denote the subsequence $(a_i, \tau_i), (a_{i+1}, \tau_{i+1}), \cdots, (a_j, \tau_j)$ by $w(i,j)$. For $t \in \mathbb{R}$ such that $-\tau_1 < t$, the *t-shift* of w is $(\overline{a}, \overline{\tau}) + t = (\overline{a}, \overline{\tau} + t)$ where $\overline{\tau} + t = \tau_1 + t, \tau_2 + t, \cdots, \tau_{|\tau|} + t$. For timed words $w = (\overline{a}, \overline{\tau})$ and $w' = (\overline{a'}, \overline{\tau'})$, their *absorbing concatenation* is $w \circ w' = (\overline{a} \circ \overline{a'}, \overline{\tau} \circ \overline{\tau'})$ where $\overline{a} \circ \overline{a'}$ and $\overline{\tau} \circ \overline{\tau'}$ are usual concatenations, and their *non-absorbing concatenation* is $w \cdot w' = w \circ (w' + \tau_{|w|})$. The concatenations on $\mathcal{T}(\Sigma)$ are also defined similarly. For a set $W \in \mathcal{T}(\Sigma)$ of timed words, its untimed projection $\text{Untimed}(W) \in \Sigma^*$ is $\{\overline{a} \mid (\overline{a}, \overline{\tau}) \in W\}$.

For a timed word $w = (\bar{a}, \bar{\tau})$ on Σ and $t, t' \in \mathbb{R}_{\geq 0}$ satisfying $t < t'$, a *timed word segment* $w|_{(t,t')}$ is defined by the timed word $(w(i, j) - t) \circ (\$, t' - t)$ on the augmented alphabet $\Sigma \sqcup \{\$\}$, where i, j are chosen so that $\tau_{i-1} \leq t < \tau_i$ and $\tau_j < t' \leq \tau_{j+1}$. Here the fresh symbol $\$$ is called the *terminal character*.

We assume a set $\mathbb{X} = \{x_1, \ldots, x_H\}$ of *clocks*, i.e., real-valued variables that evolve at the same rate. A clock valuation is $\nu : \mathbb{X} \to \mathbb{R}_{\geq 0}$. We write $\mathbf{0}$ for the clock valuation assigning 0 to all clocks. Given $d \in \mathbb{R}_{\geq 0}$, $\nu + d$ is s.t. $(\nu + d)(x) = \nu(x) + d$, for all $x \in \mathbb{X}$. Given $R \subseteq \mathbb{X}$, we define the *reset* of a valuation ν, denoted by $[\nu]_R$, as follows: $[\nu]_R(x) = 0$ if $x \in R$, and $[\nu]_R(x) = \nu(x)$ otherwise.

We assume a set $\mathbb{P} = \{p_1, \ldots, p_M\}$ of *parameters*. A parameter *valuation* v is $v : \mathbb{P} \to \mathbb{Q}_+$. We assume $\bowtie \in \{<, \leq, =, \geq, >\}$. A guard g is a constraint over $\mathbb{X} \cup \mathbb{P}$ defined by a conjunction of inequalities of the form $x \bowtie d$, or $x \bowtie p$ with $d \in \mathbb{N}$ and $p \in \mathbb{P}$. Given g, we write $\nu \models v(g)$ if the expression obtained by replacing each x with $\nu(x)$ and each p with $v(p)$ in g evaluates to true.

A linear term over $\mathbb{X} \cup \mathbb{P}$ is of the form $\sum_{1 \leq i \leq H} \alpha_i x_i + \sum_{1 \leq j \leq M} \beta_j p_j + d$, with $x_i \in \mathbb{X}$, $p_j \in \mathbb{P}$, and $\alpha_i, \beta_j, d \in \mathbb{Z}$. A *constraint* $\bar{C}$ (i.e., a convex polyhedron) over $\mathbb{X} \cup \mathbb{P}$ is a conjunction of inequalities of the form $lt \bowtie 0$, where lt is a linear term. Given a set $\mathbb{P}$ of parameters, we denote by $C\downarrow_\mathbb{P}$ the projection of C onto $\mathbb{P}$, i.e., obtained by eliminating the variables not in $\mathbb{P}$ (e.g., using Fourier-Motzkin). $\perp$ denotes the constraint over $\mathbb{P}$ representing the empty set of parameter valuations.

2.1 Parametric Timed Automata

Parametric timed automata (PTA) extend timed automata with parameters within guards in place of integer constants [2].

Definition 1 (PTA). *A PTA $\mathcal{A}$ is a tuple $\mathcal{A} = (\Sigma, L, l_0, F, \mathbb{X}, \mathbb{P}, E)$, where:*

1. *Σ is a finite set of actions,*
2. *L is a finite set of locations,*
3. *$l_0 \in L$ is the initial location,*
4. *$F \subseteq L$ is the set of accepting locations,*
5. *$\mathbb{X}$ is a finite set of clocks,*
6. *$\mathbb{P}$ is a finite set of parameters,*
7. *E is a finite set of edges $e = (l, g, a, R, l')$ where $l, l' \in L$ are the source and target locations, $a \in \Sigma$, $R \subseteq \mathbb{X}$ is a set of clocks to be reset, and g is a guard.*

Given v, we denote by $v(\mathcal{A})$ the non-parametric structure where all occurrences of a parameter p_i have been replaced by $v(p_i)$. We refer as a *timed automaton* to any structure $v(\mathcal{A})$, by assuming a rescaling of the constants: by multiplying all constants in $v(\mathcal{A})$ by the least common multiple of their denominators, we obtain an equivalent (integer-valued) TA.

Let us now recall the concrete semantics of TA.

Definition 2 (Semantics of a TA). *Given a PTA $\mathcal{A} = (\Sigma, L, l_0, F, \mathbb{X}, \mathbb{P}, E)$, and a parameter valuation v, the semantics of $v(\mathcal{A})$ is given by the timed transition system (TTS) $(S, s_0, \to)$, with*

- $S = L \times \mathbb{R}_{\geq 0}^H$
- $s_0 = (l_0, \mathbf{0})$,
- $\rightarrow$ consists of the discrete and (continuous) delay transition relations: (i) discrete transitions: $(l, \nu) \xmapsto{e} (l', \nu')$, if there exists $e = (l, g, a, R, l') \in E$, such that $\nu' = [\nu]_R$, and $\nu \models \nu(g)$. (ii) delay transitions: $(l, \nu) \xmapsto{d} (l, \nu + d)$, with $d \in \mathbb{R}_{\geq 0}$.

Moreover we write $(l, \nu) \xrightarrow{(e,d)} (l', \nu')$ for a combination of a delay and discrete transition if $\exists \nu'' : (l, \nu) \xmapsto{d} (l, \nu'') \xmapsto{e} (l', \nu')$.

Given a TA $\nu(\mathcal{A})$ with concrete semantics $(S, s_0, \rightarrow)$, we refer to the states of S as the *concrete states* of $\nu(\mathcal{A})$. A *run* of $\nu(\mathcal{A})$ is an alternating sequence of concrete states of $\nu(\mathcal{A})$ and pairs of edges and delays starting from the initial state s_0 of the form $s_0, (e_0, d_0), s_1, \cdots$ with $i = 0, 1, \ldots, e_i \in E$, $d_i \in \mathbb{R}_{\geq 0}$ and $(s_i, e_i, s_{i+1}) \in \rightarrow$. Given such a run, the associated *timed word* is $(a_1, \tau_1), (a_2, \tau_2), \cdots$, where a_i is the action of edge e_{i-1}, and $\tau_i = \sum_{0 \leq j \leq i-1} d_j$, for $i = 1, 2 \cdots$.[1] Given $s = (l, \nu)$, we say that s is reachable in $\nu(\mathcal{A})$ if s appears in a run of $\nu(\mathcal{A})$. By extension, we say that l is reachable; and by extension again, given a set T of locations, we say that T is reachable if there exists $l \in T$ such that l is reachable in $\nu(\mathcal{A})$.

A finite run is *accepting* if its last state (l, ν) is such that $l \in F$. The (timed) *language* $\mathcal{L}(\nu(\mathcal{A}))$ is defined to be the set of timed words associated with all accepting runs of $\nu(\mathcal{A})$.

2.2 Reachability Synthesis

We use here reachability synthesis to improve our new parametric timed pattern matching algorithm with a skipping optimization. This procedure, called EFsynth, takes as input a PTA $\mathcal{A}$ and a set of target locations T, and attempts to synthesize all parameter valuations v for which T is reachable in $v(\mathcal{A})$. EFsynth was formalized in e.g., [26] and is a procedure that may not terminate, but that computes an exact result (sound and complete) if it terminates. EFsynth traverses the *parametric zone graph* of $\mathcal{A}$, which is a potentially infinite extension of the well-known zone graph of TAs (see, e.g., [3, 26]).

2.3 Parametric Timed Pattern Matching

Let us recall parametric timed pattern matching [5].

> **Parametric timed pattern matching problem:**
> INPUT: a PTA $\mathcal{A}$, a timed word w over a common alphabet Σ
> PROBLEM: compute all the triples (t, t', v) for which the segment $w|_{(t,t')}$ is accepted by $v(\mathcal{A})$. That is, it requires the *match set* $\mathcal{M}(w, \mathcal{A}) = \{(t, t', v) \mid w|_{(t,t')} \in \mathcal{L}(v(\mathcal{A}))\}$.

---

[1] The "−1" in indices comes from the fact that, following usual conventions in the literature, states are numbered starting from 0 while words are numbered from 1.

The match set $\mathcal{M}(w, \mathcal{A})$ is in general uncountable; however it allows finite representation, as a finite union of special polyhedra in $|\mathbb{P}| + 2$ dimensions, i.e., the number of parameters $+ 2$ further dimensions for t and t' [5].

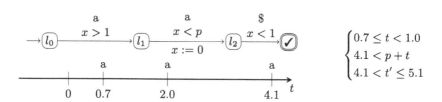

Fig. 2. Example of parametric timed pattern matching: input PTA and timed word (left); and output polyhedron (right)

3 An Online Algorithm for Parametric Timed Pattern Matching

In this section, we present an online algorithm for parametric timed pattern matching, which is our first contribution. Similarly to the online algorithm for timed pattern matching in [35], our algorithm finds all the matching triples $(t, t', v) \in \mathcal{M}(w, \mathcal{A})$ by a breadth-first search. Our algorithm is online in the following sense: after reading the i-th element (a_i, τ_i) of the timed word $w = (\overline{a}, \overline{\tau})$, it immediately outputs all the matching triples (t, t', v) over the available prefix $(a_1, \tau_1), (a_2, \tau_2), \ldots, (a_i, \tau_i)$ of w.

Firstly, we define the auxiliary for our online algorithm for parametric timed pattern matching. We introduce an additional variable t representing the absolute time of the beginning of the matching. We use a function $\rho \colon \mathbb{X} \to (\mathbb{R}_{>0} \sqcup \{t\})$ to represent the latest reset time of each clock variable $x \in \mathbb{X}$. Intuitively, $\rho(x) = \tau \in \mathbb{R}_{>0}$ means the latest reset of x is at τ, and $\rho(x) = t$ means x is not reset after the beginning of the matching.

Definition 3 $(\mathrm{eval}(\rho, \tau), \mathrm{reset}(\rho, R, \tau), \rho_\emptyset)$. *Let $\mathbb{X}$ be the set of clock variables and t be the variable for the beginning of a matching. For a function $\rho \colon \mathbb{X} \to (\mathbb{R}_{>0} \sqcup \{t\})$ and the current time $\tau \in \mathbb{R}_{>0}$, $\mathrm{eval}(\rho, \tau)$ is the constraint $\mathrm{eval}(\rho, \tau) = \bigwedge_{x \in \mathbb{X}} (x = \tau - \rho(x))$ on $\mathbb{X} \sqcup \{t\}$. For a function $\rho \colon \mathbb{X} \to (\mathbb{R}_{>0} \sqcup \{t\})$, the set $R \subseteq \mathbb{X}$ of clocks to be reset, and the current time $\tau \in \mathbb{R}_{>0}$, $\mathrm{reset}(\rho, R, \tau) \colon \mathbb{X} \to (\mathbb{R}_{>0} \sqcup \{t\})$ is the following function.*

$$\mathrm{reset}(\rho, R, \tau)(x) = \begin{cases} \tau & \text{if } x \in R \\ \rho(x) & \text{if } x \notin R \end{cases}$$

By $\rho_\emptyset \colon \mathbb{X} \to (\mathbb{R}_{>0} \sqcup \{t\})$, we denote the function mapping each $x \in \mathbb{X}$ to t.

Intuitively, $\mathrm{eval}(\rho, \tau)$ is the constraint corresponding to the clock valuation, and $\mathrm{reset}(\rho, R, \tau)$ is the operation to reset the clock variables $x \in R$ at τ.

Algorithm 1 shows our online algorithm for parametric timed pattern matching. In the pseudocode, we used *CurrConf*, *PrevConf*, and Z: *CurrConf* and *PrevConf* are finite sets of triples $(l, \rho, \mathcal{C})$ made of a location $l \in L$, a mapping $\rho \colon \mathbb{X} \to (\mathbb{R}_{>0} \sqcup \{t\})$ denoting the latest reset of each clock, and a constraint $\mathcal{C}$ over $\mathbb{P} \sqcup \{t\}$; and Z is a finite set of constraints over $\mathbb{P} \sqcup \{t, t'\}$. As a running example, we use the PTA and the timed word in Fig. 2.

Algorithm 1. Online parametric timed pattern matching without skipping

---

Require: A timed word $w = (\bar{a}, \bar{\tau})$, and a PTA $\mathcal{A} = (\Sigma, L, l_0, F, \mathbb{X}, \mathbb{P}, E)$.
Ensure: $\bigvee Z$ is the match set $\mathcal{M}(w, \mathcal{A})$
1:   *CurrConf* $\leftarrow \emptyset$; $Z \leftarrow \emptyset$
2:   **for** $i \leftarrow 1$ **to** $|w|$ **do**
3:      **push** $(l_0, \rho_\emptyset, (\tau_{i-1} \le t < \tau_i))$ **to** *CurrConf*
4:      **for** $(l, \rho, \mathcal{C}) \in$ *CurrConf* **do**   ▷ Lines 4 to 7 try to insert $\$$ in $(\tau_{i-1}, \tau_i]$.
5:         **for** $l_f \in F$ **do**
6:            **for** $(l, g, \$, R, l_f) \in E$ **do**
7:               **push** $\big(\mathcal{C} \wedge (\tau_{i-1} < t' \le \tau_i) \wedge g \wedge \mathrm{eval}(\rho, t')\big){\downarrow}_{\mathbb{P} \sqcup \{t, t'\}}$ **to** Z
8:      $(\textit{PrevConf}, \textit{CurrConf}) \leftarrow (\textit{CurrConf}, \emptyset)$
9:      **for** $(l, \rho, \mathcal{C}) \in$ *PrevConf* **do**   ▷ Lines 9 to 13 try to go forward using (a_i, τ_i).
10:        **for** $(l, g, a_i, R, l') \in E$ **do**
11:            $\mathcal{C}' \leftarrow \big(\mathcal{C} \wedge g \wedge \mathrm{eval}(\rho, \tau_i)\big){\downarrow}_{\mathbb{P} \sqcup \{t\}}$
12:            **if** $\mathcal{C}' \ne \bot$ **then**
13:               **push** $(l', \mathrm{reset}(\rho, R, \tau), \mathcal{C}')$ **to** *CurrConf*
14: **push** $(l_0, \rho_\emptyset, \{\tau_{|w|} \le t < \infty\})$ **to** *CurrConf*
15: **for** $(l, \rho, \mathcal{C}) \in$ *CurrConf* **do**   ▷ Lines 15 to 18 try to insert $\$$ in $(\tau_{|w|}, \infty)$.
16:      **for** $l_f \in F$ **do**
17:         **for** $(l, g, \$, R, l_f) \in E$ **do**
18:            **push** $\big(\mathcal{C} \wedge (\tau_{|w|} < t' < \infty) \wedge g \wedge \mathrm{eval}(\rho, t')\big){\downarrow}_{\mathbb{P} \sqcup \{t, t'\}}$ **to** Z

At first, the counter i is 1 (line 2), and we start the matching trial from $t \in [\tau_0, \tau_1)$. At line 3, we add the new configuration $(l_0, \rho_\emptyset, (\tau_0 \le t < \tau_1))$ to *CurrConf*, which means we are at the initial location l_0, we have no reset of the clock variables yet, and we can potentially start the matching from any $t \in [\tau_0, \tau_1)$. In lines 4 to 7, we try to insert $\$$ (i.e., the end of the matching) in $(\tau_0, \tau_1]$; in our running example in Fig. 2, since there is no edge from l_0 to the accepting state, we immediately jump to line 8. Then, in lines 9 to 13, we consume $(a_1, \tau_1) = (a, 0.7)$ and try to transit from l_0 to l_1. The guard $x > 1$ at the edge from l_0 to l_1 is examined at line 11. We take the conjunction of the current constraint $\mathcal{C}$, the guard g, and the constraints $\mathrm{eval}(\rho, \tau_i)$ on the clock valuations. We take the projection to $\mathbb{P} \sqcup \{t\}$ because the constraint on the clock variables changes after time passing. Since no clock variable is reset so far, the constraint on the clock valuation is $x = \tau_1 - t$. The constraint $\mathcal{C} \wedge g \wedge \mathrm{eval}(\rho, \tau_1) = (0 \le t < 0.7) \wedge (x > 1) \wedge (x = 0.7 - t)$ is unsatisfiable and we go back to line 3.

At line 3, we add the new configuration $(l_0, \rho_\emptyset, (\tau_1 \le t < \tau_2))$ to *CurrConf*. Similarly, we immediately jump to line 8, and we try the edge from l_0 to l_1 in lines 9 to 13. This time, the constraint $\mathcal{C} \wedge g \wedge \mathrm{eval}(\rho, \tau_2) = (0.7 \le t < 2.0) \wedge (x > 1) \wedge (x = 2.0 - t)$ is satisfiable at line 12, and we push the next configuration $(l_1, \rho_\emptyset, \mathcal{C}')$ to *CurrConf* at line 13.

Similarly, we keep adding and updating configurations until the end of the input timed word w. Finally, in lines 15 to 18, we try to insert $\$$ in $(\tau_3, \infty) = (4.1, \infty)$. We can use the edge from l_2 to the accepting state, and we add the constraint at the right of Fig. 2 to Z.

Algorithm 1 terminates because the size of $CurrConf$ is always finite. Algorithm 1 is correct because it symbolically keeps track of all the runs of $v(\mathcal{A})$ over $w|_{(t,t')}$ for any $v \in (\mathbb{Q}_+)^{\mathbb{P}}$ and $(t, t') \subseteq \mathbb{R}_{\geq 0}$.

4   Skipping Enhanced Parametric Timed Pattern Matching

In this section, we present automata-based skipping for Algorithm 1, which is our second contribution. In an algorithm with skipping, the counter i in Algorithm 1 is increased at line 2 by the *skip value*. The skip value can be more than 1 and, as a consequence, some unnecessary matching trials may be prevented. A large part of the skip value computation can be reused and the whole algorithm can be faster. Following [37], we employ *FJS-style* skipping [21]. An FJS-style skipping consists of two skip value functions: the KMP-style skip value function Δ_{KMP} [28] and the Quick Search-style skip value function Δ_{QS} [31]. See [36] for the proofs.

The following are auxiliary for the skip values. For a PTA $\mathcal{A}$ and a parameter valuation v, the language without the last element is denoted by $\mathcal{L}_{-\$}(v(\mathcal{A})) = \{w(1, |w| - 1) \mid w \in \mathcal{L}(v(\mathcal{A}))\}$. For a PTA $\mathcal{A} = (\Sigma, L, l_0, F, \mathbb{X}, \mathbb{P}, E)$ and $l \in L$, $\mathcal{A}_l$ denotes the PTA $\mathcal{A}_l = (\Sigma, L, l_0, \{l\}, \mathbb{X}, \mathbb{P}, E)$.

KMP-Style Skip Values. Given a location $l \in L$ and a set $V \subseteq (\mathbb{Q}_+)^{\mathbb{P}}$ of parameter valuations, the *KMP-style skip value function* Δ_{KMP} returns the skip value $\Delta_{\text{KMP}}(l, V) \in \mathbb{N}_{>0}$. The location l and the parameter valuations V present one of the configurations in the previous matching trial. We utilize the pair (l, V) to overapproximate the subsequence $w(i, j)$ of the timed word w examined in the latest matching trial.

Definition 4 (Δ_{KMP}). *Let $\mathcal{A}$ be a PTA $\mathcal{A} = (\Sigma, L, l_0, F, \mathbb{X}, \mathbb{P}, E)$. For $l \in L$ and $n \in \mathbb{N}_{>0}$, let $V_{l,n}$ be the set of parameter valuations v such that there is a parameter valuation $v' \in (\mathbb{Q}_+)^{\mathbb{P}}$ satisfying $\mathcal{L}(v(\mathcal{A}_l)) \cdot \mathcal{T}(\Sigma) \cap \mathcal{T}^n(\Sigma) \cdot \{w'' + t \mid w'' \in \mathcal{L}_{-\$}(v'(\mathcal{A})), t > 0\} \cdot \mathcal{T}(\Sigma) \neq \emptyset$. The KMP-style skip value function $\Delta_{\text{KMP}} \colon L \times \mathcal{P}((\mathbb{Q}_+)^{\mathbb{P}}) \to \mathbb{N}_{>0}$ is $\Delta_{\text{KMP}}(l, V) = \min\{n \in \mathbb{N}_{>0} \mid V \subseteq V_{l,n}\}$.*

Let l be a location we reached in the end of the matching trial from $i \in \{1, 2, \ldots, |w|\}$ for the parameter valuation v. Intuitively, $w(i, |w|)$ is overapproximated by $\mathcal{L}(v(\mathcal{A}_l)) \cdot \mathcal{T}(\Sigma)$. For $n \in \mathbb{N}_{>0}$, the matching from $i + n$ is overapproximated by $\bigcup_{v' \in (\mathbb{Q}_+)^{\mathbb{P}}} \mathcal{T}^n(\Sigma) \cdot \{w'' + t \mid w'' \in \mathcal{L}_{-\$}(v'(\mathcal{A})), t > 0\} \cdot \mathcal{T}(\Sigma)$. Therefore, $v \notin V_{l,n}$ implies that we have no matching from $i + n$, and we can skip the matching trials from $i + 1, i + 2, \ldots, i + \Delta_{\text{KMP}}(l, \{v\}) - 1$. We note that if we reached both l and l', the intersection $(\mathcal{L}(v(\mathcal{A}_l)) \cdot \mathcal{T}(\Sigma)) \cap (\mathcal{L}(v(\mathcal{A}_{l'})) \cdot \mathcal{T}(\Sigma))$ is an overapproximation of $w(i, |w|)$, and therefore, we take the maximum of $\Delta_{\text{KMP}}(l, V)$ over the reached configurations.

Since $V_{l,n}$ is independent of the timed word w, we can compute it before the matching trials by reachability synthesis of PTAs. See [36] for the construction of the PTAs. During the matching trials, only the inclusion checking $V \subseteq V_{l,n}$ is necessary. This test can be achieved thanks to convex polyhedra inclusion.

Theorem 1. *Let $\mathcal{A}$ be a PTA $\mathcal{A} = (\Sigma, L, l_0, F, \mathbb{X}, \mathbb{P}, E)$ and let $w \in \mathcal{T}(\Sigma)$. For any subsequence $w(i,j)$ of w and for any $(l,v) \in L \times (\mathbb{Q}_+)^{\mathbb{P}}$, if there exists $t \in \mathbb{R}_{\geq 0}$ satisfying $w(i,j) - t \in \mathcal{L}(v(\mathcal{A}_l))$, for any $n \in \{1, 2, \ldots, \Delta_{\mathrm{KMP}}(l, \{v\}) - 1\}$, we have $\left([\tau_{i+n-1}, \tau_{i+n}) \times \mathbb{R}_{>0} \times (\mathbb{Q}_+)^{\mathbb{P}}\right) \cap \mathcal{M}(w, \mathcal{A}) = \emptyset$.* $\square$

Although $V_{l,n}$ can be computed before the matching trials, Δ_{KMP} requires checking $V \subseteq V_{l,n}$ after each matching trial, which means a polyhedral inclusion test in $|\mathbb{P}| + 2$ dimensions. To reduce this runtime overhead, we define the *non-parametric* KMP-style skip value function $\Delta'_{\mathrm{KMP}}(l) = \min_{v \in (\mathbb{Q}_+)^{\mathbb{P}}} \Delta_{\mathrm{KMP}}(l, \{v\})$. For comparison, we refer Δ_{KMP} as the *parametric* KMP-style skip value function.

Quick Search-Style Skip Values. Given an action $a \in \Sigma$, the *Quick Search-style skip value function* Δ_{QS} returns the skip value $\Delta_{\mathrm{QS}}(a) \in \mathbb{N}_{>0}$. Before the matching trial from the i-th element (a_i, τ_i), we look ahead the action a_{i+N-1}, where N is the length of the shortest matching. If we observe that there is no matching, we also look ahead the action a_{i+N} and skip by $\Delta_{\mathrm{QS}}(a_{i+N})$. The construction of Δ_{QS} is by reachability emptiness of PTAs, i.e., the emptiness of the valuation set reaching a given location.

Definition 5 (Δ_{QS}). *For a PTA $\mathcal{A} = (\Sigma, L, l_0, F, \mathbb{X}, \mathbb{P}, E)$, the* Quick-Search-style skip value function $\Delta_{\mathrm{QS}} \colon \Sigma \to \mathbb{N}_{>0}$ *is as follows, where $N \in \mathbb{N}_{>0}$ is* $N = \min\{|w| \mid w \in \bigcup_{v \in (\mathbb{Q}_+)^{\mathbb{P}}} \mathcal{L}_{-\$}(v(\mathcal{A}))\}$.

$$\Delta_{\mathrm{QS}}(a) = \min\left\{n \in \mathbb{N}_{>0} \mid \exists v \in (\mathbb{Q}_+)^{\mathbb{P}}. \Sigma^N a \Sigma^* \cap \Sigma^n \mathrm{Untimed}(\mathcal{L}_{-\$}(v(\mathcal{A}))) \neq \emptyset\right\}$$

For $i \in \{1, 2, \ldots, |w|\}$, $w(i, |w|)$ is overapproximated by $\Sigma^N a_{i+N} \Sigma^*$. For $n \in \mathbb{N}_{>0}$, the matching from $i + n$ is overapproximated by $\bigcup_{v \in (\mathbb{Q}_+)^{\mathbb{P}}} \Sigma^n$ $\mathrm{Untimed}(\mathcal{L}_{-\$}(v(\mathcal{A})))$. Therefore, for any $n \in \{1, 2, \ldots, \Delta_{\mathrm{QS}}(a_{i+N}) - 1\}$, we have no matching from $i + n$ and we can skip these matching trials.

Theorem 2. *Let $\mathcal{A}$ be a PTA $\mathcal{A} = (\Sigma, L, l_0, F, \mathbb{X}, \mathbb{P}, E)$, let $w = (\bar{a}, \bar{\tau}) \in \mathcal{T}(\Sigma)$, and let $N = \min\{|w| \mid w \in \bigcup_{v \in (\mathbb{Q}_+)^{\mathbb{P}}} \mathcal{L}_{-\$}(v(\mathcal{A}))\}$. For any index $i \in \{1, 2, \ldots, |w|\}$ of w and for any $m \in \{1, 2, \ldots, \Delta_{\mathrm{QS}}(a_{i+N}) - 1\}$, we have $\left([\tau_{i+m-1}, \tau_{i+m}) \times \mathbb{R}_{>0} \times (\mathbb{Q}_+)^{\mathbb{P}}\right) \cap \mathcal{M}(w, \mathcal{A}) = \emptyset$.* $\square$

Algorithm 2 shows an improvement of Algorithm 1 enhanced by skipping. The loop in lines 2 to 13 of Algorithm 1 is used in the matching trial i.e., lines 7 to 9 of Algorithm 2. After reading the i-th element (a_i, τ_i) of the timed word $w = (\bar{a}, \bar{\tau})$, Algorithm 2 does not immediately output the matching over the available prefix $(a_1, \tau_1), (a_2, \tau_2), \ldots, (a_i, \tau_i)$ of w, but it still outputs the matching before obtaining the entire timed word with some delay. At line 10, it skips using the parametric KMP-style skip value $\Delta_{\mathrm{KMP}}(l, V)$. We can employ the non-parametric KMP-style skip value by replacing $\Delta_{\mathrm{KMP}}(l, V)$ with $\Delta'_{\mathrm{KMP}}(l)$.

5   Experiments

We implemented our online algorithms for parametric timed pattern matching in a tool `ParamMONAA`. We implemented the following three algorithms: the online algorithm without skipping (Algorithm 1, referred as "no skip"); the online algorithm with parametric skipping (Algorithm 2, referred as "parametric skip"); and the online algorithm with non-parametric skipping (Algorithm 2 where $\Delta_{\text{KMP}}(l, V)$ at line 10 is replaced with $\Delta'_{\text{KMP}}(l)$, referred as "non-parametric skip"). In the skip value computation, we use reachability synthesis for PTAs. Since reachability synthesis is intractable in general (the emptiness problem, i.e., the (non-)existence of a valuation reaching a given location, is undecidable [2]), we use the following overapproximation: after investigating 100 configurations, we speculate that all the inconclusive parameter valuations are reachable parameter valuations. We remark that this overapproximation does not affect the correctness of parametric timed pattern matching, as it potentially *decreases* the skip value. We conducted experiments to answer the following research questions.

Algorithm 2. Parametric timed pattern matching with parametric skipping

---

Require: A timed word w and a PTA $\mathcal{A} = (\Sigma, L, l_0, F, \mathbb{X}, \mathbb{P}, E)$
Ensure: Z is the match set $\mathcal{M}(w, \mathcal{A})$
1: $i \leftarrow 1$ ▷ i is the position in w of the beginning of the current matching trial
2: $N = \min\{|w| \mid w \in \bigcup_{v \in (\mathbb{Q}_+)^{\mathbb{P}}} \mathcal{L}_{-\$}(v(\mathcal{A}))\}$
3: **while** $i \leq |w| - N + 1$ **do**
4:   $\mid$ **while** $\forall v \in (\mathbb{Q}_+)^{\mathbb{P}}, (\overline{a'}, \overline{\tau'}) \in \mathcal{L}(v(\mathcal{A})). a_{i+N-1} \neq a'_N$ **do**
                                              ▷ Try matching the tail of $\mathcal{L}(v(\mathcal{A}))$
5:   $\mid$ $\mid$ $i \leftarrow i + \Delta_{\text{QS}}(a_{i+N})$ ▷ Quick Search-style skipping
6:   $\mid$ **if** $i > |w| - N + 1$ **then return**
7:   $\mid$ $Z \leftarrow Z \cup \{(t, t', v) \in [\tau_{i-1}, \tau_i) \times (\tau_{i-1}, \infty) \times (\mathbb{Q}_+)^{\mathbb{P}} \mid w|_{(t,t')} \in \mathcal{L}(v(\mathcal{A}))\}$ ▷ Try matching
8:   $\mid$ $j \leftarrow \max\{j \in \{i, i+1, \ldots, |w|\} \mid \exists l \in L, v \in (\mathbb{Q}_+)^{\mathbb{P}}, t \in \mathbb{R}_{>0}. w(i, j) - t \in \mathcal{L}(v(\mathcal{A}_l))\}$
9:   $\mid$ $C \leftarrow \{(l, V) \in L \times \mathcal{P}((\mathbb{Q}_+)^{\mathbb{P}}) \mid \forall v \in V, \exists t \in \mathbb{R}_{>0}. w(i, j) - t \in \mathcal{L}(v(\mathcal{A}_l))\}$
10:   $\mid$ $i \leftarrow i + \max_{(l,V) \in C} \Delta_{\text{KMP}}(l, V)$ ▷ Parametric KMP-style skipping
11: $Z \leftarrow Z \cup \{(t, t', v) \in [\tau_{|w|}, \infty) \times (\tau_{|w|}, \infty) \times (\mathbb{Q}_+)^{\mathbb{P}} \mid w|_{(t,t')} \in \mathcal{L}(v(\mathcal{A}))\}$

RQ1 Which is the fastest algorithm for parametric timed pattern matching?
RQ2 Why is parametric timed pattern matching slower than non-parametric timed pattern matching? Namely, is it purely because of the difficulty of the problem itself or is it mainly because of the general implementation and data structure required by the general problem setting?
RQ3 How large is the overhead of the skip value computation? Namely, is it small and acceptable?

We implemented `ParamMONAA` in C++ and we compiled them using GCC 7.3.0. We conducted the experiments on an Amazon EC2 c4.large instance (2.9 GHz Intel Xeon E5-2666 v3, 2 vCPUs, and 3.75 GiB RAM) that runs Ubuntu 18.04 LTS (64 bit). Experiment data can be found on https://github.com/MasWag/monaa/blob/PTPM/doc/NFM2019.md.

(a) GEAR: the parameter p is substituted to 2 in GEAR-NP.

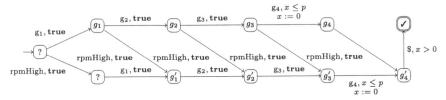

(b) ACCEL: the parameter p is substituted to 3 in ACCEL-NP.

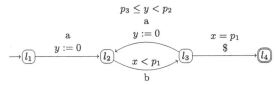

(c) BLOWUP: the parameters p_1, p_2, and p_3 are substituted to 10, 2, and 1, respectively in BLOWUP-NP.

$$\rightarrow \boxed{l_1} \xrightarrow[\ ]{\begin{array}{c}a\\x:=0\end{array}} \boxed{l_2} \xrightarrow[x:=0]{\begin{array}{c}a\\x>1\end{array}} \boxed{l_3} \xrightarrow[\ ]{\begin{array}{c}a\\x<p\end{array}} \boxed{l_4} \xrightarrow{\$} \boxed{l_5}$$

(d) ONLYTIMING: the parameter p is substituted to 1 in ONLYTIMING-NP.

Fig. 3. Pattern PTAs and their non-parametric variants in the experiments

Figure 3 shows the pattern PTAs we used in the experiments. We took the benchmarks GEAR, ACCEL, and BLOWUP from [5] as well as the new original benchmark ONLYTIMING. The timed words for GEAR and ACCEL are generated by the automatic transmission system model in [23]. BLOWUP and ONLYTIMING are toy examples. BLOWUP shows the worst case situation for parametric timed pattern matching. In ONLYTIMING, the parametric skip values are greater than the non-parametric skip values. In Sects. 5.2 and 5.3, we also used the non-parametric variants GEAR-NP, ACCEL-NP, BLOWUP-NP, and ONLYTIMING-NP where the parameters are substituted to specific concrete values.

5.1   RQ1: Overall Execution Time

To answer RQ1, we compared the total execution time of `ParamMONAA` using GEAR, ACCEL, BLOWUP, and ONLYTIMING. As a baseline, we used our previous implementation of parametric timed pattern matching based on IMITATOR [5] (version 2.10.4). Tables 2, 3, 4 and 5 and Fig. 4 show the execution time of our online algorithms compared with the IMITATOR-based implementation.

In Tables 2, 3, 4 and 5, we observe that our algorithms are faster than the IMI-TATOR-based implementation by orders of magnitude. Moreover, for BLOWUP, the IMITATOR-based implementation aborted due to out of memory. This is mainly because `ParamMONAA` is specific to parametric timed pattern matching while IMITATOR is a general tool for parametric verification. This shows the much better efficiency of our new approach compared to [5].

In Fig. 4, we observe that the curve of "no skip" has the steepest slope and the curves of either "parametric skip" or "non-parametric skip" have the gentlest slope except for BLOWUP. BLOWUP is a benchmark designed on purpose to observe exponential blowup of the execution time, and it requires much time for all of the implementations.

For GEAR and ACCEL, the execution time of "non-parametric skip" increases the most gently. This is because the parametric KMP-style skip value $\Delta_{\mathrm{KMP}}(l, V)$ and the non-parametric KMP-style skip value $\Delta'_{\mathrm{KMP}}(l)$ are equal for these benchmarks, and "parametric skip" is slower due to the inclusion checking $V \subseteq V_{l,n}$.

Table 2. Execution time for GEAR [s]

$|w|$	No skip	Non-param. skip	Param. skip	IMITATOR
1467	0.04	0.05	0.05	1.781
2837	0.0725	0.0805	0.09	3.319
4595	0.124	0.13	0.1405	5.512
5839	0.1585	0.156	0.17	7.132
7301	0.201	0.193	0.2115	8.909
8995	0.241	0.2315	0.2505	10.768
10315	0.2815	0.269	0.2875	12.778
11831	0.322	0.301	0.325	14.724
13183	0.3505	0.3245	0.353	16.453
14657	0.392	0.361	0.395	18.319

Table 3. Execution time for ACCEL [s]

$|w|$	No skip	Non-param. skip	Param. skip	IMITATOR
2559	0.03	0.0515	0.06	2.332
4894	0.0605	0.0605	0.0705	4.663
7799	0.1005	0.071	0.08	7.532
10045	0.13	0.08	0.09	9.731
12531	0.161	0.09	0.1	12.503
15375	0.1985	0.1005	0.113	15.583
17688	0.2265	0.1095	0.1215	17.754
20299	0.261	0.115	0.1325	21.040
22691	0.288	0.121	0.143	23.044
25137	0.3205	0.1315	0.159	25.815

Table 4. Execution time for BLOWUP [s]

$|w|$	No skip	Non-param. skip	Param. skip	IMITATOR
2000	66.75	68.0125	67.9735	OutOfMemory
4000	267.795	271.642	269.084	OutOfMemory
6000	601.335	611.782	607.58	OutOfMemory
8000	1081.42	1081.25	1079	OutOfMemory
10000	1678.15	1688.22	1694.53	OutOfMemory

Table 5. Execution time for ONLYTIMING [s]

$|w|$	No skip	Non-param. skip	Param. skip	IMITATOR
1000	0.0995	0.1305	0.11	1.690
2000	0.191	0.23	0.191	3.518
3000	0.2905	0.3265	0.273	5.499
4000	0.3905	0.426	0.3525	7.396
5000	0.488	0.5225	0.4325	9.123
6000	0.588	0.6235	0.517	11.005

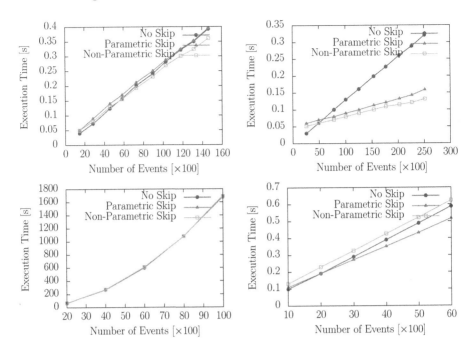

Fig. 4. Execution time for the benchmarks with parameters which MONAA cannot handle: GEAR (above left), ACCEL (above right), BLOWUP (below left), and ONLYTIMING (below right)

For ONLYTIMING, we observe that the execution time of "parametric skip" increases the most gently because the parametric KMP-style skip value $\Delta_{\mathrm{KMP}}(l, V)$ is larger than the non-parametric KMP-style skip value $\Delta'_{\mathrm{KMP}}(l)$.

We conclude that skipping usually makes parametric timed pattern matching efficient. The preference between two skipping methods depends on the pattern PTA and it is a future work to investigate the tendency. Since the computation of the skip values does not take much time, the following work flow is reasonable: *(i)* compute the skip values for both of them; and *(ii)* use "parametric skip" only if its skip values are strictly larger than that of "non-parametric skip".

5.2 RQ2: Parametric vs. Non-parametric Timed Pattern Matching

To answer RQ2, we ran ParamMONAA using the non-parametric benchmarks (ACCEL-NP, GEAR-NP, BLOWUP-NP, and ONLYTIMING-NP) and compared the execution time with a tool MONAA [38] for non-parametric timed pattern matching.

In Fig. 5, we observe that our algorithms are slower than MONAA by orders of magnitude even though we solve the same problem (non-parametric timed pattern matching). This is presumably because our implementations rely on Parma Polyhedra Library (PPL) [9] to compute symbolic states, while MONAA utilizes

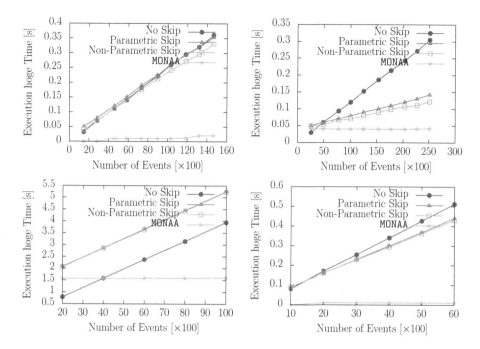

Fig. 5. Execution time for the benchmarks without parameters: GEAR-NP (above left), ACCEL-NP (above right), BLOWUP-NP (below left), and ONLYTIMING-NP (below right)

DBMs (difference bound matrices) [16]. It was shown in [11] that polyhedra may be dozens of times slower than DBMs; however, for parametric analyses, DBMs are not suitable, and parameterized extensions (e.g., in [24]) still need polyhedra in their representation.

Moreover, in Figs. 4 and 5, we observe that the execution time of our algorithms are not much different between each parametric benchmark and its non-parametric variant except BLOWUP. This observation shows that at least one additional parameter does not make the problem too difficult.

Therefore, we conclude that the lower efficiency of parametric timed pattern matching is mainly because of its general data structure required by the general problem setting.

5.3   RQ3: Overhead of Skip Value Computation

To answer RQ3, we compared the execution time of our algorithms for an empty timed word using all the benchmarks. As a baseline, we also measured the execution time of MONAA.

In Table 6, we observe that the execution time for the skip values is less than 0.05 s except for BLOWUP and BLOWUP-NP. Even for the slowest pattern

Table 6. Execution time [s] for the skip value computation

	Non-parametric skip	Parametric skip	MONAA
GEAR	0.0115	0.0175	n/a
GEAR-NP	0.01	0.01	<0.01
ACCEL	0.042	0.0435	n/a
ACCEL-NP	0.04	0.04	0.0305
ONLYTIMING	0.03	0.03	n/a
ONLYTIMING-NP	0.02	0.02	<0.01
BLOWUP	0.3665	0.381	n/a
BLOWUP-NP	1.268	1.2905	1.5455

PTA BLOWUP-NP, the execution time for the skip values is less than 1.5 s and it is faster than that of MONAA. We conclude that the overhead of the skip value computation is small and acceptable in many usage scenarios.

6 Conclusion and Perspectives

In this work, we proposed a new approach for monitoring logs given in the form of timed words using a specification given in the form of parametric timed automata. Our new approach dramatically outperforms the previous approach of [5]. In addition, we discussed an optimization using skipping.

Natural future works include more expressive specifications than (parametric) timed automata-based specifications, e.g., using more expressive logics such as [14].

References

1. Alur, R., Dill, D.L.: A theory of timed automata. Theor. Comput. Sci. **126**(2), 183–235 (1994)
2. Alur, R., Henzinger, T.A., Vardi, M.Y.: Parametric real-time reasoning. In: Kosaraju, S.R., Johnson, D.S., Aggarwal, A. (eds.) Proceedings of the Twenty-Fifth Annual ACM Symposium on Theory of Computing (STOC 1993), pp. 592–601. ACM, New York (1993)
3. André, É., Chatain, Th., Encrenaz, E., Fribourg, L.: An inverse method for parametric timed automata. Int. J. Found. Comput. Sci. **20**(5), 819–836 (2009). https://doi.org/10.1142/S0129054109006905
4. André, É., Fribourg, L., Kühne, U., Soulat, R.: IMITATOR 2.5: a tool for analyzing robustness in scheduling problems. In: Giannakopoulou, D., Méry, D. (eds.) FM 2012. LNCS, vol. 7436, pp. 33–36. Springer, Heidelberg (2012). https://doi.org/10.1007/978-3-642-32759-9_6
5. André, É., Hasuo, I., Waga, M.: Offline timed pattern matching under uncertainty. In: Lin, A.W., Sun, J. (eds.) Proceedings of the 23rd International Conference on Engineering of Complex Computer Systems (ICECCS 2018), pp. 10–20. IEEE CPS (2018). https://doi.org/10.1109/ICECCS2018.2018.00010

6. Asarin, E., Basset, N., Degorre, A.: Distance on timed words and applications. In: Jansen, D.N., Prabhakar, P. (eds.) FORMATS 2018. LNCS, vol. 11022, pp. 199–214. Springer, Cham (2018). https://doi.org/10.1007/978-3-030-00151-3_12

7. Asarin, E., Donzé, A., Maler, O., Nickovic, D.: Parametric identification of temporal properties. In: Khurshid, S., Sen, K. (eds.) RV 2011. LNCS, vol. 7186, pp. 147–160. Springer, Heidelberg (2012). https://doi.org/10.1007/978-3-642-29860-8_12

8. Asarin, E., Maler, O., Nickovic, D., Ulus, D.: Combining the temporal and epistemic dimensions for MTL monitoring. In: Abate, A., Geeraerts, G. (eds.) FORMATS 2017. LNCS, vol. 10419, pp. 207–223. Springer, Cham (2017). https://doi.org/10.1007/978-3-319-65765-3_12

9. Bagnara, R., Hill, P.M., Zaffanella, E.: The Parma Polyhedra Library: toward a complete set of numerical abstractions for the analysis and verification of hardware and software systems. Sci. Comput. Program. **72**(1–2), 3–21 (2008). https://doi.org/10.1016/j.scico.2007.08.001

10. Bakhirkin, A., Ferrère, T., Maler, O.: Efficient parametric identification for STL. In: Proceedings of the 21st International Conference on Hybrid Systems: Computation and Control (Part of CPS Week) (HSCC 2018), pp. 177–186. ACM (2018). https://doi.org/10.1145/3178126.3178132

11. Bakhirkin, A., Ferrère, T., Maler, O., Ulus, D.: On the quantitative semantics of regular expressions over real-valued signals. In: Abate, A., Geeraerts, G. (eds.) FORMATS 2017. LNCS, vol. 10419, pp. 189–206. Springer, Cham (2017). https://doi.org/10.1007/978-3-319-65765-3_11

12. Bakhirkin, A., Ferrère, T., Nickovic, D., Maler, O., Asarin, E.: Online timed pattern matching using automata. In: Jansen, D.N., Prabhakar, P. (eds.) FORMATS 2018. LNCS, vol. 11022, pp. 215–232. Springer, Cham (2018). https://doi.org/10.1007/978-3-030-00151-3_13

13. Bartocci, E., et al.: Specification-based monitoring of cyber-physical systems: a survey on theory, tools and applications. In: Bartocci, E., Falcone, Y. (eds.) Lectures on Runtime Verification. LNCS, vol. 10457, pp. 135–175. Springer, Cham (2018). https://doi.org/10.1007/978-3-319-75632-5_5

14. Basin, D.A., Klaedtke, F., Müller, S., Zalinescu, E.: Monitoring metric first-order temporal properties. J. ACM **62**(2), 15:1–15:45 (2015). https://doi.org/10.1145/2699444

15. Deshmukh, J.V., Majumdar, R., Prabhu, V.S.: Quantifying conformance using the Skorokhod metric. Formal Methods Syst. Des. **50**(2–3), 168–206 (2017). https://doi.org/10.1007/s10703-016-0261-8

16. Dill, D.L.: Timing assumptions and verification of finite-state concurrent systems. In: Sifakis, J. (ed.) CAV 1989. LNCS, vol. 407, pp. 197–212. Springer, Heidelberg (1990). https://doi.org/10.1007/3-540-52148-8_17

17. Donzé, A.: Breach, a toolbox for verification and parameter synthesis of hybrid systems. In: Touili, T., Cook, B., Jackson, P. (eds.) CAV 2010. LNCS, vol. 6174, pp. 167–170. Springer, Heidelberg (2010). https://doi.org/10.1007/978-3-642-14295-6_17

18. Donzé, A., Ferrère, T., Maler, O.: Efficient robust monitoring for STL. In: Sharygina, N., Veith, H. (eds.) CAV 2013. LNCS, vol. 8044, pp. 264–279. Springer, Heidelberg (2013). https://doi.org/10.1007/978-3-642-39799-8_19

19. Donzé, A., Maler, O.: Robust satisfaction of temporal logic over real-valued signals. In: Chatterjee, K., Henzinger, T.A. (eds.) FORMATS 2010. LNCS, vol. 6246, pp. 92–106. Springer, Heidelberg (2010). https://doi.org/10.1007/978-3-642-15297-9_9

20. Fages, F., Rizk, A.: On temporal logic constraint solving for analyzing numerical data time series. Theor. Comput. Sci. **408**(1), 55–65 (2008). https://doi.org/10.1016/j.tcs.2008.07.004

21. Franek, F., Jennings, C.G., Smyth, W.F.: A simple fast hybrid pattern-matching algorithm. J. Discret. Algorithms **5**(4), 682–695 (2007). https://doi.org/10.1016/j.jda.2006.11.004

22. Ho, H.-M., Ouaknine, J., Worrell, J.: Online monitoring of metric temporal logic. In: Bonakdarpour, B., Smolka, S.A. (eds.) RV 2014. LNCS, vol. 8734, pp. 178–192. Springer, Cham (2014). https://doi.org/10.1007/978-3-319-11164-3_15

23. Hoxha, B., Abbas, H., Fainekos, G.E.: Benchmarks for temporal logic requirements for automotive systems. In: Frehse, G., Althoff, M. (eds.) Proceedings of the 1st and 2nd International Workshops on Applied Verification for Continuous and Hybrid Systems (ARCH@CPSWeek 2014/ARCH@CPSWeek 2015). EPiC Series in Computing, vol. 34, pp. 25–30. EasyChair (2014)

24. Hune, T., Romijn, J., Stoelinga, M., Vaandrager, F.W.: Linear parametric model checking of timed automata. J. Logic Algebraic Program. **52–53**, 183–220 (2002). https://doi.org/10.1016/S1567-8326(02)00037-1

25. Jakšić, S., Bartocci, E., Grosu, R., Nguyen, T., Ničković, D.: Quantitative monitoring of STL with edit distance. Formal Methods Syst. Des. **53**(1), 83–112 (2018). https://doi.org/10.1007/s10703-018-0319-x

26. Jovanović, A., Lime, D., Roux, O.H.: Integer parameter synthesis for timed automata. IEEE Trans. Softw. Eng. **41**(5), 445–461 (2015)

27. Kane, A., Chowdhury, O., Datta, A., Koopman, P.: A case study on runtime monitoring of an autonomous research vehicle (ARV) system. In: Bartocci, E., Majumdar, R. (eds.) RV 2015. LNCS, vol. 9333, pp. 102–117. Springer, Cham (2015). https://doi.org/10.1007/978-3-319-23820-3_7

28. Knuth, D.E., Morris Jr., J.H., Pratt, V.R.: Fast pattern matching in strings. SIAM J. Comput. **6**(2), 323–350 (1977). https://doi.org/10.1137/0206024

29. Koymans, R.: Specifying real-time properties with metric temporal logic. Real-Time Syst. **2**(4), 255–299 (1990). https://doi.org/10.1007/BF01995674

30. Reinbacher, T., Függer, M., Brauer, J.: Runtime verification of embedded real-time systems. Formal Methods Syst. Des. **44**(3), 203–239 (2014). https://doi.org/10.1007/s10703-013-0199-z

31. Sunday, D.: A very fast substring search algorithm. Communun. ACM **33**(8), 132–142 (1990). https://doi.org/10.1145/79173.79184

32. Ulus, D.: MONTRE: a tool for monitoring timed regular expressions. In: Majumdar, R., Kunčak, V. (eds.) CAV 2017. LNCS, vol. 10426, pp. 329–335. Springer, Cham (2017). https://doi.org/10.1007/978-3-319-63387-9_16

33. Ulus, D., Ferrère, T., Asarin, E., Maler, O.: Timed pattern matching. In: Legay, A., Bozga, M. (eds.) FORMATS 2014. LNCS, vol. 8711, pp. 222–236. Springer, Cham (2014). https://doi.org/10.1007/978-3-319-10512-3_16

34. Ulus, D., Ferrère, T., Asarin, E., Maler, O.: Online timed pattern matching using derivatives. In: Chechik, M., Raskin, J.-F. (eds.) TACAS 2016. LNCS, vol. 9636, pp. 736–751. Springer, Heidelberg (2016). https://doi.org/10.1007/978-3-662-49674-9_47

35. Waga, M., Akazaki, T., Hasuo, I.: A Boyer-Moore type algorithm for timed pattern matching. In: Fränzle, M., Markey, N. (eds.) FORMATS 2016. LNCS, vol. 9884, pp. 121–139. Springer, Cham (2016). https://doi.org/10.1007/978-3-319-44878-7_8

36. Waga, M., André, É.: Online parametric timed pattern matching with automata-based skipping. abs/1903.07328 (2019). http://arxiv.org/abs/1903.07328

37. Waga, M., Hasuo, I., Suenaga, K.: Efficient online timed pattern matching by automata-based skipping. In: Abate, A., Geeraerts, G. (eds.) FORMATS 2017. LNCS, vol. 10419, pp. 224–243. Springer, Cham (2017). https://doi.org/10.1007/978-3-319-65765-3_13

38. Waga, M., Hasuo, I., Suenaga, K.: MONAA: a tool for timed pattern matching with automata-based acceleration. In: Proceedings of the 3rd Workshop on Monitoring and Testing of Cyber-Physical Systems (MT@CPSWeek 2018), pp. 14–15. IEEE (2018). https://doi.org/10.1109/MT-CPS.2018.00014

Author Index

Printed in the United States
By Bookmasters